WELLA RESPLANDOR

SAS® Programming 1: Essentials

Course Notes

SAS® Programming 1: Essentials Course Notes was developed by Michele Ensor and Susan Farmer. Additional contributions were made by Michelle Buchecker, Christine Dillon, Marty Hultgren, Marya Ilgen-Lieth, Mike Kalt, Natalie McGowan, Linda Mitterling, Georg Morsing, Dr. Sue Rakes, Warren Repole, and Larry Stewart. Editing and production support was provided by the Curriculum Development and Support Department.

SAS® Programming 1: Essentials Course Notes

Book code E1516, course code LWPRG1/PRG1, prepared date 18Jun2009. LWPRG1_002

ISBN 978-1-60764-194-0

Table of Contents

Course Description x

Prerequisites xi

Chapter 1 Introduction 1-1

1.1 Course Logistics 1-3

1.2 An Overview of Foundation SAS 1-7

1.3 Chapter Review 1-10

1.4 Solutions 1-11

Solutions to Chapter Review 1-11

Chapter 2 Getting Started with SAS 2-1

2.1 Introduction to SAS Programs 2-3

2.2 Submitting a SAS Program 2-11

Demonstration: Submitting a SAS Program with SAS Windowing Environment – Windows 2-16

Demonstration: Submitting a SAS Program with SAS Windowing Environment – UNIX 2-21

Demonstration: Submitting a SAS Program with SAS Windowing Environment – z/OS (OS/390) 2-25

Demonstration: Submitting a SAS Program with SAS Enterprise Guide 2-30

Exercises 2-43

2.3 Chapter Review 2-45

2.4 Solutions 2-46

Solutions to Exercises 2-46

Solutions to Student Activities (Polls/Quizzes) 2-49

Solutions to Chapter Review 2-50

Chapter 3 Working with SAS Syntax 3-1

3.1 Mastering Fundamental Concepts 3-3

3.2 Diagnosing and Correcting Syntax Errors 3-10

Demonstration: Diagnosing and Correcting Syntax Errors 3-12

Demonstration: Diagnosing and Correcting Syntax Errors 3-15

Exercises 3-19

3.3 Chapter Review 3-20

3.4 Solutions 3-21

Solutions to Exercises 3-21

Solutions to Student Activities (Polls/Quizzes) 3-23

Solutions to Chapter Review 3-25

Chapter 4 Getting Familiar with SAS Data Sets 4-1

4.1 Examining Descriptor and Data Portions 4-3

Exercises 4-13

4.2 Accessing SAS Data Libraries 4-16

Demonstration: Accessing and Browsing SAS Data Libraries – Windows 4-24

Demonstration: Accessing and Browsing SAS Data Libraries – UNIX 4-28

Demonstration: Accessing and Browsing SAS Data Libraries – z/OS (OS/390) 4-31

Exercises 4-33

4.3 Accessing Relational Databases (Self-Study) 4-35

4.4 Chapter Review 4-40

4.5 Solutions 4-41

Solutions to Exercises 4-41

Solutions to Student Activities (Polls/Quizzes) 4-45

Solutions to Chapter Review 4-48

Chapter 5 Reading SAS Data Sets 5-1

5.1 Introduction to Reading Data 5-3

5.2 Using SAS Data as Input 5-6

5.3 Subsetting Observations and Variables 5-12

Exercises 5-26

5.4 Adding Permanent Attributes 5-29

Exercises 5-41

5.5 Chapter Review 5-44

5.6 Solutions 5-45

Solutions to Exercises 5-45

Solutions to Student Activities (Polls/Quizzes) 5-50

Solutions to Chapter Review 5-54

Chapter 6 Reading Excel Worksheets 6-1

6.1 Using Excel Data as Input 6-3

Demonstration: Reading Excel Worksheets – Windows 6-15

Exercises 6-17

6.2 Doing More with Excel Worksheets (Self-Study) 6-20

Exercises 6-36

6.3 Chapter Review 6-37

6.4 Solutions 6-38

Solutions to Exercises 6-38

Solutions to Student Activities (Polls/Quizzes) 6-43

Solutions to Chapter Review 6-44

Chapter 7 Reading Delimited Raw Data Files 7-1

7.1 Using Standard Delimited Data as Input 7-3

Exercises 7-27

7.2 Using Nonstandard Delimited Data as Input 7-30

Exercises 7-44

7.3 Chapter Review 7-48

7.4 Solutions 7-49

Solutions to Exercises 7-49

Solutions to Student Activities (Polls/Quizzes) 7-52

Solutions to Chapter Review 7-55

Chapter 8 Validating and Cleaning Data 8-1

8.1 Introduction to Validating and Cleaning Data 8-3

8.2 Examining Data Errors When Reading Raw Data Files 8-9

Demonstration: Examining Data Errors 8-14

8.3 Validating Data with the PRINT and FREQ Procedures 8-19

Exercises 8-30

8.4 Validating Data with the MEANS and UNIVARIATE Procedures 8-33

Exercises 8-38

8.5 Cleaning Invalid Data 8-41

Demonstration: Using the Viewtable Window to Clean Data – Windows (Self-Study) 8-44

Demonstration: Using the Viewtable Window to Clean Data – UNIX (Self-Study) 8-47

Demonstration: Using the FSEDIT Window to Clean Data – z/OS (OS/390) (Self-Study) 8-49

Exercises 8-64

8.6 Chapter Review 8-66

8.7 Solutions 8-67

Solutions to Exercises 8-67

Solutions to Student Activities (Polls/Quizzes) 8-73

Solutions to Chapter Review 8-77

Chapter 9 Manipulating Data 9-1

9.1 Creating Variables 9-3

Exercises 9-27

9.2 Creating Variables Conditionally 9-30

Exercises 9-41

9.3 Subsetting Observations 9-44

Exercises 9-51

9.4 Chapter Review 9-53

9.5 Solutions 9-54

Solutions to Exercises 9-54

Solutions to Student Activities (Polls/Quizzes) 9-62

Solutions to Chapter Review 9-66

Chapter 10 Combining SAS Data Sets 10-1

10.1 Introduction to Combining Data Sets 10-3

10.2 Appending a Data Set (Self-Study) 10-7

Exercises 10-17

10.3 Concatenating Data Sets 10-19

Exercises 10-41

10.4 Merging Data Sets One-to-One 10-44

10.5 Merging Data Sets One-to-Many 10-53

Exercises 10-64

10.6 Merging Data Sets with Nonmatches 10-66

Exercises 10-89

10.7 Chapter Review 10-92

10.8 Solutions 10-93

Solutions to Exercises 10-93

Solutions to Student Activities (Polls/Quizzes) 10-100

Solutions to Chapter Review 10-107

Chapter 11 Enhancing Reports 11-1

11.1 Using Global Statements 11-3

Exercises 11-16

11.2 Adding Labels and Formats 11-20

Exercises 11-29

11.3 Creating User-Defined Formats 11-32

Exercises 11-43

11.4 Subsetting and Grouping Observations 11-46

Exercises 11-52

11.5 Directing Output to External Files 11-55

Demonstration: Creating HTML, PDF, and RTF Files 11-64

Demonstration: Creating Files That Open in Excel 11-77

Demonstration: Using Options with the EXCELXP Destination (Self-Study) 11-80

Exercises 11-83

11.6 Chapter Review 11-88

11.7 Solutions 11-89

Solutions to Exercises 11-89

Solutions to Student Activities (Polls/Quizzes) 11-103

Solutions to Chapter Review 11-109

Chapter 12 Producing Summary Reports 12-1

12.1 Using the FREQ Procedure 12-3

Exercises 12-21

12.2 Using the MEANS Procedure 12-27

Exercises 12-42

12.3 Using the TABULATE Procedure (Self-Study) 12-46

Exercises 12-60

12.4 Chapter Review 12-65

12.5 Solutions 12-66

Solutions to Exercises 12-66

Solutions to Student Activities (Polls/Quizzes) 12-75

Solutions to Chapter Review 12-78

Chapter 13 Introduction to Graphics Using SAS/GRAPH (Self-Study) 13-1

13.1 Introduction 13-3

13.2 Creating Bar and Pie Charts 13-9

Demonstration: Creating Bar and Pie Charts 13-10

13.3 Creating Plots 13-21

Demonstration: Creating Plots 13-22

13.4 Enhancing Output 13-25

Demonstration: Enhancing Output 13-26

Chapter 14 Learning More 14-1

14.1 SAS Resources 14-3

14.2 Beyond This Course 14-6

Appendix A Index A-1

Course Description

This course is for users who want to learn how to write SAS programs. It is the entry point to learning SAS programming and is a prerequisite to many other SAS courses. If you do not plan to write SAS programs and you prefer a point-and-click interface, you should attend the *SAS® Enterprise Guide® 1: Querying and Reporting* course.

To learn more…

A full curriculum of general and statistical instructor-based training is available at any of the Institute's training facilities. Institute instructors can also provide on-site training.

For information on other courses in the curriculum, contact the SAS Education Division at 1-800-333-7660, or send e-mail to training@sas.com. You can also find this information on the Web at support.sas.com/training/ as well as in the Training Course Catalog.

For a list of other SAS books that relate to the topics covered in this Course Notes, USA customers can contact our SAS Publishing Department at 1-800-727-3228 or send e-mail to sasbook@sas.com. Customers outside the USA, please contact your local SAS office.

Also, see the Publications Catalog on the Web at support.sas.com/pubs for a complete list of books and a convenient order form.

Prerequisites

Before attending this course, you should have experience using computer software. Specifically, you should be able to

- understand file structures and system commands on your operating systems
- access data files on your operating systems.

No prior SAS experience is needed. If you do not feel comfortable with the prerequisites or are new to programming and think that the pace of this course might be too demanding, you can take the Introduction to Programming Concepts Using SAS® Software course before attending this course. Introduction to Programming Concepts Using SAS® Software is designed to introduce you to computer programming and presents a portion of the SAS® Programming 1: Essentials material at a slower pace.

Chapter 1 Introduction

1.1 Course Logistics 1-3

1.2 An Overview of Foundation SAS 1-7

1.3 Chapter Review 1-10

1.4 Solutions 1-11

Solutions to Chapter Review 1-11

1.1 Course Logistics

Objectives

- Explain the naming convention that is used for the course files.
- Compare the three levels of exercises that are used in the course.
- Describe at a high level how data is used and stored at Orion Star Sports & Outdoors.
- Navigate to the Help facility.

3

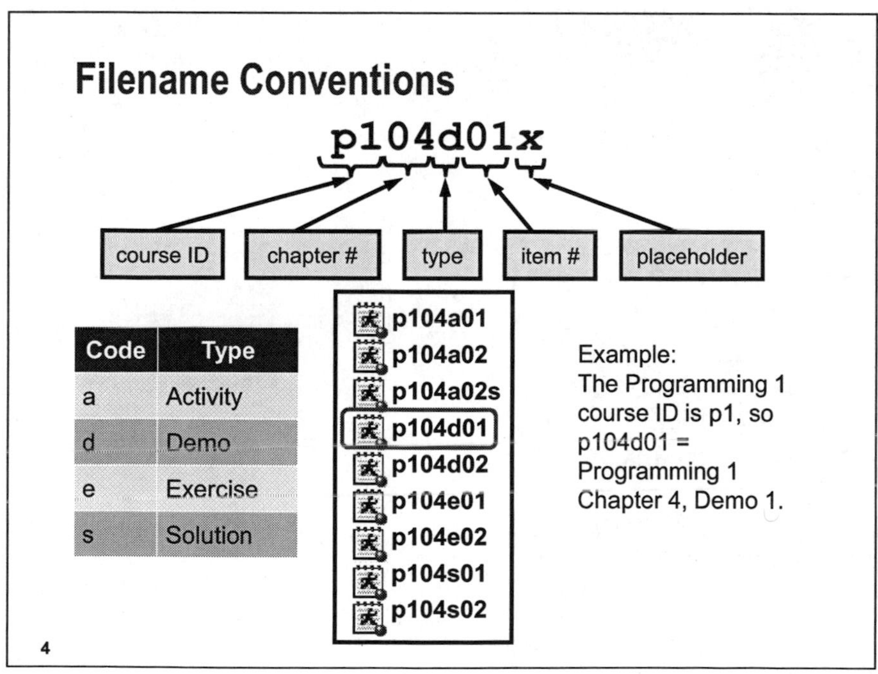

Code	Type
a	Activity
d	Demo
e	Exercise
s	Solution

Three Levels of Exercises

Level 1	The exercise mimics an example presented in the section.
Level 2	Less information and guidance are provided in the exercise instructions.
Level 3	Only the task you are to perform or the results to be obtained are provided. Typically, you will need to use the Help facility.

✎ You are not expected to complete all of the exercises in the time allotted. Choose the exercise or exercises that are at the level you are most comfortable with.

5

Orion Star Sports & Outdoors

Orion Star Sports & Outdoors is a fictitious global sports and outdoors retailer with traditional stores, an online store, and a large catalog business.

The corporate headquarters is located in the United States with offices and stores in many countries throughout the world.

Orion Star has about 1,000 employees and 90,000 customers, processes approximately 150,000 orders annually, and purchases products from 64 suppliers.

6

Orion Star Data

As is the case with most organizations, Orion Star has a large amount of data about its customers, suppliers, products, and employees. Much of this information is stored in transactional systems in various formats.

Using applications and processes such as SAS Data Integration Studio, this transactional information was extracted, transformed, and loaded into a data warehouse.

Data marts were created to meet the needs of specific departments such as Marketing.

7

The SAS Help Facility

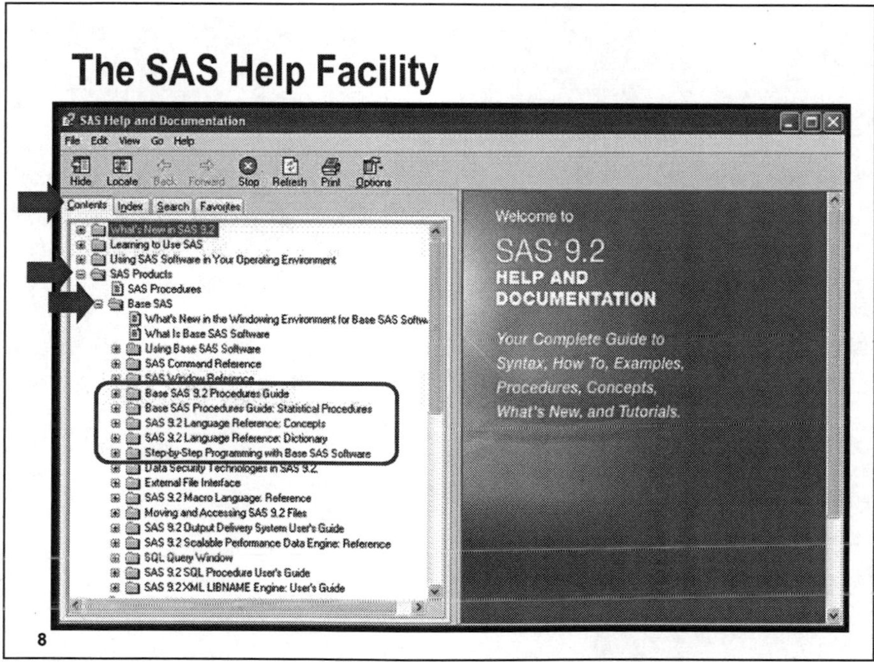

8

The Help facility can also be accessed from a Web browser at the following link:

http://support.sas.com/documentation/index.html

Setup for the Poll

- Start your SAS session.
- Open the Help facility.

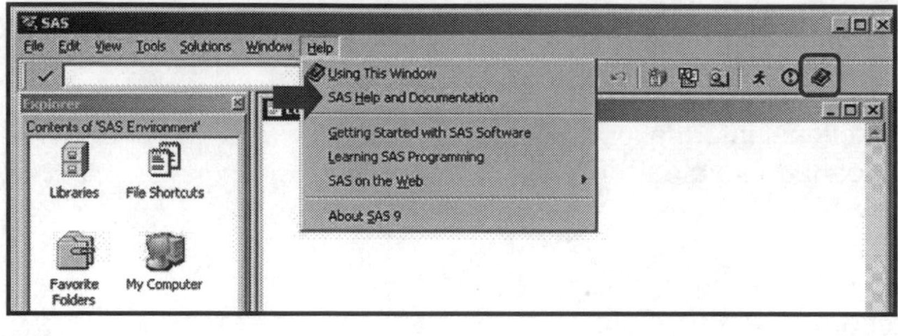

10

1.01 Poll

Were you able to open the Help facility in your SAS session?

❍ Yes

❍ No

11

1.2 An Overview of Foundation SAS

Objectives

- Describe the structure and design of Foundation SAS.
- Describe the functionality of Foundation SAS.

14

What Is Foundation SAS?

Foundation SAS is a highly flexible and integrated software environment that can be used in virtually any setting to access, manipulate, manage, store, analyze, and report on data.

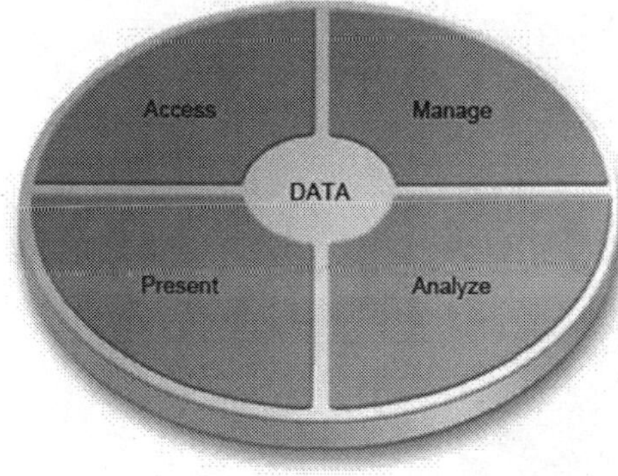

15

What Is Foundation SAS?

Foundation SAS provides the following:

- a graphical user interface for administering SAS tasks
- a highly flexible and extensible programming language
- a rich library of prewritten, ready-to-use SAS procedures
- the flexibility to run on all major operating environments such as Windows, UNIX, and z/OS (OS/390)
- the access to virtually any data source such as DB2, Oracle, SYBASE, Teradata, SAP, and Microsoft Excel
- the support for most widely used character encodings for globalization

16

What Is Foundation SAS?

At the core of Foundation SAS is Base SAS software.

Components of Foundation SAS		
Reporting and Graphics	Data Access and Management	User Interfaces
Analytics	Base SAS	Application Development
Visualization and Discovery	Business Solutions	Web Enablement

Base SAS capabilities can be extended with additional components.

17

→ It started in IBM 360

1.02 Poll

Are you currently using SAS?

- ❍ Yes
- ❍ No

19

1.3 Chapter Review

Chapter Review

1. How can you open the Help facility?

2. What is at the core of Foundation SAS?

21

1.4 Solutions

Solutions to Chapter Review

Chapter Review Answers

1. How can you open the Help facility?
   - **The Help facility can be accessed from a Web browser at http://support.sas.com/documentation/index.html.**
   - **The Help facility can be opened within your SAS session from Help ⇨ SAS Help and Documentation.**

2. What is at the core of Foundation SAS?

   Base SAS is at the core of Foundation SAS.

22

Chapter 2 Getting Started with SAS

2.1 Introduction to SAS Programs **2-3**

2.2 Submitting a SAS Program **2-11**

Demonstration: Submitting a SAS Program with SAS Windowing Environment – Windows 2-16

Demonstration: Submitting a SAS Program with SAS Windowing Environment – UNIX 2-21

Demonstration: Submitting a SAS Program with SAS Windowing Environment – z/OS (OS/390) 2-25

Demonstration: Submitting a SAS Program with SAS Enterprise Guide 2-30

Exercises 2-43

2.3 Chapter Review **2-45**

2.4 Solutions **2-46**

Solutions to Exercises 2-46

Solutions to Student Activities (Polls/Quizzes) 2-49

Solutions to Chapter Review 2-50

2.1 Introduction to SAS Programs

Objectives

- List the components of a SAS program.
- State the modes in which you can run a SAS program.

3

SAS Programs

A *SAS program* is a sequence of steps that the user submits for execution.

DATA steps are typically used to create SAS data sets.

PROC steps are typically used to process SAS data sets (that is, generate reports and graphs, manage data, and sort data).

4

PROC step - Procedure

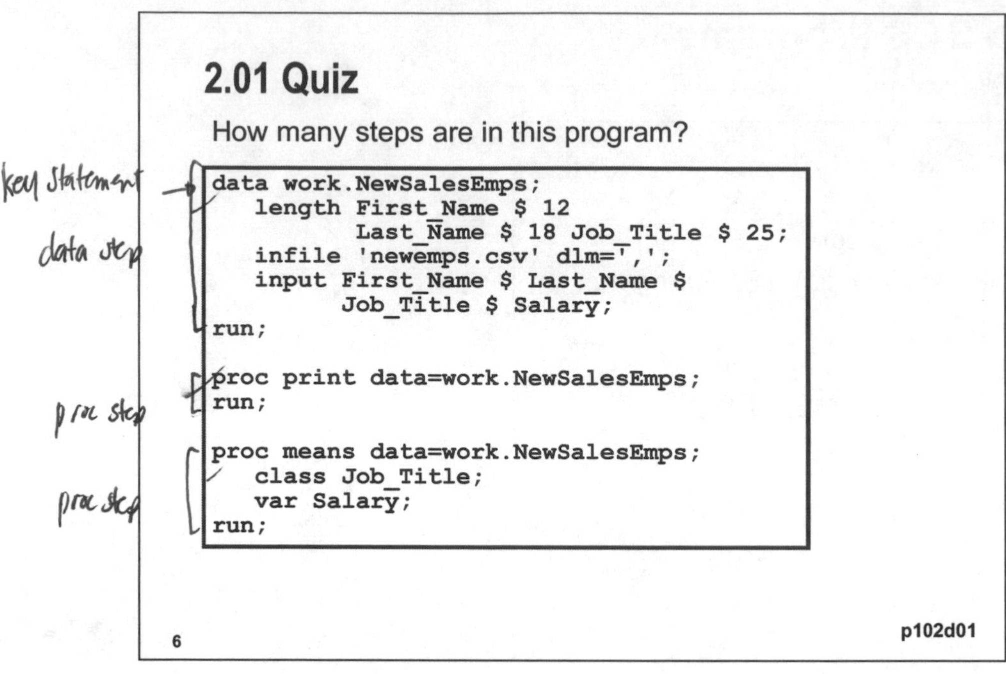

SAS Program Example

This DATA step creates a temporary SAS data set named **`Work.NewSalesEmps`** by reading four fields from a raw data file.

```
data work.NewSalesEmps;
   length First_Name $ 12
          Last_Name $ 18 Job_Title $ 25;
   infile 'newemps.csv' dlm=',';
   input First_Name $ Last_Name $
         Job_Title $ Salary;
run;

proc print data=work.NewSalesEmps;
run;

proc means data=work.NewSalesEmps;
   class Job_Title;
   var Salary;
run;
```

8

The raw data filename specified in the INFILE statement needs to be specific to your operating environment.

Examples of raw data filenames:

Windows	`s:\workshop\newemps.csv`
UNIX	`/users/`*`userid`*`/newemps.csv`
z/OS (OS/390)	*`userid`*`.workshop.rawdata(newemps)`

SAS Program Example

This PROC PRINT step creates a listing report of the **Work.NewSalesEmps** data set.

```
data work.NewSalesEmps;
   length First_Name $ 12
          Last_Name $ 18 Job_Title $ 25;
   infile 'newemps.csv' dlm=',';
   input First_Name $ Last_Name $
         Job_Title $ Salary;
run;

proc print data=work.NewSalesEmps;
run;

proc means data=work.NewSalesEmps;
   class Job_Title;
   var Salary;
run;
```

9

SAS Program Example

This PROC MEANS step creates a summary report of the **Work.NewSalesEmps** data set with statistics for the variable **Salary** for each value of **Job_Title**.

```
data work.NewSalesEmps;
   length First_Name $ 12
          Last_Name $ 18 Job_Title $ 25;
   infile 'newemps.csv' dlm=',';
   input First_Name $ Last_Name $
         Job_Title $ Salary;
run;

proc print data=work.NewSalesEmps;
run;

proc means data=work.NewSalesEmps;
   class Job_Title;
   var Salary;
run;
```

10

Step Boundaries

SAS steps begin with either of the following:

- a DATA statement
- a PROC statement

SAS detects the end of a step when it encounters one of the following:

- a RUN statement (for most steps)
- a QUIT statement (for some procedures)
- the beginning of another step (DATA statement or PROC statement)

11

A SAS program executed in batch or noninteractive mode might not require any RUN statements to execute successfully. However, this practice is not recommended.

Step Boundaries

SAS detects the end of the DATA step when it encounters the RUN statement.

```
data work.NewSalesEmps;
   length First_Name $ 12
          Last_Name $ 18 Job_Title $ 25;
   infile 'newemps.csv' dlm=',';
   input First_Name $ Last_Name $
         Job_Title $ Salary;
run;

proc print data=work.NewSalesEmps;

proc means data=work.NewSalesEmps;
   class Job_Title;
   var Salary;
```

SAS detects the end of the PROC PRINT step when it encounters the beginning of the PROC MEANS step.

12

→ SAS runs independently w/ each other

2.02 Quiz

How does SAS detect the end of the PROC MEANS step?

```
data work.NewSalesEmps;
   length First_Name $ 12
          Last_Name $ 18 Job_Title $ 25;
   infile 'newemps.csv' dlm=',';
   input First_Name $ Last_Name $
         Job_Title $ Salary;
run;

proc print data=work.NewSalesEmps;

proc means data=work.NewSalesEmps;
   class Job_Title;
   var Salary;
```

14

Step Boundaries

SAS detects the end of the PROC MEANS step when it encounters the RUN statement.

```
data work.NewSalesEmps;
   length First_Name $ 12
          Last_Name $ 18 Job_Title $ 25;
   infile 'newemps.csv' dlm=',';
   input First_Name $ Last_Name $
         Job_Title $ Salary;
run;

proc print data=work.NewSalesEmps;

proc means data=work.NewSalesEmps;
   class Job_Title;
   var Salary;
run;
```

16

Running a SAS Program

You can invoke SAS in the following ways:

- interactive mode (for example, SAS windowing environment and SAS Enterprise Guide)
- batch mode
- noninteractive mode

17

SAS Windowing Environment

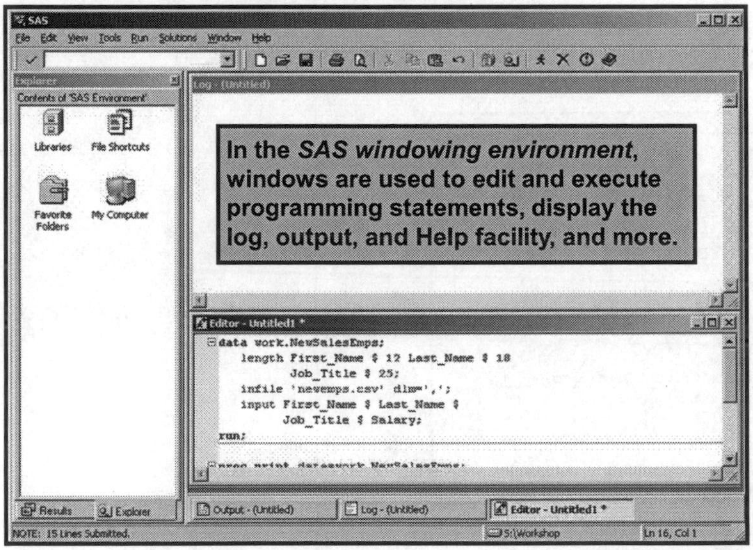
SAS
File Edit View Tools Run Solutions Window Help
Explorer
Contents of 'SAS Environment'
Libraries
File Shortcuts
Favorite Folders
My Computer
Log - (Untitled)
In the *SAS windowing environment*, windows are used to edit and execute programming statements, display the log, output, and Help facility, and more.
Editor - Untitled1 *
data work.NewSalesEmps;
length First_Name $ 12 Last_Name $ 18
Job_Title $ 25;
infile 'newemps.csv' dlm=',';
input First_Name $ Last_Name $
Job_Title $ Salary;
run;
Results
Explorer
Output - (Untitled)
Log - (Untitled)
Editor - Untitled1 *
NOTE: 15 Lines Submitted.
S:\Workshop
Ln 16, Col 1

18

SAS Enterprise Guide

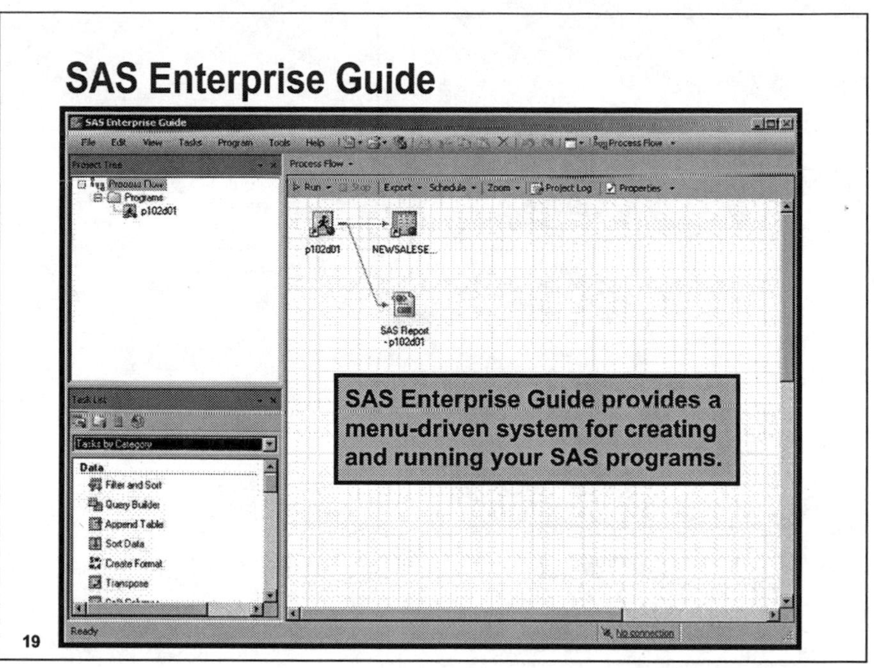

SAS Enterprise Guide provides a menu-driven system for creating and running your SAS programs.

19

Batch Mode

Batch mode is a method of running SAS programs in which you prepare a file that contains SAS statements plus any necessary operating system control statements and submit the file to the operating system.

Partial z/OS (OS/390) Example:

```
//jobname JOB accounting info,name ...
// EXEC SAS
//SYSIN DD *

data work.NewSalesEmps;
   length First_Name $ 12
          Last_Name $ 18 Job_Title $ 25;
   infile '.workshop.rawdata(newemps)' dlm=',';
   input First_Name $ Last_Name $
         Job_Title $ Salary;
run;
```

Appropriate JCL is placed before SAS statements.

20

ex. → EDW datamarts is running in batch mode

Noninteractive Mode

In *noninteractive mode*, SAS program statements are stored in an external file and are executed immediately after you issue a SAS command referencing the file.

Directory-based Example:

SAS *filename*

z/OS (OS/390) Example:

SAS INPUT(*filename***)**

21

The command for invoking SAS at your site might be different from the default shown above. Ask your SAS administrator for the command to invoke SAS at your site.

2.03 Multiple Answer Poll

Which mode(s) will you use for running SAS programs?

a. SAS windowing environment
b. SAS Enterprise Guide
c. batch mode
d. noninteractive mode
e. other
f. unknown

23

2.2 Submitting a SAS Program

Objectives

- Include a SAS program in your session.
- Submit a program and browse the results.
- Navigate the SAS windowing environment.
- Navigate SAS Enterprise Guide.

26

SAS Windowing Environment

The SAS windowing environment is used to write, include, and submit SAS programs and examine SAS results.

```
data work.NewSalesEmps;
   length First_Name $ 12 Last_Name $ 18
          Job_Title $ 25;
   infile 'newemps.csv' dlm=',';
   input First_Name $ Last_Name $
         Job_Title $ Salary;
run;
```

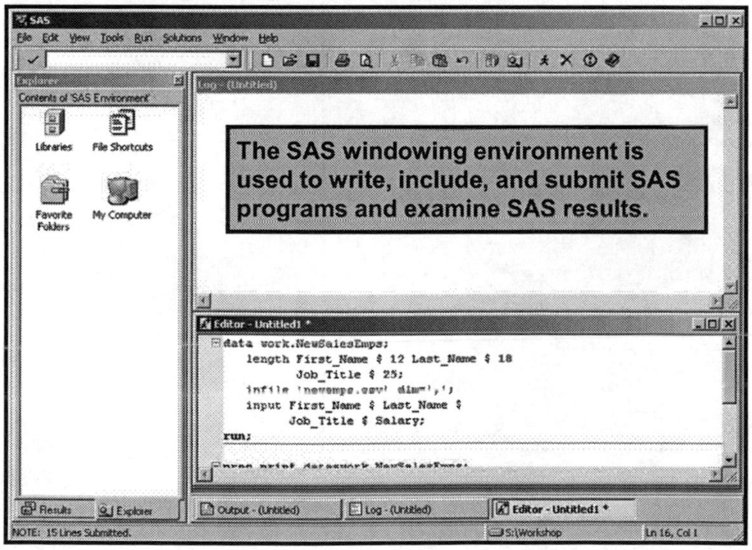

27

Three Primary Windows

In the SAS windowing environment, you submit and view the results of a SAS program using three primary windows.

Window	Description
Editor - Untitled1 Program Editor - (Untitled)	contains the SAS program to submit.
Log - (Untitled)	contains information about the processing of the SAS program, including any warning and error messages.
Output - (Untitled)	contains reports generated by the SAS program.

28

Editor Windows

Enhanced Editor Editor - Untitled1	Program Editor Program Editor - (Untitled)
Only available in the Windows operating environment	Available in all operating environments
Default editor for Windows operating environment	Default editor for all operating environments except Windows
Multiple instances of the editor can be open at one time	Only one instance of the editor can be open at one time
Code does not disappear after it is submitted	Code disappears after it is submitted
Incorporates color-coding as you type	Incorporates color-coding after you press ENTER

29

Editor Windows

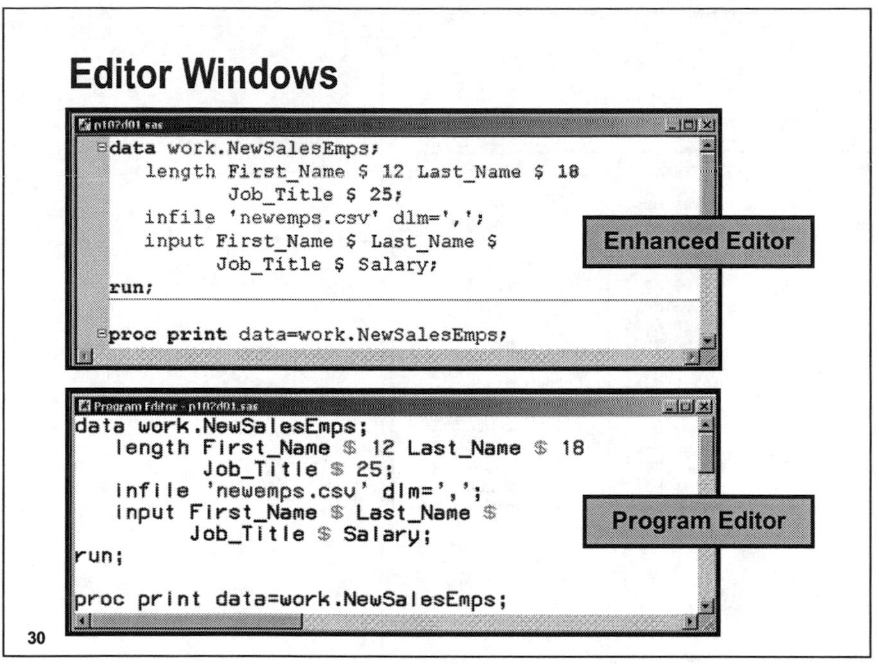

30

Log Window

Partial SAS Log

```
data work.NewSalesEmps;
   length First_Name $ 12 Last_Name $ 18
          Job_Title $ 25;
   infile 'newemps.csv' dlm=',';
   input First_Name $ Last_Name $
         Job_Title $ Salary;
run;

NOTE: The infile 'newemps.csv' is:
      File Name=S:\Workshop\newemps.csv,
      RECFM=V,LRECL=256

NOTE: 71 records were read from the infile 'newemps.csv'.
      The minimum record length was 28.
      The maximum record length was 47.
NOTE: The data set WORK.NEWSALESEMPS has 71 observations and 4 variables.


proc print data=work.NewSalesEmps;
run;

NOTE: There were 71 observations read from the data set WORK.NEWSALESEMPS.
```

31

Output Window

Partial PROC PRINT Output

Obs	First_Name	Last_Name	Job_Title	Salary
1	Satyakam	Denny	Sales Rep. II	26780
2	Monica	Kletschkus	Sales Rep. IV	30890
3	Kevin	Lyon	Sales Rep. I	26955
4	Petrea	Soltau	Sales Rep. II	27440
5	Marina	Iyengar	Sales Rep. III	29715
6	Shani	Duckett	Sales Rep. I	25795
7	Fang	Wilson	Sales Rep. II	26810
8	Michael	Minas	Sales Rep. I	26970
9	Amanda	Liebman	Sales Rep. II	27465
10	Vincent	Eastley	Sales Rep. III	29695
11	Viney	Barbis	Sales Rep. III	30265
12	Skev	Rusli	Sales Rep. II	26580
13	Narelle	James	Sales Rep. III	29990
14	Gerry	Snellings	Sales Rep. I	26445
15	Leonid	Karavdic	Sales Rep. II	27860

32

Output Window

PROC MEANS Output

The MEANS Procedure

Analysis Variable : Salary

Job_Title	N Obs	N	Mean	Std Dev	Minimum	Maximum
Sales Rep. I	21	21	26418.81	713.1898498	25275.00	27475.00
Sales Rep. II	9	9	26902.22	592.9487283	26080.00	27860.00
Sales Rep. III	11	11	29345.91	989.4311956	28025.00	30785.00
Sales Rep. IV	6	6	31215.00	545.4997709	30305.00	31865.00
Temp. Sales Rep.	24	24	26265.83	732.6480659	25020.00	27480.00

33

2.04 Multiple Answer Poll

Which operating environment(s) will you use with SAS?

a. Windows
b. UNIX
c. z/OS (OS/390)
d. other
e. unknown

35

Submitting a SAS Program with SAS Windowing Environment – Windows

p102d01

- Start a SAS session.
- Include and submit a SAS program.
- Examine the results.
- Use the Help facility.

Starting a SAS Session

1. Double-click the **SAS** icon to start your SAS session.

   The method that you use to invoke SAS varies by your operating environment and any customizations in effect at your site.

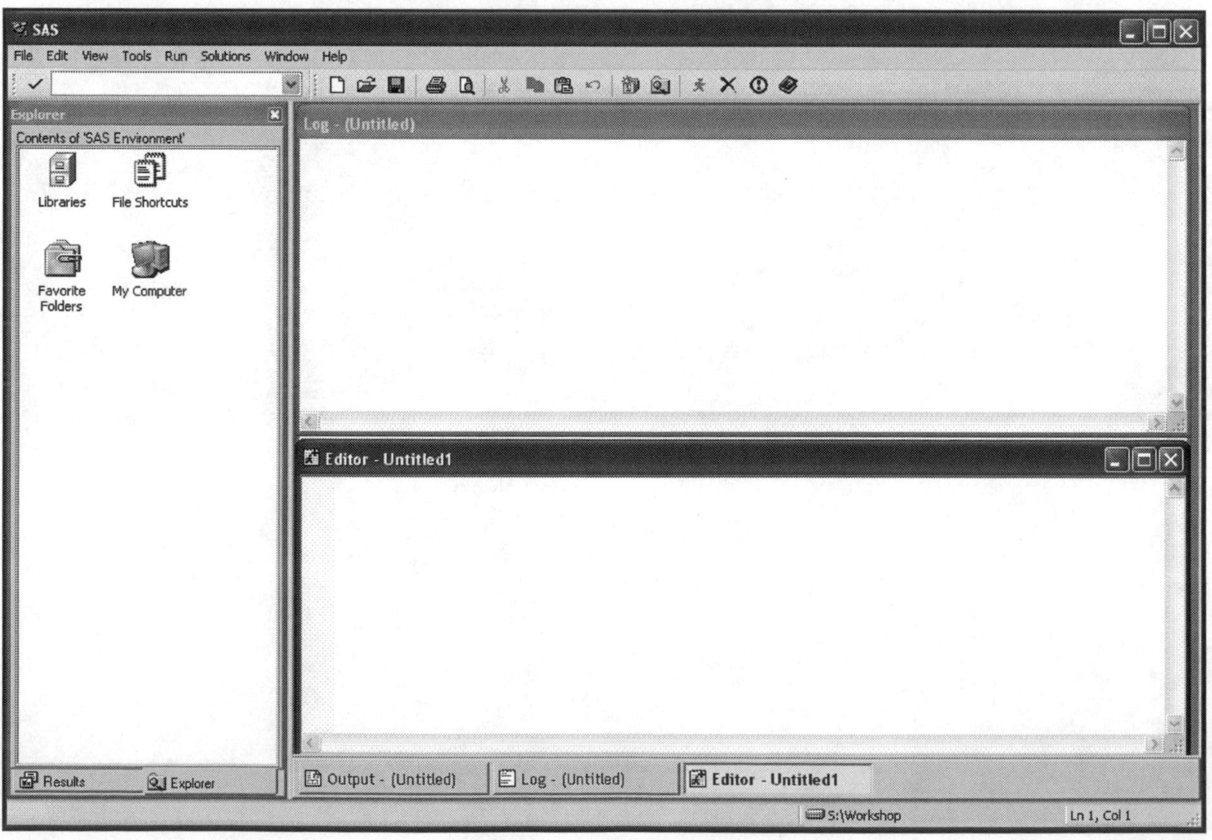

Including and Submitting a SAS Program

1. To open a SAS program into your SAS session, select **File** ⇨ **Open Program** or click [icon] and then select the file that you want to include. To open a program, your Enhanced Editor must be active.

   You can also issue the INCLUDE command to open (include) a program into your SAS session.

   a. With the Enhanced Editor active, on the command bar type `include` and the name of the file containing the program.

   b. Press ENTER.

   The program is included in the Enhanced Editor.

   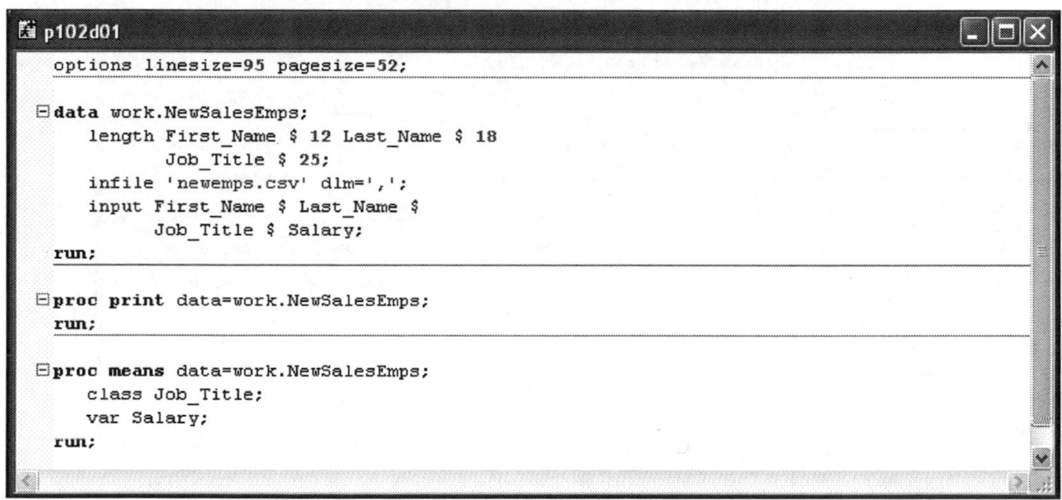

   You can use the Enhanced Editor to do the following:

   - access and edit existing SAS programs
   - write new SAS programs
   - submit SAS programs
   - save SAS programs to a file

   In the Enhanced Editor, the syntax in your program is color-coded to show these items:

   - step boundaries
   - keywords
   - variable and data set names

2. To submit the program for execution, issue the SUBMIT command, click [icon], or select **Run** ⇨ **Submit**. The output from the program is displayed in the Output window.

→ UPPERCASE, LOWERCASE program is ok

→ DATASTEP, PROC STEP _ 2 components of SAS program

Examining the Results

The Output window

- is one of the primary windows and is open by default
- becomes the active window each time that it receives output
- automatically accumulates output in the order in which it is generated.

You can issue the CLEAR command or select **Edit** ⇨ **Clear All** to clear the contents of the window, or you can click (the NEW icon).

To scroll horizontally in the Output window, use the horizontal scroll bar or issue the RIGHT and LEFT commands.

In the Windows environment, the Output window displays the last page of output generated by the submitted program.

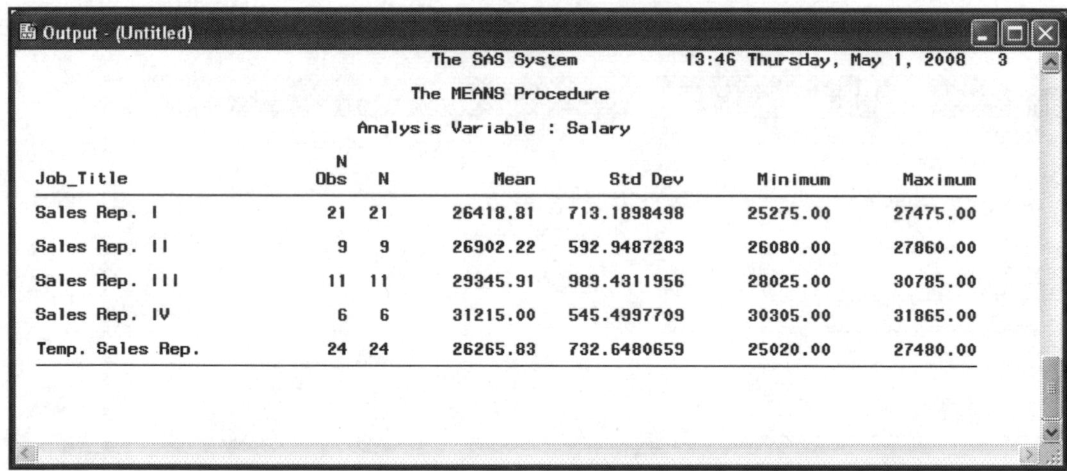

Output - (Untitled)

The SAS System 13:46 Thursday, May 1, 2008 3

The MEANS Procedure

Analysis Variable : Salary

Job_Title	N Obs	N	Mean	Std Dev	Minimum	Maximum
Sales Rep. I	21	21	26418.81	713.1898498	25275.00	27475.00
Sales Rep. II	9	9	26902.22	592.9487283	26080.00	27860.00
Sales Rep. III	11	11	29345.91	989.4311956	28025.00	30785.00
Sales Rep. IV	6	6	31215.00	545.4997709	30305.00	31865.00
Temp. Sales Rep.	24	24	26265.83	732.6480659	25020.00	27480.00

To scroll vertically in the Output window, use the vertical scroll bar, issue the FORWARD and BACKWARD commands, or use the PAGE UP or PAGE DOWN keys on the keyboard.

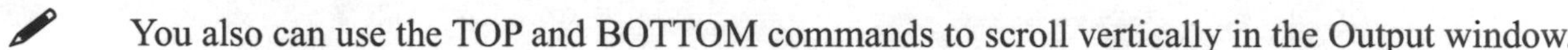

You also can use the TOP and BOTTOM commands to scroll vertically in the Output window.

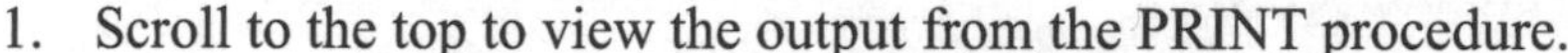

1. Scroll to the top to view the output from the PRINT procedure.

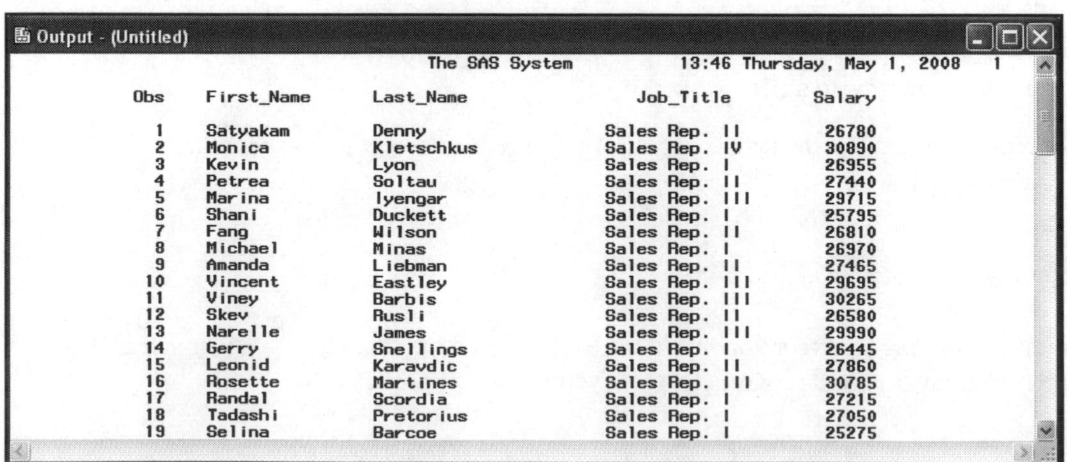

Output - (Untitled)

The SAS System 13:46 Thursday, May 1, 2008 1

Obs	First_Name	Last_Name	Job_Title	Salary
1	Satyakam	Denny	Sales Rep. II	26780
2	Monica	Kletschkus	Sales Rep. IV	30890
3	Kevin	Lyon	Sales Rep. I	26955
4	Petrea	Soltau	Sales Rep. II	27440
5	Marina	Iyengar	Sales Rep. III	29715
6	Shani	Duckett	Sales Rep. I	25795
7	Fang	Wilson	Sales Rep. II	26810
8	Michael	Minas	Sales Rep. I	26970
9	Amanda	Liebman	Sales Rep. II	27465
10	Vincent	Eastley	Sales Rep. III	29695
11	Viney	Barbis	Sales Rep. III	30265
12	Skev	Rusli	Sales Rep. II	26580
13	Narelle	James	Sales Rep. III	29990
14	Gerry	Snellings	Sales Rep. I	26445
15	Leonid	Karavdic	Sales Rep. II	27860
16	Rosette	Martines	Sales Rep. III	30785
17	Randal	Scordia	Sales Rep. I	27215
18	Tadashi	Pretorius	Sales Rep. I	27050
19	Selina	Barcoe	Sales Rep. I	25275

2. To open the Log window and browse the messages that the program generated, issue the LOG command, select **Window** ⇨ **Log**, or click on the log.

   The Log window

   - is one of the primary windows and is open by default
   - acts as an audit trail of your SAS session; messages are written to the log in the order in which they are generated by the program.

3. To clear the contents of the window, issue the CLEAR command, select **Edit** ⇨ **Clear All**, or you can click [NEW icon] (the NEW icon).

```
Log - (Untitled)
    options linesize=95 pagesize=52;

    data work.NewSalesEmps;
       length First_Name $ 12 Last_Name $ 18
              Job_Title $ 25;
       infile 'newemps.csv' dlm=',';
       input First_Name $ Last_Name $
             Job_Title $ Salary;
    run;

NOTE: The infile 'newemps.csv' is:
      Filename=S:\Workshop\newemps.csv,
      RECFM=V,LRECL=256,File Size (bytes)=2604,
      Last Modified=02Apr2008:09:10:12,
      Create Time=01May2008:13:52:50

NOTE: 71 records were read from the infile 'newemps.csv'.
      The minimum record length was 28.
      The maximum record length was 47.
NOTE: The data set WORK.NEWSALESEMPS has 71 observations and 4 variables.
NOTE: DATA statement used (Total process time):
      real time           0.00 seconds
      cpu time            0.00 seconds



    proc print data=work.NewSalesEmps;
    run;

NOTE: There were 71 observations read from the data set WORK.NEWSALESEMPS.
NOTE: PROCEDURE PRINT used (Total process time):
      real time           0.00 seconds
      cpu time            0.00 seconds



    proc means data=work.NewSalesEmps;
       class Job_Title;
       var Salary;
    run;

NOTE: There were 71 observations read from the data set WORK.NEWSALESEMPS.
NOTE: PROCEDURE MEANS used (Total process time):
      real time           0.01 seconds
      cpu time            0.01 seconds
```

The Log window contains the programming statements that are submitted, as well as notes about the following:

- any files that were read
- the records that were read
- the program execution and results

In this example, the Log window contains no warning or error messages. If the program contains errors, relevant warning and error messages are also written to the SAS log.

Using the Help Facility

1. To open the Help facility, select **Help** ⇨ **SAS Help and Documentation** or click .

2. Select the **Contents** tab.

3. From the Contents tab, select **SAS Products** ⇨ **Base SAS**.

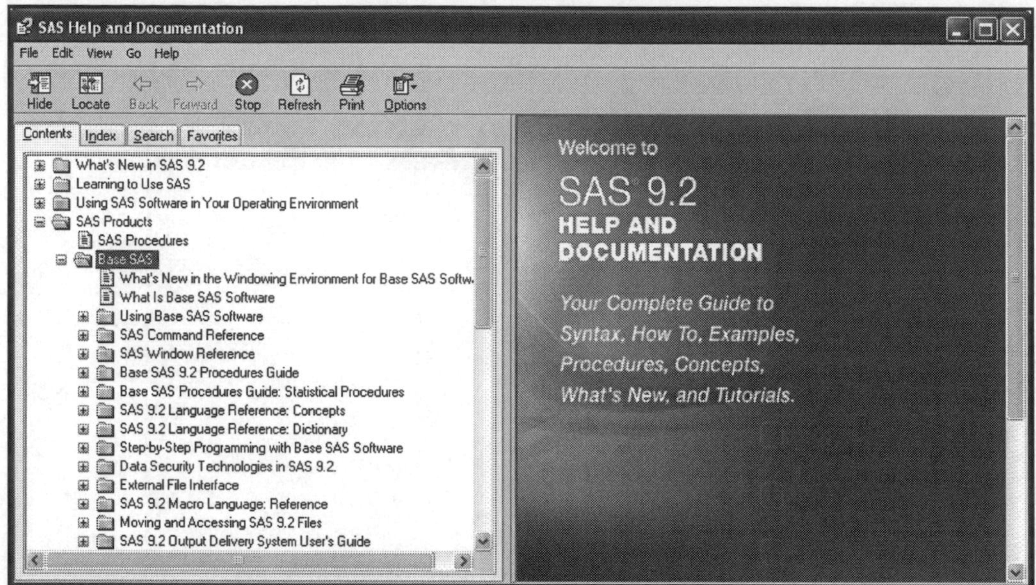

The primary Base SAS syntax books are the *Base SAS 9.2 Procedures Guide* and *SAS 9.2 Language Reference: Dictionary*. The *SAS 9.2 Language Reference: Concepts* and *Step-by-Step Programming with Base SAS Software* are recommended to learn SAS concepts.

4. For example, select **Base SAS 9.2 Procedures Guide** ⇨ **Procedures** ⇨ **The PRINT Procedure** to find the documentation for the PRINT procedure.

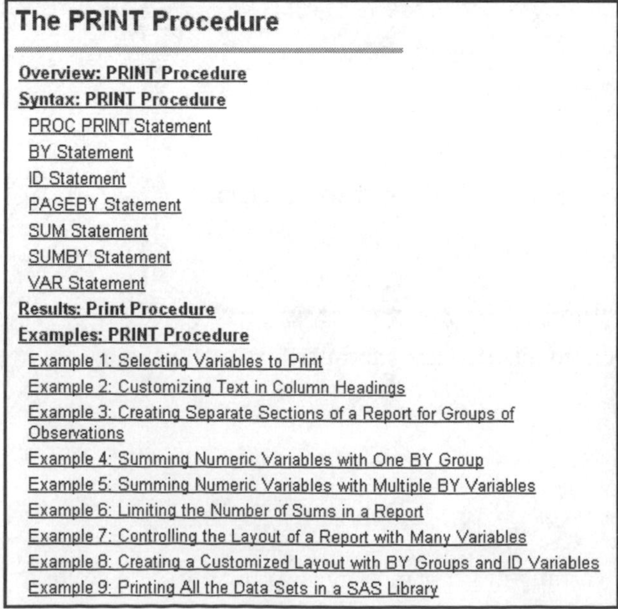

The PRINT Procedure

Overview: PRINT Procedure
Syntax: PRINT Procedure
PROC PRINT Statement
BY Statement
ID Statement
PAGEBY Statement
SUM Statement
SUMBY Statement
VAR Statement
Results: Print Procedure
Examples: PRINT Procedure
Example 1: Selecting Variables to Print
Example 2: Customizing Text in Column Headings
Example 3: Creating Separate Sections of a Report for Groups of Observations
Example 4: Summing Numeric Variables with One BY Group
Example 5: Summing Numeric Variables with Multiple BY Variables
Example 6: Limiting the Number of Sums in a Report
Example 7: Controlling the Layout of a Report with Many Variables
Example 8: Creating a Customized Layout with BY Groups and ID Variables
Example 9: Printing All the Data Sets in a SAS Library

Submitting a SAS Program with SAS Windowing Environment – UNIX

p102d01

- Start a SAS session.
- Include and submit a SAS program.
- Examine the results.
- Use the Help facility.

Starting a SAS Session

1. In your UNIX session, type the appropriate command to start a SAS session.

   The method that you use to invoke SAS varies by your operating environment and any customizations in effect at your site.

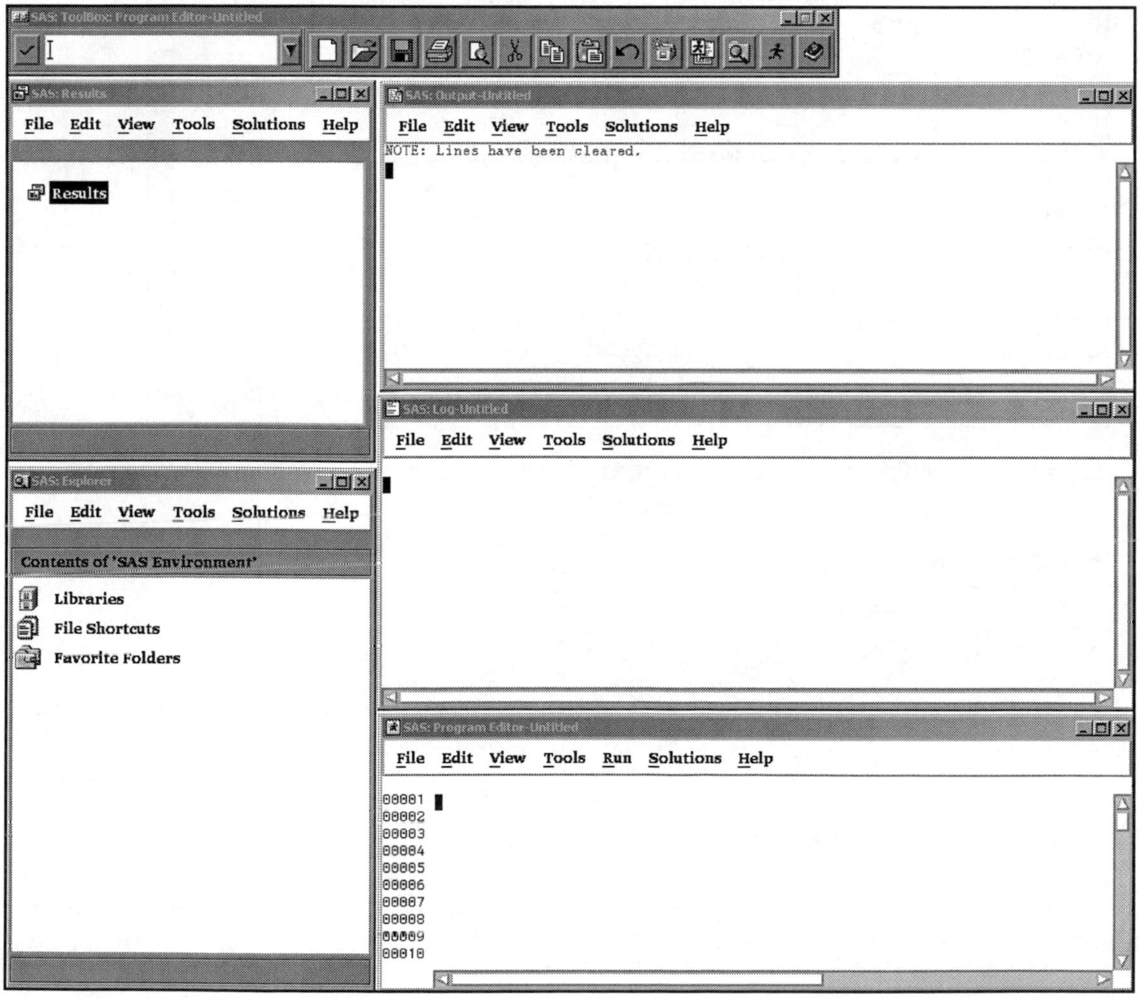

Including and Submitting a SAS Program

1. To open a SAS program into your SAS session, select **File** ⇨ **Open** or click and then select the file that you want to include. To open a program, your Program Editor must be active.

   You can also issue the INCLUDE command to open (include) a SAS program into your SAS session.

   a. With the Program Editor active, on the command bar type **`include`** and the name of the file containing the program.

   b. Press ENTER.

      The program is included in the Program Editor window.

      SAS: Program Editor-p102d01.sas

      File Edit View Tools Run Solutions Help

```
options linesize=95 pagesize=52;

data work.NewSalesEmps;
   length First_Name $ 12 Last_Name $ 18
          Job_Title $ 25;
   infile 'newemps.csv' dlm=',';
   input First_Name $ Last_Name $
         Job_Title $ Salary;
run;

proc print data=work.NewSalesEmps;
run;

proc means data=work.NewSalesEmps;
   class Job_Title;
   var Salary;
run;
```

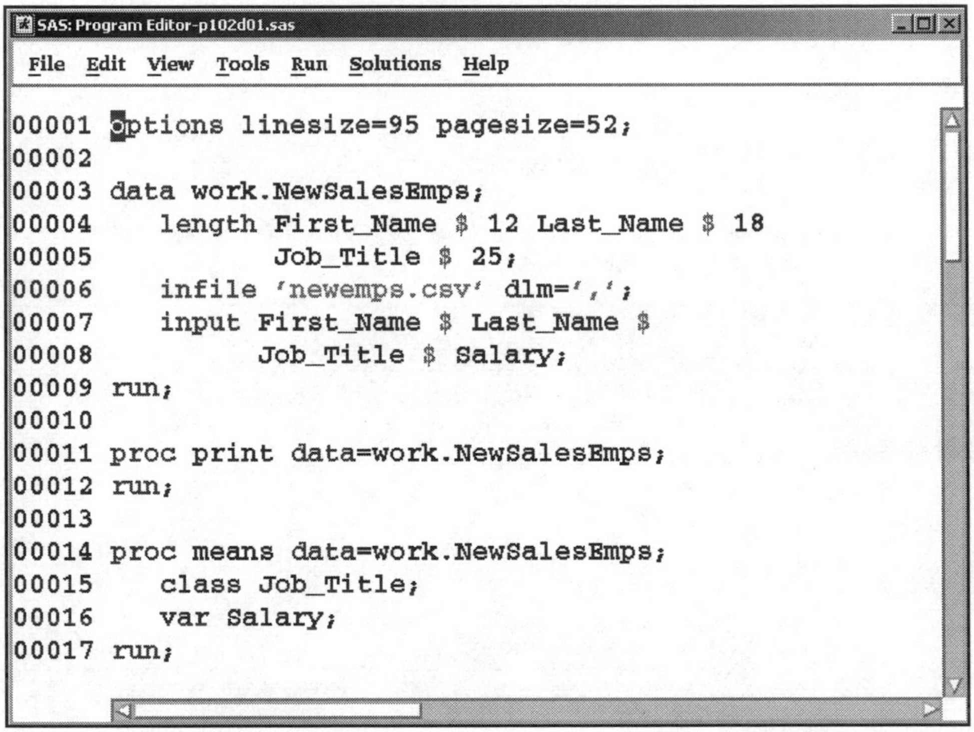

      You can use the Program Editor window to do the following:

      - access and edit existing SAS programs
      - write new SAS programs
      - submit SAS programs
      - save SAS programs to a file

      Within the Program Editor, the syntax in your program is color-coded to show these items:

      - step boundaries
      - keywords
      - variable and data set names

2. To submit the program for execution, issue the SUBMIT command, click , or select **Run** ⇨ **Submit**. The output from the program is displayed in the Output window.

Examining the Results

The Output window

- is one of the primary windows and is open by default
- becomes the active window each time that it receives output
- automatically accumulates output in the order in which it is generated.

To clear the contents of the window, issue the CLEAR command, select **Edit** ⇨ **Clear All**, or click .

To scroll horizontally in the Output window, use the horizontal scroll bar or issue the RIGHT and LEFT commands.

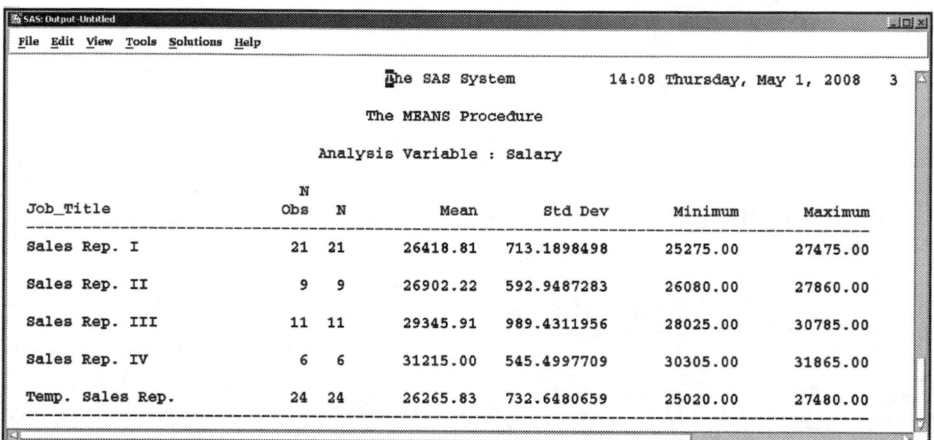

SAS: Output-Untitled

File Edit View Tools Solutions Help

The SAS System 14:08 Thursday, May 1, 2008 3

The MEANS Procedure

Analysis Variable : Salary

Job_Title	N Obs	N	Mean	Std Dev	Minimum	Maximum
Sales Rep. I	21	21	26418.81	713.1898498	25275.00	27475.00
Sales Rep. II	9	9	26902.22	592.9487283	26080.00	27860.00
Sales Rep. III	11	11	29345.91	989.4311956	28025.00	30785.00
Sales Rep. IV	6	6	31215.00	545.4997709	30305.00	31865.00
Temp. Sales Rep.	24	24	26265.83	732.6480659	25020.00	27480.00

To scroll vertically within the Output window, use the vertical scroll bar or issue the FORWARD and BACKWARD commands.

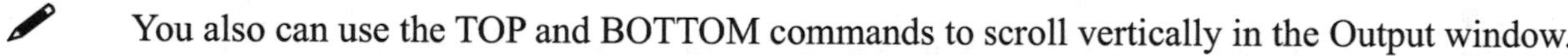

You also can use the TOP and BOTTOM commands to scroll vertically in the Output window.

1. Scroll to the top to view the output from the PRINT procedure.

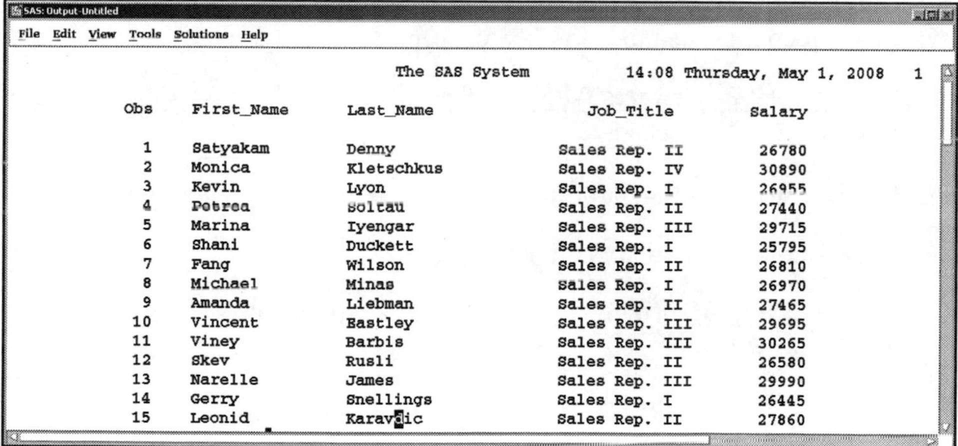

SAS: Output-Untitled

File Edit View Tools Solutions Help

The SAS System 14:08 Thursday, May 1, 2008 1

Obs	First_Name	Last_Name	Job_Title	Salary
1	Satyakam	Denny	Sales Rep. II	26780
2	Monica	Kletschkus	Sales Rep. IV	30890
3	Kevin	Lyon	Sales Rep. I	26955
4	Petrea	Soltau	Sales Rep. II	27440
5	Marina	Iyengar	Sales Rep. III	29715
6	Shani	Duckett	Sales Rep. I	25795
7	Fang	Wilson	Sales Rep. II	26810
8	Michael	Minas	Sales Rep. I	26970
9	Amanda	Liebman	Sales Rep. II	27465
10	Vincent	Eastley	Sales Rep. III	29695
11	Viney	Barbis	Sales Rep. III	30265
12	Skev	Rusli	Sales Rep. II	26580
13	Narelle	James	Sales Rep. III	29990
14	Gerry	Snellings	Sales Rep. I	26445
15	Leonid	Karavdic	Sales Rep. II	27860

2. To open the Log window and browse the messages that the program generated, issue the LOG command or select **View** ⇨ **Log**.

   The Log window

   - is one of the primary windows and is open by default
   - acts as a record of your SAS session; messages are written to the log in the order in which they are generated by the program.

3. To clear the contents of the window, issue the CLEAR command, select **Edit** ⇨ **Clear All**, or click .

   The Log window contains the programming statements that were most recently submitted, as well as notes about the following:

   - any files that were read
   - the records that were read
   - the program execution and results

   In this example, the Log window contains no warning or error messages. If your program contains errors, relevant warning and error messages are also written to the SAS log.

4. Issue the END command or select **View** ⇨ **Program Editor** to return to the Program Editor window.

Using the Help Facility

1. To open the Help facility, select **Help** ⇨ **SAS Help and Documentation** or click .

2. Select the **Contents** tab.

3. From the Contents tab, select **SAS Products** ⇨ **Base SAS**.

   The primary Base SAS syntax books are the *Base SAS 9.2 Procedures Guide* and *SAS 9.2 Language Reference: Dictionary*. The *SAS 9.2 Language Reference: Concepts* and *Step-by-Step Programming with Base SAS Software* are recommended to learn SAS concepts.

4. For example, select **Base SAS 9.2 Procedures Guide** ⇨ **Procedures** ⇨ **The PRINT Procedure** to find the documentation for the PRINT procedure.

   The Help facility can also be accessed from a Web browser at the following link:

   http://support.sas.com/documentation/index.html

   From this Web page, **Base SAS** can be selected. The SAS syntax books are available in HTML or PDF version.

Submitting a SAS Program with SAS Windowing Environment – z/OS (OS/390)

.workshop.sascode(p102d01)

- Start a SAS session.
- Include and submit a SAS program.
- Examine the results.
- Use the Help facility.

Starting a SAS Session

1. Type the appropriate command to start your SAS session.

 The method that you use to invoke SAS varies by your operating environment and any customizations in effect at your site.

Including and Submitting a SAS Program

1. To include (copy) a SAS program into your SAS session, issue the INCLUDE command.

   a. Type **`include`** and the name of the file that contains your program on the command line of the Program Editor.

   b. Press ENTER.

```
+Program Editor-------------------------------------------------------------+
 Command ===> inc '.workshop.sascode(p102d01)'
```

The program is included in the Program Editor.

```
+Program Editor-------------------------------------------------------------+
 Command ===>

options linesize=95 pagesize=52;

data work.NewSalesEmps;
   length First_Name $ 12 Last_Name $ 18
          Job_Title $ 25;
   infile '.workshop.rawdata(newemps)' dlm=',';
   input First_Name $ Last_Name $
         Job_Title $ Salary;
run;

proc print data=work.NewSalesEmps;
run;

proc means data=work.NewSalesEmps;
   class Job_Title;
   var Salary;
run;
```

You can use the Program Editor to do the following:

- access and edit existing SAS programs
- write new SAS programs
- submit SAS programs
- save programming statements in a file

The program contains three steps: a DATA step and two PROC steps.

Issue the SUBMIT command to execute your program.

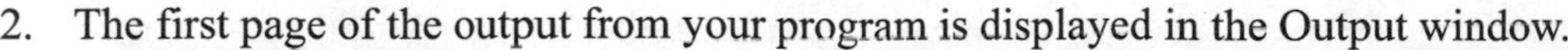

2. The first page of the output from your program is displayed in the Output window.

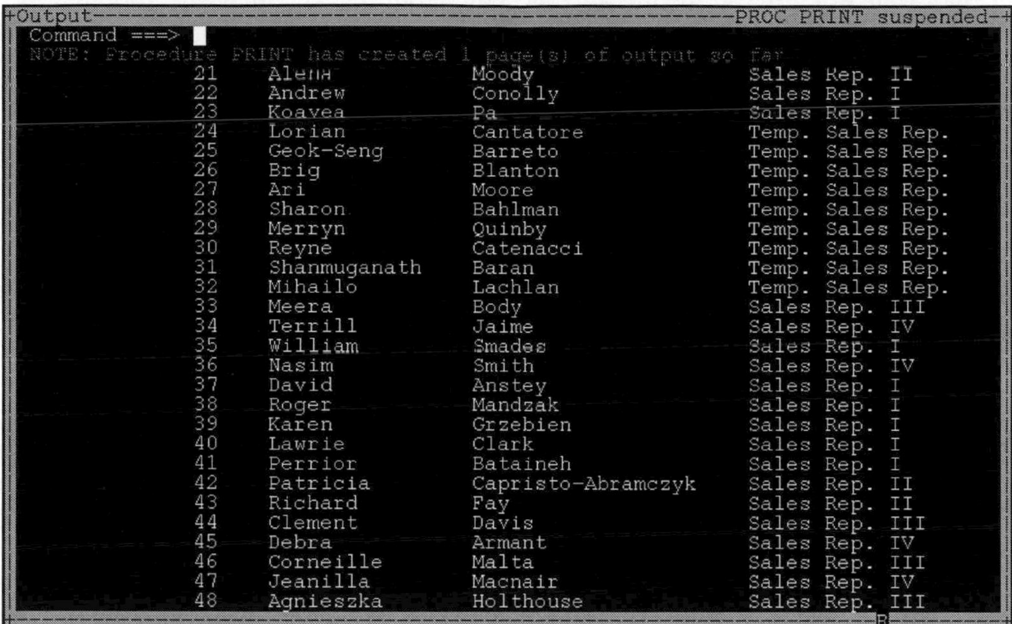

Examining the Results

The Output window

- is one of the primary windows and is open by default
- becomes the active window each time that it receives output
- automatically accumulates output in the order in which it is generated.

You can issue the CLEAR command or select **Edit** ⇨ **Clear All** to clear the contents of the window.

To scroll horizontally in the Output window, issue the RIGHT and LEFT commands.

To scroll vertically in the Output window, issue the FORWARD and BACKWARD commands.

You also can use the TOP and BOTTOM commands to scroll vertically within the Output window.

1. Issue the END command. If the PRINT procedure produces more than one page of output, you are taken to the last page of output. If the PRINT procedure produces only one page of output, the END command enables the MEANS procedure to execute and produce its output.

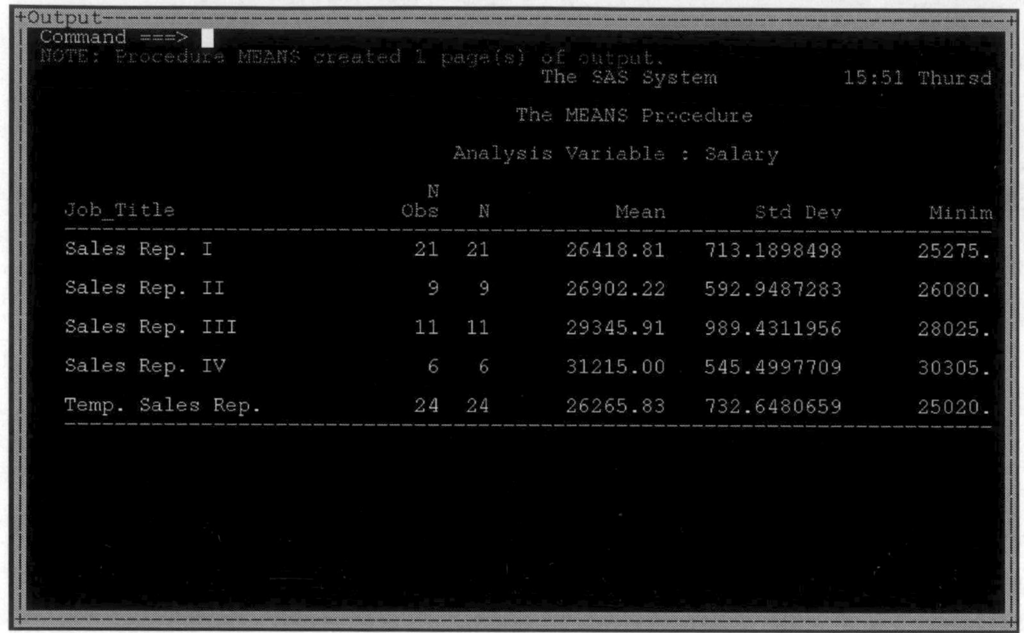

Output
Command ===>
NOTE: Procedure MEANS created 1 page(s) of output.

The SAS System 15:51 Thursd

The MEANS Procedure

Analysis Variable : Salary

Job_Title	N Obs	N	Mean	Std Dev	Minim
Sales Rep. I	21	21	26418.81	713.1898498	25275.
Sales Rep. II	9	9	26902.22	592.9487283	26080.
Sales Rep. III	11	11	29345.91	989.4311956	28025.
Sales Rep. IV	6	6	31215.00	545.4997709	30305.
Temp. Sales Rep.	24	24	26265.83	732.6480659	25020.

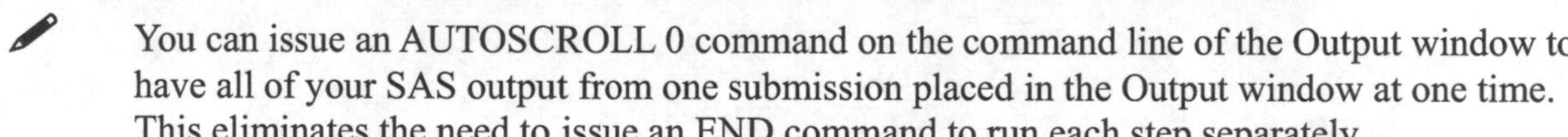

You can issue an AUTOSCROLL 0 command on the command line of the Output window to have all of your SAS output from one submission placed in the Output window at one time. This eliminates the need to issue an END command to run each step separately.

The AUTOSCROLL command is in effect for the duration of your SAS session. If you want this every time that you invoke SAS, you can save this setting by typing **`autoscroll 0; wsave`** on the command line of the Output window.

2. Issue the END command to return to the Program Editor.

   After the program executes, you can view messages in the Log window.

   The Log window

   - is one of the primary windows and is open by default.
   - acts as a record of your SAS session; messages are written to the log in the order in which they are generated by the program.

   You can issue the CLEAR command to clear the contents of the window.

   The Log window contains the programming statements that were recently submitted, as well as notes about the following:

   - any files that were read
   - the records that were read
   - the program execution and results

   In this example, the Log window contains no warning or error messages. If your program contains errors, relevant warning and error messages are also written to the SAS log.

Issue the END command to return to the Program Editor.

Using the Help Facility

1. To open the Help facility, select **Help** ⇨ **SAS Help and Documentation** or click .
2. Select the **Contents** tab.
3. From the Contents tab, select **SAS Products** ⇨ **Base SAS**.

   The primary Base SAS syntax books are the *Base SAS 9.2 Procedures Guide* and *SAS 9.2 Language Reference: Dictionary*. The *SAS 9.2 Language Reference: Concepts* and *Step-by-Step Programming with Base SAS Software* are recommended to learn SAS concepts.

4. For example, select **Base SAS 9.2 Procedures Guide** ⇨ **Procedures** ⇨ **The PRINT Procedure** to find the documentation for the PRINT procedure.

 The Help facility can also be accessed from a Web browser at the following link:

http://support.sas.com/documentation/index.html

From this Web page, **Base SAS** can be selected. The SAS syntax books are available in HTML or PDF version.

Submitting a SAS Program with SAS Enterprise Guide

p102d01

- Start SAS Enterprise Guide.
- Include and submit a SAS program.
- Examine the results.
- Manage a project (optional).
- Use the Help facility.

Starting SAS Enterprise Guide

1. Double-click the **Enterprise Guide** icon to start your SAS session.

   The method that you use to invoke Enterprise Guide varies by any customizations in effect at your site. This demo is based on Enterprise Guide 4.2.

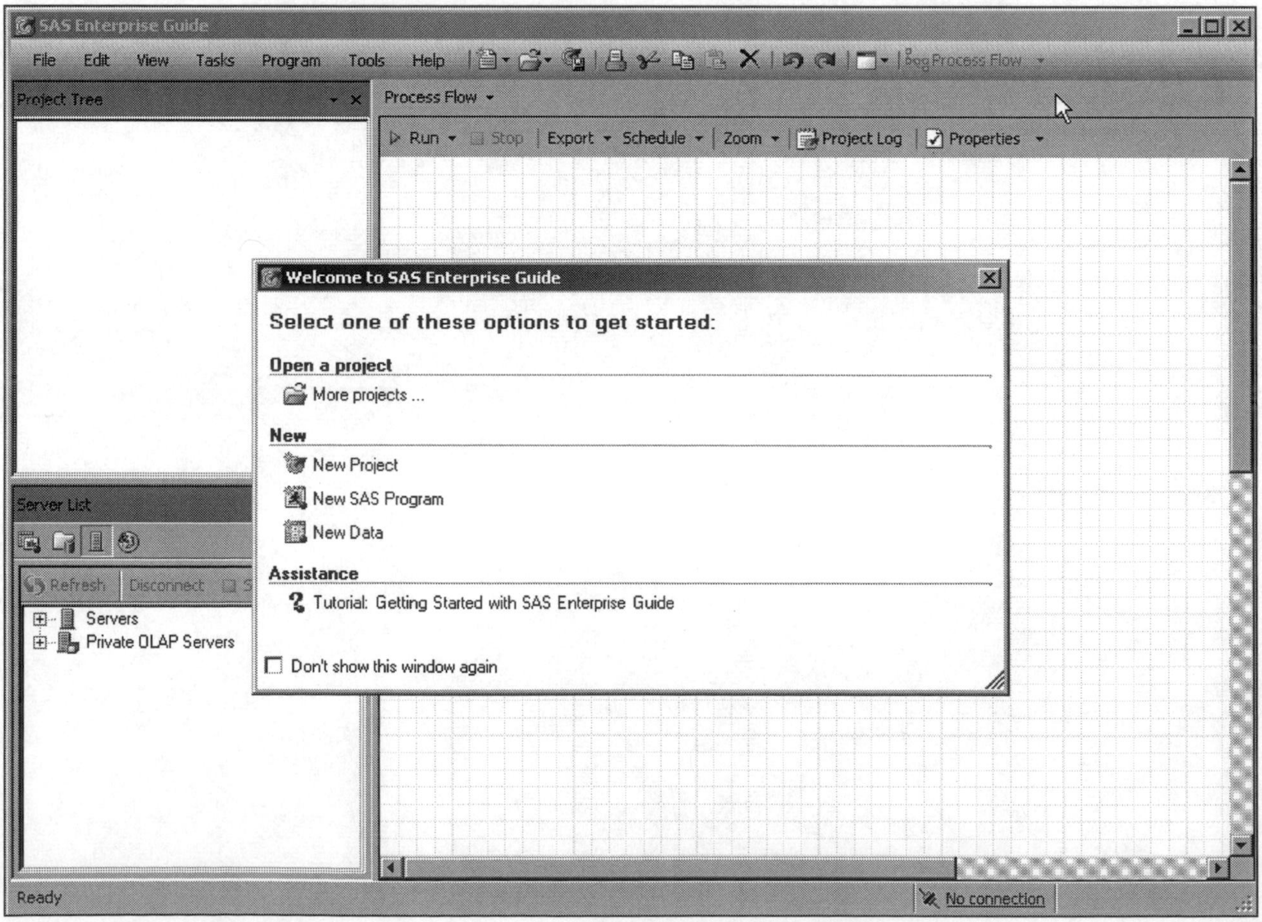

2. Close the Welcome to SAS Enterprise Guide window by selecting the  .

Including and Submitting a SAS Program

1. To open a SAS program into Enterprise Guide, select **File** ⇨ **Open** ⇨ **Program** or select [toolbar button] ⇨ **Program** and then select the file that you want to include.

   The program is included in the Program tab of the workspace area.

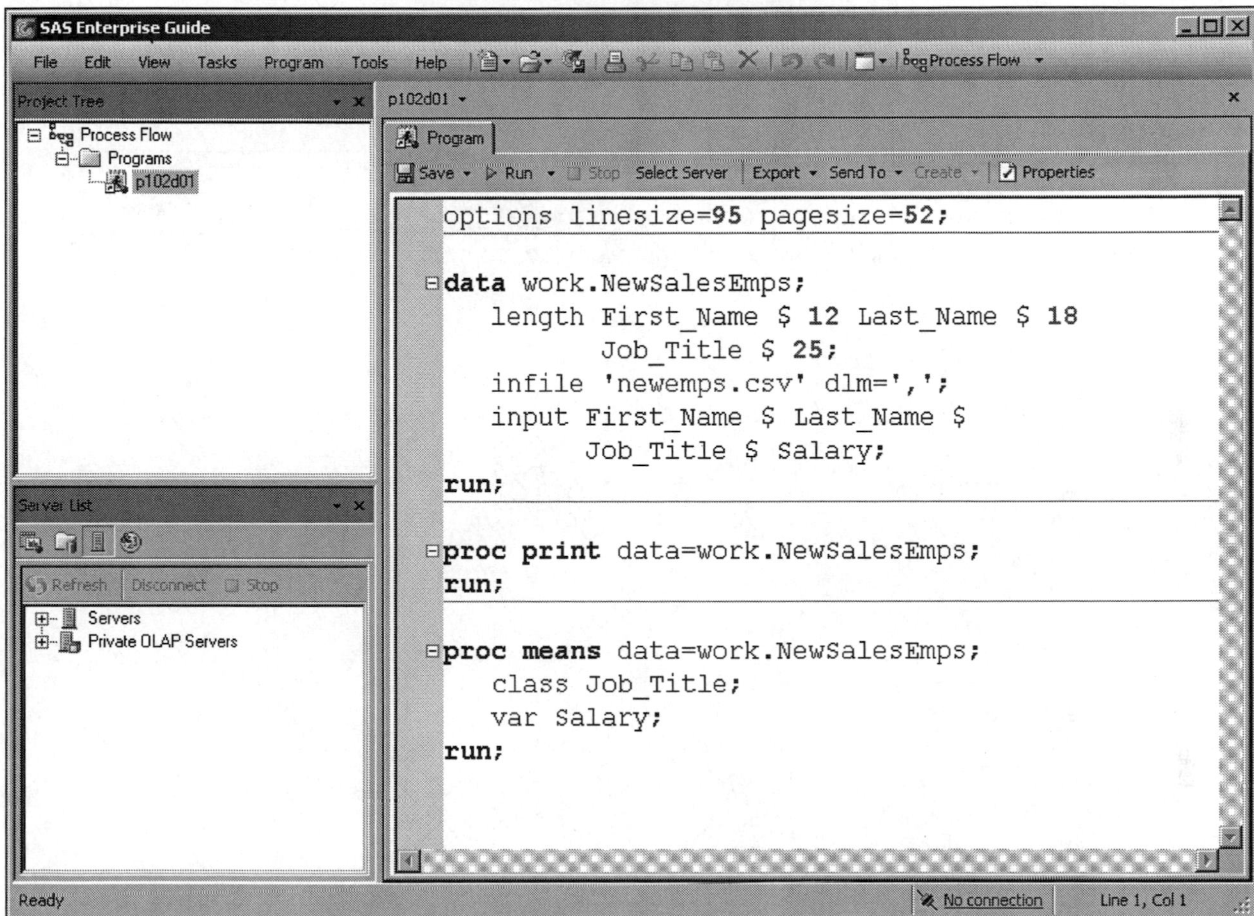

   You can use the Program tab to do the following:

   - access and edit existing SAS programs
   - write new SAS programs
   - submit SAS programs
   - save SAS programs to a file

   In the Program tab, the syntax in your program is color-coded to show these items:

   - step boundaries
   - keywords
   - variable and data set names

3. Modify the INFILE statement in the Program tab to include the path location of the CSV file.

```
data work.NewSalesEmps;
   length First_Name $ 12 Last_Name $ 18
          Job_Title $ 25;
   infile 's:\workshop\newemps.csv' dlm=',';
   input First_Name $ Last_Name $
         Job_Title $ Salary;
run;
```

4. To submit the program for execution, select **Program** ⇨ **Run On Local** or click ▷ Run in the Program tab or select the F8 key. The output from the program is displayed in the Results tab of the workspace area.

Examining the Results

The Results tab

- displays the output of the code that you run in SAS Enterprise Guide
- becomes the active tab each time that it receives output.

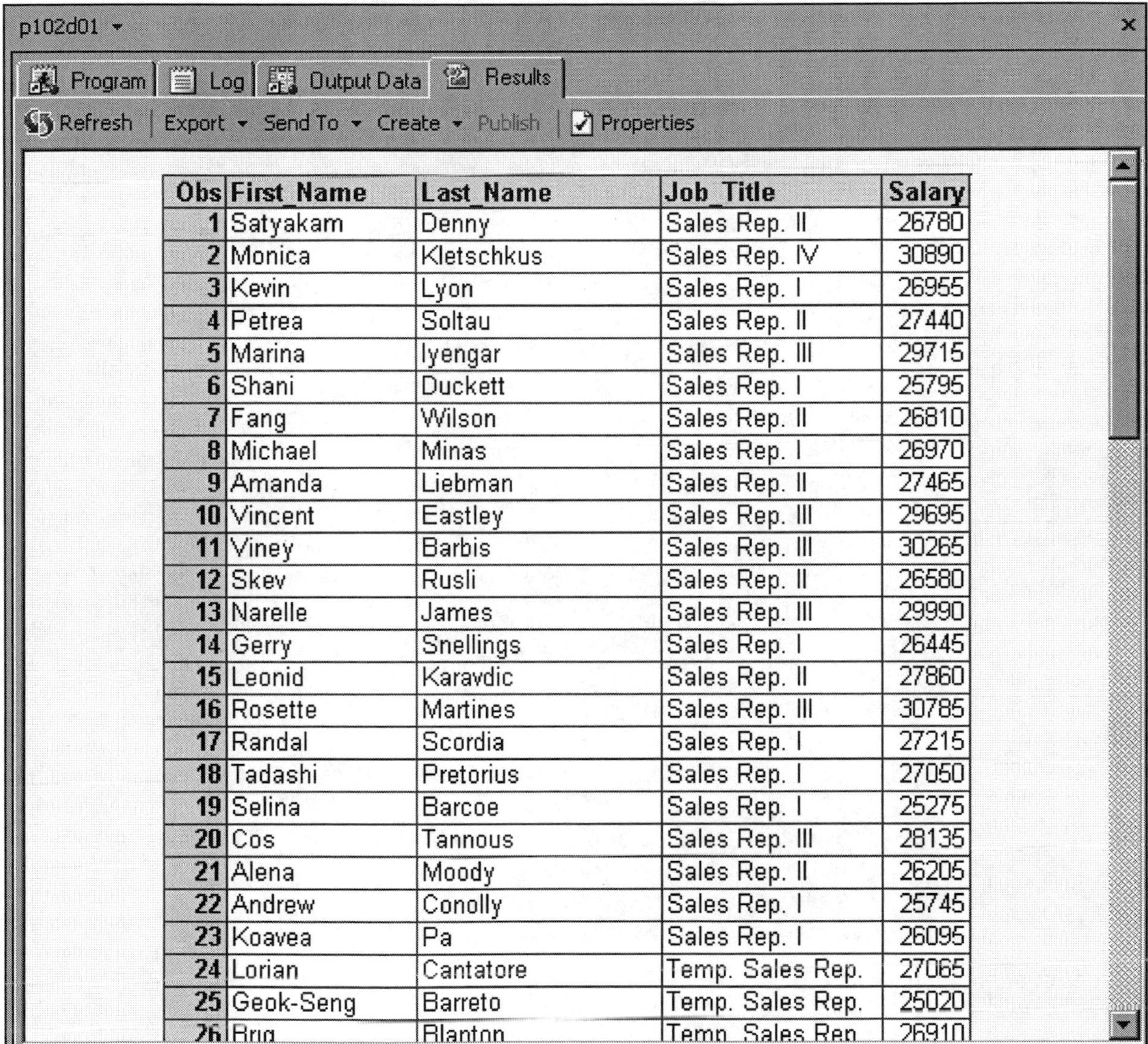

Obs	First_Name	Last_Name	Job_Title	Salary
1	Satyakam	Denny	Sales Rep. II	26780
2	Monica	Kletschkus	Sales Rep. IV	30890
3	Kevin	Lyon	Sales Rep. I	26955
4	Petrea	Soltau	Sales Rep. II	27440
5	Marina	Iyengar	Sales Rep. III	29715
6	Shani	Duckett	Sales Rep. I	25795
7	Fang	Wilson	Sales Rep. II	26810
8	Michael	Minas	Sales Rep. I	26970
9	Amanda	Liebman	Sales Rep. II	27465
10	Vincent	Eastley	Sales Rep. III	29695
11	Viney	Barbis	Sales Rep. III	30265
12	Skev	Rusli	Sales Rep. II	26580
13	Narelle	James	Sales Rep. III	29990
14	Gerry	Snellings	Sales Rep. I	26445
15	Leonid	Karavdic	Sales Rep. II	27860
16	Rosette	Martines	Sales Rep. III	30785
17	Randal	Scordia	Sales Rep. I	27215
18	Tadashi	Pretorius	Sales Rep. I	27050
19	Selina	Barcoe	Sales Rep. I	25275
20	Cos	Tannous	Sales Rep. III	28135
21	Alena	Moody	Sales Rep. II	26205
22	Andrew	Conolly	Sales Rep. I	25745
23	Koavea	Pa	Sales Rep. I	26095
24	Lorian	Cantatore	Temp. Sales Rep.	27065
25	Geok-Seng	Barreto	Temp. Sales Rep.	25020
26	Brig	Blanton	Temp. Sales Rep.	26910

To scroll vertically in the Results tab, use the vertical scroll bar or use the PAGE UP or PAGE DOWN keys on the keyboard.

By default, the result format is set to SAS Report (an XML file specific to SAS) in SAS Enterprise Guide 4.2.

1. To change the result format, select **Tools** ⇨ **Options** ⇨ **Results** ⇨ **Results General**.
2. Select the desired result formats such as HTML and Text Output and select **OK**.

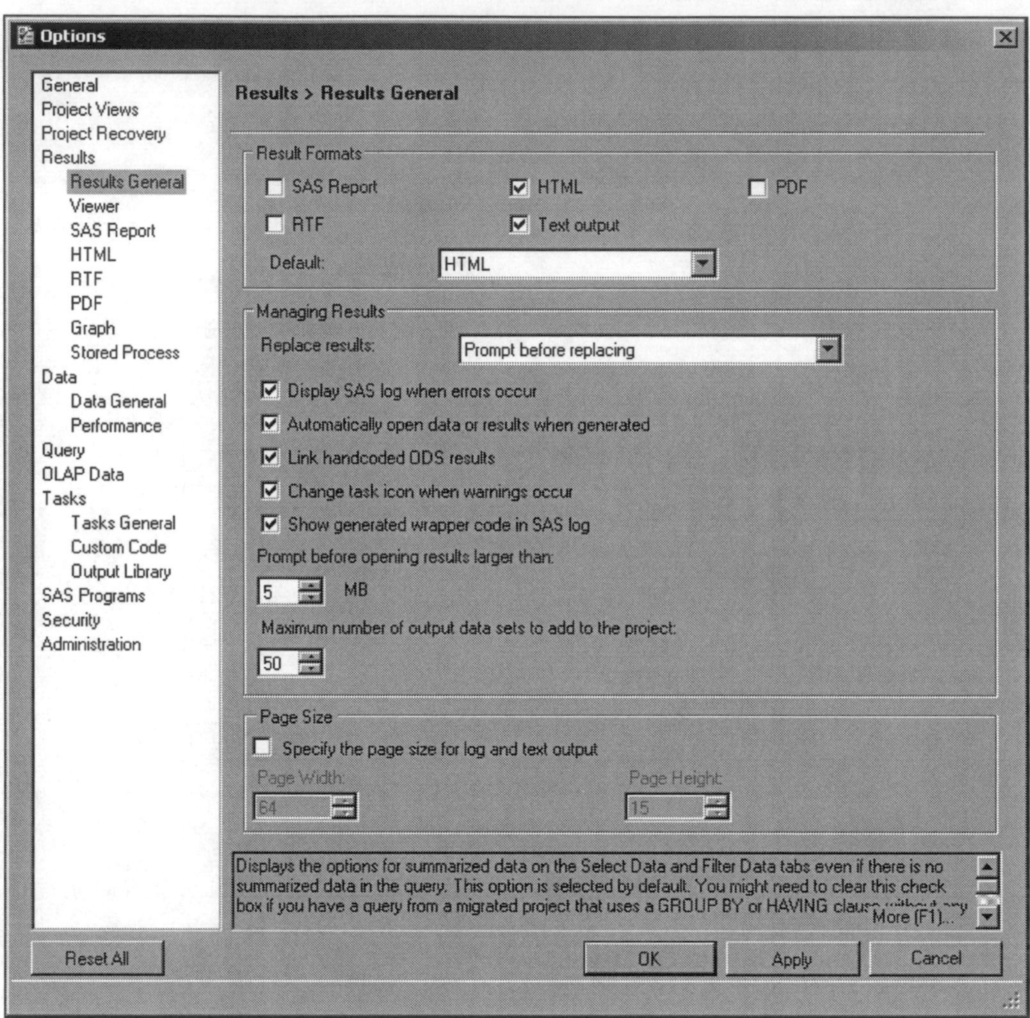

3. Resubmit the program.

4. Select **Yes** to replace the results from the previous run.

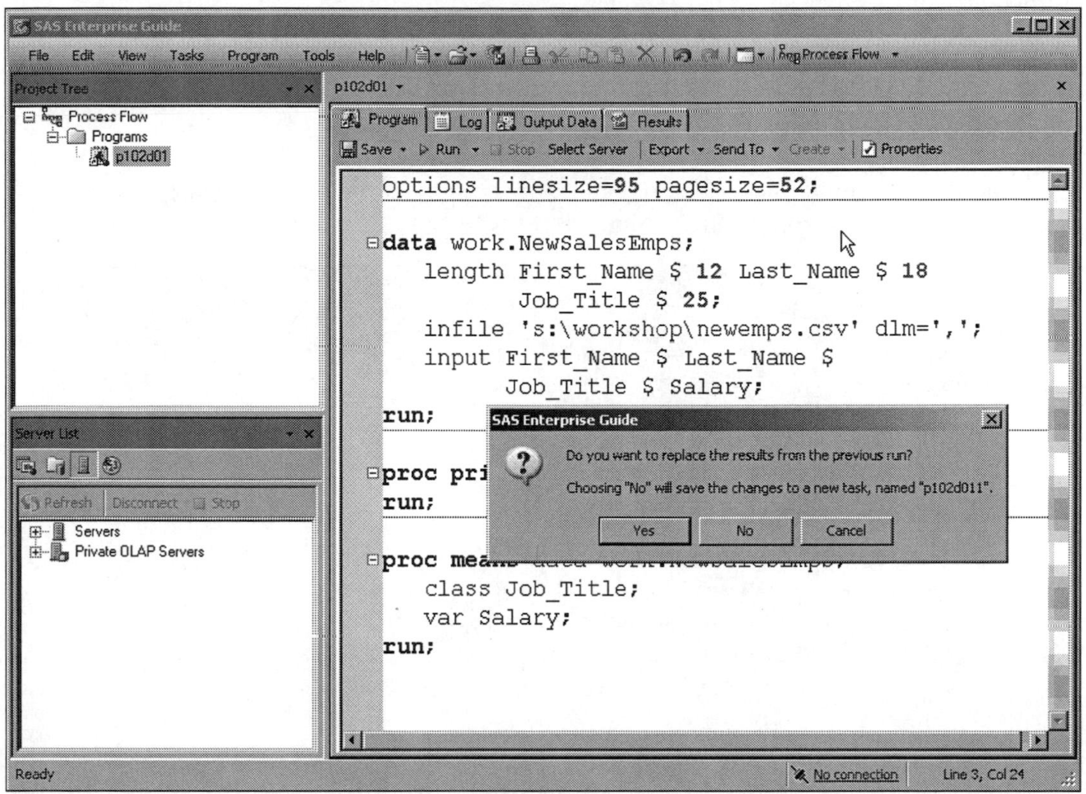

5. View the multiple Results tabs to view the different result formats.

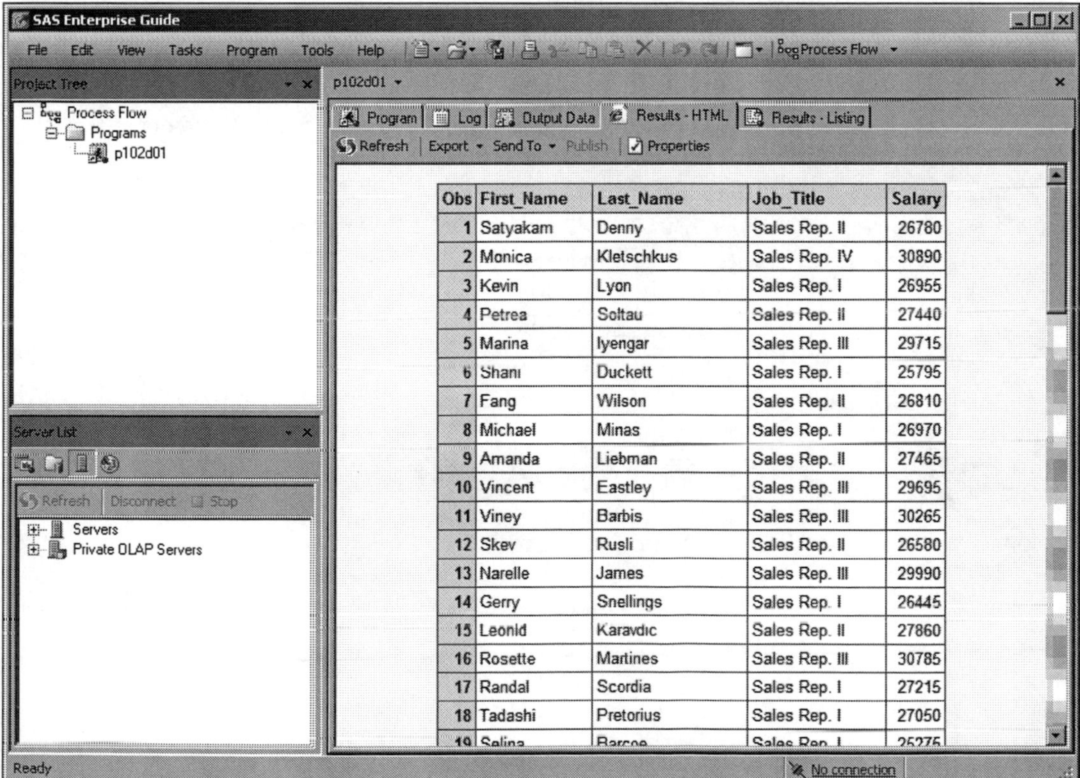

The Log tab contains the statements specific to SAS Enterprise Guide and the programming statements that are submitted as well as notes about the following:

- any files that were read
- the records that were read
- the program execution and results.

In this example, the Log tab contains no warning or error messages. If the program contains errors, relevant warning and error messages are also written to the SAS log.

p102d01

Program | Log | Output Data | Results - HTML | Results - Listing

Export Send To Create | Project Log | Properties

```
       options linesize=95 pagesize=52;

       data work.NewSalesEmps;
          length First_Name $ 12 Last_Name $ 18
                 Job_Title $ 25;
          infile 's:\workshop\newemps.csv' dlm=',';
          input First_Name $ Last_Name $
                Job_Title $ Salary;
       run;

NOTE: The infile 's:\workshop\newemps.csv' is:
      Filename=s:\workshop\newemps.csv,
      RECFM=V,LRECL=256,File Size (bytes)=2604,
      Last Modified=31Mar2009:14:30:42,
      Create Time=15Jun2009:09:21:54

NOTE: 71 records were read from the infile 's:\workshop\newemps.csv'
      The minimum record length was 28.
      The maximum record length was 47.
NOTE: The data set WORK.NEWSALESEMPS has 71 observations and 4 varia
NOTE: DATA statement used (Total process time):
      real time           0.29 seconds
      cpu time            0.01 seconds
```

To scroll horizontally in the Log tab, use the horizontal scroll bar.

To scroll vertically in the Log tab, use the vertical scroll bar or use the PAGE UP or PAGE DOWN keys on the keyboard.

Managing a Project (Optional)

The Project Tree window displays the active project and its associated programs. SAS Enterprise Guide uses *projects* to manage each collection of related data, tasks, code, and results.

Multiple programs can be added to one project.

1. To add a new program to the existing project, select **New** ⇨ **Program**.
2. Enter a PROC FREQ step on the Program tab.

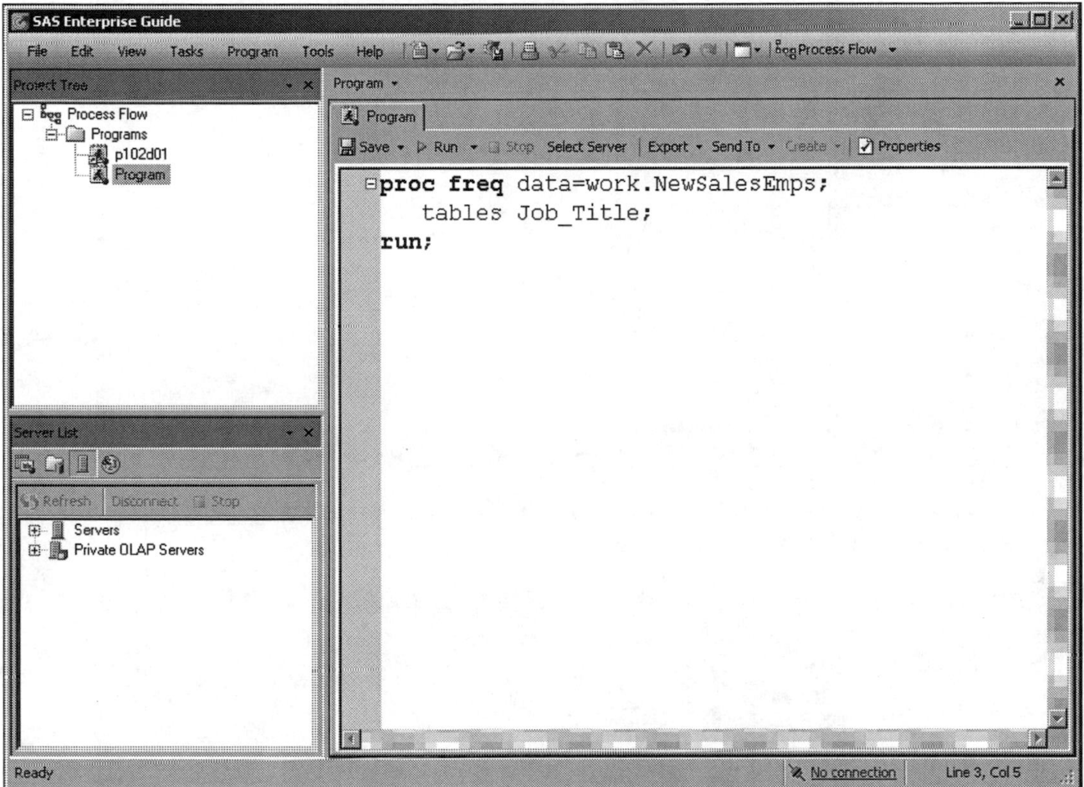

3. Submit the program and review the results.

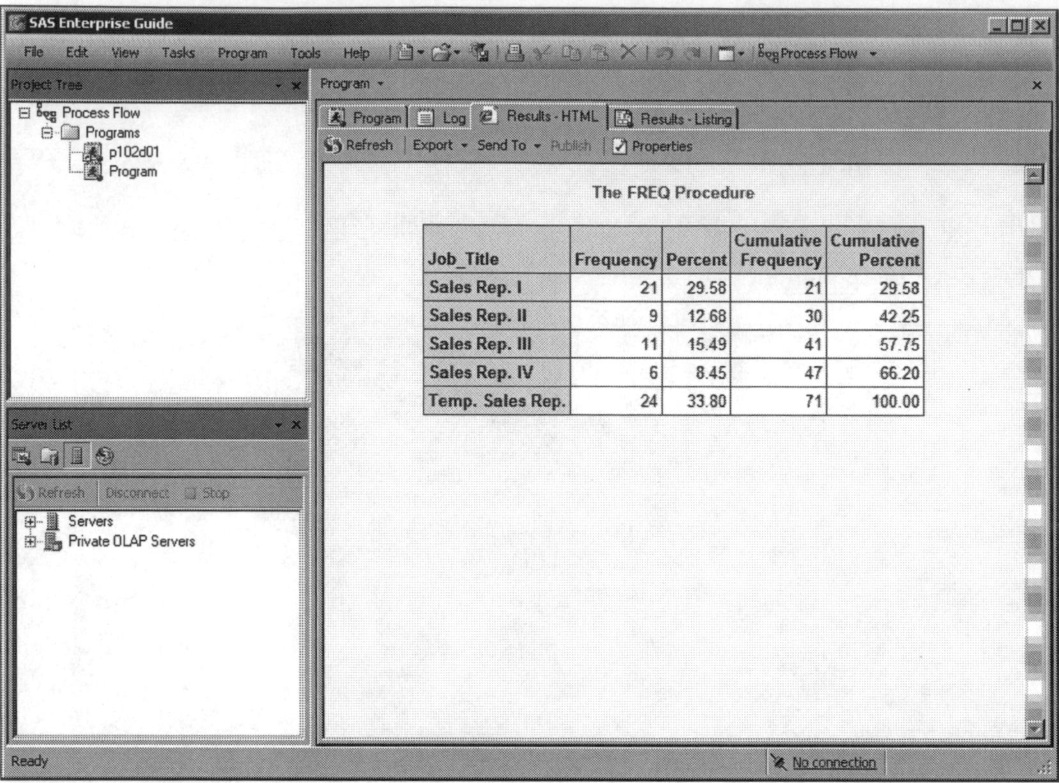

4. To save the program, right-click on **Program** in the Project Tree and select **Save Program As…**. Then, supply a location and name for the program.

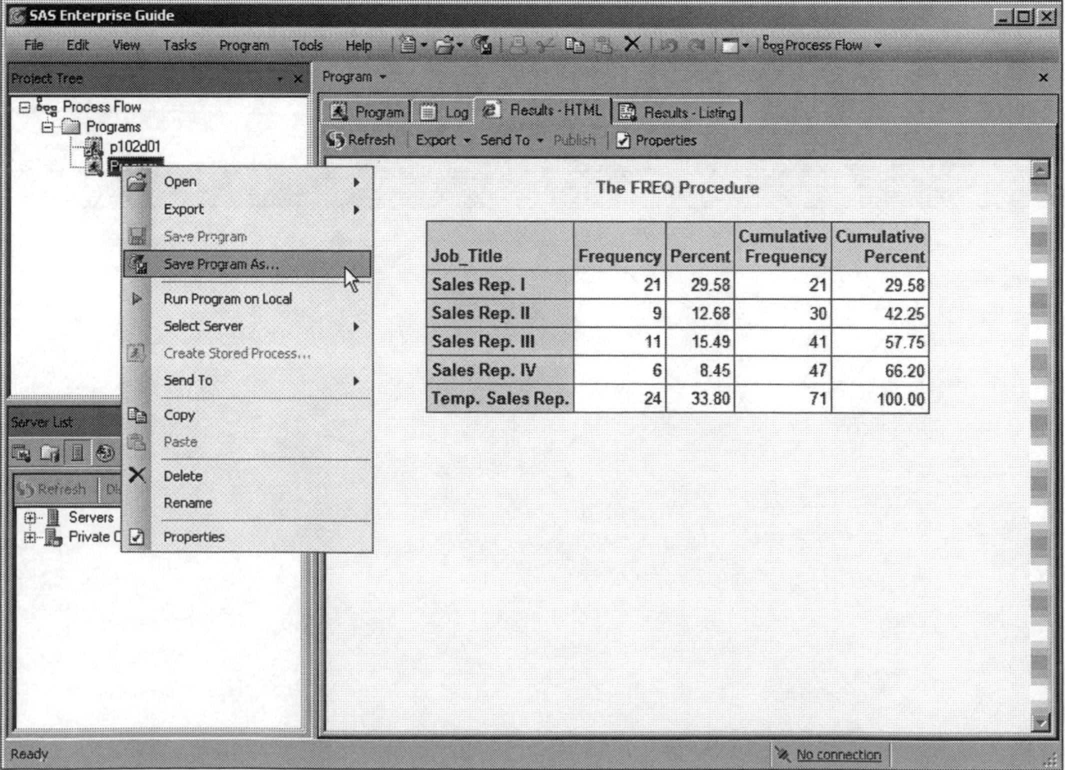

5. To save the project, select **File** ⇨ **Save Project As …**. Then, supply a location and name for the project.

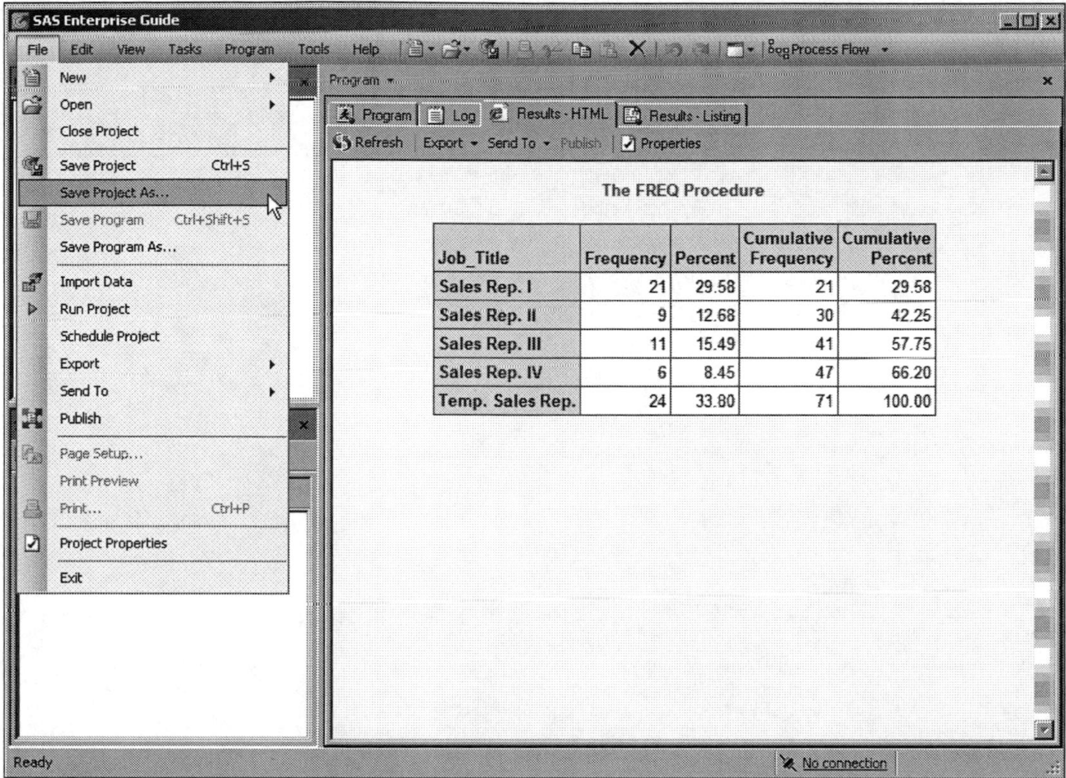

Job_Title	Frequency	Percent	Cumulative Frequency	Cumulative Percent
Sales Rep. I	21	29.58	21	29.58
Sales Rep. II	9	12.68	30	42.25
Sales Rep. III	11	15.49	41	57.75
Sales Rep. IV	6	8.45	47	66.20
Temp. Sales Rep.	24	33.80	71	100.00

6. To maneuver between programs, double-click the desired program in the Project Tree.

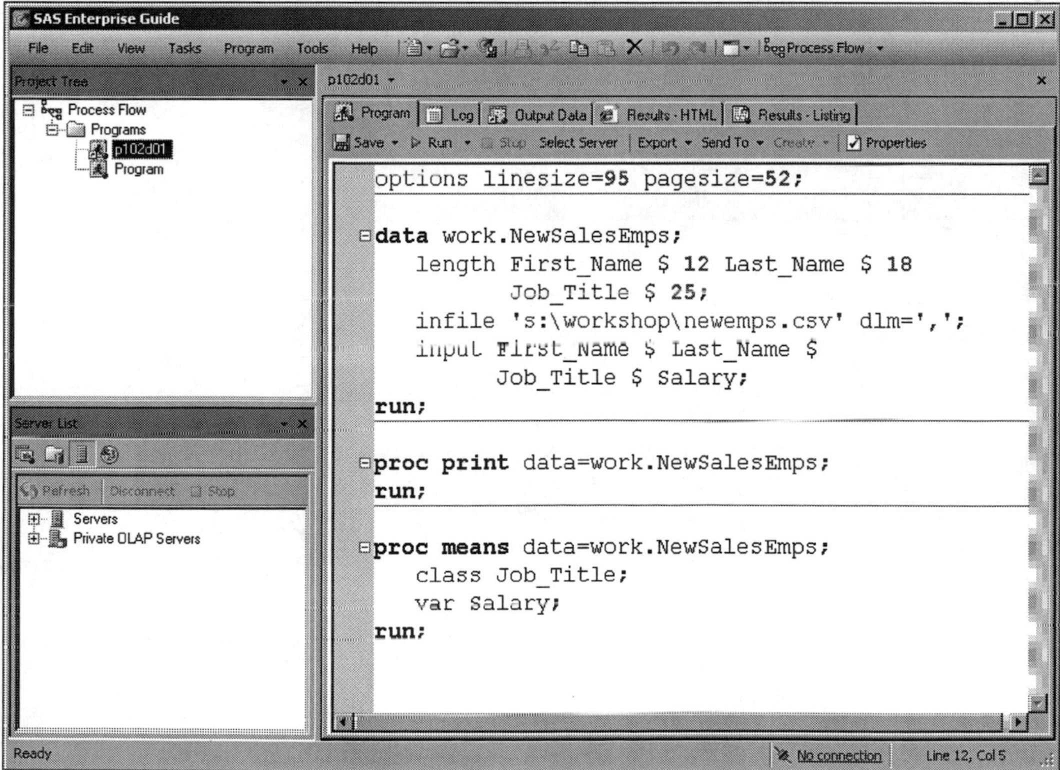


```
options linesize=95 pagesize=52;

data work.NewSalesEmps;
   length First_Name $ 12 Last_Name $ 18
          Job_Title $ 25;
   infile 's:\workshop\newemps.csv' dlm=',';
   input First_Name $ Last_Name $
         Job_Title $ Salary;
run;

proc print data=work.NewSalesEmps;
run;

proc means data=work.NewSalesEmps;
   class Job_Title;
   var Salary;
run;
```

7. To delete a program, right-click on the program in the Project Tree and select **Delete**.

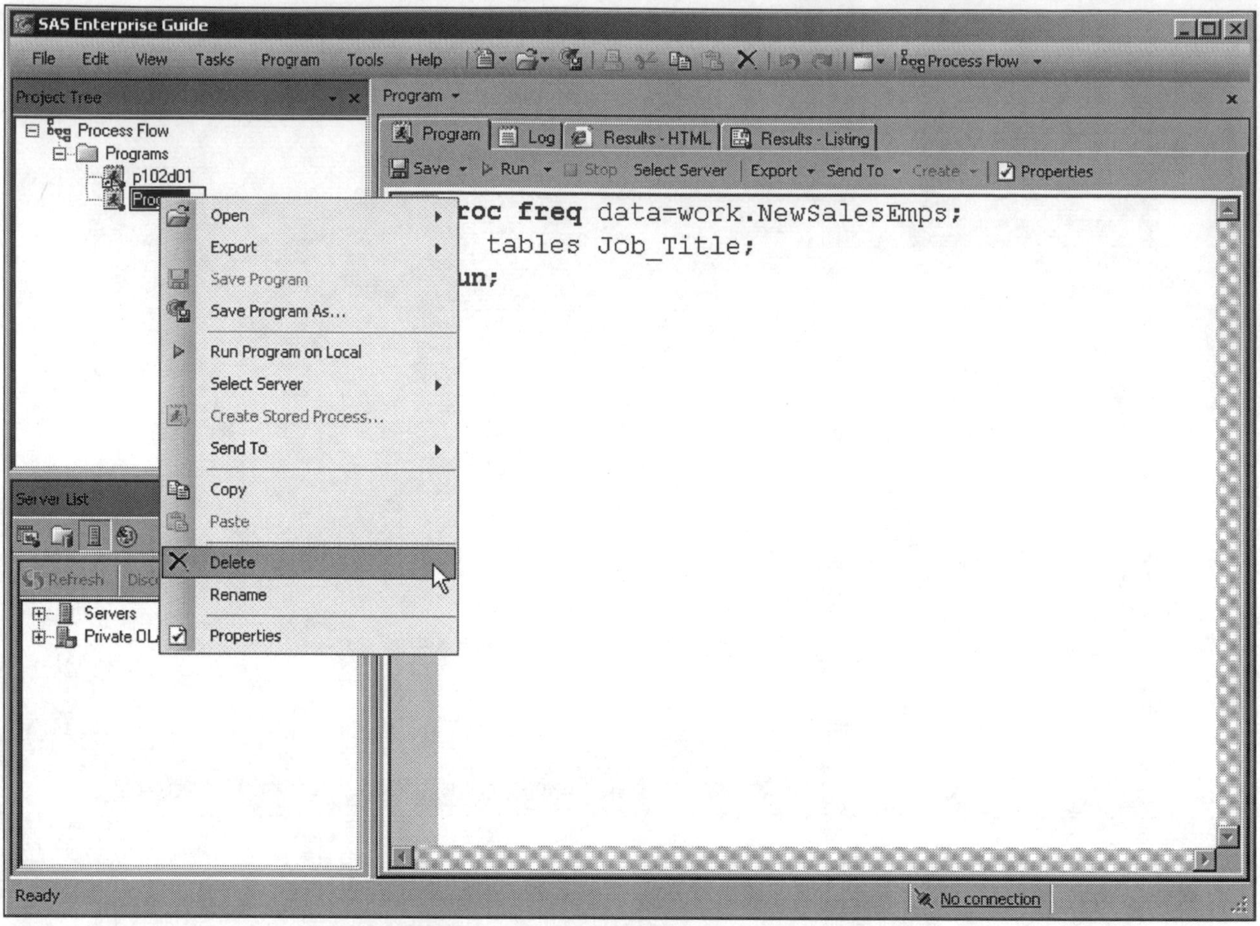

You will need to select **Yes** to delete all the items associated with the program.

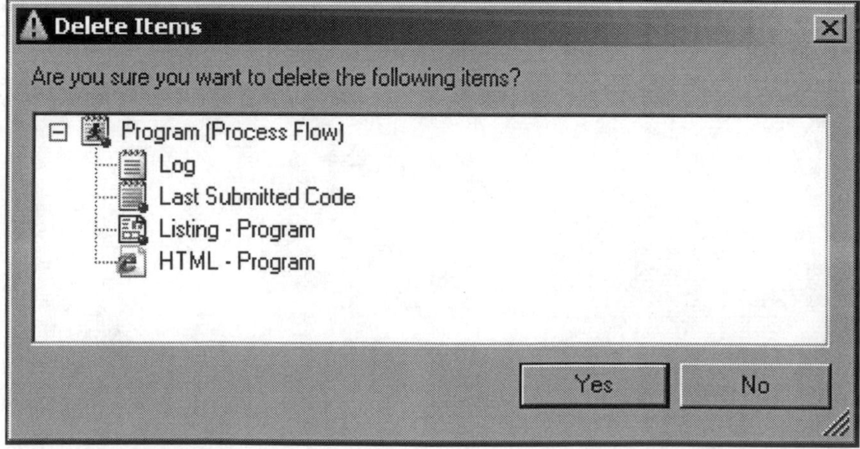

Using the Help Facility

1. To open the Help facility for SAS Enterprise Guide, select **Help** ⇨ **SAS Enterprise Guide Help**.

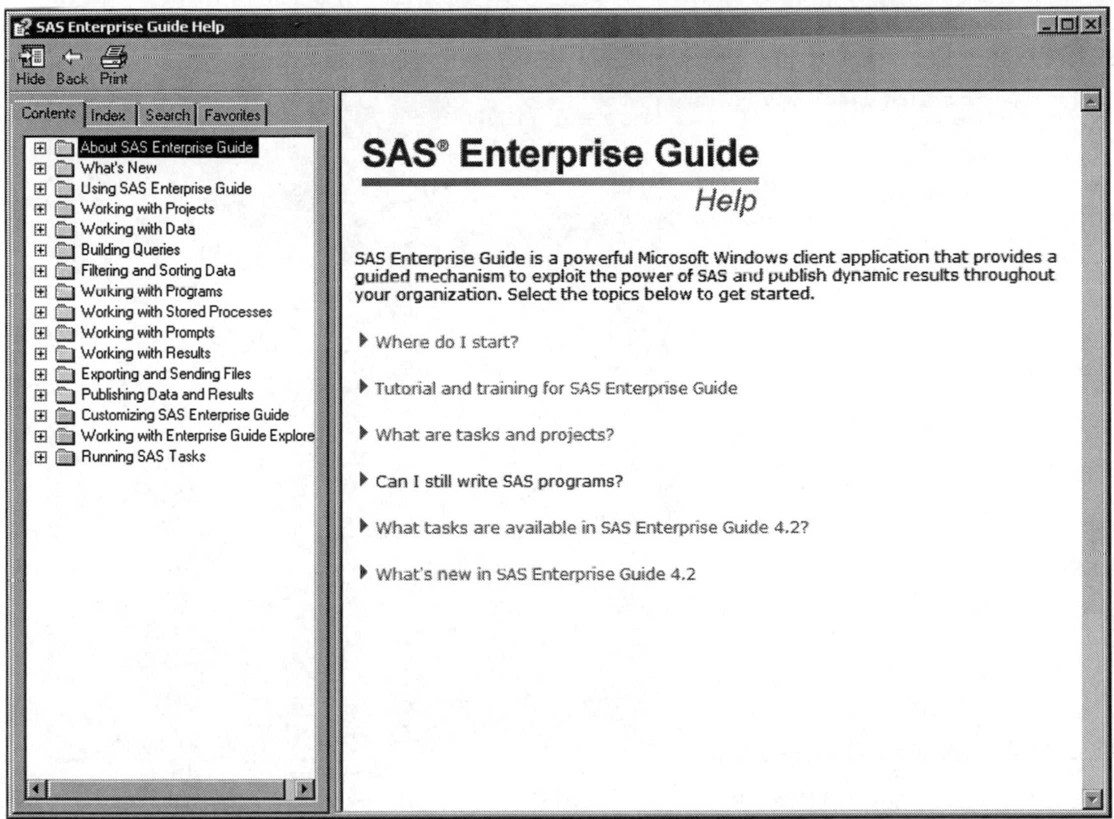

2. To open the Help facility for SAS Syntax, select **Help** ⇨ **SAS Syntax Help**.

3. Select the **Contents** tab.

4. From the Contents tab, select **SAS Products** ⇨ **Base SAS**.

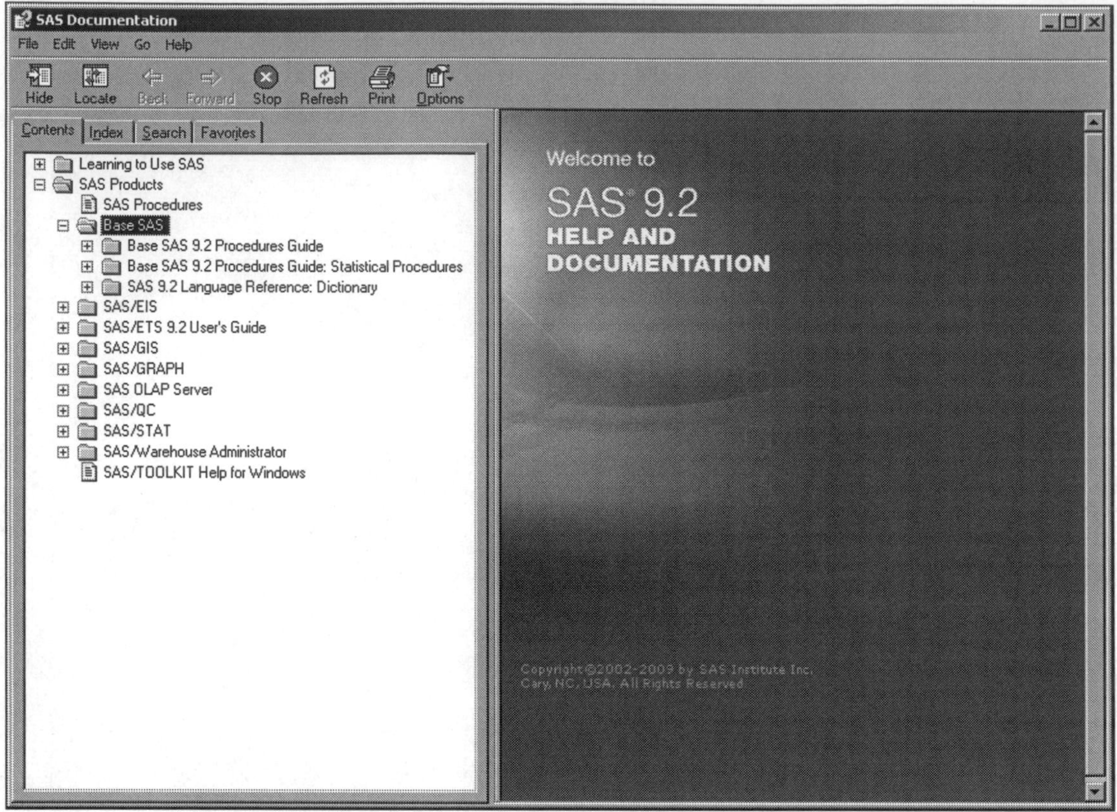

5. For example, select **Base SAS 9.2 Procedures Guide** ⇨ **Procedures** ⇨ **The PRINT Procedure** to find the documentation for the PRINT procedure.

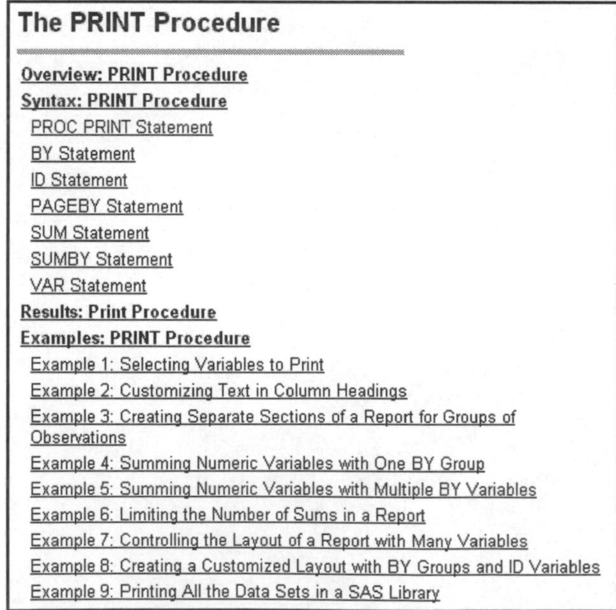

The PRINT Procedure

Overview: PRINT Procedure
Syntax: PRINT Procedure
PROC PRINT Statement
BY Statement
ID Statement
PAGEBY Statement
SUM Statement
SUMBY Statement
VAR Statement
Results: Print Procedure
Examples: PRINT Procedure
Example 1: Selecting Variables to Print
Example 2: Customizing Text in Column Headings
Example 3: Creating Separate Sections of a Report for Groups of Observations
Example 4: Summing Numeric Variables with One BY Group
Example 5: Summing Numeric Variables with Multiple BY Variables
Example 6: Limiting the Number of Sums in a Report
Example 7: Controlling the Layout of a Report with Many Variables
Example 8: Creating a Customized Layout with BY Groups and ID Variables
Example 9: Printing All the Data Sets in a SAS Library

Exercises

Level 1

1. Submitting a Program and Using the Help Facility

a. With the appropriate Editor window active, include a SAS program.

Windows	Select **File** ⇨ **Open Program** and select the **p102e01.sas** program.
UNIX	Select **File** ⇨ **Open** and select the **p102e01.sas** program.
z/OS (OS/390)	Issue the command: `include '.workshop.sascode(p102e01)'`.

b. Submit the program for execution. Based on the report in the Output window, how many rows and columns are in the report?

rows: __________ columns: __________

c. Examine the Log window. Based on the log notes, how many observations and variables are in the `Work.country` data set?

observations: __________ variables: __________

d. Clear the Log and Output windows.

e. Use the Help facility to find documentation about the LINESIZE= option.

Go to the CONTENTS tab in the SAS Help and Documentation. Select **SAS Products** ⇨ **Base SAS** ⇨ **SAS 9.2 Language Reference: Dictionary** ⇨ **Dictionary of Language Elements** ⇨ **SAS System Options** ⇨ **LINESIZE= System Option**.

What is an alias for the LINESIZE= system option? ____________________

Level 2

2. Identifying SAS Components

a. With the appropriate Editor window active, type the following SAS program:

```
proc setinit;
run;
```

b. Submit the program for execution, and then look at the results in the Log window.

✎ The SETINIT procedure produces a list of the SAS components licensed at a given site.

c. If you see SAS/GRAPH in the list of components in the log, include a SAS program.

Windows	Select **File** ⇨ **Open Program** and select the **p102e02.sas** program.
UNIX	Select **File** ⇨ **Open** and select the **p102e02.sas** program.
z/OS (OS/390)	Issue the command: `include '.workshop.sascode(p102e02)'`.

d. Submit the program for execution. View the results in the GRAPH window.

e. Close the GRAPH window.

3. **Setting Up Function Keys**

a. Issue the KEYS command or select **Tools** ⇨ **Options** ⇨ **Keys** to open the KEYS window.

> The KEYS window is a secondary window used to browse or change function key definitions.

b. Add the following commands to the F12 key:

```
clear log; clear output
```

c. Close the KEYS window.

d. Press the F12 key and confirm that the Log and Output windows are cleared.

Level 3

4. **Exploring Your SAS Environment – Windows**

a. Customize the appearance and functionality of the Enhanced Editor by selecting **Tools** ⇨ **Options** ⇨ **Enhanced Editor**. For example, select the Appearance tab to modify the font size.

b. In the Help facility, look up the documentation for the Enhanced Editor.

From the Contents tab, select **Using SAS Software in Your Operating Environment** ⇨ **SAS 9.2 Companion for Windows** ⇨ **Running SAS under Windows** ⇨ **Using the SAS Editors** ⇨ **Using the Enhanced Editor**.

5. **Exploring Your SAS Environment – UNIX and z/OS (OS/390)**

a. From a Web browser, access the following link: http://support.sas.com/documentation/.

b. Select **Base SAS**.

c. Select the HTML version of **Step-by-Step Programming with Base SAS Software**.

d. On the Contents tab, select **Understanding Your SAS Environment** ⇨ **Using the SAS Windowing Environment** ⇨ **Working with SAS Programs**.

e. Refer to **Command Line Commands and the Editor** and **Line Commands and the Editor**.

2.3 Chapter Review

Chapter Review

1. What are the two components of a SAS program?
2. In which modes can you run a SAS program?
3. How can you include a program in the SAS windowing environment?
4. How can you submit a program in the SAS windowing environment?
5. What are the three primary windows in the SAS windowing environment?

39

2.4 Solutions

Solutions to Exercises

1. Submitting a Program and Using the Help Facility

a. Include a SAS program.

```
options linesize=95 pagesize=52;

data work.country;
   length Country_Code $ 2 Country_Name $ 48;
   infile 'country.dat' dlm='!';
   input Country_Code $ Country_Name $;
run;

proc print data=work.country;
run;
```

b. Submit the program.

rows: **238** columns: **3**

c. Examine the Log window.

observations: **238** variables: **2**

d. Clear the Log and Output windows.

e. Use the Help facility.

What is an alias for the LINESIZE= system option? **LS=**

2. Identifying SAS Components

a. Type the following SAS program:

```
proc setinit;
run;
```

b. Submit the program.

Partial SAS Log

```
                                    Product expiration dates:
---Base Product                                                                 31DEC2008
---SAS/STAT                                                                     31DEC2008
---SAS/GRAPH                                                                    31DEC2008
---SAS/ETS                                                                      31DEC2008
```

c. Include a SAS program.

```
data work.SalesEmps;
   length Job_Title $ 25;
   infile 'sales.csv' dlm=',';
   input Employee_ID First_Name $ Last_Name $
         Gender $ Salary Job_Title $ Country $;
run;

goptions reset=all;
proc gchart data=work.SalesEmps;
   vbar3d Job_Title / sumvar=Salary type=mean;
   hbar Job_Title / group=Gender sumvar=Salary
                    patternid=midpoint;
   pie3d Job_Title / noheading;
   where Job_Title contains 'Sales Rep';
   label Job_Title='Job Title';
   format Salary dollar12.;
   title 'Orion Star Sales Employees';
run;
quit;
```

d. Submit the program.

e. Close the GRAPH window.

3. Setting Up Function Keys

a. Issue the KEYS command.

b. Add a command to the F12 key.

Keys Window (Windows):

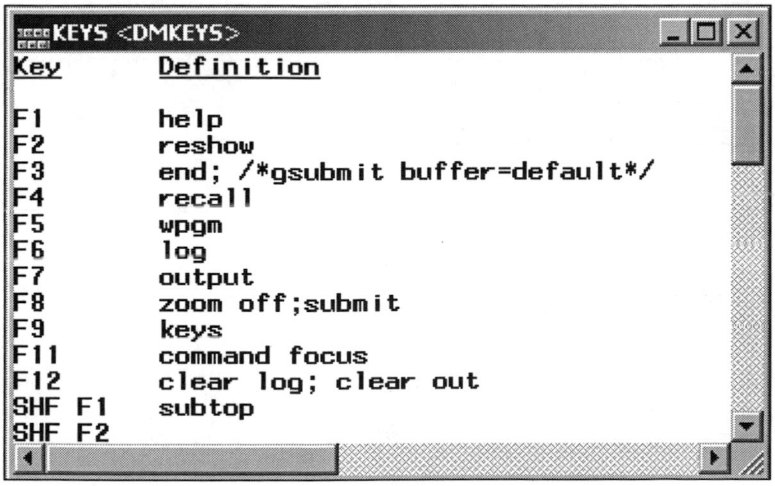

KEYS <DMKEYS>

Key	Definition
F1	help
F2	reshow
F3	end; /*gsubmit buffer=default*/
F4	recall
F5	wpgm
F6	log
F7	output
F8	zoom off;submit
F9	keys
F11	command focus
F12	clear log; clear out
SHF F1	subtop
SHF F2	

c. Close the KEYS window.

d. Press the F12 key.

4. Exploring Your SAS Environment – Windows

a. Customize the appearance and functionality of the Enhanced Editor.

b. Use the Help facility.

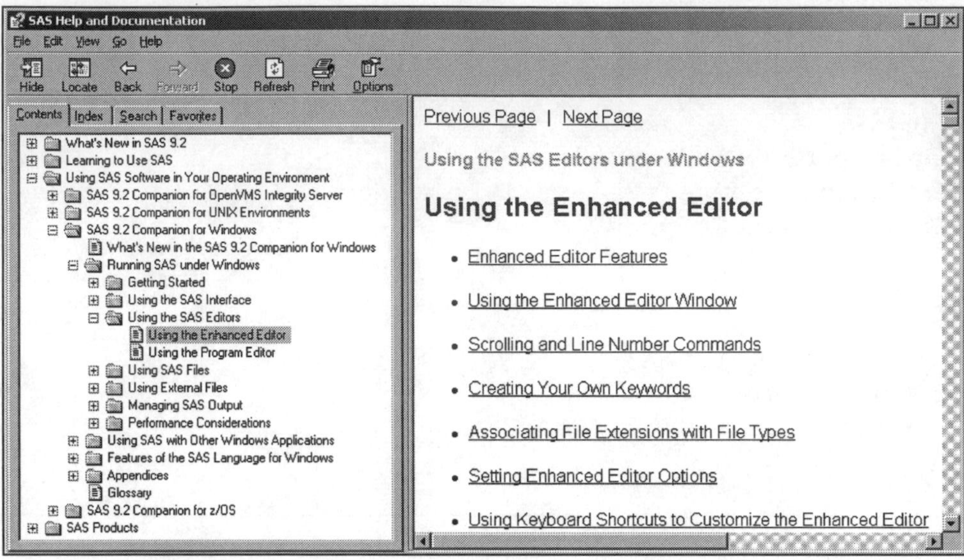

5. Exploring Your SAS Environment – UNIX and z/OS (OS/390)

a. From a Web browser, access the following link: http://support.sas.com/documentation/.

b. Select **Base SAS**.

c. Select the HTML version of **Step-by-Step Programming with Base SAS Software**.

d. On the Contents tab, select **Understanding Your SAS Environment** ⇨ **Using the SAS Windowing Environment** ⇨ **Working with SAS Programs**.

e. Refer to **Command Line Commands and the Editor** and **Line Commands and the Editor**.

Partial Documentation

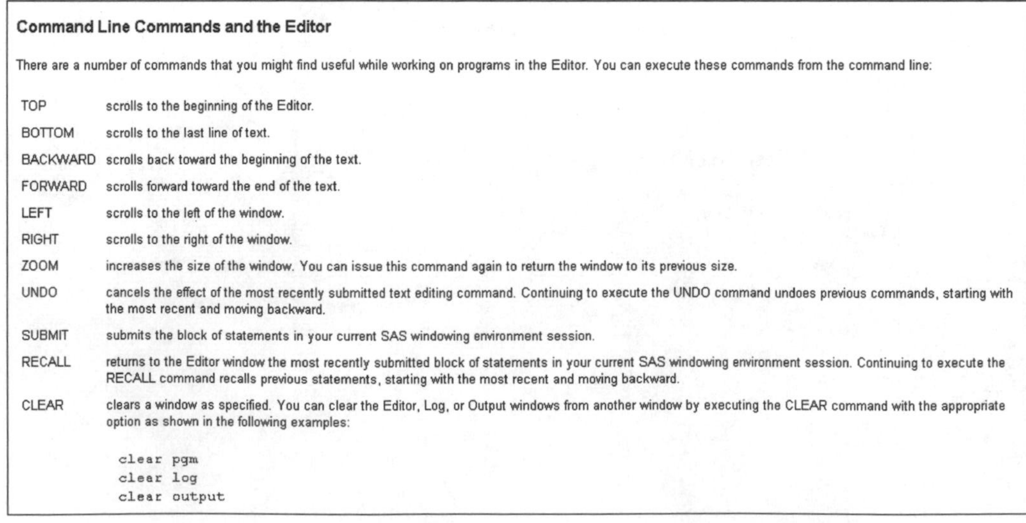

Command Line Commands and the Editor

There are a number of commands that you might find useful while working on programs in the Editor. You can execute these commands from the command line:

TOP	scrolls to the beginning of the Editor.
BOTTOM	scrolls to the last line of text.
BACKWARD	scrolls back toward the beginning of the text.
FORWARD	scrolls forward toward the end of the text.
LEFT	scrolls to the left of the window.
RIGHT	scrolls to the right of the window.
ZOOM	increases the size of the window. You can issue this command again to return the window to its previous size.
UNDO	cancels the effect of the most recently submitted text editing command. Continuing to execute the UNDO command undoes previous commands, starting with the most recent and moving backward.
SUBMIT	submits the block of statements in your current SAS windowing environment session.
RECALL	returns to the Editor window the most recently submitted block of statements in your current SAS windowing environment session. Continuing to execute the RECALL command recalls previous statements, starting with the most recent and moving backward.
CLEAR	clears a window as specified. You can clear the Editor, Log, or Output windows from another window by executing the CLEAR command with the appropriate option as shown in the following examples:

```
clear pgm
clear log
clear output
```

Solutions to Student Activities (Polls/Quizzes)

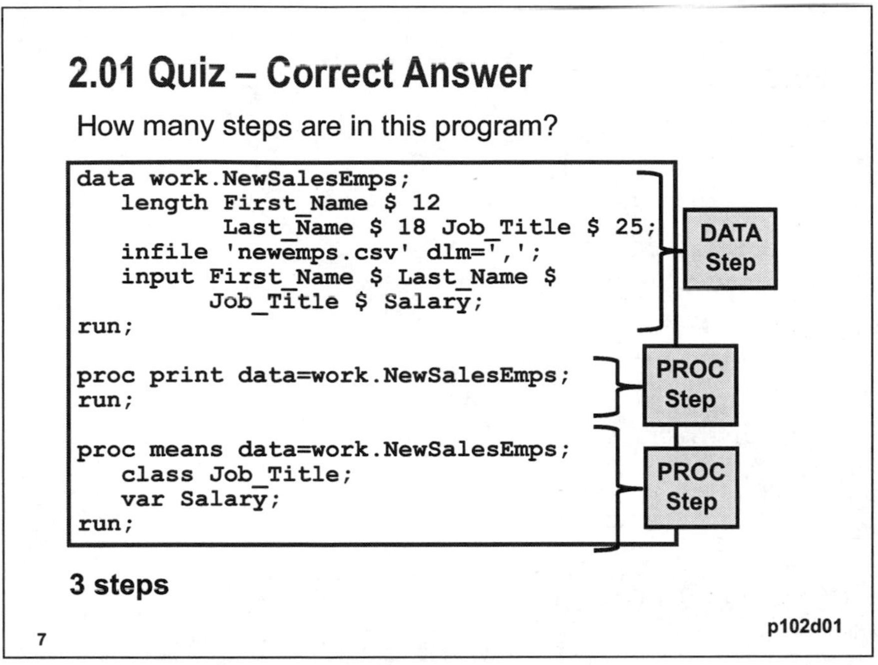
2.01 Quiz – Correct Answer
How many steps are in this program?
data work.NewSalesEmps;
length First_Name $ 12
Last_Name $ 18 Job_Title $ 25;
infile 'newemps.csv' dlm=',';
input First_Name $ Last_Name $
Job_Title $ Salary;
run;
proc print data=work.NewSalesEmps;
run;
proc means data=work.NewSalesEmps;
class Job_Title;
var Salary;
run;
DATA Step
PROC Step
PROC Step
3 steps
7
p102d01

2.02 Quiz – Correct Answer

How does SAS detect the end of the PROC MEANS step?

```
data work.NewSalesEmps;
   length First_Name $ 12
          Last_Name $ 18 Job_Title $ 25;
   infile 'newemps.csv' dlm=',';
   input First_Name $ Last_Name $
         Job_Title $ Salary;
run;

proc print data=work.NewSalesEmps;

proc means data=work.NewSalesEmps;
   class Job_Title;
   var Salary;
```

SAS does not detect the end of the PROC MEANS step.
SAS needs a RUN statement to detect the end.

15

Solutions to Chapter Review

Chapter Review Answers

1. What are the two components of a SAS program?
   DATA step and PROC step

2. In which modes can you run a SAS program?
   Batch, noninteractive, and interactive modes

3. How can you include a program in the SAS windowing environment?
   INCLUDE command, <u>File</u> ⇨ <u>Open</u>, or [open icon]

4. How can you submit a program in the SAS windowing environment?
   SUBMIT command, <u>Run</u> ⇨ <u>Submit</u>, or [submit icon]

40

continued...

Chapter Review Answers

5. What are the three primary windows in the SAS windowing environment?
   LOG, OUTPUT, and EDITOR windows

41

Chapter 3 Working with SAS Syntax

3.1 Mastering Fundamental Concepts 3-3

3.2 Diagnosing and Correcting Syntax Errors 3-10

Demonstration: Diagnosing and Correcting Syntax Errors 3-12

Demonstration: Diagnosing and Correcting Syntax Errors 3-15

Exercises 3-19

3.3 Chapter Review 3-20

3.4 Solutions 3-21

Solutions to Exercises 3-21

Solutions to Student Activities (Polls/Quizzes) 3-23

Solutions to Chapter Review 3-25

LINE SIZE – width of the report

PAGE SIZE – length of the report

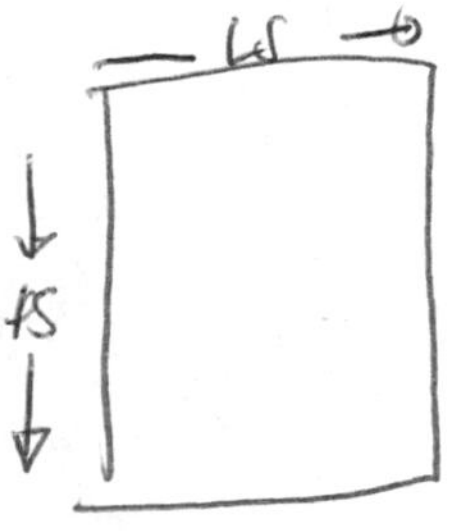

keys → shortcut keys (command line)

ex. F1, F2, etc.

3.1 Mastering Fundamental Concepts

Objectives

- Identify the characteristics of SAS statements.
- Explain SAS syntax rules.
- Insert SAS comments using two methods.

3

SAS Programs

A *SAS program* is a sequence of steps.

```
data work.NewSalesEmps;
   length First_Name $ 12
          Last_Name $ 18 Job_Title $ 25;
   infile 'newemps.csv' dlm=',';
   input First_Name $ Last_Name $
         Job_Title $ Salary;
run;

proc print data=work.NewSalesEmps;
run;

proc means data=work.NewSalesEmps;
   class Job_Title;
   var Salary;
run;
```

DATA Step

PROC Step

PROC Step

A *step* is a sequence of SAS statements.

4

Statements

SAS statements have these characteristics:

- usually begin with an **identifying keyword**
- always end with a **semicolon**

```
data work.NewSalesEmps;
   length First_Name $ 12
          Last_Name $ 18 Job_Title $ 25;
   infile 'newemps.csv' dlm=',';
   input First_Name $ Last_Name $
         Job_Title $ Salary;
run;

proc print data=work.NewSalesEmps;
run;

proc means data=work.NewSalesEmps;
   class Job_Title;
   var Salary;
run;
```

5 p103d01

3.01 Quiz

How many statements are in the DATA step?

a. 1

b. 3

c. 5

d. 7

```
data work.NewSalesEmps;
   length First_Name $ 12
          Last_Name $ 18 Job_Title $ 25;
   infile 'newemps.csv' dlm=',';
   input First_Name $ Last_Name $
         Job_Title $ Salary;
run;
```

7

SAS Syntax Rules

-- Indentional

Structured, consistent spacing makes a SAS program easier to read.

Conventional Formatting

```
data work.NewSalesEmps;
   length First_Name $ 12
          Last_Name $ 18 Job_Title $ 25;
   infile 'newemps.csv' dlm=',';
   input First_Name $ Last_Name $
         Job_Title $ Salary;
run;

proc print data=work.NewSalesEmps;
run;

proc means data=work.NewSalesEmps;
   class Job_Title;
   var Salary;
run;
```

9

SAS programming statements are easier to read if you begin DATA, PROC, and RUN statements in column one and indent the other statements.

SAS Syntax Rules

- SAS statements are free-format.
- One or more blanks or special characters can be used to separate words.
- They can begin and end in any column.
- A single statement can span multiple lines.
- Several statements can be on the same line.

Unconventional Formatting

```
data work.NewSalesEmps;
length First_Name $ 12
Last_Name $ 18 Job_Title $ 25;
infile 'newemps.csv' dlm=',';
input First_Name $ Last_Name $
Job_Title $ Salary;
run;
proc print data=work.NewSalesEmps; run;
   proc means data  =work.NewSalesEmps;
class Job_Title;  var Salary;run;
```

10

→ ALWAYS COMMENT /* COMMENT HERE */

SAS Syntax Rules

- SAS statements are free-format.
- One or more blanks or special characters can be used to separate words.
- They can begin and end in any column.
- A single statement can span multiple lines.
- Several statements can be on the same line.

Unconventional Formatting

```
data work.NewSalesEmps;
length First_Name $ 12
Last_Name $ 18 Job_Title $ 25;
infile 'newemps.csv' dlm=',';
input First_Name $ Last_Name $
Job_Title $ Salary;
run;
proc print data=work.NewSalesEmps; run;
   proc means data  =work.NewSalesEmps;
class Job_Title;  var Salary;run;
```

11

SAS Syntax Rules

- SAS statements are free-format.
- One or more blanks or special characters can be used to separate words.
- They can begin and end in any column.
- A single statement can span multiple lines.
- Several statements can be on the same line.

Unconventional Formatting

```
data work.NewSalesEmps;
length First_Name $ 12
Last_Name $ 18 Job_Title $ 25;
infile 'newemps.csv' dlm=',';
input First_Name $ Last_Name $
Job_Title $ Salary;
run;
proc print data=work.NewSalesEmps; run;
   proc means data  =work.NewSalesEmps;
class Job_Title;  var Salary;run;
```

12

SAS Syntax Rules

- SAS statements are free-format.
- One or more blanks or special characters can be used to separate words.
- They can begin and end in any column.
- A single statement can span multiple lines.
- Several statements can be on the same line.

Unconventional Formatting

```
data work.NewSalesEmps;
length First_Name $ 12
Last_Name $ 18 Job_Title $ 25;
infile 'newemps.csv' dlm=',';
input First_Name $ Last_Name $
Job_Title $ Salary;
run;
proc print data=work.NewSalesEmps; run;
   proc means data  =work.NewSalesEmps;
class Job_Title;  var Salary;run;
```

13

SAS Syntax Rules

- SAS statements are free-format.
- One or more blanks or special characters can be used to separate words.
- They can begin and end in any column.
- A single statement can span multiple lines.
- Several statements can be on the same line.

Unconventional Formatting

```
data work.NewSalesEmps;
length First_Name $ 12
Last_Name $ 18 Job_Title $ 25;
infile 'newemps.csv' dlm=',';
input First_Name $ Last_Name $
Job_Title $ Salary;
run;
proc print data=work.NewSalesEmps; run;
   proc means data  =work.NewSalesEmps;
class Job_Title;  var Salary;run;
```

14

SAS Comments

SAS comments are text that SAS ignores during processing. You can use comments anywhere in a SAS program to document the purpose of the program, explain segments of the program, or mark SAS code as non-executing text.

Two methods of commenting:

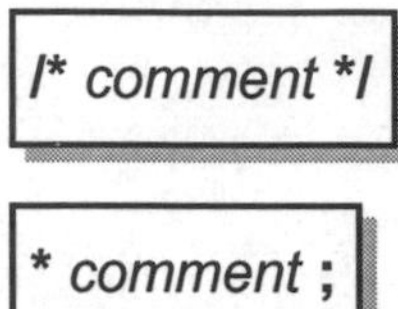

15

Avoid placing the /* comment symbols in columns 1 and 2. On some operating environments, SAS might interpret these symbols as a request to end the SAS job or session.

SAS Comments

This program contains four comments.

```
*-----------------------------------------*
|   This program creates and uses the     |
|   data set called work.NewSalesEmps.    |
*-----------------------------------------*;
data work.NewSalesEmps;
   length First_Name $ 12 Last_Name $ 18
          Job_Title $ 25;
   infile 'newemps.csv' dlm=',';
   input First_Name $ Last_Name $
         Job_Title $ Salary /*numeric*/;
run;
/*
proc print data=work.NewSalesEmps;
run;
*/
proc means data=work.NewSalesEmps;
   *class Job_Title;
   var Salary;
run;
```

16 p103d02

Setup for the Poll

- Retrieve program **p103a01**.
- Read the comment concerning DATALINES.
- Submit the program and view the log to confirm that the PROC CONTENTS step did not execute.

18

3.02 Multiple Choice Poll

Which statement is true concerning the DATALINES statement based on reading the comment?

a. The DATALINES statement is used when reading data located in a raw data file.
b. The DATALINES statement is used when reading data located directly in the program.

19

3.2 Diagnosing and Correcting Syntax Errors

Objectives

- Identify SAS syntax errors.
- Diagnose and correct a program with errors.
- Save the corrected program.

23

Syntax Errors

Syntax errors occur when program statements do not conform to the rules of the SAS language.

Examples of syntax errors:

- misspelled keywords
- unmatched quotation marks
- missing semicolons
- invalid options

When SAS encounters a syntax error, SAS prints a warning or an error message to the log.

```
ERROR 22-322: Syntax error, expecting one of the following:
              a name, a quoted string, (, /, ;, _DATA_, _LAST_,
              _NULL_.
```

24

When SAS encounters a syntax error, SAS underlines the error and the following information is written to the SAS log:

- the word ERROR or WARNING
- the location of the error
- an explanation of the error

3.03 Quiz

This program has three syntax errors.

What are the errors?

```
daat work.NewSalesEmps;
   length First_Name $ 12
          Last_Name $ 18 Job_Title $ 25;
   infile 'newemps.csv' dlm=',';
   input First_Name $ Last_Name $
         Job_Title $ Salary;
run;

proc print data=work.NewSalesEmps
run;

proc means data=work.NewSalesEmps average max;
   class Job_Title;
   var Salary;
run;
```

26 p103d03

Diagnosing and Correcting Syntax Errors

p103d03

- Submit a SAS program with errors.
- Diagnose and correct the errors.
- Save the corrected program.

Submitting a SAS Program with Errors

```
daat work.NewSalesEmps;
   length First_Name $ 12
          Last_Name $ 18 Job_Title $ 25;
   infile 'newemps.csv' dlm=',';
   input First_Name $ Last_Name $
         Job_Title $ Salary;
run;

proc print data=work.NewSalesEmps
run;

proc means data=work.NewSalesEmps average max;
   class Job_Title;
   var Salary;
run;
```

For z/OS (OS/390), the following INFILE statement is used:

```
   infile '.workshop.rawdata(newemps)' dlm=',';
```

The SAS log contains error messages and warnings.

```
36   daat work.NewSalesEmps;
     ----
     14
WARNING 14-169: Assuming the symbol DATA was misspelled as daat.

37      length First_Name $ 12
38             Last_Name $ 18 Job_Title $ 25;
39      infile 'newemps.csv' dlm=',';
40      input First_Name $ Last_Name $
41            Job_Title $ Salary;
42   run;

NOTE: The infile 'newemps.csv' is:
      Filename=S:\Workshop\newemps.csv,
      RECFM=V,LRECL=256,File Size (bytes)=2604,
      Last Modified=02Apr2008:09:10:12,
      Create Time=02Apr2008:09:10:12
```

(Continued on the next page.)

```
NOTE: 71 records were read from the infile 'newemps.csv'.
      The minimum record length was 28.
      The maximum record length was 47.
NOTE: The data set WORK.NEWSALESEMPS has 71 observations and 4 variables.


43
44   proc print data=work.NewSalesEmps
45   run;
     ---
     22
     202
ERROR 22-322: Syntax error, expecting one of the following: ;, (, BLANKLINE, DATA, DOUBLE,
              HEADING, LABEL, N, NOOBS, OBS, ROUND, ROWS, SPLIT, STYLE, SUMLABEL, UNIFORM,
              WIDTH.
ERROR 202-322: The option or parameter is not recognized and will be ignored.
46

NOTE: The SAS System stopped processing this step because of errors.


47   proc means data=work.NewSalesEmps average max;
                                       -------
                                       22
                                       202
ERROR 22-322: Syntax error, expecting one of the following: ;, (, ALPHA, CHARTYPE, CLASSDATA,
              CLM, COMPLETETYPES, CSS, CV, DATA, DESCEND, DESCENDING, DESCENDTYPES, EXCLNPWGT,
              EXCLNPWGTS, EXCLUSIVE, FW, IDMIN, KURTOSIS, LCLM, MAX, MAXDEC, MEAN, MEDIAN, MIN,
              MISSING, MODE, N, NDEC, NMISS, NOLABELS, NONOBS, NOPRINT, NOTHREADS, NOTRAP,
              NWAY, ORDER, P1, P10, P25, P5, P50, P75, P90, P95, P99, PCTLDEF, PRINT, PRINTALL,
              PRINTALLTYPES, PRINTIDS, PRINTIDVARS, PROBT, Q1, Q3, QMARKERS, QMETHOD, QNTLDEF,
              QRANGE, RANGE, SKEWNESS, STDDEV, STDERR, SUM, SUMSIZE, SUMWGT, T, THREADS, UCLM,
              USS, VAR, VARDEF.
ERROR 202-322: The option or parameter is not recognized and will be ignored.
48      class Job_Title;
49      var Salary;
50   run;

NOTE: The SAS System stopped processing this step because of errors.
```

Diagnosing and Correcting the Errors

The log indicates that SAS

- assumed that the keyword DATA was misspelled and executed the DATA step
- interpreted the word RUN as an option in the PROC PRINT statement (because there was a missing semicolon), so PROC PRINT was not executed
- did not recognize the word AVERAGE as a valid option in the PROC MEANS statement, so the PROC MEANS step was not executed.

1. If you are using the Enhanced Editor, the program remains in the editor.

   However, if you use the Program Editor, the code disappears with each submission. Use the RECALL command or select **Run** ⇨ **Recall Last Submit** to recall the program that you submitted. The original program is copied into the Program Editor.

2. Edit the program.

   a. Correct the spelling of DATA.

   b. Put a semicolon at the end of the PROC PRINT statement.

   c. Change the word AVERAGE to MEAN in the PROC MEANS statement.

```
data work.NewSalesEmps;
   length First_Name $ 12
          Last_Name $ 18 Job_Title $ 25;
   infile 'newemps.csv' dlm=',';
   input First_Name $ Last_Name $
         Job_Title $ Salary;
run;

proc print data=work.NewSalesEmps;
run;

proc means data=work.NewSalesEmps mean max;
   class Job_Title;
   var Salary;
run;
```

3. Submit the program. It runs successfully without errors and generates output.

Saving the Corrected Program

You can use the FILE command to save your program to a file. The program must be in the Enhanced Editor or Program Editor before you issue the FILE command. If the code is not in the Program Editor, recall your program before saving the program.

Windows or UNIX	`file 'myprog.sas'`
z/OS (OS/390)	`file '.workshop.sascode(myprog)'`

You can also select **File** ⇨ **Save As**.

A note appears that indicates that the statements are saved to the file.

Diagnosing and Correcting Syntax Errors

p103d04

- Submit a SAS program that contains unbalanced quotation marks.
- Diagnose and correct the error.
- Resubmit the program.

Submitting a SAS Program that Contains Unbalanced Quotation Marks

The closing quotation mark for the DLM= option in the INFILE statement is missing.

```
data work.NewSalesEmps;
   length First_Name $ 12 Last_Name $ 18
          Job_Title $ 25;
   infile 'newemps.csv' dlm=',;
   input First_Name $ Last_Name $
         Job_Title $ Salary;
run;

proc print data=work.NewSalesEmps;
run;

proc means data=work.NewSalesEmps;
   class Job_Title;
   var Salary;
run;
```

SAS Log

```
data work.NewSalesEmps;
   length First_Name $ 12 Last_Name $ 18
          Job_Title $ 25;
   infile 'newemps.csv' dlm=',;
   input First_Name $ Last_Name $
         Job_Title $ Salary;
run;

proc print data=work.NewSalesEmps;
run;

proc means data=work.NewSalesEmps;
   class Job_Title;
   var Salary;
run;
```

Diagnosing and Correcting the Errors

There are no notes in the SAS log because all of the SAS statements after the DLM= option became part of the quoted delimiter.

 The banner in the window indicates that the DATA step is still running, and it is still running because the RUN statement was not recognized.

You can correct the unbalanced quotation marks programmatically by adding the following code before your previous statements:

```
*';*";run;
```

If the quotation mark counter within SAS has an uneven number of quotation marks, as seen in the above program, SAS reads the quotation mark in the code above as the matching quotation mark in the quotation mark counter. SAS then has an even number of quotation marks in the quotation mark counter and runs successfully, assuming no other errors occur. Both single quotation marks and double quotation marks are used in case you submitted double quotation marks instead of single quotation marks.

Point-and-Click Approaches to Balancing Quotation Marks

Windows

1. To correct the problem in the Windows environment, click the break icon or press the **CTRL** and **Break** keys.
2. Select **1. Cancel Submitted Statements** in the Tasking Manager window and select **OK**.

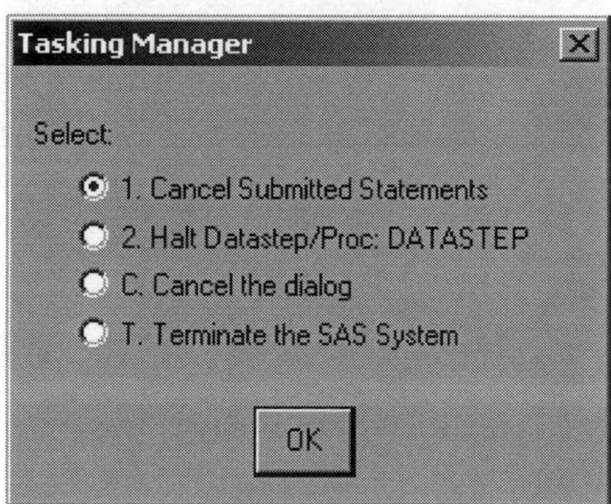

3. Select **Y to cancel submitted statements,** ⇨ **OK**.

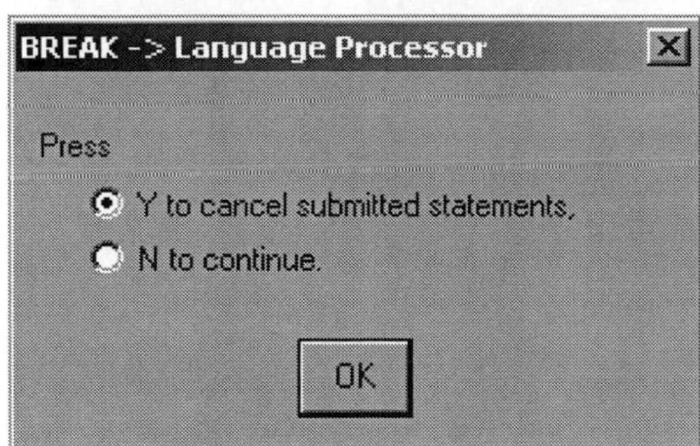

UNIX

1. To correct the problem in the UNIX operating environment, open the SAS: Session Management window and select **Interrupt**.

2. Select **1** in the SAS: Tasking Manager window.

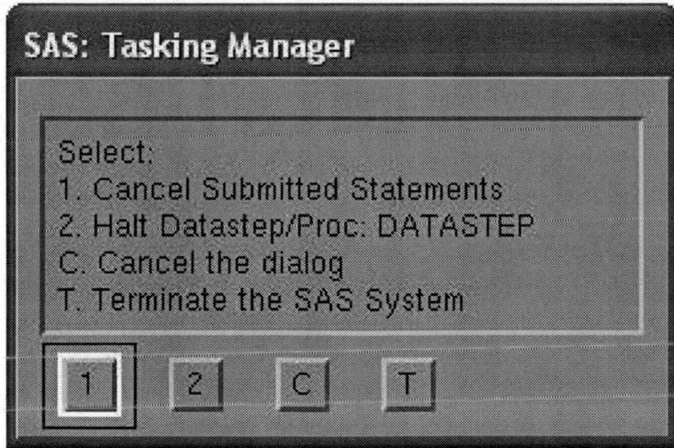

3. Select **Y**.

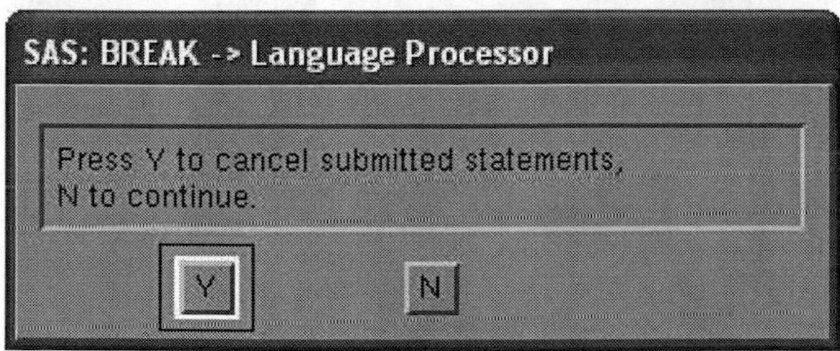

z/OS (OS/390)

1. To correct the problem in the z/OS (OS/390) operating environment, press the **Attention** key or issue the ATTENTION command.

2. Type **1** to select **1. Cancel Submitted Statements** and press the ENTER key.

```
Tasking Manager
 Select:
 1 1. Cancel Submitted Statements
   2. Halt Datastep/Proc: DATASTEP
   C. Cancel the dialog
   T. Terminate the SAS System
```

3. Type **Y** and press ENTER.

```
BREAK -> Language Processor
 Press Y to cancel submitted statements, N to continue.  y
```

Resubmitting the Program

1. In the appropriate Editor window, add a closing quotation mark to the DLM= option in the INFILE statement.

```
data work.NewSalesEmps;
   length First_Name $ 12 Last_Name $ 18
          Job_Title $ 25;
   infile 'newemps.csv' dlm=',';
   input First_Name $ Last_Name $
         Job_Title $ Salary;
run;

proc print data=work.NewSalesEmps;
run;

proc means data=work.NewSalesEmps;
   class Job_Title;
   var Salary;
run;
```

2. Resubmit the program.

When you make changes to the program in the Enhanced Editor and did not save the new version of the program, the window bar and the top border of the window reflect that you changed the program without saving it by putting an asterisk (*) beside the window name. When you save the program, the * disappears.

Exercises

Level 1

1. Diagnosing and Correcting a Misspelled Word

a. With the appropriate Editor window active, include the SAS program **p103e01**.

b. Submit the program.

c. Use the notes in the SAS log to identify the error. – mis pelled PRNNT, it should be print

d. Correct the error and resubmit the program.

Level 2

2. Diagnosing and Correcting a Missing Statement

a. With the appropriate Editor window active, include the SAS program **p103e02**.

b. Submit the program.

c. Are there any errors in the SAS log? yes

d. Notice the message in the title bar of the Editor window.

e. Why is PROC PRINT running? no RUN; statement

f. Add the missing statement to execute the PROC PRINT step.

g. Submit the added statement. –added RUN; statement

h. Confirm that the output was created for the program by viewing the Log and Output windows.

Level 3

3. Using the Help Facility to Determine the Types of Errors in SAS

a. In the Help facility, type **`syntax errors`** on the Index tab.

b. Double-click **syntax errors** in the results box.

c. In the Topics Found pop-up box, select **Error Processing and Debugging: Types of Errors in SAS**.

d. Name the five types of errors.

____

3.3 Chapter Review

Chapter Review

1. With what do SAS statements usually begin?

   -reserved word

2. With what do SAS statements always end?

   semicolon

3. What are two methods of commenting?

   - /* */

4. Name four types of syntax errors.

   -misspelled keywork
   -unmatched quotation mark
   -missing semicolon
   -invalid options

5. How do you save a program?

   → File, Save As

31

3.4 Solutions

Solutions to Exercises

1. **Diagnosing and Correcting a Misspelled Word**

   a. Include the SAS program.

   b. Submit the program.

   c. Use the notes in the SAS log to identify the error.

   d. Correct the error.

```
data work.country;
   length Country_Code $ 2 Country_Name $ 48;
   infile 'country.dat' dlm='!';
   input Country_Code $ Country_Name $;
run;

proc print data=work.country;
run;
```

2. **Diagnosing and Correcting a Missing Statement**

   a. Include the SAS program.

   b. Submit the program.

   c. Are there any errors in the SAS log? **No**

   d. Notice the message in the title bar.

   e. Why is PROC PRINT running? **The PROC PRINT step is missing a RUN statement.**

   f. Add the missing statement.

```
data work.donations;
   infile 'donation.dat';
   input Employee_ID Qtr1 Qtr2 Qtr3 Qtr4;
   Total=sum(Qtr1,Qtr2,Qtr3,Qtr4);
run;

proc print data=work.donations;
run;
```

   g. Submit the added statement.

   h. Confirm that the output was created.

3. Using the Help Facility to Determine the Types of Errors in SAS

a. In the Help facility, type `syntax errors` on the Index tab.

b. Double-click **syntax errors** in the results box.

c. Select **Error Processing and Debugging: Type of Errors in SAS**.

d. Name the five types of errors.

Syntax: when programming statements do not conform to the rules of the SAS language compile time

Semantic: when the language element is correct, but the element might not be valid for a particular usage compile time

Execution-time: when SAS attempts to execute a program and execution fails execution time

Data: when data values are invalid execution time

Macro-related: when you use the macro facility incorrectly

Solutions to Student Activities (Polls/Quizzes)

3.01 Quiz – Correct Answer

How many statements are in the DATA step?

a. 1
b. 3
c. 5 (circled)
d. 7

```
data work.NewSalesEmps;
   length First_Name $ 12
          Last_Name $ 18 Job_Title $ 25;
   infile 'newemps.csv' dlm=',';
   input First_Name $ Last_Name $
         Job_Title $ Salary;
run;
```

8

3.02 Multiple Choice Poll – Correct Answer

Which statement is true concerning the DATALINES statement based on reading the comment?

a. The DATALINES statement is used when reading data located in a raw data file.
b. The DATALINES statement is used when reading data located directly in the program. (circled)

20

3.03 Quiz – Correct Answer

This program has three syntax errors.

What are the errors?

```
daat work.NewSalesEmps;
   length First_Name $ 12
          Last_Name $ 18 Job_Title $ 25;
   infile 'newemps.csv' dlm=',';
   input First_Name $ Last_Name $
         Job_Title $ Salary;
run;

proc print data=work.NewSalesEmps
run;

proc means data=work.NewSalesEmps average max;
   class Job_Title;
   var Salary;
run;
```

27

p103d03

Solutions to Chapter Review

Chapter Review Answers

1. With what do SAS statements usually begin?
   identifying keyword

2. With what do SAS statements always end?
   semicolon

3. What are two methods of commenting?
   - ***/* comment */***
   - **** comment;***

32

continued...

Chapter Review Answers

4. Name four types of syntax errors.
   - **misspelled keywords**
   - **unmatched quotation marks**
   - **missing semicolons**
   - **invalid options**

5. How do you save a program?
   - **Issue the FILE command.**
   - **Select File ⇨ Save As.**

33

Chapter 4 Getting Familiar with SAS Data Sets

4.1 Examining Descriptor and Data Portions 4-3

Exercises 4-13

4.2 Accessing SAS Data Libraries 4-16

Demonstration: Accessing and Browsing SAS Data Libraries – Windows 4-24

Demonstration: Accessing and Browsing SAS Data Libraries – UNIX 4-28

Demonstration: Accessing and Browsing SAS Data Libraries – z/OS (OS/390) 4-31

Exercises 4-33

4.3 Accessing Relational Databases (Self-Study) 4-35

4.4 Chapter Review 4-40

4.5 Solutions 4-41

Solutions to Exercises 4-41

Solutions to Student Activities (Polls/Quizzes) 4-45

Solutions to Chapter Review 4-48

4.1 Examining Descriptor and Data Portions

Objectives

- Define the components of a SAS data set.
- Define a SAS variable.
- Identify a missing value and a SAS date value.
- State the naming conventions for SAS data sets and variables.
- Browse the descriptor portion of SAS data sets by using the CONTENTS procedure.
- Browse the data portion of SAS data sets by using the PRINT procedure.

METADATA – data about your data

3

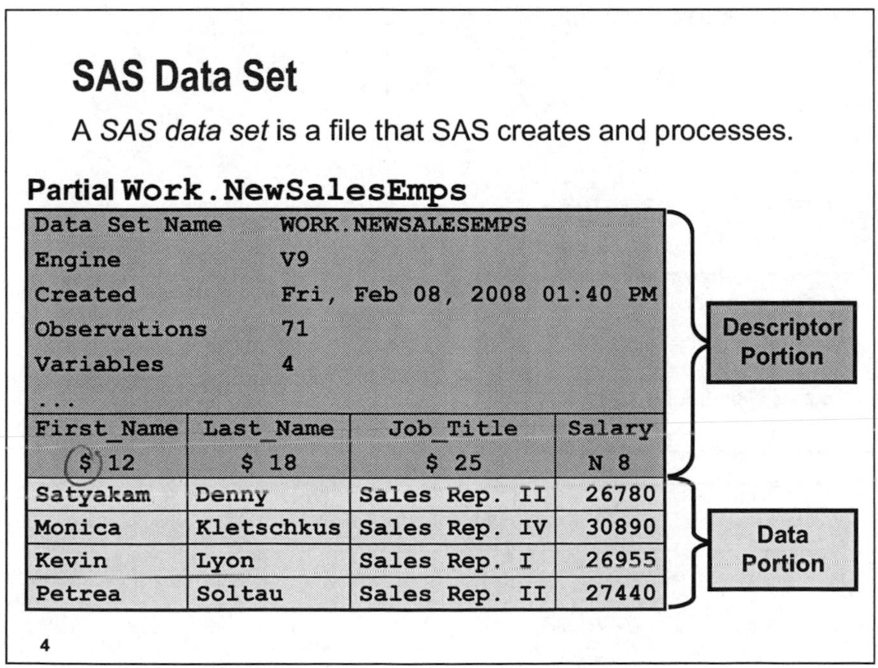
SAS Data Set
A *SAS data set* is a file that SAS creates and processes.
Partial Work.NewSalesEmps
Descriptor Portion
Data Portion
4

Data Set Name	WORK.NEWSALESEMPS		
Engine	V9		
Created	Fri, Feb 08, 2008 01:40 PM		
Observations	71		
Variables	4		
...			
First_Name	Last_Name	Job_Title	Salary
$ 12	$ 18	$ 25	N 8
Satyakam	Denny	Sales Rep. II	26780
Monica	Kletschkus	Sales Rep. IV	30890
Kevin	Lyon	Sales Rep. I	26955
Petrea	Soltau	Sales Rep. II	27440

Data must be in the form of a SAS data set to be processed by many SAS procedures and some DATA step statements.

A SAS data set is a specially structured file that contains data values.

$ – indicates the type

2 types:
① numeric data type – $
② character data type

Descriptor Portion

The *descriptor portion* of a SAS data set contains the following:

- general information about the SAS data set (such as data set name and number of observations)
- variable information (such as name, type, and length)

Partial `Work.NewSalesEmps`

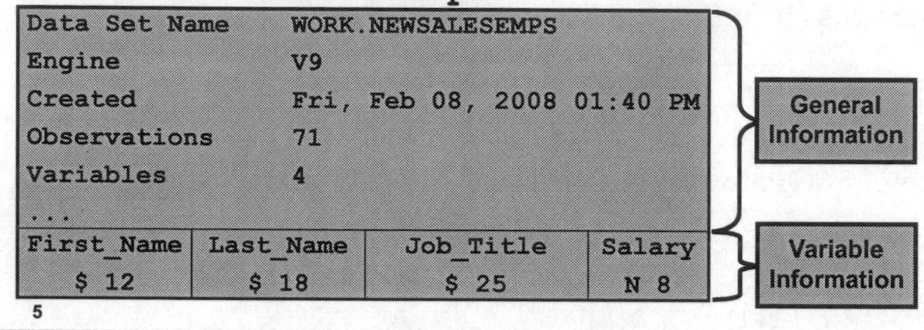

Data Set Name	WORK.NEWSALESEMPS
Engine	V9
Created	Fri, Feb 08, 2008 01:40 PM
Observations	71
Variables	4
...	

First_Name	Last_Name	Job_Title	Salary
$ 12	$ 18	$ 25	N 8

5

Browsing the Descriptor Portion

The *CONTENTS procedure* displays the descriptor portion of a SAS data set.

General form of the CONTENTS procedure:

> **PROC CONTENTS** DATA=*SAS-data-set*;
> **RUN;**

Example:

```
proc contents data=work.NewSalesEmps;
run;
```

6

p104d01

Browsing the Descriptor Portion

Partial PROC CONTENTS Output

```
                          The CONTENTS Procedure

Data Set Name          WORK.NEWSALESEMPS           Observations          71
Member Type            DATA                        Variables             4
Engine                 V9                          Indexes               0
Created                Wed, Jan 16, 2008           Observation Length    64
                       02:14:20 PM
Last Modified          Wed, Jan 16, 2008           Deleted Observations  0
                       02:14:20 PM
Protection                                         Compressed            NO
Data Set Type                                      Sorted                NO
Label


              Alphabetic List of Variables and Attributes

                    #    Variable      Type    Len

                    1    First_Name    Char     12
                    3    Job_Title     Char     25
                    2    Last_Name     Char     18
                    4    Salary        Num       8
```

7

This is a partial view of the default PROC CONTENTS output. PROC CONTENTS output also contains information about the physical location of the file and other data set information.

The descriptor portion contains the metadata of the data set.

4.01 Quiz

How many observations are in the data set **Work.donations**?

- Retrieve program **p104a01**.
- After the DATA step, add a PROC CONTENTS step to view the descriptor portion of **Work.donations**.
- Submit the program and review the results.

9

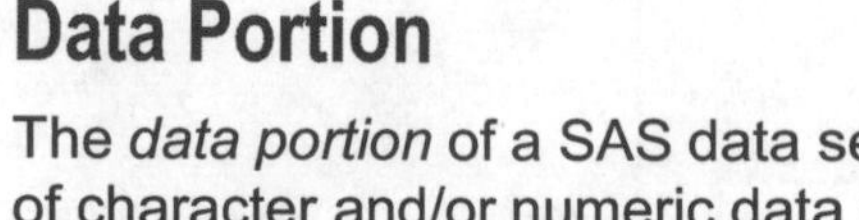

Data Portion

The *data portion* of a SAS data set is a rectangular table of character and/or numeric data values.

Partial `Work.NewSalesEmps`

First_Name	Last_Name	Job_Title	Salary
Satyakam	Denny	Sales Rep. II	26780
Monica	Kletschkus	Sales Rep. IV	30890
Kevin	Lyon	Sales Rep. I	26955
Petrea	Soltau	Sales Rep. II	27440

Variable names

Variable values

Character values

Numeric values

The data values are organized as a table of observations (rows) and variables (columns).

11

Variable names are part of the descriptor portion, not the data portion.

SAS Variable Values

There are two types of variables: ONLY !

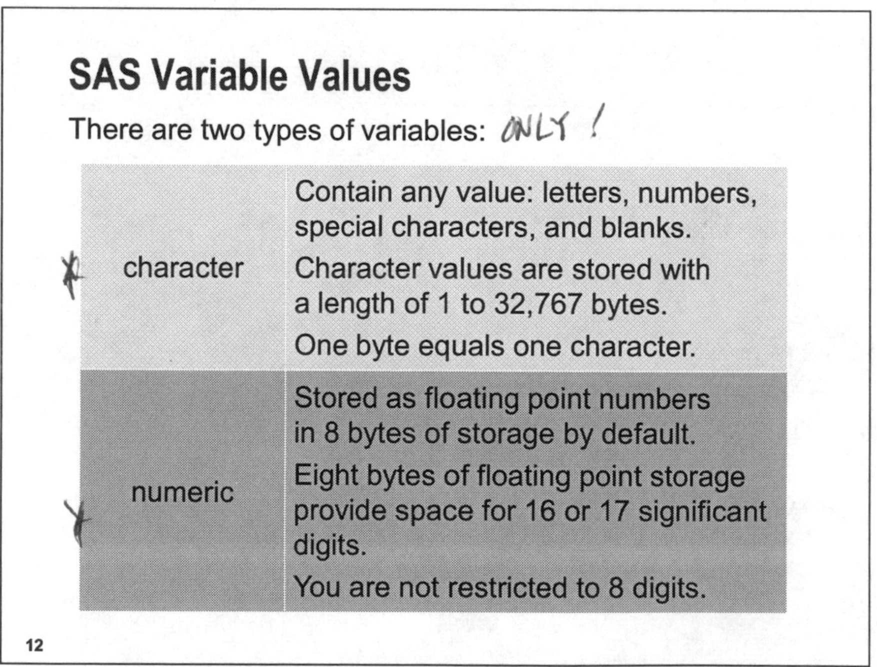

* character	Contain any value: letters, numbers, special characters, and blanks. Character values are stored with a length of 1 to 32,767 bytes. One byte equals one character.
* numeric	Stored as floating point numbers in 8 bytes of storage by default. Eight bytes of floating point storage provide space for 16 or 17 significant digits. You are not restricted to 8 digits.

12

Ex. 2009IRS —should be _2009IRS (underscore)

3 attributes of variables:
① name
② type
③ length

4.02 Multiple Choice Poll

Which variable type do you think SAS uses to store date values?

a. character

b. numeric

14

SAS Date Values

SAS stores date values as numeric values.

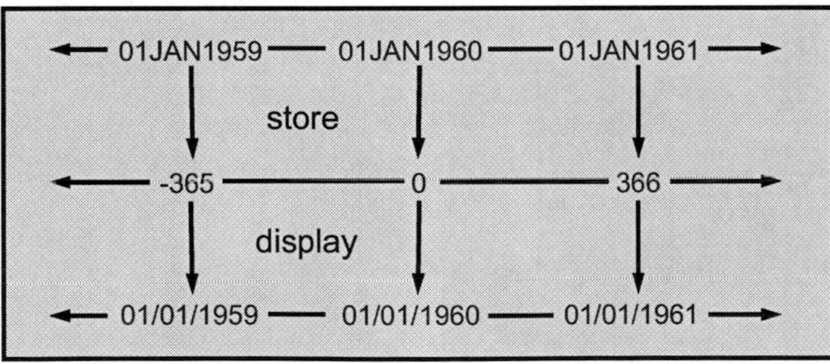

A *SAS date value* is stored as the number of days between January 1, 1960, and a specific date.

18

SAS can perform calculations on dates starting from 1582 A.D.

SAS can read either two- or four-digit year values. If SAS encounters a two-digit year, the YEARCUTOFF= system option is used to specify to which 100-year span the two-digit year should be attributed. For example, by setting the option YEARCUTOFF= option to 1950, the 100-year span from 1950 to 2049 is used for two-digit year values.

4.03 Quiz

What is the numeric value for today's date?

- Submit program **p104a02**.
- View the output to retrieve the current date as a numeric value referencing January 1, 1960.

(18315)

CurrentDate = today();

– gets current data

20

Missing Data Values

A value must exist for every variable for each observation. Missing values are valid values in a SAS data set.

Partial `Work.NewSalesEmps`

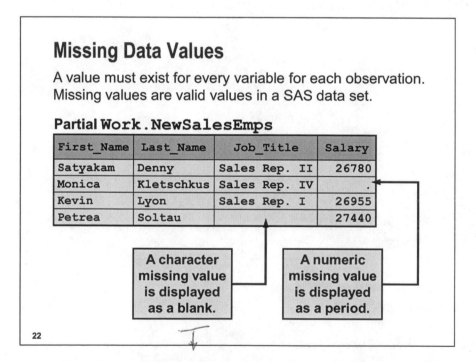

First_Name	Last_Name	Job_Title	Salary
Satyakam	Denny	Sales Rep. II	26780
Monica	Kletschkus	Sales Rep. IV	.
Kevin	Lyon	Sales Rep. I	26955
Petrea	Soltau		27440

A character missing value is displayed as a blank.

A numeric missing value is displayed as a period.

22

A period is the default display for a missing numeric value. The default display can be altered by changing the MISSING= SAS system option.

SAS Data Set and Variable Names

SAS names have these characteristics:

- can be 32 characters long.
- must start with a letter or underscore. Subsequent characters can be letters, underscores, or numerals.
- can be uppercase, lowercase, or mixed case.
- are not case sensitive.

23

Special characters can be used in variable names if you put the name in quotation marks followed immediately by the letter N.

Example: **`class 'Flight#'n;`**

In order to use special characters in variable names, the VALIDVARNAME option must be set to ANY.

Example: **`options validvarname=any;`**

4.04 Multiple Answer Poll

Which variable names are valid?

a. **`data5mon`**
b. **`5monthsdata`**
c. **`data#5`**
d. **`five months data`**
e. **`five_months_data`**
f. **`FiveMonthsData`**

25

SAS Data Set Terminology

Comparable Terminology:

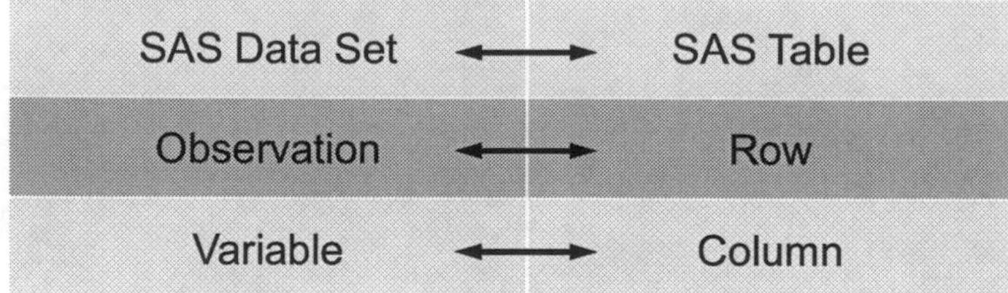

- The terminology of data set, observation, and variable is specific to SAS.
- The terminology of table, row, and column is common among databases.

27

Browsing the Data Portion

The *PRINT procedure* displays the data portion of a SAS data set.

By default, PROC PRINT displays the following:

- all observations
- all variables
- an Obs column on the left side

28

Browsing the Data Portion

General form of the PRINT procedure:

PROC PRINT DATA=*SAS-data-set*;
RUN;

PRINT = show

Example:

```
proc print data=work.NewSalesEmps;
run;
```

29

p104d02

Browsing the Data Portion

Partial PROC PRINT Output

Obs	First_Name	Last_Name	Job_Title	Salary
1	Satyakam	Denny	Sales Rep. II	26780
2	Monica	Kletschkus	Sales Rep. IV	30890
3	Kevin	Lyon	Sales Rep. I	26955
4	Petrea	Soltau	Sales Rep. II	27440
5	Marina	Iyengar	Sales Rep. III	29715
6	Shani	Duckett	Sales Rep. I	25795
7	Fang	Wilson	Sales Rep. II	26810
8	Michael	Minas	Sales Rep. I	26970
9	Amanda	Liebman	Sales Rep. II	27465
10	Vincent	Eastley	Sales Rep. III	29695
11	Viney	Barbis	Sales Rep. III	30265
12	Skev	Rusli	Sales Rep. II	26580
13	Narelle	James	Sales Rep. III	29990
14	Gerry	Snellings	Sales Rep. I	26445
15	Leonid	Karavdic	Sales Rep. II	27860

30

Browsing the Data Portion

Options and statements can be added to the PRINT procedure.

```
PROC PRINT DATA=SAS-data-set NOOBS;
      VAR variable(s);
RUN;
```

- The NOOBS option suppresses the observation numbers on the left side of the report.
- The VAR statement selects variables that appear in the report and determines their order.

31

Browsing the Data Portion

```
proc print data=work.NewSalesEmps noobs;
   var Last_Name First_Name Salary;
run;
```

Partial PROC PRINT Output

Last_Name	First_Name	Salary
Denny	Satyakam	26780
Kletschkus	Monica	30890
Lyon	Kevin	26955
Soltau	Petrea	27440
Iyengar	Marina	29715
Duckett	Shani	25795
Wilson	Fang	26810
Minas	Michael	26970
Liebman	Amanda	27465
Eastley	Vincent	29695

32 p104d03

Exercises

Level 1

1. Examining the Data Portion

a. Retrieve the starter program **p104e01**.

b. After the PROC CONTENTS step, add a PROC PRINT step to display all observations, all variables, and the Obs column for the data set named **`Work.donations`**.

c. Submit the program to create the following PROC PRINT report:

Partial PROC PRINT Output (First 10 of 124 Observations)

Obs	Employee_ ID	Qtr1	Qtr2	Qtr3	Qtr4	Total
1	120265	.	.	.	25	25
2	120267	15	15	15	15	60
3	120269	20	20	20	20	80
4	120270	20	10	5	.	35
5	120271	20	20	20	20	80
6	120272	10	10	10	10	40
7	120275	15	15	15	15	60
8	120660	25	25	25	25	100
9	120662	10	.	5	5	20
10	120663	.	.	5	.	5

d. In the PROC PRINT step, add a VAR statement and the NOOBS option to display only the **`Employee_ID`** and **`Total`** variables.

e. Submit the program to create the following PROC PRINT report:

Partial PROC PRINT Output (First 10 of 124 Observations)

proc print data=work.donation
noobs;
var Employee ID Total;
Run;

Employee_ ID	Total
120265	25
120267	60
120269	80
120270	35
120271	80
120272	40
120275	60
120660	100
120662	20
120663	5

Level 2

2. Examining the Descriptor and Data Portions

a. Retrieve the starter program **p104e02**.

b. After the DATA step, add a PROC CONTENTS step to display the descriptor portion of **`Work.newpacks`**.

c. Submit the program and answer the following questions:

How many observations are in the data set? 15

How many variables are in the data set? 3

What is the length (byte-size) of the variable **`Product_Name`**? 28-40

d. After the PROC CONTENTS step, add a PROC PRINT step with appropriate statements and options to display part of the data portion of **`Work.newpacks`**.

e. Submit the program to create the following PROC PRINT report:

```
Product_Name                                    Supplier_Name

Black/Black                                     Top Sports
X-Large Bottlegreen/Black                       Top Sports
Commanche Women's 6000 Q Backpack. Bark         Top Sports
Expedition Camp Duffle Medium Backpack          Miller Trading Inc
Feelgood 55-75 Litre Black Women's Backpack     Toto Outdoor Gear
Jaguar 50-75 Liter Blue Women's Backpack        Toto Outdoor Gear
Medium Black/Bark Backpack                      Top Sports
Medium Gold Black/Gold Backpack                 Top Sports
Medium Olive Olive/Black Backpack               Top Sports
Trekker 65 Royal Men's Backpack                 Toto Outdoor Gear
Victor Grey/Olive Women's Backpack              Top Sports
Deer Backpack                                   Luna sastreria S.A.
Deer Waist Bag                                  Luna sastreria S.A.
Hammock Sports Bag                              Luna sastreria S.A.
Sioux Men's Backpack 26 Litre.                  Miller Trading Inc
```

Level 3

3. Working with Times and Datetimes

a. Retrieve and submit the starter program **p104e03**.

b. Notice the values of **`CurrentTime`** and **`CurrentDateTime`** in the PROC PRINT output.

c. Use the Help facility to find documentation on how times and datetimes are stored in SAS.

Go to the CONTENTS tab in the SAS Help and Documentation and select **SAS Products** ⇨ **Base SAS** ⇨ **SAS 9.2 Language Reference: Concepts** ⇨ **SAS System Concepts** ⇨ **Dates, Times, and Intervals** ⇨ **About SAS Date, Time, and Datetime Values**.

d. Complete the following sentences:

A SAS time value is a value representing the number of seconds since midnight of the current day.

A SAS datetime value is a value representing the number of seconds between Jan. 1, 1960 and an hour/minute/second w/in a specified date.

4.2 Accessing SAS Data Libraries

Objectives

- Explain the concept of a SAS data library.
- Assign a library reference name to a SAS data library by using the LIBNAME statement.
- State the difference between a permanent library and a temporary library.
- Browse the contents of a SAS data library by using the SAS Explorer window.
- Investigate a SAS data library by using the CONTENTS procedure.

36

SAS Data Libraries

A *SAS data library* is a collection of SAS files that are recognized as a unit by SAS.

Directory-based System	A SAS data library is a directory.
Windows Example:	`s:\workshop`
UNIX Example:	`/users/`*`userid`*

z/OS (OS/390)	A SAS data library is an operating system file.
z/OS (OS/390) Example:	*`userid`*`.workshop.sasdata`

37

SAS Data Libraries

You can think of a SAS data library as a drawer in a filing cabinet and a SAS data set as one of the file folders in the drawer.

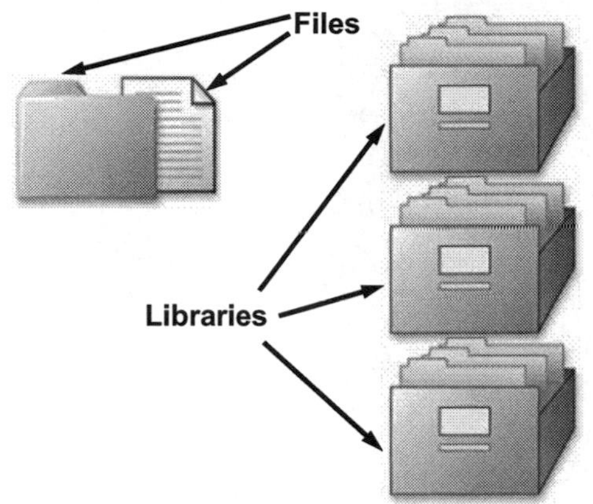

38

Assigning a Libref

Regardless of which host operating system you use, you identify SAS data libraries by assigning a *library reference name (libref)* to each library.

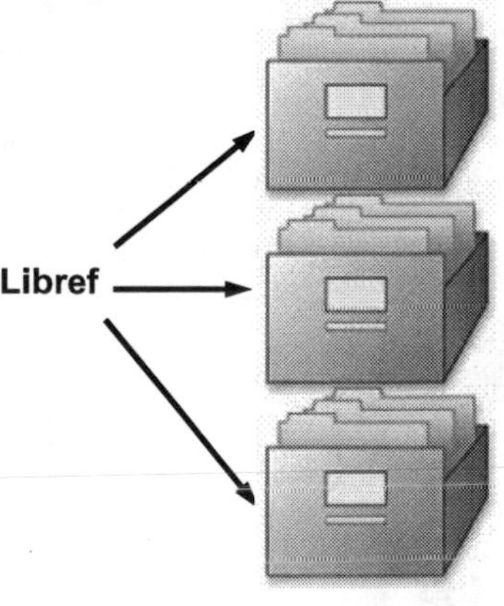

39

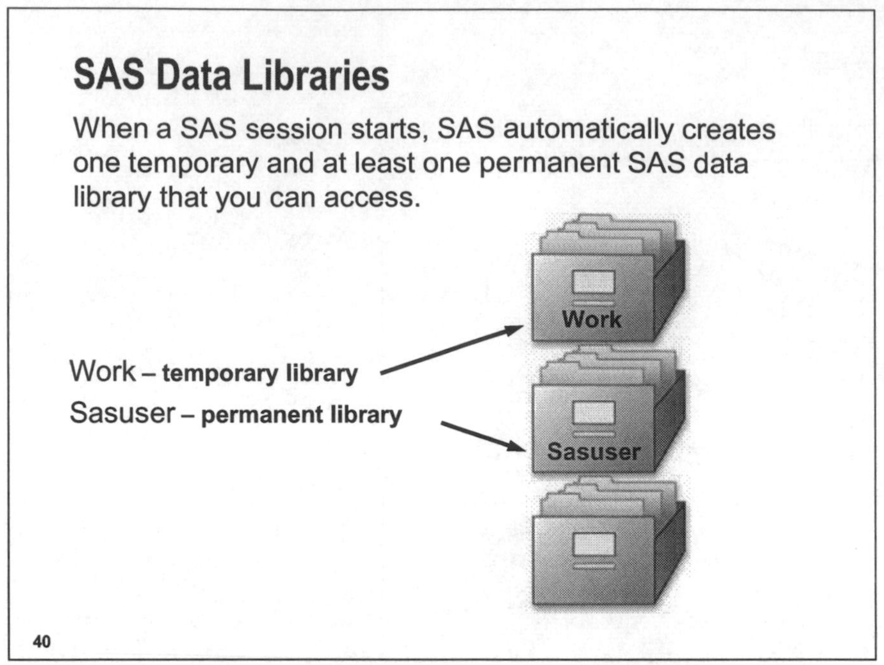

SAS Data Libraries
When a SAS session starts, SAS automatically creates one temporary and at least one permanent SAS data library that you can access.
Work – temporary library
Sasuser – permanent library
Work
Sasuser
40

The Work library and its SAS data files are deleted after your SAS session ends.

SAS data sets in permanent libraries such as the Sasuser library are saved after your SAS session ends.

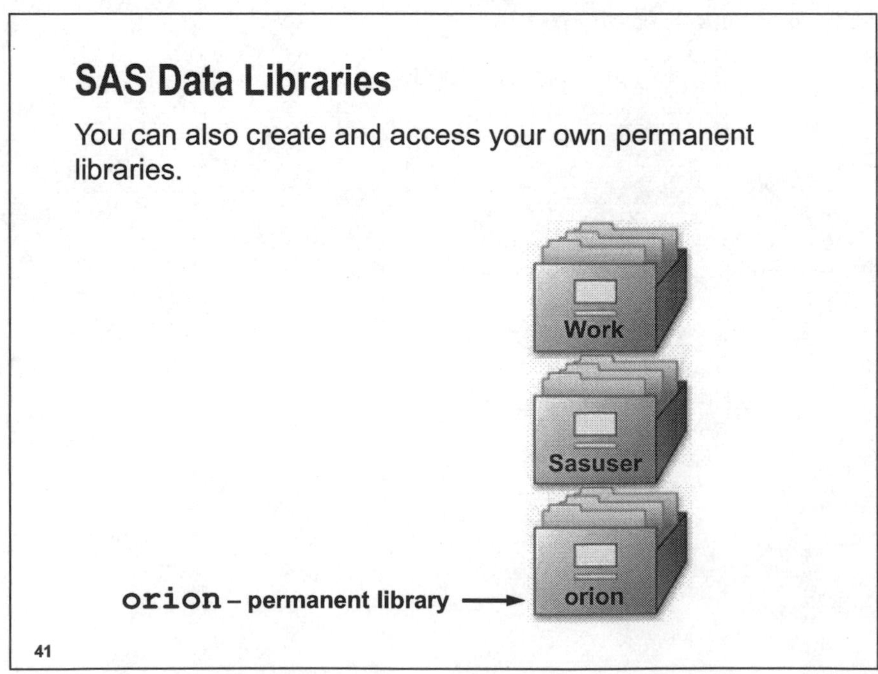

SAS Data Libraries
You can also create and access your own permanent libraries.
Work
Sasuser
orion – permanent library
orion
41

Assigning a Libref

You can use the *LIBNAME statement* to assign a library reference name (libref) to a SAS data library.

General form of the LIBNAME statement:

LIBNAME *libref* *'SAS-data-library'* *<options>*;

Rules for naming a libref:

- The name must be 8 characters or less.
- The name must begin with a letter or underscore.
- The remaining characters must be letters, numerals, or underscores.

42

For Windows and UNIX, SAS can only make an association between a libref and an existing directory. The LIBNAME statement does not create a new directory.

z/OS (OS/390) users can use a DD statement or TSO ALLOCATE command instead of issuing a LIBNAME statement.

Assigning a Libref

Examples:

Windows

```
libname orion 's:\workshop';
```

UNIX

```
libname orion '/users/userid';
```

z/OS (OS/390)

```
libname orion 'userid.workshop.sasdata';
```

43

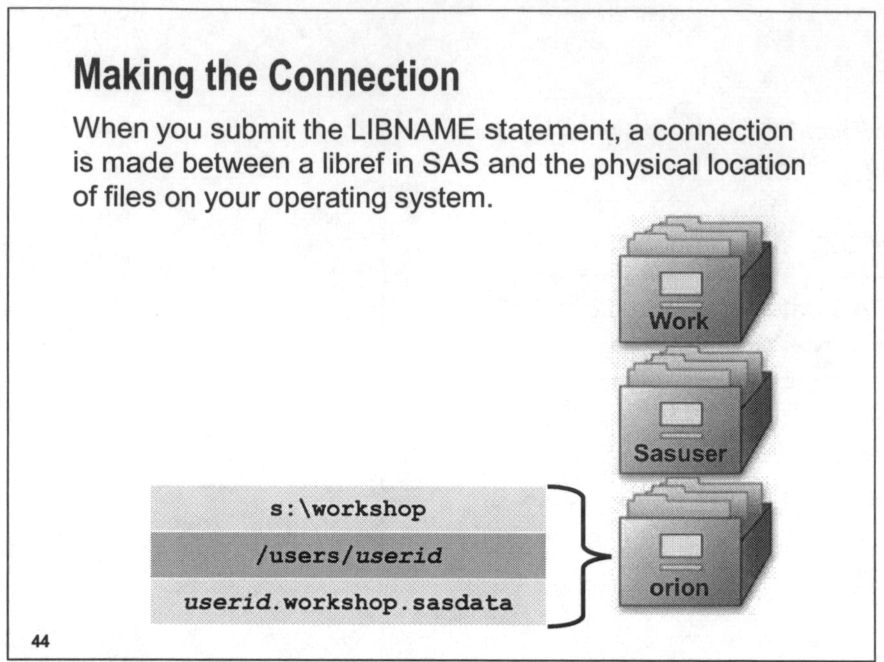

Making the Connection
When you submit the LIBNAME statement, a connection is made between a libref in SAS and the physical location of files on your operating system.
Work
Sasuser
s:\workshop
/users/userid
userid.workshop.sasdata
orion
44

When your session ends, the link between the libref and the physical location of your files is broken.

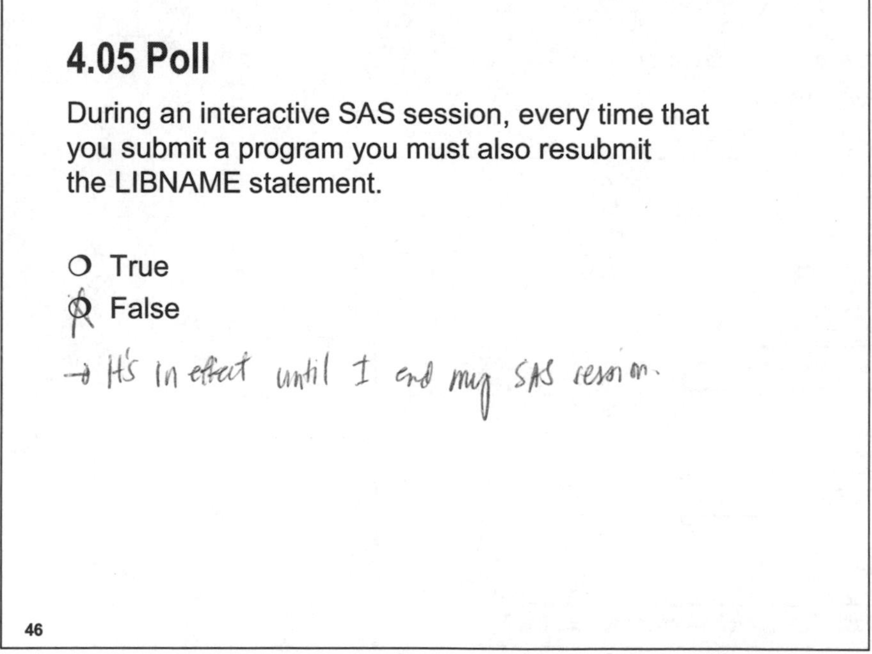

4.05 Poll
During an interactive SAS session, every time that you submit a program you must also resubmit the LIBNAME statement.
True
False
46

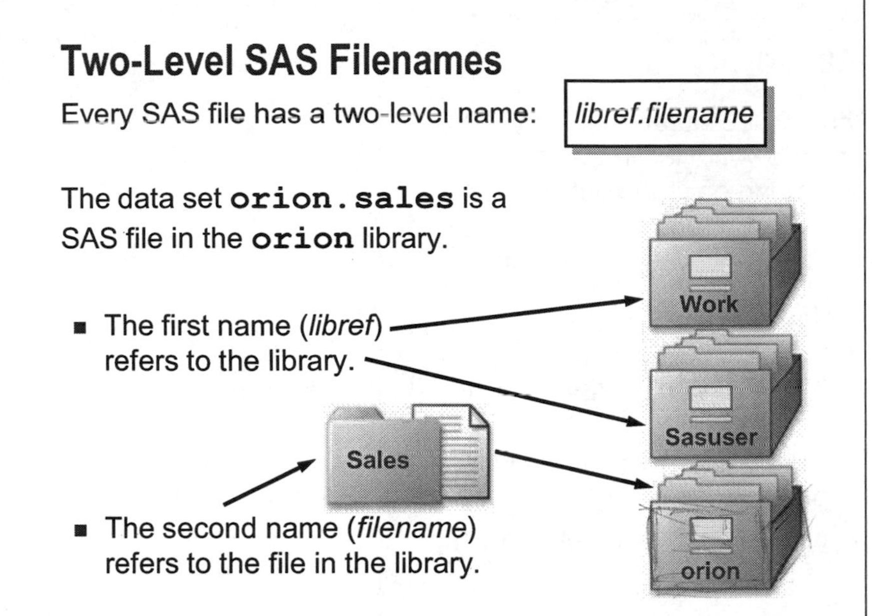

Two-Level SAS Filenames
Every SAS file has a two-level name:
libref.filename
The data set orion.sales is a SAS file in the orion library.
The first name (libref) refers to the library.
The second name (filename) refers to the file in the library.
Work
Sasuser
Sales
orion
48

Temporary SAS Filename

The default libref is Work if the libref is omitted.

`NewSalesEmps` ⟷ `work.NewSalesEmps`

```
data NewSalesEmps;
   length First_Name $ 12
          Last_Name $ 18 Job_Title $ 25;
   infile 'newemps.csv' dlm=',';
   input First_Name $ Last_Name $
         Job_Title $ Salary;
run;

proc print data=work.NewSalesEmps;
run;
```

49

Browsing a SAS Data Library

The *SAS Explorer* enables you to manage your files in the windowing environment.

In the SAS Explorer, you can do the following:

- view a list of all the libraries available during your current SAS session
- navigate to see all members of a specific library
- display the descriptor portion of a SAS data set

50

The SAS windowing environment opens the SAS Explorer by default on many hosts. You can issue the SAS EXPLORER command to invoke this window if it does not appear by default.

The SAS Explorer can be opened by selecting

- **View** ⇨ **Contents Only**

or

- **View** ⇨ **Explorer**.

In the Contents Only view, the SAS Explorer is a single-paned window that contains the contents of your SAS environment. As you open folders, the folder contents replace the previous contents in the same window.

In the Explorer view of the SAS Explorer window, folders appear in the tree view on the left and folder contents appear in the list view on the right.

Browsing a SAS Data Library

The CONTENTS procedure with the _ALL_ keyword produces a list of all the SAS files in the data library.

```
PROC CONTENTS DATA=libref._ALL_ NODS;
RUN;
```

- The NODS option suppresses the descriptor portions of the data sets.
- NODS is only used in conjunction with the keyword _ALL_.

51

If you are using a noninteractive or batch SAS session, the CONTENTS procedure is an alternative to the EXPLORER command.

Accessing and Browsing SAS Data Libraries – Windows

p104d04

1. Retrieve and submit the program **p104d04**.

```
libname orion 's:\workshop';

proc contents data=orion._all_ nods;
run;
```

2. Check the log to confirm that the `orion` libref was assigned.

```
1    libname orion 's:\workshop';
NOTE: Libref ORION was successfully assigned as follows:
      Engine:        V9
      Physical Name: s:\workshop
```

3. View the PROC CONTENTS output in the Output window.

Partial PROC CONTENTS Output

```
                              The CONTENTS Procedure

                                    Directory

                            Libref          ORION
                            Engine          V9
                            Physical Name   s:\workshop
                            File Name       s:\workshop


                                      Member      File
            #  Name                   Type        Size  Last Modified

            1  BUDGET                 DATA        5120  12Feb08:00:57:25
            2  COUNTRY                DATA       17408  12Feb08:00:57:25
               COUNTRY                INDEX      17408  12Feb08:00:57:25
            3  CUSTOMER               DATA       33792  12Feb08:00:57:25
            4  CUSTOMER_DIM           DATA       33792  12Feb08:00:57:25
            5  CUSTOMER_TYPE          DATA       17408  12Feb08:00:57:25
               CUSTOMER_TYPE          INDEX       9216  12Feb08:00:57:25
            6  EMPLOYEE_ADDRESSES     DATA       74752  12Feb08:00:57:25
            7  EMPLOYEE_DONATIONS     DATA       25600  12Feb08:00:57:25
            8  EMPLOYEE_ORGANIZATION  DATA       41984  12Feb08:00:57:25
            9  EMPLOYEE_PAYROLL       DATA       33792  12Feb08:00:57:25
           10  LOOKUP_COUNTRY         DATA       37888  12Feb08:00:57:25
           11  MNTH7_2007             DATA        5120  12Feb08:00:57:25
           12  MNTH8_2007             DATA        5120  12Feb08:00:57:25
           13  MNTH9_2007             DATA        5120  12Feb08:00:57:25
           14  NONSALES               DATA       33792  12Feb08:00:57:25
```

4. Select the Explorer tab on the SAS window bar to activate the SAS Explorer or sclcct **View** ⇨ **Contents Only**.

5. Double-click **Libraries** to show all available libraries.

6. Double-click on the **Orion** library to show all members of that library.

7. Right-click on the **Sales** data set and select **Properties**.

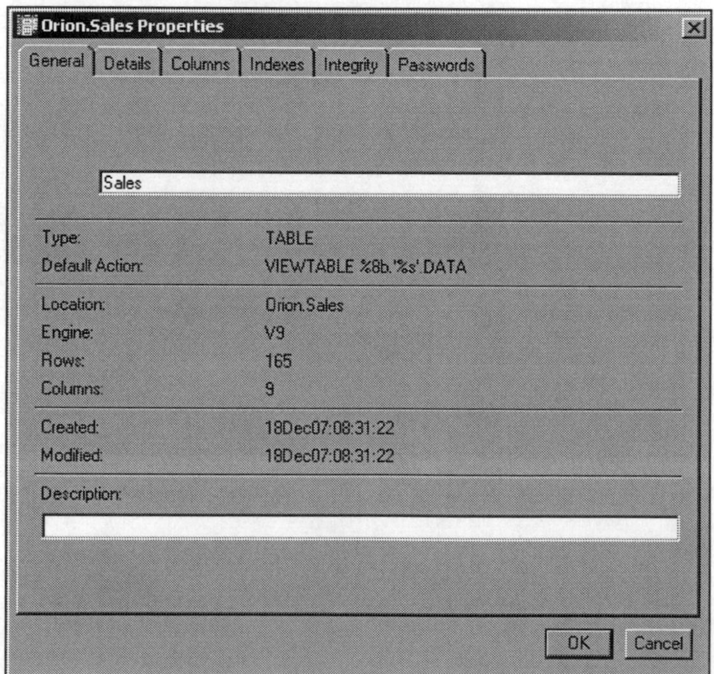

This default view provides general information about the data set, such as the library in which it is stored, the type of information it contains, its creation date, the number of observations and variables, and so on. You can request specific information about the columns in the data table by selecting the **Columns** tab at the top of the Properties window.

8. Select [X] to close the Properties window.

9. Double-click on the **Sales** data set or right-click on the file and select **Open**.

   This opens the data set in a VIEWTABLE window. A view of `orion.sales` is shown below.

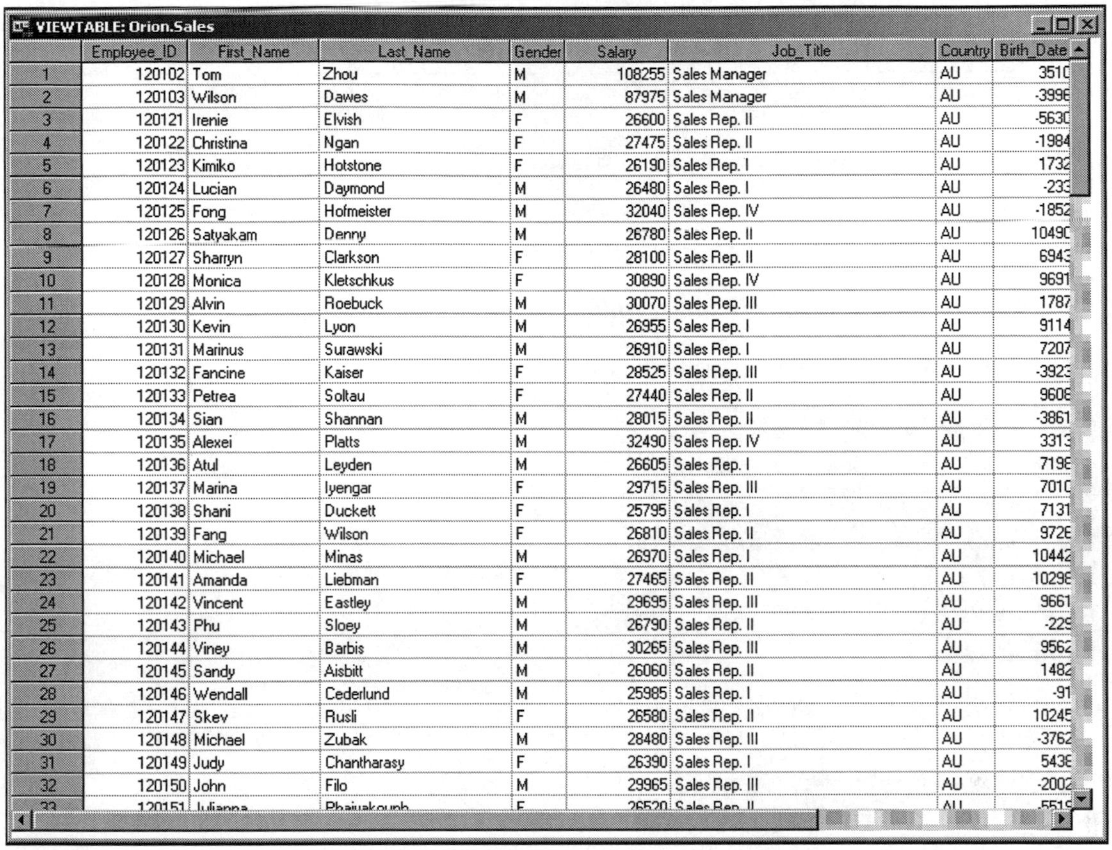

VIEWTABLE: Orion.Sales

	Employee_ID	First_Name	Last_Name	Gender	Salary	Job_Title	Country	Birth_Date
1	120102	Tom	Zhou	M	108255	Sales Manager	AU	3510
2	120103	Wilson	Dawes	M	87975	Sales Manager	AU	-3996
3	120121	Irenie	Elvish	F	26600	Sales Rep. II	AU	-5630
4	120122	Christina	Ngan	F	27475	Sales Rep. II	AU	-1984
5	120123	Kimiko	Hotstone	F	26190	Sales Rep. I	AU	1732
6	120124	Lucian	Daymond	M	26480	Sales Rep. I	AU	-233
7	120125	Fong	Hofmeister	M	32040	Sales Rep. IV	AU	-1852
8	120126	Satyakam	Denny	M	26780	Sales Rep. II	AU	10490
9	120127	Sharryn	Clarkson	F	28100	Sales Rep. II	AU	6943
10	120128	Monica	Kletschkus	F	30890	Sales Rep. IV	AU	9691
11	120129	Alvin	Roebuck	M	30070	Sales Rep. III	AU	1787
12	120130	Kevin	Lyon	M	26955	Sales Rep. I	AU	9114
13	120131	Marinus	Surawski	M	26910	Sales Rep. I	AU	7207
14	120132	Fancine	Kaiser	F	28525	Sales Rep. III	AU	-3923
15	120133	Petrea	Soltau	F	27440	Sales Rep. II	AU	9608
16	120134	Sian	Shannan	M	28015	Sales Rep. II	AU	-3861
17	120135	Alexei	Platts	M	32490	Sales Rep. IV	AU	3313
18	120136	Atul	Leyden	M	26605	Sales Rep. I	AU	7198
19	120137	Marina	Iyengar	F	29715	Sales Rep. III	AU	7010
20	120138	Shani	Duckett	F	25795	Sales Rep. I	AU	7131
21	120139	Fang	Wilson	F	26810	Sales Rep. II	AU	9726
22	120140	Michael	Minas	M	26970	Sales Rep. I	AU	10442
23	120141	Amanda	Liebman	F	27465	Sales Rep. II	AU	10298
24	120142	Vincent	Eastley	M	29695	Sales Rep. III	AU	9661
25	120143	Phu	Sloey	M	26790	Sales Rep. II	AU	-229
26	120144	Viney	Barbis	M	30265	Sales Rep. III	AU	9562
27	120145	Sandy	Aisbitt	M	26060	Sales Rep. II	AU	1482
28	120146	Wendall	Cederlund	M	25985	Sales Rep. I	AU	-91
29	120147	Skev	Rusli	F	26580	Sales Rep. II	AU	10245
30	120148	Michael	Zubak	M	28480	Sales Rep. III	AU	-3762
31	120149	Judy	Chantharasy	F	26390	Sales Rep. I	AU	5438
32	120150	John	Filo	M	29965	Sales Rep. III	AU	-2002
33	120151	Julianna	Phaiyakounh	F	26520	Sales Rep. II	AU	-5519

In addition to browsing SAS data sets, you can use the VIEWTABLE window to edit data sets, create data sets, and customize your view of a SAS data set. For example, you can do the following:

- sort your data
- change the color and fonts of variables
- display variable labels versus variable names
- remove and add variables

Variable labels are displayed by default. Display variable names instead of variable labels by selecting **View** ⇨ **Column Names**.

10. Select [X] to close the VIEWTABLE window.

11. With the Explorer window active, select [Up One Level] to return to **Libraries**.

Accessing and Browsing SAS Data Libraries – UNIX

p104d04

1. Retrieve and submit the program **p104d04**.

```
libname orion '/users/userid';

proc contents data=orion._all_ nods;
run;
```

2. Check the log to confirm that the `orion` libref was assigned.
3. View the PROC CONTENTS output in the Output window.
4. Select **View** ⇨ **Contents Only** to activate the SAS Explorer.

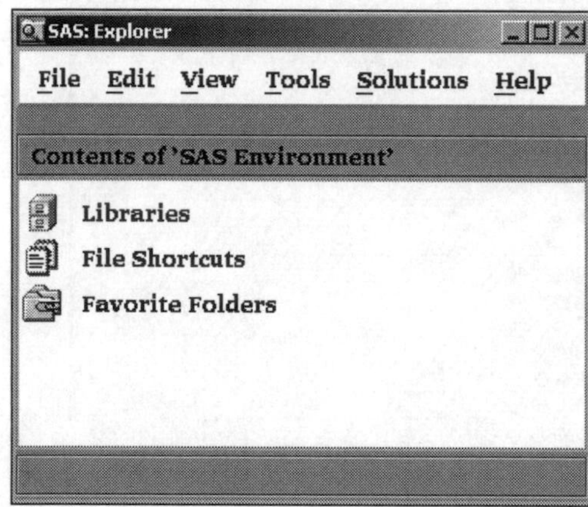

5. Double-click **Libraries** to show all available libraries.

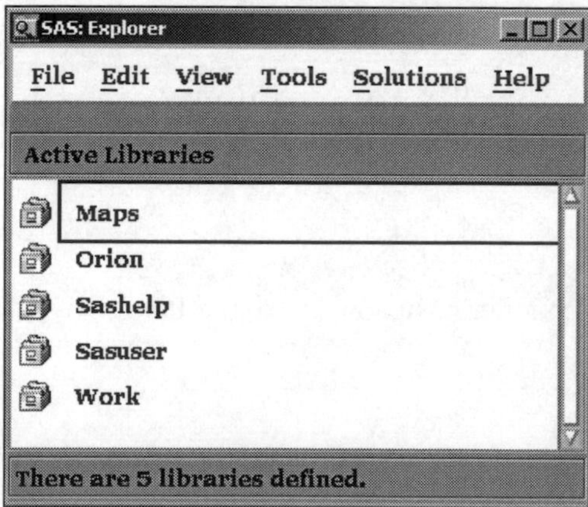

6. Double-click on the **Orion** library to show all members of that library.

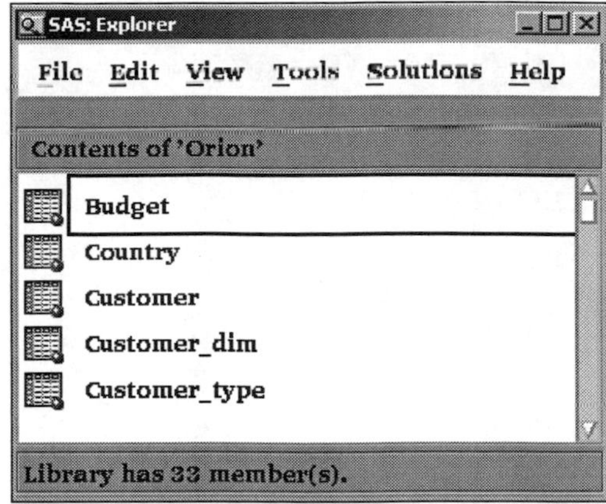

7. Right-click on the **Sales** data set and select **Properties**.

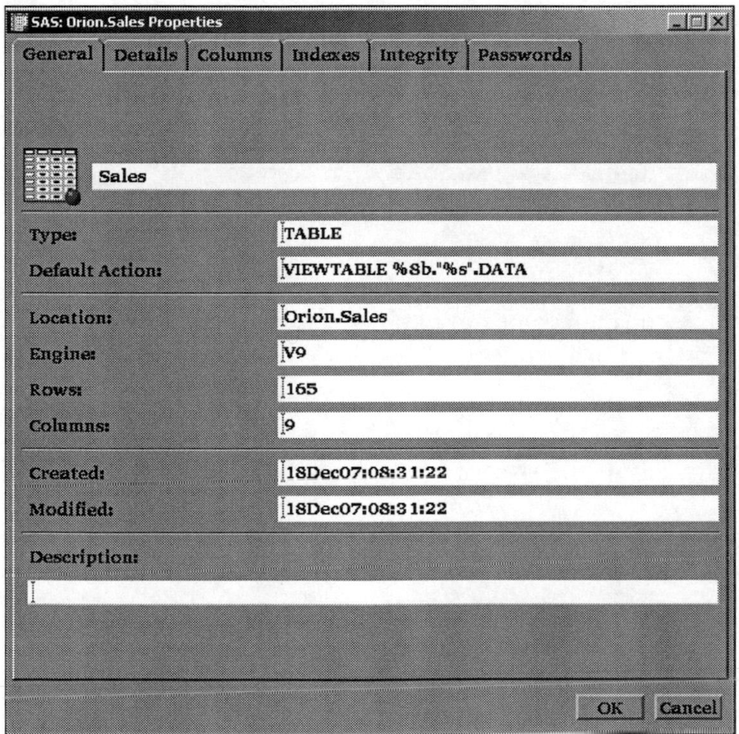

8. Select X to close the Properties window.

9. Double-click on the **Sales** data set or right-click on the file and select **Open**.

   This opens the data set in a VIEWTABLE window. A view of `orion.sales` is shown below.

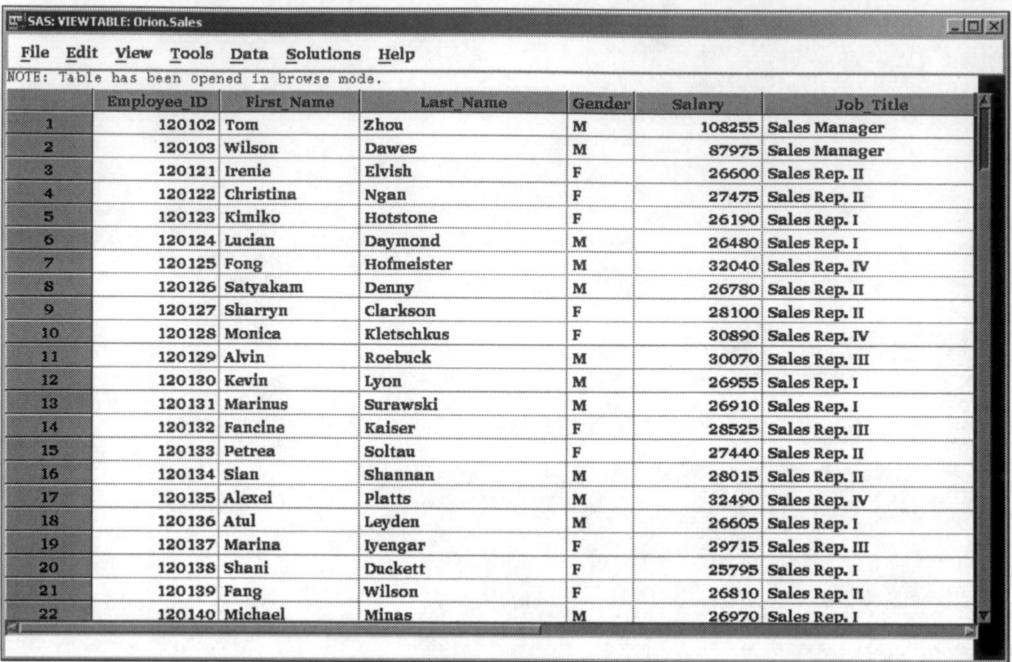

	Employee_ID	First_Name	Last_Name	Gender	Salary	Job_Title
1	120102	Tom	Zhou	M	108255	Sales Manager
2	120103	Wilson	Dawes	M	87975	Sales Manager
3	120121	Irenie	Elvish	F	26600	Sales Rep. II
4	120122	Christina	Ngan	F	27475	Sales Rep. II
5	120123	Kimiko	Hotstone	F	26190	Sales Rep. I
6	120124	Lucian	Daymond	M	26480	Sales Rep. I
7	120125	Fong	Hofmeister	M	32040	Sales Rep. IV
8	120126	Satyakam	Denny	M	26780	Sales Rep. II
9	120127	Sharryn	Clarkson	F	28100	Sales Rep. II
10	120128	Monica	Kletschkus	F	30890	Sales Rep. IV
11	120129	Alvin	Roebuck	M	30070	Sales Rep. III
12	120130	Kevin	Lyon	M	26955	Sales Rep. I
13	120131	Marinus	Surawski	M	26910	Sales Rep. I
14	120132	Fancine	Kaiser	F	28525	Sales Rep. III
15	120133	Petrea	Soltau	F	27440	Sales Rep. II
16	120134	Sian	Shannan	M	28015	Sales Rep. II
17	120135	Alexei	Platts	M	32490	Sales Rep. IV
18	120136	Atul	Leyden	M	26605	Sales Rep. I
19	120137	Marina	Iyengar	F	29715	Sales Rep. III
20	120138	Shani	Duckett	F	25795	Sales Rep. I
21	120139	Fang	Wilson	F	26810	Sales Rep. II
22	120140	Michael	Minas	M	26970	Sales Rep. I

10. Select [X] to close the VIEWTABLE window.

11. With the SAS Explorer active, select [up-folder icon] on the Toolbox to return to **Libraries**.

Accessing and Browsing SAS Data Libraries – z/OS (OS/390)

.workshop.sascode(p104d04)

1. Retrieve and submit the program **p104d04**.

```
libname orion '.workshop.sasdata';

proc contents data=orion._all_ nods;
run;
```

2. Check the log to confirm that the **orion** libref was assigned.

3. View the PROC CONTENTS output in the Output window.

4. Type **explorer** on the command line and press ENTER to activate the SAS Explorer.

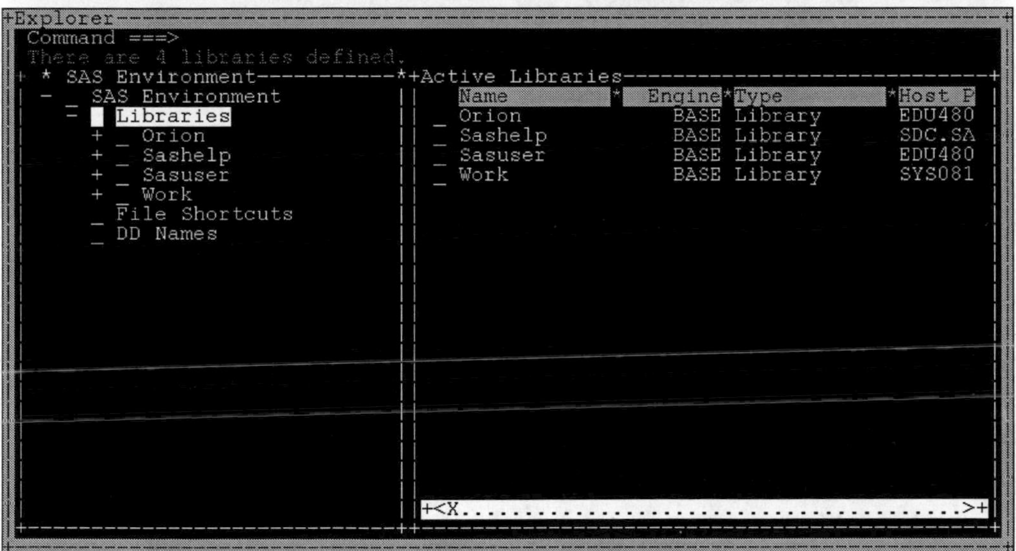

5. Type **s** beside **Orion** and press ENTER to show all members of that library.

libname orion 's:\workshop'; – created orion folder under S:\workshop

6. Type **s** beside **Sales** and press ENTER to display the properties.

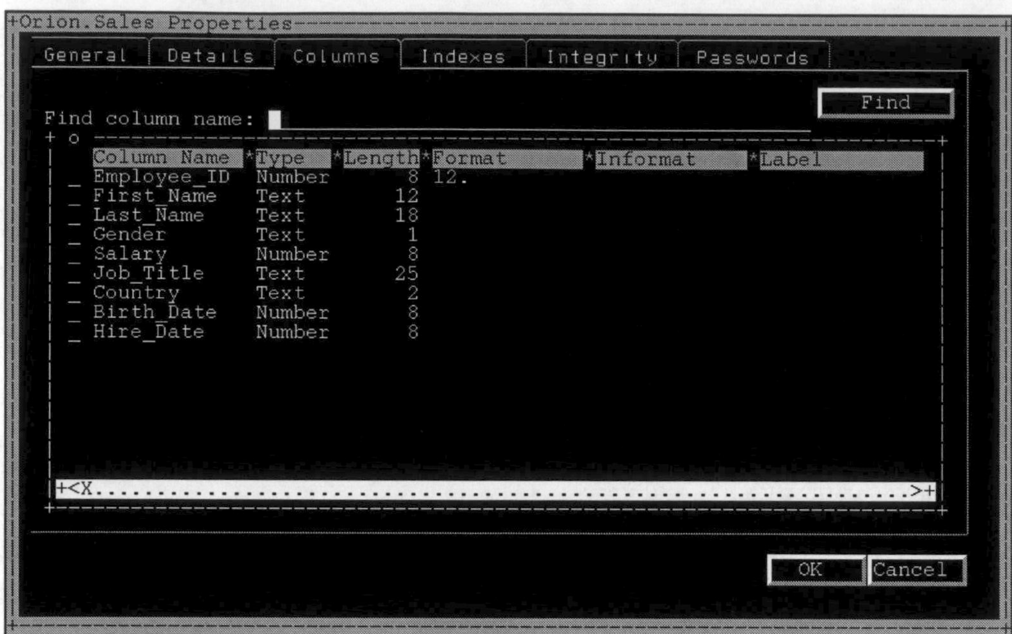

7. Select **OK** to close the Properties window.

8. Type **?** beside **Sales** and press ENTER.

9. Select **Open** to open the FSVIEW window.

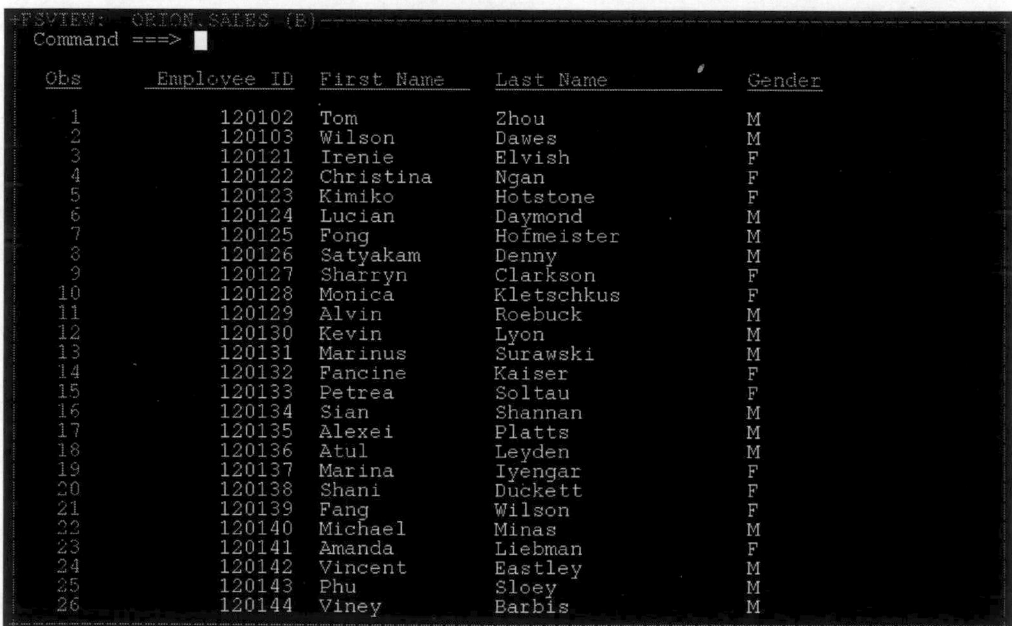

10. Type **end** to close the FSVIEW window.

11. Type **end** to close the SAS Explorer.

Exercises

Level 1

4. Accessing a SAS Data Library

a. Write and submit the appropriate LIBNAME statement to provide access to the **orion** libref.

Fill in the blank with the location of your SAS data library.
libname orion ' s:\workshop **';**

Possible location of your SAS data library:

Windows	**s:\workshop**
UNIX	**/users/*userid***
z/OS (OS/390)	**.workshop.sasdata**

b. Check the log to confirm that the SAS data library was assigned.

```
NOTE: Libref ORION was successfully assigned as follows:
```

c. Add a PROC CONTENTS step to list all the SAS data sets in the **orion** library. Do not display the descriptor portions of the individual data sets.

d. Add another PROC CONTENTS step to display the descriptor portion of the data set **orion.sales**.

e. Use the SAS Explorer window to view the contents of the **orion** library.

Level 2

5. Reviewing Concepts

a. SAS statements usually begin with a(n) reserved word / identifying keyword.

b. Every SAS statement ends with a Semi-colon.

c. The descriptor portion of a SAS data set can be viewed using the CONTENTS procedure.

d. Character variable values can be up to 32,767 characters long and use 1 byte(s) of storage per character.

e. By default, numeric variables are stored in 8 bytes of storage.

f. The internally stored SAS date value for January 3, 1960, is 2.

Jan 1 - 0
Jan 2 - 1
Jan 3 - 2

g. A SAS variable name has ____________ to ____________ characters and begins with a ____________ or an ____________.

h. A missing character value is displayed as a ____________.

i. A missing numeric value is displayed as a ____________.

j. When a SAS session starts, SAS automatically creates the temporary library called ____________.

k. A libref name must be ____________ characters or less.

l. What are the two kinds of steps? ____________

m. What are the three primary windows in the SAS windowing environment? ____________

n. What are the two portions of every SAS data set? ____________

o. What are the two types of variables? ____________

p. True or False: If a SAS program produces output, then the program ran successfully and there is no need to check the SAS log.

q. True or False: There are two methods for commenting in a SAS program.

r. True or False: Omitting a semicolon never causes errors.

s. True or False: A library reference name (libref) references a particular data set.

t. True or False: If a data set is referenced with a one level name, **Work** is the implied libref.

u. True or False: The _ALL_ keyword is used with the PRINT procedure.

Level 3

6. Investigating the LIBNAME Statement

a. Use the Help facility to find documentation about the LIBNAME statement.

Go to the CONTENTS tab in the SAS Help and Documentation and select **SAS Products** ⇨ **Base SAS** ⇨ **SAS 9.2 Language Reference: Dictionary** ⇨ **Dictionary of Language Elements** ⇨ **Statements** ⇨ **LIBNAME Statement**.

b. Answer the following questions:

What argument disassociates one or more currently assigned librefs? ____________

What system option provides you the convenience of specifying only a one-level name for permanent SAS files? ____________

c. Write and submit a LIBNAME statement that shows the attributes of all currently assigned SAS libraries in the SAS log. ____________

4.3 Accessing Relational Databases (Self-Study)

Objectives

- Assign a library reference name to a relational database by using the LIBNAME statement.
- Reference a relational database table using a SAS two-level name.

62

The LIBNAME Statement (Review)

The *LIBNAME statement* assigns a library reference name (libref) to a SAS data library.

General form of the LIBNAME statement:

LIBNAME *libref 'SAS-data-library' <options>*;

63

The SAS/ACCESS LIBNAME Statement

The *SAS/ACCESS LIBNAME statement* assigns a library reference name (libref) to a relational database.

General form of the SAS/ACCESS LIBNAME statement:

LIBNAME *libref engine-name <SAS/ACCESS-options>;*

After a database is associated with a libref, you can use a SAS two-level name to specify any table in the database and then work with the table as you would with a SAS data set.

64

The SAS/ACCESS interface to relational databases is a family of interfaces (each of which is licensed separately) that enable you to interact with data in other vendors' databases from within SAS.

The *engine-name* such as Oracle or DB2 is the SAS/ACCESS component that reads from and writes to your DBMS. The engine name is required. Because the SAS/ACCESS LIBNAME statement associates a libref with a SAS/ACCESS engine that supports connections to a particular DBMS, it requires a DBMS-specific engine name.

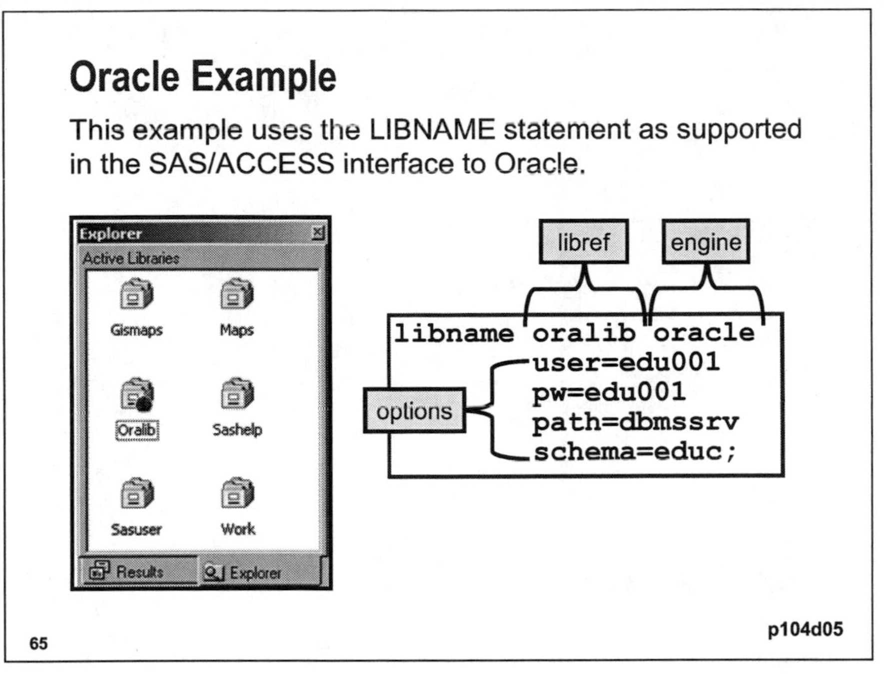

USER= specifies an optional Oracle user name. If the user name contains blanks or national characters, enclose it in quotation marks. USER= must be used with PASSWORD=.

PASSWORD= or *PW*= specifies an optional Oracle password that is associated with the Oracle user name.

PATH= specifies the Oracle driver, node, and database. SAS/ACCESS uses the same Oracle path designation that you use to connect to Oracle directly. See your database administrator to determine the databases that are set up in your operating environment, and to determine the default values if you do not specify a database.

SCHEMA= enables you to read database objects, such as tables and views, in the specified schema. If this option is omitted, you connect to the default schema for your DBMS. The values for SCHEMA= are usually case sensitive, so use care when you specify this option.

Oracle Example

Any table in this Oracle database can be referenced using a SAS two-level name.

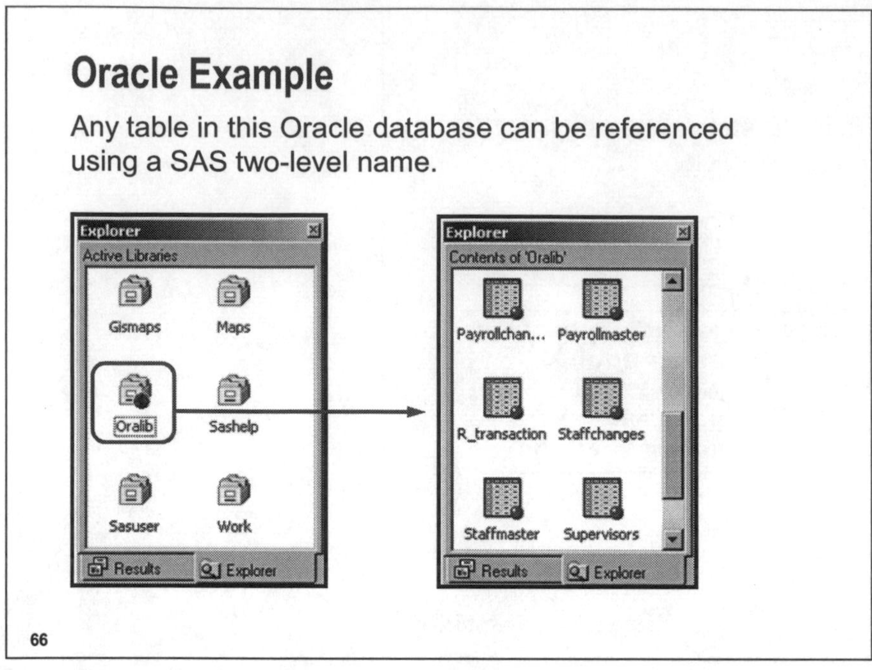

66

Oracle Example

```
libname oralib oracle
        user=edu001 pw=edu001
        path=dbmssrv schema=educ;

proc print data=oralib.supervisors;
run;

data work.staffpay;
   merge oralib.staffmaster
         oralib.payrollmaster;
   by empid;
run;

libname oralib clear;
```

67 p104d05

The CLEAR option in the LIBNAME statement disassociates the libref. Disassociating the libref disconnects the database engine from the database and closes any resources that are associated with that libref's connection.

4.06 Quiz

Which option in the LIBNAME statement specifies a user's password when accessing an Informix database?

Documentation on SAS/ACCESS for Informix can be found in the SAS Help and Documentation from the Contents tab (**SAS Products** ⇨ **SAS/ACCESS** ⇨ **SAS/ACCESS 9.2 for Relational Databases Reference** ⇨ **DBMS-Specific Reference** ⇨ **SAS/ACCESS for Informix** ⇨ **LIBNAME Statement Specifics for Informix**).

69

4.4 Chapter Review

Chapter Review

1. What structure is a SAS data library in UNIX or Windows?
2. What structure is a SAS data library in z/OS (OS/390)?
3. What is the name of the permanent SAS data library that SAS creates for you?
4. What can you do with the SAS Explorer?
5. What window enables you to interactively browse a SAS data set?

72

4.5 Solutions

Solutions to Exercises

1. Examining the Data Portion

a. Retrieve the starter program.

b. After the PROC CONTENTS step, add a PROC PRINT step.

```
data work.donations;
   infile 'donation.dat';
   input Employee_ID Qtr1 Qtr2 Qtr3 Qtr4;
   Total=sum(Qtr1,Qtr2,Qtr3,Qtr4);
run;

proc contents data=work.donations;
run;

proc print data=work.donations;
run;
```

c. Submit the program.

d. In the PROC PRINT step, add a VAR statement and the NOOBS option.

```
proc print data=work.donations noobs;
   var Employee_ID Total;
run;
```

e. Submit the program.

2. Examining the Descriptor and Data Portions

a. Retrieve the starter program.

b. After the DATA step, add a PROC CONTENTS step.

```
data work.newpacks;
   input Supplier_Name $ 1-20 Supplier_Country $ 23-24
         Product_Name $ 28-70;
   datalines;
Top Sports             DK    Black/Black
Top Sports             DK    X-Large Bottlegreen/Black
Top Sports             DK    Commanche Women's 6000 Q Backpack. Bark
Miller Trading Inc     US    Expedition Camp Duffle Medium Backpack
Toto Outdoor Gear      AU    Feelgood 55-75 Litre Black Women's Backpack
Toto Outdoor Gear      AU    Jaguar 50-75 Liter Blue Women's Backpack
Top Sports             DK    Medium Black/Bark Backpack
Top Sports             DK    Medium Gold Black/Gold Backpack
Top Sports             DK    Medium Olive Olive/Black Backpack
Toto Outdoor Gear      AU    Trekker 65 Royal Men's Backpack
Top Sports             DK    Victor Grey/Olive Women's Backpack
Luna sastreria S.A.    ES    Deer Backpack
Luna sastreria S.A.    ES    Deer Waist Bag
Luna sastreria S.A.    ES    Hammock Sports Bag
Miller Trading Inc     US    Sioux Men's Backpack 26 Litre.
;
run;

proc contents data=work.newpacks;
run;
```

c. Submit the program and answer the following questions:

How many observations are in the data set? **15**

How many variables are in the data set? **3**

What is the length (byte-size) of the variable **`Product_Name`**? **43**

d. After the PROC CONTENTS step, add a PROC PRINT step.

```
proc print data=work.newpacks noobs;
   var Product_Name Supplier_Name;
run;
```

e. Submit the program.

3. **Working with Times and Datetimes**

   a. Retrieve and submit the starter program.

   b. Notice the values of **CurrentTime** and **CurrentDateTime** in the PROC PRINT output.

   c. Use the Help facility to find documentation on how times and datetimes are stored in SAS.

   d. Complete the following sentences:

   A SAS time value is a value representing the number of **seconds since midnight of the current day**.

   A SAS datetime value is a value representing the number of **seconds between January 1, 1960, and an hour/minute/second within a specified date**.

4. **Accessing a SAS Data Library**

   a. Write and submit the appropriate LIBNAME statement.

```
libname orion 'SAS-data-library';
```

   b. Check the log to confirm that the SAS data library was assigned.

   c. Add a PROC CONTENTS step to list all the SAS data sets in the **orion** library.

```
proc contents data=orion._all_ nods;
run;
```

   d. Add another PROC CONTENTS step to display the descriptor portion of **orion.sales**.

```
proc contents data=orion.sales;
run;
```

   e. Use the SAS Explorer window to view the contents of the **orion** library.

5. **Reviewing Concepts**

   a. SAS statements usually begin with an **identifying keyword**.

   b. Every SAS statement ends with a **semicolon**.

   c. The descriptor portion of a SAS data set can be viewed using the **CONTENTS** procedure.

   d. Character variable values can be up to **32,767** characters long and use **1** byte(s) of storage per character.

   e. By default, numeric variables are stored in **8** bytes of storage.

   f. The internally stored SAS date value for January 3, 1960, is **2**.

   g. A SAS variable name has **1** to **32** characters and begins with a **letter** or an **underscore**.

   h. A missing character value is displayed as a **blank**.

   i. A missing numeric value is displayed as a **period**.

   j. When a SAS session starts, SAS automatically creates the temporary library called **Work**.

   k. A libref name must be **8** characters or less.

l. What are the two kinds of steps? **DATA and PROC**

m. What are the three primary windows in the SAS windowing environment? **Editor, Log, and Output**

n. What are the two portions of every SAS data set? **Descriptor and Data**

o. What are the two types of variables? **Character and Numeric**

p. True or False: If a SAS program produces output, then the program ran successfully and there is no need to check the SAS log. **False**

q. True or False: There are two methods for commenting in a SAS program. **True**

r. True or False: Omitting a semicolon never causes errors. **False**

s. True or False: A library reference name (libref) references a particular data set. **False**

t. True or False: If a data set is referenced with a one level name, `Work` is the implied libref. **True**

u. True or False: The _ALL_ keyword is used with the PRINT procedure. **False**

6. Investigating the LIBNAME Statement

a. Use the Help facility.

b. Answer the following questions:

What argument disassociates one or more currently assigned librefs? **CLEAR**

What system option provides you the convenience of specifying only a one-level name for permanent SAS files? **USER=**

c. Write and submit a LIBNAME statement.

```
libname _all_ list;
```

Solutions to Student Activities (Polls/Quizzes)

4.01 Quiz – Correct Answer

How many observations are in the data set **Work.donations**?

124 observations

```
data work.donations;
   infile 'donation.dat';
   input Employee_ID Qtr1 Qtr2 Qtr3 Qtr4;
   Total=sum(Qtr1,Qtr2,Qtr3,Qtr4);
run;

proc contents data=work.donations;
run;
```

10 **p104a01s**

4.02 Multiple Choice Poll – Correct Answer

Which variable type do you think SAS uses to store date values?

a. character

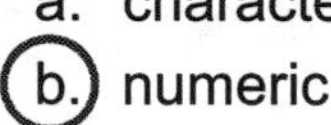

numeric

15

4.03 Quiz – Correct Answer

What is the numeric value for today's date?

The answer depends on the current date.

Example:

If the current date is February 1, 2008, the numeric value is 17563.

21

4.04 Multiple Answer Poll – Correct Answer

Which variable names are valid?

a. `data5mon`
b. `5monthsdata`
c. `data#5`
d. `five months data`
e. `five_months_data`
f. `FiveMonthsData`

26

4.05 Poll – Correct Answer

During an interactive SAS session, every time that you submit a program you must also resubmit the LIBNAME statement.

❍ True

False

The LIBNAME statement remains in effect until canceled, changed, or your SAS session ends.

47

4.06 Quiz – Correct Answer

Which option in the LIBNAME statement specifies a user's password when accessing an Informix database?

The USING= option specifies the password that is associated with the Informix user. USING= can also be specified with the PASSWORD= and PWD= aliases.

70

Solutions to Chapter Review

Chapter Review Answers

1. What structure is a SAS data library in UNIX or Windows?

   a directory

2. What structure is a SAS data library in z/OS (OS/390)?

   an operating system file

3. What is the name of the permanent SAS data library that SAS creates for you?

   Sasuser

73

continued...

Chapter Review Answers

4. What can you do with the SAS Explorer?
   - **view a list of all the libraries available to your SAS session**
   - **navigate to see all members of a specific library**
   - **display the descriptor portion of a SAS data set**

5. What window enables you to interactively browse a SAS data set?

   the VIEWTABLE window

74

Chapter 5 Reading SAS Data Sets

5.1 Introduction to Reading Data **5-3**

5.2 Using SAS Data as Input **5-6**

5.3 Subsetting Observations and Variables **5-12**

Exercises 5-26

5.4 Adding Permanent Attributes **5-29**

Exercises 5-41

5.5 Chapter Review **5-44**

5.6 Solutions **5-45**

Solutions to Exercises 5-45

Solutions to Student Activities (Polls/Quizzes) 5-50

Solutions to Chapter Review 5-54

5.1 Introduction to Reading Data

Objectives

- Define the concept of reading from a data source to create a SAS data set.
- Define the business scenario that will be used when reading from a SAS data set, an Excel worksheet, and a raw data file.

3

Business Scenario

An existing data source contains information on Orion Star sales employees from Australia and the United States.

A new SAS data set needs to be created that contains a subset of this existing data source.

This new SAS data set must contain the following:

- only the employees from Australia who are Sales Representatives
- the employee's first name, last name, salary, job title, and hired date
- labels and formats in the descriptor portion

4

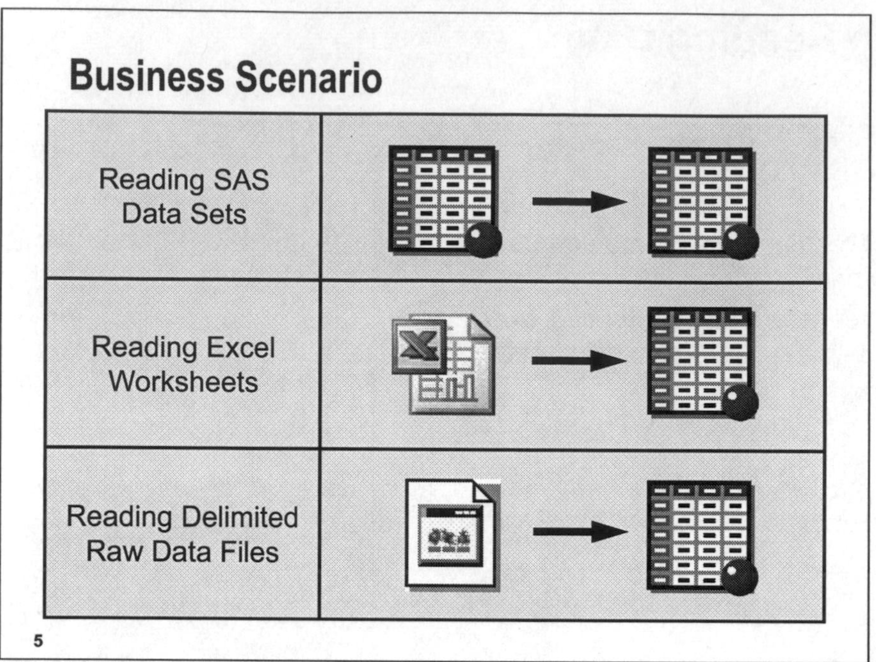

Three different input data sources are used to create the new SAS data set.

First, a SAS data set is used as the input data source.

Second, an Excel workbook is used as the input data source.

Third, a raw data file is used as the input data source.

Business Scenario

Reading SAS Data Sets	`libname ____________________;`
	`data ______________;`
	`   set ______________;`
	`   ...`
	`run;`

Reading Excel Worksheets	`libname ____________________;`
	`data ______________;`
	`   set ______________;`
	`   ...`
	`run;`

Reading Delimited Raw Data Files	`data ______________;`
	`   infile ____________;`
	`   input ____________;`
	`   ...`
	`run;`

6

The DATA step is used to accomplish the scenario regardless of the input data source. Additional statements are added to the DATA step to complete all of the requirements.

The LIBNAME statement references a SAS data library when reading a SAS data set, and an Excel workbook when reading an Excel worksheet.

5.01 Multiple Answer Poll

Which types of files will you read into SAS?

a. SAS data sets
b. Excel worksheets
c. raw data files
d. other
e. not sure

8

5.2 Using SAS Data as Input

Objectives

- Use the DATA step to create a SAS data set from an existing SAS data set.

10

Business Scenario

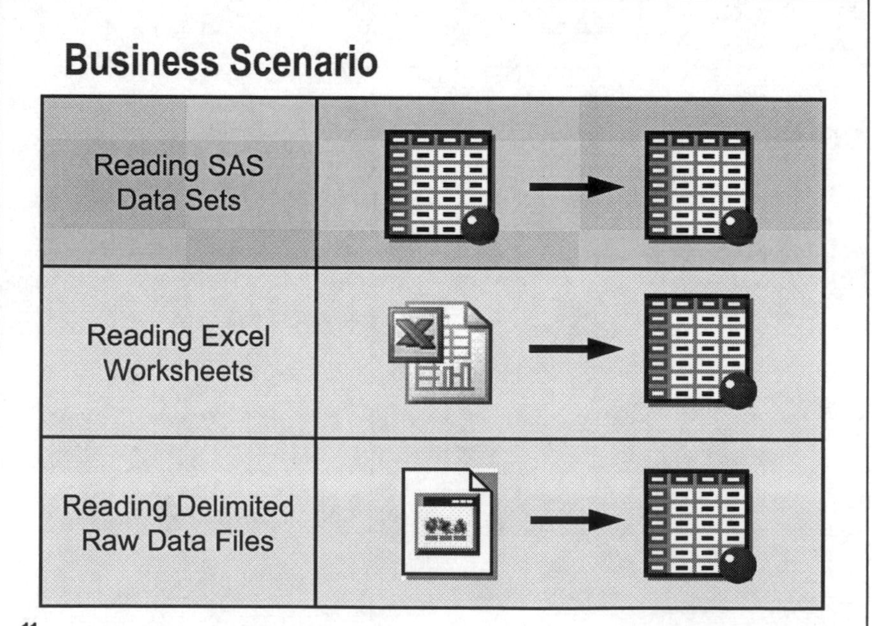

11

Business Scenario

Reading SAS Data Sets	`libname ____________;`
	`data ________;`
	`   set ________;`
	`   ...`
	`run;`

Reading Excel Worksheets	`libname ____________;`
	`data ________;`
	`   set ________;`
	`   ...`
	`run;`

Reading Delimited Raw Data Files	`data ________;`
	`   infile ________;`
	`   input ________;`
	`   ...`
	`run;`

12

Business Scenario Syntax

Use the following statements to complete the scenario:

LIBNAME *libref* '*SAS-data-library*';

DATA *output-SAS-data-set*;
  SET *input-SAS-data-set*;
  WHERE *where-expression*;
  KEEP *variable-list*;
  LABEL *variable* = '*label*'
    variable = '*label*'
    variable = '*label*';
  FORMAT *variable(s) format*;
RUN;

13

continued...

Read from any file (permanent or temp. file) to any file (permanent or temp file)

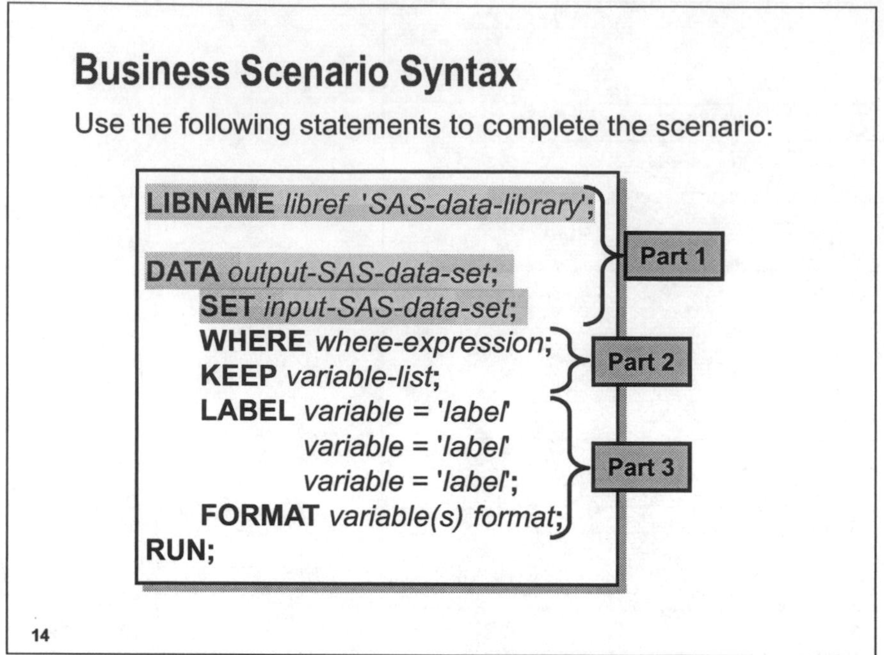
Business Scenario Syntax
Use the following statements to complete the scenario:
LIBNAME libref 'SAS-data-library';
DATA output-SAS-data-set;
SET input-SAS-data-set;
WHERE where-expression;
KEEP variable-list;
LABEL variable = 'label'
variable = 'label'
variable = 'label';
FORMAT variable(s) format;
RUN;
Part 1
Part 2
Part 3
14

Instead of writing the program all at once, break the program into three parts. Test each part before you move to the next part.

The LIBNAME Statement (Review)

A library reference name (libref) is needed if a permanent data set is being read or created.

```
LIBNAME libref 'SAS-data-library';

DATA output-SAS-data-set;
     SET input-SAS-data-set;
     <additional SAS statements>
RUN;
```

The *LIBNAME statement* assigns a libref to a SAS data library.

15

The DATA Statement

The *DATA statement* begins a DATA step and provides the name of the SAS data set being created.

```
LIBNAME libref 'SAS-data-library';

DATA output-SAS-data-set;
     SET input-SAS-data-set;
     <additional SAS statements>
RUN;
```

The DATA statement can create temporary or permanent data sets.

16

The SET Statement

The *SET statement* reads observations from a SAS data set for further processing in the DATA step.

```
LIBNAME libref 'SAS-data-library';

DATA output-SAS-data-set;
     SET input-SAS-data-set;
     <additional SAS statements>
RUN;
```

- By default, the SET statement reads all observations and all variables from the input data set.
- The SET statement can read temporary or permanent data sets.

17

Business Scenario Part 1

Create a temporary SAS data set named **Work.subset1** from the permanent SAS data set named **orion.sales**.

```
libname orion 's:\workshop';

data work.subset1;
   set orion.sales;
run;
```

Partial SAS Log

```
data work.subset1;
   set orion.sales;
run;

NOTE: There were 165 observations read from the data set ORION.SALES.
NOTE: The data set WORK.SUBSET1 has 165 observations and 9 variables.
```

Both data sets contain 165 observations and 9 variables

18 p105d01

The LIBNAME statement needs to reference a SAS data library specific to your operating environment.

For example:

Windows	`libname orion 's:\workshop';`
UNIX	`libname orion '/users/userid';`
z/OS (OS/390)	`libname orion '.workshop.sasdata';`

Business Scenario Part 1

```
proc print data=work.subset1;
run;
```

Partial PROC PRINT Output

Obs	Employee_ID	First_ Name	Last_Name	Gender	Salary	Job_Title	Country	Birth_ Date	Hire_ Date
1	120102	Tom	Zhou	M	108255	Sales Manager	AU	3510	10744
2	120103	Wilson	Dawes	M	87975	Sales Manager	AU	-3996	5114
3	120121	Irenie	Elvish	F	26600	Sales Rep. II	AU	-5630	5114
4	120122	Christina	Ngan	F	27475	Sales Rep. II	AU	-1984	6756
5	120123	Kimiko	Hotstone	F	26190	Sales Rep. I	AU	1732	9405
6	120124	Lucian	Daymond	M	26480	Sales Rep. I	AU	-233	6999
7	120125	Fong	Hofmeister	M	32040	Sales Rep. IV	AU	-1852	6999
8	120126	Satyakam	Denny	M	26780	Sales Rep. II	AU	10490	17014
9	120127	Sharryn	Clarkson	F	28100	Sales Rep. II	AU	6943	14184
10	120128	Monica	Kletschkus	F	30890	Sales Rep. IV	AU	9691	17106
11	120129	Alvin	Roebuck	M	30070	Sales Rep. III	AU	1787	9405
12	120130	Kevin	Lyon	M	26955	Sales Rep. I	AU	9114	16922
13	120131	Marinus	Surawski	M	26910	Sales Rep. I	AU	7207	15706
14	120132	Fancine	Kaiser	F	28525	Sales Rep. III	AU	-3923	6848
15	120133	Petrea	Soltau	F	27440	Sales Rep. II	AU	9608	17075

19 p105d01

Setup for the Poll

- Retrieve program **p105a01**.
- Submit the program and confirm that a new SAS data set was created with 77 observations and 12 variables.

21

5.02 Poll

The DATA step reads a temporary SAS data set to create a permanent SAS data set.

❍ True
❍ False

22

5.3 Subsetting Observations and Variables

Objectives

- Subset observations by using the WHERE statement.
- Subset variables by using the DROP and KEEP statements.

26

Business Scenario Syntax

Use the following statements to complete the scenario:

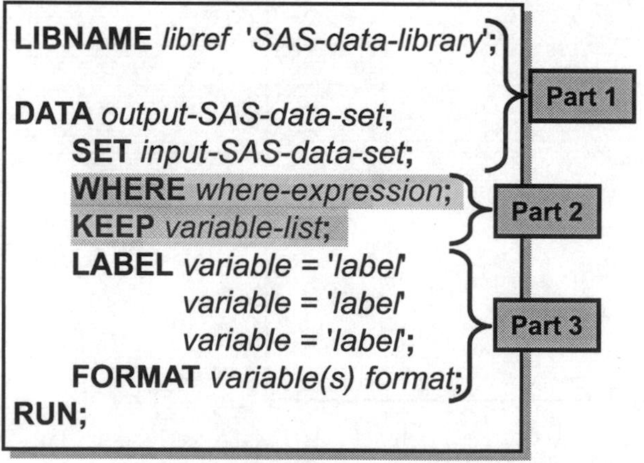
LIBNAME libref 'SAS-data-library';
DATA output-SAS-data-set;
SET input-SAS-data-set;
WHERE where-expression;
KEEP variable-list;
LABEL variable = 'label'
variable = 'label'
variable = 'label';
FORMAT variable(s) format;
RUN;
Part 1
Part 2
Part 3

27

Subsetting Observations and Variables

By default, the SET statement reads **all observations** and **all variables** from the input data set.

```
data work.subset1;
   set orion.sales;
run;

NOTE: There were 165 observations read from the data set ORION.SALES.
NOTE: The data set WORK.SUBSET1 has 165 observations and 9 variables.
```

By adding statements to the DATA step, the number of observations and variables can be reduced.

```
NOTE: The data set WORK.SUBSET1 has 61 observations and 5 variables.
```

28

The WHERE Statement

The *WHERE statement* subsets observations that meet a particular condition.

General form of the WHERE statement:

WHERE *where-expression* ;

The *where-expression* is a sequence of operands and operators that form a set of instructions that define a condition for selecting observations.

- Operands include constants and variables.
- Operators are symbols that request a comparison, arithmetic calculation, or logical operation.

29

Operands

A *constant operand* is a fixed value.

- Character values must be enclosed in quotation marks and are case sensitive.
- Numeric values do not use quotation marks.

A *variable operand* must be a variable coming from an input data set.

Examples:

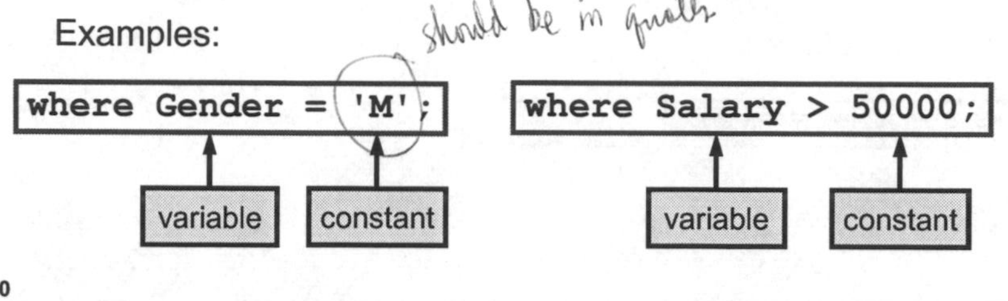
where Gender = 'M';
variable
constant
where Salary > 50000;
variable
constant

30

Comparison Operators

Comparison operators compare a variable with a value or with another variable.

Symbol	Mnemonic	Definition
=	EQ	equal to
^= ¬= ~=	NE	not equal to
>	GT	greater than
<	LT	less than
>=	GE	greater than or equal
<=	LE	less than or equal
	IN	equal to one of a list

31

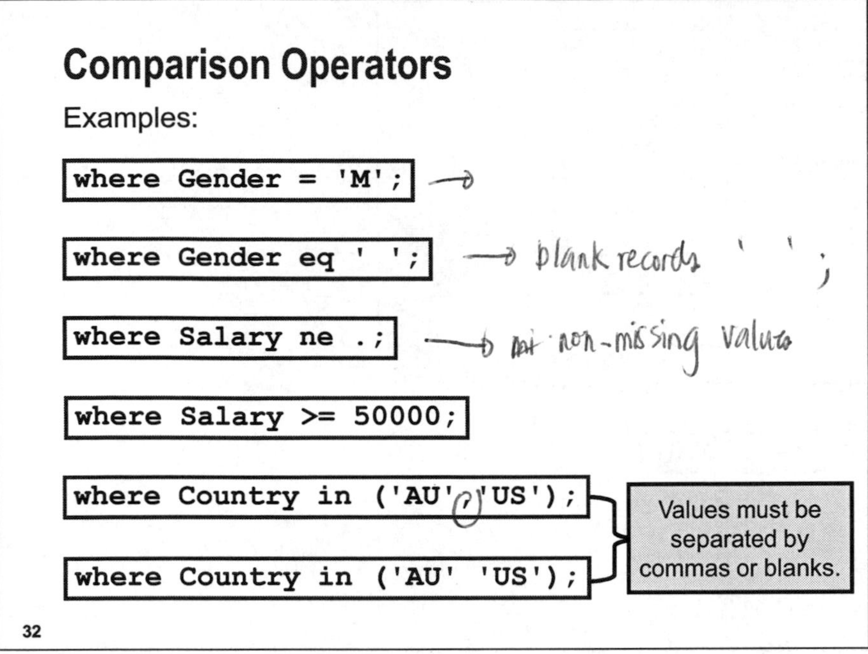

Comparison Operators
Examples:
where Gender = 'M';
where Gender eq ' ';
where Salary ne .;
where Salary >= 50000;
where Country in ('AU','US');
where Country in ('AU' 'US');
Values must be separated by commas or blanks.
32

Arithmetic Operators

Arithmetic operators indicate that an arithmetic calculation is performed.

Symbol	Definition
**	exponentiation
*	multiplication
/	division
+	addition
-	subtraction

33

Arithmetic Operators

Examples:

```
where Salary / 12 < 6000;
```

```
where Salary / 12 * 1.10 >= 7500;
```

```
where (Salary / 12 ) * 1.10 >= 7500;
```

```
where Salary + Bonus <= 10000;
```

34

Logical Operators

Logical operators combine or modify expressions.

Symbol	Mnemonic	Definition
&	AND	logical and
|	OR	logical or
^ ¬ ~	NOT	logical not

35

Logical Operators

Examples:

```
where Gender ne 'M' and Salary >=50000;
```

```
where Gender ne 'M' or Salary >= 50000;
```

```
where Country = 'AU' or Country = 'US';
```

```
where Country not in ('AU' 'US');
```

36

5.03 Quiz

Which WHERE statement correctly subsets the numeric values for May, June, or July and missing character names?

a.
```
where Months in (5-7)
      and Names = .;
```

b.
```
where Months in (5,6,7)
      and Names = ' ';
```

c.
```
where Months in ('5','6','7')
      and Names = '.';
```

→ numeric?

38

Special WHERE Operators

Special WHERE operators are operators that can only be used in a where-expression.

Symbol	Mnemonic	Definition
	BETWEEN-AND	an inclusive range
	IS NULL	missing value
	IS MISSING	missing value
?	CONTAINS	a character string
	LIKE	a character pattern

null and blank are the same

40

BETWEEN-AND Operator

The *BETWEEN-AND operator* selects observations in which the value of a variable falls within an inclusive range of values.

Examples:

```
where salary between 50000 and 100000;
```

```
where salary not between 50000 and 100000;
```

Equivalent Expressions:

```
where salary between 50000 and 100000;
```

```
where 50000 <= salary <= 100000;
```

41

IS NULL and IS MISSING Operators

The *IS NULL* and *IS MISSING operators* select observations in which the value of a variable is missing.

- The operator can be used for both character and numeric variables.
- You can combine the NOT logical operator with IS NULL or IS MISSING to select nonmissing values.

Examples:

```
where Employee_ID is null;
```

```
where Employee_ID is missing;
```

42

CONTAINS Operator

The *CONTAINS (?) operator* selects observations that include the specified substring.

- The position of the substring within the variable's values is not important.
- The operator is case sensitive when you make comparisons.

Example:

```
where Job_Title contains 'Rep';
```

43

5.04 Quiz

Which value will not be returned based on the WHERE statement?

a. Office Rep
b. Sales Rep. IV
c. service rep III
d. Representative

```
where Job_Title contains 'Rep';
```

45

LIKE Operator

The *LIKE operator* selects observations by comparing character values to specified patterns.

There are two special characters available for specifying a pattern:

- A percent sign (%) replaces any number of characters.
- An underscore (_) replaces one character.

Consecutive underscores can be specified.

A percent sign and an underscore can be specified in the same pattern.

The operator is case sensitive.

47

LIKE Operator

Examples:

```
where Name like '%N';
```

This WHERE statement selects observations that begin with any number of characters and end with an N.

```
where Name like 'T_M%';
```

This WHERE statement selects observations that begin with a T, followed by a single character, followed by an M, followed by any number of characters.

48

Starting in SAS 9.2, the LIKE operator supports an escape character, which enables you to search for the percent sign (%) and the underscore (_) characters in values.

An escape character is a single character that in a sequence of characters signifies that what is to follow takes an alternative meaning. For the LIKE operator, an escape character signifies to search for literal instances of the % and _ characters in the variable's values instead of performing the special-character function.

To specify an escape character, you include the character in the pattern-matching expression and then the keyword ESCAPE followed by the escape character expression. When you include an escape character, the pattern-matching expression must be enclosed in quotation marks and it cannot contain a column name. The escape character expression is an expression that evaluates to a single character. The operands must be character or string literals. If it is a single character, it must be enclosed in quotation marks.

For example, if the variable **X** contains the values abc, a_b, and axb, the following LIKE operator using an escape character selects only the value a_b. The escape character (/) specifies that the pattern search for a '_' instead of matching any single character:

```
where x like 'a/_b' escape '/';
```

Without an escape character, the following LIKE operator would select the values a_b and axb. The special character underscore in the search pattern matches any single character, including the value with the underscore:

```
where x like 'a_b';
```

5.05 Quiz

Which WHERE statement will return all the observations that have a first name starting with the letter M for the given values?

a. `where Name like '_, M_';`

b. `where Name like '%, M%';`

c. `where Name like '_, M%';`

d. `where Name like '%, M_';`

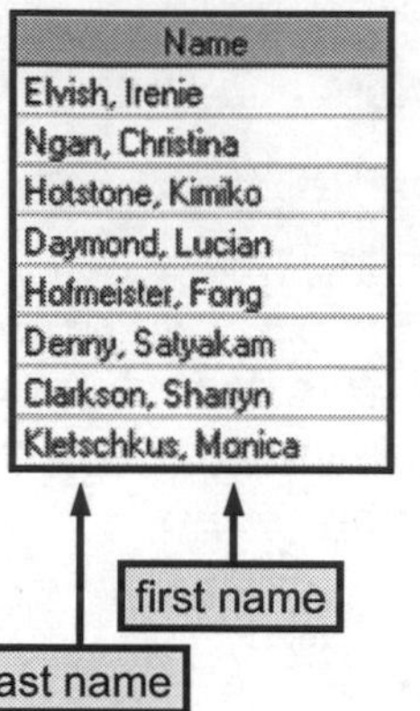

Name
Elvish, Irenie
Ngan, Christina
Hotstone, Kimiko
Daymond, Lucian
Hofmeister, Fong
Denny, Satyakam
Clarkson, Sharryn
Kletschkus, Monica

50

Business Scenario Part 2

Include only the employees from Australia who have the word `Rep` in their job title.

```
data work.subset1;
   set orion.sales;
   where Country='AU' and
         Job_Title contains 'Rep';
run;
```

Partial SAS Log

```
NOTE: There were 61 observations read from the data set ORION.SALES.
      WHERE (Country='AU') and Job_Title contains 'Rep';
NOTE: The data set WORK.SUBSET1 has 61 observations and 9 variables.
```

52 p105d02

ex. ' AU' → it's looking for space AU country
space

'AU ' → it's still ok

→ space after no letter is still ok

Business Scenario Part 2

```
proc print data=work.subset1;
run;
```

Partial PROC PRINT Output

Obs	Employee_ID	First_ Name	Last_Name	Gender	Salary	Job_Title	Country	Birth_ Date	Hire_ Date
1	120121	Irenie	Elvish	F	26600	Sales Rep. II	AU	-5630	5114
2	120122	Christina	Ngan	F	27475	Sales Rep. II	AU	-1984	6756
3	120123	Kimiko	Hotstone	F	26190	Sales Rep. I	AU	1732	9405
4	120124	Lucian	Daymond	M	26480	Sales Rep. I	AU	-233	6999
5	120125	Fong	Hofmeister	M	32040	Sales Rep. IV	AU	-1852	6999
6	120126	Satyakam	Denny	M	26780	Sales Rep. II	AU	10490	17014
7	120127	Sharryn	Clarkson	F	28100	Sales Rep. II	AU	6943	14184
8	120128	Monica	Kletschkus	F	30890	Sales Rep. IV	AU	9691	17106
9	120129	Alvin	Roebuck	M	30070	Sales Rep. III	AU	1787	9405
10	120130	Kevin	Lyon	M	26955	Sales Rep. I	AU	9114	16922
11	120131	Marinus	Surawski	M	26910	Sales Rep. I	AU	7207	15706
12	120132	Fancine	Kaiser	F	28525	Sales Rep. III	AU	-3923	6848
13	120133	Petrea	Soltau	F	27440	Sales Rep. II	AU	9608	17075
14	120134	Sian	Shannan	M	28015	Sales Rep. II	AU	-3861	5114
15	120135	Alexei	Platts	M	32490	Sales Rep. IV	AU	3313	13788

53

p105d02

The DROP and KEEP Statements

The *DROP statement* specifies the names of the variables to omit from the output data set(s).

DROP *variable-list*;

The *KEEP statement* specifies the names of the variables to write to the output data set(s).

KEEP *variable-list*;

The *variable-list* specifies the variables to drop or keep, respectively, in the output data set.

55

The DROP and KEEP Statements

Examples:

```
drop Employee_ID Gender
     Country Birth_Date;
```

```
keep First_Name Last_Name
     Salary Job_Title
     Hire_Date;
```

– do not use KEEP and DROP in the same procedure

56

Business Scenario Part 2

Include only the employee's first name, last name, salary, job title, and hired date in the data set **Work.subset1**.

```
data work.subset1;   – DATASET
   set orion.sales;
   where Country='AU' and
         Job_Title contains 'Rep';
   keep First_Name Last_Name Salary
        Job_Title Hire_Date;
run;
```

Partial SAS Log

```
NOTE: There were 61 observations read from the data set ORION.SALES.
      WHERE (Country='AU') and Job_Title contains 'Rep';
NOTE: The data set WORK.SUBSET1 has 61 observations and 5 variables.
```

57 p105d03

Business Scenario Part 2

```
proc print data=work.subset1;
run;
```

Partial PROC PRINT Output

Obs	First_ Name	Last_Name	Salary	Job_Title	Hire_ Date
1	Irenie	Elvish	26600	Sales Rep. II	5114
2	Christina	Ngan	27475	Sales Rep. II	6756
3	Kimiko	Hotstone	26190	Sales Rep. I	9405
4	Lucian	Daymond	26480	Sales Rep. I	6999
5	Fong	Hofmeister	32040	Sales Rep. IV	6999
6	Satyakam	Denny	26780	Sales Rep. II	17014
7	Sharryn	Clarkson	28100	Sales Rep. II	14184
8	Monica	Kletschkus	30890	Sales Rep. IV	17106
9	Alvin	Roebuck	30070	Sales Rep. III	9405
10	Kevin	Lyon	26955	Sales Rep. I	16922
11	Marinus	Surawski	26910	Sales Rep. I	15706
12	Fancine	Kaiser	28525	Sales Rep. III	6848

58 p105d03

proc print data = clothing

options nonumber nodate;
(global)
→ suppress page #, date
options number date, dtreset pageno=1;
(resubmit the page #, date)
(dtreset = reset the date)
(pageno = clear the page # to 1)

→ Only 1 where statement
per step – NO multiple WHERE statements
use AND OR OR
(&)

NAME] Required
TYPE
LENGTH

Label] optional
Format

FIRST THING TO DO: (ex. get SAS file from CD)
libname stuff 'f:\'; → to create a physical file in SAS from CD (ex)

proc CONTENTS data = stuff.product_dim VARNUM; → to view the SAS descriptor CONTENTS of file
(stuff → library reference; product_dim → file)
run;

proc print data = stuff.product_dim → to view the data
var product-id product-group → to view only specified variables
(Keep or drop don't work in procedure, only in datastep)

proc print data = stuff.product-dim (obs = 20); → to view first 20 observations only
run;

data clothing;
set stuff.product-dim
] to create a permanent/temporary file from CD data
where product-group contains 'Clothes'; — conditions to manipulate the data
drop product-id; — keep or drop variables/fields
run;

Exercises

Level 1

1. **Subsetting Observations and Variables Using the WHERE and KEEP Statements**

   a. Retrieve and submit the starter program **p105e01**.

      What is the variable name that contains gender values? ______________________

      What are the two possible gender values? ______________________

   b. Add a DATA step before the PROC PRINT step to read the data set **`orion.customer_dim`** to create a new data set called **`Work.youngadult`**.

   c. Modify the PROC PRINT step to refer to the new data set.

   d. Submit the program and confirm that **`Work.youngadult`** was created with 77 observations and 11 variables.

   e. Add a WHERE statement to the DATA step to subset for female customers.

   f. Submit the program and confirm that **`Work.youngadult`** was created with 30 observations and 11 variables.

   g. Modify the WHERE statement to subset for female customers whose **`Customer_Age`** is between 18 and 36.

   h. Submit the program and confirm that **`Work.youngadult`** was created with 15 observations and 11 variables.

   i. Modify the WHERE statement to subset for female 18- to 36-year-old customers who have the word `Gold` in their **`Customer_Group`**.

   j. Submit the program and confirm that **`Work.youngadult`** was created with 5 observations and 11 variables.

   k. Modify the DATA step so that **`Work.youngadult`** contains only **`Customer_Name`**, **`Customer_Age`**, **`Customer_BirthDate`**, **`Customer_Gender`**, and **`Customer_Group`**.

   l. Submit the program and confirm that **`Work.youngadult`** was created with 5 observations and 5 variables.

Level 2

2. Subsetting Observations and Variables Using the WHERE and DROP Statements

a. Write a DATA step to read the data set **orion.product_dim** to create a new data set called **Work.sports**.

   Work.sports should include only those observations with **Supplier_Country** from Great Britain (GB), Spain (ES), or Netherlands (NL) and **Product_Category** values that end in the word Sports.

   Work.sports should not include the following variables: **Product_ID**, **Product_Line**, **Product_Group**, **Supplier_Name**, and **Supplier_ID**.

b. Write a PROC PRINT step to create the following report:

   Partial PROC PRINT Output (First 10 of 30 Observations)

Obs	Product_ Category	Product_Name	Supplier_ Country
1	Children Sports	Butch T-Shirt with V-Neck	ES
2	Children Sports	Children's Knit Sweater	ES
3	Children Sports	Gordon Children's Tracking Pants	ES
4	Children Sports	O'my Children's T-Shirt with Logo	ES
5	Children Sports	Strap Pants BBO	ES
6	Indoor Sports	Abdomen Shaper	NL
7	Indoor Sports	Fitness Dumbbell Foam 0.90	NL
8	Indoor Sports	Letour Heart Bike	NL
9	Indoor Sports	Letour Trimag Bike	NL
10	Indoor Sports	Weight 5.0 Kg	NL

Level 3

3. Using the SOUNDS-LIKE Operator and the KEEP= Option

a. Write a DATA step to read the data set **orion.customer_dim** to create a new data set called **Work.tony**.

b. Add a WHERE statement to the DATA step to subset the observations with the **Customer_FirstName** value that sounds like Tony.

   ✏ Documentation on the SOUNDS-LIKE operator can be found in the SAS Help and Documentation from the Index tab by typing **sounds-like operator**.

c. Add a KEEP= data set option in the SET statement to read only the **Customer_FirstName** and **Customer_LastName** variables.

   ✏ Documentation on the KEEP= data set option can be found in the SAS Help and Documentation from the Contents tab. (Select **SAS Products** ⇨ **Base SAS** ⇨ **SAS 9.2 Language Reference: Dictionary** ⇨ **Dictionary of Language Elements** ⇨ **SAS Data Set Options** ⇨ **KEEP= Data Set Option**.)

d. Write a PROC PRINT step to create the following report:

```
                 Customer_     Customer_
         Obs     FirstName     LastName

           1       Tonie       Asmussen
           2       Tommy       Mcdonald
```

5.4 Adding Permanent Attributes

Objectives

- Add labels to the descriptor portion of a SAS data set by using the LABEL statement.
- Add formats to the descriptor portion of a SAS data set by using the FORMAT statement.

61

Business Scenario Syntax

Use the following statements to complete the scenario:

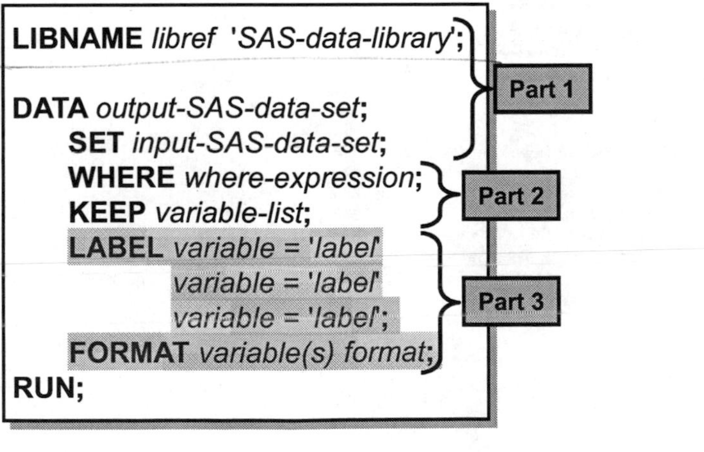

```
LIBNAME libref 'SAS-data-library';

DATA output-SAS-data-set;
     SET input-SAS-data-set;
     WHERE where-expression;
     KEEP variable-list;
     LABEL variable = 'label'
           variable = 'label'
           variable = 'label';
     FORMAT variable(s) format;
RUN;
```


62

Adding Permanent Attributes

The descriptor portion of the SAS data set stores variable attributes including the name, type (character or numeric), and length of the variable.

Labels and formats can also be stored in the descriptor portion.

Partial PROC CONTENTS Output

Alphabetic List of Variables and Attributes

#	Variable	Type	Len	Format	Label
1	First_Name	Char	12		
5	Hire_Date	Num	8	DDMMYY10.	Date Hired
4	Job_Title	Char	25		Sales Title
2	Last_Name	Char	18		
3	Salary	Num	8	COMMAX8.	

63

Adding Permanent Attributes

When displaying reports,

- a *label* changes the appearance of a variable name
- a *format* changes the appearance of variable value.

Partial PROC PRINT Output

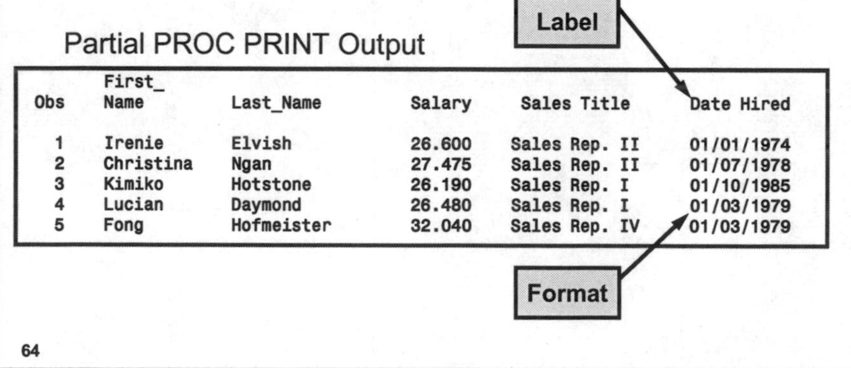

Obs	First_ Name	Last_Name	Salary	Sales Title	Date Hired
1	Irenie	Elvish	26.600	Sales Rep. II	01/01/1974
2	Christina	Ngan	27.475	Sales Rep. II	01/07/1978
3	Kimiko	Hotstone	26.190	Sales Rep. I	01/10/1985
4	Lucian	Daymond	26.480	Sales Rep. I	01/03/1979
5	Fong	Hofmeister	32.040	Sales Rep. IV	01/03/1979

64

The LABEL Statement

— COLUMN headers

The *LABEL statement* assigns descriptive labels to variable names.

General form of the LABEL statement:

> **LABEL** *variable* = '*label*'
> *variable* = '*label*'
> *variable* = '*label*';

- A label can have as many as 256 characters.
- Any number of variables can be associated with labels in a single LABEL statement.
- Using a LABEL statement in a DATA step permanently associates labels with variables by storing the label in the descriptor portion of the SAS data set.

65

Business Scenario Part 3

Include labels in the descriptor portion of **Work.subset1**.

```
data work.subset1;
   set orion.sales;
   where Country='AU' and
         Job_Title contains 'Rep';
   keep First_Name Last_Name Salary
        Job_Title Hire_Date;
   label Job_Title='Sales Title'
         Hire_Date='Date Hired';
run;
```

66

p105d04

Business Scenario Part 3

```
proc contents data=work.subset1;
run;
```

Partial PROC CONTENTS Output

Alphabetic List of Variables and Attributes

#	Variable	Type	Len	Label
1	First_Name	Char	12	
5	Hire_Date	Num	8	Date Hired
4	Job_Title	Char	25	Sales Title
2	Last_Name	Char	18	
3	Salary	Num	8	

67 p105d04

Business Scenario Part 3

In order to use labels in the PRINT procedure, a LABEL option needs to be added to the PROC PRINT statement.

```
proc print data=work.subset1 label;
run;
```

Partial PROC PRINT Output

Obs	First_ Name	Last_Name	Salary	Sales Title	Date Hired
1	Irenie	Elvish	26600	Sales Rep. II	5114
2	Christina	Ngan	27475	Sales Rep. II	6756
3	Kimiko	Hotstone	26190	Sales Rep. I	9405
4	Lucian	Daymond	26480	Sales Rep. I	6999
5	Fong	Hofmeister	32040	Sales Rep. IV	6999
6	Satyakam	Denny	26780	Sales Rep. II	17014
7	Sharryn	Clarkson	28100	Sales Rep. II	14184
8	Monica	Kletschkus	30890	Sales Rep. IV	17106
9	Alvin	Roebuck	30070	Sales Rep. III	9405
10	Kevin	Lyon	26955	Sales Rep. I	16922

68 p105d04

The FORMAT Statement

The *FORMAT statement* assigns formats to variable values.

General form of the FORMAT statement:

FORMAT *variable(s) format*;

- A *format* is an instruction that SAS uses to write data values.
- Using a FORMAT statement in a DATA step permanently associates formats with variables by storing the format in the descriptor portion of the SAS data set.

69

SAS Formats

SAS formats have the following form:

<$>*format*<*w*>.<*d*>

$	indicates a character format.
format	names the SAS format or user-defined format.
w	specifies the total format width including decimal places and special characters.
.	is a required delimiter.
d	specifies the number of decimal places in numeric formats.

70

SAS Formats

Selected SAS formats:

Format	Definition
$*w*.	writes standard character data.
w.d	writes standard numeric data.
COMMA*w.d*	writes numeric values with a comma that separates every three digits and a period that separates the decimal fraction.
COMMAX*w.d*	writes numeric values with a period that separates every three digits and a comma that separates the decimal fraction.
DOLLAR*w.d*	writes numeric values with a leading dollar sign, a comma that separates every three digits, and a period that separates the decimal fraction.
EUROX*w.d*	writes numeric values with a leading euro symbol (€), a period that separates every three digits, and a comma that separates the decimal fraction.

71

SAS Formats

Selected SAS formats:

Format	Stored Value	Displayed Value
$4.	`Programming`	`Prog`
12.	`27134.2864`	`27134`
12.2	`27134.2864`	`27134.29`
COMMA12.2	`27134.2864`	`27,134.29`
COMMAX12.2	`27134.2864`	`27.134,29`
DOLLAR12.2	`27134.2864`	`$27,134.29`
EUROX12.2	`27134.2864`	`€27.134,29`

72

SAS Formats

If you do not specify a format width that is large enough to accommodate a numeric value, the displayed value is automatically adjusted to fit into the width.

Format	Stored Value	Displayed Value
DOLLAR12.2	27134.2864	$27,134.29
DOLLAR9.2	27134.2864	$27134.29
DOLLAR8.2	27134.2864	27134.29
DOLLAR5.2	27134.2864	27134
DOLLAR4.2	27134.2864	27E3

73

5.06 Quiz

Which numeric format writes standard numeric data with leading zeros?

Documentation on formats can be found in the SAS Help and Documentation from the Contents tab (**SAS Products** ⇨ **Base SAS** ⇨ **SAS 9.2 Language Reference: Dictionary** ⇨ **Dictionary of Language Elements** ⇨ **Formats** ⇨ **Formats by Category**).

75

SAS Date Formats

SAS date formats display SAS date values in standard date forms.

Format	Stored Value	Displayed Value
MMDDYY6.	0	010160
MMDDYY8.	0	01/01/60
MMDDYY10.	0	01/01/1960
DDMMYY6.	365	311260
DDMMYY8.	365	31/12/60
DDMMYY10.	365	31/12/1960

78

SAS Date Formats

Additional date formats:

Format	Stored Value	Displayed Value
DATE7.	-1	31DEC59
DATE9.	-1	31DEC1959
WORDDATE.	0	January 1, 1960
WEEKDATE.	0	Friday, January 1, 1960
MONYY7.	0	JAN1960
YEAR4.	0	1960

79

5.07 Quiz

Which FORMAT statement creates the output?

a.
```
format Birth_Date Hire_Date ddmmyy9.
         Term_Date mmyy7.;
```

b.
```
format Birth_Date Hire_Date ddmmyyyy.
         Term_Date mmmyyyy.;
```

c.
```
format Birth_Date Hire_Date ddmmyy10.
         Term_Date monyy7.;
```

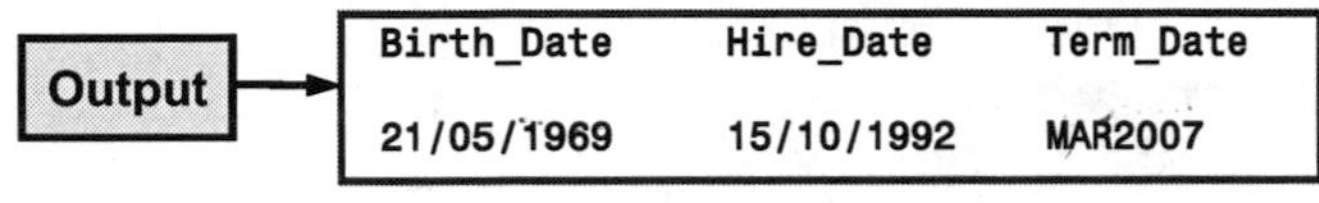

Birth_Date	Hire_Date	Term_Date
21/05/1969	15/10/1992	MAR2007

81

SAS Date Formats

The SAS National Language Support (NLS) date formats convert SAS date values to a locale-sensitive date string.

Format	Locale	Example
NLDATE*w.*	English_UnitedStates	January 01, 1960
	German_Germany	01. Januar 1960
NLDATEMN*w.*	English_UnitedStates	January
	German_Germany	Januar
NLDATEW*w.*	English_UnitedStates	Fri, Jan 01, 60
	German_Germany	Fr, 01. Jan 60
NLDATEWN*w.*	English_UnitedStates	Friday
	German_Germany	Freitag

83 p105d05

National Language Support (NLS) is a set of features that enable a software product to function properly in every global market for which the product is targeted. SAS contains NLS features to ensure that SAS applications conform to local language conventions.

A locale reflects the language, local conventions, and culture for a geographical region. Local conventions might include specific formatting rules for dates. Dates have many representations, depending on the conventions that are accepted in a culture.

The LOCALE= system option is used to specify the locale, which reflects the local conventions, language, and culture of a geographical region. For example, a locale value of `English_Canada` represents the country of Canada with a language of English, and a locale value of `French_Canada` represents the country of Canada with a language of French. `English_UnitedStates` represents the country of United States with a language of English. `German_Germany` represents the country of Germany with a language of German.

The LOCALE= system option can be specified in a configuration file, at SAS invocation, in the OPTIONS statement, or in the SAS System Options window.

For more information, refer to the *SAS 9.2 National Language Support Reference Guide* in SAS Help and Documentation.

5.08 Quiz

How many date and time formats start with EUR?

Documentation on NLS formats can be found in the SAS Help and Documentation from the Contents tab (**SAS Products** ⇨ **Base SAS** ⇨ **SAS 9.2 Language Reference: Dictionary** ⇨ **Dictionary of Language Elements** ⇨ **Formats** ⇨ **Formats Documented in Other SAS Publications**).

85

Business Scenario Part 3

Include formats in the descriptor portion of **Work.subset1**.

```
data work.subset1;
   set orion.sales;
   where Country='AU' and
         Job_Title contains 'Rep';
   keep First_Name Last_Name Salary
        Job_Title Hire_Date;
   label Job_Title='Sales Title'
         Hire_Date='Date Hired';
   format Salary commax8. Hire_Date ddmmyy10.;
run;
```

87

p105d06

Business Scenario Part 3

```
proc contents data=work.subset1;
run;
```

Partial PROC CONTENTS Output

Alphabetic List of Variables and Attributes

#	Variable	Type	Len	Format	Label
1	First_Name	Char	12		
5	Hire_Date	Num	8	DDMMYY10.	Date Hired
4	Job_Title	Char	25		Sales Title
2	Last_Name	Char	18		
3	Salary	Num	8	COMMAX8.	

88 p105d06

Business Scenario Part 3

```
proc print data=work.subset1 label;
run;
```

Partial PROC PRINT Output

Obs	First_ Name	Last_Name	Salary	Sales Title	Date Hired
1	Irenie	Elvish	26.600	Sales Rep. II	01/01/1974
2	Christina	Ngan	27.475	Sales Rep. II	01/07/1978
3	Kimiko	Hotstone	26.190	Sales Rep. I	01/10/1985
4	Lucian	Daymond	26.480	Sales Rep. I	01/03/1979
5	Fong	Hofmeister	32.040	Sales Rep. IV	01/03/1979
6	Satyakam	Denny	26.780	Sales Rep. II	01/08/2006
7	Sharryn	Clarkson	28.100	Sales Rep. II	01/11/1998
8	Monica	Kletschkus	30.890	Sales Rep. IV	01/11/2006
9	Alvin	Roebuck	30.070	Sales Rep. III	01/10/1985
10	Kevin	Lyon	26.955	Sales Rep. I	01/05/2006
11	Marinus	Surawski	26.910	Sales Rep. I	01/01/2003
12	Fancine	Kaiser	28.525	Sales Rep. III	01/10/1978

89 p105d06

Exercises

Level 1

4. Adding Permanent Attributes to `Work.youngadult`

a. Retrieve and submit the starter program **p105e04**.

Notice the format and labels stored in the descriptor portion of **`Work.youngadult`**.

b. Add a LABEL statement and a FORMAT statement to the DATA step to create the following PROC PRINT report:

```
                                                                                  Customer
Obs   Gender     Customer Name              Date of Birth          Member Level       Age

 1      F      Sandrina Stephano              July 9, 1979     Orion Club Gold members    28
 2      F      Cornelia Krahl             February 27, 1974     Orion Club Gold members    33
 3      F      Dianne Patchin                  May 6, 1979     Orion Club Gold members    28
 4      F      Annmarie Leveille             July 16, 1984     Orion Club Gold members    23
 5      F      Sanelisiwe Collier             July 7, 1988     Orion Club Gold members    19
```

The labels need to be changed for **`Customer_Gender`**, **`Customer_BirthDate`**, and **`Customer_Group`**.

The format needs to be changed for **`Customer_BirthDate`**.

Hint: Do not forget the option in the PROC PRINT step that enables the labels to appear.

Why do **`Customer_Name`** and **`Customer_Age`** appear with a space in the column header but do not need labels? ____

Level 2

5. Adding Permanent Attributes to `Work.sports`

a. Retrieve the starter program **p105e05**.

b. Add a LABEL statement to the DATA step and a LABEL option to the PROC PRINT step to add the following labels:

Variable	Label
`Product_Category`	`Sports Category`
`Product_Name`	`Product Name (Abbrev)`
`Supplier_Name`	`Supplier Name (Abbrev)`

c. Add a FORMAT statement to the DATA step to display only the first 15 letters of **Product_Name** and **Supplier_Name**.

d. Submit the program to create the following PROC PRINT report:

Partial PROC PRINT Output (First 10 of 30 Observations)

```
                                 Product Name      Supplier    Supplier Name
       Obs    Sports Category    (Abbrev)          Country     (Abbrev)

         1    Children Sports    Butch T-Shirt w      ES       Luna sastreria
         2    Children Sports    Children's Knit      ES       Luna sastreria
         3    Children Sports    Gordon Children      ES       Luna sastreria
         4    Children Sports    O'my Children's      ES       Luna sastreria
         5    Children Sports    Strap Pants BBO      ES       Sportico
         6    Indoor Sports      Abdomen Shaper       NL       TrimSport B.V.
         7    Indoor Sports      Fitness Dumbbel      NL       TrimSport B.V.
         8    Indoor Sports      Letour Heart Bi      NL       TrimSport B.V.
         9    Indoor Sports      Letour Trimag B      NL       TrimSport B.V.
        10    Indoor Sports      Weight  5.0 Kg       NL       TrimSport B.V.
```

e. Add a PROC CONTENTS step to the end of the program to verify that the labels and formats are stored in the descriptor portion.

Level 3

6. Using the $UPCASE*w*. Format and the SPLIT= Option

a. Retrieve the starter program **p105e06**.

b. Add a FORMAT statement to display **Customer_FirstName** and **Customer_LastName** in uppercase values.

> Documentation on the $UPCASE*w*. format can be found in the SAS Help and Documentation from the Contents tab (**SAS Products** ⇨ **Base SAS** ⇨ **SAS 9.2 Language Reference: Dictionary** ⇨ **Dictionary of Language Elements** ⇨ **Formats** ⇨ **$UPCASE*w*. Format**).

c. Add a LABEL statement to add the following labels:

Variable	Label
Customer_FirstName	CUSTOMER*FIRST NAME
Customer_LastName	CUSTOMER*LAST NAME

d. In the PROC PRINT statement, replace the LABEL option with the SPLIT= option and reference the asterisk as the split character.

> Documentation on the SPLIT= option can be found in the SAS Help and Documentation from the Contents tab (**SAS Products** ⇨ **Base SAS** ⇨ **Base SAS 9.2 Procedures Guide** ⇨ **Procedures** ⇨ **The PRINT Procedure**).

e. Submit the program to create the following PROC PRINT report:

```
            CUSTOMER       CUSTOMER
    Obs    FIRST NAME      LAST NAME

     1       TONIE         ASMUSSEN
     2       TOMMY         MCDONALD
```

5.5 Chapter Review

Chapter Review

1. What statement is used to read from a SAS data set in the DATA step?

2. What statement is used to write to a SAS data set in the DATA step?

3. What does the WHERE statement do?

4. What are examples of logical operators?

5. How can you limit the variables written to an output data set in the DATA step?

92

5.6 Solutions

Solutions to Exercises

1. **Subsetting Observations and Variables Using the WHERE and KEEP Statements**

   a. Retrieve and submit the program.

   What is the variable name that contains gender values? **Customer_Gender**

   What are the two possible gender values? **F** and **M**

   b. Add a DATA step.

```
data work.youngadult;
   set orion.customer_dim;
run;

proc print data=orion.customer_dim;
run;
```

   c. Modify the PROC PRINT step.

```
proc print data=work.youngadult;
run;
```

   d. Submit the program.

   e. Add a WHERE statement to subset for female customers.

```
data work.youngadult;
   set orion.customer_dim;
   where Customer_Gender='F';
run;
```

   f. Submit the program.

   g. Modify the WHERE statement to subset for female 18- to 36-year-old customers.

```
data work.youngadult;
   set orion.customer_dim;
   where Customer_Gender='F' and
         Customer_Age between 18 and 36;
run;
```

   h. Submit the program.

i. Modify the WHERE statement to subset for female 18- to 36-year-old customers who have the word `Gold` in their **Customer_Group**.

```
data work.youngadult;
   set orion.customer_dim;
   where Customer_Gender='F' and
         Customer_Age between 18 and 36 and
         Customer_Group contains 'Gold';
run;
```

j. Submit the program.

k. Keep only five variables.

```
data work.youngadult;
   set orion.customer_dim;
   where Customer_Gender='F' and
         Customer_Age between 18 and 36 and
         Customer_Group contains 'Gold';
   keep Customer_Name Customer_Age Customer_BirthDate
        Customer_Gender Customer_Group;
run;
```

l. Submit the program.

2. Subsetting Observations and Variables Using the WHERE and DROP Statements

a. Write a DATA step.

```
data work.sports;
   set orion.product_dim;
   where Supplier_Country in ('GB','ES','NL') and
         Product_Category like '%Sports';
   drop Product_ID Product_Line Product_Group
        Supplier_Name Supplier_ID;
run;
```

b. Write a PROC PRINT step.

```
proc print data=work.sports;
run;
```

3. Using the SOUNDS-LIKE Operator and the KEEP= Option

a. Write a DATA step.

```
data work.tony;
   set orion.customer_dim;
run;
```

b. Add a WHERE statement to the DATA step.

```
data work.tony;
   set orion.customer_dim;
   where Customer_FirstName =* 'Tony';
run;
```

c. Add a KEEP= data set option in the SET statement.

```
data work.tony;
   set orion.customer_dim(keep=Customer_FirstName Customer_LastName);
   where Customer_FirstName =* 'Tony';
run;
```

d. Write a PROC PRINT step.

```
proc print data=work.tony;
run;
```

4. **Adding Permanent Attributes to `Work.youngadult`**

a. Retrieve and submit the starter program.

b. Add a LABEL statement and a FORMAT statement to the DATA step.

```
data work.youngadult;
   set orion.customer_dim;
   where Customer_Gender='F' and
         Customer_Age between 18 and 35 and
         Customer_Group contains 'Gold';
   keep Customer_Name Customer_Age Customer_BirthDate
        Customer_Gender Customer_Group;
   label Customer_Gender='Gender'
         Customer_BirthDate='Date of Birth'
         Customer_Group='Member Level';
   format Customer_BirthDate worddate.;
run;

proc contents data=work.youngadult;
run;

proc print data=work.youngadult label;
run;
```

Why do **`Customer_Name`** and **`Customer_Age`** appear with a space in the column header but do not need labels? **These variables already have permanent labels assigned in the data set descriptor portion.**

5. **Adding Permanent Attributes to `Work.sports`**

a. Retrieve the starter program.

b. Add a LABEL statement to the DATA step and a LABEL option to PROC PRINT.

```
data work.sports;
   set orion.product_dim;
   where Supplier_Country in ('GB','ES','NL') and
         Product_Category like '%Sports';
   drop Product_ID Product_Line Product_Group Supplier_ID;
   label Product_Category='Sports Category'
         Product_Name='Product Name (Abbrev)'
         Supplier_Name='Supplier Name (Abbrev)';
run;

proc print data=work.sports label;
run;
```

c. Add a FORMAT statement to the DATA step.

```
data work.sports;
   set orion.product_dim;
   where Supplier_Country in ('GB','ES','NL') and
         Product_Category like '%Sports';
   drop Product_ID Product_Line Product_Group Supplier_ID;
   label Product_Category='Sports Category'
         Product_Name='Product Name (Abbrev)'
         Supplier_Name='Supplier Name (Abbrev)';
   format Product_Name Supplier_Name $15.;
run;
```

d. Submit the program.

e. Add a PROC CONTENTS step.

```
proc contents data=work.sports;
run;
```

6. Using the $UPCASE*w*. Format and the SPLIT= Option

a. Retrieve the starter program.

b. Add a FORMAT statement.

```
data work.tony;
   set orion.customer_dim(keep=Customer_FirstName Customer_LastName);
   where Customer_FirstName =* 'Tony';
   format Customer_FirstName Customer_LastName $upcase.;
run;

proc print data=work.tony label;
run;
```

c. Add a LABEL statement.

```
data work.tony;
   set orion.customer_dim(keep=Customer_FirstName Customer_LastName);
   where Customer_FirstName =* 'Tony';
   format Customer_FirstName Customer_LastName $upcase.;
   label Customer_FirstName='CUSTOMER*FIRST NAME'
         Customer_LastName='CUSTOMER*LAST NAME';
run;
```

d. Replace the LABEL option with the SPLIT= option.

```
proc print data=work.tony split='*';
run;
```

e. Submit the program.

Solutions to Student Activities (Polls/Quizzes)

5.02 Poll – Correct Answer

The DATA step reads a temporary SAS data set to create a permanent SAS data set.

- ❍ True
- (❍) False

```
data work.mycustomers;
   set orion.customer;
run;

proc print data=work.mycustomers;
   var Customer_ID Customer_Name
       Customer_Address;
run;
```

23

5.03 Quiz – Correct Answer

Which WHERE statement correctly subsets the numeric values for May, June, or July and missing character names?

a.
```
where Months in (5-7)
      and Names = .;
```

(b.)
```
where Months in (5,6,7)
      and Names = ' ';
```

c.
```
where Months in ('5','6','7')
      and Names = '.';
```

39

5.04 Quiz – Correct Answer

Which value will not be returned based on the WHERE statement?

a. Office Rep
b. Sales Rep. IV
(c.) service rep III
d. Representative

```
where Job_Title contains 'Rep';
```

46

5.05 Quiz – Correct Answer

Which WHERE statement will return all the observations that have a first name starting with the letter M for the given values?

a. `where Name like '_, M_';`

(b.) `where Name like '%, M%';`

c. `where Name like '_, M%';`

d. `where Name like '%, M_';`

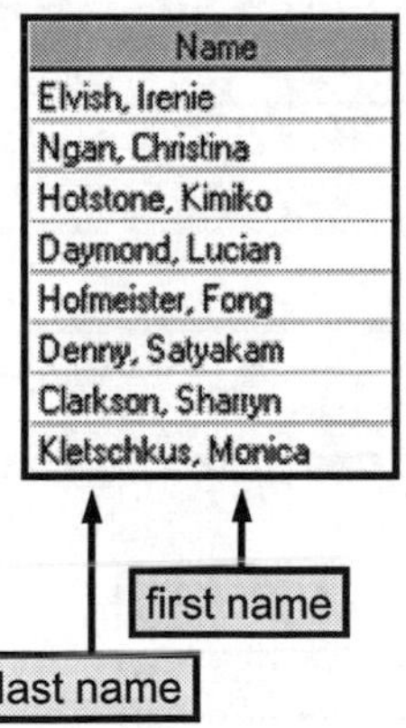

Name
Elvish, Irenie
Ngan, Christina
Hotstone, Kimiko
Daymond, Lucian
Hofmeister, Fong
Denny, Satyakam
Clarkson, Sharryn
Kletschkus, Monica
first name
last name

51

5.06 Quiz – Correct Answer

Which numeric format writes standard numeric data with leading zeros?

Zw.d

The Z*w.d* format is similar to the *w.d* format except that Z*w.d* pads right-aligned output with zeros instead of blanks.

76

5.07 Quiz – Correct Answer

Which FORMAT statement creates the output?

a.
```
format Birth_Date Hire_Date ddmmyy9.
       Term_Date mmyy7.;
```

b.
```
format Birth_Date Hire_Date ddmmyyyy.
       Term_Date mmmyyyy.;
```

(c.)
```
format Birth_Date Hire_Date ddmmyy10.
       Term_Date monyy7.;
```

Output →

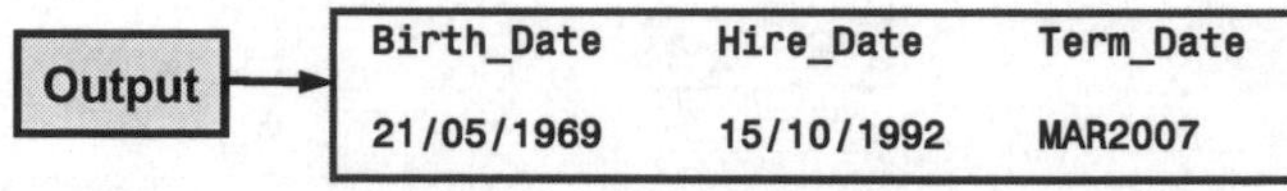

Birth_Date	Hire_Date	Term_Date
21/05/1969	15/10/1992	MAR2007

82

5.08 Quiz – Correct Answer

How many date and time formats start with EUR?

Nine

Example:

The EURDFDD*w*. format writes international SAS date values in the form dd.mm.yy or dd.mm.yyyy.

86

Solutions to Chapter Review

Chapter Review Answers

1. What statement is used to read from a SAS data set in the DATA step?

   SET statement

2. What statement is used to write to a SAS data set in the DATA step?

   DATA statement

3. What does the WHERE statement do?

   The WHERE statement subsets observations that meet a certain condition.

93

continued...

Chapter Review Answers

4. What are examples of logical operators?
   - **AND**
   - **OR**
   - **NOT**

5. How can you limit the variables written to an output data set in the DATA step?

   DROP or KEEP statement

94

Chapter 6 Reading Excel Worksheets

6.1 Using Excel Data as Input **6-3**

Demonstration: Reading Excel Worksheets – Windows 6-15

Exercises 6-17

6.2 Doing More with Excel Worksheets (Self-Study) **6-20**

Exercises 6-36

6.3 Chapter Review **6-37**

6.4 Solutions **6-38**

Solutions to Exercises 6-38

Solutions to Student Activities (Polls/Quizzes) 6-43

Solutions to Chapter Review 6-44

6.1 Using Excel Data as Input

Objectives

- Use the DATA step to create a SAS data set from an Excel worksheet.
- Use the SAS/ACCESS LIBNAME statement to read from an Excel worksheet as though it were a SAS data set.

3

Business Scenario

An existing data source contains information on Orion Star sales employees from Australia and the United States.

A new SAS data set needs to be created that contains a subset of this existing data source.

This new SAS data set must contain the following:

- only the employees from Australia who are Sales Representatives
- the employee's first name, last name, salary, job title, and hired date
- labels and formats in the descriptor portion

4

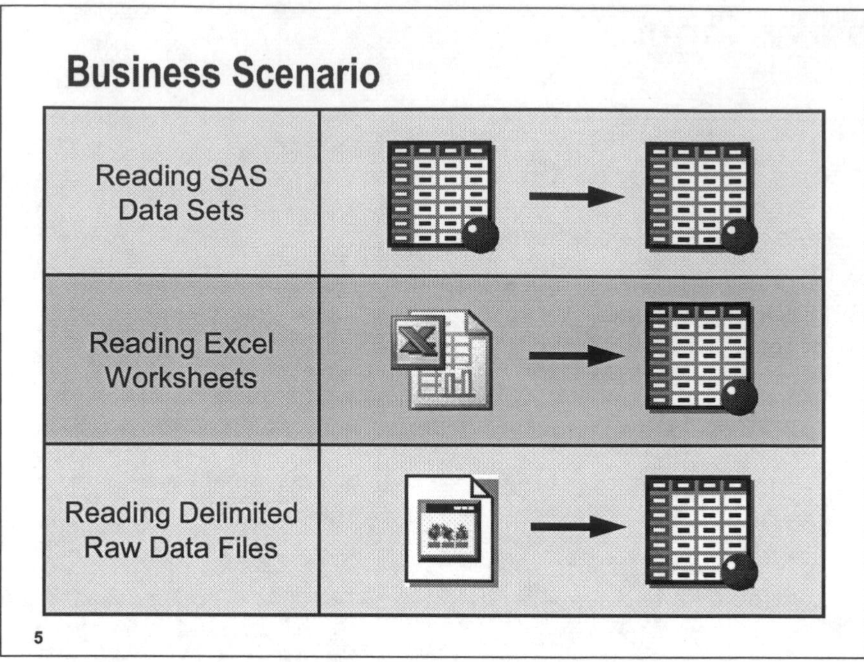

Business Scenario

Reading SAS Data Sets	`libname ________;`
	`data ________;`
	`   set ________;`
	`   ...`
	`run;`

Reading Excel Worksheets	`libname ________;`
	`data ________;`
	`   set ________;`
	`   ...`
	`run;`

Reading Delimited Raw Data Files	`data ________;`
	`   infile ________;`
	`   input ________;`
	`   ...`
	`run;`

6

The LIBNAME statement references a SAS data library when reading a SAS data set and an Excel workbook when reading an Excel worksheet.

Business Scenario Syntax

Use the following statements to complete the scenario:

```
LIBNAME libref 'physical-file-name';

DATA output-SAS-data-set;
     SET input-SAS-data-set;
     WHERE where-expression;
     KEEP variable-list;
     LABEL variable = 'label'
               variable = 'label'
               variable = 'label';
     FORMAT variable(s) format ;
RUN;
```

7

sales.xls

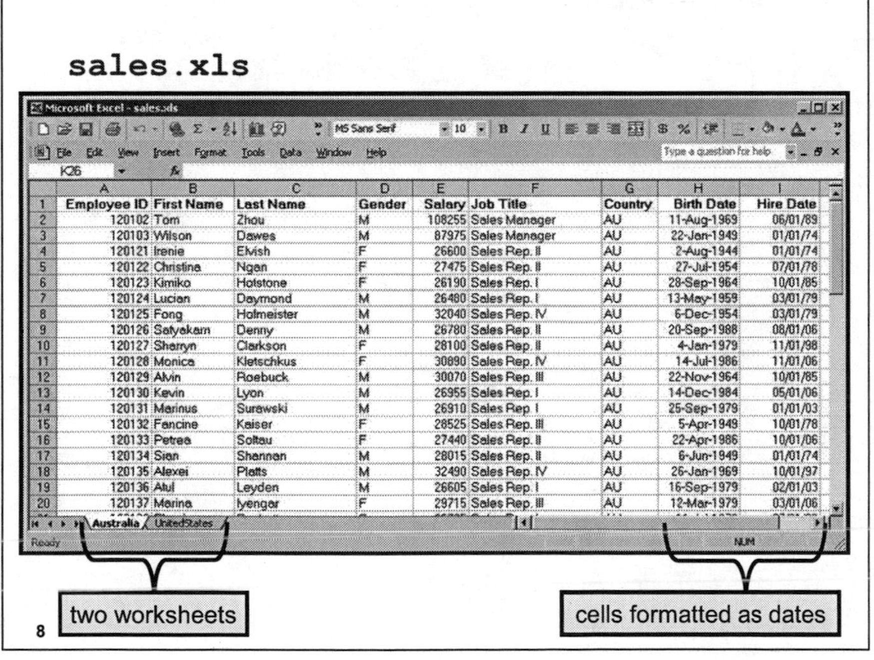

	A	B	C	D	E	F	G	H	I
1	Employee ID	First Name	Last Name	Gender	Salary	Job Title	Country	Birth Date	Hire Date
2	120102	Tom	Zhou	M	108255	Sales Manager	AU	11-Aug-1969	06/01/89
3	120103	Wilson	Dawes	M	87975	Sales Manager	AU	22-Jan-1949	01/01/74
4	120121	Irenie	Elvish	F	26600	Sales Rep. II	AU	2-Aug-1944	01/01/74
5	120122	Christina	Ngan	F	27475	Sales Rep. II	AU	27-Jul-1954	07/01/78
6	120123	Kimiko	Hotstone	F	26190	Sales Rep. I	AU	28-Sep-1964	10/01/85
7	120124	Lucian	Daymond	M	26480	Sales Rep. I	AU	13-May-1959	03/01/79
8	120125	Fong	Hofmeister	M	32040	Sales Rep. IV	AU	6-Dec-1954	03/01/79
9	120126	Satyakam	Denny	M	26780	Sales Rep. II	AU	20-Sep-1988	08/01/06
10	120127	Sharryn	Clarkson	F	28100	Sales Rep. II	AU	4-Jan-1979	11/01/98
11	120128	Monica	Kletschkus	F	30890	Sales Rep. IV	AU	14-Jul-1986	11/01/06
12	120129	Alvin	Roebuck	M	30070	Sales Rep. III	AU	22-Nov-1964	10/01/85
13	120130	Kevin	Lyon	M	26955	Sales Rep. I	AU	14-Dec-1984	05/01/06
14	120131	Marinus	Surawski	M	26910	Sales Rep. I	AU	25-Sep-1979	01/01/03
15	120132	Fancine	Kaiser	F	28525	Sales Rep. III	AU	5-Apr-1949	10/01/78
16	120133	Petrea	Soltau	F	27440	Sales Rep. II	AU	22-Apr-1986	10/01/06
17	120134	Sian	Shannan	M	28015	Sales Rep. II	AU	6-Jun-1949	01/01/74
18	120135	Alexei	Platts	M	32490	Sales Rep. IV	AU	26-Jan-1969	10/01/97
19	120136	Atul	Leyden	M	26605	Sales Rep. I	AU	16-Sep-1979	02/01/03
20	120137	Marina	Iyengar	F	29715	Sales Rep. III	AU	12-Mar-1979	03/01/06

8

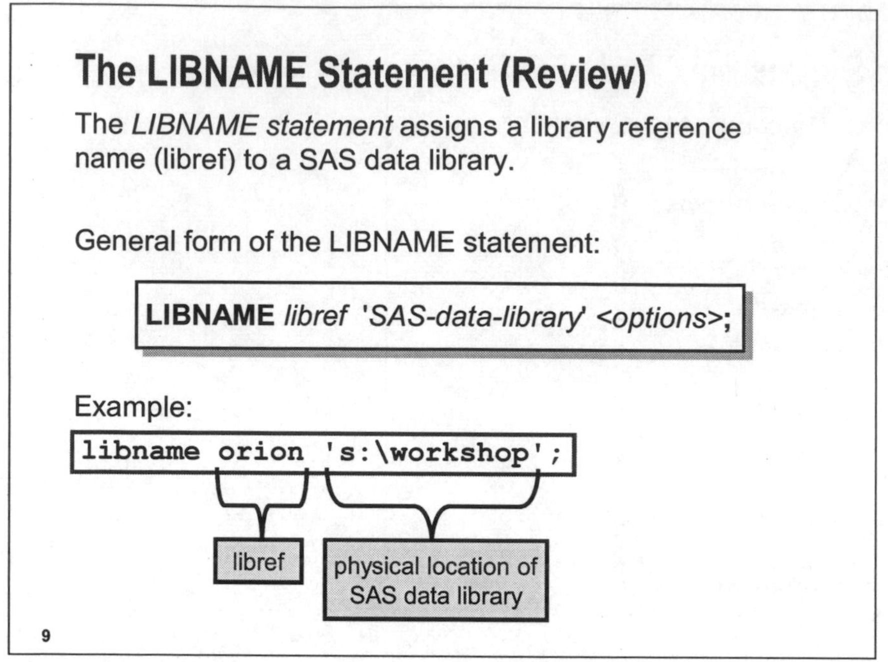

The LIBNAME statement needs to reference a SAS data library specific to your operating environment.

The SAS/ACCESS LIBNAME Statement

The *SAS/ACCESS LIBNAME statement* extends the LIBNAME statement to support assigning a library reference name (libref) to Microsoft Excel workbooks.

General form of the SAS/ACCESS LIBNAME statement:

LIBNAME *libref 'physical-file-name' <options>*;

This enables you to reference worksheets directly in a DATA step or SAS procedure, and to read from and write to a Microsoft Excel worksheet as though it were a SAS data set.

10

SAS/ACCESS options can be used in the LIBNAME statement.

For example,

MIXED=YES | NO

specifies whether to convert numeric data values into character data values for a column with mixed data types.

The default is NO, which means that numeric data will be imported as missing values in a character column. If MIXED=YES, the engine assigns a SAS character type for the column and converts all numeric data values to character data.

The following Technical Support Usage Note addresses column data that is imported as missing:

http://support.sas.com/kb/6/123.html

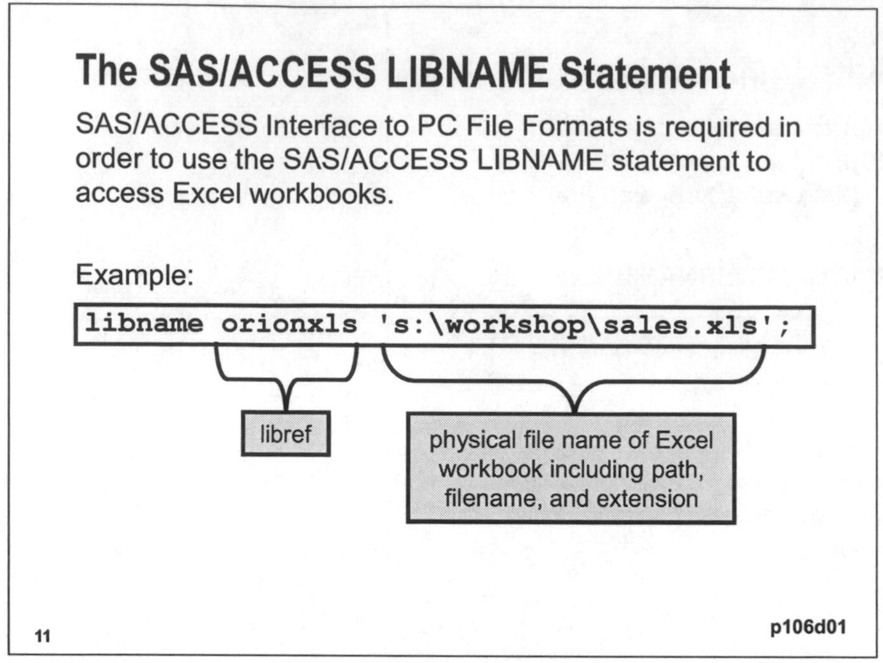

SAS/ACCESS Interface to PC File Formats enables you to read data from PC files, to use that data in SAS reports or applications, and to use SAS data sets to create PC files in various formats.

SAS/ACCESS Interface to PC File Formats gives access to Microsoft Excel, Microsoft Access, dBase, JMP, Lotus 1-2-3, SPSS, Stata, and Paradox.

To determine if you have a license for SAS/ACCESS Interface to PC File Formats, submit the following step:

```
proc setinit;
run;
```

After submitting, look in the SAS log for the products that are licensed for your site.

 SAS/ACCESS Interface to PC File Formats on Linux and UNIX enables access to PC files from the Linux and UNIX operating environments. A PC Files Server is used to access the PC data. The PC Files Server runs on a Microsoft Windows server, and SAS/ACCESS Interface to PC File Formats runs on a Linux or UNIX client server.

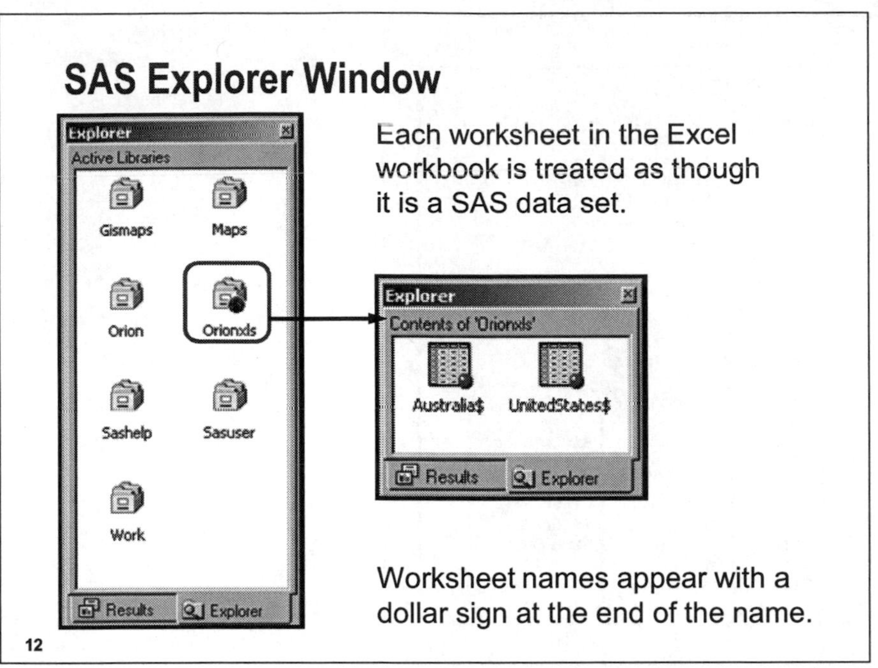
SAS Explorer Window
Explorer
Active Libraries
Gismaps
Maps
Orion
Orionxls
Sashelp
Sasuser
Work
Results
Explorer
Each worksheet in the Excel workbook is treated as though it is a SAS data set.
Explorer
Contents of 'Orionxls'
Australia$
UnitedStates$
Results
Explorer
Worksheet names appear with a dollar sign at the end of the name.
12

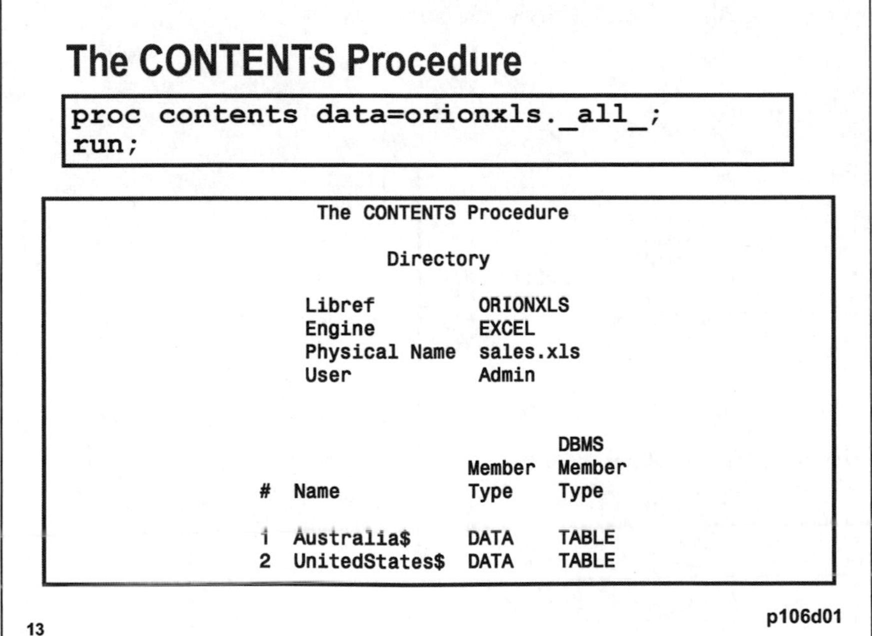
The CONTENTS Procedure
proc contents data=orionxls._all_;
run;
The CONTENTS Procedure
Directory
Libref ORIONXLS
Engine EXCEL
Physical Name sales.xls
User Admin
DBMS
Member Member
Name Type Type
1 Australia$ DATA TABLE
2 UnitedStates$ DATA TABLE
13
p106d01

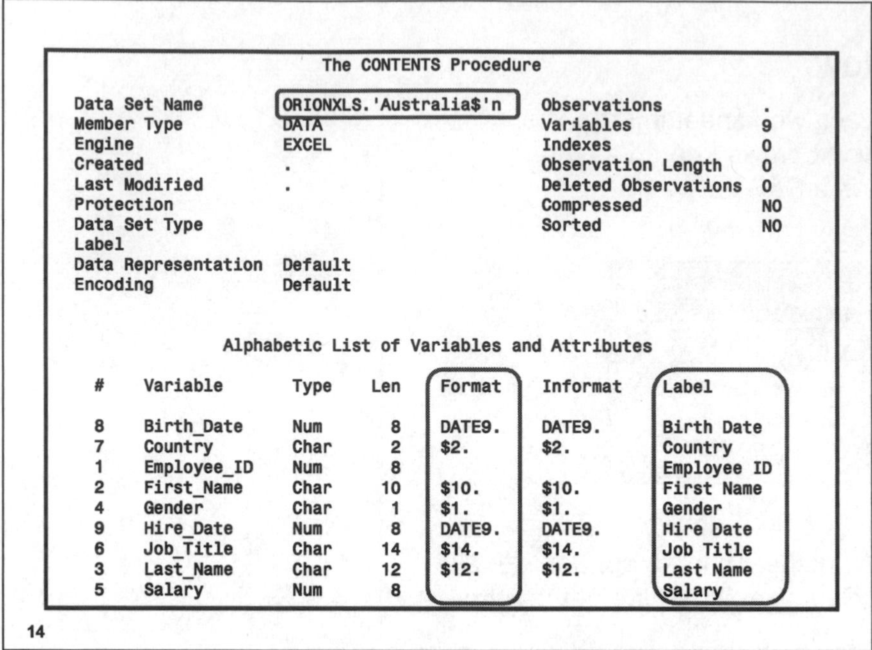

The CONTENTS Procedure

```
Data Set Name          ORIONXLS.'Australia$'n    Observations           .
Member Type            DATA                      Variables              9
Engine                 EXCEL                     Indexes                0
Created                .                         Observation Length     0
Last Modified          .                         Deleted Observations   0
Protection                                       Compressed             NO
Data Set Type                                    Sorted                 NO
Label
Data Representation    Default
Encoding               Default
```

Alphabetic List of Variables and Attributes

#	Variable	Type	Len	Format	Informat	Label
8	Birth_Date	Num	8	DATE9.	DATE9.	Birth Date
7	Country	Char	2	$2.	$2.	Country
1	Employee_ID	Num	8			Employee ID
2	First_Name	Char	10	$10.	$10.	First Name
4	Gender	Char	1	$1.	$1.	Gender
9	Hire_Date	Num	8	DATE9.	DATE9.	Hire Date
6	Job_Title	Char	14	$14.	$14.	Job Title
3	Last_Name	Char	12	$12.	$12.	Last Name
5	Salary	Num	8			Salary

14

The Excel LIBNAME engine converts worksheet dates to SAS date values and assigns the DATE9. format.

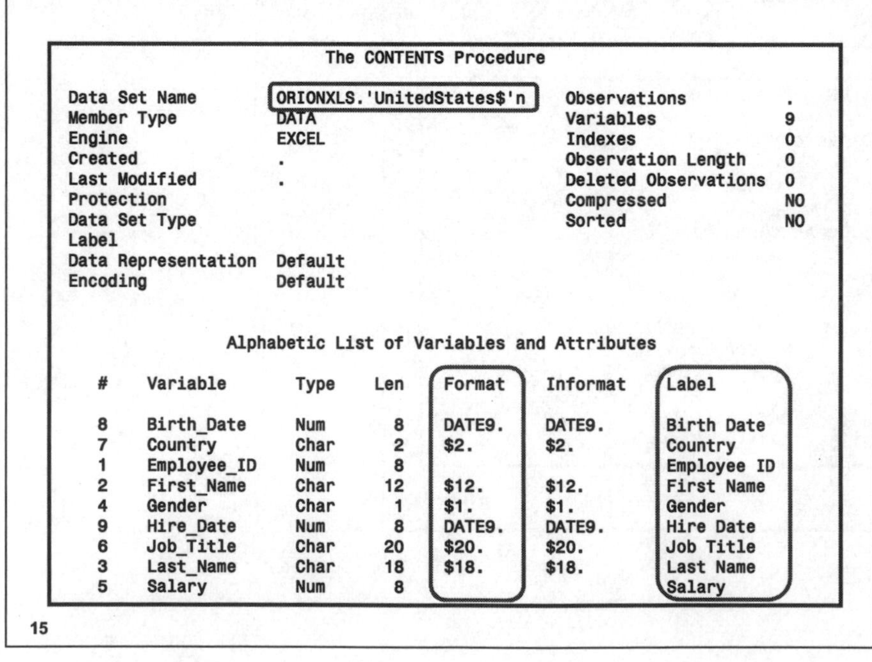

The CONTENTS Procedure

```
Data Set Name          ORIONXLS.'UnitedStates$'n    Observations           .
Member Type            DATA                         Variables              9
Engine                 EXCEL                        Indexes                0
Created                .                            Observation Length     0
Last Modified          .                            Deleted Observations   0
Protection                                          Compressed             NO
Data Set Type                                       Sorted                 NO
Label
Data Representation    Default
Encoding               Default
```

Alphabetic List of Variables and Attributes

#	Variable	Type	Len	Format	Informat	Label
8	Birth_Date	Num	8	DATE9.	DATE9.	Birth Date
7	Country	Char	2	$2.	$2.	Country
1	Employee_ID	Num	8			Employee ID
2	First_Name	Char	12	$12.	$12.	First Name
4	Gender	Char	1	$1.	$1.	Gender
9	Hire_Date	Num	8	DATE9.	DATE9.	Hire Date
6	Job_Title	Char	20	$20.	$20.	Job Title
3	Last_Name	Char	18	$18.	$18.	Last Name
5	Salary	Num	8			Salary

15

SAS Name Literals

By default, special characters such as the $ are not allowed in data set names.

SAS name literals enable special characters to be included in data set names.

A *SAS name literal* is a name token that is expressed as a string within quotation marks, followed by the letter n.

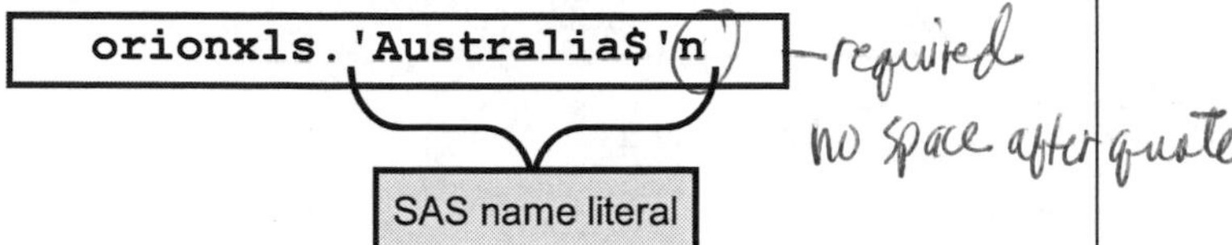

16

The PRINT Procedure

```
proc print data=orionxls.'Australia$'n;
run;
```

Partial PROC PRINT Output

Obs	Employee_ ID	First_Name	Last_Name	Gender	Salary	Job_Title	Country	Birth_ Date	Hire_Date
1	120102	Tom	Zhou	M	108255	Sales Manager	AU	11AUG1969	01JUN1989
2	120103	Wilson	Dawes	M	87975	Sales Manager	AU	22JAN1949	01JAN1974
3	120121	Irenie	Elvish	F	26600	Sales Rep. II	AU	02AUG1944	01JAN1974
4	120122	Christina	Ngan	F	27475	Sales Rep. II	AU	27JUL1954	01JUL1978
5	120123	Kimiko	Hotstone	F	26190	Sales Rep. I	AU	28SEP1964	01OCT1985
6	120124	Lucian	Daymond	M	26480	Sales Rep. I	AU	13MAY1959	01MAR1979
7	120125	Fong	Hofmeister	M	32040	Sales Rep. IV	AU	06DEC1954	01MAR1979
8	120126	Satyakam	Denny	M	26780	Sales Rep. II	AU	20SEP1988	01AUG2006
9	120127	Sharryn	Clarkson	F	28100	Sales Rep. II	AU	04JAN1979	01NOV1998
10	120128	Monica	Kletschkus	F	30890	Sales Rep. IV	AU	14JUL1986	01NOV2006
11	120129	Alvin	Roebuck	M	30070	Sales Rep. III	AU	22NOV1964	01OCT1985
12	120130	Kevin	Lyon	M	26955	Sales Rep. I	AU	14DEC1984	01MAY2006
13	120131	Marinus	Surawski	M	26910	Sales Rep. I	AU	25SEP1979	01JAN2003
14	120132	Fancine	Kaiser	F	28525	Sales Rep. III	AU	05APR1949	01OCT1978
15	120133	Petrea	Soltau	F	27440	Sales Rep. II	AU	22APR1986	01OCT2006

17 p106d01

6.01 Quiz

Which PROC PRINT step displays the worksheet containing employees from the United States?

a.
```
proc print data=orionxls.'UnitedStates';
run;
```

b.
```
proc print data=orionxls.'UnitedStates$';
run;
```

c.
```
proc print data=orionxls.'UnitedStates'n;
run;
```

d.
```
proc print data=orionxls.'UnitedStates$'n;
run;
```

19

Business Scenario

Create a temporary SAS data set named **Work.subset2** from the Excel workbook named **sales.xls**.

```
libname orionxls 's:\workshop\sales.xls';

data work.subset2;
   set orionxls.'Australia$'n;
   where Job_Title contains 'Rep';
   keep First_Name Last_Name Salary
        Job_Title Hire_Date;
   label Job_Title='Sales Title'
         Hire_Date='Date Hired';
   format Salary comma10. Hire_Date weekdate.;
run;
```

21 p106d02

→ You have to declare which worksheet you are importing / using

Business Scenario

```
proc contents data=work.subset2;
run;
```

Partial PROC CONTENTS Output

Alphabetic List of Variables and Attributes

#	Variable	Type	Len	Format	Informat	Label
1	First_Name	Char	10	$10.	$10.	First Name
5	Hire_Date	Num	8	WEEKDATE.	DATE9.	Date Hired
4	Job_Title	Char	14	$14.	$14.	Sales Title
2	Last_Name	Char	12	$12.	$12.	Last Name
3	Salary	Num	8	COMMA10.		Salary

22 p106d02

Business Scenario

```
proc print data=work.subset2 label;
run;
```

Partial PROC PRINT Output

Obs	First Name	Last Name	Salary	Sales Title	Date Hired
1	Irenie	Elvish	26,600	Sales Rep. II	Tuesday, January 1, 1974
2	Christina	Ngan	27,475	Sales Rep. II	Saturday, July 1, 1978
3	Kimiko	Hotstone	26,190	Sales Rep. I	Tuesday, October 1, 1985
4	Lucian	Daymond	26,480	Sales Rep. I	Thursday, March 1, 1979
5	Fong	Hofmeister	32,040	Sales Rep. IV	Thursday, March 1, 1979
6	Satyakam	Denny	26,780	Sales Rep. II	Tuesday, August 1, 2006
7	Sharryn	Clarkson	28,100	Sales Rep. II	Sunday, November 1, 1998
8	Monica	Kletschkus	30,890	Sales Rep. IV	Wednesday, November 1, 2006
9	Alvin	Roebuck	30,070	Sales Rep. III	Tuesday, October 1, 1985
10	Kevin	Lyon	26,955	Sales Rep. I	Monday, May 1, 2006
11	Marinus	Surawski	26,910	Sales Rep. I	Wednesday, January 1, 2003
12	Fancine	Kaiser	28,525	Sales Rep. III	Sunday, October 1, 1978

23 p106d02

→ you have to clear the physical file you created so you don't lock the file

Disassociating a Libref

If SAS has a libref assigned to an Excel workbook, the workbook cannot be opened in Excel. To disassociate a libref, use a LIBNAME statement and specify the libref and the CLEAR option.

```
libname orionxls 's:\workshop\sales.xls';

data work.subset2;
   set orionxls.'Australia$'n;
   ...
run;

libname orionxls clear;
```

SAS disconnects from the data source and closes any resources that are associated with that libref's connection.

24 p106d02

Reading Excel Worksheets – Windows

p106d02

1. Submit the following program except for the last LIBNAME statement.

```
libname orionxls 'sales.xls';

data work.subset2;
   set orionxls.'Australia$'n;
   where Job_Title contains 'Rep';
   keep First_Name Last_Name Salary
        Job_Title Hire_Date;
   label Job_Title='Sales Title'
         Hire_Date='Date Hired';
   format Salary comma10. Hire_Date weekdate.;
run;

proc contents data=work.subset2;
run;

proc print data=work.subset2 label;
run;

libname orionxls clear;
```

2. Review the PROC CONTENTS and PROC PRINT results in the Output window.

3. Select the **Explorer** tab on the SAS window bar to activate the SAS Explorer or select **View** ⇨ **Contents Only**.

4. Double-click **Libraries** to show all available libraries.

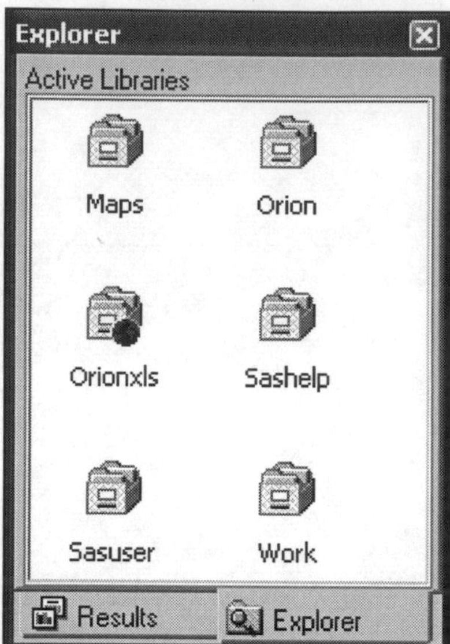

5. Double-click on the **Orionxls** library to show all Excel worksheets of that library.

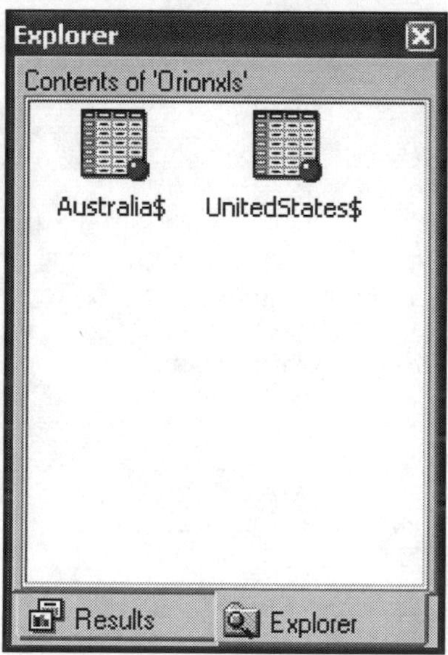

6. Submit the last LIBNAME statement to disassociate the libref.

Exercises

Level 1

1. Reading an Excel Worksheet

a. Retrieve the starter program **p106e01**.

b. Add a LIBNAME statement before the PROC CONTENTS step to create a libref called CUSTFM that references the Excel workbook named custfm.xls.

c. Submit the LIBNAME statement and the PROC CONTENTS step to create the following partial PROC CONTENTS report:

Page 1 of 3

```
                    The CONTENTS Procedure

                           Directory

                 Libref          CUSTFM
                 Engine          EXCEL
                 Physical Name   custfm.xls
                 User            Admin


                                        DBMS
                              Member    Member
                 #   Name     Type      Type

                 1   Females$ DATA      TABLE
                 2   Males$   DATA      TABLE
```

d. Add a SET statement in the DATA step to read the worksheet containing the male data.

e. Add a KEEP statement in the DATA step to include only the **`First_Name`**, **`Last_Name`**, and **`Birth_Date`** variables.

f. Add a FORMAT statement in the DATA step to display the **`Birth_Date`** as a four-digit year.

g. Add a LABEL statement to change the column header of **`Birth_Date`** to **`Birth Year`**.

h. Submit the program including the last LIBNAME statement and create the following PROC PRINT report:

Partial PROC PRINT Output (First 5 of 47 Observations)

```
                                                  Birth
          Obs    First Name     Last Name         Year

            1    James          Kvarniq           1974
            2    David          Black             1969
            3    Markus         Sepke             1988
            4    Ulrich         Heyde             1939
            5    Jimmie         Evans             1954
```

Level 2

2. Reading an Excel Worksheet

a. Write a LIBNAME statement to create a libref called PROD that references the Excel workbook named products.xls.

b. Write a PROC CONTENTS step to view all of the contents of PROD.

c. Submit the program to determine the names of the four worksheets in products.xls.

d. Write a DATA step to read the worksheet containing sports data to create a new data set called **`Work.golf`**.

The data set **`Work.golf`** should

- include only the observations where **`Category`** is equal to `Golf`
- not include the **`Category`** variable
- include a label of `Golf Products` for the **`Name`** variable.

e. Write a LIBNAME to clear the PROD libref.

f. Write a PROC PRINT step to create the following report:

Partial PROC PRINT Output (First 10 of 56 Observations)

```
Obs    Golf Products

  1    Ball Bag
  2    Red/White/Black Staff 9 Bag
  3    Tee Holder
  4    Bb Softspikes - Xp 22-pack
  5    Bretagne Performance Tg Men's Golf Shoes L.
  6    Bretagne Soft-Tech Men's Glove, left
  7    Bretagne St2 Men's Golf Glove, left
  8    Bretagne Stabilites 2000 Goretex Shoes
  9    Bretagne Stabilities Tg Men's Golf Shoes
 10    Bretagne Stabilities Women's Golf Shoes
```

Level 3

3. Reading a Range of an Excel Worksheet

a. Write a LIBNAME statement to create a libref called XLSDATA that references the Excel workbook named custcaus.xls. The worksheets in this Excel workbook do not have column names. Add the appropriate option to the LIBNAME statement that specifies not to use the first row of data as column names.

Documentation on the appropriate option can be found in the SAS Help and Documentation from the Contents tab (**SAS Products** ⇨ **SAS/ACCESS** ⇨ **SAS/ACCESS 9.2 for PC Files: Reference** ⇨ **LIBNAME Statement and Pass-Through Facility on 32-Bit Microsoft Windows** ⇨ **File-Specific Reference** ⇨ **Microsoft Excel Workbook Files**).

b. Write a PROC CONTENTS step to view all of the contents of XLSDATA.

c. Submit the program. Any member not containing a dollar sign in the name is an Excel range.

d. Write a DATA step to read the range containing Germany (DE) data to create a new data set called **`Work.germany`**. Add appropriate labels and formats based on the desired report.

e. Write a LIBNAME to clear the XLSDATA libref.

f. Write a PROC PRINT step to create the following report:

```
             Customer                                                                   Birth
     Obs        ID       Country    Gender    First Name     Last Name        Date

       1         9          DE         F       Cornelia       Krahl         27/02/74
       2        11          DE         F       Elke           Wallstab      16/08/74
       3        13          DE         M       Markus         Sepke         21/07/88
       4        16          DE         M       Ulrich         Heyde         16/01/39
       5        19          DE         M       Oliver S.      Füßling       23/02/64
       6        33          DE         M       Rolf           Robak         24/02/39
       7        42          DE         M       Thomas         Leitmann      09/02/79
       8        50          DE         M       Gert-Gunter    Mendler       16/01/34
       9        61          DE         M       Carsten        Maestrini     08/07/44
      10        65          DE         F       Ines           Deisser       20/07/69
```

Level 2 code:

```
libname PROD 's:\workshop\products.xls';
proc contents data=PROD._all_;
run;
data work.golf
    set prod.'Sports$'n;   → workshet/tab
    where Category='Golf';
    drop Category;
    label Name='Golf Products';
run;
proc print data=work.golf label;
run;
libname PROD clear;   → clearing the physical file
```

6.2 Doing More with Excel Worksheets (Self-Study)

Objectives

- Use the DATA step to create an Excel worksheet from a SAS data set.
- Use the COPY procedure to create an Excel worksheet from a SAS data set.
- Use the IMPORT Wizard and procedure to read an Excel worksheet.
- Use the EXPORT Wizard and procedure to create an Excel worksheet.

29

Creating Excel Worksheets

In addition to reading an Excel worksheet, the SAS/ACCESS LIBNAME statement with the DATA step can be used to create an Excel worksheet.

```
libname orionxls
        's:\workshop\qtr2007a.xls';

data orionxls.qtr1_2007;
   set orion.qtr1_2007;
run;

data orionxls.qtr2_2007;
   set orion.qtr2_2007;
run;

proc contents data=orionxls._all_;
run;

libname orionxls clear;
```

30 p106d03

Creating Excel Worksheets

Partial SAS Log

```
70   data orionxls.qtr1_2007;
71      set orion.qtr1_2007;
72
73   run;

NOTE: SAS variable labels, formats, and lengths are not written to DBMS tables.
NOTE: There were 22 observations read from the data set ORION.QTR1_2007.
NOTE: The data set ORIONXLS.qtr1_2007 has 22 observations and 5 variables.


74   data orionxls.qtr2_2007;
75      set orion.qtr2_2007;
76   run;

NOTE: SAS variable labels, formats, and lengths are not written to DBMS tables.
NOTE: There were 36 observations read from the data set ORION.QTR2_2007.
NOTE: The data set ORIONXLS.qtr2_2007 has 36 observations and 6 variables.
```

31

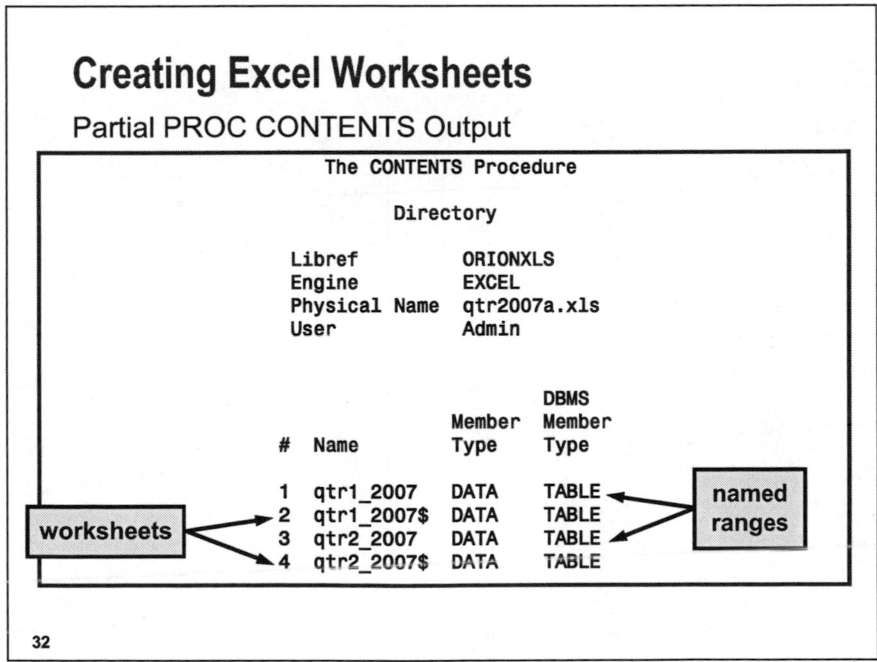

Creating Excel Worksheets
Partial PROC CONTENTS Output
The CONTENTS Procedure
Directory
Libref ORIONXLS
Engine EXCEL
Physical Name qtr2007a.xls
User Admin
Name Member Type DBMS Member Type
1 qtr1_2007 DATA TABLE
2 qtr1_2007$ DATA TABLE
3 qtr2_2007 DATA TABLE
4 qtr2_2007$ DATA TABLE
worksheets
named ranges
32

In Excel, a named range is a descriptive name for a range of cells.

3 WAYS TO IMPORT .XLS FILE TO SAS:
(1) LIBNAME
(2) PROC COPY — efficient way to copy/import data
(3) IMPORT TABLE directly into SAS

Creating Excel Worksheets

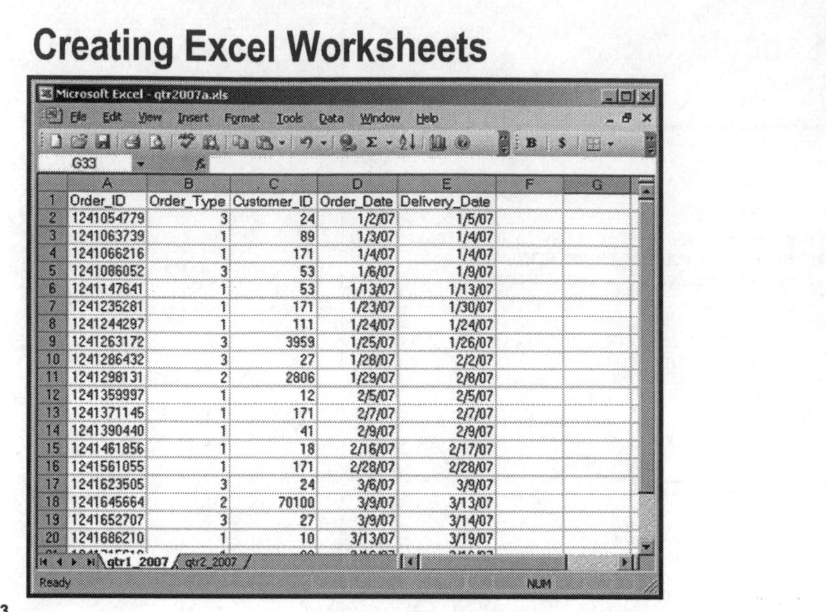

	A	B	C	D	E	F	G
1	Order_ID	Order_Type	Customer_ID	Order_Date	Delivery_Date		
2	1241054779	3	24	1/2/07	1/5/07		
3	1241063739	1	89	1/3/07	1/4/07		
4	1241066216	1	171	1/4/07	1/4/07		
5	1241086052	3	53	1/6/07	1/9/07		
6	1241147641	1	53	1/13/07	1/13/07		
7	1241235281	1	171	1/23/07	1/30/07		
8	1241244297	1	111	1/24/07	1/24/07		
9	1241263172	3	3959	1/25/07	1/26/07		
10	1241286432	3	27	1/28/07	2/2/07		
11	1241298131	2	2806	1/29/07	2/8/07		
12	1241359997	1	12	2/5/07	2/5/07		
13	1241371145	1	171	2/7/07	2/7/07		
14	1241390440	1	41	2/9/07	2/9/07		
15	1241461856	1	18	2/16/07	2/17/07		
16	1241561055	1	171	2/28/07	2/28/07		
17	1241623505	3	24	3/6/07	3/9/07		
18	1241645664	2	70100	3/9/07	3/13/07		
19	1241652707	3	27	3/9/07	3/14/07		
20	1241686210	1	10	3/13/07	3/19/07		

33

Creating Excel Worksheets

As an alternative to the DATA step, the COPY procedure can be used to create an Excel worksheet.

```
libname orionxls
        's:\workshop\qtr2007b.xls';

proc copy  in=orion out=orionxls;
   select qtr1_2007 qtr2_2007;
run;

proc contents data=orionxls._all_;
run;

libname orionxls clear;
```

34 p106d03

Creating Excel Worksheets

Partial SAS Log

```
proc copy  in=orion out=orionxls;
   select qtr1_2007 qtr2_2007;
run;

NOTE: Copying ORION.QTR1_2007 to ORIONXLS.QTR1_2007 (memtype=DATA).
NOTE: SAS variable labels, formats, and lengths are not written to DBMS tables.
NOTE: There were 22 observations read from the data set ORION.QTR1_2007.
NOTE: The data set ORIONXLS.QTR1_2007 has 22 observations and 5 variables.
NOTE: Copying ORION.QTR2_2007 to ORIONXLS.QTR2_2007 (memtype=DATA).
NOTE: SAS variable labels, formats, and lengths are not written to DBMS tables.
NOTE: There were 36 observations read from the data set ORION.QTR2_2007.
NOTE: The data set ORIONXLS.QTR2_2007 has 36 observations and 6 variables.
```

35

Import/Export Wizards and Procedures

The Import/Export Wizards and IMPORT/EXPORT procedures enable you to read and write data between SAS data sets and external PC files.

The Import/Export Wizards and procedures are part of Base SAS and enable access to delimited files. If you have a license to SAS/ACCESS Interface to PC File Formats, you can also access Microsoft Excel, Microsoft Access, dBASE, JMP, Lotus 1-2-3, SPSS, Stata, and Paradox files.

36

Census data (ex) .csv - IMPORTING from CD (ex.)

```
options pageno=1;
data census;
   length citystate $ 30 state $ 2;
   infile f:\census90_99.csv dsd;
   input citystate $
         pop99 : comma.
         pop90 : comma.;
   label citystate='Metro Area'
         pop99 = '1999 population'
         pop90 = '1990 population'
```

→ if the file has quotation mark, dsd will ignore the " " quotation to read it.

→ you need informat so SAS will strip the comma in the number (ex. 136,800) raw file

Import/Export Wizards and Procedures

The wizards and procedures have similar capabilities; the wizards are point-and-click interfaces and the procedures are code-based.

To invoke the wizards from the SAS windowing environment, select **File** and **Import Data** or **Export Data**.

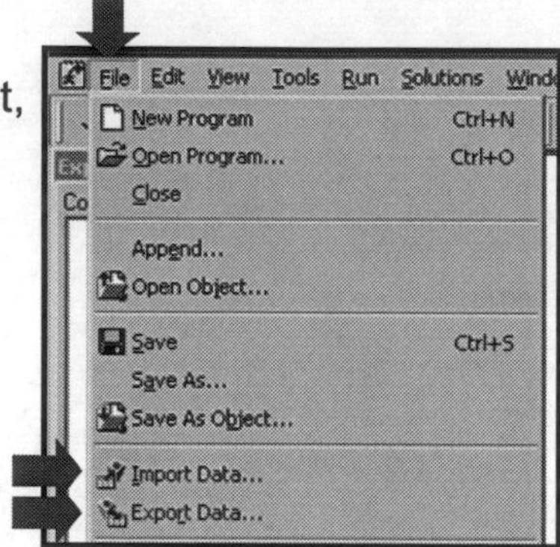

37

The Import Wizard

The Import Wizard enables you to read data from an external data source and write it to a SAS data set.

Steps of the Import Wizard:

1. Select the type of file you are importing.
2. Locate the input file.
3. Select the table range or worksheet from which to import data.
4. Select a location to store the imported file.
5. Save the generated PROC IMPORT code. (Optional)

38

format pop 90 pop 99 comma11.; (to put comma in numbers)
state = left, etc. →

proc print data= orion.census label;
var citystate state growthrate pop 90 pop 99 → VAR (to re-organize the order of fields in view)

The Import Wizard

1. Select the type of file you are importing.

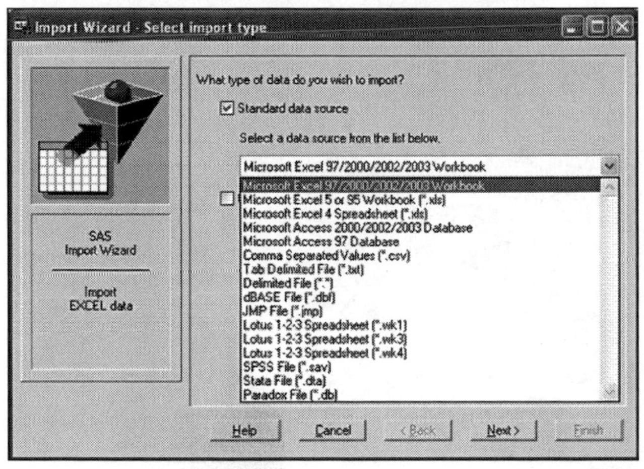

39

The Import Wizard

2. Locate the input file.

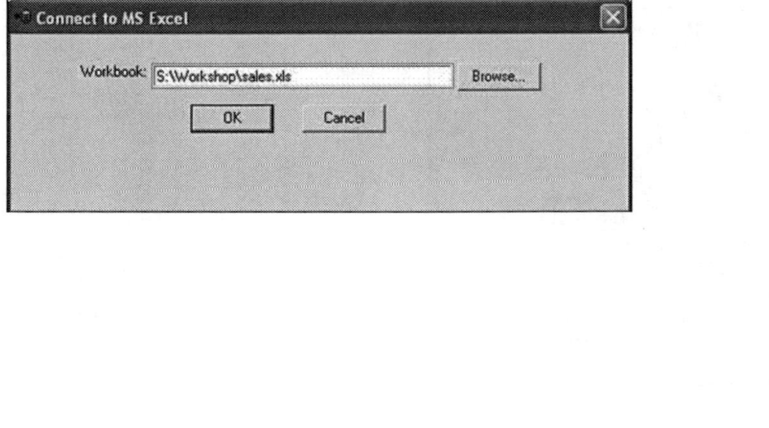

40

SCAN Function - ex. separate one variable SAN FRANCISCO, CA (1) (2)

→ state = scan(citystate, 2, ',');

LEFT FUNCTION → ex. | CA | will pad the space on the left

→ state = left(scan(citystate, 2, ','));
growthrate = (pop90 - pop90)/pop90;
citystate = left(scan(citystate, 1, ',')); → to get the city, strip off the state

The Import Wizard

3. Select the table range or worksheet from which to import data.

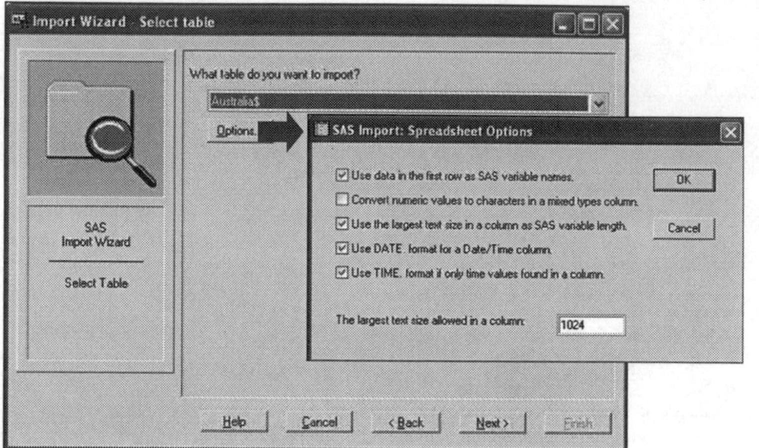

41

The Import Wizard

4. Select a location to store the imported file.

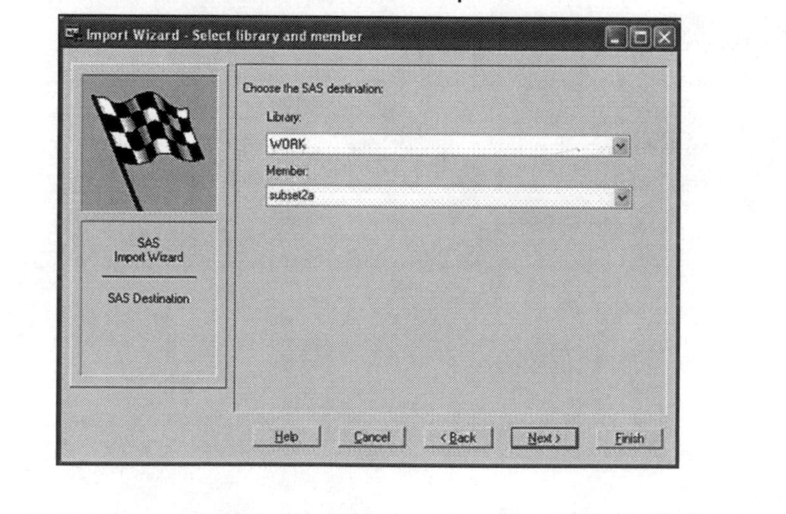

42

proc sort data= census; out = orion-census;
(SAS Sorts Ascending - default)
by ~~growthrate~~ descending growthrate;

The Import Wizard

5. Save the generated PROC IMPORT code. (Optional)

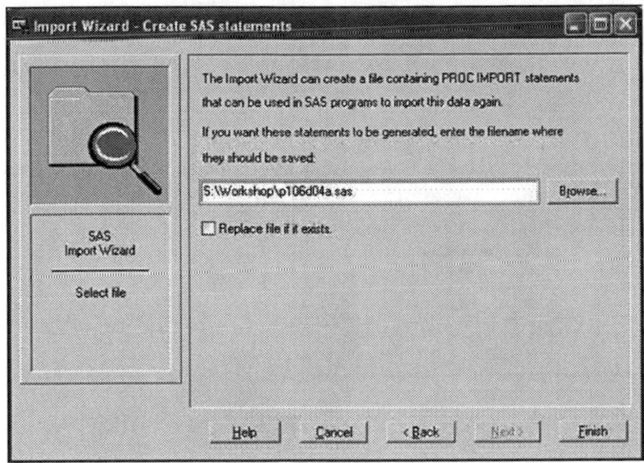

43

The Import Wizard

SAS Log

```
NOTE: WORK.SUBSET2A data set was successfully created.
```

```
proc print data=work.subset2a;
run;
```

Partial PROC PRINT Output

Obs	Employee_ ID	First_Name	Last_Name	Gender	Salary	Job_Title	Country	Birth_ Date	Hire_Date
1	120102	Tom	Zhou	M	108255	Sales Manager	AU	11AUG1969	01JUN1989
2	120103	Wilson	Dawes	M	87975	Sales Manager	AU	22JAN1949	01JAN1974
3	120121	Irenie	Elvish	F	26600	Sales Rep. II	AU	02AUG1944	01JAN1974
4	120122	Christina	Ngan	F	27475	Sales Rep. II	AU	27JUL1954	01JUL1978
5	120123	Kimiko	Hotstone	F	26190	Sales Rep. I	AU	28SEP1964	01OCT1985

44

p106d04

The Import Wizard

```
proc contents data=work.subset2a;
run;
```

Partial PROC CONTENTS Output

```
               Alphabetic List of Variables and Attributes

 #    Variable       Type    Len    Format    Informat    Label

 8    Birth_Date     Num       8    DATE9.    DATE9.      Birth Date
 7    Country        Char      2    $2.       $2.         Country
 1    Employee_ID    Num       8                          Employee ID
 2    First_Name     Char     10    $10.      $10.        First Name
 4    Gender         Char      1    $1.       $1.         Gender
 9    Hire_Date      Num       8    DATE9.    DATE9.      Hire Date
 6    Job_Title      Char     14    $14.      $14.        Job Title
 3    Last_Name      Char     12    $12.      $12.        Last Name
 5    Salary         Num       8                          Salary
```

45

p106d04

The IMPORT Procedure

The program **p106d04a** was created from the Import Wizard.

```
PROC IMPORT OUT= WORK.subset2a
            DATAFILE= "S:\Workshop\sales.xls"
            DBMS=EXCEL REPLACE;
     RANGE="Australia$";
     GETNAMES=YES;
     MIXED=NO;
     SCANTEXT=YES;
     USEDATE=YES;
     SCANTIME=YES;
RUN;
```

46 p106d04a

OUT=<*libref.*>*SAS-data-set*

identifies the output SAS data set.

DATAFILE="*filename*"

specifies the complete path and filename or a fileref for the input PC file, spreadsheet, or delimited external file.

DBMS=*identifier*

specifies the type of data to import. To import a DBMS table, you must specify DBMS= using a valid database identifier. For example, DBMS=EXCEL specifies to import a Microsoft Excel worksheet.

REPLACE

overwrites an existing SAS data set. If you do not specify REPLACE, PROC IMPORT does not overwrite an existing data set.

RANGE="*range-name* | *absolute-range*"

subsets a spreadsheet by identifying the rectangular set of cells to import from the specified spreadsheet.

GETNAMES=YES | NO

for spreadsheets and delimited external files, determines whether to generate SAS variable names from the column names in the input file's first row of data. Note that if a column name contains special characters that are not valid in a SAS name, such as a blank, SAS converts the character to an underscore.

MIXED=YES | NO

converts numeric data values into character data values for a column that contains mixed data types. The default is NO, which means that numeric data will be imported as missing values in a character column. If MIXED=YES, then the engine will assign a SAS character type for the column and convert all numeric data values to character data values.

SCANTEXT=YES | NO

scans the length of text data for a data source column and uses the longest string data that is found as the SAS column width.

USEDATE=YES | NO

specifies which format to use. If USEDATE=YES, then the DATE. format is used for date/time columns in the data source table while importing data from Excel workbook. If USEDATE=NO, then a DATETIME. format is used for date/time.

SCANTIME=YES | NO

scans all row values for a DATETIME data type field and automatically determines the TIME data type if only time values (that is, no date or datetime values) exist in the column.

The Export Wizard

The Export Wizard reads data from a SAS data set and writes it to an external file source.

Steps of the Export Wizard:

1. Select the data set from which you want to export data.
2. Select the type of data source to which you want to export files.
3. Assign the output file.
4. Assign the table name.
5. Save the generated PROC EXPORT code. (Optional)

47

The Export Wizard

1. Select the data set from which you want to export data.

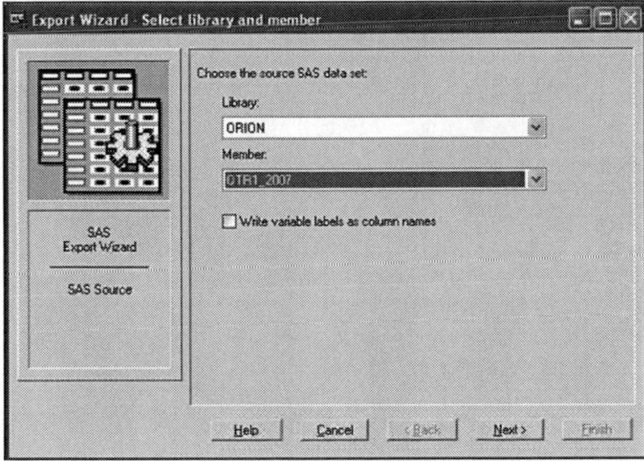

48

The Export Wizard

2. Select the type of data source to which you want to export files.

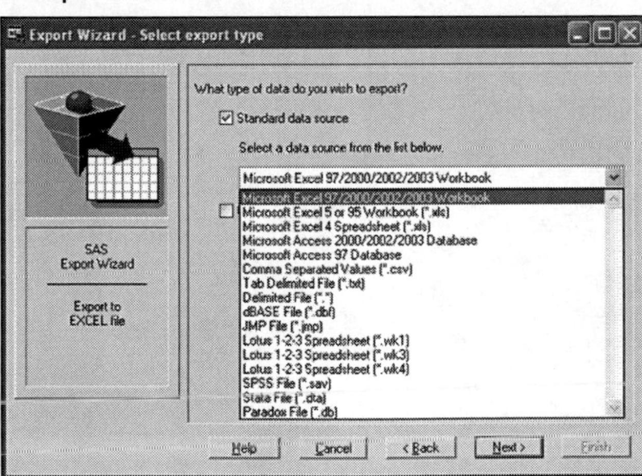

49

The Export Wizard

3. Assign the output file.

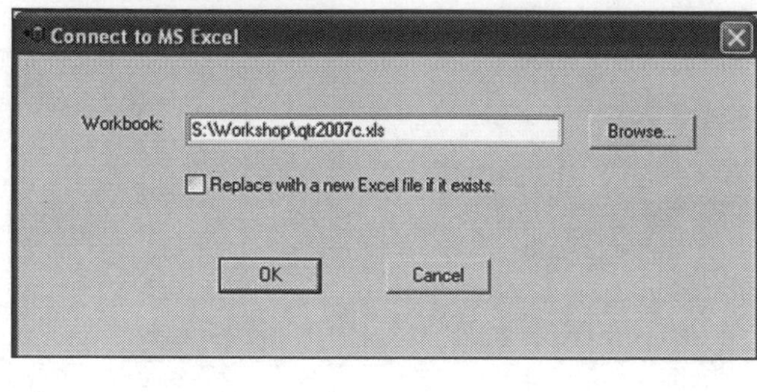

50

The Export Wizard

4. Assign the table name.

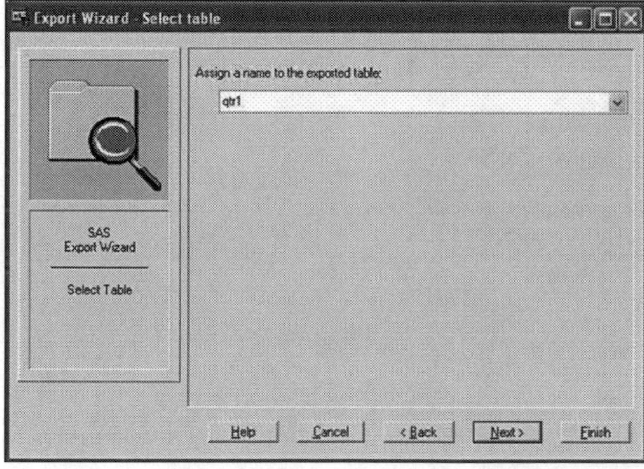

51

The Export Wizard

5. Save the generated PROC EXPORT code. (Optional)

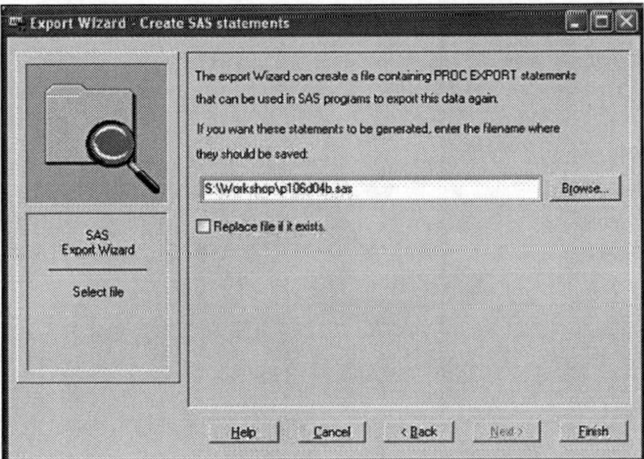

52

The Export Wizard

SAS Log

```
NOTE: File "S:\Workshop\qtr2007c.xls" will be created if the export
      process succeeds.
NOTE: "qtr1" table was successfully created.
```

53

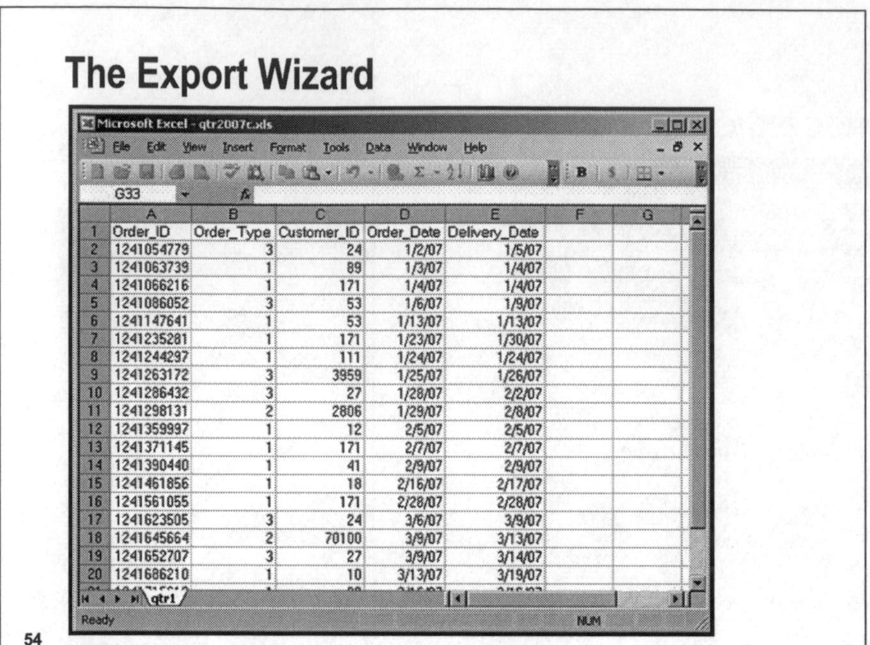

	A	B	C	D	E	F	G
1	Order_ID	Order_Type	Customer_ID	Order_Date	Delivery_Date		
2	1241054779	3	24	1/2/07	1/5/07		
3	1241063739	1	89	1/3/07	1/4/07		
4	1241066216	1	171	1/4/07	1/4/07		
5	1241086052	3	53	1/6/07	1/9/07		
6	1241147641	1	53	1/13/07	1/13/07		
7	1241235281	1	171	1/23/07	1/30/07		
8	1241244297	1	111	1/24/07	1/24/07		
9	1241263172	3	3959	1/25/07	1/26/07		
10	1241286432	3	27	1/28/07	2/2/07		
11	1241298131	2	2806	1/29/07	2/8/07		
12	1241359997	1	12	2/5/07	2/5/07		
13	1241371145	1	171	2/7/07	2/7/07		
14	1241390440	1	41	2/9/07	2/9/07		
15	1241461856	1	18	2/16/07	2/17/07		
16	1241561055	1	171	2/28/07	2/28/07		
17	1241623505	3	24	3/6/07	3/9/07		
18	1241645664	2	70100	3/9/07	3/13/07		
19	1241652707	3	27	3/9/07	3/14/07		
20	1241686210	1	10	3/13/07	3/19/07		

The EXPORT Procedure

The program **p106d04b** was created from the Export Wizard.

```
PROC EXPORT DATA= ORION.QTR1_2007
            OUTFILE= "S:\Workshop\qtr2007c.xls"
            DBMS=EXCEL REPLACE;
     RANGE="qtr1";
RUN;
```

✎ The RANGE statement is not supported and is ignored in the EXPORT procedure.

55 **p106d04b**

DATA=*<libref.>SAS-data-set*

identifies the input SAS data set.

OUTFILE="*filename*"

specifies the complete path and filename or a fileref for the output PC file, spreadsheet, or delimited external file.

DBMS=*identifier*

specifies the type of data to export. To export a DBMS table, you must specify DBMS= by using a valid database identifier. For example, DBMS=EXCEL specifies to export a table into a Microsoft Excel worksheet.

Exercises

Level 1

4. Using PROC COPY to Create an Excel Worksheet

a. Write a LIBNAME statement to create a libref called MNTH that references a new Excel workbook named mnth2007.xls.

b. Write a PROC COPY step that copies **`orion.mnth7_2007`**, **`orion.mnth8_2007`**, and **`orion.mnth9_2007`** to the new Excel workbook.

c. Write a PROC CONTENTS step to view all of the contents of **`MNTH`**.

d. Write a LIBNAME statement to clear the MNTH libref.

Level 2

5. Using the Import Wizard to Read an Excel Worksheet

a. Use the Import Wizard to read the products.xls workbook.

1) Select the worksheet containing children data.

2) Name the new data set **`Work.children`**.

3) Save the generated PROC IMPORT code to a file called **children.sas**.

b. Write a PROC PRINT step to create a report of the new data set.

c. Open **children.sas** to view the PROC IMPORT code.

Level 3

6. Using the EXPORT Procedure to Create an Excel Worksheet

a. Write a PROC EXPORT step to export the data set **`orion.mnth7_2007`** to an Excel workbook called mnth7.xls.

b. Submit the program and confirm in the log that the mnth_2007 worksheet was successfully created in mnth7.xls.

6.3 Chapter Review

Chapter Review

1. What statement is used to point to a physical filename including the path, filename, and extension of an Excel workbook ?
2. What character appears at the end of an Excel worksheet name in the SAS Explorer?
3. What is an example of a SAS name literal?
4. How do you disassociate a libref?

58

6.4 Solutions

Solutions to Exercises

1. **Reading an Excel Worksheet**

   a. Retrieve the starter program.

   b. Add a LIBNAME statement.

```
libname custfm 'custfm.xls';

proc contents data=custfm._all_;
run;

data work.males;

run;

proc print data=work.males label;
run;

libname custfm clear;
```

   c. Submit the LIBNAME statement and the PROC CONTENTS step.

   d. Add a SET statement in the DATA step.

```
data work.males;
   set custfm.'Males$'n;
run;
```

   e. Add a KEEP statement in the DATA step.

```
data work.males;
   set custfm.'Males$'n;
   keep First_Name Last_Name Birth_Date;
run;
```

   f. Add a FORMAT statement in the DATA step.

```
data work.males;
   set custfm.'Males$'n;
   keep First_Name Last_Name Birth_Date;
   format Birth_Date year4.;
run;
```

   g. Add a LABEL statement.

```
data work.males;
   set custfm.'Males$'n;
   keep First_Name Last_Name Birth_Date;
   format Birth_Date year4.;
   label Birth_Date='Birth Year';
run;
```

   h. Submit the program.

2. **Reading an Excel Worksheet**

   a. Write a LIBNAME statement.

```
libname prod 'products.xls';
```

   b. Write a PROC CONTENTS step.

```
proc contents data=prod._all_;
run;
```

   c. Submit the program.

   d. Write a DATA step.

```
data work.golf;
   set prod.'Sports$'n;
   where Category='Golf';
   drop Category;
   label Name='Golf Products';
run;
```

   e. Write a LIBNAME statement.

```
libname prod clear;
```

   f. Write a PROC PRINT step.

```
proc print data=work.golf label;
run;
```

3. **Reading a Range of an Excel Worksheet**

   a. Write a LIBNAME statement.

```
libname xlsdata 'custcaus.xls' header=no;
```

   b. Write a PROC CONTENTS step.

```
proc contents data=xlsdata._all_;
run;
```

   c. Submit the program.

   d. Write a DATA step.

```
data work.germany;
   set xlsdata.DE;
   label F1='Customer ID'
         F2='Country'
         F3='Gender'
         F4='First Name'
         F5='Last Name'
         F6='Birth Date';
   format F6 ddmmyy8.;
run;
```

   e. Write a LIBNAME statement.

```
libname xlsdata clear;
```

f. Write a PROC PRINT step.

```
proc print data=work.germany label;
run;
```

4. Using PROC COPY to Create an Excel Worksheet

a. Write a LIBNAME statement.

```
libname mnth 'mnth2007.xls';
```

b. Write a PROC COPY step.

```
proc copy  in=orion out=mnth;
   select mnth7_2007 mnth8_2007 mnth9_2007;
run;
```

c. Write a PROC CONTENTS step.

```
proc contents data=mnth._all_;
run;
```

d. Write a LIBNAME statement.

```
libname mnth clear;
```

5. Using the Import Wizard to Read an Excel Worksheet

a. Use the Import Wizard.

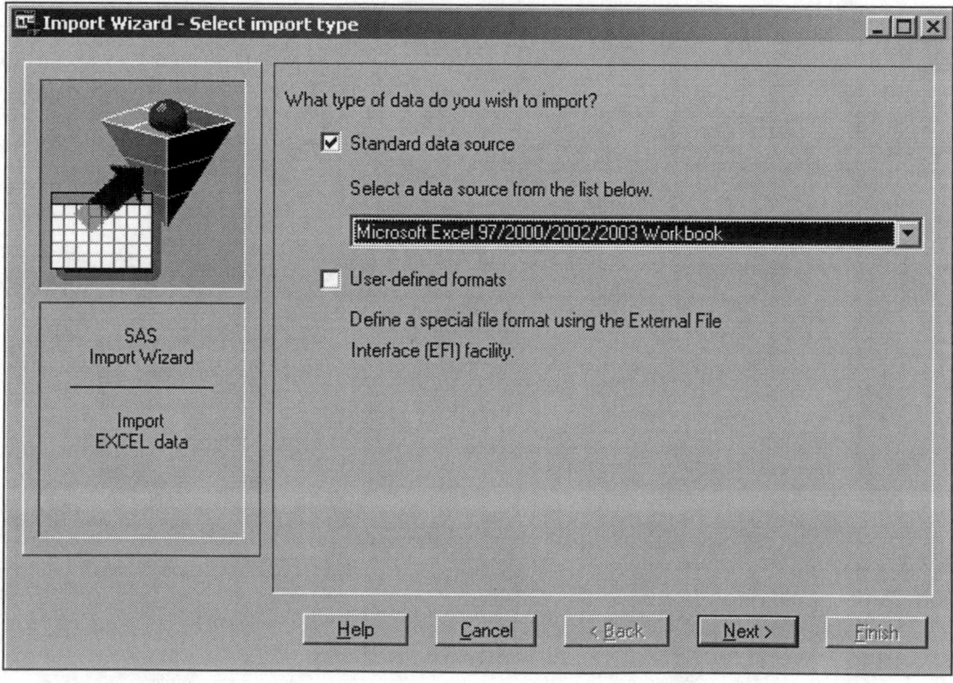

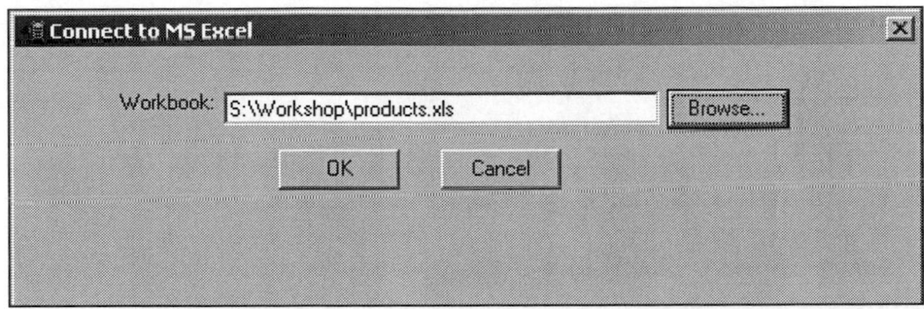
Connect to MS Excel
Workbook: S:\Workshop\products.xls
Browse...
OK
Cancel

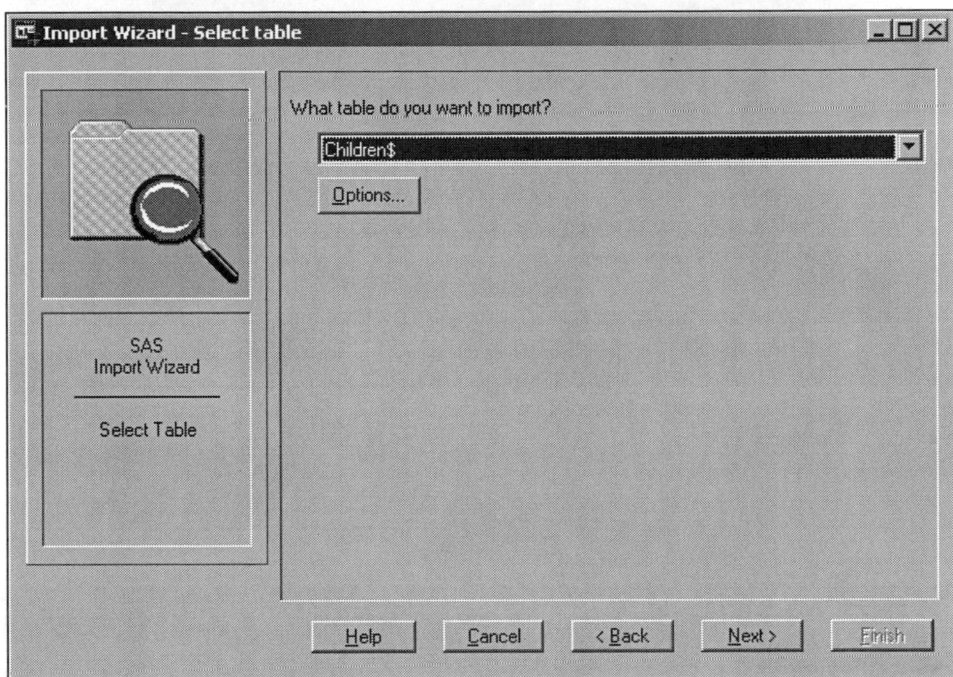
Import Wizard - Select table
What table do you want to import?
Children$
Options...
SAS
Import Wizard
Select Table
Help
Cancel
< Back
Next >
Finish

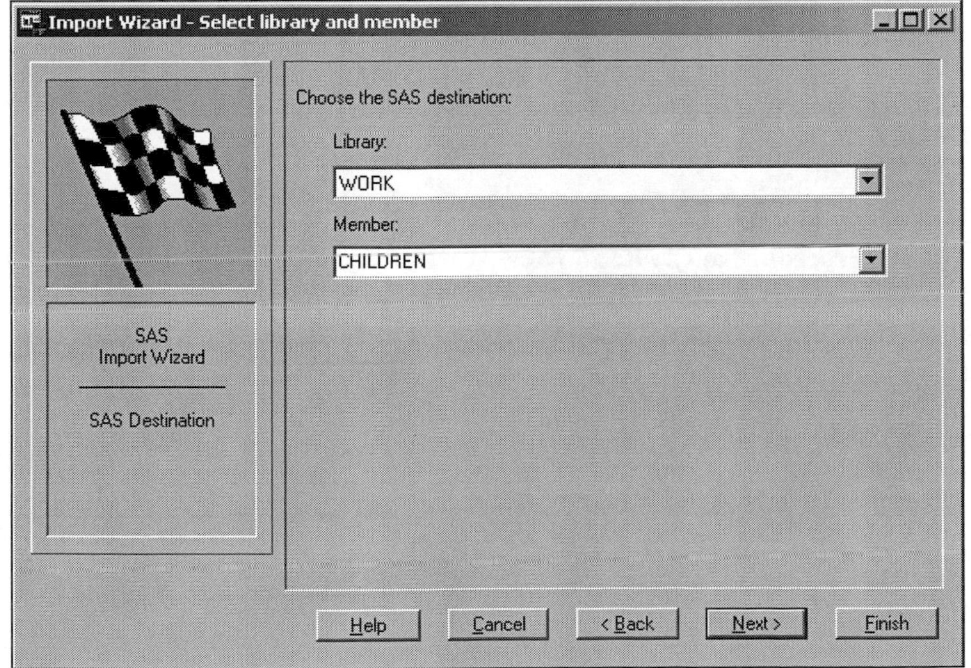
Import Wizard - Select library and member
Choose the SAS destination:
Library:
WORK
Member:
CHILDREN
SAS
Import Wizard
SAS Destination
Help
Cancel
< Back
Next >
Finish

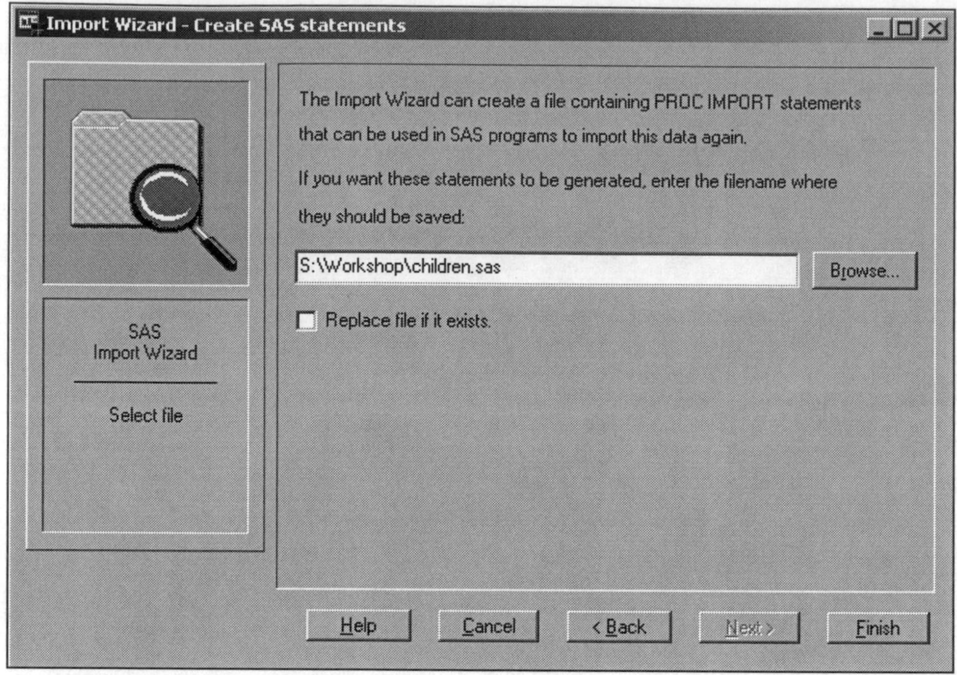

b. Write a PROC PRINT step.

```
proc print data=work.children;
run;
```

c. Open **children.sas.**

```
PROC IMPORT OUT= WORK.children
            DATAFILE= "S:\Workshop\products.xls"
            DBMS=EXCEL REPLACE;
     RANGE="Children$";
     GETNAMES=YES;
     MIXED=NO;
     SCANTEXT=YES;
     USEDATE=YES;
     SCANTIME=YES;
RUN;
```

6. Using the EXPORT Procedure to Create an Excel Worksheet

a. Write a PROC EXPORT step.

```
proc export data=orion.mnth7_2007
            outfile='mnth7.xls'
            dbms=excel replace;
run;
```

b. Submit the program.

Solutions to Student Activities (Polls/Quizzes)

6.01 Quiz – Correct Answer

Which PROC PRINT step displays the worksheet containing employees from the United States?

a.
```
proc print data=orionxls.'UnitedStates';
run;
```

b.
```
proc print data=orionxls.'UnitedStates$';
run;
```

c.
```
proc print data=orionxls.'UnitedStates'n;
run;
```

(d.)
```
proc print data=orionxls.'UnitedStates$'n;
run;
```

20

Solutions to Chapter Review

Chapter Review Answers

1. What statement is used to point to a physical filename including the path, filename, and extension of an Excel workbook ?

   a LIBNAME statement

2. What character appears at the end of an Excel worksheet name in the SAS Explorer?

   $

3. What is an example of a SAS name literal?

   `orionxls.'Australia$'n`

59

continued...

Chapter Review Answers

4. How do you disassociate a libref?

   CLEAR option

60

Chapter 7 Reading Delimited Raw Data Files

7.1 Using Standard Delimited Data as Input..7-3

Exercises 7-27

7.2 Using Nonstandard Delimited Data as Input...7-30

Exercises 7-44

7.3 Chapter Review...7-48

7.4 Solutions 7-49

Solutions to Exercises 7-49

Solutions to Student Activities (Polls/Quizzes) 7-52

Solutions to Chapter Review 7-55

7.1 Using Standard Delimited Data as Input

Objectives

- Use the DATA step to create a SAS data set from a delimited raw data file.
- Examine the compilation and execution phases of the DATA step when reading a raw data file.
- Explicitly define the length of a variable by using the LENGTH statement.

3

Business Scenario

An existing data source contains information on Orion Star sales employees from Australia and the United States.

A new SAS data set needs to be created that contains a subset of this existing data source.

This new SAS data set must contain the following:

- only the employees from Australia who are Sales Representatives
- the employee's first name, last name, salary, job title, and hired date
- labels and formats in the descriptor portion

4

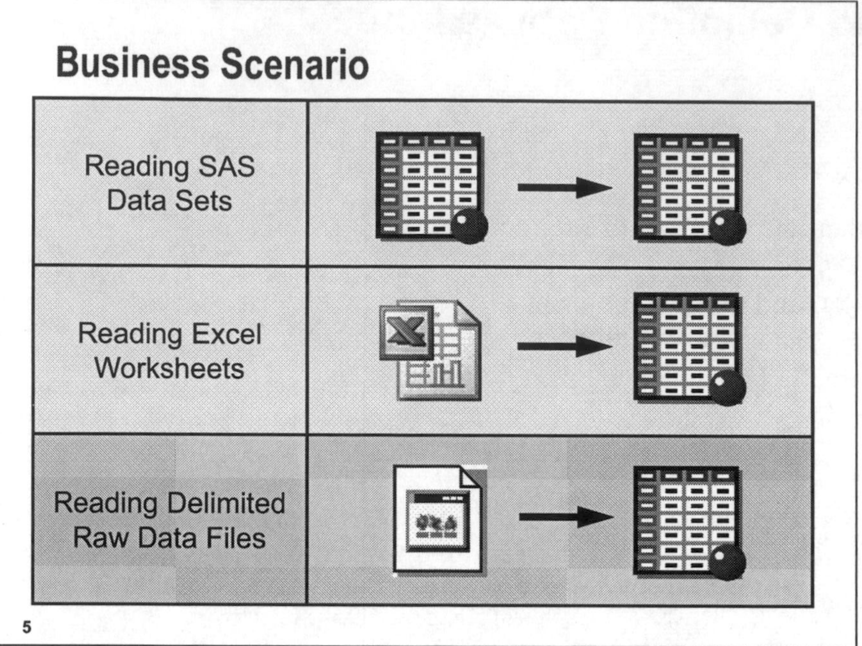

Business Scenario

Reading SAS Data Sets

```
libname ____________________;
data ________________;
   set ________________;
   ...
run;
```

Reading Excel Worksheets

```
libname ____________________;
data ________________;
   set ________________;
   ...
run;
```

Reading Delimited Raw Data Files

```
data ________________;
   infile ________________;
   input ________________;
   ...
run;
```

6

sales.csv

Partial sales.csv

comma delimited

```
120102,Tom,Zhou,M,108255,Sales Manager,AU,11AUG1969,
120103,Wilson,Dawes,M,87975,Sales Manager,AU,22JAN1949,01/01/1974
120121,Irenie,Elvish,F,26600,Sales Rep. II,AU,02AUG1944,01/01/1974
120122,Christina,Ngan,F,27475,Sales Rep. II,AU,27JUL1954,07/01/1978
120123,Kimiko,Hotstone,F,26190,Sales Rep. I,AU,28SEP1964,10/01/1985
120124,Lucian,Daymond,M,26480,Sales Rep. I,AU,13MAY1959,03/01/1979
120125,Fong,Hofmeister,M,32040,Sales Rep. IV,AU,06DEC1954,03/01/1979
120126,Satyakam,Denny,M,26780,Sales Rep. II,AU,20SEP1988,08/01/2006
120127,Sharryn,Clarkson,F,28100,Sales Rep. II,AU,04JAN1979,11/01/1998
120128,Monica,Kletschkus,F,30890,Sales Rep. IV,AU,14JUL1986,11/01/2006
120129,Alvin,Roebuck,M,30070,Sales Rep. III,AU,22NOV1964,10/01/1985
120130,Kevin,Lyon,M,26955,Sales Rep. I,AU,14DEC1984,05/01/2006
120131,Marinus,Surawski,M,26910,Sales Rep. I,AU,25SEP1979,01/01/2003
120132,Fancine,Kaiser,F,28525,Sales Rep. III,AU,05APR1949,10/01/1978
120133,Petrea,Soltau,F,27440,Sales Rep. II,AU,22APR1986,10/01/2006
120134,Sian,Shannan,M,28015,Sales Rep. II,AU,06JUN1949,01/01/1974
120135,Alexei,Platts,M,32490,Sales Rep. IV,AU,26JAN1969,10/01/1997
```

7

The raw data filename needs to be specific to your operating environment.

Business Scenario Syntax

Use the following statements to complete the scenario:

DATA *output-SAS-data-set*;
  LENGTH *variable(s)* $ *length*;
  INFILE '*raw-data-file-name*'; → identify name and location of raw file
  INPUT *specifications*; → describes the organization of data you imported.
  KEEP *variable-list*;
  LABEL *variable* = '*label*'
    variable = '*label*'
    variable = '*label*';
  FORMAT *variable(s) format*;
RUN;

8

— for raw data, you need to assign name, type, length

The DATA Statement (Review)

The *DATA statement* begins a DATA step and provides the name of the SAS data set being created.

```
DATA output-SAS-data-set;
     INFILE 'raw-data-file-name';
     INPUT specifications;
     <additional SAS statements>
RUN;
```

The DATA statement can create temporary or permanent data sets.

9

The INFILE Statement

The *INFILE statement* identifies the physical name of the raw data file to read with an INPUT statement.

```
DATA output-SAS-data-set;
     INFILE 'raw-data-file-name';
     INPUT specifications;
     <additional SAS statements>
RUN;
```

The physical name is the name that the operating environment uses to access the file.

10

The INFILE Statement

Examples:

Windows	`infile 's:\workshop\sales.csv';`
UNIX	`infile '/users/userid/sales.csv';`
z/OS (OS/390)	`infile '.workshop.rawdata(sales)';`

11

The INPUT Statement

The *INPUT statement* describes the arrangement of values in the raw data file and assigns input values to the corresponding SAS variables.

```
DATA output-SAS-data-set;
     INFILE 'raw-data-file-name';
     INPUT specifications;
     <additional SAS statements>
RUN;
```

The following are input specifications:

- column input
- formatted input
- list input — delimited data

12

Column input enables you to read standard data values that are aligned in columns in the raw data file.

Formatted input combines the flexibility of using informats with many of the features of column input. By using formatted input, you can read nonstandard data for which SAS requires additional instructions.

List input uses a scanning method for locating data values. Data values are not required to be aligned in columns, but must be separated by at least one blank or other defined delimiter.

7.01 Multiple Answer Poll

Which types of raw data files do you read?

a. delimited raw data files
b. raw data files aligned in columns
c. other
d. none
e. not sure

14

List Input

To read with list input, data values

- must be separated with a delimiter
- can be in standard or nonstandard form.

Partial **sales.csv**

```
120102,Tom,Zhou,M,108255,Sales Manager,AU,11AUG1969,06/01/1989
120103,Wilson,Dawes,M,87975,Sales Manager,AU,22JAN1949,01/01/1974
120121,Irenie,Elvish,F,26600,Sales Rep. II,AU,02AUG1944,01/01/1974
120122,Christina,Ngan,F,27475,Sales Rep. II,AU,27JUL1954,07/01/1978
120123,Kimiko,Hotstone,F,26190,Sales Rep. I,AU,28SEP1964,10/01/1985
120124,Lucian,Daymond,M,26480,Sales Rep. I,AU,13MAY1959,03/01/1979
120125,Fong,Hofmeister,M,32040,Sales Rep. IV,AU,06DEC1954,03/01/1979
120126,Satyakam,Denny,M,26780,Sales Rep. II,AU,20SEP1988,08/01/2006
120127,Sharryn,Clarkson,F,28100,Sales Rep. II,AU,04JAN1979,11/01/1998
```

15

Delimiter

A space (blank) is the default delimiter.

The *DLM= option* can be added to the INFILE statement to specify an alternate delimiter.

```
DATA output-SAS-data-set;
     INFILE 'raw-data-file-name' DLM='delimiter';
     INPUT specifications;
     <additional SAS statements>
RUN;
```

Syntax

16

The DLM= option is an alias for the DELIMITER= option.

To specify a tab delimiter on Windows or UNIX, type **`dlm='09'x`**.

To specify a tab delimiter on z/OS (OS/390), type **`dlm='05'x`**.

The DSD (delimiter-sensitive data) option changes how SAS treats delimiters when you use LIST input and sets the default delimiter to a comma. When you specify **`DSD`**, SAS treats two consecutive delimiters as a missing value and removes quotation marks from character values. The DSD option specifies that when data values are enclosed in quotation marks, delimiters within the value be treated as character data.

Standard and Nonstandard Data

- *Standard data* is data that SAS can read without any special instructions.

  Examples of standard numeric data:
  58 -23 67.23 00.99 5.67E5 1.2E-2

- *Nonstandard data* is any data that SAS cannot read without a special instruction.

  Examples of nonstandard numeric data:
  5,823 (23) $67.23 01/12/1999 12MAY2006

17

List Input for Standard Data

List input specification:

INPUT *variable* <$>;

- Variables must be specified in the order that they appear in the raw data file, left to right.
- $ indicates to store a variable value as a character value rather than as a numeric value.
- The default length for character and numeric variables is eight bytes.

18

List Input for Standard Data

Partial **sales.csv**

```
120102,Tom,Zhou,M,108255,Sales Manager,AU,11AUG1969,06/01/1989
120103,Wilson,Dawes,M,87975,Sales Manager,AU,22JAN1949,01/01/1974
120121,Irenie,Elvish,F,26600,Sales Rep. II,AU,02AUG1944,01/01/1974
120122,Christina,Ngan,F,27475,Sales Rep. II,AU,27JUL1954,07/01/1978
120123,Kimiko,Hotstone,F,26190,Sales Rep. I,AU,28SEP1964,10/01/1985
120124,Lucian,Daymond,M,26480,Sales Rep. I,AU,13MAY1959,03/01/1979
120125,Fong,Hofmeister,M,32040,Sales Rep. IV,AU,06DEC1954,03/01/1979
120126,Satyakam,Denny,M,26780,Sales Rep. II,AU,20SEP1988,08/01/2006
120127,Sharryn,Clarkson,F,28100,Sales Rep. II,AU,04JAN1979,11/01/1998
```

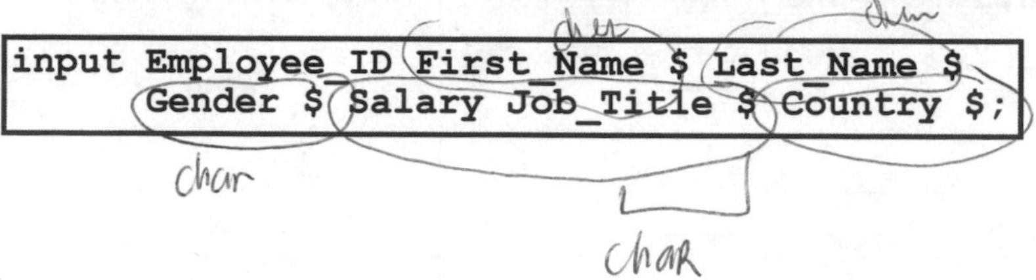

```
input Employee_ID First_Name $ Last_Name $
      Gender $ Salary Job_Title $ Country $;
```

19

Business Scenario

Create a temporary SAS data set named **Work.subset3** from the delimited raw data file named **sales.csv**.

```
data work.subset3;
   infile 'sales.csv' dlm=',';
   input Employee_ID First_Name $ Last_Name $
         Gender $ Salary Job_Title $ Country $;
run;
```

20 p107d01

Business Scenario

```
data work.subset3;
   infile 'sales.csv' dlm=',';
   input Employee_ID First_Name $ Last_Name $
         Gender $ Salary Job_Title $ Country $;
run;

NOTE: The infile 'sales.csv' is:
      File Name=S:\Workshop\sales.csv,
      RECFM=V,LRECL=256

NOTE: 165 records were read from the infile 'sales.csv'.
      The minimum record length was 61.
      The maximum record length was 80.
NOTE: The data set WORK.SUBSET3 has 165 observations and 7 variables.
```

21

LIST INPUT:

1. must have a delimiter (default delimiter is a blank)
2. must read vars in order, left → right. can't skip variables.
3. default length of ALL variables is 8 bytes.
4. Consecutive delimiter (ex. 2 ,, commas) is treated as a single delimiter

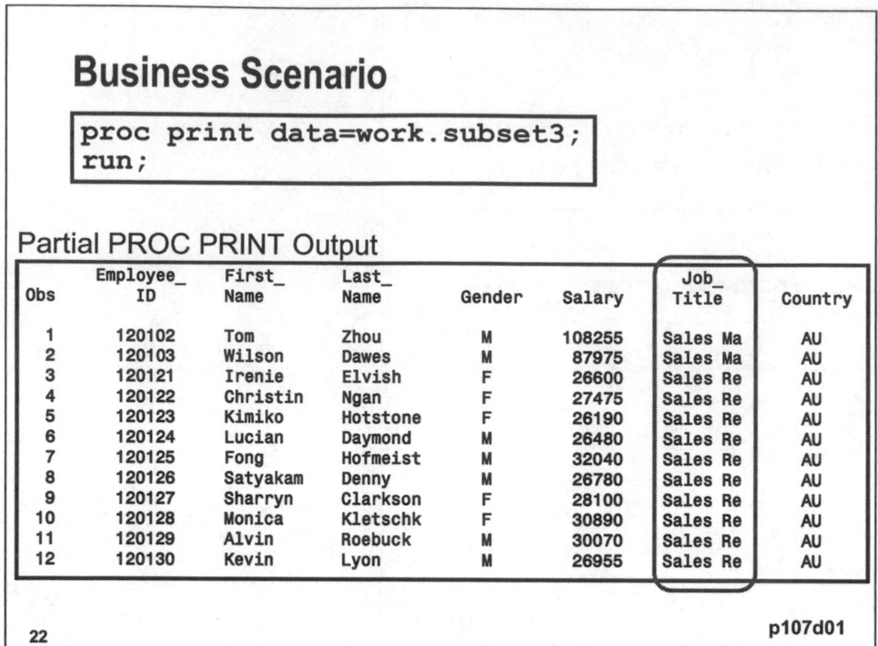

Business Scenario

```
proc print data=work.subset3;
run;
```

Partial PROC PRINT Output

Obs	Employee_ ID	First_ Name	Last_ Name	Gender	Salary	Job_ Title	Country
1	120102	Tom	Zhou	M	108255	Sales Ma	AU
2	120103	Wilson	Dawes	M	87975	Sales Ma	AU
3	120121	Irenie	Elvish	F	26600	Sales Re	AU
4	120122	Christin	Ngan	F	27475	Sales Re	AU
5	120123	Kimiko	Hotstone	F	26190	Sales Re	AU
6	120124	Lucian	Daymond	M	26480	Sales Re	AU
7	120125	Fong	Hofmeist	M	32040	Sales Re	AU
8	120126	Satyakam	Denny	M	26780	Sales Re	AU
9	120127	Sharryn	Clarkson	F	28100	Sales Re	AU
10	120128	Monica	Kletschk	F	30890	Sales Re	AU
11	120129	Alvin	Roebuck	M	30070	Sales Re	AU
12	120130	Kevin	Lyon	M	26955	Sales Re	AU

22 p107d01

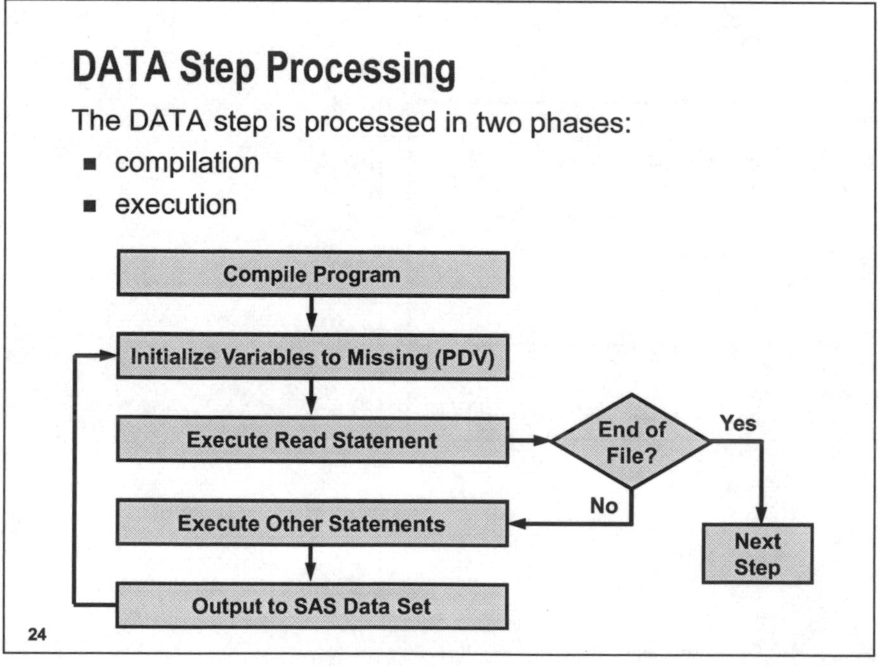

DATA Step Processing

The DATA step is processed in two phases:

- compilation
- execution

24

Compilation

During the compilation phase, SAS

- checks the syntax of the DATA step statements
- creates an input buffer to hold the current raw data file record that is being processed
- creates a program data vector (PDV) to hold the current SAS observation
- creates the descriptor portion of the output data set.

→ converts the program to machine language (1, 0)

25

Compilation

```
data work.subset3;
   infile 'sales.csv' dlm=',';
   input Employee_ID First_Name $ Last_Name $
         Gender $ Salary Job_Title $ Country $;
run;
```

26 ...

60

Compilation

```
data work.subset3;
   infile 'sales.csv' dlm=',';
   input Employee_ID First_Name $ Last_Name $
         Gender $ Salary Job_Title $ Country $;
run;
```

Input Buffer

```
                  1                   2
1 2 3 4 5 6 7 8 9 0 1 2 3 4 5 6 7 8 9 0 1 2 3 4 5
```

27

Compilation

```
data work.subset3;
   infile 'sales.csv' dlm=',';
   input Employee_ID First_Name $ Last_Name $
         Gender $ Salary Job_Title $ Country $;
run;
```

Input Buffer

```
                  1                   2
1 2 3 4 5 6 7 8 9 0 1 2 3 4 5 6 7 8 9 0 1 2 3 4 5
```

PDV

Employee_ID N 8

The default length for numeric variables is eight bytes.

28

Compilation

```
data work.subset3;
   infile 'sales.csv' dlm=',';
   input Employee_ID First_Name $ Last_Name $
         Gender $ Salary Job_Title $ Country $;
run;
```

Input Buffer

1 2 3 4 5 6 7 8 9 0 1 2 3 4 5 6 7 8 9 0 1 2 3 4 5 (1 above the 10th position, 2 above the 20th)

PDV

Employee _ID N 8	First_ Name $ 8

For list input, the default length for character variables is eight bytes.

29 ...

Compilation

```
data work.subset3;
   infile 'sales.csv' dlm=',';
   input Employee_ID First_Name $ Last_Name $
         Gender $ Salary Job_Title $ Country $;
run;
```

Input Buffer

1 2 3 4 5 6 7 8 9 0 1 2 3 4 5 6 7 8 9 0 1 2 3 4 5 (1 above the 10th position, 2 above the 20th)

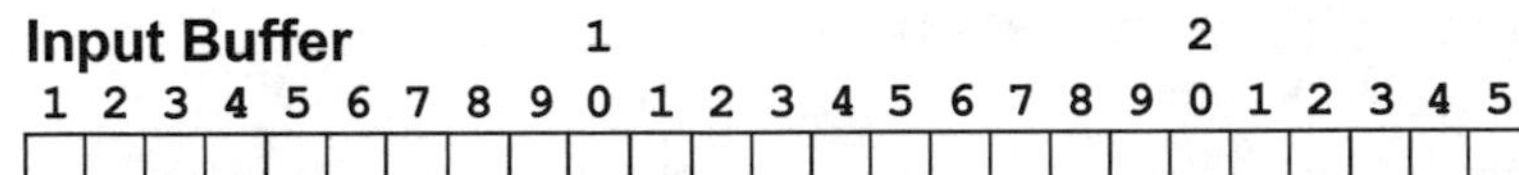

PDV

Employee _ID N 8	First_ Name $ 8	Last _Name $ 8	Gender $ 8	Salary N 8	Job_ Title $ 8	Country $ 8

30 ...

Compilation

```
data work.subset3;
   infile 'sales.csv' dlm=',';
   input Employee_ID First_Name $ Last_Name $
         Gender $ Salary Job_Title $ Country $;
run;
```

Descriptor Portion `Work.subset3`

Employee_ID N 8	First_Name $ 8	Last_Name $ 8	Gender $ 8	Salary N 8	Job_Title $ 8	Country $ 8

31

7.02 Multiple Choice Poll

Which statement is true?

a. An input buffer is only created if you are reading data from a raw data file. → If SAS reads an input statement, it will create an input buffer

b. The PDV at compile time holds the variable name, type, byte size, and initial value. → no data is read yet

c. The descriptor portion is the first item that is created at compile time. – last time to do

33

Execution

Partial sales.csv

```
120102,Tom,Zhou, ...
120103,Wilson,Dawes, ...
120121,Irenie,Elvish, ...
120122,Christina,Ngan, ...
120123,Kimiko,Hotstone, ...
120124,Lucian,Daymond, ...
120125,Fong,Hofmeister, ...
```

```
data work.subset3;
  infile 'sa[...]dlm=',';
  input Empl[...]Name $
        Las[...] $
        Salary Job_Title $
        Country $;
run;
```

Initialize PDV

Input Buffer

1	2	3	4	5	6	7	8	9	10	1	2	3	4	5	6	7	8	9	20	1	2	3	4	5

PDV

Employee_ID N 8	First_Name $ 8	Last_Name $ 8	Gender $ 8	Salary N 8	Job_Title $ 8	Country $ 8
.				.		

35 ...

Execution

Partial sales.csv

```
120102,Tom,Zhou, ...
120103,Wilson,Dawes, ...
120121,Irenie,Elvish, ...
120122,Christina,Ngan, ...
120123,Kimiko,Hotstone, ...
120124,Lucian,Daymond, ...
120125,Fong,Hofmeister, ...
```

```
data work.subset3;
  infile 'sales.csv' dlm=',';
  input Employee_ID First_Name $
        Last_Name $ Gender $
        Salary Job_Title $
        Country $;
run;
```

Input Buffer

1	2	3	4	5	6	7	8	9	10	1	2	3	4	5	6	7	8	9	20	1	2	3	4	5

PDV

Employee_ID N 8	First_Name $ 8	Last_Name $ 8	Gender $ 8	Salary N 8	Job_Title $ 8	Country $ 8
.				.		

36 ...

Execution

Partial sales.csv

```
120102,Tom,Zhou, ...
120103,Wilson,Dawes, ...
120121,Irenie,Elvish, ...
120122,Christina,Ngan, ...
120123,Kimiko,Hotstone, ...
120124,Lucian,Daymond, ...
120125,Fong,Hofmeister, ...
```

```
data work.subset3;
  infile 'sales.csv' dlm=',';
  input Employee_ID First_Name $
        Last_Name $ Gender $
        Salary Job_Title $
        Country $;
run;
```

Input Buffer

1	2	3	4	5	6	7	8	9	10	1	2	3	4	5	6	7	8	9	20	1	2	3	4	5
1	2	0	1	0	2	,	T	o	m	,	Z	h	o	u	,	M	,	1	0	8	2	5	5	,

PDV

Employee _ID N 8	First_ Name $ 8	Last _Name $ 8	Gender $ 8	Salary N 8	Job_ Title $ 8	Country $ 8
.				.		

37 ...

Execution

Partial sales.csv

```
120102,Tom,Zhou, ...
120103,Wilson,Dawes, ...
120121,Irenie,Elvish, ...
120122,Christina,Ngan, ...
120123,Kimiko,Hotstone, ...
120124,Lucian,Daymond, ...
120125,Fong,Hofmeister, ...
```

```
data work.subset3;
  infile 'sales.csv' dlm=',';
  input Employee_ID First_Name $
        Last_Name $ Gender $
        Salary Job_Title $
        Country $;
run;
```

Input Buffer

1	2	3	4	5	6	7	8	9	10	1	2	3	4	5	6	7	8	9	20	1	2	3	4	5
1	2	0	1	0	2	,	T	o	m	,	Z	h	o	u	,	M	,	1	0	8	2	5	5	,

PDV

Employee _ID N 8	First_ Name $ 8	Last _Name $ 8	Gender $ 8	Salary N 8	Job_ Title $ 8	Country $ 8
120102	Tom	Zhou	M	108255	Sales Ma	AU

38 ...

– delimiter is where SAS stops and puts the value in the variables.

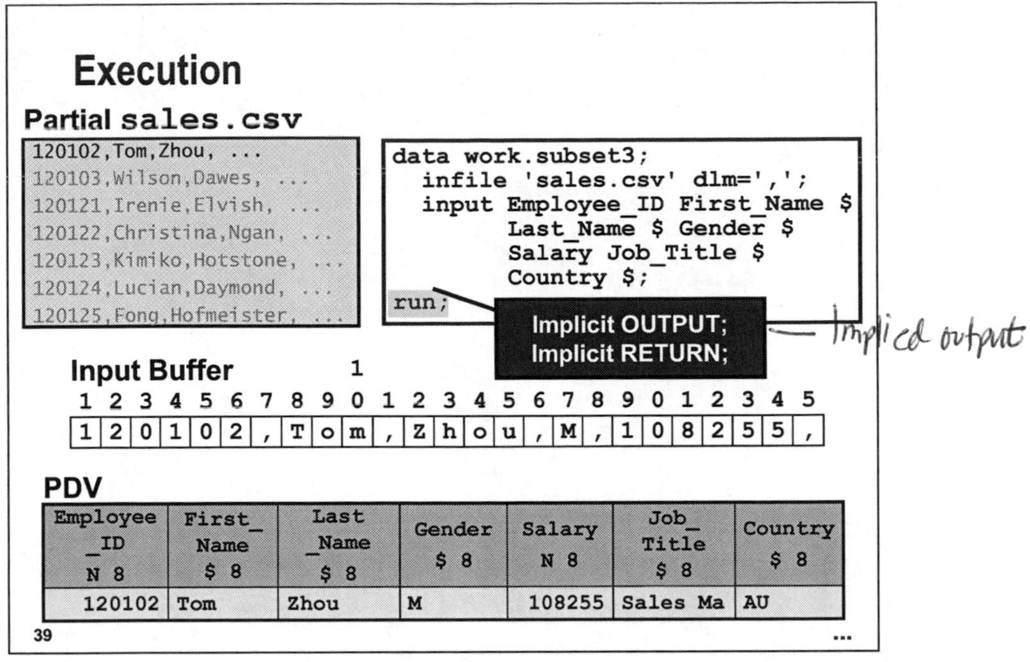
Execution
Partial sales.csv
120102,Tom,Zhou, ...
120103,Wilson,Dawes, ...
120121,Irenie,Elvish, ...
120122,Christina,Ngan, ...
120123,Kimiko,Hotstone, ...
120124,Lucian,Daymond, ...
120125,Fong,Hofmeister, ...
data work.subset3;
infile 'sales.csv' dlm=',';
input Employee_ID First_Name $
Last_Name $ Gender $
Salary Job_Title $
Country $;
run;
Implicit OUTPUT;
Implicit RETURN;
Implied output
Input Buffer
1
1 2 3 4 5 6 7 8 9 0 1 2 3 4 5 6 7 8 9 0 1 2 3 4 5
1 2 0 1 0 2 , T o m , Z h o u , M , 1 0 8 2 5 5 ,
PDV
Employee _ID N 8
First_ Name $ 8
Last _Name $ 8
Gender $ 8
Salary N 8
Job_ Title $ 8
Country $ 8
120102
Tom
Zhou
M
108255
Sales Ma
AU
39
...

Execution

Output SAS Data Set after First Iteration of DATA Step

Work.subset3

Employee _ID	First_ Name	Last _Name	Gender	Salary	Job_ Title	Country
120102	Tom	Zhou	M	108255	Sales Ma	AU

40 ...

Execution

Partial sales.csv

```
120102,Tom,Zhou, ...
120103,Wilson,Dawes, ...
120121,Irenie,Elvish, ...
120122,Christina,Ngan, ...
120123,Kimiko,Hotstone, ...
120124,Lucian,Daymond, ...
120125,Fong,Hofmeister, ...
```

```
data work.subset3;
  infile 'sa...dlm=',';
  input Empl...me $
        Last...
        Salary Job_Title $
        Country $;
run;
```

Reinitialize PDV

Input Buffer

```
                   1                   2
 1 2 3 4 5 6 7 8 9 0 1 2 3 4 5 6 7 8 9 0 1 2 3 4 5
|1|2|0|1|0|2|,|T|o|m|,|Z|h|o|u|,|M|,|1|0|8|2|5|5|,|
```

PDV

Employee _ID N 8	First_ Name $ 8	Last _Name $ 8	Gender $ 8	Salary N 8	Job_ Title $ 8	Country $ 8
.				.		

41 ...

Execution

Partial sales.csv

```
120102,Tom,Zhou, ...
120103,Wilson,Dawes, ...
120121,Irenie,Elvish, ...
120122,Christina,Ngan, ...
120123,Kimiko,Hotstone, ...
120124,Lucian,Daymond, ...
120125,Fong,Hofmeister, ...
```

```
data work.subset3;
  infile 'sales.csv' dlm=',';
  input Employee_ID First_Name $
        Last_Name $ Gender $
        Salary Job_Title $
        Country $;
run;
```

Input Buffer

```
                   1                   2
 1 2 3 4 5 6 7 8 9 0 1 2 3 4 5 6 7 8 9 0 1 2 3 4 5
|1|2|0|1|0|2|,|T|o|m|,|Z|h|o|u|,|M|,|1|0|8|2|5|5|,|
```

PDV

Employee _ID N 8	First_ Name $ 8	Last _Name $ 8	Gender $ 8	Salary N 8	Job_ Title $ 8	Country $ 8
.				.		

42 ...

Execution

Partial sales.csv

```
120102,Tom,Zhou, ...
120103,Wilson,Dawes, ...
120121,Irenie,Elvish, ...
120122,Christina,Ngan, ...
120123,Kimiko,Hotstone, ...
120124,Lucian,Daymond, ...
120125,Fong,Hofmeister, ...
```

```
data work.subset3;
  infile 'sales.csv' dlm=',';
  input Employee_ID First_Name $
        Last_Name $ Gender $
        Salary Job_Title $
        Country $;
run;
```

Input Buffer

1	2	3	4	5	6	7	8	9	10	1	2	3	4	5	6	7	8	9	20	1	2	3	4	5
1	2	0	1	0	3	,	W	i	l	s	o	n	,	D	a	w	e	s	,	M	,	8	7	9

PDV

Employee _ID N 8	First_ Name $ 8	Last _Name $ 8	Gender $ 8	Salary N 8	Job_ Title $ 8	Country $ 8
.				.		

43 ...

Execution

Partial sales.csv

```
120102,Tom,Zhou, ...
120103,Wilson,Dawes, ...
120121,Irenie,Elvish, ...
120122,Christina,Ngan, ...
120123,Kimiko,Hotstone, ...
120124,Lucian,Daymond, ...
120125,Fong,Hofmeister, ...
```

```
data work.subset3;
  infile 'sales.csv' dlm=',';
  input Employee_ID First_Name $
        Last_Name $ Gender $
        Salary Job_Title $
        Country $;
run;
```

Input Buffer

1	2	3	4	5	6	7	8	9	10	1	2	3	4	5	6	7	8	9	20	1	2	3	4	5
1	2	0	1	0	3	,	W	i	l	s	o	n	,	D	a	w	e	s	,	M	,	8	7	9

PDV

Employee ID N 8	First_ Name $ 8	Last _Name $ 8	Gender $ 8	Salary N 8	Job_ Title $ 8	Country $ 8
120103	Wilson	Dawes	M	87975	Sales Ma	AU

44 ...

Execution

Partial sales.csv

```
120102,Tom,Zhou, ...
120103,Wilson,Dawes, ...
120121,Irenie,Elvish, ...
120122,Christina,Ngan, ...
120123,Kimiko,Hotstone, ...
120124,Lucian,Daymond, ...
120125,Fong,Hofmeister, ...
```

```
data work.subset3;
  infile 'sales.csv' dlm=',';
  input Employee_ID First_Name $
        Last_Name $ Gender $
        Salary Job_Title $
        Country $;
run;
```

Implicit OUTPUT;
Implicit RETURN;

Input Buffer

```
                   1
1 2 3 4 5 6 7 8 9 0 1 2 3 4 5 6 7 8 9 0 1 2 3 4 5
1 2 0 1 0 3 , W i l s o n , D a w e s , M , 8 7 9
```

PDV

Employee _ID N 8	First_ Name $ 8	Last _Name $ 8	Gender $ 8	Salary N 8	Job_ Title $ 8	Country $ 8
120103	Wilson	Dawes	M	87975	Sales Ma	AU

45 ...

Execution

Output SAS Data Set after Second Iteration of DATA Step

Work.subset3

Employee _ID	First_ Name	Last _Name	Gender	Salary	Job_ Title	Country
120102	Tom	Zhou	M	108255	Sales Ma	AU
120103	Wilson	Dawes	M	87975	Sales Ma	AU

46 ...

Execution

Partial sales.csv

```
120102,Tom,Zhou, ...
120103,Wilson,Dawes, ...
120121,Irenie,Elvish, ...
120122,Christina,Ngan, ...
120123,Kimiko,Hotstone, ...
120124,Lucian,Daymond, ...
120125,Fong,Hofmeister, ...
```

Continue until EOF

```
   infile 'sales.csv' dlm=',';
   input Employee_ID First_Name $
         Last_Name $ Gender $
         Salary Job_Title $
         Country $;
run;
```

EOF - would be the semi-colon

Input Buffer

1	2	3	4	5	6	7	8	9	10	1	2	3	4	5	6	7	8	9	20	1	2	3	4	5
1	2	0	1	0	3	,	W	i	l	s	o	n	,	D	a	w	e	s	,	M	,	8	7	9

PDV

Employee_ID N 8	First_Name $ 8	Last_Name $ 8	Gender $ 8	Salary N 8	Job_Title $ 8	Country $ 8
120103	Wilson	Dawes	M	87975	Sales Ma	AU

47

7.03 Multiple Choice Poll

Which statement is true?

a. Data is read directly from the raw data file to the PDV. X – Input buffer

b. At the bottom of the DATA step, the contents of the PDV are output to the output SAS data set. — run statement, whatever is on the PDV is the output dataset

c. When SAS returns to the top of the DATA step, any variable coming from a SAS data set is set to missing.

49

The LENGTH Statement

The *LENGTH statement* defines the length of a variable explicitly.

General form of the LENGTH statement:

LENGTH *variable(s)* $ *length*;

Example:

```
length First_Name Last_Name $ 12
       Gender $ 1;
```

↳ to change the LENGTH from the raw file.

52

Business Scenario

Create a temporary SAS data set named **Work.subset3** from the delimited raw data file named **sales.csv**.

```
data work.subset3;
   length First_Name $ 12 Last_Name $ 18
          Gender $ 1 Job_Title $ 25
          Country $ 2;
   infile 'sales.csv' dlm=',';
   input Employee_ID First_Name $ Last_Name $
         Gender $ Salary Job_Title $ Country $;
run;
```

53 p107d02

→ don't set length w/ numeric variable

→ Char – 8 bytes is 8 char.

Numeric – 8 bytes

Business Scenario

```
proc print data=work.subset3;
run;
```

Partial PROC PRINT Output

Obs	First_ Name	Last_Name	Gender	Job_Title	Country	Employee_ ID	Salary
1	Tom	Zhou	M	Sales Manager	AU	120102	108255
2	Wilson	Dawes	M	Sales Manager	AU	120103	87975
3	Irenie	Elvish	F	Sales Rep. II	AU	120121	26600
4	Christina	Ngan	F	Sales Rep. II	AU	120122	27475
5	Kimiko	Hotstone	F	Sales Rep. I	AU	120123	26190
6	Lucian	Daymond	M	Sales Rep. I	AU	120124	26480
7	Fong	Hofmeister	M	Sales Rep. IV	AU	120125	32040
8	Satyakam	Denny	M	Sales Rep. II	AU	120126	26780
9	Sharryn	Clarkson	F	Sales Rep. II	AU	120127	28100
10	Monica	Kletschkus	F	Sales Rep. IV	AU	120128	30890
11	Alvin	Roebuck	M	Sales Rep. III	AU	120129	30070
12	Kevin	Lyon	M	Sales Rep. I	AU	120130	26955

54

p107d02

Compilation

```
data work.subset3;
   length First_Name $ 12 Last_Name $ 18
          Gender $ 1 Job_Title $ 25
          Country $ 2;
   infile 'sales.csv' dlm=',';
   input Employee_ID First_Name $ Last_Name $
         Gender $ Salary Job_Title $ Country $;
run;
```

PDV

First _Name $ 12	Last _Name $ 18	Gender $ 1	Job_Title $ 25	Country $ 2

55

...

Compilation

```
data work.subset3;
   length First_Name $ 12 Last_Name $ 18
          Gender $ 1 Job_Title $ 25
          Country $ 2;
   infile 'sales.csv' dlm=',';
   input Employee_ID First_Name $ Last_Name $
         Gender $ Salary Job_Title $ Country $;
run;
```

PDV

First _Name $ 12	Last _Name $ 18	Gender $ 1	Job_Title $ 25	Country $ 2	Employee _ID N 8	Salary N 8

56

Exercises

Level 1

1. Reading a Comma-Delimited Raw Data File

a. Retrieve the starter program **p107e01**.

b. Add the appropriate LENGTH, INFILE, and INPUT statements to read the comma-delimited raw data file named the following:

Windows or UNIX	**newemps.csv**
z/OS (OS/390)	**.workshop.rawdata(newemps)**

Partial Raw Data File

```
Satyakam,Denny,Sales Rep. II,26780
Monica,Kletschkus,Sales Rep. IV,30890
Kevin,Lyon,Sales Rep. I,26955
Petrea,Soltau,Sales Rep. II,27440
Marina,Iyengar,Sales Rep. III,29715
```

The following variables should be read into the program data vector:

Name	Type	Length
First	Character	12
Last	Character	18
Title	Character	25
Salary	Numeric	8

c. Submit the program to create the following PROC PRINT report:

Partial PROC PRINT Output (First 5 of 71 Observations)

```
Obs    First       Last          Title              Salary

 1     Satyakam    Denny         Sales Rep. II       26780
 2     Monica      Kletschkus    Sales Rep. IV       30890
 3     Kevin       Lyon          Sales Rep. I        26955
 4     Petrea      Soltau        Sales Rep. II       27440
 5     Marina      Iyengar       Sales Rep. III      29715
```

```
data work.NewEmployees;
  length first $ 12 Last $18 title$25;
  infile 'newemps.csv' dlm=',';
  input first $ Last $ title $ Salary;
run;
  proc print data=work.NewEmployees;
  run;
```

Level 2

2. Reading a Space-Delimited Raw Data File

a. Write a DATA step to create a new data set named **`Work.QtrDonation`** by reading the space-delimited raw data file named the following:

Windows or UNIX	**`donation.dat`**
z/OS (OS/390)	**`.workshop.rawdata(donation)`**

Partial Raw Data File

```
120265 . . . 25
120267 15 15 15 15
120269 20 20 20 20
120270 20 10 5 .
120271 20 20 20 20
```

The following variables should be read into the program data vector:

Name	Type	Length
`IDNum`	Character	6
`Qtr1`	Numeric	8
`Qtr2`	Numeric	8
`Qtr3`	Numeric	8
`Qtr4`	Numeric	8

b. Write a PROC PRINT step to create the following report:

Partial PROC PRINT Output (First 10 of 124 Observations)

```
 Obs    IDNum     Qtr1    Qtr2    Qtr3    Qtr4

   1    120265      .       .       .      25
   2    120267     15      15      15      15
   3    120269     20      20      20      20
   4    120270     20      10       5       .
   5    120271     20      20      20      20
   6    120272     10      10      10      10
   7    120275     15      15      15      15
   8    120660     25      25      25      25
   9    120662     10       .       5       5
  10    120663      .       .       5       .
```

Level 3

3. Using Column Input to Read a Fixed Column Raw Data File

a. Write a DATA step to create a new data set named **Work.supplier_info** by reading the fixed column raw data file named the following:

Windows or UNIX	**supplier.dat**
z/OS (OS/390)	**.workshop.rawdata(supplier)**

Use column input in the INPUT statement to read the fixed column data.

Documentation on column input can be found in the SAS Help and Documentation from the Contents tab (**SAS Products** ⇨ **Base SAS** ⇨ **SAS 9.2 Language Reference: Dictionary** ⇨ **Dictionary of Language Elements** ⇨ **Statements** ⇨ **INPUT Statement, Column**).

Partial Raw Data File

```
50     Scandinavian Clothing A/S        NO
109    Petterson AB                     SE
316    Prime Sports Ltd                 GB
755    Top Sports                       DK
772    AllSeasons Outdoor Clothing      US
```

The following is the layout of the raw data file:

Name	Starting Column	Ending Column
ID	1	5
Name	8	37
Country	40	41

b. Write a PROC PRINT step to create the following report:

Partial PROC PRINT Output (First 10 of 52 Observations)

```
                     Obs     ID     Name                            Country

                       1     50     Scandinavian Clothing A/S         NO
                       2    109     Petterson AB                      SE
                       3    316     Prime Sports Ltd                  GB
                       4    755     Top Sports                        DK
                       5    772     AllSeasons Outdoor Clothing       US
                       6    798     Sportico                          ES
                       7   1280     British Sports Ltd                GB
                       8   1303     Eclipse Inc                       US
                       9   1684     Magnifico Sports                  PT
                      10   1747     Pro Sportswear Inc                US
```

7.2 Using Nonstandard Delimited Data as Input

Objectives

- Use informats to read nonstandard data.
- Add additional SAS statements to perform further processing in the DATA step.
- Use the DSD option with list input to read consecutive delimiters as missing values.
- Use the MISSOVER option to recognize missing values at the end of a record (Self-Study).

60

Standard and Nonstandard Data

- *Standard data* is data that SAS can read without any special instructions.

  Examples of standard numeric data:
  58 -23 67.23 00.99 5.67E5 1.2E-2

- *Nonstandard data* is any data that SAS cannot read without a special instruction.

  Examples of nonstandard numeric data:
  5,823 (23) $67.23 01/12/1999 12MAY2006

61

List Input for Nonstandard Data

List input specification:

INPUT *variable* <$> *variable* < *:informat* >;

- The : format modifier enables you to use an informat to read nonstandard delimited data.
- An *informat* is an instruction that SAS uses to read data values into a variable.
- The width of the informat can be eliminated.
- For character variables, the width of the informat determines the variable length, if it has not been previously defined.

62

SAS Informats

SAS informats have the following form:

<$>*informat*<*w*>.<*d*>

$	indicates a character informat.
informat	names the SAS informat or user-defined informat.
w	specifies the number of columns to read in the input data.
.	is a required delimiter.
d	specifies an optional decimal scaling factor in the numeric informats.

63

SAS Informats

Selected SAS Informats:

Informat	Definition
$*w*.	reads standard character data.
w.d	reads standard numeric data.
COMMA*w.d* DOLLAR*w.d*	reads nonstandard numeric data and removes embedded commas, blanks, dollar signs, percent signs, and dashes.
COMMAX*w.d* DOLLARX*w.d*	reads nonstandard numeric data and removes embedded periods, blanks, dollar signs, percent signs, and dashes.
EUROX*w.d*	reads nonstandard numeric data and removes embedded characters in European currency.

64

SAS Informats

In list input, informats are used to convert nonstandard numeric data to SAS numeric values.

Informat	Raw Data Value	SAS Data Value
COMMA. DOLLAR.	`$12,345`	`12345`
COMMAX. DOLLARX.	`$12.345`	`12345`
EUROX.	`€12.345`	`12345`

65

SAS Informats

SAS uses date informats to read and convert dates to SAS date values.

Informat	Raw Data Value	SAS Data Value
MMDDYY.	010160 01/01/60 01/01/1960	0
DDMMYY.	311260 31/12/60 31/12/1960	365
DATE.	31DEC59 31DEC1959	-1

66

List Input for Nonstandard Data

Partial **sales.csv**

```
120102,Tom,Zhou,M,108255,Sales Manager,AU,11AUG1969,06/01/1989
120103,Wilson,Dawes,M,87975,Sales Manager,AU,22JAN1949,01/01/1974
120121,Irenie,Elvish,F,26600,Sales Rep. II,AU,02AUG1944,01/01/1974
120122,Christina,Ngan,F,27475,Sales Rep. II,AU,27JUL1954,07/01/1978
120123,Kimiko,Hotstone,F,26190,Sales Rep. I,AU,28SEP1964,10/01/1985
120124,Lucian,Daymond,M,26480,Sales Rep. I,AU,13MAY1959,03/01/1979
120125,Fong,Hofmeister,M,32040,Sales Rep. IV,AU,06DEC1954,03/01/1979
120126,Satyakam,Denny,M,26780,Sales Rep. II,AU,20SEP1988,08/01/2006
120127,Sharryn,Clarkson,F,28100,Sales Rep. II,AU,04JAN1979,11/01/1998
```

translate these dates to a readable format

```
input Employee_ID First_Name $ Last_Name $
      Gender $ Salary Job_Title $ Country $
      Birth_Date :date.
      Hire_Date :mmddyy.;
```

67

7.04 Quiz

Which INPUT statement correctly uses list input to read the space-delimited raw data file?

Raw Data

```
Donny 5MAY2008 25 FL $43,132.50
Margaret 20FEB2008 43 NC 65,150
```

a.
```
input name $ hired date. age
      state $ salary comma.;
```

b.
```
input name $ hired :date. age
      state $ salary :comma.;
```

69

Business Scenario

Create a temporary SAS data set named **Work.subset3** from the delimited raw data file named **sales.csv**.

```
data work.subset3;
   length First_Name $ 12 Last_Name $ 18
          Gender $ 1 Job_Title $ 25
          Country $ 2;
   infile 'sales.csv' dlm=',';
   input Employee_ID First_Name $ Last_Name $
         Gender $ Salary Job_Title $ Country $
         Birth_Date :date.
         Hire_Date :mmddyy.;
run;
```

71 p107d03

Business Scenario

```
proc print data=work.subset3;
run;
```

Partial PROC PRINT Output

Obs	First_ Name	Last_Name	Gender	Job_Title	Country	Employee_ ID	Salary	Birth_ Date	Hire_ Date
1	Tom	Zhou	M	Sales Manager	AU	120102	108255	3510	10744
2	Wilson	Dawes	M	Sales Manager	AU	120103	87975	-3996	5114
3	Irenie	Elvish	F	Sales Rep. II	AU	120121	26600	-5630	5114
4	Christina	Ngan	F	Sales Rep. II	AU	120122	27475	-1984	6756
5	Kimiko	Hotstone	F	Sales Rep. I	AU	120123	26190	1732	9405
6	Lucian	Daymond	M	Sales Rep. I	AU	120124	26480	-233	6999
7	Fong	Hofmeister	M	Sales Rep. IV	AU	120125	32040	-1852	6999
8	Satyakam	Denny	M	Sales Rep. II	AU	120126	26780	10490	17014
9	Sharryn	Clarkson	F	Sales Rep. II	AU	120127	28100	6943	14184
10	Monica	Kletschkus	F	Sales Rep. IV	AU	120128	30890	9691	17106
11	Alvin	Roebuck	M	Sales Rep. III	AU	120129	30070	1787	9405
12	Kevin	Lyon	M	Sales Rep. I	AU	120130	26955	9114	16922
13	Marinus	Surawski	M	Sales Rep. I	AU	120131	26910	7207	15706
14	Fancine	Kaiser	F	Sales Rep. III	AU	120132	28525	-3923	6848

72

p107d03

Additional SAS Statements

Additional SAS statements can be added to perform further processing in the DATA step.

```
data work.subset3;
   length First_Name $ 12 Last_Name $ 18
          Gender $ 1 Job_Title $ 25
          Country $ 2;
   infile 'sales.csv' dlm=',';
   input Employee_ID First_Name $ Last_Name $
         Gender $ Salary Job_Title $ Country $
         Birth_Date :date.
         Hire_Date :mmddyy.;
   keep First_Name Last_Name Salary
        Job_Title Hire_Date;
   label Job_Title='Sales Title'
         Hire_Date='Date Hired';
   format Salary dollar12. Hire_Date monyy7.;
run;
```

p107d04

Additional SAS Statements

```
proc print data=work.subset3 label;
run;
```

Partial PROC PRINT Output

Obs	First_ Name	Last_Name	Sales Title	Salary	Date Hired
1	Tom	Zhou	Sales Manager	$108,255	JUN1989
2	Wilson	Dawes	Sales Manager	$87,975	JAN1974
3	Irenie	Elvish	Sales Rep. II	$26,600	JAN1974
4	Christina	Ngan	Sales Rep. II	$27,475	JUL1978
5	Kimiko	Hotstone	Sales Rep. I	$26,190	OCT1985
6	Lucian	Daymond	Sales Rep. I	$26,480	MAR1979
7	Fong	Hofmeister	Sales Rep. IV	$32,040	MAR1979
8	Satyakam	Denny	Sales Rep. II	$26,780	AUG2006
9	Sharryn	Clarkson	Sales Rep. II	$28,100	NOV1998
10	Monica	Kletschkus	Sales Rep. IV	$30,890	NOV2006

74

p107d04

Additional SAS Statements

- The WHERE statement is used to obtain a subset of observations from an input data set.
- The WHERE statement cannot be used to select records from a raw data file.

The subsetting IF can subset data that is in the PDV.

75

Missing Values in the Middle of the Record

Each record in **phone2.csv** has a contact name, phone number, and a mobile number. The phone number is missing from some of the records.

Missing data is indicated by two consecutive delimiters.

phone2.csv

```
         1    1    2    2    3    3    4    4
1---5----0----5----0----5----0----5----0----5
James Kvarniq,(704) 293-8126,(701) 281-8923
Sandrina Stephano,,(919) 271-4592
Cornelia Krahl,(212) 891-3241,(212) 233-5413
Karen Ballinger,,(714) 644-9090
Elke Wallstab,(910) 763-5561,(910) 545-3421
```

77

7.05 Quiz

- Open and submit **p107a01**.
- Examine the SAS log.
- How many input records were read and how many observations were created?

```
data contacts;
   length Name $ 20 Phone Mobile $ 14;
   infile 'phone2.csv' dlm=',';
   input Name $ Phone $ Mobile $;
run;

proc print data=contacts noobs;
run;
```

79

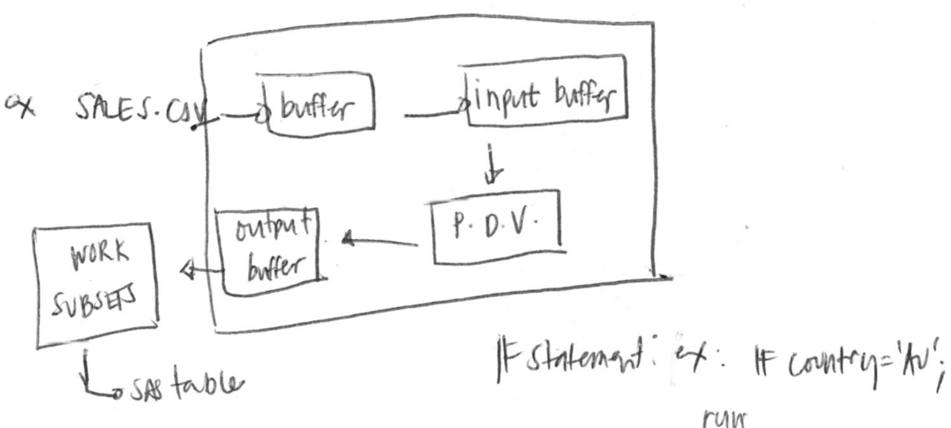

Unexpected Results

The missing phone numbers caused unexpected results in the output.

PROC PRINT Output

```
       Name                  Phone              Mobile

James Kvarniq          (704) 293-8126     (701) 281-8923
Sandrina Stephano      (919) 871-7830     Cornelia Krahl
Karen Ballinger        (714) 344-4321     Elke Wallstab
```

Partial SAS Log

```
NOTE: 5 records were read from the infile 'phone2.csv'.
      The minimum record length was 31.
      The maximum record length was 44.
NOTE: SAS went to a new line when INPUT statement reached
past the end of a line.
NOTE: The data set WORK.CONTACTS has 3 observations and 3
variables.
```

81

Consecutive Delimiters in List Input

By default, list input treats two or more consecutive delimiters as a single delimiter and not treated as a missing value.

The two consecutive commas are not being read as a missing value.

phone2.csv

```
         1    1    2    2    3    3    4    4
1---5----0----5----0----5----0----5----0----5
James Kvarniq,(704) 293-8126,(701) 281-8923
Sandrina Stephano,,(919) 271-4592
Cornelia Krahl,(212) 891-3241,(212) 233-5413
Karen Ballinger,,(714) 644-9090
Elke Wallstab,(910) 763-5561,(910) 545-3421
```

82

The DSD Option

The DSD option for the INFILE statement

- sets the default delimiter to a comma
- treats consecutive delimiters as missing values
- enables SAS to read values with embedded delimiters if the value is surrounded by quotation marks.

General form of a DSD option in an INFILE statement:

INFILE '*raw-data-file-name*' DSD;

83

Using the DSD Option

Adding the DSD option will correctly read the **phone2.csv** data file.

```
data contacts;
   length Name $ 20 Phone Mobile $ 14;
   infile 'phone2.csv' dsd;
   input Name $ Phone $ Mobile $;
run;

proc print data=contacts noobs;
run;
```

The DLM=',' option is no longer needed in the INFILE statement because the DSD option sets the default delimiter to a comma.

84

p107d05

Results

Adding the DSD option gives the expected results.

PROC PRINT Output

```
        Name                  Phone              Mobile

  James Kvarniq        (704) 293-8126     (701) 281-8923
  Sandrina Stephano                       (919) 271-4592
  Cornelia Krahl       (212) 891-3241     (212) 233-5413
  Karen Ballinger                         (714) 644-9090
  Elke Wallstab        (910) 763-5561     (910) 545-3421
```

Partial SAS Log

```
NOTE: 5 records were read from the infile 'phone2.csv'.
      The minimum record length was 31.
      The maximum record length was 44.
NOTE: The data set WORK.CONTACTS has 5 observations and
3 variables.
```

85

Missing Values at the End of a Record (Self-Study)

The data values in **phone.csv** are separated by commas. Each record has a contact name, and then a phone number, and finally a mobile number.

phone.csv

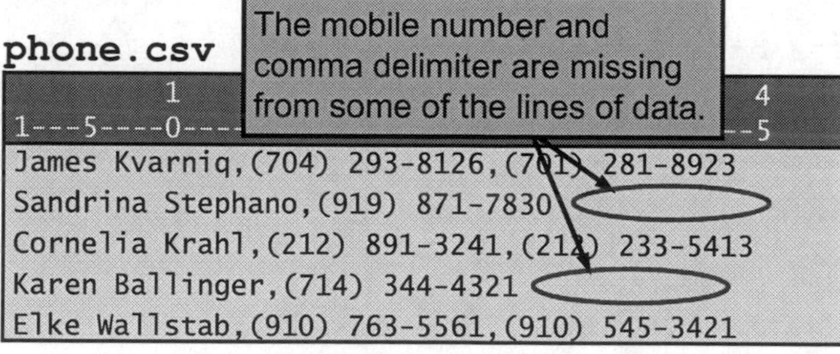

```
1---5----0---
James Kvarniq,(704) 293-8126,(701) 281-8923
Sandrina Stephano,(919) 871-7830
Cornelia Krahl,(212) 891-3241,(212) 233-5413
Karen Ballinger,(714) 344-4321
Elke Wallstab,(910) 763-5561,(910) 545-3421
```

1
4
--5
The mobile number and comma delimiter are missing from some of the lines of data.

87

7.06 Quiz (Self-Study)

Open and submit **p107a02**. Examine the SAS log. How many input records were read and how many observations were created?

```
data contacts;
   length Name $ 20 Phone Mobile $ 14;
   infile 'phone.csv' dsd;
   input Name $ Phone $ Mobile $;
run;

proc print data=contacts noobs;
run;
```

89

Unexpected Results (Self-Study)

The missing mobile phone numbers caused unexpected results in the output.

PROC PRINT Output

Name	Phone	Mobile
James Kvarniq	(704) 293-8126	(701) 281-8923
Sandrina Stephano	(919) 871-7830	Cornelia Krahl
Karen Ballinger	(714) 344-4321	Elke Wallstab

Partial SAS Log

```
NOTE: 5 records were read from the infile 'phone.csv'.
      The minimum record length was 31.
      The maximum record length was 44.
NOTE: SAS went to a new line when INPUT statement
reached past the end of a line.
NOTE: The data set WORK.CONTACTS has 3 observations and
3 variables.
```

91

Missing Values at the End of a Record (Self-Study)

By default, when there is missing data at the end of a row, SAS does the following:

- loads the next record to finish the observation
- writes a note to the log

92

The MISSOVER Option (Self-Study)

The MISSOVER option prevents SAS from loading a new record when the end of the current record is reached.

General form of an INFILE statement with a MISSOVER option:

INFILE '*raw-data-file-name*' MISSOVER;

If SAS reaches the end of the row without finding values for all fields, variables without values are set to missing.

93

7.07 Quiz (Self-Study)

Open **p107a03** and add the MISSOVER option to the INFILE statement. Submit the program and examine the SAS log. How many input records were read and how many observations were created?

```
data contacts;
   length Name $ 20 Phone Mobile $ 14;
   infile 'phone.csv' dsd;
   input Name $ Phone $ Mobile $;
run;

proc print data=contacts noobs;
run;
```

95

Results (Self-Study)

Adding the MISSOVER option gives the expected results.

PROC PRINT Output

Name	Phone	Mobile
James Kvarniq	(704) 293-8126	(701) 281-8923
Sandrina Stephano	(919) 871-7830	
Cornelia Krahl	(212) 891-3241	(212) 233-5413
Karen Ballinger	(714) 344-4321	
Elke Wallstab	(910) 763-5561	(910) 545-3421

Partial SAS Log

```
NOTE: 5 records were read from the infile 'phone.csv'.
      The minimum record length was 31.
      The maximum record length was 44.
NOTE: The data set WORK.CONTACTS has 5 observations and
3 variables.
```

97

Exercises

Level 1

4. Reading a Comma-Delimited Raw Data File

a. Retrieve the starter program **p107e04**.

b. Add the appropriate LENGTH, INFILE, and INPUT statements to read the comma-delimited raw data file named the following:

Windows or UNIX	`custca.csv`
z/OS (OS/390)	`.workshop.rawdata(custca)`

Partial Raw Data File

```
Bill,Cuddy,11171,M,16/10/1986,21,15-30 years
Susan,Krasowski,17023,F,09/07/1959,48,46-60 years
Andreas,Rennie,26148,M,18/07/1934,73,61-75 years
Lauren,Krasowski,46966,F,24/10/1986,21,15-30 years
Lauren,Marx,54655,F,18/08/1969,38,31-45 years
```

The following variables should be read into the program data vector:

Name	Type	Length
`First`	Character	20
`Last`	Character	20
`ID`	Numeric	8
`Gender`	Character	1
`BirthDate`	Numeric	8
`Age`	Numeric	8
`AgeGroup`	Character	12

c. Add a FORMAT statement and a DROP statement in the DATA step to create a data set that resembles the following when used in the PROC PRINT step:

Partial PROC PRINT Output (First 5 of 15 Observations)

```
                                                              Birth
  Obs    First      Last         Gender    AgeGroup            Date

   1     Bill       Cuddy          M       15-30 years      OCT1986
   2     Susan      Krasowski      F       46-60 years      JUL1959
   3     Andreas    Rennie         M       61-75 years      JUL1934
   4     Lauren     Krasowski      F       15-30 years      OCT1986
   5     Lauren     Marx           F       31-45 years      AUG1969
```

Level 2

5. Reading a Space-Delimited Raw Data File with Spaces in Data Values

a. Write a DATA step to create a new data set named **Work.us_customers** by reading the space-delimited raw data named the following:

Windows or UNIX	**custus.dat**
z/OS (OS/390)	**.workshop.rawdata(custus)**

Some of the data values contain spaces. Use an option in the INFILE statement to specify that when data values are enclosed in quotation marks, delimiters within the value are treated as part of the data value.

Partial Raw Data File

```
"James Kvarniq" 4 M 27JUN1974 33 "31-45 years"
"Sandrina Stephano" 5 F 09JUL1979 28 "15-30 years"
"Karen Ballinger" 10 F 18OCT1984 23 "15-30 years"
"David Black" 12 M 12APR1969 38 "31-45 years"
"Jimmie Evans" 17 M 17AUG1954 53 "46-60 years"
```

The following variables should be created in the data set **Work.us_customers**:

Name	Type	Length
Name	Character	20
ID	Numeric	8
Gender	Character	1
BirthDate	Numeric	8
Age	Numeric	8
AgeGroup	Character	12

b. Add a FORMAT statement in the DATA step to make the **BirthDate** resemble a three-character month with a four-digit year.

c. Write a PROC PRINT step with a VAR statement to create the following report:

Partial PROC PRINT Output (First 7 of 28 Observations)

```
                                                    Birth
 Obs    Name                      Gender           Date      AgeGroup        Age

   1    James Kvarniq               M            JUN1974    31-45 years      33
   2    Sandrina Stephano           F            JUL1979    15-30 years      28
   3    Karen Ballinger             F            OCT1984    15-30 years      23
   4    David Black                 M            APR1969    31-45 years      38
   5    Jimmie Evans                M            AUG1954    46-60 years      53
   6    Tonie Asmussen              M            FEB1954    46-60 years      53
   7    Michael Dineley             M            APR1959    46-60 years      48
```

Level 3

6. Reading Missing Values at the End of a Record

a. Write a DATA step to create a new data set named **Work.prices** by reading the asterisk-delimited raw data file named the following:

Windows or UNIX	**prices.dat**
z/OS (OS/390)	**.workshop.rawdata(prices)**

Some of the records do not have a value for **UnitSalesPrice** and the last delimiter is missing.

Documentation on the INFILE statement options can be found in the SAS Help and Documentation from the Contents tab (**SAS Products** ⇨ **Base SAS** ⇨ **SAS 9.2 Language Reference: Dictionary** ⇨ **Dictionary of Language Elements** ⇨ **Statements** ⇨ **INFILE Statement**).

Partial Raw Data File

```
210200100009*09JUN2007*31DEC9999*$15.50*$34.70
210200100017*24JAN2007*31DEC9999*$17.80
210200200023*04JUL2007*31DEC9999*$8.25*$19.80
210200600067*27OCT2007*31DEC9999*$28.90
210200600085*28AUG2007*31DEC9999*$17.85*$39.40
```

The following variables should be read into the program data vector:

Name	Type	Length
`ProductID`	Numeric	8
`StartDate`	Numeric	8
`EndDate`	Numeric	8
`UnitCostPrice`	Numeric	8
`UnitSalesPrice`	Numeric	8

b. Write a PROC PRINT step and add a LABEL and a FORMAT statement in the DATA step to create a data set that resembles the following when used in the PROC PRINT step:

Partial PROC PRINT Output (First 10 of 259 Observations)

```
                                                                  Sales
                            Start of       End of     Cost Price  Price per
 Obs     Product ID        Date Range    Date Range    per Unit     Unit

   1    210200100009      06/09/2007    12/31/9999      15.50      34.70
   2    210200100017      01/24/2007    12/31/9999      17.80        .
   3    210200200023      07/04/2007    12/31/9999       8.25      19.80
   4    210200600067      10/27/2007    12/31/9999      28.90        .
   5    210200600085      08/28/2007    12/31/9999      17.85      39.40
   6    210200600112      01/04/2007    12/31/9999       9.25      21.80
   7    210200900033      09/17/2007    12/31/9999       6.45      14.20
   8    210200900038      02/01/2007    12/31/9999       9.30      20.30
   9    210201000050      04/02/2007    12/31/9999       9.00      19.60
  10    210201000126      04/22/2007    12/31/9999       2.30       6.50
```

7.3 Chapter Review

Chapter Review

1. What statement identifies the physical filename of the raw data file to read?
2. What statement describes the arrangement of values in the raw data file?
3. What is the default delimiter when the DLM= option is used?
4. What are the two phases of DATA step processing?
5. What is a program data vector (PDV)?

100

continued...

Chapter Review

6. Why would you use a LENGTH statement?
7. What is an instruction that SAS uses to read data values into a variable?
8. When would you use a : modifier?

101

7.4 Solutions

Solutions to Exercises

1. **Reading a Comma-Delimited Raw Data File**

   a. Retrieve the starter program.

   b. Add the appropriate LENGTH, INFILE, and INPUT statements.

```
data work.NewEmployees;
   length First $ 12 Last $ 18 Title $ 25;
   infile 'newemps.csv' dlm=',';
   input First $ Last $ Title $ Salary;
run;

proc print data=work.NewEmployees;
run;
```

   For z/OS (OS/390), the following INFILE statement is used:

```
   infile '.workshop.rawdata(newemps)' dlm=',';
```

   c. Submit the program.

2. **Reading a Space-Delimited Raw Data File**

   a. Write a DATA step.

```
data work.QtrDonation;
   length IDNum $ 6;
   infile 'donation.dat';
   input IDNum $ Qtr1 Qtr2 Qtr3 Qtr4;
run;
```

   For z/OS (OS/390), the following INFILE statement is used:

```
   infile '.workshop.rawdata(donation)';
```

   b. Write a PROC PRINT step.

```
proc print data=work.QtrDonation;
run;
```

3. **Using Column Input to Read a Fixed Column Raw Data File**

   a. Write a DATA step.

```
data work.supplier_info;
   infile 'supplier.dat';
   input ID 1-5 Name $ 8-37 Country $ 40-41;
run;
```

   For z/OS (OS/390), the following INFILE statement is used:

```
   infile '.workshop.rawdata(supplier)';
```

b. Write a PROC PRINT step.

```
proc print data=work.supplier_info;
run;
```

4. Reading a Comma-Delimited Raw Data File

a. Retrieve the starter program.

b. Add the appropriate LENGTH, INFILE, and INPUT statements.

```
data work.canada_customers;
   length First Last $ 20 Gender $ 1 AgeGroup $ 12;
   infile 'custca.csv' dlm=',';
   input First $ Last $ ID Gender $
         BirthDate :ddmmyy. Age AgeGroup $;
run;

proc print data=work.canada_customers;
run;
```

For z/OS (OS/390), the following INFILE statement is used:

```
   infile '.workshop.rawdata(custca)' dlm=',';
```

c. Add a FORMAT statement and a DROP statement.

```
data work.canada_customers;
   length First Last $ 20 Gender $ 1 AgeGroup $ 12;
   infile 'custca.csv' dlm=',';
   input First $ Last $ ID Gender $
         BirthDate :ddmmyy. Age AgeGroup $;
   format BirthDate monyy7.;
   drop ID Age;
run;
```

5. Reading a Space-Delimited Raw Data File with Spaces in Data Values

a. Write a DATA step.

```
data work.us_customers;
   length Name $ 20 Gender $ 1 AgeGroup $ 12;
   infile 'custus.dat' dlm=' ' dsd;
   input Name $ ID Gender $ BirthDate :date.
         Age AgeGroup $;
run;
```

For z/OS (OS/390), the following INFILE statement is used:

```
   infile '.workshop.rawdata(custus)' dlm=' ' dsd;
```

b. Add a FORMAT statement.

```
data work.us_customers;
   length Name $ 20 Gender $ 1 AgeGroup $ 12;
   infile 'custus.dat' dlm=' ' dsd;
   input Name $ ID Gender $ BirthDate :date.
         Age AgeGroup $;
   format BirthDate monyy7.;
run;
```

c. Write a PROC PRINT step.

```
proc print data=work.us_customers;
   var Name Gender BirthDate AgeGroup Age;
run;
```

6. Reading Missing Values at the End of a Record

a. Write a DATA step.

```
data work.prices;
   infile 'prices.dat' dlm='*' missover;
   input ProductID StartDate :date. EndDate :date.
         UnitCostPrice :dollar. UnitSalesPrice :dollar.;
run;
```

For z/OS (OS/390), the following INFILE statement is used:

```
   infile '.workshop.rawdata(prices)' dlm='*' missover;
```

b. Write a PROC PRINT step and add a LABEL and a FORMAT statement in the DATA step.

```
data work.prices;
   infile 'prices.dat' dlm='*' missover;
   input ProductID StartDate :date. EndDate :date.
         UnitCostPrice :dollar. UnitSalesPrice :dollar.;
   label ProductID='Product ID'
         StartDate='Start of Date Range'
         EndDate='End of Date Range'
         UnitCostPrice='Cost Price per Unit'
         UnitSalesPrice='Sales Price per Unit';
   format StartDate EndDate mmddyy10.
          UnitCostPrice UnitSalesPrice 8.2;
run;

proc print data=work.prices label;
run;
```

Solutions to Student Activities (Polls/Quizzes)

7.02 Multiple Choice Poll – Correct Answer

Which statement is true?

(a.) An input buffer is only created if you are reading data from a raw data file.

b. The PDV at compile time holds the variable name, type, byte size, and initial value.

c. The descriptor portion is the first item that is created at compile time.

34

7.03 Multiple Choice Poll – Correct Answer

Which statement is true?

a. Data is read directly from the raw data file to the PDV.

(b.) At the bottom of the DATA step, the contents of the PDV are output to the output SAS data set.

c. When SAS returns to the top of the DATA step, any variable coming from a SAS data set is set to missing.

50

7.04 Quiz – Correct Answer

Which INPUT statement correctly uses list input to read the space-delimited raw data file?

Raw Data

```
Donny 5MAY2008 25 FL $43,132.50
Margaret 20FEB2008 43 NC 65,150
```

a.
```
input name $ hired date. age
      state $ salary comma.;
```

(b.)
```
input name $ hired :date. age
      state $ salary :comma.;
```

70

7.05 Quiz – Correct Answer

- Open and submit **p107a01**.
- Examine the SAS log.
- How many input records were read and how many observations were created?

Five records were read from the input file and three observations were created.

80

7.06 Quiz – Correct Answer (Self-Study)

Open and submit **p107a02**. Examine the SAS log. How many input records were read and how many observations were created?

Five records were read from the input file, and three observations were created.

90

7.07 Quiz – Correct Answer (Self-Study)

Open **p107a03** and add the MISSOVER option to the INFILE statement. Submit the program and examine the SAS log. How many input records were read and how many observations were created?

```
data contacts;
   length Name $ 20 Phone Mobile $ 14;
   infile 'phone.csv' dsd missover;
   input Name $ Phone $ Mobile $;
run;

proc print data=contacts noobs;
run;
```

Five input records were read and five observations created.

96

p107a03s

Solutions to Chapter Review

Chapter Review Answers

1. What statement identifies the physical filename of the raw data file to read?

   an INFILE statement

2. What statement describes the arrangement of values in the raw data file?

   an INPUT statement

3. What is the default delimiter when the DLM= option is used?

   a blank delimiter

102

continued...

Chapter Review Answers

4. What are the two phases of DATA step processing?
   - **compilation**
   - **execution**

5. What is a program data vector (PDV)?

   A logical area in memory where SAS holds the current observation

6. Why would you use a LENGTH statement?

   A LENGTH statement is used to define a variable length when the default length is not adequate.

103

continued...

Chapter Review Answers

7. What is an instruction that SAS uses to read data values into a variable?

   an informat

8. When would you use a : modifier?

   You use a : modifier with nonstandard raw data that requires list input and an informat.

104

Chapter 8 Validating and Cleaning Data

8.1 Introduction to Validating and Cleaning Data 8-3

8.2 Examining Data Errors When Reading Raw Data Files 8-9

Demonstration: Examining Data Errors 8-14

8.3 Validating Data with the PRINT and FREQ Procedures 8-19

Exercises 8-30

8.4 Validating Data with the MEANS and UNIVARIATE Procedures 8-33

Exercises 8-38

8.5 Cleaning Invalid Data 8-41

Demonstration: Using the Viewtable Window to Clean Data – Windows (Self-Study) 8-44

Demonstration: Using the Viewtable Window to Clean Data – UNIX (Self-Study) 8-47

Demonstration: Using the FSEDIT Window to Clean Data – z/OS (OS/390) (Self-Study) 8-49

Exercises 8-64

8.6 Chapter Review 8-66

8.7 Solutions 8-67

Solutions to Exercises 8-67

Solutions to Student Activities (Polls/Quizzes) 8-73

Solutions to Chapter Review 8-77

8.1 Introduction to Validating and Cleaning Data

Objectives

- Define data errors in a raw data file.
- Identify procedures for validating data.
- Identify techniques for cleaning data.
- Define the business scenario that will be used with validating and cleaning data.

3

Business Scenario

A delimited raw data file containing information on Orion Star non-sales employees from Australia and the United States needs to be read to create a data set.

Requirements of non-sales employee data:

- **Employee_ID**, **Salary**, **Birth_Date**, and **Hire_Date** must be numeric variables.
- **First**, **Last**, **Gender**, **Job_Title**, and **Country** must be character variables.

4

8.01 Quiz

What problems will SAS have reading the numeric data **Salary** and **Hire_Date**?

Partial **nonsales.csv**

```
120101,Patrick,Lu,M,163040,Director,AU,18AUG1976,01JUL2003
120104,Kareen,Billington,F,46230,Administration Manager,au,11MAY1954,01JAN1981
120105,Liz,Povey,F,27110,Secretary I,AU,21DEC1974,01MAY1999
120106,John,Hornsey,M,unknown,Office Assistant II,AU,23DEC1944,01JAN1974
120107,Sherie,Sheedy,F,30475,Office Assistant III,AU,01FEB1978,21JAN1953
120108,Gladys,Gromek,F,27660,Warehouse Assistant II,AU,23FEB1984,01AUG2006
120108,Gabriele,Baker,F,26495,Warehouse Assistant I,AU,15DEC1986,01OCT2006
120110,Dennis,Entwisle,M,28615,Warehouse Assistant III,AU,20NOV1949,01NOV1979
120111,Ubaldo,Spillane,M,26895,Security Guard II,AU,23JUL1949,99NOV1978
120112,Ellis,Glattback,F,26550, ,AU,17FEB1969,01JUL1990
120113,Riu,Horsey,F,26870,Security Guard II,AU,10MAY1944,01JAN1974
120114,Jeannette,Buddery,G,31285,Security Manager,AU,08FEB1944,01JAN1974
120115,Hugh,Nichollas,M,2650,Service Assistant I,AU,08MAY1984,01AUG2005
.,Austen,Ralston,M,29250,Service Assistant II,AU,13JUN1959,01FEB1980
120117,Bill,Mccleary,M,31670,Cabinet Maker III,AU,11SEP1964,01APR1986
```

6

Data Errors

Data errors occur when data values are not appropriate for the SAS statements that are specified in a program.

- SAS detects data errors during program execution.
- When a data error is detected, SAS continues to execute the program.

```
NOTE: Invalid data for Salary in line 4 23-29.
RULE:      ----+----1----+----2----+----3----+----4----+----5----+----6
4          120106,John,Hornsey,M,unknown,Office Assistant II,AU,23DEC19
     61    44,01JAN1974 72
Employee_ID=120106 First=John Last=Hornsey Gender=M Salary=.
Job_Title=Office Assistant II Country=AU Birth_Date=23/12/1944
Hire_Date=01/01/1974 _ERROR_=1 _N_=4
NOTE: Invalid data for Hire_Date in li
9          120111,Ubaldo,Spillane,M,2689                       94
     61    9,99NOV1978 71
Employee_ID=120111 First=Ubaldo Last=S
Job_Title=Security Guard II Country=AU
Hire_Date=. _ERROR_=1 _N_=9
```

A data error example is defining a variable as numeric, but the data value is actually character.

8

Business Scenario

Additional requirements of non-sales employee data:

- **Employee_ID** must be unique and not missing.
- **Gender** must have a value of F or M.
- **Salary** must be in the numeric range of 24000 – 500000.
- **Job_Title** must not be missing.
- **Country** must have a value of AU or US.
- **Birth_Date** value must occur before **Hire_Date** value.
- **Hire_Date** must have a value of 01/01/1974 or later.

9

8.02 Quiz

What problems exist with the data in this partial data set?

	Employee_ID	First	Last	Gender	Salary	Job_Title	Country	Birth_Date	Hire_Date
1	120101	Patrick	Lu	M	163E3	Director	AU	18/08/1976	01/07/2003
2	120104	Kareen	Billington	F	46230	Administration Manager	au	11/05/1954	01/01/1981
3	120105	Liz	Povey	F	27110	Secretary I	AU	21/12/1974	01/05/1999
4	120106	John	Hornsey	M	.	Office Assistant II	AU	23/12/1944	01/01/1974
5	120107	Sherie	Sheedy	F	30475	Office Assistant III	AU	01/02/1978	21/01/1953
6	120108	Gladys	Gromek	F	27660	Warehouse Assistant II	AU	23/02/1984	01/08/2006
7	120108	Gabriele	Baker	F	26495	Warehouse Assistant I	AU	15/12/1986	01/10/2006
8	120110	Dennis	Entwisle	M	28615	Warehouse Assistant III	AU	20/11/1949	01/11/1979
9	120111	Ubaldo	Spillane	M	26895	Security Guard II	AU	23/07/1949	.
10	120112	Ellis	Glattback	F	26550		AU	17/02/1969	01/07/1990
11	120113	Riu	Horsey	F	26870	Security Guard II	AU	10/05/1944	01/01/1974
12	120114	Jeannette	Buddery	G	31285	Security Manager	AU	08/02/1944	01/01/1974
13	120115	Hugh	Nichollas	M	2650	Service Assistant I	AU	08/05/1984	01/08/2005
14	.	Austen	Ralston	M	29250	Service Assistant II	AU	13/06/1959	01/02/1980
15	120117	Bill	Mccleary	M	31670	Cabinet Maker III	AU	11/09/1964	01/04/1986

Hint: There are nine data problems.

11

Validating the Data

In general, SAS procedures analyze data, produce output, or manage SAS files.

In addition, SAS procedures can be used to detect invalid data.

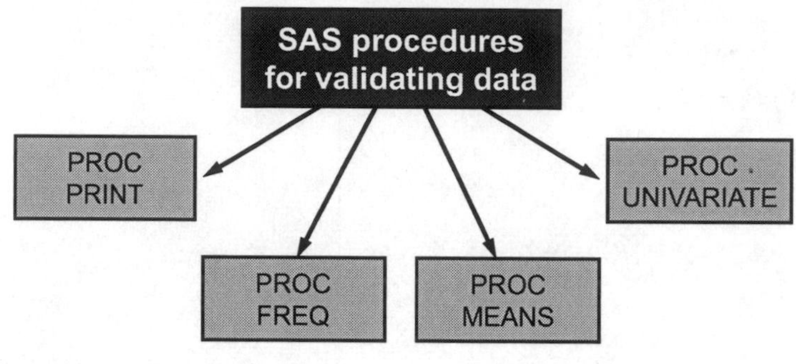

13

The PRINT Procedure

The PRINT procedure can show the job titles that are missing and the hire dates that occur before the birth dates.

Obs	Employee_ ID	Job_Title	Birth_Date	Hire_Date
5	120107	Office Assistant III	01/02/1978	21/01/1953
9	120111	Security Guard II	23/07/1949	.
10	120112		17/02/1969	01/07/1990

14 p108d01

The FREQ Procedure

The FREQ procedure can show if any genders are not `F` or `M` and if any countries are not `AU` or `US`.

The FREQ Procedure

Gender	Frequency	Percent	Cumulative Frequency	Cumulative Percent
F	110	47.01	110	47.01
G	1	0.43	111	47.44
M	123	52.56	234	100.00

Frequency Missing = 1

Country	Frequency	Percent	Cumulative Frequency	Cumulative Percent
AU	33	14.04	33	14.04
US	196	83.40	229	97.45
au	3	1.28	232	98.72
us	3	1.28	235	100.00

15

The MEANS Procedure

The MEANS procedure can show if any salaries are not in the range of 24000 to 500000.

The MEANS Procedure

Analysis Variable : Salary

N	N Miss	Minimum	Maximum
234	1	2401.00	433800.00

16

p108d01

The UNIVARIATE Procedure

The UNIVARIATE procedure can show if any salaries are not in the range of 24000 to 500000.

Partial PROC UNIVARIATE Output

```
                The UNIVARIATE Procedure
                   Variable:  Salary

                 Extreme Observations

     -----Lowest----          -----Highest----

     Value       Obs           Value       Obs

      2401        20          163040         1
      2650        13          194885       231
     24025        25          207885        28
     24100        19          268455        29
     24390       228          433800        27
```

17 p108d01

Cleaning the Data

After the data is validated, the invalid data needs to be cleaned.

Techniques for cleaning data:

- Editing raw data file outside of SAS
- Interactively editing data set using VIEWTABLE
- Programmatically editing data set using the DATA step
- Programmatically editing data set using the SQL procedure
- Using the SAS DataFlux product dfPower Studio

18

Ideally, invalid data should be cleaned in the original data source and not in the SAS data set.

Integrity constraints can be placed on a data set to eliminate the possibility of invalid data in the data set. Integrity constraints are a set of data validation rules that you can specify in order to restrict the data values that can be stored for a variable in a SAS data file. Integrity constraints help you preserve the validity and consistency of your data. SAS enforces the integrity constraints when the values associated with an integrity constraint variable are added, updated, or deleted.

Section 8.5 addresses the situation where you have no choice but to correct the data in the SAS data set.

8.2 Examining Data Errors When Reading Raw Data Files

Objectives

- Identify data errors.
- Demonstrate what happens when a data error is encountered.
- Direct the observations with data errors to a different data set than the observations without data errors. (Self-Study)

21

Business Scenario

A delimited raw data file containing information on Orion Star non-sales employees from Australia and the United States needs to be read to create a data set.

Requirements of non-sales employee data:

- **`Employee_ID`**, **`Salary`**, **`Birth_Date`**, and **`Hire_Date`** must be numeric variables.
- **`First`**, **`Last`**, **`Gender`**, **`Job_Title`**, and **`Country`** must be character variables.

22

8.03 Multiple Choice Poll

Which statements are used to read a delimited raw data file and create a SAS data set?

a. DATA and SET only
b. DATA and INFILE only
c. DATA, SET, and INPUT only
d. DATA, INFILE, and INPUT only

24

Data Errors

One type of data error is when the INPUT statement encounters invalid data in a field.

When SAS encounters a data error, these events occur:

- A note that describes the error is printed in the SAS log.
- The input record (contents of the input buffer) being read is displayed in the SAS log.
- The values in the SAS observation (contents of the PDV) being created are displayed in the SAS log.
- A missing value is assigned to the appropriate SAS variable.
- Execution continues.

26

Data Errors

A note that describes the error is printed in the SAS log.

Partial SAS Log

```
NOTE: Invalid data for Salary in line 4 23-29.
RULE:      ----+----1----+----2----+----3----+----4----+----5----+----6
4          120106,John,Hornsey,M,unknown,Office Assistant II,AU,23DEC19
      61   44,01JAN1974 72
Employee_ID=120106 First=John Last=Hornsey Gender=M Salary=.
Job_Title=Office Assistant II Country=AU Birth_Date=23/12/1944
Hire_Date=01/01/1974 _ERROR_=1 _N_=4
```

This note indicates that invalid data was found for variable **Salary** in line 4 of the raw data file in columns 23-29.

27

Data Errors

The input record (contents of the input buffer) being read is displayed in the SAS log.

Partial SAS Log

```
NOTE: Invalid data for Salary in line 4 23-29.
RULE:      ----+----1----+----2----+----3----+----4----+----5----+----6
4          120106,John,Hornsey,M,unknown,Office Assistant II,AU,23DEC19
      61   44,01JAN1974 72
Employee_ID=120106 First=John Last=Hornsey Gender=M Salary=.
Job_Title=Office Assistant II Country=AU Birth_Date=23/12/1944
Hire_Date=01/01/1974 _ERROR_=1 _N_=4
```

A ruler is drawn above the raw data record that contains the invalid data.

28

Data Errors

The values in the SAS observation (contents of the PDV) being created are displayed in the SAS log.

Partial SAS Log

```
NOTE: Invalid data for Salary in line 4 23-29.
RULE:      ----+----1----+----2----+----3----+----4----+----5----+----6
4          120106,John,Hornsey,M,unknown,Office Assistant II,AU,23DEC19
     61    44,01JAN1974 72
Employee_ID=120106 First=John Last=Hornsey Gender=M Salary=.
Job_Title=Office Assistant II Country=AU Birth_Date=23/12/1944
Hire_Date=01/01/1974 _ERROR_=1 _N_=4
```

29

Data Errors

A missing value is assigned to the appropriate SAS variable.

Partial SAS Log

```
NOTE: Invalid data for Salary in line 4 23-29.
RULE:      ----+----1----+----2----+----3----+----4----+----5----+----6
4          120106,John,Hornsey,M,unknown,Office Assistant II,AU,23DEC19
     61    44,01JAN1974 72
Employee_ID=120106 First=John Last=Hornsey Gender=M Salary=.
Job_Title=Office Assistant II Country=AU Birth_Date=23/12/1944
Hire_Date=01/01/1974 _ERROR_=1 _N_=4
```

30

Data Errors

During the processing of every DATA step, SAS automatically creates the following temporary variables:

- the _N_ variable, which counts the number of times the DATA step begins to iterate
- the _ERROR_ variable, which signals the occurrence of an error caused by the data during execution

  0 indicates that no errors exist.

  1 indicates that one or more errors occurred.

```
NOTE: Invalid data for Salary in line 4 23-29.
RULE:      ----+----1----+----2----+----3----+----4----+----5----+----6
4          120106,John,Hornsey,M,unknown,Office Assistant II,AU,23DEC19
      61   44,01JAN1974 72
Employee_ID=120106 First=John Last=Hornsey Gender=M Salary=.
Job_Title=Office Assistant II Country=AU Birth_Date=23/12/1944
Hire_Date=01/01/1974 _ERROR_=1 _N_=4
```

31

Examining Data Errors

p108d02

Submit the following program and review the results in the Output and Log windows.

```
data work.nonsales;
   length Employee_ID 8 First $ 12 Last $ 18
          Gender $ 1 Salary 8 Job_Title $ 25 Country $ 2
          Birth_Date Hire_Date 8;
   infile 'nonsales.csv' dlm=',';
   input Employee_ID First $ Last $
         Gender $ Salary Job_Title $ Country $
         Birth_Date :date9.
         Hire_Date :date9.;
   format Birth_Date Hire_Date ddmmyy10.;
run;

proc print data=work.nonsales;
run;
```

For z/OS (OS/390), the following INFILE statement is used:

```
   infile '.workshop.rawdata(nonsales)' dlm=',';
```

Partial PROC PRINT Output

Obs	Employee_ID	First	Last	Gender	Salary	Job_Title	Country	Birth_Date	Hire_Date
1	120101	Patrick	Lu	M	163040	Director	AU	18/08/1976	01/07/2003
2	120104	Kareen	Billington	F	46230	Administration Manager	au	11/05/1954	01/01/1981
3	120105	Liz	Povey	F	27110	Secretary I	AU	21/12/1974	01/05/1999
4	120106	John	Hornsey	M	.	Office Assistant II	AU	23/12/1944	01/01/1974
5	120107	Sherie	Sheedy	F	30475	Office Assistant III	AU	01/02/1978	21/01/1953
6	120108	Gladys	Gromek	F	27660	Warehouse Assistant II	AU	23/02/1984	01/08/2006
7	120108	Gabriele	Baker	F	26495	Warehouse Assistant I	AU	15/12/1986	01/10/2006
8	120110	Dennis	Entwisle	M	28615	Warehouse Assistant III	AU	20/11/1949	01/11/1979
9	120111	Ubaldo	Spillane	M	26895	Security Guard II	AU	23/07/1949	.
10	120112	Ellis	Glattback	F	26550		AU	17/02/1969	01/07/1990
11	120113	Riu	Horsey	F	26870	Security Guard II	AU	10/05/1944	01/01/1974
12	120114	Jeannette	Buddery	G	31285	Security Manager	AU	08/02/1944	01/01/1974
13	120115	Hugh	Nichollas	M	2650	Service Assistant I	AU	08/05/1984	01/08/2005
14	.	Austen	Ralston	M	29250	Service Assistant II	AU	13/06/1959	01/02/1980
15	120117	Bill	Mccleary	M	31670	Cabinet Maker III	AU	11/09/1964	01/04/1986

Partial SAS Log

```
data work.nonsales;
   length Employee_ID 8 First $ 12 Last $ 18
          Gender $ 1 Salary 8 Job_Title $ 25 Country $ 2
          Birth_Date Hire_Date 8;
   infile 'nonsales.csv' dlm=',';
   input Employee_ID First $ Last $
         Gender $ Salary Job_Title $ Country $
         Birth_Date :date9.
         Hire_Date :date9.;
   format Birth_Date Hire_Date ddmmyy10.;
run;

NOTE: The infile 'nonsales.csv' is:
      File Name=s:\workshop\nonsales.csv,
      RECFM=V,LRECL=256

NOTE: Invalid data for Salary in line 4 23-29.
RULE:      ----+----1----+----2----+----3----+----4----+----5----+----6----+----7----+----8----+
4          120106,John,Hornsey,M,unknown,Office Assistant II,AU,23DEC1944,01JAN1974 72
Employee_ID=120106 First=John Last=Hornsey Gender=M Salary=. Job_Title=Office Assistant II
Country=AU Birth_Date=23/12/1944 Hire_Date=01/01/1974 _ERROR_=1 _N_=4
NOTE: Invalid data for Hire_Date in line 9 63-71.
9          120111,Ubaldo,Spillane,M,26895,Security Guard II,AU,23JUL1949,99NOV1978 71
Employee_ID=120111 First=Ubaldo Last=Spillane Gender=M Salary=26895 Job_Title=Security Guard II
Country=AU Birth_Date=23/07/1949 Hire_Date=. _ERROR_=1 _N_=9
NOTE: 235 records were read from the infile 'nonsales.csv'.
      The minimum record length was 55.
      The maximum record length was 82.
NOTE: The data set WORK.NONSALES has 235 observations and 9 variables.
```

Setup for the Poll

- Submit program **p108a01**.
- Determine the reason for the invalid data that appears in the SAS log.

34

8.04 Multiple Choice Poll

Which statement best describes the invalid data?

a. The data in the raw data file is bad.
b. The programmer incorrectly read the data.

35

Outputting to Multiple Data Sets (Self-Study)

The DATA statement can specify multiple output data sets.

```
data work.baddata work.gooddata;
   length Employee_ID 8 First $ 12 Last $ 18
          Gender $ 1 Salary 8 Job_Title $ 25
          Country $ 2 Birth_Date Hire_Date 8;
   infile 'nonsales.csv' dlm=',';
   input Employee_ID First $ Last $
         Gender $ Salary Job_Title $ Country $
         Birth_Date :date9.
         Hire_Date :date9.;
   format Birth_Date Hire_Date ddmmyy10.;
   if _error_=1 then output work.baddata;
   else output work.gooddata;
run;
```

38 p108d03

The raw data filename specified in the INFILE statement must be specific to your operating environment.

Outputting to Multiple Data Sets (Self-Study)

An OUTPUT statement can be used in a conditional statement to write the current observation to a specific data set that is listed in the DATA statement.

```
data work.baddata work.gooddata;
   length Employee_ID 8 First $ 12 Last $ 18
          Gender $ 1 Salary 8 Job_Title $ 25
          Country $ 2 Birth_Date Hire_Date 8;
   infile 'nonsales.csv' dlm=',';
   input Employee_ID First $ Last $
         Gender $ Salary Job_Title $ Country $
         Birth_Date :date9.
         Hire_Date :date9.;
   format Birth_Date Hire_Date ddmmyy10.;
   if _error_=1 then output work.baddata;
   else output work.gooddata;
run;
```

39 p108d03

Outputting to Multiple Data Sets (Self-Study)

Partial SAS Log

```
NOTE: Invalid data for Salary in line 4 23-29.
RULE:      ----+----1----+----2----+----3----+----4----+----5----+----6
4          120106,John,Hornsey,M,unknown,Office Assistant II,AU,23DEC19
      61   44,01JAN1974 72
Employee_ID=120106 First=John Last=Hornsey Gender=M Salary=.
Job_Title=Office Assistant II Country=AU Birth_Date=23/12/1944
Hire_Date=01/01/1974 _ERROR_=1 _N_=4
NOTE: Invalid data for Hire_Date in line 9 63-71.
9          120111,Ubaldo,Spillane,M,26895,Security Guard II,AU,23JUL194
      61   9,99NOV1978 71
Employee_ID=120111 First=Ubaldo Last=Spillane Gender=M Salary=26895
Job_Title=Security Guard II Country=AU Birth_Date=23/07/1949
Hire_Date=. _ERROR_=1 _N_=9
NOTE: 235 records were read from the infile
      's:\workshop\nonsales.csv'.
      The minimum record length was 55.
      The maximum record length was 82.
NOTE: The data set WORK.BADDATA has 2 observations and 9 variables.
NOTE: The data set WORK.GOODDATA has 233 observations and 9 variables.
```

40

8.3 Validating Data with the PRINT and FREQ Procedures

Objectives

- Validate data by using the PRINT procedure with the WHERE statement.
- Validate data by using the FREQ procedure with the TABLES statement.

42

Business Scenario

Additional requirements of non-sales employee data:

- **Employee_ID** must be unique and not missing.
- **Gender** must have a value of F or M.
- **Salary** must be in the numeric range of 24000 – 500000.
- **Job_Title** must not be missing.
- **Country** must have a value of AU or US.
- **Birth_Date** value must occur before **Hire_Date** value.
- **Hire_Date** must have a value of 01/01/1974 or later.

43

SAS Procedures for Validating Data

SAS procedures can be used to detect invalid data.

PROC PRINT step with **VAR** and **WHERE** statements	detects invalid character and numeric values by subsetting observations based on conditions.
PROC FREQ step with **TABLES** statement	detects invalid character and numeric values by looking at distinct values.
PROC MEANS step with **VAR** statement	detects invalid numeric values by using summary statistics.
PROC UNIVARIATE step with **VAR** statement	detects invalid numeric values by looking at extreme values.

44

The PRINT Procedure

The PRINT procedure produces detail reports based on SAS data sets.

General form of the PRINT procedure:

```
PROC PRINT DATA=SAS-data-set ;
      VAR variable(s) ;
      WHERE where-expression ;
RUN;
```

- The VAR statement selects variables to include in the report and determines their order in the report.
- The WHERE statement is used to obtain a subset of observations.

45

where can be placed inside the procedure or data step

The WHERE Statement

For validating data, the WHERE statement is used to retrieve the observations that do not meet the data requirements.

General form of the WHERE statement:

> **WHERE** *where-expression* ;

The *where-expression* is a sequence of operands and operators that form a set of instructions that define a condition for selecting observations.

- Operands include constants and variables.
- Operators are symbols that request a comparison, arithmetic calculation, or logical operation.

46

The WHERE Statement

The following PROC PRINT step retrieves observations that have missing values for **Job_Title**.

```
proc print data=orion.nonsales;
   var Employee_ID Last Job_Title;
   where Job_Title = ' ';
run;
```

```
              Employee_                  Job_
       Obs       ID          Last        Title

        10     120112      Glattback
```

47 p108d04

The WHERE Statement

A WHERE statement might need to reference a SAS date value.

For example, the PRINT procedure needs to retrieve observations that have values of **`Hire_Date`** less than January 1, 1974.

What is the numeric SAS date value for January 1, 1974?

A *SAS date constant* is used to convert a calendar date to a SAS date value.

48

SAS Date Constant

To write a SAS date constant, enclose a date in quotation marks in the form ***ddMMMyyyy*** and immediately follow the final quotation mark with the letter **d**.

dd	is a one- or two-digit value for the day.
MMM	is a three-letter abbreviation for the month.
yyyy	is a four-digit value for the year.
d	is required to convert the quoted string to a SAS date.

Example:
The date constant for January 1, 1974, is **`'01JAN1974'd`**.

49

SAS Date Constant

The following PROC PRINT step retrieves observations that have values of **Hire_Date** that are less than January 1, 1974.

```
proc print data=orion.nonsales;
   var Employee_ID Birth_Date Hire_Date;
   where Hire_Date < '01JAN1974'd;
run;
```

or
where Hire_date mdy(1,1,1974);
↓
month, date, year function

Obs	Employee_ ID	Birth_Date	Hire_Date
5	120107	01/02/1978	21/01/1953
9	120111	23/07/1949	.
214	121011	11/03/1944	01/01/1968

50

p108d04

8.05 Multiple Choice Poll

Which data requirement cannot be achieved with the PRINT procedure using a WHERE statement?

a. **Employee_ID** must be unique and not missing.
b. **Gender** must have a value of F or M.
c. **Salary** must be in the numeric range of 24000 – 500000.
d. **Job_Title** must not be missing.
e. **Country** must have a value of AU or US.
f. **Birth_Date** value must occur before **Hire_Date** value.
g. **Hire_Date** must have a value of 01/01/1974 or later.

52

Data Requirements

Data Requirement	*where-expression* to obtain invalid data
`Employee_ID` must be unique and not missing.	`Employee_ID = .` **Does not account for uniqueness.**
`Gender` must have a value of `F` or `M`.	`Gender not in ('F','M')`
`Salary` must be in the range of 24000 – 500000.	`Salary not between 24000 and 500000`
`Job_Title` must not be missing.	`Job_Title = ' '`
`Country` must have a value of `AU` or `US`.	`Country not in ('AU','US')`
`Birth_Date` must occur before `Hire_Date`.	`Birth_Date > Hire_Date`
`Hire_Date` must have a value of 01/01/1974 or later.	`Hire_Date < '01JAN1974'd`

54

Data Requirements

The following PROC PRINT step accounts for all of the data requirements except the **`Employee_ID`** being unique.

```
proc print data=orion.nonsales;
   var Employee_ID Gender Salary Job_Title
       Country Birth_Date Hire_Date;
   where Employee_ID = . or
         Gender not in ('F','M') or
         Salary not between 24000 and 500000 or
         Job_Title = ' ' or
         Country not in ('AU','US') or
         Birth_Date > Hire_Date or
         Hire_Date < '01JAN1974'd;
run;
```

The OR operator is used between expressions. Only one expression needs to be true to account for an observation with invalid data.

55 p108d04

Data Requirements

Sixteen observations need the data cleaned.

Obs	Employee_ID	Gender	Salary	Job_Title	Country	Birth_Date	Hire_Date
2	120104	F	46230	Administration Manager	au	11/05/1954	01/01/1981
4	120106	M	.	Office Assistant II	AU	23/12/1944	01/01/1974
5	120107	F	30475	Office Assistant III	AU	01/02/1978	21/01/1953
9	120111	M	26895	Security Guard II	AU	23/07/1949	.
10	120112	F	26550		AU	17/02/1969	01/07/1990
12	120114	G	31285	Security Manager	AU	08/02/1944	01/01/1974
13	120115	M	2650	Service Assistant I	AU	08/05/1984	01/08/2005
14	.	M	29250	Service Assistant II	AU	13/06/1959	01/02/1980
20	120191	F	2401	Trainee	AU	17/01/1959	01/01/2003
84	120695	M	28180	Warehouse Assistant II	au	13/07/1964	01/07/1989
87	120698	M	26160	Warehouse Assistant I	au	17/05/1954	01/08/1976
101	120723		33950	Corp. Comm. Specialist II	US	10/08/1949	01/01/1974
125	120747	F	43590	Financial Controller I	us	20/06/1974	01/08/1995
197	120994	F	31645	Office Administrator I	us	16/06/1974	01/11/1994
200	120997	F	27420	Shipping Administrator I	us	21/11/1974	01/09/1996
214	121011	M	25735	Service Assistant I	US	11/03/1944	01/01/1968

56

The FREQ Procedure

The FREQ procedure produces one-way to *n*-way frequency tables.

General form of the FREQ procedure:

```
PROC FREQ DATA=SAS-data-set <NLEVELS>;
    TABLES variable(s);
RUN;
```

- The TABLES statement specifies the frequency tables to produce.
- The NLEVELS option displays a table that provides the number of distinct values for each variable named in the TABLES statement.

57

The FREQ Procedure

The following PROC FREQ step will show whether there are any invalid values for **Gender** and **Country**.

```
proc freq data=orion.nonsales;
   tables Gender Country;
run;
```

✎ Without the TABLES statement, PROC FREQ produces a frequency table for each variable.

58 p108d05

The FREQ Procedure

Two observations need the data cleaned for **Gender** and six observations need the data cleaned for **Country**.

The FREQ Procedure

Gender	Frequency	Percent	Cumulative Frequency	Cumulative Percent
F	110	47.01	110	47.01
G	1	0.43	111	47.44
M	123	52.56	234	100.00

Frequency Missing = 1

Country	Frequency	Percent	Cumulative Frequency	Cumulative Percent
AU	33	14.04	33	14.04
US	196	83.40	229	97.45
au	3	1.28	232	98.72
us	3	1.28	235	100.00

59

If a format is permanently assigned to a variable, PROC FREQ automatically groups the report by the formatted values.

The FREQ Procedure

This PROC FREQ step will show whether there are any duplicates for **Employee_ID**.

```
proc freq data=orion.nonsales;
   tables Employee_ID;
run;
```

60 p108d05

proc freq data=orion.nonsales noprint;
tables employee_ID / out=rich;
proc print data = rich (ex);
where count > 1;
run

The FREQ Procedure

Partial PROC FREQ Output

The FREQ Procedure

Employee_ID	Frequency	Percent	Cumulative Frequency	Cumulative Percent
120101	1	0.43	1	0.43
120104	1	0.43	2	0.86
120105	1	0.43	3	1.29
120106	1	0.43	4	1.72
120107	1	0.43	5	2.15
120108	2	0.85	7	2.99
120110	1	0.43	8	3.43
120111	1	0.43	9	3.86
120112	1	0.43	10	4.29
120113	1	0.43	11	4.72

121146	1	0.43	232	99.14
121147	1	0.43	233	99.57
121148	1	0.43	234	100.00

Frequency Missing = 1

61

The NLEVELS Option

If the number of desired distinct values is known, the NLEVELS option can help to determine whether there are any duplicates.

```
proc freq data=orion.nonsales nlevels;
   tables Gender Country Employee_ID;
run;
```

The *NLEVELS option* displays a table that provides the number of distinct values for each variable named in the TABLES statement.

62 p108d05

To display the number of levels without displaying the frequency counts, add the NOPRINT option to the TABLES statement.

```
proc freq data=orion.nonsales nlevels;
   tables Gender Country Employee_ID / noprint;
run;
```

To display the number of levels for all variables without displaying any frequency counts, use the _ALL_ keyword and the NOPRINT option in the TABLES statement.

```
proc freq data=orion.nonsales nlevels;
   tables _all_ / noprint;
run;
```

The NLEVELS Option

The Number of Variable Levels table appears before the individual frequency tables.

Partial PROC FREQ Output

```
                 The FREQ Procedure

             Number of Variable Levels

                                   Missing    Nonmissing
Variable              Levels        Levels        Levels
--------------------------------------------------------
Gender                     4             1             3
Country                    4             0             4
Employee_ID              234             1           233
```

There are 235 employees but there are only 234 distinct **`Employee_ID`** values. Therefore, there is one duplicate value for **`Employee_ID`**.

63

Exercises

Level 1

1. Validating orion.shoes_tracker with the PRINT and FREQ Procedures

a. Retrieve the starter program **p108e01**.

b. The data in **orion.shoes_tracker** should meet the following requirements:

- **Product_Category** must not be missing.
- **Supplier_Country** must have a value of GB or US.

Add a WHERE statement to the PROC PRINT step to find any observations that do **not** meet the above requirements.

c. Add a VAR statement to create the following PROC PRINT report:

Obs	Product_ Category	Supplier_Name	Supplier_ Country	Supplier_ID
1	Shoes	3Top Sports	us	.
2		3Top Sports	US	2963
5	Shoes	3Top Sports	UT	2963
10	Shoes	Greenline Sports Ltd	gB	14682

How many observations have missing **Product_Category**? ____________________

How many observations have invalid values of **Supplier_Country**? ______________

d. Add a PROC FREQ step with a TABLES statement to create frequency tables for **Supplier_Name** and **Supplier_ID** of **orion.shoes_tracker**. Include the NLEVELS option.

The data in **orion.shoes_tracker** should meet the following requirements:

- **Supplier_Name** must be 3Top Sports or Greenline Sports Ltd.
- **Supplier_ID** must be 2963 or 14682.

What invalid data exist for **Supplier_Name** and **Supplier_ID**? ________________

Level 2

2. Validating orion.qtr2_2007 with the PRINT and FREQ Procedures

a. Write a PROC PRINT step with a WHERE statement to validate the data in **orion.qtr2_2007**.

The data in **orion.qtr2_2007** should meet the following requirements:

- **Delivery_Date** values must be equal to or greater than **Order_Date** values.
- **Order_Date** values must be in the range of April 1, 2007 – June 30, 2007.

The WHERE statement should find any observations that do **not** meet the above requirements.

b. Submit the program to create the following PROC PRINT report:

Obs	Order_ID	Order_ Type	Employee_ID	Customer_ID	Order_ Date	Delivery_ Date
5	1242012259	1	121040	10	18APR2007	12APR2007
22	1242449327	3	99999999	27	26JUL2007	26JUL2007

How many observations have **Delivery_Date** values occurring before **Order_Date** values?

____

How many observations have **Order_Date** values out of the range of April 1, 2007 – June 30, 2007? ______________________________

c. Add a PROC FREQ step with a TABLES statement to create frequency tables for **Order_ID** and **Order_Type** of **orion.qtr2_2007**. Include the NLEVELS option.

d. Submit the PROC FREQ step.

The data in **orion.qtr2_2007** should meet the following requirements:

- **Order_ID** must be unique (36 distinct values) and not missing.
- **Order_Type** must have a value of 1, 2, or 3.

What invalid data exists for **Order_ID** and **Order_Type**? ______________________________

Level 3

3. Using the PROPCASE Function, Two-Way Frequency Table, and MISSING Option

a. Write a PROC PRINT step with a WHERE statement to validate the data in **orion.shoes_tracker**. All **Product_Name** values should be written in proper case.

> Documentation on the PROPCASE function can be found in the SAS Help and Documentation from the Contents tab (**SAS Products** ⇨ **Base SAS** ⇨ **SAS 9.2 Language Reference: Dictionary** ⇨ **Dictionary of Language Elements** ⇨ **Functions and CALL Routines** ⇨ **PROPCASE Function**).

b. Add a VAR statement to create the following PROC PRINT report:

Obs	Product_ID	Product_Name
3	220200300015	men's running shoes piedmont
6	220200300096	Mns.raptor Precision Sg Football

c. Add a PROC FREQ step with a TABLES statement to create the following two-way frequency table with **`Supplier_Name`** and **`Supplier_ID`** of **`orion.shoes_tracker`**:

The FREQ Procedure

Table of Supplier_Name by Supplier_ID

Supplier_Name(Supplier Name)	Supplier_ID(Supplier ID)			
Frequency Percent Row Pct Col Pct	.	2963	14682	Total
3Top Sports	1 10.00 14.29 100.00	5 50.00 71.43 71.43	1 10.00 14.29 50.00	7 70.00
3op Sports	0 0.00 0.00 0.00	2 20.00 100.00 28.57	0 0.00 0.00 0.00	2 20.00
Greenline Sports Ltd	0 0.00 0.00 0.00	0 0.00 0.00 0.00	1 10.00 100.00 50.00	1 10.00
Total	1 10.00	7 70.00	2 20.00	10 100.00

Documentation on two-way frequency tables and the MISSING option can be found in the SAS Help and Documentation from the Contents tab (**SAS Products** ⇨ **Base SAS** ⇨ **Base SAS Procedures Guide: Statistical Procedures** ⇨ **The FREQ Procedure** ⇨ **Syntax: FREQ Procedure** ⇨ **TABLES Statement**).

The data in **`orion.shoes_tracker`** should meet the following requirements:

- A **`Supplier_Name`** of `3Top Sports` must have a **`Supplier_ID`** of `2963`.
- A **`Supplier_Name`** of `Greenline Sports Ltd` must have a **`Supplier_ID`** of `14682`.

What invalid data exists for **`Supplier_Name`** and **`Supplier_ID`**? ____________________

8.4 Validating Data with the MEANS and UNIVARIATE Procedures

Objectives

- Validate data by using the MEANS procedure with the VAR statement.
- Validate data by using the UNIVARIATE procedure with the VAR statement.

67

The MEANS Procedure

The MEANS procedure produces summary reports that display descriptive statistics.

General form of the MEANS procedure:

```
PROC MEANS DATA=SAS-data-set <statistics>;
      VAR variable(s);
RUN;
```

- The VAR statement specifies the analysis variables and their order in the results.
- The statistics to display can be specified in the PROC MEANS statement.

68

The MEANS Procedure

This PROC MEANS step shows default descriptive statistics for **Salary**.

```
proc means data=orion.nonsales;
   var Salary;
run;
```

The MEANS Procedure

Analysis Variable : Salary

N	Mean	Std Dev	Minimum	Maximum
234	43954.60	38354.77	2401.00	433800.00

Without the VAR statement, PROC MEANS analyzes all numeric variables in the data set.

69 p108d06

The MEANS Procedure

By default, the MEANS procedure creates a report with N (number of nonmissing values), MEAN, STDDEV, MIN, and MAX.

For validating data, the following descriptive statistics are beneficial:

- N, number of nonmissing values
- NMISS, number of missing values
- MIN
- MAX

70

The MEANS Procedure

The following PROC MEANS step shows whether there are any **Salary** values not in the range of 24000 through 500000.

```
proc means data=orion.nonsales n nmiss min max;
   var Salary;
run;
```

The MEANS Procedure

Analysis Variable : Salary

N	N Miss	Minimum	Maximum
234	1	2401.00	433800.00

71

p108d06

The UNIVARIATE Procedure

The UNIVARIATE procedure produces summary reports that display descriptive statistics.

General form of the UNIVARIATE procedure:

> **PROC UNIVARIATE DATA=***SAS-data-set***;**
> **VAR** *variable(s)***;**
> **RUN;**

The VAR statement specifies the analysis variables and their order in the results.

72

The UNIVARIATE Procedure

The following PROC UNIVARIATE step shows default descriptive statistics for **Salary**.

```
proc univariate data=orion.nonsales;
   var Salary;
run;
```

Without the VAR statement, SAS will analyze all numeric variables.

73 p108d06

The UNIVARIATE Procedure

The UNIVARIATE procedure can produce the following sections of output:

- Moments
- Basic Statistical Measures
- Tests for Locations
- Quantiles

- Extreme Observations
- Missing Values

For validating data, the Extreme Observations and Missing Values sections are beneficial.

74

The UNIVARIATE Procedure

Partial PROC UNIVARIATE Output

Extreme Observations

-----Lowest----		-----Highest----	
Value	Obs	Value	Obs
2401	20	163040	1
2650	13	194885	231
24025	25	207885	28
24100	19	268455	29
24390	228	433800	27

Missing Values

Missing Value	Count	-----Percent Of----- All Obs	Missing Obs
.	1	0.43	100.00

75

NEXTROBS=*n*

specifies the number of extreme observations that PROC UNIVARIATE lists in the table of extreme observations. The table lists the *n* lowest observations and the *n* highest observations. The default value is 5, and *n* can range between 0 and half the maximum number of observations. You can specify NEXTROBS=0 to suppress the table of extreme observations.

For example:

```
proc univariate data=orion.nonsales nextrobs=8;
   var Salary;
run;
```

Exercises

Level 1

4. Validating `orion.price_current` with the MEANS and UNIVARIATE Procedures

a. Retrieve the starter program **p108e04**.

b. Add a VAR statement to the PROC MEANS step to validate **`Unit_Cost_Price`**, **`Unit_Sales_Price`**, and **`Factor`**.

c. Add statistics to the PROC MEANS statement to create the following PROC MEANS report:

```
                              The MEANS Procedure

Variable            Label                         N         Minimum         Maximum
-----------------------------------------------------------------------------------
Unit_Cost_Price     Unit Cost Price             171       2.3000000     315.1500000
Unit_Sales_Price    Unit Sales Price            170       6.5000000         5730.00
Factor              Yearly increase in Price    171       0.0100000     100.0000000
-----------------------------------------------------------------------------------
```

The data in **`orion.price_current`** should meet the following requirements:

- **`Unit_Cost_Price`** must be in the numeric range of 1 – 400.
- **`Unit_Sales_Price`** must be in the numeric range of 3 – 800.
- **`Factor`** must be in the numeric range of 1 – 1.05.

What variables have invalid data? ______________________________

d. Add a PROC UNIVARIATE step with a VAR statement to validate **`Unit_Sales_Price`** and **`Factor`**.

e. Submit the PROC UNIVARIATE step and find the Extreme Observations output.

How many values of **`Unit_Sales_Price`** are over the maximum of 800? ______________

How many values of **`Factor`** are under the minimum of 1? ______________

How many values of **`Factor`** are over the maximum of 1.05? ______________

Level 2

5. Validating `orion.shoes_tracker` with the MEANS and UNIVARIATE Procedures

a. Write a PROC MEANS step with a VAR statement to validate **`Product_ID`** of **`orion.shoes_tracker`**.

b. Add the MIN, MAX, and RANGE statistics to the PROC MEANS statement.

c. Add **FW=15** to the PROC MEANS statement. The FW= option specifies the field width to display the statistics in printed or displayed output.

d. Add the following CLASS statement to group the data by **Supplier_Name**:

```
class Supplier_Name;
```

Documentation on the FW= option and the CLASS statement can be found in the SAS Help and Documentation from the Contents tab (**SAS Products** ⇨ **Base SAS** ⇨ **Base SAS 9.2 Procedures Guide** ⇨ **Procedures** ⇨ **The MEANS Procedure**).

e. Submit the program to create the following PROC MEANS report:

```
                         The MEANS Procedure

              Analysis Variable : Product_ID Product ID

                                  N
Supplier Name                   Obs        Minimum         Maximum            Range
-----------------------------------------------------------------------------------
3Top Sports                       7    22020030007   2202003001290    2179982971283

3op Sports                        2   220200300015    220200300116     101.00000000

Greenline Sports Ltd              1   220200300157    220200300157                0
-----------------------------------------------------------------------------------
```

Which **Supplier_Name** has invalid **Product_ID** values assuming **Product_ID** must have only twelve digits? ______________________________

f. Add a PROC UNIVARIATE step with a VAR statement to validate **Product_ID** of **orion.shoes_tracker**.

g. Submit the PROC UNIVARIATE step and find the Extreme Observations output.

How many values of **Product_ID** are too small? ______________________________

How many values of **Product_ID** are too large? ______________________________

Level 3

6. Selecting Only the Extreme Observations Output from the UNIVARIATE Procedure

a. Write a PROC UNIVARIATE step with a VAR statement to validate **Product_ID** of **orion.shoes_tracker**.

b. Before the PROC UNIVARIATE step, add the following ODS statement:

```
ods trace on;
```

c. After the PROC UNIVARIATE step add, the following ODS statement:

```
ods trace off;
```

d. Submit the program and notice the trace information in the SAS log.

What is the name of the last Output Added in the SAS log? ________________________

e. Add an ODS SELECT statement immediately before the PROC UNIVARIATE step to select only the Extreme Observation output object.

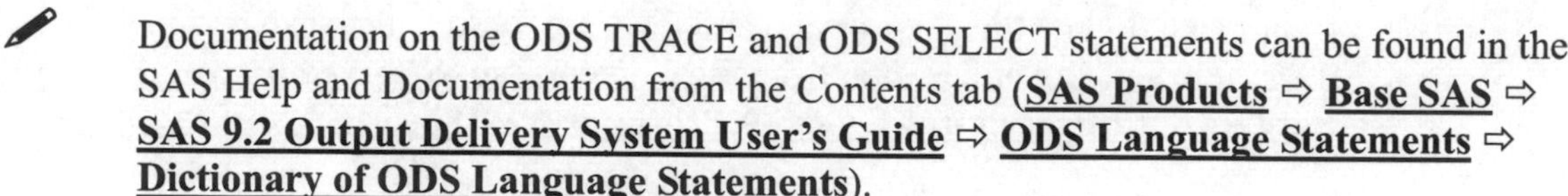

Documentation on the ODS TRACE and ODS SELECT statements can be found in the SAS Help and Documentation from the Contents tab (**SAS Products** ⇨ **Base SAS** ⇨ **SAS 9.2 Output Delivery System User's Guide** ⇨ **ODS Language Statements** ⇨ **Dictionary of ODS Language Statements**).

f. Submit the program to create the following PROC UNIVARIATE report:

```
                    The UNIVARIATE Procedure
                 Variable:  Product_ID  (Product ID)

                      Extreme Observations

        --------Lowest------          -------Highest------

              Value      Obs                Value      Obs

        2.20200E+10        4          2.2020E+11         6
        2.20200E+11        1          2.2020E+11         7
        2.20200E+11        2          2.2020E+11         9
        2.20200E+11        3          2.2020E+11        10
        2.20200E+11        5          2.2020E+12         8
```

8.5 Cleaning Invalid Data

Objectives

- Clean data by using the Viewtable window. (Self-Study)
- Clean data by using assignment statements in the DATA step.
- Clean data by using IF-THEN/ELSE statements in the DATA step.

79

Invalid Data to Clean

The **orion.nonsales** data set contains invalid data that needs to be cleaned.

	Employee_ID	First	Last	Gender	Salary	Job_Title	Country	Birth_Date	Hire_Date
1	120101	Patrick	Lu	M	163E3	Director	AU	18/08/1976	01/07/2003
2	120104	Kareen	Billington	F	46230	Administration Manager	au	11/05/1954	01/01/1981
3	120105	Liz	Povey	F	27110	Secretary I	AU	21/12/1974	01/05/1999
4	120106	John	Hornsey	M	.	Office Assistant II	AU	23/12/1944	01/01/1974
5	120107	Sherie	Sheedy	F	30475	Office Assistant III	AU	01/02/1978	21/01/1953
6	120108	Gladys	Gromek	F	27660	Warehouse Assistant II	AU	23/02/1984	01/08/2006
7	120108	Gabriele	Baker	F	26495	Warehouse Assistant I	AU	15/12/1986	01/10/2006
8	120110	Dennis	Entwisle	M	28615	Warehouse Assistant III	AU	20/11/1949	01/11/1979
9	120111	Ubaldo	Spillane	M	26895	Security Guard II	AU	23/07/1949	.
10	120112	Ellis	Glattback	F	2655[illegible]		AU	[illegible]	[illegible]
11	120113	Riu	Horsey	F	26870	Security Guard II	AU	10/05/1944	01/01/1974
12	120114	Jeannette	Buddery	G	31285	Security Manager	AU	08/02/1944	01/01/1974
13	120115	Hugh	Nichollas	M	2650	Service Assistant I	AU	08/05/1984	01/08/2005
14	.	Austen	Ralston	M	29250	Service Assistant II	AU	13/06/1959	01/02/1980
15	120117	Bill	Mccleary	M	31670	Cabinet Maker III	AU	11/09/1964	01/04/1986
16	[illegible]	[illegible]	[illegible]	[illegible]	[illegible]	[illegible]	[illegible]	[illegible]	[illegible]

After you validate the data and find the invalid data, the correct data values are needed.

80

Variable	Obs	Invalid Value	Correct Value
Employee_ID	7	120108	120109
	14	.	120116
Gender	12	G	F
	101		F
Job_Title	10		Security Guard I
Country	2, 84, 87, 125, 197, and 200	au or us	AU or US
Salary	4	.	26960
	13	2650	26500
	20	2401	24015
Hire_Date	5	21/01/1953	21/01/1995
	9	.	01/11/1978
	214	01/01/1968	01/01/1998

81

Interactively Cleaning Data (Self-Study)

If you are using the SAS windowing environment, the Viewtable window can be used to interactively clean data.

Use the Viewtable window to interactively clean the following five observations:

Variable	Obs	Invalid Value	Correct Value
Employee_ID	7	120108	120109
	14	.	120116
Gender	12	G	F
	101		F
Job_Title	10		Security Guard I

82

For z/OS (OS/390), the FSEDIT window is used to clean data. If FSEDIT is not available, the data can be cleaned programmatically instead of interactively. If you use batch mode, cleaning the data interactively is not an option.

Interactively Cleaning Data (Self-Study)

The Viewtable window enables you to browse, edit, or create SAS data sets.

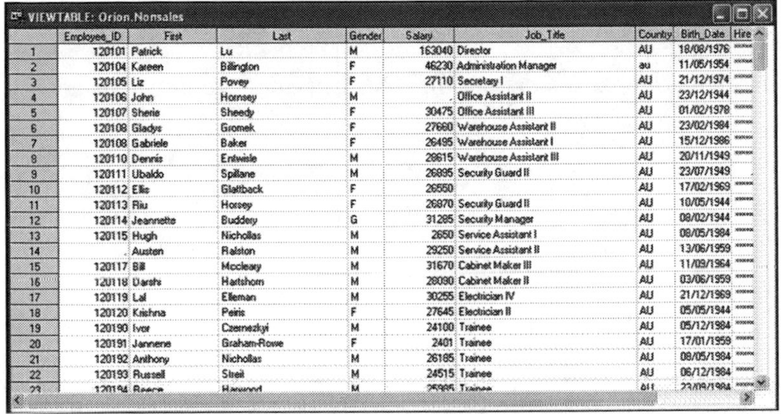

VIEWTABLE: Orion.Nonsales

	Employee_ID	First	Last	Gender	Salary	Job_Title	Country	Birth_Date	Hire
1	120101	Patrick	Lu	M	163040	Director	AU	18/08/1976	*****
2	120104	Kareen	Billington	F	46230	Administration Manager	au	11/05/1954	*****
3	120105	Liz	Povey	F	27110	Secretary I	AU	21/12/1974	*****
4	120106	John	Hornsey	M	.	Office Assistant II	AU	23/12/1944	*****
5	120107	Sherie	Sheedy	F	30475	Office Assistant III	AU	01/02/1978	*****
6	120108	Gladys	Gromek	F	27660	Warehouse Assistant II	AU	23/02/1984	*****
7	120108	Gabriele	Baker	F	26495	Warehouse Assistant I	AU	15/12/1986	*****
8	120110	Dennis	Entwisle	M	28615	Warehouse Assistant III	AU	20/11/1949	*****
9	120111	Ubaldo	Spillane	M	26895	Security Guard II	AU	23/07/1949	.
10	120112	Ellis	Glattback	F	26550		AU	17/02/1969	*****
11	120113	Riu	Horsey	F	26870	Security Guard II	AU	10/05/1944	*****
12	120114	Jeannette	Buddery	G	31285	Security Manager	AU	08/02/1944	*****
13	120115	Hugh	Nichollas	M	2650	Service Assistant I	AU	08/05/1984	*****
14	.	Austen	Ralston	M	29250	Service Assistant II	AU	13/06/1959	*****
15	120117	Bill	Mccleary	M	31670	Cabinet Maker III	AU	11/09/1964	*****
16	120118	Darshi	Hartshorn	M	28090	Cabinet Maker II	AU	03/06/1959	*****
17	120119	Lal	Elleman	M	30255	Electrician IV	AU	21/12/1969	*****
18	120120	Krishna	Peiris	F	27645	Electrician II	AU	05/05/1944	*****
19	120190	Ivor	Czernezkyi	M	24100	Trainee	AU	05/12/1984	*****
20	120191	Jannene	Graham-Rowe	F	2401	Trainee	AU	17/01/1959	*****
21	120192	Anthony	Nichollas	M	26185	Trainee	AU	08/05/1984	*****
22	120193	Russell	Streit	M	24515	Trainee	AU	06/12/1984	*****
23	120194	Reece	Harwood	M	25985	Trainee	AU	23/09/1984	*****

83

Using the Viewtable Window to Clean Data – Windows (Self-Study)

1. Select the **Explorer** tab on the SAS window bar to activate the SAS Explorer window or select **View** ⇨ **Contents Only**.

2. Double-click **Libraries** to show all available libraries.

3. Double-click on the **Orion** library to show all members of that library.

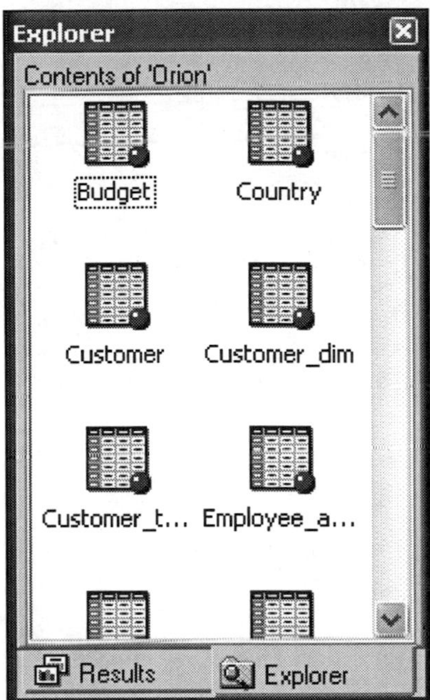

4. Double-click on the **Nonsales** data set to open the data set in the Viewtable window.

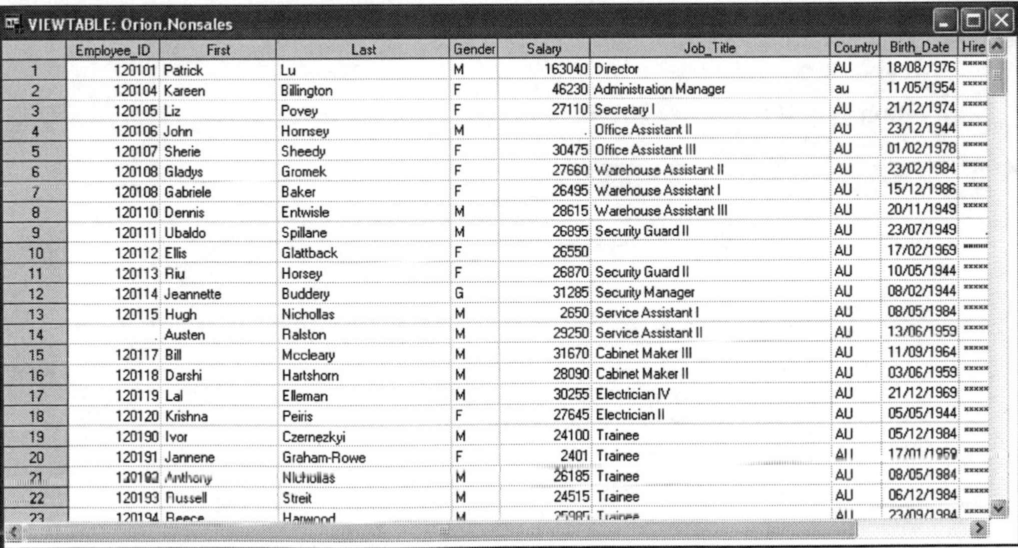

VIEWTABLE: Orion.Nonsales

	Employee_ID	First	Last	Gender	Salary	Job_Title	Country	Birth_Date	Hire
1	120101	Patrick	Lu	M	163040	Director	AU	18/08/1976	*****
2	120104	Kareen	Billington	F	46230	Administration Manager	au	11/05/1954	*****
3	120105	Liz	Povey	F	27110	Secretary I	AU	21/12/1974	*****
4	120106	John	Hornsey	M	.	Office Assistant II	AU	23/12/1944	*****
5	120107	Sherie	Sheedy	F	30475	Office Assistant III	AU	01/02/1978	*****
6	120108	Gladys	Gromek	F	27660	Warehouse Assistant II	AU	23/02/1984	*****
7	120108	Gabriele	Baker	F	26495	Warehouse Assistant I	AU	15/12/1986	*****
8	120110	Dennis	Entwisle	M	28615	Warehouse Assistant III	AU	20/11/1949	*****
9	120111	Ubaldo	Spillane	M	26895	Security Guard II	AU	23/07/1949	.
10	120112	Ellis	Glattback	F	26550		AU	17/02/1969	*****
11	120113	Riu	Horsey	F	26870	Security Guard II	AU	10/05/1944	*****
12	120114	Jeannette	Buddery	G	31285	Security Manager	AU	08/02/1944	*****
13	120115	Hugh	Nichollas	M	2650	Service Assistant I	AU	08/05/1984	*****
14	.	Austen	Ralston	M	29250	Service Assistant II	AU	13/06/1959	*****
15	120117	Bill	Mccleary	M	31670	Cabinet Maker III	AU	11/09/1964	*****
16	120118	Darshi	Hartshorn	M	28090	Cabinet Maker II	AU	03/06/1959	*****
17	120119	Lal	Elleman	M	30255	Electrician IV	AU	21/12/1969	*****
18	120120	Krishna	Peiris	F	27645	Electrician II	AU	05/05/1944	*****
19	120190	Ivor	Czernezkyi	M	24100	Trainee	AU	05/12/1984	*****
20	120191	Jannene	Graham-Rowe	F	2401	Trainee	AU	17/01/1959	*****
21	120192	Anthony	Nichollas	M	26185	Trainee	AU	08/05/1984	*****
22	120193	Russell	Streit	M	24515	Trainee	AU	06/12/1984	*****
23	120194	Reece	Harwood	M	25985	Trainee	AU	23/09/1984	*****

5. Select **Edit Mode** from the Edit menu.

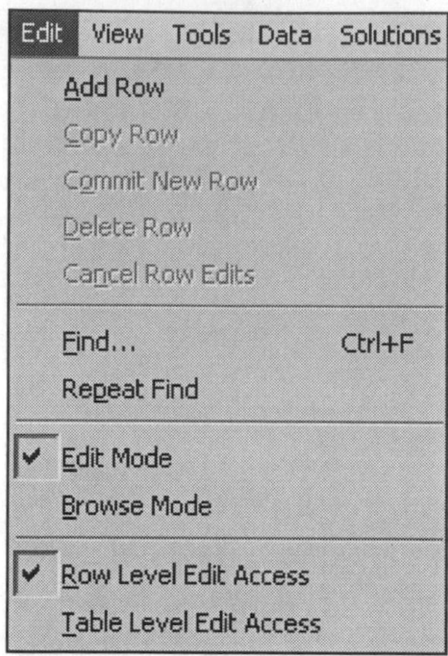

6. Go to the following observations and make the desired changes:

Obs	Variable	Correct Value
7	Employee_ID	120109
12	Gender	F
14	Employee_ID	120116
101	Gender	F

7. Select [X] to close the Viewtable window. The changes are saved to the data set.

Using the Viewtable Window to Clean Data – UNIX (Self-Study)

1. Select **View** ⇨ **Contents Only** to activate the SAS Explorer.

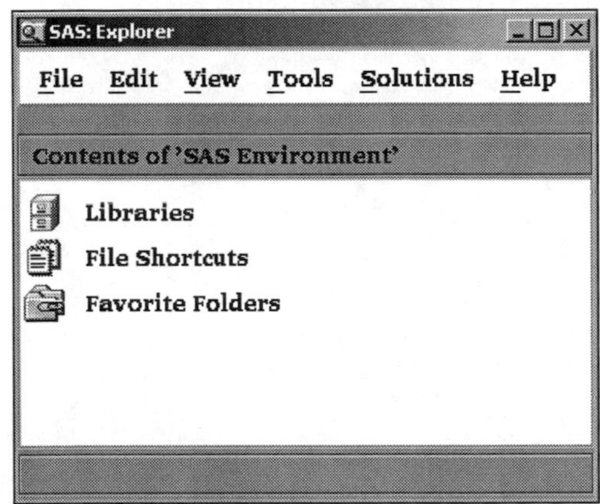

2. Double-click **Libraries** to show all available libraries.

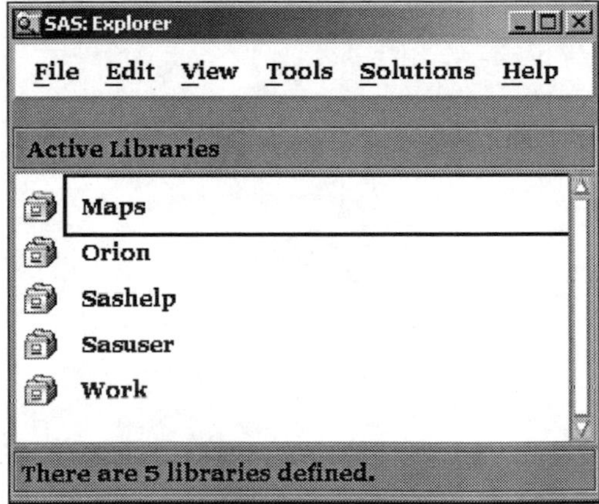

3. Double-click on the **Orion** library to show all members of that library.

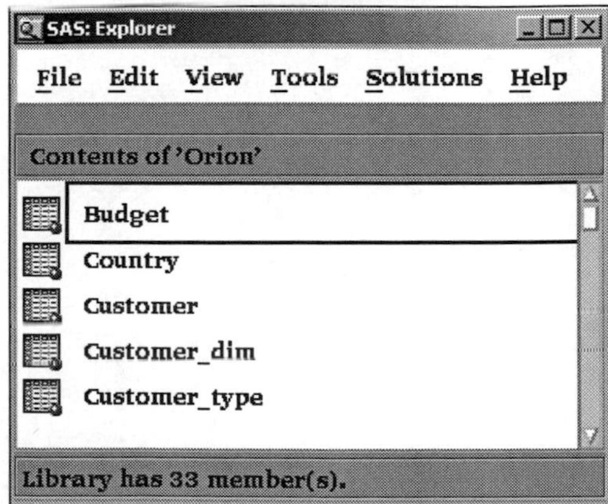

4. Double-click on the **Nonsales** data set to open the data set in the Viewtable window.

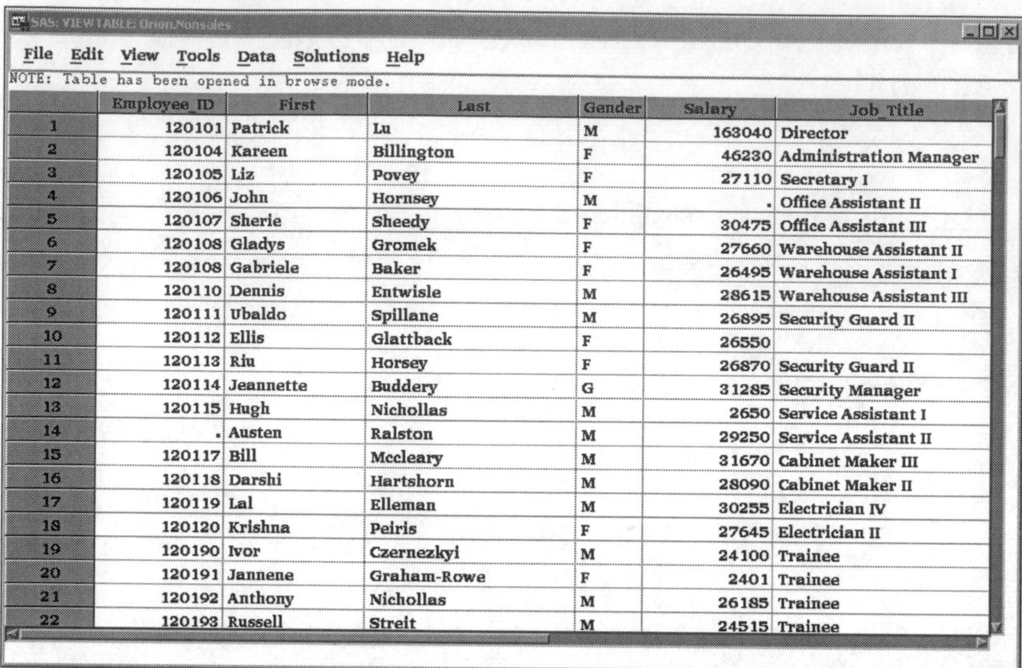

	Employee_ID	First	Last	Gender	Salary	Job_Title
1	120101	Patrick	Lu	M	163040	Director
2	120104	Kareen	Billington	F	46230	Administration Manager
3	120105	Liz	Povey	F	27110	Secretary I
4	120106	John	Hornsey	M	.	Office Assistant II
5	120107	Sherie	Sheedy	F	30475	Office Assistant III
6	120108	Gladys	Gromek	F	27660	Warehouse Assistant II
7	120108	Gabriele	Baker	F	26495	Warehouse Assistant I
8	120110	Dennis	Entwisle	M	28615	Warehouse Assistant III
9	120111	Ubaldo	Spillane	M	26895	Security Guard II
10	120112	Ellis	Glattback	F	26550	
11	120113	Riu	Horsey	F	26870	Security Guard II
12	120114	Jeannette	Buddery	G	31285	Security Manager
13	120115	Hugh	Nichollas	M	2650	Service Assistant I
14	.	Austen	Ralston	M	29250	Service Assistant II
15	120117	Bill	Mccleary	M	31670	Cabinet Maker III
16	120118	Darshi	Hartshorn	M	28090	Cabinet Maker II
17	120119	Lal	Elleman	M	30255	Electrician IV
18	120120	Krishna	Peiris	F	27645	Electrician II
19	120190	Ivor	Czernezkyi	M	24100	Trainee
20	120191	Jannene	Graham-Rowe	F	2401	Trainee
21	120192	Anthony	Nichollas	M	26185	Trainee
22	120193	Russell	Streit	M	24515	Trainee

5. Select **Edit Mode** from the Edit menu.

6. Go to the following observations and make the desired changes:

Obs	Variable	Correct Value
7	`Employee_ID`	120109
12	`Gender`	F
14	`Employee_ID`	120116
101	`Gender`	F

7. Select [X] to close the Viewtable window. The changes are saved to the data set.

Using the FSEDIT Window to Clean Data – z/OS (OS/390) (Self-Study)

1. Type **`fsedit orion.nonsales`** on the command line and press ENTER to activate the FSEDIT window.

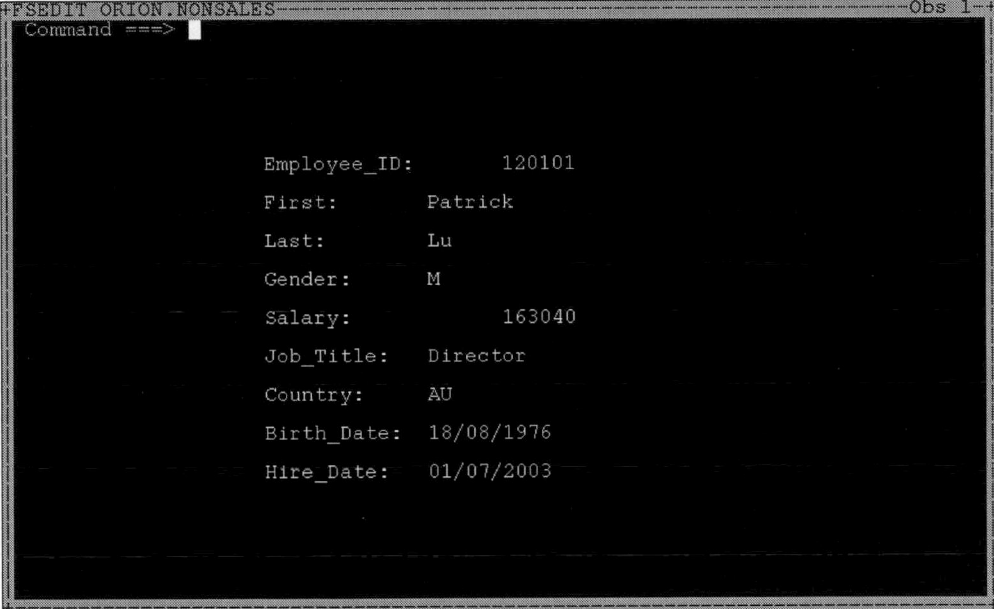

2. Go to the following observations and make the desired changes:

Obs	Variable	Correct Value
7	**`Employee_ID`**	120109
12	**`Gender`**	F
14	**`Employee_ID`**	120116
101	**`Gender`**	F

   Type the observation number on the command line and press ENTER to go to an observation.

3. Type **`end`** on the command line and press ENTER to close the FSEDIT window. The changes are saved to the data set.

8.06 Quiz (Self-Study)

- Open the VIEWTABLE window for `orion.nonsales`.
- Use the VIEWTABLE window to interactively clean the following observation:

Variable	Obs	Invalid Value	Correct Value
Job_Title	10		Security Guard I

86

Programmatically Cleaning Data

The DATA step can be used to programmatically clean the invalid data.

Use the DATA step to clean the following observations:

Variable	Obs	Invalid Value	Correct Value
`Country`	2, 84, 87, 125, 197, and 200	au or us	AU or US
`Salary`	4	.	26960
	13	2650	26500
	20	2401	24015
`Hire_Date`	5	21/01/1953	21/01/1995
	9	.	01/11/1978
	214	01/01/1968	01/01/1998

89

The Assignment Statement

The *assignment statement* evaluates an expression and assigns the resulting value to a variable.

General form of the assignment statement:

```
variable = expression;
```

- *variable* names an existing or new variable.
- *expression* is a sequence of operands and operators that form a set of instructions that produce a value.

90

Assignment statements evaluate the expression on the right side of the equal sign and store the result in the variable that is specified on the left side of the equal sign.

The Assignment Statement Expression

Operands are

- character constants
- numeric constants
- date constants
- character variables
- numeric variables.

Operators are

- symbols that represent an arithmetic calculation
- SAS functions.

91

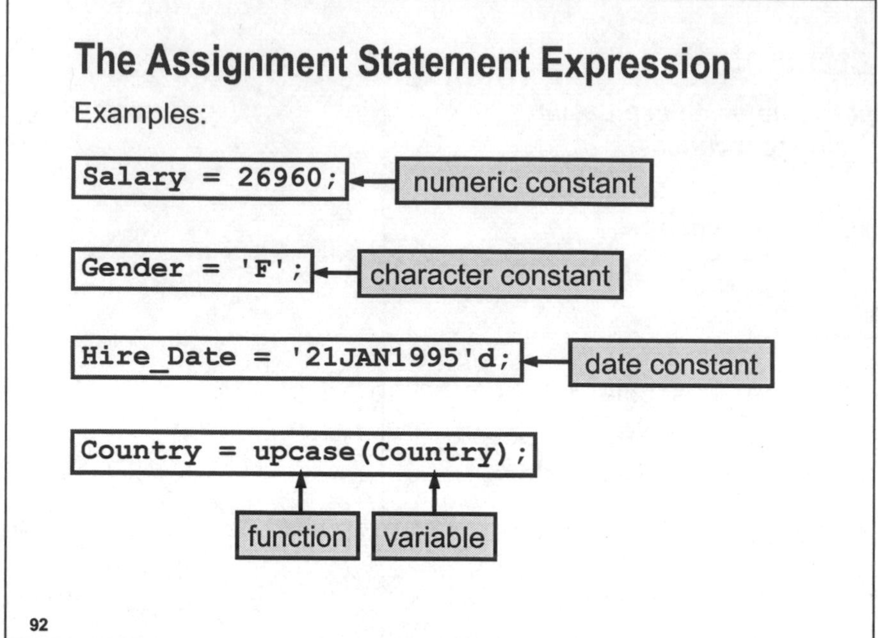
The Assignment Statement Expression
Examples:
Salary = 26960;
numeric constant
Gender = 'F';
character constant
Hire_Date = '21JAN1995'd;
date constant
Country = upcase(Country);
function
variable
92

SAS Functions

A SAS *function* is a routine that returns a value that is determined from specified arguments.

The *UPCASE function* converts all letters in an argument to uppercase.

General form of the UPCASE function:

UPCASE(*argument***)**

The *argument* specifies any SAS character expression.

93

The Assignment Statement

All the values of **Country** in the data set **orion.nonsales** need to be uppercase.

```
data work.clean;
   set orion.nonsales;
   Country=upcase(Country);
run;
```

PDV

Employee_ID		Job_Title	Country	
120101	...	Director	AU	...

94

p108d07

...

The Assignment Statement

All the values of **Country** in the data set **orion.nonsales** need to be uppercase.

```
data work.clean;
   set orion.nonsales;
   Country=upcase(Country);
run;
```

PDV

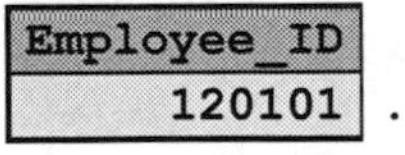

...
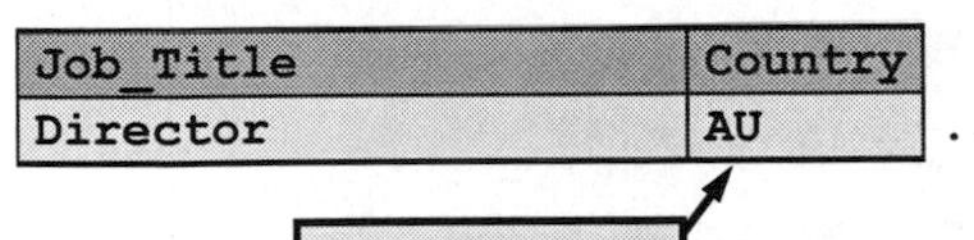

...

95

...

The Assignment Statement

All the values of **`Country`** in the data set **`orion.nonsales`** need to be uppercase.

```
data work.clean;
   set orion.nonsales;
   Country=upcase(Country);
run;
```

PDV

Employee_ID
120104

...

Job_Title	Country
Administration Manager	au

...

96 ...

The Assignment Statement

All the values of **`Country`** in the data set **`orion.nonsales`** need to be uppercase.

```
data work.clean;
   set orion.nonsales;
   Country=upcase(Country);
run;
```

PDV

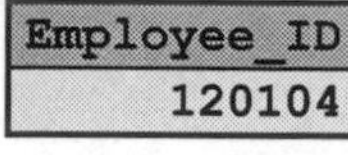

Employee_ID
120104

...

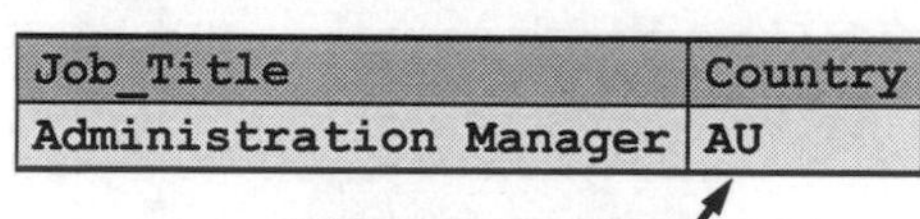

Job_Title	Country
Administration Manager	AU

...

`upcase(au)`

97

The Assignment Statement

```
proc print data=work.clean;
   var Employee_ID Job_Title Country;
run;
```

Partial PROC PRINT Output

```
            Employee_
    Obs         ID        Job_Title                      Country

     84     120695        Warehouse Assistant II           AU
     85     120696        Warehouse Assistant I            AU
     86     120697        Warehouse Assistant IV           AU
     87     120698        Warehouse Assistant I            AU
     88     120710        Business Analyst II              US
     89     120711        Business Analyst III             US
     90     120712        Marketing Manager                US
     91     120713        Marketing Assistant III          US
```

The assignment statement executed for every observation regardless of whether the value needed to be uppercased or not.

98

Programmatically Cleaning Data

The DATA step can be used to programmatically clean the invalid data.

Use the DATA step to clean the following observations:

Variable	Obs	Invalid Value	Correct Value
Country			
Salary	4	.	26960
	13	2650	26500
	20		
Hire_Date	5		
	9	.	01/11/1978
	214	01/01/1968	01/01/1998

The assignment statement was applied to all observations.

The assignment statement needs to be applied to specific observations.

99

8.07 Quiz

Which variable can be used to specifically identify the observations with invalid salary values?

```
Obs  Employee_ID Gender Salary Job_Title                  Country Birth_Date  Hire_Date

  2       120104   F     46230 Administration Manager       au    11/05/1954 01/01/1981
  4       120106   M         . Office Assistant II          AU    23/12/1944 01/01/1974
  5       120107   F     30475 Office Assistant III         AU    01/02/1978 21/01/1953
  9       120111   M     26895 Security Guard II            AU    23/07/1949          .
 10       120112   F     26550                              AU    17/02/1969 01/07/1990
 12       120114   G     31285 Security Manager             AU    08/02/1944 01/01/1974
 13       120115   M      2650 Service Assistant I          AU    08/05/1984 01/08/2005
 14            .   M     29250 Service Assistant II         AU    13/06/1959 01/02/1980
 20       120191   F      2401 Trainee                      AU    17/01/1959 01/01/2003
 84       120695   M     28180 Warehouse Assistant II       au    13/07/1964 01/07/1989
 87       120698   M     26160 Warehouse Assistant I        au    17/05/1954 01/08/1976
101       120723         33950 Corp. Comm. Specialist II    US    10/08/1949 01/01/1974
125       120747   F     43590 Financial Controller I       us    20/06/1974 01/08/1995
197       120994   F     31645 Office Administrator I       us    16/06/1974 01/11/1994
200       120997   F     27420 Shipping Administrator I     us    21/11/1974 01/09/1996
214       121011   M     25735 Service Assistant I          US    11/03/1944 01/01/1968
```

101

Programmatically Cleaning Data

The DATA step can be used to programmatically clean the invalid data.

Use the DATA step to clean the following observations:

Variable	Obs	Invalid Value	Correct Value
Country	2, 84, 87, 125, 197, and 200	au or us	AU or US
Salary	4	.	26960
	13	2650	26500
	20	2401	24015
Hire_Date	5	21/01/1953	21/01/1995
	9	.	01/11/1978
	214	01/01/1968	01/01/1998

103

IF-THEN Statements

The *IF-THEN statement* executes a SAS statement for observations that meet specific conditions.

General form of the IF-THEN statement:

IF *expression* **THEN** *statement* **;**

- *expression* is a sequence of operands and operators that form a set of instructions that define a condition for selecting observations.
- *statement* is any executable statement such as the assignment statement.

104

If the condition in the IF clause is met, the IF-THEN statement executes a SAS statement for that observation.

IF-THEN Statements

All the values of **Salary** must be in the range of 24000 – 500000.

```
data work.clean;
   set orion.nonsales;
   if Employee_ID=120106 then Salary=26960;
   if Employee_ID=120115 then Salary=26500;
   if Employee_ID=120191 then Salary=24015;
run;
```

PDV

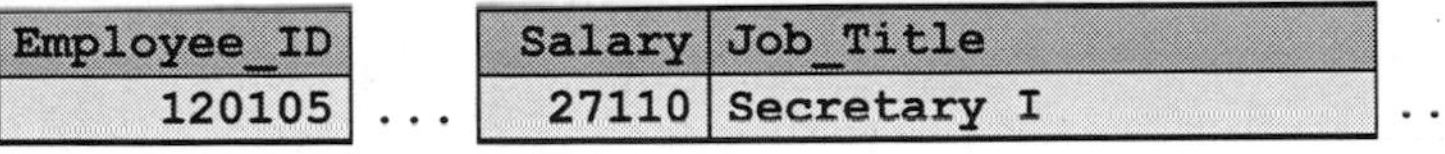

Employee_ID	...	Salary	Job_Title	...
120105	...	27110	Secretary I	...

105 p108d07

IF-THEN Statements

All the values of **Salary** must be in the range of 24000 – 500000.

```
data work.clean;
   set orion.nonsales;
   if Employee_ID=120106 then Salary=26960;
   if Employee_ID=120115 then Salary=26500;
   if Employee_ID=120191 then Salary=24015;
run;
```

FALSE

PDV

Employee_ID		Salary	Job_Title	
120105	...	27110	Secretary I	...

106 ...

IF-THEN Statements

All the values of **Salary** must be in the range of 24000 – 500000.

```
data work.clean;
   set orion.nonsales;
   if Employee_ID=120106 then Salary=26960;
   if Employee_ID=120115 then Salary=26500;
   if Employee_ID=120191 then Salary=24015;
run;
```

FALSE

PDV

Employee_ID		Salary	Job_Title	
120105	...	27110	Secretary I	...

107 ...

IF-THEN Statements

All the values of **Salary** must be in the range of 24000 – 500000.

FALSE

```
data work.clean;
   set orion.nonsales;
   if Employee_ID=120106 then Salary=26960;
   if Employee_ID=120115 then Salary=26500;
   if Employee_ID=120191 then Salary=24015;
run;
```

PDV

Employee_ID
120105

...

Salary	Job_Title
27110	Secretary I

...

108 ...

IF-THEN Statements

All the values of **Salary** must be in the range of 24000 – 500000.

```
data work.clean;
   set orion.nonsales;
   if Employee_ID=120106 then Salary=26960;
   if Employee_ID=120115 then Salary=26500;
   if Employee_ID=120191 then Salary=24015;
run;
```

PDV

Employee_ID
120106

...

Salary	Job_Title
.	Office Assistant II

...

109 ...

IF-THEN Statements

All the values of **Salary** must be in the range of 24000 – 500000.

TRUE

```
data work.clean;
   set orion.nonsales;
   if Employee_ID=120106 then Salary=26960;
   if Employee_ID=120115 then Salary=26500;
   if Employee_ID=120191 then Salary=24015;
run;
```

PDV

Employee_ID		Salary	Job_Title	
120106	...	26960	Office Assistant II	...

110 ...

IF-THEN Statements

All the values of **Salary** must be in the range of 24000 – 500000.

FALSE

```
data work.clean;
   set orion.nonsales;
   if Employee_ID=120106 then Salary=26960;
   if Employee_ID=120115 then Salary=26500;
   if Employee_ID=120191 then Salary=24015;
run;
```

PDV

Employee_ID		Salary	Job_Title	
120106	...	26960	Office Assistant II	...

111 ...

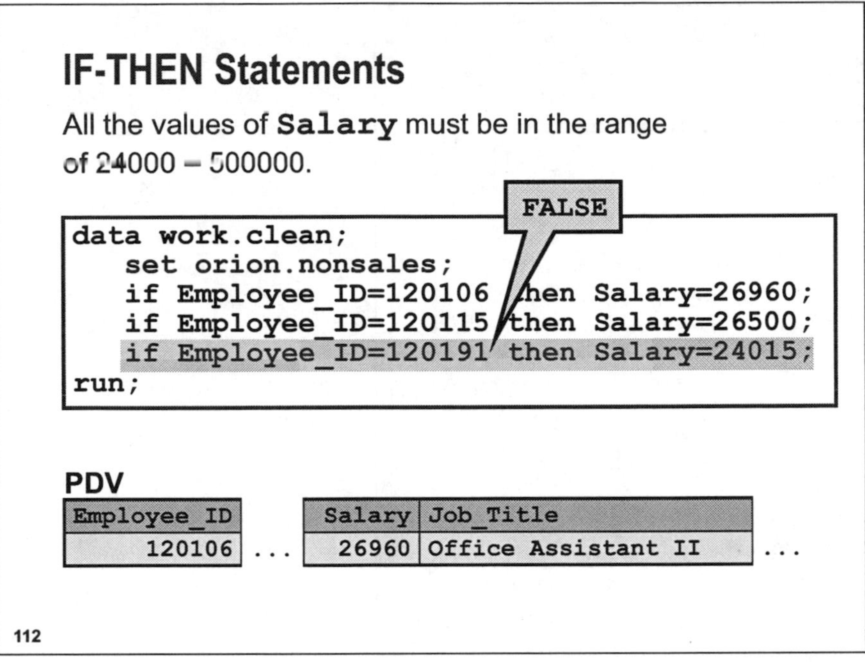
IF-THEN Statements
All the values of Salary must be in the range of 24000 – 500000.
FALSE
data work.clean;
set orion.nonsales;
if Employee_ID=120106 then Salary=26960;
if Employee_ID=120115 then Salary=26500;
if Employee_ID=120191 then Salary=24015;
run;
PDV
Employee_ID
120106
...
Salary
Job_Title
26960
Office Assistant II
...
112

IF-THEN Statements

When an IF expression is TRUE in this IF-THEN statement series, there is no reason to check the remaining IF-THEN statements when checking **`Employee_ID`**.

TRUE

```
data work.clean;
   set orion.nonsales;
   if Employee_ID=120106 then Salary=26960;
   if Employee_ID=120115 then Salary=26500;
   if Employee_ID=120191 then Salary=24015;
run;
```

The word ELSE can be placed before the word IF, causing SAS to execute conditional statements until it encounters the first true statement.

113

When a series of IF expressions represent mutually exclusive events, then it is not necessary to check all expressions when one is found to be true.

IF-THEN/ELSE Statements

All the values of **Salary** must be in the range of 24000 – 500000.

```
data work.clean;
  set orion.nonsales;
  if Employee_ID=120106 then Salary=26960;
  else if Employee_ID=120115 then Salary=26500;
  else if Employee_ID=120191 then Salary=24015;
run;
```

PDV

Employee_ID	...	Salary	Job_Title	...
120106	...	.	Office Assistant II	...

114 p108d07

IF-THEN/ELSE Statements

All the values of **Salary** must be in the range of 24000 – 500000.


```
data work.clean;
  set orion.nonsales;
  if Employee_ID=120106 then Salary=26960;
  else if Employee_ID=120115 then Salary=26500;
  else if Employee_ID=120191 then Salary=24015;
run;
```

PDV

Employee_ID	...	Salary	Job_Title	...
120106	...	26960	Office Assistant II	...

115

Programmatically Cleaning Data

The DATA step can be used to programmatically clean the invalid data.

Use the DATA step to clean the following observations:

Variable	Obs	Invalid Value	Correct Value
Country	2, 84, 87, 125, 197, and 200	au or us	AU or US
Salary	4	.	26960
	13	2650	26500
	20	2401	24015
Hire_Date	5	21/01/1953	21/01/1995
	9	.	01/11/1978
	214	01/01/1968	01/01/1998

116

IF-THEN/ELSE Statements

All the values of **Hire_Date** must have a value of 01/01/1974 or later.

```
data work.clean;
  set orion.nonsales;
  Country=upcase(Country);
  if Employee_ID=120106 then Salary=26960;
  else if Employee_ID=120115 then Salary=26500;
  else if Employee_ID=120191 then Salary=24015;
  else if Employee_ID=120107 then
          Hire_Date='21JAN1995'd;
  else if Employee_ID=120111 then
          Hire_Date='01NOV1978'd;
  else if Employee_ID=121011 then
          Hire_Date='01JAN1998'd;
run;
```

117 p108d07

Exercises

Level 1

7. Cleaning Data from `orion.qtr2_2007`

a. Retrieve the starter program **p108e07**.

b. Add two conditional statements to the DATA step to correct the following invalid data:

Variable	Obs	Invalid Value	Correct Value	Reference Variable
`Delivery_Date`	5	`12APR2007`	`12MAY2007`	**`Order_ID=1242012259`**
`Order_Date`	22	`26JUL2007`	`26JUN2007`	**`Order_ID=1242449327`**

c. Submit the program. Verify that zero observations were returned from the PROC PRINT step.

Level 2

8. Cleaning Data from `orion.price_current`

a. Retrieve the starter program **p108e08**.

b. Add a DATA step prior to the PROC steps to read **`orion.price_current`** to create **`Work.price_current`**. In the DATA step, include two conditional IF-THEN statements to correct the following invalid data:

Variable	Obs	Invalid Value	Correct Value	Reference Variable
`Unit_Sales_Price`	41	`5730`	`57.30`	**`Product_ID=220200200022`**
`Unit_Sales_Price`	103	`.`	`41.20`	**`Product_ID=240200100056`**

c. Submit the program. Verify that **`Unit_Sales_Price`** is in the numeric range of 3 – 800.

Level 3

9. Cleaning Data from orion.shoes_tracker

a. Retrieve the starter program **p108e09**.

b. Add a DATA step prior to the PROC steps to read **orion.shoes_tracker** to create **Work.shoes_tracker**. In the DATA step, include statements to correct the following invalid data:

Variable	Obs	Invalid Value	Correct Value	Reference Variable
Supplier_Country		*mixed case*	*upper case*	
Supplier_Country	5	UT	US	Supplier_Country='UT'
Product_Category	2		Shoes	Product_Category=' '
Supplier_ID	1	.	2963	Supplier_ID=.
Supplier_Name	3, 7	3op Sports	3Top Sports	Supplier_Name = '3op Sports'
Product_ID	4	22020030007	220200300079	_N_=4
Product_ID	8	2202003001290	220200300129	_N_=8
Product_Name		*not proper case*	*proper case*	
Supplier_Name	9	3Top Sports	Greenline Sports Ltd	Supplier_ID=14682 and Supplier_Name = '3Top Sports'

c. Submit the program. Verify that the data requirements are all met.

- **Product_Category** must not be missing.
- **Supplier_Country** must have a value of GB or US.
- **Supplier_Name** must be 3Top Sports or Greenline Sports Ltd.
- **Supplier_ID** must be 2963 or 14682.
- A **Supplier_Name** of 3Top Sports must have a **Supplier_ID** of 2963.
- A **Supplier_Name** of Greenline Sports Ltd must have a **Supplier_ID** of 14682.
- **Product_ID** must have only 12 digits.

8.6 Chapter Review

Chapter Review

1. What procedures can be used to detect invalid data?
2. What happens when SAS encounters a data error?
3. Why would you need a SAS date constant?
4. How can you clean invalid data?
5. What symbol is required in an assignment statement?
6. Why would you use IF-THEN/ELSE statements instead of IF-THEN statements?

120

(1) PRINT
FREQ
MEANS
UNIVARIATE

8.7 Solutions

Solutions to Exercises

1. **Validating `orion.shoes_tracker` with the PRINT and FREQ Procedures**

   a. Retrieve the starter program.

   b. Add a WHERE statement to the PROC PRINT step.

```
proc print data=orion.shoes_tracker;
   where Product_Category=' ' or
         Supplier_Country not in ('GB','US');
run;
```

   c. Add a VAR statement.

```
proc print data=orion.shoes_tracker;
   where Product_Category=' ' or
         Supplier_Country not in ('GB','US');
   var Product_Category Supplier_Name Supplier_Country Supplier_ID;
run;
```

   How many observations have missing **`Product_Category`**? **One (observation 2)**

   How many observations have invalid values of **`Supplier_Country`**? **Three (observations 1, 5, and 10)**

   d. Add a PROC FREQ step with a TABLES statement.

```
proc freq data=orion.shoes_tracker nlevels;
   tables Supplier_Name Supplier_ID;
run;
```

   What invalid data exists for **`Supplier_Name`** and **`Supplier_ID`**?

   - **two invalid values for `Supplier_Name` (`3op Sports`)**
   - **one missing value for `Supplier_ID`**

2. **Validating `orion.qtr2_2007` with the PRINT and FREQ Procedures**

   a. Write a PROC PRINT step with a WHERE statement.

```
proc print data=orion.qtr2_2007;
   where Order_Date>Delivery_Date or
         Order_Date<'01APR2007'd or
         Order_Date>'30JUN2007'd;
run;
```

   b. Submit the program.

   How many observations have **`Delivery_Date`** values occurring before **`Order_Date`** values? **One (observation 5)**

   How many observations have **`Order_Date`** values out of the range of April 1, 2007 – June 30, 2007? **One (observation 22)**

c. Add a PROC FREQ step with a TABLES statement.

```
proc freq data=orion.qtr2_2007 nlevels;
   tables Order_ID Order_Type;
run;
```

d. Submit the PROC FREQ step.

What invalid data exists for `Order_ID` and `Order_Type`?

- **two missing values for `Order_ID`**
- **one value of 0 for `Order_Type`**
- **one value of 4 for `Order_Type`**

3. Using the PROPCASE Function, Two-Way Frequency Table, and MISSING Option

a. Write a PROC PRINT step with a WHERE statement.

```
proc print data=orion.shoes_tracker;
   where propcase(Product_Name) ne Product_Name;
run;
```

b. Add a VAR statement.

```
proc print data=orion.shoes_tracker;
   where propcase(Product_Name) ne Product_Name;
   var Product_ID Product_Name;
run;
```

c. Add a PROC FREQ step with a TABLES statement.

```
proc freq data=orion.shoes_tracker;
   tables Supplier_Name*Supplier_ID / missing;
run;
```

What invalid data exists for `Supplier_Name` and `Supplier_ID`?

- **two invalid values for `Supplier_Name` (`3op Sports` should be `3Top Sports`)**
- **one missing value for `Supplier_ID` (`.` should be `2963`)**
- **one wrong value for `Supplier_ID` (`14682` should be `2963`)**

4. Validating `orion.price_current` with the MEANS and UNIVARIATE Procedures

a. Retrieve the starter program.

b. Add a VAR statement to the PROC MEANS step.

```
proc means data=orion.price_current;
   var Unit_Cost_Price Unit_Sales_Price Factor;
run;
```

c. Add statistics to the PROC MEANS statement.

```
proc means data=orion.price_current n min max;
   var Unit_Cost_Price Unit_Sales_Price Factor;
run;
```

What variables have invalid data?

- **The maximum value of Unit_Sales_Price is out of range and one value of Unit_Sales_Price is missing.**
- **The minimum and maximum values of Factor are out of range.**

d. Add a PROC UNIVARIATE step with a VAR statement.

```
proc univariate data=orion.price_current;
   var Unit_Sales_Price Factor;
run;
```

e. Find the Extreme Observations output.

How many values of **Unit_Sales_Price** are over the maximum of 800? **One (5730)**

How many values of **Factor** are under the minimum of 1? **One (0.01)**

How many values of **Factor** are over the maximum of 1.05? **Two (10.20 and 100.00)**

5. Validating orion.shoes_tracker with the MEANS and UNIVARIATE Procedures

a. Write a PROC MEANS step with a VAR statement.

```
proc means data=orion.shoes_tracker;
   var Product_ID;
run;
```

b. Add the MIN, MAX, and RANGE statistics to the PROC MEANS statement.

```
proc means data=orion.shoes_tracker min max range;
   var Product_ID;
run;
```

c. Add FW=15 to the PROC MEANS statement.

```
proc means data=orion.shoes_tracker min max range fw=15;
   var Product_ID;
run;
```

d. Add the CLASS statement.

```
proc means data=orion.shoes_tracker min max range fw=15;
   var Product_ID;
   class Supplier_Name;
run;
```

e. Submit the program.

Which **Supplier_Name** has invalid **Product_ID** values assuming **Product_ID** must have only twelve digits? **3Top Sports**

f. Add a PROC UNIVARIATE step with a VAR statement.

```
proc univariate data=orion.shoes_tracker;
   var Product_ID;
run;
```

g. Submit the PROC UNIVARIATE step.

How many values of **Product_ID** are too small? **One (2.20200E+10)**

How many values of **Product_ID** are too large? **One (2.2020E+12)**

6. Selecting Only the Extreme Observations Output from the UNIVARIATE Procedure

a. Write a PROC UNIVARIATE step with a VAR statement.

```
proc univariate data=orion.shoes_tracker;
   var Product_ID;
run;
```

b. Before the PROC UNIVARIATE step, add an ODS statement.

```
ods trace on;

proc univariate data=orion.shoes_tracker;
   var Product_ID;
run;
```

c. After the PROC UNIVARIATE step, add an ODS statement.

```
ods trace on;

proc univariate data=orion.shoes_tracker;
   var Product_ID;
run;

ods trace off;
```

d. Submit the program.

What is the name of the last Output Added in the SAS log? **ExtremeObs**

e. Add an ODS SELECT statement.

```
ods trace on;

ods select ExtremeObs;
proc univariate data=orion.shoes_tracker;
   var Product_ID;
run;

ods trace off;
```

f. Submit the program.

7. Cleaning Data from `orion.qtr2_2007`

a. Retrieve the starter program.

b. Add two conditional statements to the DATA step.

```
data work.qtr2_2007;
   set orion.qtr2_2007;
   if Order_ID=1242012259 then Delivery_Date='12MAY2007'd;
   else if Order_ID=1242449327 then Order_Date='26JUN2007'd;
run;

proc print data=work.qtr2_2007;
   where Order_Date>Delivery_Date or
         Order_Date<'01APR2007'd or
         Order_Date>'30JUN2007'd;
run;
```

c. Submit the program.

8. Cleaning Data from `orion.price_current`

a. Retrieve the starter program.

b. Add a DATA step.

```
data work.price_current;
   set orion.price_current;
   if Product_ID=220200200022 then Unit_Sales_Price=57.30;
   else if Product_ID=240200100056 then Unit_Sales_Price=41.20;
run;

proc means data=work.price_current n min max;
   var Unit_Sales_Price;
run;

proc univariate data=work.price_current;
   var Unit_Sales_Price;
run;
```

c. Submit the program.

9. Cleaning Data from `orion.shoes_tracker`

a. Retrieve the starter program.

b. Add a DATA step.

```
data work.shoes_tracker;
   set orion.shoes_tracker;
   Supplier_Country=upcase(Supplier_Country);
   if Supplier_Country='UT' then Supplier_Country='US';
   if Product_Category=' ' then Product_Category='Shoes';
   if Supplier_ID=. then Supplier_ID=2963;
   if Supplier_Name='3op Sports' then Supplier_Name='3Top Sports';
   if _n_=4 then Product_ID=220200300079;
   else if _n_=8 then Product_ID=220200300129;
   Product_Name=propcase(Product_Name);
   if Supplier_ID=14682 and Supplier_Name='3Top Sports'
      then Supplier_Name='Greenline Sports Ltd';
run;

proc print data=work.shoes_tracker;
   where Product_Category=' ' or
         Supplier_Country not in ('GB','US') or
         propcase(Product_Name) ne Product_Name;
run;

proc freq data=work.shoes_tracker;
   tables Supplier_Name*Supplier_ID / missing;
run;

proc means data=work.shoes_tracker min max range fw=15;
   var Product_ID;
   class Supplier_Name;
run;

proc univariate data=work.shoes_tracker;
   var Product_ID;
run;
```

c. Submit the program.

Solutions to Student Activities (Polls/Quizzes)

8.01 Quiz – Correct Answer

What problems will SAS have reading the numeric data **Salary** and **Hire_Date**?

Partial **nonsales.csv**

```
120101,Patrick,Lu,M,163040,Director,AU,18AUG1976,01JUL2003
120104,Kareen,Billington,F,46230,Administration Manager,au,11MAY1954,01JAN1981
120105,Liz,Povey,F,27110,Secretary I,AU,21DEC1974,01MAY1999
120106,John,Hornsey,M,unknown,Office Assistant II,AU,23DEC1944,01JAN1974
120107,Sherie,Sheedy,F,30475,Office Assistant III,AU,01FEB1978,21JAN1953
120108,Gladys,Gromek,F,27660,Warehouse Assistant II,AU,23FEB1984,01AUG2006
120108,Gabriele,Baker,F,26495,Warehouse Assistant I,AU,15DEC1986,01OCT2006
120110,Dennis,Entwisle,M,28615,Warehouse Assistant III,AU,20NOV1949,01NOV1979
120111,Ubaldo,Spillane,M,26895,Security Guard II,AU,23JUL1949,99NOV1978
120112,Ellis,Glattback,F,26550, ,AU,17FEB1969,01JUL1990
120113,Riu,Horsey,F,26870,Security Guard II,AU,10MAY1944,01JAN1974
120114,Jeannette,Buddery,G,31285,Security Manager,AU,08FEB1944,01JAN1974
120115,Hugh,Nichollas,M,2650,Service Assistant I,AU,08MAY1984,01AUG2005
.,Austen,Ralston,M,29250,Service Assistant II,AU,13JUN1959,01FEB1980
120117,Bill,Mccleary,M,31670,Cabinet Maker III,AU,11SEP1964,01APR1986
```

7

8.02 Quiz – Correct Answer

What problems exist with the data in this partial data set?

	Employee_ID	First	Last	Gender	Salary	Job_Title	Country	Birth_Date	Hire_Date
1	120101	Patrick	Lu	M	163E3	Director	AU	18/08/1976	01/07/2003
2	120104	Kareen	Billington	F	46230	Administration Manager	au	11/05/1954	01/01/1981
3	120105	Liz	Povey	F	27110	Secretary I	AU	21/12/1974	01/05/1999
4	120106	John	Hornsey	M	.	Office Assistant II	AU	23/12/1944	01/01/1974
5	120107	Sherie	Sheedy	F	30475	Office Assistant III	AU	01/02/1978	21/01/1953
6	120108	Gladys	Gromek	F	27660	Warehouse Assistant II	AU	23/02/1984	01/08/2006
7	120108	Gabriele	Baker	F	26495	Warehouse Assistant I	AU	15/12/1986	01/10/2006
8	120110	Dennis	Entwisle	M	28615	Warehouse Assistant III	AU	20/11/1949	01/11/1979
9	120111	Ubaldo	Spillane	M	26895	Security Guard II	AU	23/07/1949	.
10	120112	Ellis	Glattback	F	2655		AU	17/02/1969	01/07/1990
11	120113	Riu	Horsey	F	26870	Security Guard II	AU	10/05/1944	01/01/1974
12	120114	Jeannette	Buddery	G	31285	Security Manager	AU	08/02/1944	01/01/1974
13	120115	Hugh	Nichollas	M	2650	Service Assistant I	AU	08/05/1984	01/08/2005
14	.	Austen	Ralston	M	29250	Service Assistant II	AU	13/06/1959	01/02/1980
15	120117	Bill	Mccleary	M	31670	Cabinet Maker III	AU	11/09/1964	01/04/1986

Hint: There are nine data problems.

12

8.03 Multiple Choice Poll – Correct Answer

Which statements are used to read a delimited raw data file and create a SAS data set?

a. DATA and SET only
b. DATA and INFILE only
c. DATA, SET, and INPUT only
(d.) DATA, INFILE, and INPUT only

25

8.04 Multiple Choice Poll – Correct Answer

Which statement best describes the invalid data?

a. The data in the raw data file is bad.
(b.) The programmer incorrectly read the data.

Partial SAS Log

```
404      input Employee_ID First $ Last;
405  run;

NOTE: Invalid data for Last in line 1 16-17.
RULE:      ----+----1----+----2----+----3----+----4----+----5----+----6
1          120101,Patrick,Lu,M,163040,Director,AU,18AUG1976,01JUL2003 58
Employee_ID=120101 First=Patrick Last=. _ERROR_=1 _N_=1
NOTE: Invalid data for Last in line 2 15-24.
2          120104,Kareen,Billington,F,46230,Administration Manager,au,1
      61   1MAY1954,01JAN1981 78
Employee_ID=120104 First=Kareen Last=. _ERROR_=1 _N_=2
```

`Last` was read as numeric but needs to be read as character.

36

8.05 Multiple Choice Poll – Correct Answer

Which data requirement cannot be achieved with the PRINT procedure using a WHERE statement?

(a.) **`Employee_ID`** must be unique and not missing.
b. **`Gender`** must have a value of `F` or `M`.
c. **`Salary`** must be in the numeric range of 24000 – 500000.
d. **`Job_Title`** must not be missing.
e. **`Country`** must have a value of `AU` or `US`.
f. **`Birth_Date`** value must occur before **`Hire_Date`** value.
g. **`Hire_Date`** must have a value of 01/01/1974 or later.

53

8.06 Quiz – Correct Answer (Self-Study)

- Open the VIEWTABLE window for **`orion.nonsales`**.
- Use the VIEWTABLE window to interactively clean the following observation:

VIEWTABLE: Orion.Nonsales

	Employee_ID	First	Last	Gender	Salary	Job_Title
1	120101	Patrick	Lu	M	163040	Director
2	120104	Kareen	Billington	F	46230	Administration Manager
3	120105	Liz	Povey	F	27110	Secretary I
4	120106	John	Hornsey	M	.	Office Assistant II
5	120107	Sherie	Sheedy	F	30475	Office Assistant III
6	120108	Gladys	Gromek	F	27660	Warehouse Assistant II
7	120109	Gabriele	Baker	F	26495	Warehouse Assistant I
8	120110	Dennis	Entwisle	M	28615	Warehouse Assistant III
9	120111	Ubaldo	Spillane	M	26895	Security Guard II
10	120112	Ellis	Glattback	F	26550	Security Guard I

87

8.07 Quiz – Correct Answer

Which variable can be used to specifically identify the observations with invalid salary values?

Obs	Employee_ID	Gender	Salary	Job_Title	Country	Birth_Date	Hire_Date
2	120104	F	46230	Administration Manager	au	11/05/1954	01/01/1981
4	120106	M	.	Office Assistant II	AU	23/12/1944	01/01/1974
5	120107	F	30475	Office Assistant III	AU	01/02/1978	21/01/1953
9	120111	M	26895	Security Guard II	AU	23/07/1949	.
10	120112	F	26550		AU	17/02/1969	01/07/1990
12	120114	G	31285	Security Manager	AU	08/02/1944	01/01/1974
13	120115	M	2650	Service Assistant I	AU	08/05/1984	01/08/2005
14	.	M	29250	Service Assistant II	AU	13/06/1959	01/02/1980
20	120191	F	2401	Trainee	AU	17/01/1959	01/01/2003
84	120695	M	28180	Warehouse Assistant II	au	13/07/1964	01/07/1989
87	120698	M	26160	Warehouse Assistant I	au	17/05/1954	01/08/1976
101	120723		33950	Corp. Comm. Specialist II	US	10/08/1949	01/01/1974
125	120747	F	43590	Financial Controller I	us	20/06/1974	01/08/1995
197	120994	F	31645	Office Administrator I	us	16/06/1974	01/11/1994
200	120997	F	27420	Shipping Administrator I	us	21/11/1974	01/09/1996
214	121011	M	25735	Service Assistant I	US	11/03/1944	01/01/1968

102

`Employee_ID` because the values are unique.

Solutions to Chapter Review

Chapter Review Answers

1. What procedures can be used to detect invalid data?
   - **PRINT**
   - **FREQ**
   - **MEANS**
   - **UNIVARIATE**

121

continued...

Chapter Review Answers

2. What happens when SAS encounters a data error?
   - **A note that describes the error is printed in the SAS log.**
   - **The input record (contents of the input buffer) being read is displayed in the SAS log.**
   - **The values in the SAS observation (contents of the PDV) being created are displayed in the SAS log.**
   - **A missing value is assigned to the appropriate SAS variable.**
   - **Execution continues.**

122

continued...

Chapter Review Answers

3. Why would you need a SAS date constant?

   You use a SAS date constant when you want to convert a calendar date to a SAS date value.

4. How can you clean invalid data?

   - **the VIEWTABLE window**
   - **assignment statements in the DATA step**
   - **IF-THEN/ELSE statements in the DATA step**

5. What symbol is required in an assignment statement?

   = (Equal sign)

123

continued...

Chapter Review Answers

6. Why would you use IF-THEN/ELSE statements instead of IF-THEN statements?

   If a series of IF expressions are mutually exclusive, it is not necessary to check all expressions when one is found to be true.

124

Chapter 9 Manipulating Data

9.1 Creating Variables 9-3

Exercises 9-27

9.2 Creating Variables Conditionally 9-30

Exercises 9-41

9.3 Subsetting Observations 9-44

Exercises 9-51

9.4 Chapter Review 9-53

9.5 Solutions 9-54

Solutions to Exercises 9-54

Solutions to Student Activities (Polls/Quizzes) 9-62

Solutions to Chapter Review 9-66

9.1 Creating Variables

Objectives

- Create SAS variables with the assignment statement in the DATA step.
- Create data values by using operators including SAS functions.
- Subset variables by using the DROP and KEEP statements.
- Examine the compilation and execution phases of the DATA step when you read a SAS data set.
- Subset variables by using the DROP= and KEEP= options. (Self-Study)

3

Business Scenario

A new SAS data set named **`Work.comp`** needs to be created by reading the **`orion.sales`** data set.

`Work.comp` must include the following new variables:

- **`Bonus`**, which is equal to a constant 500
- **`Compensation`**, which is the combination of the employee's salary and bonus
- **`BonusMonth`**, which is equal to the month that the employee was hired

`Work.comp` must not include the **`Gender`**, **`Salary`**, **`Job_Title`**, **`Country`**, **`Birth_Date`**, and **`Hire_Date`** variables from **`orion.sales`**.

4

Business Scenario

Partial **orion.sales**

Employee_ ID	First_ Name	Last_ Name	Gender	Salary	Job_ Title	Country	Birth_ Date	Hire_ Date
120102	Tom	Zhou	M	108255	Sales Manager	AU	3510	10744
120103	Wilson	Dawes	M	87975	Sales Manager	AU	-3996	5114
120121	Irenie	Elvish	F	26600	Sales Rep. II	AU	-5630	5114

Partial **Work.comp**

Employee_ ID	First_ Name	Last_ Name	Bonus	Compensation	Bonus Month
120102	Tom	Zhou	500	108755	6
120103	Wilson	Dawes	500	88475	1
120121	Irenie	Elvish	500	27100	1

5

Assignment Statements (Review)

Assignment statements are used in the DATA step to update existing variables or create new variables.

```
DATA output-SAS-data-set;
     SET input-SAS-data-set;
     variable = expression;
RUN;
```

```
DATA output-SAS-data-set;
     INFILE 'raw-data-file-name';
     INPUT specifications;
     variable = expression;
RUN;
```

6

Assignment Statements (Review)

The *assignment statement* evaluates an expression and assigns the resulting value to a variable.

General form of the assignment statement:

```
variable = expression;
```

- *variable* names an existing or new variable.
- *expression* is a sequence of operands and operators that form a set of instructions that produce a value.

7

An assignment statement evaluates the expression on the right side of the equal sign and stores the result in the variable that is specified on the left side of the equal sign.

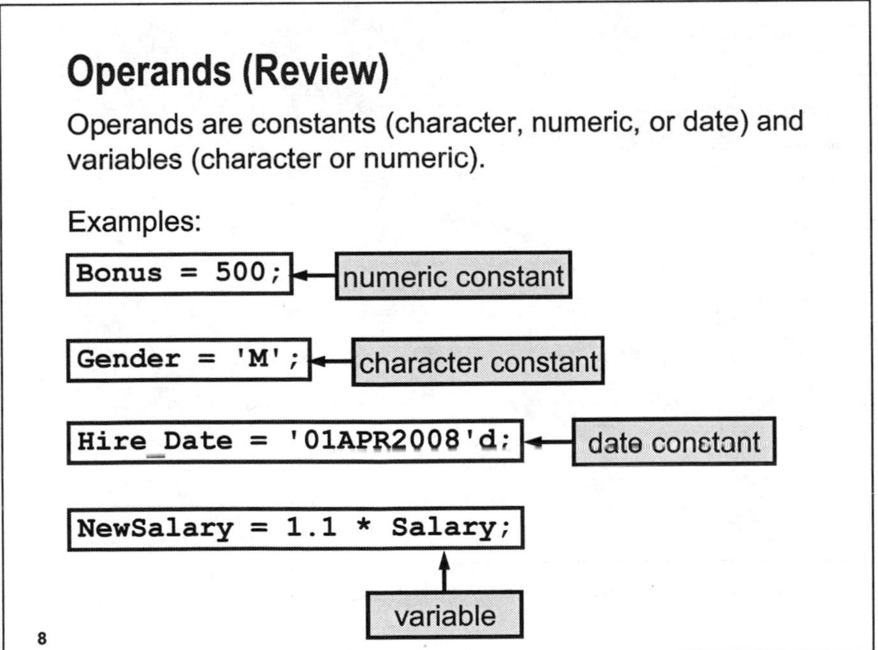
Operands (Review)
Operands are constants (character, numeric, or date) and variables (character or numeric).
Examples:
Bonus = 500;
numeric constant
Gender = 'M';
character constant
Hire_Date = '01APR2008'd;
date constant
NewSalary = 1.1 * Salary;
variable
8

Operators (Review)

Operators are symbols that represent an arithmetic calculation and SAS functions.

Examples:

```
Revenue = Quantity * Price;
```

```
NewCountry = upcase(Country);
```

9

Arithmetic Operators

Arithmetic operators indicate that an arithmetic calculation is performed.

Symbol	Definition	Priority
**	exponentiation	I
-	negative prefix	I
*	multiplication	II
/	division	II
+	addition	III
-	subtraction	III

If a missing value is an operand for an arithmetic operator, the result is a missing value.

10

Rules for Operators

- Operations of priority I are performed before operations of priority II, and so on.
- Consecutive operations with the same priority are performed in this sequence:
  - from right to left within priority I
  - from left to right within priorities II and III
- Parentheses can be used to control the order of operations.

9.01 Quiz

What is the result of the assignment statement?

a. . (missing)
b. 0
c. 7
d. 9

```
num = 4 + 10 / 2;
```

12

9.02 Quiz

What is the result of the assignment statement given the values of **var1** and **var2**?

a. . (missing)
b. 0
c. 5
d. 10

```
num = var1 + var2 / 2;
```

var1	var2
.	10

15

SAS Functions (Review)

A SAS *function* is a routine that returns a value that is determined from specified arguments.

Some SAS functions manipulate character values, compute descriptive statistics, or manipulate SAS date values.

General form of a SAS function:

function-name(*argument1*, *argument2*, ...)

- Depending on the function, zero, one, or many arguments are used.
- Arguments are separated with commas.

17

Descriptive Statistics Function

The *SUM function* returns the sum of the arguments.

General form of the SUM function:

SUM(*argument1*,*argument2*, ...)

- The arguments must be numeric values.
- Missing values are ignored by some of the descriptive statistics functions.

Example:

```
Compensation=sum(Salary,Bonus);
```

18

* most arithmetic function ignore the missing values

Date Functions

SAS date functions can be used to

- extract information from SAS date values
- create SAS date values.

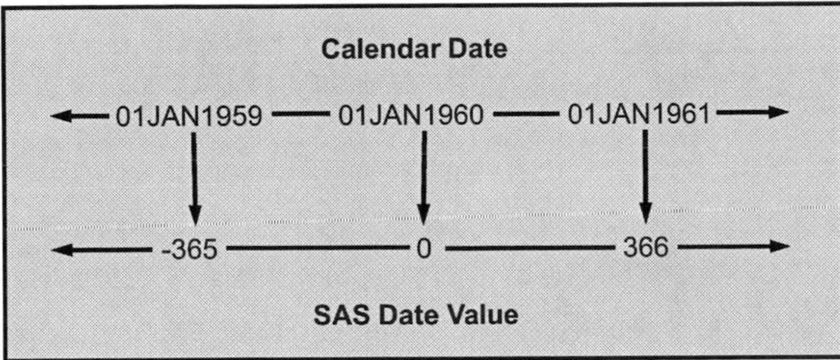

19

Date Functions – Extracting Information

Function	Description
YEAR(*SAS-date*)	extracts the year from a SAS date and returns a four-digit value for year.
QTR(*SAS-date*)	extracts the quarter from a SAS date and returns a number from 1 to 4.
MONTH(*SAS-date*)	extracts the month from a SAS date and returns a number from 1 to 12.
DAY(*SAS-date*)	extracts the day of the month from a SAS date and returns a number from 1 to 31.
WEEKDAY(*SAS-date*)	extracts the day of the week from a SAS date and returns a number from 1 to 7, where 1 represents Sunday, and so on.

Example:

```
BonusMonth=month(Hire_Date);
```

20

ex: X = month (32).
(2) ← Feb 1, 1960 (32 days after Jan 1, 1960)

ex:
```
data _null_;
lisa = weekday(mdy(11, 26,1963));
put lisa=;
run;
```
to get the day of the DATE inside ( )

Date Functions – Creating SAS Dates

TODAY()	returns the current date as a SAS date value.
MDY(*month,day,year*)	returns a SAS date value from numeric month, day, and year values.

Example:

```
AnnivBonus=mdy(month(Hire_Date),15,2008);
```

21

Business Scenario

Create **Bonus**, **Compensation**, and **BonusMonth**.

```
data work.comp;
   set orion.sales;
   Bonus=500;
   Compensation=sum(Salary,Bonus);
   BonusMonth=month(Hire_Date);
run;
```

```
data work.comp;
   set orion.sales;
   Bonus=500;
   Compensation=sum(Salary,Bonus);
   BonusMonth=month(Hire_Date);
run;

NOTE: There were 165 observations read from the data set ORION.SALES.
NOTE: The data set WORK.COMP has 165 observations and 12 variables.
```

orion.sales has 9 variables.

23

p109d01

9.03 Quiz

What statement needs to be added to the DATA step to eliminate six of the 12 variables?

Keep or Drop

25

The DROP and KEEP Statements (Review)

The *DROP statement* specifies the names of the variables to omit from the output data set(s).

DROP *variable-list* ;

The *KEEP statement* specifies the names of the variable to write to the output data set(s).

KEEP *variable-list* ;

The *variable-list* specifies the variables to drop or keep, respectively, in the output data set.

27

Business Scenario

Drop **Gender**, **Salary**, **Job_Title**, **Country**, **Birth_Date**, and **Hire_Date**.

```
data work.comp;
   set orion.sales;
   Bonus=500;
   Compensation=sum(Salary,Bonus);
   BonusMonth=month(Hire_Date);
   drop Gender Salary Job_Title
        Country Birth_Date Hire_Date;
run;
```

Partial SAS Log

```
NOTE: There were 165 observations read from the data set ORION.SALES.
NOTE: The data set WORK.COMP has 165 observations and 6 variables.
```

28

p109d01

Business Scenario

```
proc print data=work.comp;
run;
```

Partial PROC PRINT Output

Obs	Employee_ID	First_ Name	Last_Name	Bonus	Compensation	Bonus Month
1	120102	Tom	Zhou	500	108755	6
2	120103	Wilson	Dawes	500	88475	1
3	120121	Irenie	Elvish	500	27100	1
4	120122	Christina	Ngan	500	27975	7
5	120123	Kimiko	Hotstone	500	26690	10
6	120124	Lucian	Daymond	500	26980	3
7	120125	Fong	Hofmeister	500	32540	3
8	120126	Satyakam	Denny	500	27280	8
9	120127	Sharryn	Clarkson	500	28600	11
10	120128	Monica	Kletschkus	500	31390	11

29

p109d01

Setup for the Poll

- Submit program **p109a01**.
- Verify the results.

```
data work.comp;
   set orion.sales;
   drop Gender Salary Job_Title
        Country Birth_Date Hire_Date;
   Bonus=500;
   Compensation=sum(Salary,Bonus);
   BonusMonth=month(Hire_Date);
run;
```

31

9.04 Poll

Are the correct results produced when the DROP statement is placed after the SET statement?

❍ Yes

❍ No

32

DROP - COMPILE TIME statement

- it is still in the program data vector but it doesn't output, so it's still being computed

- it will just flag the variables

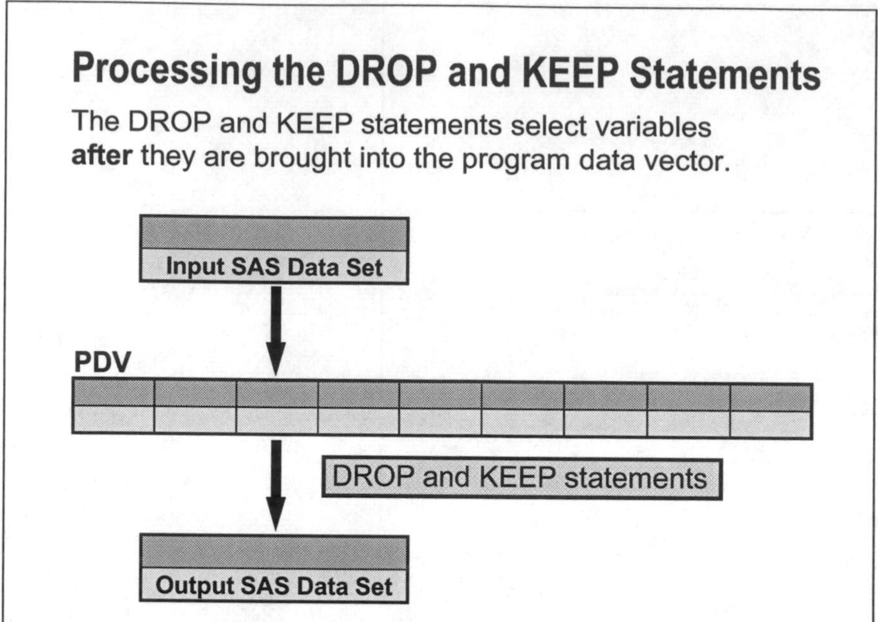

Processing the DROP and KEEP Statements
The DROP and KEEP statements select variables **after** they are brought into the program data vector.
Input SAS Data Set
PDV
DROP and KEEP statements
Output SAS Data Set
34

Compilation

```
data work.comp;
   set orion.sales;
   drop Gender Salary Job_Title
        Country Birth_Date Hire_Date;
   Bonus=500;
   Compensation=sum(Salary,Bonus);
   BonusMonth=month(Hire_Date);
run;
```

35

...

Compilation

```
data work.comp;
   set orion.sales;
   drop Gender Salary Job_Title
        Country Birth_Date Hire_Date;
   Bonus=500;
   Compensation=sum(Salary,Bonus);
   BonusMonth=month(Hire_Date);
run;
```

PDV

Employee_ID N 8	First_Name $ 12	Last_Name $ 18	Gender $ 1	Salary N 8	Job_Title $ 25

Country $ 2	Birth_Date N 8	Hire_Date N 8

36 ...

Compilation

```
data work.comp;
   set orion.sales;
   drop Gender Salary Job_Title
        Country Birth_Date Hire_Date;
   Bonus=500;
   Compensation=sum(Salary,Bonus);
   BonusMonth=month(Hire_Date);
run;
```

PDV

Employee_ID N 8	First_Name $ 12	Last_Name $ 18	Gender $ 1	Salary N 8	Job_Title $ 25

Country $ 2	Birth_Date N 8	Hire_Date N 8	Bonus N 8

37 ...

Compilation

```
data work.comp;
   set orion.sales;
   drop Gender Salary Job_Title
        Country Birth_Date Hire_Date;
   Bonus=500;
   Compensation=sum(Salary,Bonus);
   BonusMonth=month(Hire_Date);
run;
```

PDV

Employee_ID N 8	First_Name $ 12	Last_Name $ 18	Gender $ 1	Salary N 8	Job_Title $ 25

Country $ 2	Birth_Date N 8	Hire_Date N 8	Bonus N 8	Compensation N 8

38 ...

Compilation

```
data work.comp;
   set orion.sales;
   drop Gender Salary Job_Title
        Country Birth_Date Hire_Date;
   Bonus=500;
   Compensation=sum(Salary,Bonus);
   BonusMonth=month(Hire_Date);
run;
```

PDV

Employee_ID N 8	First_Name $ 12	Last_Name $ 18	Gender $ 1	Salary N 8	Job_Title $ 25

Country $ 2	Birth_Date N 8	Hire_Date N 8	Bonus N 8	Compensation N 8	BonusMonth N 8

39 ...

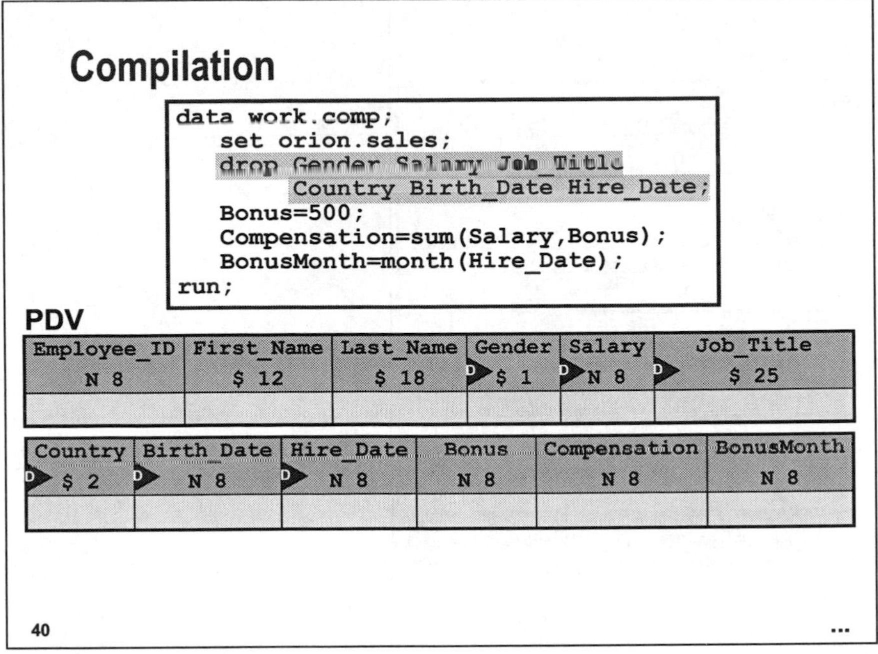
Compilation
data work.comp;
set orion.sales;
drop Gender Salary Job_Title
Country Birth_Date Hire_Date;
Bonus=500;
Compensation=sum(Salary,Bonus);
BonusMonth=month(Hire_Date);
run;
PDV
Employee_ID N 8
First_Name $ 12
Last_Name $ 18
Gender $ 1
Salary N 8
Job_Title $ 25
Country $ 2
Birth_Date N 8
Hire_Date N 8
Bonus N 8
Compensation N 8
BonusMonth N 8
40

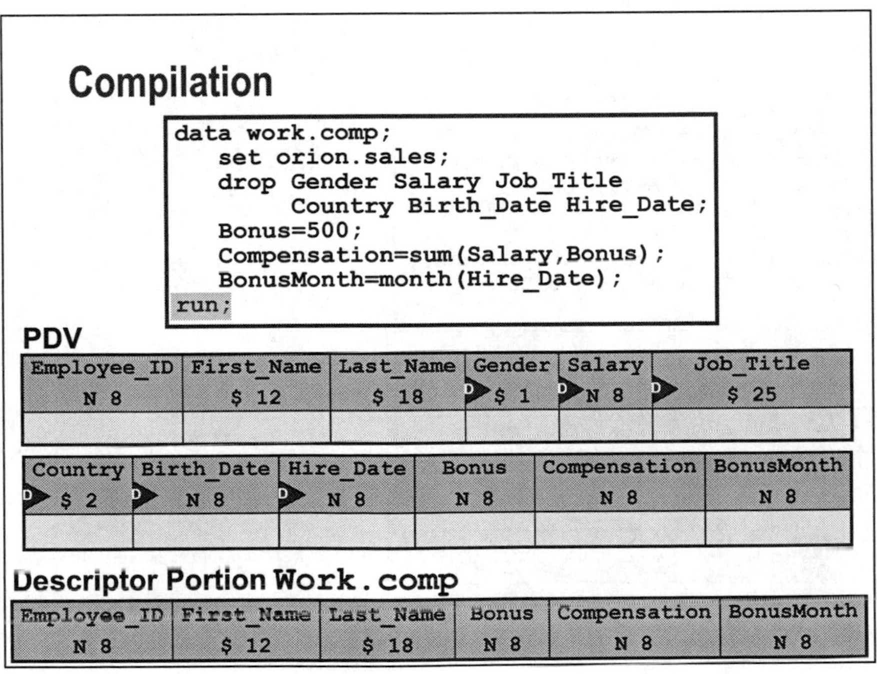
Compilation
data work.comp;
set orion.sales;
drop Gender Salary Job_Title
Country Birth_Date Hire_Date;
Bonus=500;
Compensation=sum(Salary,Bonus);
BonusMonth=month(Hire_Date);
run;
PDV
Employee_ID N 8
First_Name $ 12
Last_Name $ 18
Gender $ 1
Salary N 8
Job_Title $ 25
Country $ 2
Birth_Date N 8
Hire_Date N 8
Bonus N 8
Compensation N 8
BonusMonth N 8
Descriptor Portion Work.comp
Employee_ID N 8
First_Name $ 12
Last_Name $ 18
Bonus N 8
Compensation N 8
BonusMonth N 8

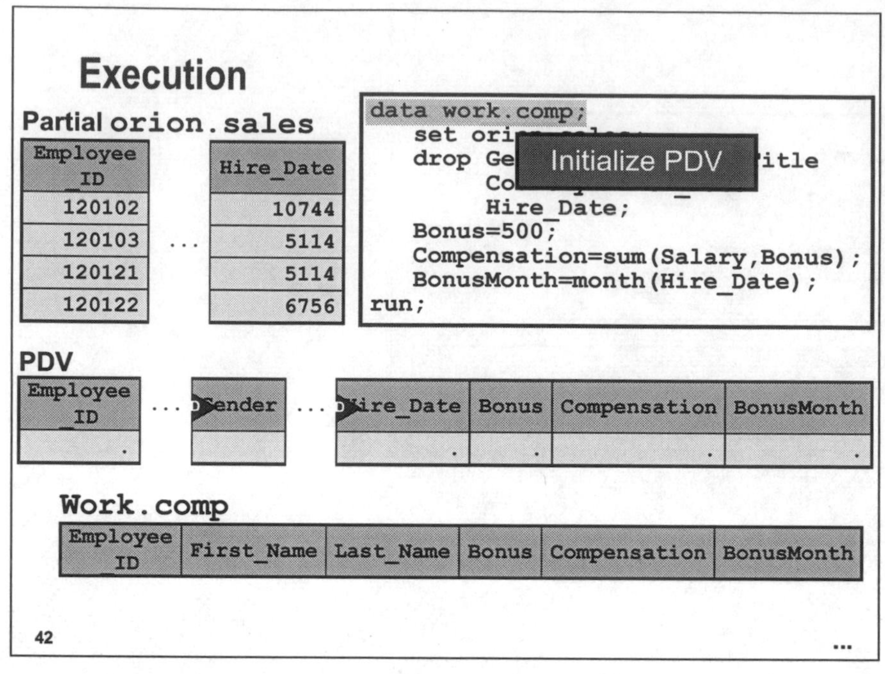
Execution
Partial orion.sales
Employee_ID
120102
120103
120121
120122
...
Hire_Date
10744
5114
5114
6756
data work.comp;
set ori
drop Ge
Initialize PDV
itle
Co
Hire_Date;
Bonus=500;
Compensation=sum(Salary,Bonus);
BonusMonth=month(Hire_Date);
run;
PDV
Employee_ID
...
ender
...
ire_Date
Bonus
Compensation
BonusMonth
Work.comp
Employee_ID
First_Name
Last_Name
Bonus
Compensation
BonusMonth
42
...

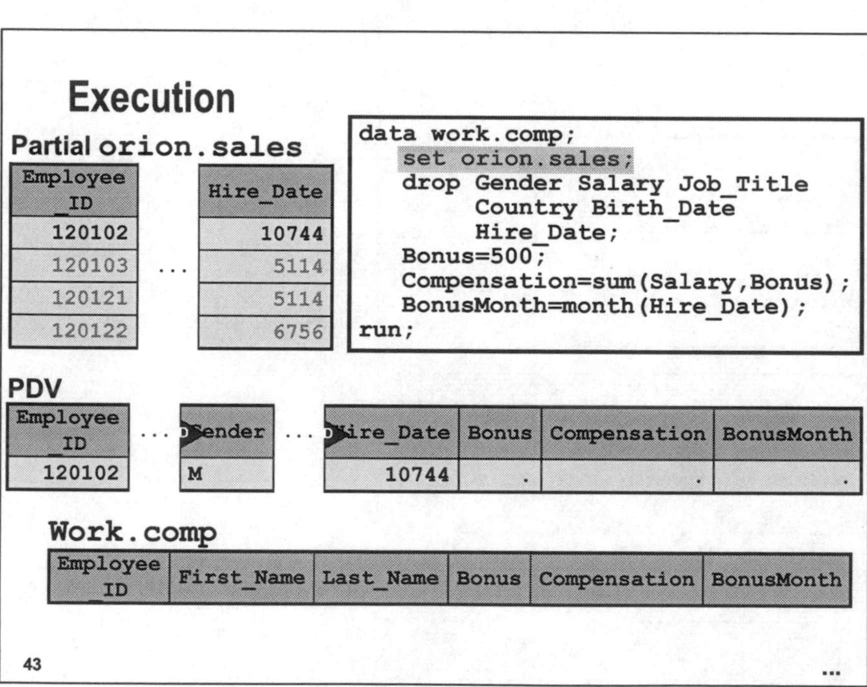
Execution
Partial orion.sales
Employee_ID
120102
120103
120121
120122
...
Hire_Date
10744
5114
5114
6756
data work.comp;
set orion.sales;
drop Gender Salary Job_Title
Country Birth_Date
Hire_Date;
Bonus=500;
Compensation=sum(Salary,Bonus);
BonusMonth=month(Hire_Date);
run;
PDV
Employee_ID
120102
...
ender
M
...
ire_Date
10744
Bonus
Compensation
BonusMonth
Work.comp
Employee_ID
First_Name
Last_Name
Bonus
Compensation
BonusMonth
43
...

Execution

Partial orion.sales

Employee_ID	...	Hire_Date
120102		10744
120103	...	5114
120121		5114
120122		6756

```
data work.comp;
   set orion.sales;
   drop Gender Salary Job_Title
        Country Birth_Date
        Hire_Date;
   Bonus=500;
   Compensation=sum(Salary,Bonus);
   BonusMonth=month(Hire_Date);
run;
```

PDV

Employee_ID	...	D Gender	...	D Hire_Date	Bonus	Compensation	BonusMonth
120102		M		10744	500	.	.

Work.comp

Employee_ID	First_Name	Last_Name	Bonus	Compensation	BonusMonth

44 ...

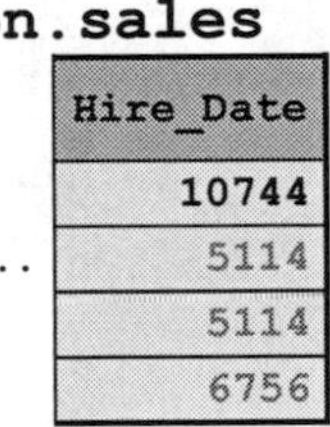

Execution

Partial orion.sales

Employee_ID	...	Hire_Date
120102		10744
120103	...	5114
120121		5114
120122		6756

```
data work.comp;
   set orion.sales;
   drop Gender Salary Job_Title
        Country Birth_Date
        Hire_Date;
   Bonus=500;
   Compensation=sum(Salary,Bonus);
   BonusMonth=month(Hire_Date);
run;
```

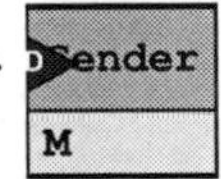

PDV

Employee_ID	...	D Gender	...	D Hire_Date	Bonus	Compensation	BonusMonth
120102		M		10744	500	108755	.

Work.comp

Employee_ID	First_Name	Last_Name	Bonus	Compensation	BonusMonth

45 ...

Execution

Partial orion.sales

Employee_ID	...	Hire_Date
120102		10744
120103	...	5114
120121		5114
120122		6756

```
data work.comp;
   set orion.sales;
   drop Gender Salary Job_Title
        Country Birth_Date
        Hire_Date;
   Bonus=500;
   Compensation=sum(Salary,Bonus);
   BonusMonth=month(Hire_Date);
run;
```

PDV

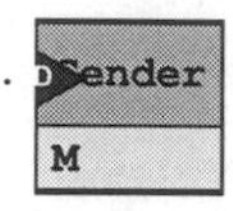

Employee_ID	...	Gender	...	Hire_Date	Bonus	Compensation	BonusMonth
120102		M		10744	500	108755	6

Work.comp

Employee_ID	First_Name	Last_Name	Bonus	Compensation	BonusMonth

46 ...

Execution

Partial orion.sales

Employee_ID	...	Hire_Date
120102		10744
120103	...	5114
120121		5114
120122		6756

```
data work.comp;
   set orion.sales;
   drop Gender Salary Job_Title
        Country Birth_Date
        Hire_Date;
   Bonus=500;
   Compensation=sum(Salary,Bonus);
   BonusMon                    ;
run;
```

Implicit OUTPUT;
Implicit RETURN;

PDV

Employee_ID	...	Gender	...	Hire_Date	Bonus	Compensation	BonusMonth
120102		M		10744	500	108755	6

Work.comp

Employee_ID	First_Name	Last_Name	Bonus	Compensation	BonusMonth
120102	Tom	Zhou	500	108755	6

47 ...

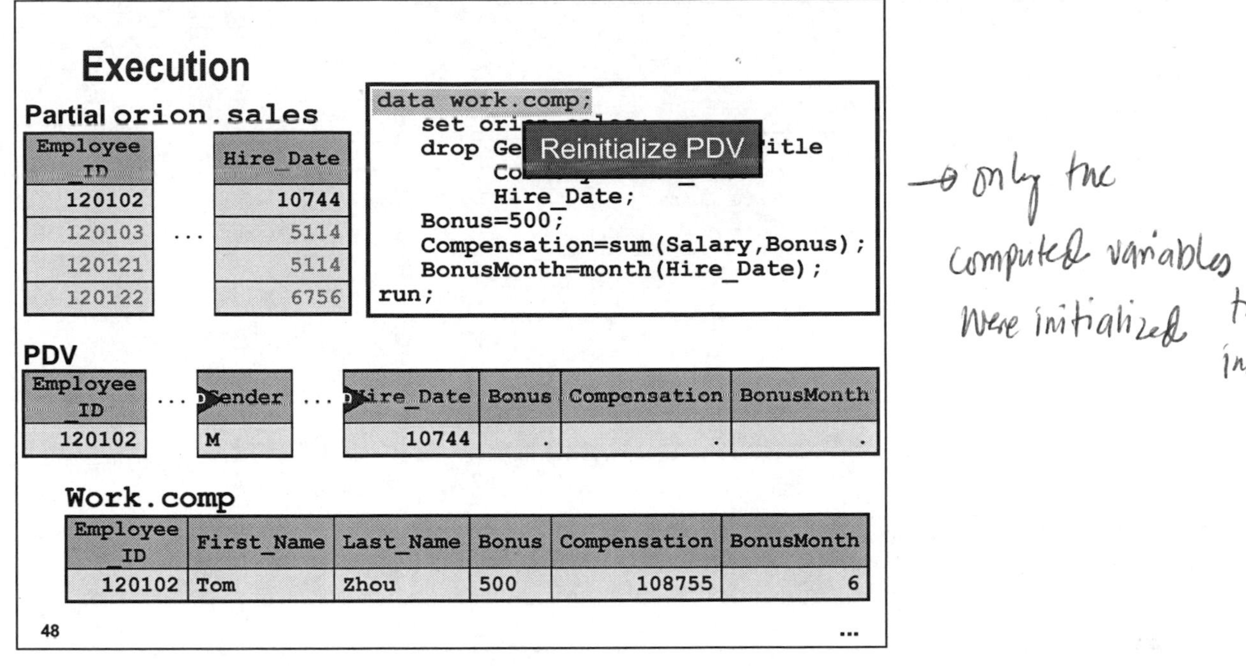

SAS reinitializes variables in the PDV at the start of every DATA step iteration. Variables created by an assignment statement are reset to missing, but variables that are read with a SET statement are not reset to missing.

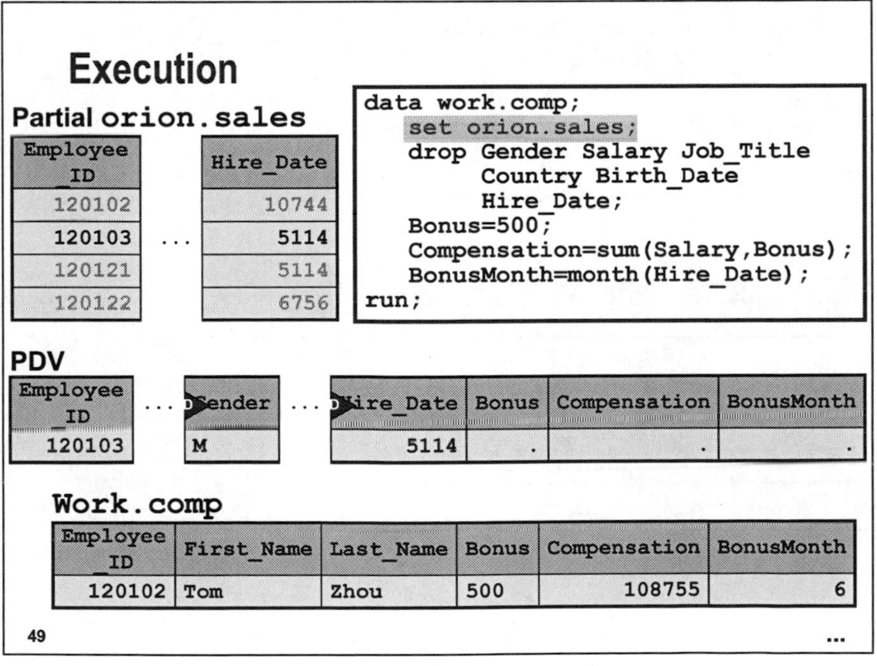

Execution

Partial orion.sales

Employee_ID	...	Hire_Date
120102		10744
120103	...	5114
120121		5114
120122		6756

```
data work.comp;
   set orion.sales;
   drop Gender Salary Job_Title
        Country Birth_Date
        Hire_Date;
   Bonus=500;
   Compensation=sum(Salary,Bonus);
   BonusMonth=month(Hire_Date);
run;
```

PDV

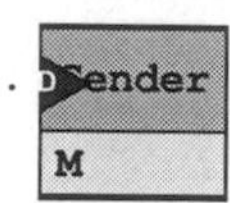

Employee_ID	...	Gender	...	Hire_Date	Bonus	Compensation	BonusMonth
120103		M		5114	500	.	.

Work.comp

Employee_ID	First_Name	Last_Name	Bonus	Compensation	BonusMonth
120102	Tom	Zhou	500	108755	6

50

...

Execution

Partial orion.sales

Employee_ID	...	Hire_Date
120102		10744
120103	...	5114
120121		5114
120122		6756

```
data work.comp;
   set orion.sales;
   drop Gender Salary Job_Title
        Country Birth_Date
        Hire_Date;
   Bonus=500;
   Compensation=sum(Salary,Bonus);
   BonusMonth=month(Hire_Date);
run;
```

PDV

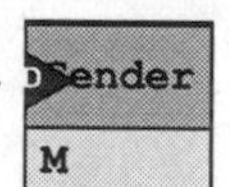

Employee_ID	...	Gender	...	Hire_Date	Bonus	Compensation	BonusMonth
120103		M		5114	500	88475	.

Work.comp

Employee_ID	First_Name	Last_Name	Bonus	Compensation	BonusMonth
120102	Tom	Zhou	500	108755	6

51

...

Execution

Partial `orion.sales`

Employee _ID	...	Hire_Date
120102		10744
120103	...	5114
120121		5114
120122		6756

```
data work.comp;
   set orion.sales;
   drop Gender Salary Job_Title
        Country Birth_Date
        Hire_Date;
   Bonus=500;
   Compensation=sum(Salary,Bonus);
   BonusMonth=month(Hire_Date);
run;
```

PDV

Employee _ID	...	D Gender	...	D Hire_Date	Bonus	Compensation	BonusMonth
120103		M		5114	500	88475	1

`Work.comp`

Employee _ID	First_Name	Last_Name	Bonus	Compensation	BonusMonth
120102	Tom	Zhou	500	108755	6

52 ...

Execution

Partial `orion.sales`

Employee _ID	...	Hire_Date
120102		10744
120103	...	5114
120121		5114
120122		6756

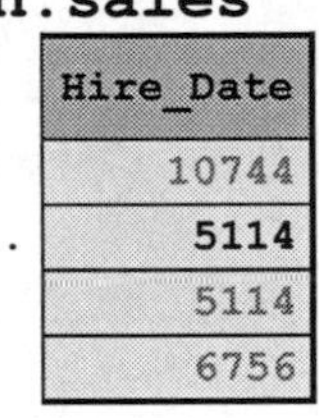

```
data work.comp;
   set orion.sales;
   drop Gender Salary Job_Title
        Country Birth_Date
        Hire_Date;
   Bonus=500;
   Compensation=sum(Salary,Bonus);
   BonusMon                       ;
run;
```

Implicit OUTPUT;
Implicit RETURN;

PDV

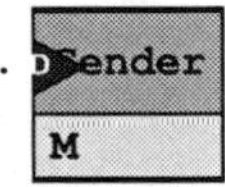

Employee _ID	...	D Gender	...	D Hire_Date	Bonus	Compensation	BonusMonth
120103		M		5114	500	88475	1

`Work.comp`

Employee _ID	First_Name	Last_Name	Bonus	Compensation	BonusMonth
120102	Tom	Zhou	500	108755	6
120103	Wilson	Dawes	500	88475	1

53

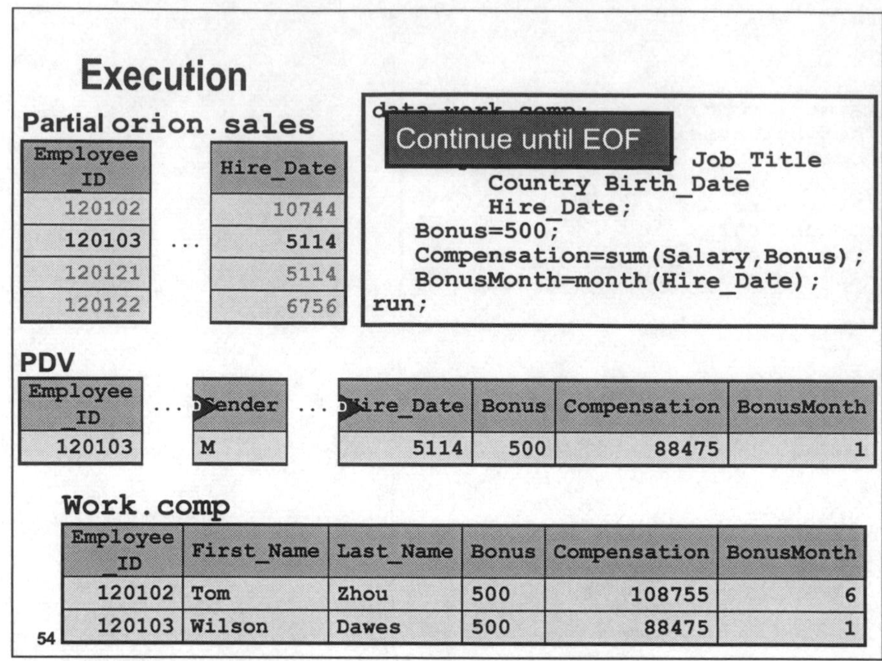

DROP= and KEEP= Options (Self-Study)

Alternatives to the DROP and KEEP statements are the DROP= and KEEP= data set options placed in the DATA statement.

- The *DROP= data set option* in the DATA statement excludes the variables for writing to the output data set.

  DATA *output-SAS-data-set* (DROP = *variable-list*) ;

- The *KEEP= data set option* in the DATA statement specifies the variables for writing to the output data set.

  DATA *output-SAS-data-set* (KEEP = *variable-list*) ;

56

When specified for a data set named in the DATA statement, the DROP= and KEEP= data set options are similar to DROP and KEEP statements. However, the DROP= and KEEP= data set options can be used in situations where the DROP and KEEP statements cannot. For example, the DROP= and KEEP= data set options can be used in a PROC step to control which variables are available for processing by the procedure.

DROP= and KEEP= Options (Self-Study)

The DROP= and KEEP= data set options can also be placed in the SET statement to control which variables are read from the input data set.

- The *DROP= data set option* in the SET statement excludes the variables for processing in the PDV.

SET *input-SAS-data-set* (DROP = *variable-list*) ;

- The *KEEP= data set option* in the SET statement specifies the variables for processing in the PDV.

SET *input-SAS-data-set* (KEEP = *variable-list*) ;

57

DROP= and KEEP= Options (Self-Study)

```
data work.comp(drop=Salary Hire_Date);
   set orion.sales(keep=Employee_ID First_Name
                        Last_Name Salary Hire_Date);
   Bonus=500;
   Compensation=sum(Salary,Bonus);
   BonusMonth=month(Hire_Date);
run;
```

orion.sales

Employee_ ID	First_ Name	Last_ Name	Gender	Salary	Job_ Title	Country	Birth_ Date	Hire_ Date

PDV

Employee_ ID	First_ Name	Last_ Name	Salary	Hire_ Date	Bonus	Compensation	BonusMonth

Work.comp

Employee_ ID	First_ Name	Last_ Name	Bonus	Compensation	BonusMonth

58 p109d02

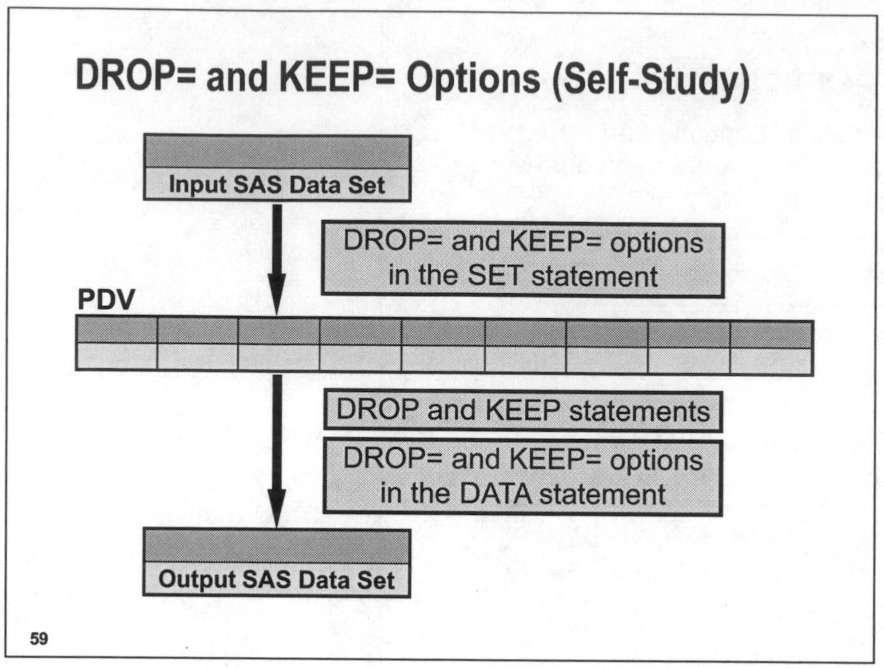
DROP= and KEEP= Options (Self-Study)
Input SAS Data Set
DROP= and KEEP= options in the SET statement
PDV
DROP and KEEP statements
DROP= and KEEP= options in the DATA statement
Output SAS Data Set
59

Exercises

Level 1

1. Creating Two New Variables

a. Retrieve the starter program **p109e01**.

b. In the DATA step, create two new variables, **`Increase`** and **`NewSalary`**.
   - **`Increase`** is the **`Salary`** multiplied by 0.10.
   - **`NewSalary`** is **`Salary`** added with **`Increase`**.

c. Include only the following variables: **`Employee_ID`**, **`Salary`**, **`Increase`**, and **`NewSalary`**.

d. Store formats displaying commas for **`Salary`**, **`Increase`**, and **`NewSalary`**.

e. Submit the program to create the following PROC PRINT report:

Partial PROC PRINT Output (First 10 of 424 Observations)

Obs	Employee_ID	Employee Annual Salary	Increase	NewSalary
1	120101	163,040	16,304	179,344
2	120102	108,255	10,826	119,081
3	120103	87,975	8,798	96,773
4	120104	46,230	4,623	50,853
5	120105	27,110	2,711	29,821
6	120106	26,960	2,696	29,656
7	120107	30,475	3,048	33,523
8	120108	27,660	2,766	30,426
9	120109	26,495	2,650	29,145
10	120110	28,615	2,862	31,477

Level 2

2. Creating Three New Variables

a. Write a DATA step to read **`orion.customer`** to create **`Work.birthday`**.

b. In the DATA step, create three new variables, **`Bday2009`**, **`BdayDOW2009`**, and **`Age2009`**.
   - **`Bday2009`** is the combination of the month of **`Birth_Date`**, the day of **`Birth_Date`**, and the constant of `2009` in the MDY function.
   - **`BdayDOW2009`** is the day of the week of **`Bday2009`**.
   - **`Age2009`** is the age of the customer in 2009. Subtract **`Birth_Date`** from **`Bday2009`** and then divide by **`365.25`**.

c. Include only the following variables: **Customer_Name**, **Birth_Date**, **Bday2009**, **BdayDOW2009**, and **Age2009**.

d. Format **Bday2009** to resemble a two-digit day, a three-letter month, and a four-digit year. **Age2009** should be formatted to appear with no digits after the decimal point.

e. Write a PROC PRINT step to create the following report:

Partial PROC PRINT Output (First 10 of 77 Observations)

Obs	Customer_Name	Birth_ Date	Bday2009	Bday DOW2009	Age2009
1	James Kvarniq	27JUN1974	27JUN2009	7	35
2	Sandrina Stephano	09JUL1979	09JUL2009	5	30
3	Cornelia Krahl	27FEB1974	27FEB2009	6	35
4	Karen Ballinger	18OCT1984	18OCT2009	1	25
5	Elke Wallstab	16AUG1974	16AUG2009	1	35
6	David Black	12APR1969	12APR2009	1	40
7	Markus Sepke	21JUL1988	21JUL2009	3	21
8	Ulrich Heyde	16JAN1939	16JAN2009	6	70
9	Jimmie Evans	17AUG1954	17AUG2009	2	55
10	Tonie Asmussen	02FEB1954	02FEB2009	2	55

Level 3

3. Using the CATX and INTCK Functions to Create Variables

a. Write a DATA step to read **orion.sales** to create **Work.employees**.

b. In the DATA step, create the new variable **FullName**, which is the combination of **First_Name**, a space, and **Last_Name**. Use the CATX function.

> ✎ Documentation on the CATX function can be found in the SAS Help and Documentation from the Contents tab (**SAS Products** ⇨ **Base SAS** ⇨ **SAS 9.2 Language Reference: Dictionary** ⇨ **Dictionary of Language Elements** ⇨ **Functions and CALL Routines** ⇨ **CATX Function**).

c. In the DATA step, create the new variable **Yrs2012**, which is the number of years between January 1, 2012, and **Hire_Date**. Use the INTCK function.

> ✎ Documentation on the INTCK function can be found in the SAS Help and Documentation from the Contents tab (**SAS Products** ⇨ **Base SAS** ⇨ **SAS 9.2 Language Reference: Dictionary** ⇨ **Dictionary of Language Elements** ⇨ **Functions and CALL Routines** ⇨ **INTCK Function**).

d. Format **Hire_Date** to resemble a two-digit day, a two-digit month, and a four-digit year.

e. Give **Yrs2012** a label of **Years of Employment in 2012**.

f. Write a PROC PRINT step with a VAR statement to crcate the following report:

Partial PROC PRINT Output (First 10 of 165 Observations)

Obs	FullName	Hire_Date	Years of Employment in 2012
1	Tom Zhou	01/06/1989	23
2	Wilson Dawes	01/01/1974	38
3	Irenie Elvish	01/01/1974	38
4	Christina Ngan	01/07/1978	34
5	Kimiko Hotstone	01/10/1985	27
6	Lucian Daymond	01/03/1979	33
7	Fong Hofmeister	01/03/1979	33
8	Satyakam Denny	01/08/2006	6
9	Sharryn Clarkson	01/11/1998	14
10	Monica Kletschkus	01/11/2006	6

9.2 Creating Variables Conditionally

Objectives

- Execute statements conditionally by using IF-THEN and IF-THEN DO statements.
- Give alternate actions if the previous THEN clause is not executed by using the ELSE statement.
- Control the length of character variables by using the LENGTH statement.

62

Business Scenario

A new SAS data set named **`Work.bonus`** needs to be created by reading the **`orion.sales`** data set.

`Work.bonus` must include a new variable named **`Bonus`** that is equal to

- 500 for United States employees
- 300 for Australian employees.

63

IF-THEN Statements (Review)

The *IF-THEN statement* executes a SAS statement for observations that meet specific conditions.

General form of the IF-THEN statement:

IF *expression* **THEN** *statement*;

- *expression* is a sequence of operands and operators that form a set of instructions that define a condition for selecting observations.
- *statement* is any executable statement such as the assignment statement.

64

If the condition in the IF clause is met, the IF-THEN statement executes a SAS statement for that observation.

IF-THEN/ELSE Statements (Review)

The optional *ELSE statement* gives an alternate action if the previous THEN clause is not executed.

General form of the IF-THEN/ELSE statements:

IF *expression* **THEN** *statement*;
ELSE IF *expression* **THEN** *statement*;

- Using IF-THEN statements **without** the ELSE statement causes SAS to evaluate all IF-THEN statements.
- Using IF-THEN statements **with** the ELSE statement causes SAS to execute IF-THEN statements until it encounters the first true statement.

65

Conditional logic can include one or more ELSE IF statements.

For greater efficiency, construct your IF-THEN/ELSE statements with conditions of decreasing probability.

Business Scenario

Create the new variable **Bonus**.

```
data work.bonus;
   set orion.sales;
   if Country='US' then Bonus=500;
   else if Country='AU' then Bonus=300;
run;
```

```
data work.bonus;
   set orion.sales;
   if Country='US' then Bonus=500;
   else if Country='AU' then Bonus=300;
run;

NOTE: There were 165 observations read from the data set ORION.SALES.
NOTE: The data set WORK.BONUS has 165 observations and 10 variables
```

66

p109d03

Business Scenario

```
proc print data=work.bonus;
   var First_Name Last_Name Country Bonus;
run;
```

Partial PROC PRINT Output

Obs	First_Name	Last_Name	Country	Bonus
60	Billy	Plested	AU	300
61	Matsuoka	Wills	AU	300
62	Vino	George	AU	300
63	Meera	Body	AU	300
64	Harry	Highpoint	US	500
65	Julienne	Magolan	US	500
66	Scott	Desanctis	US	500
67	Cherda	Ridley	US	500
68	Priscilla	Farren	US	500
69	Robert	Stevens	US	500

67

p109d03

9.05 Quiz

Why are some of the **Bonus** values missing in the PROC PRINT output for **orion.nonsales**?

- Submit program **p109a02**.
- Review the results.

69

ELSE Statements

The conditional clause does not have to be in an ELSE statement.

For example:

```
data work.bonus;
   set orion.sales;
   if Country='US' then Bonus=500;
   else Bonus=300;
run;
```

 All observations not equal to US get a bonus of 300.

71 p109d03

Business Scenario

A new SAS data set named **Work.bonus** needs to be created by reading the **orion.sales** data set.

Work.bonus must include a new variable named **Bonus** that is equal to

- 500 for United States employees
- 300 for Australian employees.

Work.bonus must include another new variable named **Freq** that is equal to

- **Once a Year** for United States employees
- **Twice a Year** for Australian employees.

72

IF-THEN/ELSE Statements

Only **one** executable statement is allowed in IF-THEN/ELSE statements.

IF *expression* **THEN** *statement*;
ELSE IF *expression* **THEN** *statement*;
ELSE *statement*;

For the given business scenario, two statements need to be executed per each true expression.

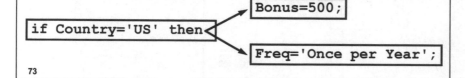

```
if Country='US' then
    Bonus=500;
    Freq='Once per Year';
```

73

IF-THEN DO/ELSE DO Statements

Multiple executable statements are allowed in IF-THEN DO/ELSE DO statements.

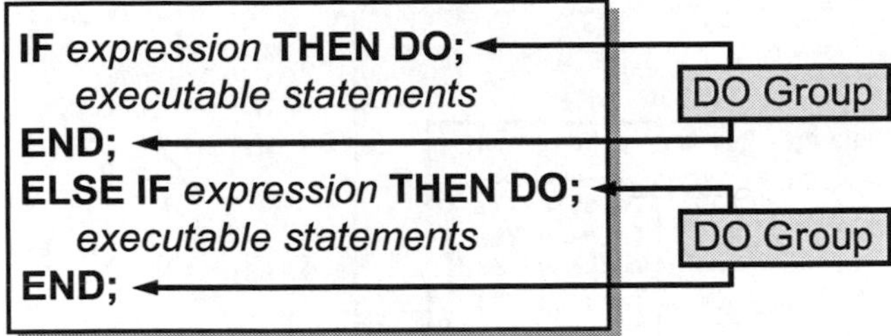

- Each DO group can contain multiple statements that apply to the expression.
- Each DO group ends with an END statement.

74

Business Scenario

Create another new variable named **Freq**.

```
data work.bonus;
   set orion.sales;
   if Country='US' then do;
      Bonus=500;
      Freq='Once a Year';
   end;
   else if Country='AU' then do;
      Bonus=300;
      Freq='Twice a Year';
   end;
run;
```

75 p109d04

Business Scenario

```
proc print data=work.bonus;
   var First_Name Last_Name
       Country Bonus Freq;
run;
```

Partial PROC PRINT Output

Obs	First_Name	Last_Name	Country	Bonus	Freq
60	Billy	Plested	AU	300	Twice a Yea
61	Matsuoka	Wills	AU	300	Twice a Yea
62	Vino	George	AU	300	Twice a Yea
63	Meera	Body	AU	300	Twice a Yea
64	Harry	Highpoint	US	500	Once a Year
65	Julienne	Magolan	US	500	Once a Year
66	Scott	Desanctis	US	500	Once a Year
67	Cherda	Ridley	US	500	Once a Year
68	Priscilla	Farren	US	500	Once a Year
69	Robert	Stevens	US	500	Once a Year

76

p109d04

Compilation

```
data work.bonus;
   set orion.sales;
   if Country='US' then do;
      Bonus=500;
      Freq='Once a Year';
   end;
   else if Country='AU' then do;
      Bonus=300;
      Freq='Twice a Year';
   end;
run;
```

PDV

Employee_ID N 8	First_Name $ 12	...	Hire_Date N 8

77

...

Compilation

```
data work.bonus;
   set orion.sales;
   if Country='US' then do;
      Bonus=500;
      Freq='Once a Year';
   end;
   else if Country='AU' then do;
      Bonus=300;
      Freq='Twice a Year';
   end;
run;
```

PDV

Employee_ID	First_Name	...	Hire_Date	Bonus
N 8	$ 12		N 8	N 8

78 ...

Compilation

```
data work.bonus;
   set orion.sales;
   if Country='US' then do;
      Bonus=500;
      Freq='Once a Year';
   end;
   else if Country='AU' then do;
      Bonus=300;
      Freq='Twice a Year';
   end;
run;
```

11 characters

PDV

Employee_ID	First_Name	...	Hire_Date	Bonus	Freq
N 8	$ 12		N 8	N 8	$ 11

79

9.06 Quiz

How would you prevent **Freq** from being truncated?

81

The LENGTH Statement (Review)

The *LENGTH statement* defines the length of a variable explicitly.

General form of the LENGTH statement:

LENGTH *variable(s)* $ *length*;

Example:

```
length First_Name Last_Name $ 12
       Gender $ 1;
```

83

Business Scenario

Set the length of the variable **Freq** to avoid truncation.

```
data work.bonus;
   set orion.sales;
   length Freq $ 12;
   if Country='US' then do;
      Bonus=500;
      Freq='Once a Year';
   end;
   else if Country='AU' then do;
      Bonus=300;
      Freq='Twice a Year';
   end;
run;
```

84 p109d04

Business Scenario

```
proc print data=work.bonus;
   var First_Name Last_Name
       Country Bonus Freq;
run;
```

Partial PROC PRINT Output

Obs	First_Name	Last_Name	Country	Bonus	Freq
60	Billy	Plested	AU	300	Twice a Year
61	Matsuoka	Wills	AU	300	Twice a Year
62	Vino	George	AU	300	Twice a Year
63	Meera	Body	AU	300	Twice a Year
64	Harry	Highpoint	US	500	Once a Year
65	Julienne	Magolan	US	500	Once a Year
66	Scott	Desanctis	US	500	Once a Year
67	Cherda	Ridley	US	500	Once a Year
68	Priscilla	Farren	US	500	Once a Year
69	Robert	Stevens	US	500	Once a Year

85 p109d04

ELSE Statements

The conditional clause does not have to be in an ELSE statement.

```
data work.bonus;
   set orion.sales;
   length Freq $ 12;
   if Country='US' then do;
      Bonus=500;
      Freq='Once a Year';
   end;
   else do;
      Bonus=300;
      Freq='Twice a Year';
   end;
run;
```

⚠ All observations not equal to US execute the statements in the second DO group.

86 p109d04

Exercises

Level 1

4. Creating Variables Conditionally

a. Retrieve the starter program **p109e04**.

b. In the DATA step, create three new variables, **Discount**, **DiscountType**, and **Region**.

If **Country** is equal to `CA` or `US`,

- **Discount** is equal to `0.10`
- **DiscountType** is equal to `Required`
- **Region** is equal to `North America`.

If **Country** is equal to any other value,

- **Discount** is equal to `0.05`
- **DiscountType** is equal to `Optional`
- **Region** is equal to `Not North America`.

c. Include only the following variables: **Supplier_Name**, **Country**, **Discount**, **DiscountType**, and **Region**.

d. Submit the program to create the following PROC PRINT report:

Partial PROC PRINT Output (First 10 of 52 Observations)

Obs	Supplier_Name	Country	Region	Discount	Discount Type
1	Scandinavian Clothing A/S	NO	Not North America	0.05	Optional
2	Petterson AB	SE	Not North America	0.05	Optional
3	Prime Sports Ltd	GB	Not North America	0.05	Optional
4	Top Sports	DK	Not North America	0.05	Optional
5	AllSeasons Outdoor Clothing	US	North America	0.10	Required
6	Sportico	ES	Not North America	0.05	Optional
7	British Sports Ltd	GB	Not North America	0.05	Optional
8	Eclipse Inc	US	North America	0.10	Required
9	Magnifico Sports	PT	Not North America	0.05	Optional
10	Pro Sportswear Inc	US	North America	0.10	Required

Level 2

5. Creating Variables Unconditionally and Conditionally

a. Write a DATA step to read **orion.orders** to create **Work.ordertype**.

b. Create the new variable **DayOfWeek**, which is equal to the week day of **Order_Date**.

c. Create the new variable **Type**, which is equal to
- `Catalog Sale` if **Order_Type** is equal to `1`
- `Internet Sale` if **Order_Type** is equal to `2`
- `Retail Sale` if **Order_Type** is equal to `3`.

d. Create the new variable **SaleAds**, which is equal to
- `Mail` if **Order_Type** is equal to `1`
- `Email` if **Order_Type** is equal to `2`.

e. Do not include **Order_Type, Employee_ID**, and **Customer_ID**.

f. Write a PROC PRINT step to create the following report:

Partial PROC PRINT Output (First 20 of 490 Observations)

Obs	Order_ID	Order_ Date	Delivery_ Date	Type	Sale Ads	Day Of Week
1	1230058123	11JAN2003	11JAN2003	Catalog Sale	Mail	7
2	1230080101	15JAN2003	19JAN2003	Internet Sale	Email	4
3	1230106883	20JAN2003	22JAN2003	Internet Sale	Email	2
4	1230147441	28JAN2003	28JAN2003	Catalog Sale	Mail	3
5	1230315085	27FEB2003	27FEB2003	Catalog Sale	Mail	5
6	1230333319	02MAR2003	03MAR2003	Internet Sale	Email	1
7	1230338566	03MAR2003	08MAR2003	Internet Sale	Email	2
8	1230371142	09MAR2003	11MAR2003	Internet Sale	Email	1
9	1230404278	15MAR2003	15MAR2003	Catalog Sale	Mail	7
10	1230440481	22MAR2003	22MAR2003	Catalog Sale	Mail	7
11	1230450371	24MAR2003	26MAR2003	Internet Sale	Email	2
12	1230453723	24MAR2003	25MAR2003	Internet Sale	Email	2
13	1230455630	25MAR2003	25MAR2003	Catalog Sale	Mail	3
14	1230478006	28MAR2003	30MAR2003	Internet Sale	Email	6
15	1230498538	01APR2003	01APR2003	Catalog Sale	Mail	3
16	1230500669	02APR2003	03APR2003	Retail Sale		4
17	1230503155	02APR2003	03APR2003	Internet Sale	Email	4
18	1230591673	18APR2003	23APR2003	Internet Sale	Email	6
19	1230591675	18APR2003	20APR2003	Retail Sale		6
20	1230591684	18APR2003	18APR2003	Catalog Sale	Mail	6

Level 3

6. Using WHEN Statements in a SELECT Group to Create Variables Conditionally

a. Write a DATA step to read `orion.nonsales` to create `Work.gifts`.

b. Create two new variables, **Gift1** and **Gift2**, using a SELECT group with WHEN statements.

If **Gender** is equal to `F`,

- **Gift1** is equal to `Perfume`
- **Gift2** is equal to `Cookware`.

If **Gender** is equal to `M`,

- **Gift1** is equal to `Cologne`
- **Gift2** is equal to `Lawn Equipment`.

If **Gender** is not equal to `F` or `M`,

- **Gift1** is equal to `Coffee`
- **Gift2** is equal to `Calendar`.

Documentation on the SELECT group with WHEN statements can be found in the SAS Help and Documentation from the Contents tab (**SAS Products** ⇨ **Base SAS** ⇨ **SAS 9.2 Language Reference: Dictionary** ⇨ **Dictionary of Language Elements** ⇨ **Statements** ⇨ **SELECT Statement**).

c. Include only the following variables: **Employee_ID**, **First**, **Last**, **Gift1**, and **Gift2**.

d. Write a PROC PRINT step to create the following report:

Partial PROC PRINT Output (First 15 of 235 Observations)

Obs	Employee_ID	First	Last	Gift1	Gift2
1	120101	Patrick	Lu	Cologne	Lawn Equipment
2	120104	Kareen	Billington	Perfume	Cookware
3	120105	Liz	Povey	Perfume	Cookware
4	120106	John	Hornsey	Cologne	Lawn Equipment
5	120107	Sherie	Sheedy	Perfume	Cookware
6	120108	Gladys	Gromek	Perfume	Cookware
7	120108	Gabriele	Baker	Perfume	Cookware
8	120110	Dennis	Entwisle	Cologne	Lawn Equipment
9	120111	Ubaldo	Spillane	Cologne	Lawn Equipment
10	120112	Ellis	Glattback	Perfume	Cookware
11	120113	Riu	Horsey	Perfume	Cookware
12	120114	Jeannette	Buddery	Coffee	Calendar
13	120115	Hugh	Nichollas	Cologne	Lawn Equipment
14	.	Austen	Ralston	Cologne	Lawn Equipment
15	120117	Bill	Mccleary	Cologne	Lawn Equipment

9.3 Subsetting Observations

Objectives

- Subset observations by using the WHERE statement.
- Subset observations by using the subsetting IF statement.
- Subset observations by using the IF-THEN DELETE statement. (Self-Study)

90

Business Scenario

A new SAS data set named **`Work.december`** needs to be created by reading the **`orion.sales`** data set.

`Work.december` must include the following new variables:

- **`Bonus`**, which is equal to a constant 500.
- **`Compensation`**, which is the combination of the employee's salary and bonus.
- **`BonusMonth`**, which is equal to the month the employee was hired.

`Work.december` must include only the employees from Australia who have a bonus month in December.

91

The WHERE Statement (Review)

The *WHERE statement* subsets observations that meet a particular condition.

General form of the WHERE statement:

WHERE *where-expression*;

The *where-expression* is a sequence of operands and operators that form a set of instructions that define a condition for selecting observations.

- Operands include constants and variables.
- Operators are symbols that request a comparison, arithmetic calculation, or logical operation.

92

Processing the WHERE Statement

The WHERE statement selects observations **before** they are brought into the program data vector.

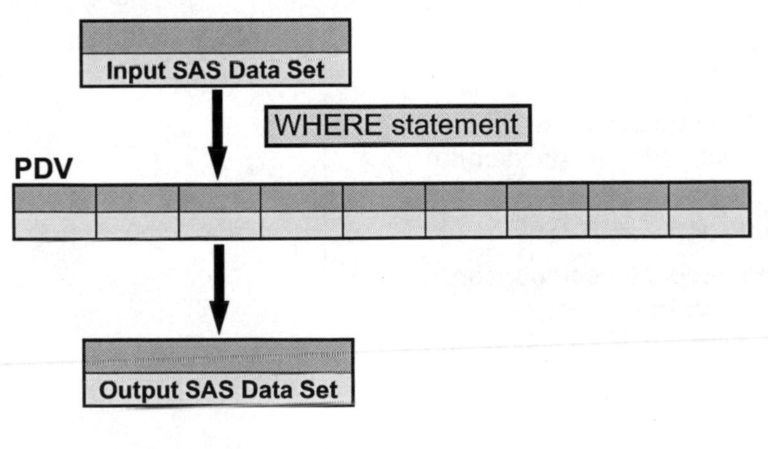

93

NO COMPUTED VARIABLE IN THE WHERE STATEMENT

9.07 Quiz

Why does the WHERE statement not work in this DATA step?

```
data work.december;
   set orion.sales;
   BonusMonth=month(Hire_Date);
   Bonus=500;
   Compensation=sum(Salary,Bonus);
   where Country='AU' and BonusMonth=12;
run;
```

ERROR

* NO COMPUTED VARIABLE/S IN THE WHERE STATEMENT *

— SAS is computing 0 or missing, too early

95

p109d05

The Subsetting IF Statement

The *subsetting IF statement* continues processing only those observations that meet the condition.

General form of the subsetting IF statement:

IF *expression*;

The *expression* is a sequence of operands and operators that form a set of instructions that define a condition for selecting observations.

- Operands include constants and variables.
- Operators are symbols that request a comparison, arithmetic calculation, or logical operation.

97

The Subsetting IF Statement

Examples:

```
if Salary > 50000;
```

```
if Last_Name='Smith' and First_Name='Joe';
```

```
if Country not in ('GB', 'FR', 'NL');
```

```
if Hire_Date = '15APR2008'd;
```

```
if BirthMonth = 5 or BirthMonth = 6;
```

```
if upcase(Gender)='M';
```

```
if 40000 <= Compensation <= 80000;
```

```
if sum(Salary,Bonus) < 43000;
```

98

Special WHERE operators such as BETWEEN-AND, IS NULL, IS MISSING, CONTAINS, and LIKE cannot be used with the subsetting IF statement.

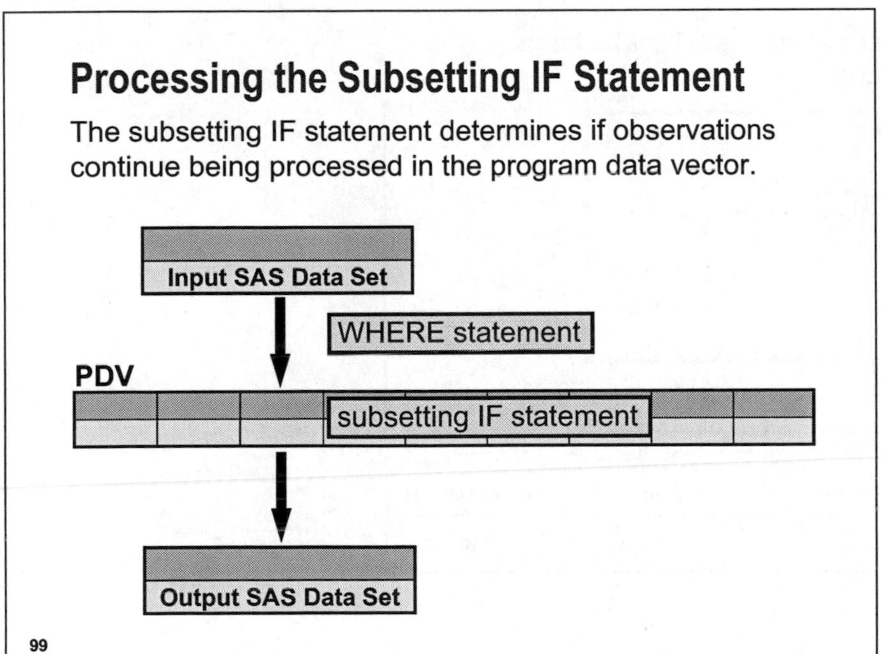

Processing the Subsetting IF Statement
The subsetting IF statement determines if observations continue being processed in the program data vector.
Input SAS Data Set
WHERE statement
PDV
subsetting IF statement
Output SAS Data Set
99

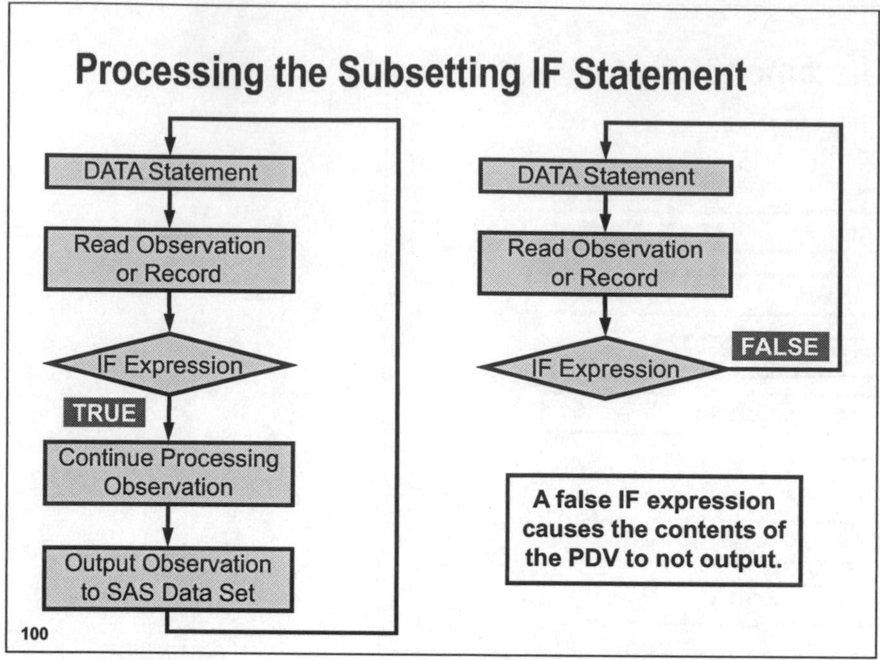

Business Scenario

Include only the employees from Australia who have a bonus month in December.

```
data work.december;
   set orion.sales;
   where Country='AU';
   BonusMonth=month(Hire_Date);
   if BonusMonth=12;
   Bonus=500;
   Compensation=sum(Salary,Bonus);
run;
```

Partial SAS Log

```
NOTE: There were 63 observations read from the data set ORION.SALES.
      WHERE Country='AU';
NOTE: The data set WORK.DECEMBER has 3 observations and 12 variables.
```

101 p109d05

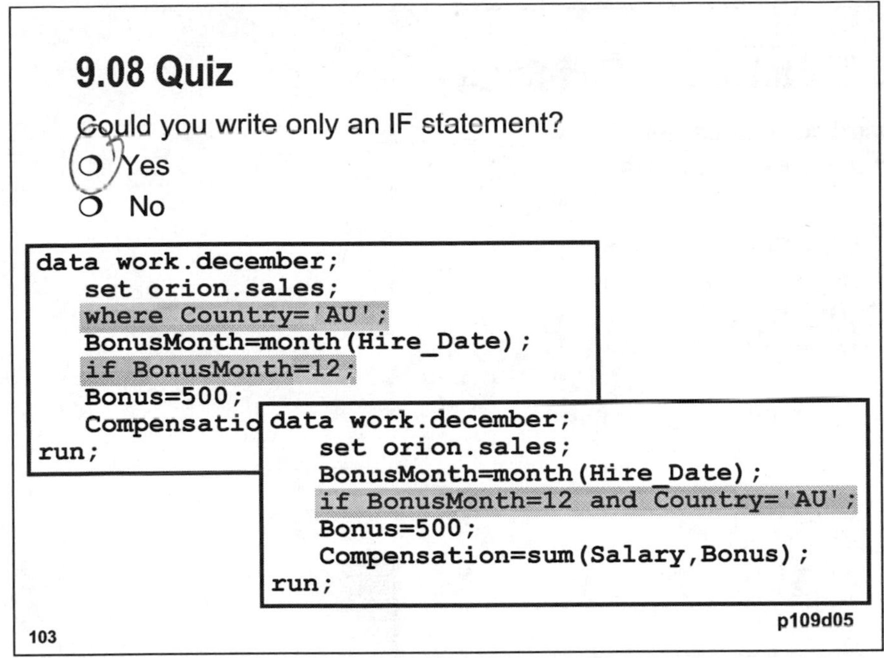
9.08 Quiz
Could you write only an IF statement?
Yes
No
data work.december;
set orion.sales;
where Country='AU';
BonusMonth=month(Hire_Date);
if BonusMonth=12;
Bonus=500;
Compensatio
run;
data work.december;
set orion.sales;
BonusMonth=month(Hire_Date);
if BonusMonth=12 and Country='AU';
Bonus=500;
Compensation=sum(Salary,Bonus);
run;
103
p109d05

WHERE Statement versus Subsetting IF Statement

Step and Usage	WHERE	IF
PROC step	Yes	No
DATA step (source of variable)		
INPUT statement	No	Yes
assignment statement	No	Yes
SET statement (single data set)	Yes	Yes
SET/MERGE statement (multiple data sets)		
Variable in ALL data sets	Yes	Yes
Variable not in ALL data sets	No	Yes

105

The IF-THEN DELETE Statement (Self-Study)

An alternative to the subsetting IF statement is the DELETE statement in an IF-THEN statement.

General form of the IF-THEN DELETE statement:

IF *expression* **THEN DELETE;**

The *DELETE statement* stops processing the current observation.

107

When the DELETE statement executes, the current observation is not written to a data set, and SAS returns immediately to the beginning of the DATA step for the next iteration.

The IF-THEN DELETE Statement (Self-Study)

```
data work.december;
   set orion.sales;
   where Country='AU';
   BonusMonth=month(Hire_Date);
   if BonusMonth ne 12 then delete;
   Bonus=500;
   Compensation=sum(Salary,Bonus);
run;
```

equivalent

```
data work.december;
   set orion.sales;
   where Country='AU';
   BonusMonth=month(Hire_Date);
   if BonusMonth=12;
   Bonus=500;
   Compensation=sum(Salary,Bonus);
run;
```

108 p109d06

Exercises

Level 1

7. Subsetting Observations Based on Two Conditions

a. Retrieve the starter program **p109e07**.

b. In the DATA step, write a statement to select only the observations that have **Emp_Hire_Date** greater than or equal to July 1, 2006. Subset the observations as they are being read into the program data vector.

c. In the DATA step, write another statement to select only the observations that have an increase greater than 3000.

d. Submit the program to create the following PROC PRINT report:

Obs	Employee ID	Employee Annual Salary	Employee Hire Date	Increase	NewSalary
1	120128	30,890	01NOV2006	3,089	33,979
2	120144	30,265	01OCT2006	3,027	33,292
3	120161	30,785	01OCT2006	3,079	33,864
4	120264	37,510	01DEC2006	3,751	41,261
5	120761	30,960	01JUL2006	3,096	34,056
6	120995	34,850	01AUG2006	3,485	38,335
7	121055	30,185	01AUG2006	3,019	33,204
8	121062	30,305	01AUG2006	3,031	33,336
9	121085	32,235	01JAN2007	3,224	35,459
10	121107	31,380	01JUL2006	3,138	34,518

Level 2

8. Subsetting Observations Based on Three Conditions

a. Write a DATA step to read **orion.orders** to create **Work.delays**.

b. Create the new variable **Order_Month**, which is equal to the month of **Order_Date**.

c. Use a WHERE statement and a subsetting IF statement to select only the observations that meet all of the following conditions:

- **Delivery_Date** values that are more than four days beyond **Order_Date**
- **Employee_ID** values that are equal to 99999999
- **Order_Month** values occurring in August

d. Write a PROC PRINT step to create the following report:

Obs	Order_ID	Order_ Type	Employee_ID	Customer_ID	Order_ Date	Delivery_ Date	Order_ Month
1	1231227910	2	99999999	70187	13AUG2003	18AUG2003	8
2	1231270767	3	99999999	52	20AUG2003	26AUG2003	8
3	1231305521	2	99999999	16	27AUG2003	04SEP2003	8
4	1231317443	2	99999999	61	29AUG2003	03SEP2003	8
5	1233484749	3	99999999	2550	10AUG2004	15AUG2004	8
6	1233514453	3	99999999	70201	15AUG2004	20AUG2004	8
7	1236673732	3	99999999	9	10AUG2005	15AUG2005	8
8	1240051245	3	99999999	71	30AUG2006	05SEP2006	8
9	1243165497	3	99999999	70201	24AUG2007	29AUG2007	8

Level 3

9. Using an IF-THEN DELETE Statement to Subset Observations

a. Write a DATA step to read `orion.employee_donations` to create `Work.bigdonations`.

b. Create the new variable `Total`, which is equal to the sum of `Qtr1`, `Qtr2`, `Qtr3`, and `Qtr4`.

c. Create the new variable `NoDonation`, which is equal to the count of missing values in `Qtr1`, `Qtr2`, `Qtr3`, and `Qtr4`. Use the NMISS function.

> Documentation on the NMISS function can be found in the SAS Help and Documentation from the Contents tab (**SAS Products** ⇨ **Base SAS** ⇨ **SAS 9.2 Language Reference: Dictionary** ⇨ **Dictionary of Language Elements** ⇨ **Functions and CALL Routines** ⇨ **NMISS Function**).

d. The final data set should contain only observations meeting the following two conditions:

- `Total` values greater than or equal to 50
- `NoDonation` values equal to 0.

Use an IF-THEN DELETE statement to eliminate the observations where the conditions are not met.

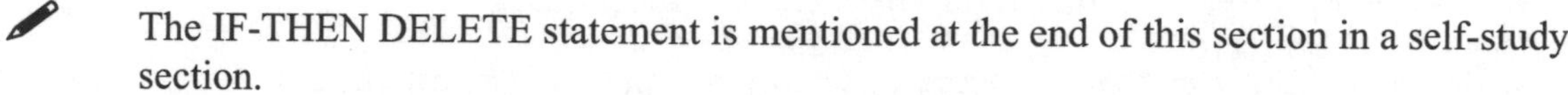

> The IF-THEN DELETE statement is mentioned at the end of this section in a self-study section.

e. Write a PROC PRINT step with a VAR statement to create the following report:

Partial PROC PRINT Output (First 7 of 50 Observations)

Obs	Employee_ID	Qtr1	Qtr2	Qtr3	Qtr4	Total	No Donation
1	120267	15	15	15	15	60	0
2	120269	20	20	20	20	80	0
3	120271	20	20	20	20	80	0
4	120275	15	15	15	15	60	0
5	120660	25	25	25	25	100	0
6	120669	15	15	15	15	60	0
7	120671	20	20	20	20	80	0

9.4 Chapter Review

Chapter Review

1. What is an advantage in using the SUM function instead of an arithmetic operator?

2. Do the DROP/KEEP statements eliminate variables from the input or output data set in the DATA step?

3. When would you use DO group statements in the DATA step?

4. What is the default length of a numeric variable created in an assignment statement?

110

9.5 Solutions

Solutions to Exercises

1. **Creating Two New Variables**

   a. Retrieve the starter program.

   b. Create two new variables.

```
data work.increase;
   set orion.staff;
   Increase=Salary*0.10;
   NewSalary=sum(Salary,Increase);
run;

proc print data=work.increase label;
run;
```

   c. Include only four variables.

```
data work.increase;
   set orion.staff;
   Increase=Salary*0.10;
   NewSalary=sum(Salary,Increase);
   keep Employee_ID Salary Increase NewSalary;
run;

proc print data=work.increase label;
run;
```

   d. Format three variables.

```
data work.increase;
   set orion.staff;
   Increase=Salary*0.10;
   NewSalary=sum(Salary,Increase);
   keep Employee_ID Salary Increase NewSalary;
   format Salary Increase NewSalary comma10.;
run;

proc print data=work.increase label;
run;
```

   e. Submit the program.

2. **Creating Three New Variables**

   a. Write a DATA step.

```
data work.birthday;
   set orion.customer;
run;
```

b. Create three new variables.

```
data work.birthday;
   set orion.customer;
   Bday2009=mdy(month(Birth_Date),day(Birth_Date),2009);
   BdayDOW2009=weekday(Bday2009);
   Age2009=(Bday2009-Birth_Date)/365.25;
run;
```

c. Include only five variables.

```
data work.birthday;
   set orion.customer;
   Bday2009=mdy(month(Birth_Date),day(Birth_Date),2009);
   BdayDOW2009=weekday(Bday2009);
   Age2009=(Bday2009-Birth_Date)/365.25;
   keep Customer_Name Birth_Date Bday2009 BdayDOW2009 Age2009;
run;
```

d. Format two variables.

```
data work.birthday;
   set orion.customer;
   Bday2009=mdy(month(Birth_Date),day(Birth_Date),2009);
   BdayDOW2009=weekday(Bday2009);
   Age2009=(Bday2009-Birth_Date)/365.25;
   keep Customer_Name Birth_Date Bday2009 BdayDOW2009 Age2009;
   format Bday2009 date9. Age2009 3.;
run;
```

e. Write a PROC PRINT step.

```
proc print data=work.birthday;
run;
```

3. Using the CATX and INTCK Functions to Create Variables

a. Write a DATA step.

```
data work.employees;
   set orion.sales;
run;
```

b. Create the new variable `FullName`.

```
data work.employees;
   set orion.sales;
   FullName=catx(' ',First_Name,Last_Name);
run;
```

c. Create the new variable `Yrs2012`.

```
data work.employees;
   set orion.sales;
   FullName=catx(' ',First_Name,Last_Name);
   Yrs2012=intck('year',Hire_Date,'01JAN2012'd);
run;
```

d. Format **Hire_Date**.

```
data work.employees;
   set orion.sales;
   FullName=catx(' ',First_Name,Last_Name);
   Yrs2012=intck('year',Hire_Date,'01JAN2012'd);
   format Hire_Date ddmmyy10.;
run;
```

e. Add a label.

```
data work.employees;
   set orion.sales;
   FullName=catx(' ',First_Name,Last_Name);
   Yrs2012=intck('year',Hire_Date,'01JAN2012'd);
   format Hire_Date ddmmyy10.;
   label Yrs2012='Years of Employment in 2012';
run;
```

f. Write a PROC PRINT step.

```
proc print data=work.employees label;
   var FullName Hire_Date Yrs2012;
run;
```

4. Creating Variables Conditionally

a. Retrieve the starter program.

b. Create three new variables.

```
data work.region;
   set orion.supplier;
   length Region $ 17;
   if Country in ('CA','US') then do;
      Discount=0.10;
      DiscountType='Required';
      Region='North America';
   end;
   else do;
      Discount=0.05;
      DiscountType='Optional';
      Region='Not North America';
   end;
run;

proc print data=work.region;
run;
```

c. Include only five variables.

```
data work.region;
   set orion.supplier;
   length Region $ 17;
   if Country in ('CA','US') then do;
      Discount=0.10;
      DiscountType='Required';
      Region='North America';
   end;
   else do;
      Discount=0.05;
      DiscountType='Optional';
      Region='Not North America';
   end;
   keep Supplier_Name Country
        Discount DiscountType Region ;
run;

proc print data=work.region;
run;
```

d. Submit the program.

5. **Creating Variables Unconditionally and Conditionally**

a. Write a DATA step.

```
data work.ordertype;
   set orion.orders;
run;
```

b. Create the new variable **DayOfWeek**.

```
data work.ordertype;
   set orion.orders;
   DayOfWeek=weekday(Order_Date);
run;
```

c. Create the new variable **Type**.

```
data work.ordertype;
   set orion.orders;
   length Type $ 13;
   DayOfWeek=weekday(Order_Date);
   if Order_Type=1 then do;
      Type='Catalog Sale';
   end;
   else if Order_Type=2 then do;
      Type='Internet Sale';
   end;
   else if Order_Type=3 then do;
      Type='Retail Sale';
   end;
run;
```

d. Create the new variable **SaleAds**.

```
data work.ordertype;
   set orion.orders;
   length Type $ 13 SaleAds $ 5;
   DayOfWeek=weekday(Order_Date);
   if Order_Type=1 then do;
      Type='Catalog Sale';
      SaleAds='Mail';
   end;
   else if Order_Type=2 then do;
      Type='Internet Sale';
      SaleAds='Email';
   end;
   else if Order_Type=3 then do;
      Type='Retail Sale';
   end;
run;
```

e. Do not include three variables.

```
data work.ordertype;
   set orion.orders;
   length Type $ 13 SaleAds $ 5;
   DayOfWeek=weekday(Order_Date);
   if Order_Type=1 then do;
      Type='Catalog Sale';
      SaleAds='Mail';
   end;
   else if Order_Type=2 then do;
      Type='Internet Sale';
      SaleAds='Email';
   end;
   else if Order_Type=3 then do;
      Type='Retail Sale';
   end;
   drop Order_Type Employee_ID Customer_ID;
run;
```

f. Write a PROC PRINT step.

```
proc print data=work.ordertype;
run;
```

6. Using WHEN Statements in a SELECT Group to Create Variables Conditionally

a. Write a DATA step.

```
data work.gifts;
   set orion.nonsales;
run;
```

b. Create two new variables.

```
data work.gifts;
   set orion.nonsales;
   length Gift1 Gift2 $ 15;
   select(Gender);
      when('F') do;
         Gift1='Perfume';
         Gift2='Cookware';
      end;
      when('M') do;
         Gift1='Cologne';
         Gift2='Lawn Equipment';
      end;
      otherwise do;
         Gift1='Coffee';
         Gift2='Calendar';
      end;
   end;
run;
```

c. Include only five variables.

```
data work.gifts;
   set orion.nonsales;
   length Gift1 Gift2 $ 15;
   select(Gender);
      when('F') do;
         Gift1='Perfume';
         Gift2='Cookware';
      end;
      when('M') do;
         Gift1='Cologne';
         Gift2='Lawn Equipment';
      end;
      otherwise do;
         Gift1='Coffee';
         Gift2='Calendar';
      end;
   end;
   keep Employee_ID First Last Gift1 Gift2;
run;
```

d. Write a PROC PRINT step.

```
proc print data=gifts;
run;
```

7. **Subsetting Observations Based on Two Conditions**

   a. Retrieve the starter program.

   b. Write a statement to select only the observations based on **Emp_Hire_Date**.

```
data work.increase;
   set orion.staff;
   where Emp_Hire_Date>='01JUL2006'd;
   Increase=Salary*0.10;
   NewSalary=sum(Salary,Increase);
   keep Employee_ID Emp_Hire_Date Salary Increase NewSalary;
   format Salary Increase NewSalary comma10.;
run;

proc print data=work.increase label;
run;
```

   c. Write another statement to select only the observations based on **Increase**.

```
data work.increase;
   set orion.staff;
   where Emp_Hire_Date>='01JUL2006'd;
   Increase=Salary*0.10;
   if Increase>3000;
   NewSalary=sum(Salary,Increase);
   keep Employee_ID Emp_Hire_Date Salary Increase NewSalary;
   format Salary Increase NewSalary comma10.;
run;

proc print data=work.increase label;
run;
```

   d. Submit the program.

8. **Subsetting Observations Based on Three Conditions**

   a. Write a DATA step.

```
data work.delays;
   set orion.orders;
run;
```

   b. Create a new variable.

```
data work.delays;
   set orion.orders;
   Order_Month=month(Order_Date);
run;
```

c. Use a WHERE statement and a subsetting IF statement.

```
data work.delays;
   set orion.orders;
   where Order_Date+4<Delivery_Date
         and Employee_ID=99999999;
   Order_Month=month(Order_Date);
   if Order_Month=8;
run;
```

d. Write a PROC PRINT step.

```
proc print data=work.delays;
run;
```

9. **Using an IF-THEN DELETE Statement to Subset Observations**

a. Write a DATA step.

```
data work.bigdonations;
   set orion.employee_donations;
run;
```

b. Create the new variable `Total`.

```
data work.bigdonations;
   set orion.employee_donations;
   Total=sum(Qtr1,Qtr2,Qtr3,Qtr4);
run;
```

c. Create the new variable `NoDonation`.

```
data work.bigdonations;
   set orion.employee_donations;
   Total=sum(Qtr1,Qtr2,Qtr3,Qtr4);
   NoDonation=nmiss(Qtr1,Qtr2,Qtr3,Qtr4);
run;
```

d. Use an IF-THEN DELETE statement.

```
data work.bigdonations;
   set orion.employee_donations;
   Total=sum(Qtr1,Qtr2,Qtr3,Qtr4);
   NoDonation=nmiss(Qtr1,Qtr2,Qtr3,Qtr4);
   if Total < 50 or NoDonation > 0 then delete;
run;
```

e. Write a PROC PRINT step.

```
proc print data=work.bigdonations;
   var Employee_ID Qtr1 Qtr2 Qtr3 Qtr4 Total NoDonation;
run;
```

Solutions to Student Activities (Polls/Quizzes)

9.01 Quiz – Correct Answer

What is the result of the assignment statement?

a. . (missing)
b. 0
c. 7
d. 9 (circled)

```
num = 4 + 10 / 2;
```

The order of operations from left to right is division and multiplication followed by addition and subtraction.

Parentheses can be used to control the order of operations.

```
num = (4 + 10) / 2;
```

13

9.02 Quiz – Correct Answer

What is the result of the assignment statement given the values of **var1** and **var2**?

a. . (missing) (circled)
b. 0
c. 5
d. 10

```
num = var1 + var2 / 2;
```

var1	var2
.	10

If an operand is missing for an arithmetic operator, the result is missing.

16

9.03 Quiz – Correct Answer

What statement needs to be added to the DATA step to eliminate six of the 12 variables?

the DROP or KEEP statement

26

9.04 Poll – Correct Answer

Are the correct results produced when the DROP statement is placed after the SET statement?

- ❍ Yes (circled)
- ❍ No

Yes, the DROP statement specifies the names of the variables to omit from the output data set.

33

9.05 Quiz – Correct Answer

Why are some of the `Bonus` values missing in the PROC PRINT output for `orion.nonsales`?

`Country` has mixed case values in the `orion.nonsales` data set.

The UPCASE function will correct the issue.

```
data work.bonus;
   set orion.nonsales;
   if upcase(Country)='US'
      then Bonus=500;
   else if upcase(Country)='AU'
        then Bonus=300;
run;
```

70 p109a02s

9.06 Quiz – Correct Answer

How would you prevent `Freq` from being truncated?

Possible solutions:

- **Pad the first occurrence of the `Freq` value with blanks to be the length of the longest possible value.**
- **Switch conditional statements to place the longest value of `Freq` in the first conditional statement.**
- **Add a LENGTH statement to declare the byte size of the variable up front.**

82

9.07 Quiz – Correct Answer

Why does the WHERE statement not work in this DATA step?

```
data work.december;
   set orion.sales;
   BonusMonth=month(Hire_Date);
   Bonus=500;
   Compensation=sum(Salary,Bonus);
   where Country='AU' and BonusMonth=12;
run;
```

The WHERE statement can only subset variables that are coming from an existing data set.

```
ERROR: Variable BonusMonth is not on file ORION.SALES.
```

96

p109d05

9.08 Quiz – Correct Answer

Could you write only an IF statement?

- (O) Yes (circled)
- O No

Yes, but the program using both the WHERE and IF statements is more efficient.

Both methods create a data set with three observations. The program using both statements reads 63 observations into the PDV. The program using only the IF statement reads 165 observations into the PDV.

104

p109d05

Solutions to Chapter Review

Chapter Review Answers

1. What is an advantage in using the SUM function instead of an arithmetic operator?

   The SUM function ignores missing values.

2. Do the DROP/KEEP statements eliminate variables from the input or output data set in the DATA step?

   the output data set

3. When would you use DO group statements in the DATA step?

   Use DO group statements when you want to execute multiple statements as a result of a true IF expression in an IF-THEN statement.

111

continued...

Chapter Review Answers

4. What is the default length of a numeric variable created in an assignment statement?

   8 bytes

112

Chapter 10 Combining SAS Data Sets

10.1 Introduction to Combining Data Sets 10-3

10.2 Appending a Data Set (Self-Study) 10-7

Exercises 10-17

10.3 Concatenating Data Sets 10-19

Exercises 10-41

10.4 Merging Data Sets One-to-One 10-44

10.5 Merging Data Sets One-to-Many 10-53

Exercises 10-64

10.6 Merging Data Sets with Nonmatches 10-66

Exercises 10-89

10.7 Chapter Review 10-92

10.8 Solutions 10-93

Solutions to Exercises 10-93

Solutions to Student Activities (Polls/Quizzes) 10-100

Solutions to Chapter Review 10-107

10.1 Introduction to Combining Data Sets

Objectives

- Define the methods for combining SAS data sets.

3

Appending and Concatenating

Appending and concatenating involves combining SAS data sets, one after the other, into a single SAS data set.

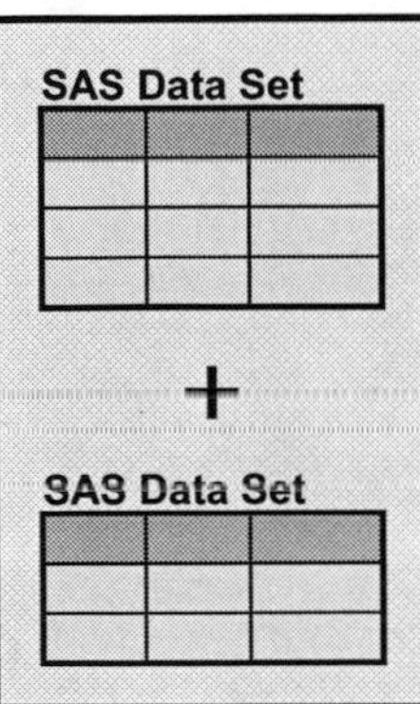

- *Appending* adds the observations in the second data set directly to the end of the original data set.
- *Concatenating* copies all observations from the first data set and then copies all observations from one or more successive data sets into a new data set.

—creating a brand-new dataset

ex. 100 + 100 = 200 records

4

Merging

Merging involves combining observations from two or more SAS data sets into a single observation in a new SAS data set.

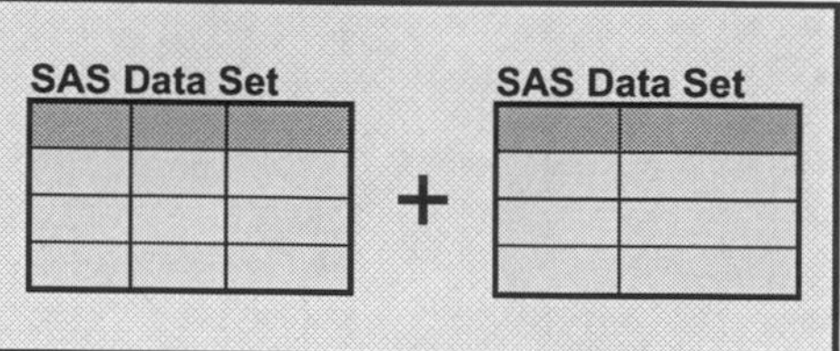

Observations can be merged based on their positions in the original data sets or merged by one or more common variables.

5

Example: Appending a Data Set

One data set is appended to a master data set.

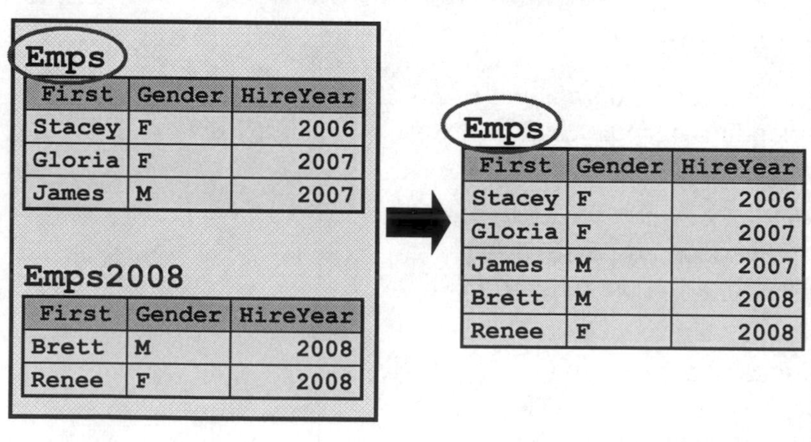

Emps

First	Gender	HireYear
Stacey	F	2006
Gloria	F	2007
James	M	2007

Emps2008

First	Gender	HireYear
Brett	M	2008
Renee	F	2008

Emps

First	Gender	HireYear
Stacey	F	2006
Gloria	F	2007
James	M	2007
Brett	M	2008
Renee	F	2008

6

Example: Concatenating Data Sets

Two data sets are concatenated to create a new data set.

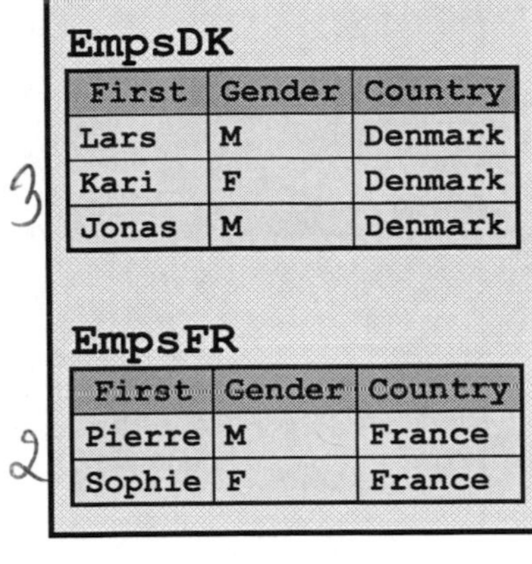

EmpsDK

First	Gender	Country
Lars	M	Denmark
Kari	F	Denmark
Jonas	M	Denmark

EmpsFR

First	Gender	Country
Pierre	M	France
Sophie	F	France

EmpsAll

First	Gender	Country
Lars	M	Denmark
Kari	F	Denmark
Jonas	M	Denmark
Pierre	M	France
Sophie	F	France

7

Example: Merging Data Sets

Two data sets are merged to create a new data set.

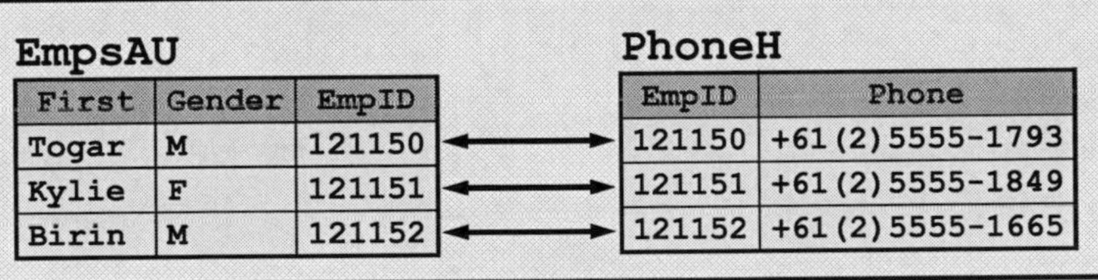

EmpsAU

First	Gender	EmpID
Togar	M	121150
Kylie	F	121151
Birin	M	121152

PhoneH

EmpID	Phone
121150	+61(2)5555-1793
121151	+61(2)5555-1849
121152	+61(2)5555-1665

EmpsAUH

First	Gender	EmpID	Phone
Togar	M	121150	+61(2)5555-1793
Kylie	F	121151	+61(2)5555-1849
Birin	M	121152	+61(2)5555-1665

8

10.01 Quiz

Which method (appending, concatenating, or merging) should be used for the given business scenario?

	Business Scenario	Method
1	The **JanSales**, **FebSales**, and **MarSales** data sets need to be combined to create the **Qtr1Sales** data set.	
2	The **Sales** data set needs to be combined with the **Target** data set by **month** to compare the sales data to the target data.	
3	The **OctSales** data set needs to be added to the **YTD** data set.	

10

10.2 Appending a Data Set (Self-Study)

Objectives

- Append one SAS data set to another SAS data set by using the APPEND procedure.
- Append a SAS data set containing additional variables to another SAS data set by using the FORCE option with the APPEND procedure.

14

Appending and Concatenating

Appending and concatenating involves combining SAS data sets, one after the other, into a single SAS data set.

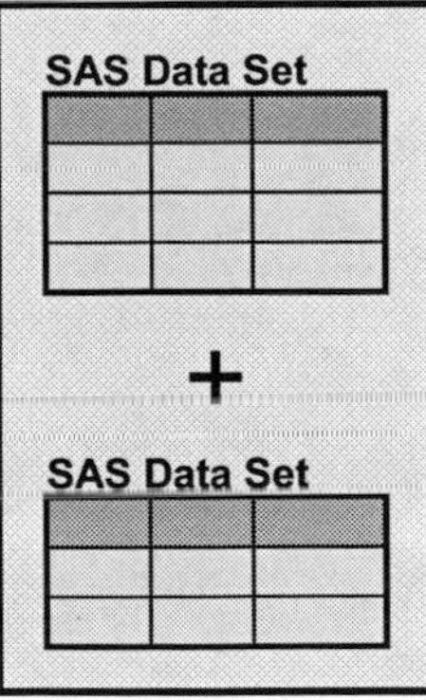

- Appending adds the observations in the second data set directly to the end of the original data set.
- Concatenating copies all observations from the first data set and then copies all observations from one or more successive data sets into a new data set.

15

The APPEND Procedure

The *APPEND procedure* adds the observations from one SAS data set to the end of another SAS data set.

General form of the APPEND procedure:

```
PROC APPEND  BASE = SAS-data-set
             DATA = SAS-data-set;
RUN;
```

BASE= names the data set to which observations are added.

DATA= names the data set containing observations that are added to the base data set.

16

The APPEND Procedure

Requirements:

- Only two data sets can be used at a time in one step.
- The observations in the base data set are not read.
- The variable information in the descriptor portion of the base data set cannot change.

17

Business Scenario

Emps is a master data set that contains employees hired in 2006 and 2007.

Emps

First	Gender	HireYear
Stacey	F	2006
Gloria	F	2007
James	M	2007

18

Business Scenario

Emps is a master data set that contains employees hired in 2006 and 2007.

Emps

First	Gender	HireYear
Stacey	F	2006
Gloria	F	2007
James	M	2007

The employees hired in 2008, 2009, and 2010 need to be appended.

Emps2008

First	Gender	HireYear
Brett	M	2008
Renee	F	2008

Emps2009

First	HireYear
Sara	2009
Dennis	2009

Emps2010

First	HireYear	Country
Rose	2010	Spain
Eric	2010	Spain

19

10.02 Quiz

How many observations will be in **Emps** after appending the three data sets?

Emps

First	Gender	HireYear
Stacey	F	2006
Gloria	F	2007
James	M	2007

Emps2008

First	Gender	HireYear
Brett	M	2008
Renee	F	2008

Emps2009

First	HireYear
Sara	2009
Dennis	2009

Emps2010

First	HireYear	Country
Rose	2010	Spain
Eric	2010	Spain

21

10.03 Quiz

How many variables will be in **Emps** after appending the three data sets?

Emps

First	Gender	HireYear
Stacey	F	2006
Gloria	F	2007
James	M	2007

Emps2008

First	Gender	HireYear
Brett	M	2008
Renee	F	2008

Emps2009

First	HireYear
Sara	2009
Dennis	2009

Emps2010

First	HireYear	Country
Rose	2010	Spain
Eric	2010	Spain

24

Like-Structured Data Sets

Emps

First	Gender	HireYear
Stacey	F	2006
Gloria	F	2007
James	M	2007

Emps2008

First	Gender	HireYear
Brett	M	2008
Renee	F	2008

The data sets contain the same variables.

```
proc append base=Emps
            data=Emps2008;
run;
```

26

p110d01

Like-Structured Data Sets

```
proc append base=Emps
            data=Emps2008;
run;

NOTE: Appending WORK.EMPS2008 to WORK.EMPS.
NOTE: There were 2 observations read from the data set
      WORK.EMPS2008.
NOTE: 2 observations added.
NOTE: The data set WORK.EMPS has 5 observations and 3 variables.
```

Emps

First	Gender	HireYear
Stacey	F	2006
Gloria	F	2007
James	M	2007
Brett	M	2008
Renee	F	2008

27

Unlike-Structured Data Sets

Emps

First	Gender	HireYear
Stacey	F	2006
Gloria	F	2007
James	M	2007
Brett	M	2008
Renee	F	2008

Emps2009

First	HireYear
Sara	2009
Dennis	2009

The BASE= data set has a variable that is not in the DATA= data set.

```
proc append base=Emps
            data=Emps2009;
run;
```

28

p110d01

Unlike-Structured Data Sets

```
proc append base=Emps
                  data=Emps2009;
run;

NOTE: Appending WORK.EMPS2009 to WORK.EMPS.
WARNING: Variable Gender was not found on DATA file.
NOTE: There were 2 observations read from the data set
      WORK.EMPS2009.
NOTE: 2 observations added.
NOTE: The data set WORK.EMPS has 7 observations and 3 variables.
```

Emps

First	Gender	HireYear
Stacey	F	2006
Gloria	F	2007
James	M	2007
Brett	M	2008
Renee	F	2008
Sara		2009
Dennis		2009

29

Unlike-Structured Data Sets

Emps

First	Gender	HireYear
Stacey	F	2006
Gloria	F	2007
James	M	2007
Brett	M	2008
Renee	F	2008
Sara		2009
Dennis		2009

Emps2010

First	HireYear	Country
Rose	2010	Spain
Eric	2010	Spain

The DATA= data set has a variable that is not in the BASE= data set.

```
proc append base=Emps
            data=Emps2010;
run;
```

p110d01

30

Unlike-Structured Data Sets

```
96   proc append base=Emps
97               data=Emps2010;
98   run;

NOTE: Appending WORK.EMPS2010 to WORK.EMPS.
WARNING: Variable Country was not found on BASE file. The
         variable will not be added to the BASE file.
WARNING: Variable Gender was not found on DATA file.
ERROR: No appending done because of anomalies listed above.
       Use FORCE option to append these files.
NOTE: 0 observations added.
NOTE: The data set WORK.EMPS has 7 observations and 3 variables.
NOTE: Statements not processed because of errors noted above.

NOTE: The SAS System stopped processing this step because of
      errors.
```

31

Unlike-Structured Data Sets

The *FORCE option* forces the observations to be appended when the DATA= data set contains variables that are not in the BASE= data set.

General form of the FORCE option:

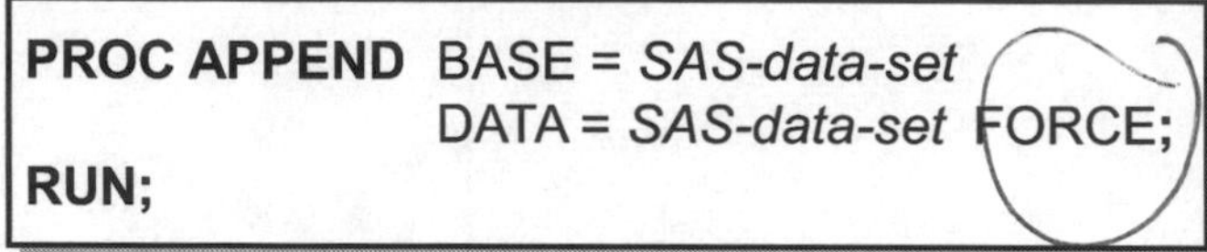

```
PROC APPEND BASE = SAS-data-set
            DATA = SAS-data-set FORCE;
RUN;
```

The FORCE option causes the extra variables to be dropped and issues a warning message.

```
proc append base=Emps
            data=Emps2010 force;
run;
```

32 p110d01

The FORCE option is needed when the DATA= data set contains variables that either

- are not in the BASE= data set
- do not have the same type as the variables in the BASE= data set
- are longer than the variables in the BASE= data set.

If the length of a variable is longer in the DATA= data set than in the BASE= data set, SAS truncates values from the DATA= data set to fit them into the length that is specified in the BASE= data set.

If the type of a variable in the DATA= data set is different than in the BASE= data set, SAS replaces all values for the variable in the DATA= data set with missing values and keeps the variable type of the variable specified in the BASE= data set.

Unlike-Structured Data Sets

```
proc append base=Emps
            data=Emps2010 force;
run;

NOTE: Appending WORK.EMPS2010 to WORK.EMPS.
WARNING: Variable Country was not found on BASE file. The
         variable will not be added to the BASE file.
WARNING: Variable Gender was not found on DATA file.
NOTE: FORCE is specified, so dropping/truncating will occur.
NOTE: There were 2 observations read from the data set
      WORK.EMPS2010.
NOTE: 2 observations added.
NOTE: The data set WORK.EMPS has 9 observations and 3 variables.
```

33

Unlike-Structured Data Sets

Emps

First	Gender	HireYear
Stacey	F	2006
Gloria	F	2007
James	M	2007
Brett	M	2008
Renee	F	2008
Sara		2009
Dennis		2009
Rose		2010
Eric		2010

34

Unlike-Structured Data Sets

Situation	Action
BASE= data set contains a variable that is not in the DATA= data set.	The observations are appended, but the observations from the DATA= data set have a missing value for the variable that was not present in the DATA= data set. The FORCE option is not necessary in this case.
DATA= data set contains a variable that is not in the BASE= data set.	Use the FORCE option in the PROC APPEND statement to force the concatenation of the two data sets. The statement drops the extra variable and issues a warning message.

35

10.04 Quiz

How many observations will be in **Emps** if the program is submitted a second time?

Submitting this program once appends six observations to the **Emps** data set, which results in a total of nine observations.

```
proc append base=Emps
            data=Emps2008;
run;
proc append base=Emps
            data=Emps2009;
run;
proc append base=Emps
            data=Emps2010 force;
run;
```

3 obs + 2 obs = 5 obs

5 obs + 2 obs = 7 obs

7 obs + 2 obs = 9 obs

37

Exercises

Level 1

1. Appending Like-Structured Data Sets

a. Retrieve the starter program **p110e01**.

b. Submit the two PROC CONTENTS steps to compare the variables in the two data sets.

   How many variables are in `orion.price_current`? ______________________

   How many variables are in `orion.price_new`? ______________________

   Does `orion.price_new` contain any variables that are not in `orion.price_current`? ______________________

c. Add a PROC APPEND step after the PROC CONTENTS steps to append `orion.price_new` to `orion.price_current`. The FORCE option is not needed.

   Why is the FORCE option not needed? ______________________

d. Submit the program and confirm that 88 observations from `orion.price_new` were added to `orion.price_current`, which should now have 259 observations (171 original observations plus 88 appended observations).

Level 2

2. Appending Unlike-Structured Data Sets

a. Write and submit two PROC CONTENTS steps to compare the variables in `orion.qtr1_2007` and `orion.qtr2_2007`.

   How many variables are in `orion.qtr1_2007`? ______________________

   How many variables are in `orion.qtr2_2007`? ______________________

   Which variable is not in both data sets? ______________________

b. Write a PROC APPEND step to append `orion.qtr1_2007` to a non-existing data set called `Work.ytd`.

c. Submit the PROC APPEND step and confirm that 22 observations were copied to `Work.ytd`.

d. Write another PROC APPEND step to append `orion.qtr2_2007` to `Work.ytd`. The FORCE option is needed.

   Why is the FORCE option needed? ______________________

e. Submit the second PROC APPEND step and confirm that 36 observations from **`orion.qtr2_2007`** were added to **`Work.ytd`**, which should now have 58 observations.

Level 3

3. Using the Append Statement

a. Write and submit three PROC CONTENTS steps to compare the variables in **`orion.shoes_eclipse`**, **`orion.shoes_tracker`**, and **`orion.shoes`**.

b. Write a PROC DATASETS step with two APPEND statements to append **`orion.shoes_eclipse`** and **`orion.shoes_tracker`** to **`orion.shoes`**.

> Documentation on the DATASETS procedure can be found in the SAS Help and Documentation from the Contents tab (**SAS Products** ⇨ **Base SAS** ⇨ **Base SAS 9.2 Procedures Guide** ⇨ **Procedures** ⇨ **The DATASETS Procedure**).

c. Submit the PROC DATASETS step and confirm that **`orion.shoes`** contains 34 observations (10 original observations plus 14 observations from **`orion.shoes_eclipse`** and 10 observations from **`orion.shoes_tracker`**).

10.3 Concatenating Data Sets

Objectives

- Concatenate two or more SAS data sets by using the SET statement in a DATA step.
- Change the names of variables by using the RENAME= data set option.
- Compare the APPEND procedure to the SET statement. (Self-Study)
- Interleave two or more SAS data sets by using the SET and BY statements in a DATA step. (Self-Study)

42

Appending and Concatenating

Appending and concatenating involves combining SAS data sets, one after the other, into a single SAS data set.

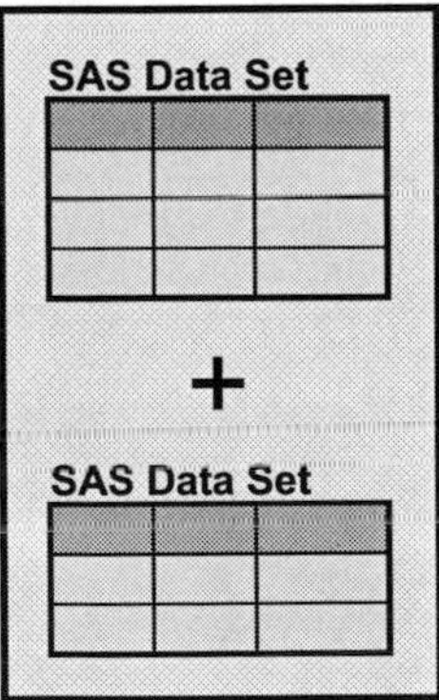

- Appending adds the observations in the second data set directly to the end of the original data set.
- Concatenating copies all observations from the first data set and then copies all observations from one or more successive data sets into a new data set.

43

The SET Statement

The *SET statement* in a DATA step reads observations from one or more SAS data sets.

```
DATA SAS-data-set;
   SET SAS-data-set1 SAS-data-set2 . . .;
   <additional SAS statements>
RUN;
```

- Any number of data sets can be in the SET statement.
- The observations from the first data set in the SET statement appear first in the new data set. The observations from the second data set follow those from the first data set, and so on.

44

You must know your data. By default, a compile-time error occurs if the same variable is not the same type in all SAS data sets in the SET statement.

Like-Structured Data Sets

Concatenate **EmpsDK** and **EmpsFR** to create a new data set named **EmpsAll1**.

EmpsDK

First	Gender	Country
Lars	M	Denmark
Kari	F	Denmark
Jonas	M	Denmark

EmpsFR

First	Gender	Country
Pierre	M	France
Sophie	F	France

The data sets contain the same variables.

```
data EmpsAll1;
   set EmpsDK EmpsFR;
run;
```

45 p110d02

Compilation

EmpsDK

First	Gender	Country
Lars	M	Denmark
Kari	F	Denmark
Jonas	M	Denmark

EmpsFR

First	Gender	Country
Pierre	M	France
Sophie	F	France

```
data EmpsAll1;
   set EmpsDK EmpsFR;
run;
```

PDV

First	Gender	Country

EmpsAll1

First	Gender	Country

46 ...

Execution

EmpsDK

First	Gender	Country
Lars	M	Denmark
Kari	F	Denmark
Jonas	M	Denmark

EmpsFR

First	Gender	Country
Pierre	M	France
Sophie	F	France

```
data EmpsAll1;
   set EmpsD
run;
```

Initialize PDV

PDV

First	Gender	Country

EmpsAll1

First	Gender	Country

47 ...

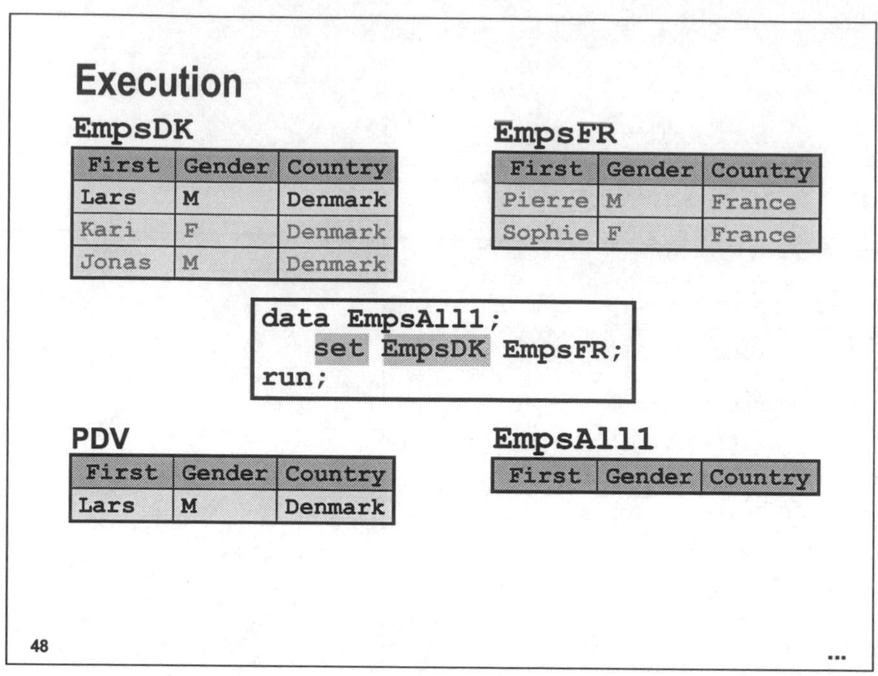

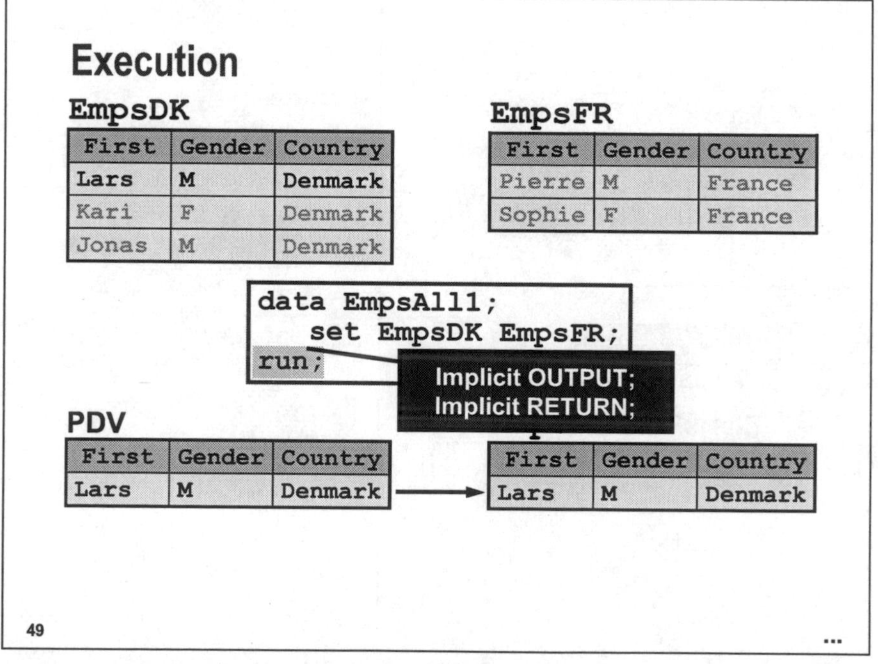

SAS reinitializes variables in the PDV at the start of every DATA step iteration. Variables created by assignment statements are reset to missing, but variables that are read with a SET statement are not reset to missing until the input SAS data set changes.

Execution

EmpsDK

First	Gender	Country
Lars	M	Denmark
Kari	F	Denmark
Jonas	M	Denmark

EmpsFR

First	Gender	Country
Pierre	M	France
Sophie	F	France

```
data EmpsAll1;
   set EmpsDK EmpsFR;
run;
```

PDV

First	Gender	Country
Kari	F	Denmark

EmpsAll1

First	Gender	Country
Lars	M	Denmark

50 ...

Execution

EmpsDK

First	Gender	Country
Lars	M	Denmark
Kari	F	Denmark
Jonas	M	Denmark

EmpsFR

First	Gender	Country
Pierre	M	France
Sophie	F	France

```
data EmpsAll1;
   set EmpsDK EmpsFR;
run;
```

Implicit OUTPUT;
Implicit RETURN;

PDV

First	Gender	Country
Kari	F	Denmark

First	Gender	Country
Lars	M	Denmark
Kari	F	Denmark

51 ...

Execution

EmpsDK

First	Gender	Country
Lars	M	Denmark
Kari	F	Denmark
Jonas	M	Denmark

EmpsFR

First	Gender	Country
Pierre	M	France
Sophie	F	France

```
data EmpsAll1;
   set EmpsDK EmpsFR;
run;
```

PDV

First	Gender	Country
Jonas	M	Denmark

EmpsAll1

First	Gender	Country
Lars	M	Denmark
Kari	F	Denmark

52 ...

Execution

EmpsDK

First	Gender	Country
Lars	M	Denmark
Kari	F	Denmark
Jonas	M	Denmark

EmpsFR

First	Gender	Country
Pierre	M	France
Sophie	F	France

```
data EmpsAll1;
   set EmpsDK EmpsFR;
run;
```

Implicit OUTPUT;
Implicit RETURN;

PDV

First	Gender	Country
Jonas	M	Denmark

First	Gender	Country
Lars	M	Denmark
Kari	F	Denmark
Jonas	M	Denmark

53 ...

Execution

EmpsDK

First	Gender	Country
Lars	M	Denmark
Kari	F	Denmark
Jonas	M	Denmark

EOF

EmpsFR

First	Gender	Country
Pierre	M	France
Sophie	F	France

```
data EmpsAll1;
   set EmpsDK EmpsFR;
run;
```

PDV

First	Gender	Country
Jonas	M	Denmark

EmpsAll1

First	Gender	Country
Lars	M	Denmark
Kari	F	Denmark
Jonas	M	Denmark

54 ...

Execution

EmpsDK

First	Gender	Country
Lars	M	Denmark
Kari	F	Denmark
Jonas	M	Denmark

EmpsFR

First	Gender	Country
Pierre	M	France
Sophie	F	France

```
data EmpsAll1;
   set EmpsD
run;
```

Reinitialize PDV

PDV

First	Gender	Country

EmpsAll1

First	Gender	Country
Lars	M	Denmark
Kari	F	Denmark
Jonas	M	Denmark

55 ...

Execution

EmpsDK

First	Gender	Country
Lars	M	Denmark
Kari	F	Denmark
Jonas	M	Denmark

EmpsFR

First	Gender	Country
Pierre	M	France
Sophie	F	France

```
data EmpsAll1;
   set EmpsDK EmpsFR;
run;
```

PDV

First	Gender	Country
Pierre	M	France

EmpsAll1

First	Gender	Country
Lars	M	Denmark
Kari	F	Denmark
Jonas	M	Denmark

56 ...

Execution

EmpsDK

First	Gender	Country
Lars	M	Denmark
Kari	F	Denmark
Jonas	M	Denmark

EmpsFR

First	Gender	Country
Pierre	M	France
Sophie	F	France

```
data EmpsAll1;
   set EmpsDK EmpsFR;
run;
```

Implicit OUTPUT;
Implicit RETURN;

PDV

First	Gender	Country
Pierre	M	France

First	Gender	Country
Lars	M	Denmark
Kari	F	Denmark
Jonas	M	Denmark
Pierre	M	France

57 ...

Execution

EmpsDK

First	Gender	Country
Lars	M	Denmark
Kari	F	Denmark
Jonas	M	Denmark

EmpsFR

First	Gender	Country
Pierre	M	France
Sophie	F	France

```
data EmpsAll1;
   set EmpsDK EmpsFR;
run;
```

PDV

First	Gender	Country
Sophie	F	France

EmpsAll1

First	Gender	Country
Lars	M	Denmark
Kari	F	Denmark
Jonas	M	Denmark
Pierre	M	France

58 ...

Execution

EmpsDK

First	Gender	Country
Lars	M	Denmark
Kari	F	Denmark
Jonas	M	Denmark

EmpsFR

First	Gender	Country
Pierre	M	France
Sophie	F	France

```
data EmpsAll1;
   set EmpsDK EmpsFR;
run;
```

Implicit OUTPUT;
Implicit RETURN;

PDV

First	Gender	Country
Sophie	F	France

First	Gender	Country
Lars	M	Denmark
Kari	F	Denmark
Jonas	M	Denmark
Pierre	M	France
Sophie	F	France

59 ...

Execution

EmpsDK

First	Gender	Country
Lars	M	Denmark
Kari	F	Denmark
Jonas	M	Denmark

EmpsFR

First	Gender	Country
Pierre	M	France
Sophie	F	France

EOF

```
data EmpsAll1;
   set EmpsDK EmpsFR;
run;
```

PDV

First	Gender	Country
Sophie	F	France

EmpsAll1

First	Gender	Country
Lars	M	Denmark
Kari	F	Denmark
Jonas	M	Denmark
Pierre	M	France
Sophie	F	France

60

Unlike-Structured Data Sets

Concatenate **EmpsCN** and **EmpsJP** to create a new data set named **EmpsAll2**.

EmpsCN

First	Gender	Country
Chang	M	China
Li	M	China
Ming	F	China

EmpsJP

First	Gender	Region
Cho	F	Japan
Tomi	M	Japan

The data sets do not contain the same variables.

```
data EmpsAll2;
   set EmpsCN EmpsJP;
run;
```

61 p110d03

10.05 Quiz

How many variables will be in **EmpsAll2** after concatenating **EmpsCN** and **EmpsJP**?

EmpsCN

First	Gender	Country
Chang	M	China
Li	M	China
Ming	F	China

EmpsJP

First	Gender	Region
Cho	F	Japan
Tomi	M	Japan

```
data EmpsAll2;
   set EmpsCN EmpsJP;
run;
```

63

Compilation

EmpsCN

First	Gender	Country
Chang	M	China
Li	M	China
Ming	F	China

EmpsJP

First	Gender	Region
Cho	F	Japan
Tomi	M	Japan

```
data EmpsAll2;
   set EmpsCN EmpsJP;
run;
```

PDV

First	Gender	Country

65

...

Compilation

EmpsCN

First	Gender	Country
Chang	M	China
Li	M	China
Ming	F	China

EmpsJP

First	Gender	Region
Cho	F	Japan
Tomi	M	Japan

```
data EmpsAll2;
   set EmpsCN EmpsJP;
run;
```

PDV

First	Gender	Country	Region

66

Final Results

EmpsAll2

First	Gender	Country	Region
Chang	M	China	
Li	M	China	
Ming	F	China	
Cho	F		Japan
Tomi	M		Japan

67

The RENAME= Data Set Option

The *RENAME= data set option* changes the name of a variable.

General form of the RENAME= data set option:

```
SAS-data-set (RENAME = (old-name-1 = new-name-1
                        old-name-2 = new-name-2
                        ...
                        old-name-n = new-name-n))
```

- The RENAME= option must be specified in parentheses immediately after the appropriate SAS data set name.
- If the RENAME= option is associated with an input data set in the SET statement, the action applies to the data set that is being read.

68

The RENAME= Data Set Option

SET statement examples:

```
set EmpsCN(rename=(Country=Region))
    EmpsJP;
```

```
set EmpsCN(rename=(First=Fname
                   Country=Region))
    EmpsJP(rename=(First=Fname));
```

```
set EmpsCN
    EmpsJP(rename=(Region=Country));
```

69

10.06 Quiz

Which statement has correct syntax?

a.
```
set EmpsCN(rename(Country=Location))
    EmpsJP(rename(Region=Location));
```

b.
```
set EmpsCN(rename=(Country=Location))
    EmpsJP(rename=(Region=Location));
```

c.
```
set EmpsCN rename=(Country=Location)
    EmpsJP rename=(Region=Location);
```

71

Compilation

EmpsCN

First	Gender	Country
Chang	M	China
Li	M	China
Ming	F	China

EmpsJP

First	Gender	Region
Cho	F	Japan
Tomi	M	Japan

```
data EmpsAll2;
   set EmpsCN EmpsJP(rename=(Region=Country));
run;
```

PDV

First	Gender	Country

73

p110d03

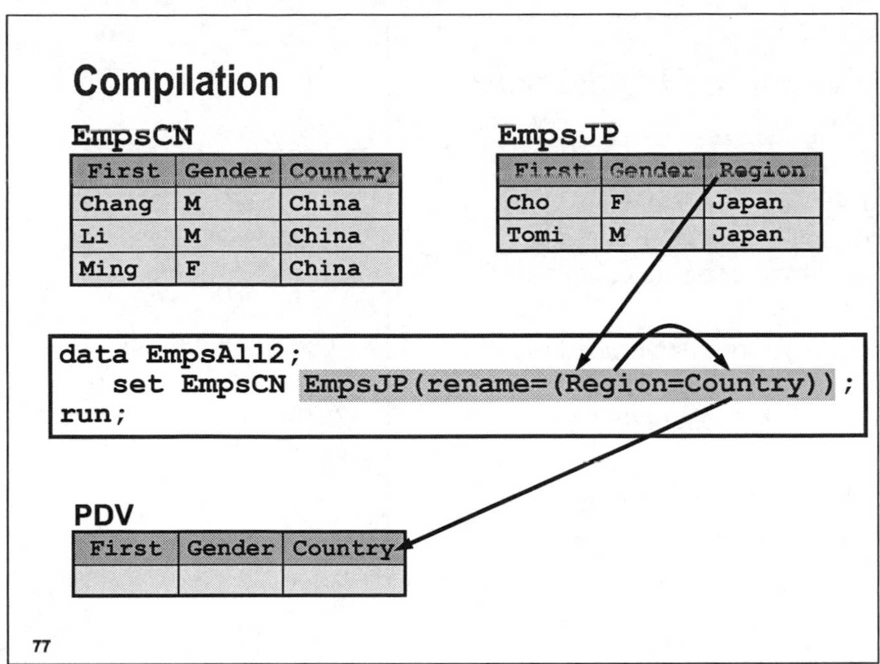

Final Results

EmpsAll2

First	Gender	Country
Chang	M	China
Li	M	China
Ming	F	China
Cho	F	Japan
Tomi	M	Japan

78

APPEND Procedure versus SET Statement (Self-Study)

- The data set that results from concatenating two data sets with the SET statement is the same data set that results from concatenating them with the APPEND procedure if the two data sets contain the same variables.
- The APPEND procedure concatenates much faster than the SET statement because the APPEND procedure does not process the observations from the BASE= data set.
- The two methods are significantly different when the variables differ between data sets.

80

APPEND Procedure versus SET Statement (Self-Study)

Criterion	APPEND Procedure	SET Statement
Number of data sets that you can concatenate	Uses two data sets.	Uses any number of data sets.
Handling of data sets that contain different variables	Uses all variables in the BASE= data set and assigns missing values to observations from the DATA= data set where appropriate; cannot include variables found only in the DATA= data set.	Uses all variables and assigns missing values where appropriate.

81

10.07 Multiple Choice Poll (Self-Study)

Which method would you use if you wanted to create a new variable at the time of concatenation?

a. APPEND procedure
b. SET statement

83

Interleaving (Self-Study)

Interleaving intersperses observations from two or more data sets, based on one or more common variables.

The SET statement with a BY statement in a DATA step interleaves SAS data sets.

```
DATA SAS-data-set;
     SET SAS-data-set1 SAS-data-set2 . . .;
     BY <DESCENDING> by-variable(s);
     <additional SAS statements>
RUN;
```

The data sets must be sorted by the BY *variable*.

Use the SORT procedure to sort the data sets by the BY variable.

85

Typically, it is more efficient to sort small SAS data sets and then interleave them as opposed to concatenating several SAS data sets and then sorting the resultant larger file.

Interleaving (Self-Study)

EmpsCN

First	Gender	Country
Chang	M	China
Li	M	China
Ming	F	China

EmpsJP

First	Gender	Region
Cho	F	Japan
Tomi	M	Japan

Which value comes first?

Chang

```
data EmpsAll2;
   set EmpsCN EmpsJP(rename=(Region=Country));
   by First;
run;
```

PDV

First	Gender	Country
Chang	M	China

86

p110d03

Interleaving (Self-Study)

EmpsCN

First	Gender	Country
Chang	M	China
Li	M	China
Ming	F	China

EmpsJP

First	Gender	Region
Cho	F	Japan
Tomi	M	Japan

Which value comes first?

Cho

```
data EmpsAll2;
   set EmpsCN                  (Region=Country));
   by First;
run;
```

PDV

First	Gender	Country

87

Interleaving (Self-Study)

EmpsCN

First	Gender	Country
Chang	M	China
Li	M	China
Ming	F	China

EmpsJP

First	Gender	Region
Cho	F	Japan
Tomi	M	Japan

Which value comes first?

```
data EmpsAll2;
   set EmpsCN EmpsJP(rename=(Region=Country));
   by First;
run;
```

PDV

First	Gender	Country
Cho	F	Japan

88 ...

Interleaving (Self-Study)

EmpsCN

First	Gender	Country
Chang	M	China
Li	M	China
Ming	F	China

EmpsJP

First	Gender	Region
Cho	F	Japan
Tomi	M	Japan

Which value comes first?

```
data EmpsAll2;
   set EmpsCN [Reinitialize PDV] (Region=Country));
   by First;
run;
```

PDV

First	Gender	Country

89 ...

Interleaving (Self-Study)

EmpsCN

First	Gender	Country
Chang	M	China
Li	M	China
Ming	F	China

EmpsJP

First	Gender	Region
Cho	F	Japan
Tomi	M	Japan

Which value comes first?

```
data EmpsAll2;
   set EmpsCN EmpsJP(rename=(Region=Country));
   by First;
run;
```

PDV

First	Gender	Country
Li	M	China

90

...

Interleaving (Self-Study)

EmpsCN

First	Gender	Country
Chang	M	China
Li	M	China
Ming	F	China

EmpsJP

First	Gender	Region
Cho	F	Japan
Tomi	M	Japan

Which value comes first?

Ming

```
data EmpsAll2;
   set EmpsCN EmpsJP(rename=(Region=Country));
   by First;
run;
```

PDV

First	Gender	Country
Ming	F	China

91

...

Interleaving (Self-Study)

EmpsCN

First	Gender	Country
Chang	M	China
Li	M	China
[illegible]ng	F	China

EOF

EmpsJP

First	Gender	Region
Cho	F	Japan
Tomi	M	Japan

Which value comes first?

Tomi

```
data EmpsAll2;
   set EmpsCN                    (Region=Country));
   by First;
run;
```

Reinitialize PDV

PDV

First	Gender	Country

92 ...

Interleaving (Self-Study)

EmpsCN

First	Gender	Country
Chang	M	China
Li	M	China
[illegible]ng	F	China

EOF

EmpsJP

First	Gender	Region
Cho	F	Japan
Tomi	M	Japan

Which value comes first?

Tomi

```
data EmpsAll2;
   set EmpsCN EmpsJP(rename=(Region=Country));
   by First;
run;
```

PDV

First	Gender	Country
Tomi	M	Japan

93 ...

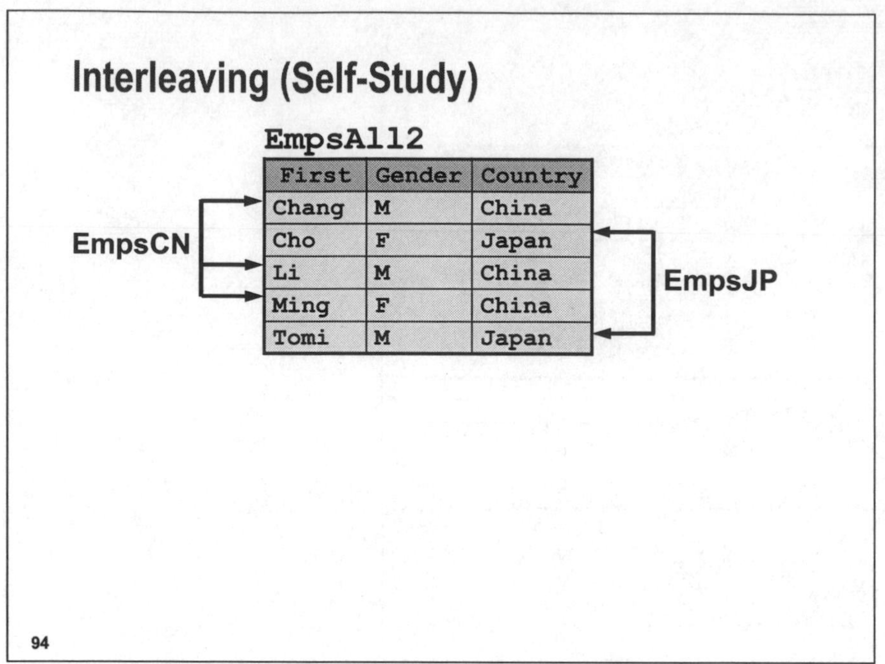

First	Gender	Country
Chang	M	China
Cho	F	Japan
Li	M	China
Ming	F	China
Tomi	M	Japan

In the case where the data values are equal, the observation is always read first from the first data set listed in the SET statement.

Exercises

Level 1

4. Concatenating Like-Structured Data Sets

a. Write and submit a DATA step to concatenate **orion.mnth7_2007**, **orion.mnth8_2007**, and **orion.mnth9_2007** to create a new data set called **Work.thirdqtr**.

How many observations in **Work.thirdqtr** are from **orion.mnth7_2007**? 10

How many observations in **Work.thirdqtr** are from **orion.mnth8_2007**? 12

How many observations in **Work.thirdqtr** are from **orion.mnth9_2007**? 10

b. Write and submit a PROC PRINT step to create the following report:

Partial PROC PRINT Output (First 10 of 32 Observations)

Obs	Order_ID	Order_ Type	Employee_ID	Customer_ID	Order_ Date	Delivery_ Date
1	1242691897	2	99999999	90	02JUL2007	04JUL2007
2	1242736731	1	121107	10	07JUL2007	07JUL2007
3	1242773202	3	99999999	24	11JUL2007	14JUL2007
4	1242782701	3	99999999	27	12JUL2007	17JUL2007
5	1242827683	1	121105	10	17JUL2007	17JUL2007
6	1242836878	1	121027	10	18JUL2007	18JUL2007
7	1242838815	1	120195	41	19JUL2007	19JUL2007
8	1242848557	2	99999999	2806	19JUL2007	23JUL2007
9	1242923327	3	99999999	70165	28JUL2007	29JUL2007
10	1242938120	1	120124	171	30JUL2007	30JUL2007

Level 2

5. Concatenating Unlike-Structured Data Sets

a. Retrieve the starter program **p110e05**.

b. Submit the two PROC CONTENTS steps to compare the variables in the two data sets.

What are the names of the two variables that are different in the two data sets?

orion.sales	orion.nonsales
FIRST_NAME	FIRST
LAST_NAME	LAST

c. Add a DATA step after the PROC CONTENTS steps to concatenate **orion.sales** and **orion.nonsales** to create a new data set called **Work.allemployees**.

   Use a RENAME= data set option to change the names of the different variables in **orion.nonsales**.

   Include only the following five variables: **Employee_ID**, **First_Name**, **Last_Name**, **Job_Title**, and **Salary**.

d. Add a PROC PRINT step to create the following report:

   Partial PROC PRINT Output (First 10 of 400 Observations)

Obs	Employee_ID	First_ Name	Last_Name	Salary	Job_Title
1	120102	Tom	Zhou	108255	Sales Manager
2	120103	Wilson	Dawes	87975	Sales Manager
3	120121	Irenie	Elvish	26600	Sales Rep. II
4	120122	Christina	Ngan	27475	Sales Rep. II
5	120123	Kimiko	Hotstone	26190	Sales Rep. I
6	120124	Lucian	Daymond	26480	Sales Rep. I
7	120125	Fong	Hofmeister	32040	Sales Rep. IV
8	120126	Satyakam	Denny	26780	Sales Rep. II
9	120127	Sharryn	Clarkson	28100	Sales Rep. II
10	120128	Monica	Kletschkus	30890	Sales Rep. IV

Level 3

6. Interleaving Data Sets

> Interleaving data sets is mentioned at the end of this section in a self-study section. Further documentation can be found in the SAS Help and Documentation from the Index tab by typing **interleaving data sets**.

a. Retrieve the starter program **p110e06**.

b. Add a PROC SORT step after the PROC SORT step in the starter program. The PROC SORT step needs to sort **orion.shoes_tracker** by **Product_Name** to create a new data set called **Work.trackersort**.

   > Documentation on the SORT procedure can be found in the SAS Help and Documentation from the Contents tab (**SAS Products** ⇨ **Base SAS** ⇨ **Base SAS 9.2 Procedures Guide** ⇨ **Procedures** ⇨ **The SORT Procedure**).

c. Add a DATA step after the two PROC SORT steps to interleave the two sorted data sets by **Product_Name** to create a new data set called **Work.e_t_shoes**.

   Include only the following three variables: **Product_Group**, **Product_Name**, and **Supplier_ID**.

d. Add a PROC PRINT step to create the following report:

Partial PROC PRINT Output (First 10 of 24 Observations)

Obs	Product_Group	Product_Name	Supplier_ID
1	Eclipse Shoes	Atmosphere Imara Women's Running Shoes	1303
2	Eclipse Shoes	Atmosphere Shatter Mid Shoes	1303
3	Eclipse Shoes	Big Guy Men's Air Deschutz Viii Shoes	1303
4	Eclipse Shoes	Big Guy Men's Air Terra Reach Shoes	1303
5	Eclipse Shoes	Big Guy Men's Air Terra Sebec Shoes	1303
6	Eclipse Shoes	Big Guy Men's International Triax Shoes	1303
7	Eclipse Shoes	Big Guy Men's Multicourt Ii Shoes	1303
8	Eclipse Shoes	Cnv Plus Men's Off Court Tennis	1303
9	Tracker Shoes	Hardcore Junior/Women's Street Shoes Large	14682
10	Tracker Shoes	Hardcore Men's Street Shoes Large	14682

The order of the observations will be different for z/OS (OS/390).

10.4 Merging Data Sets One-to-One

Objectives

- Define the different types of match-merging.
- Prepare data sets for merging using the SORT procedure.
- Merge SAS data sets one-to-one based on a common variable by using the MERGE and BY statements in a DATA step.
- Eliminate duplicate observations using the SORT procedure. (Self-Study)

97

Merging

Merging involves combining observations from two or more SAS data sets into a single observation in a new SAS data set.

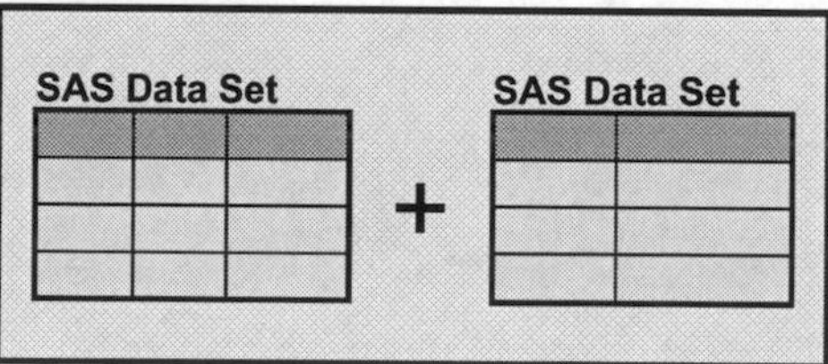

Observations can be merged based on their positions in the original data sets or merged by one or more common variables.

98

Match-Merging

Match-merging combines observations from two or more SAS data sets into a single observation in a new data set based on the values of one or more common variables.

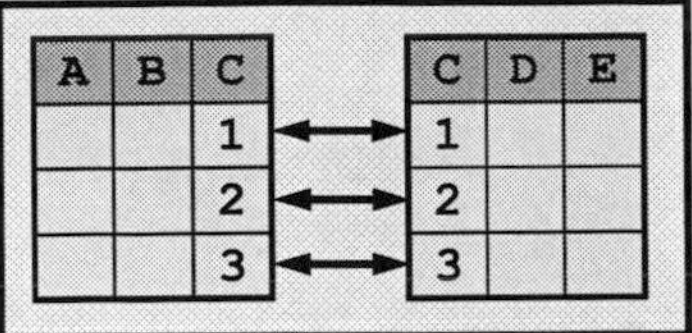
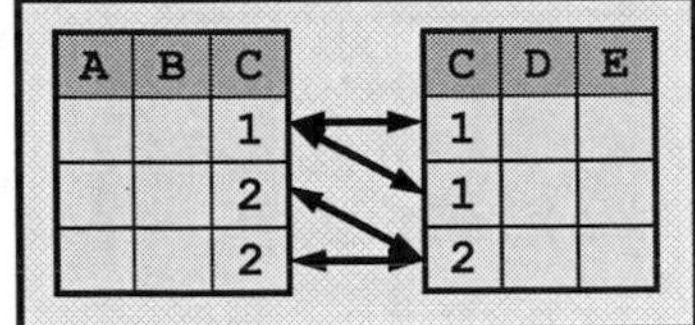
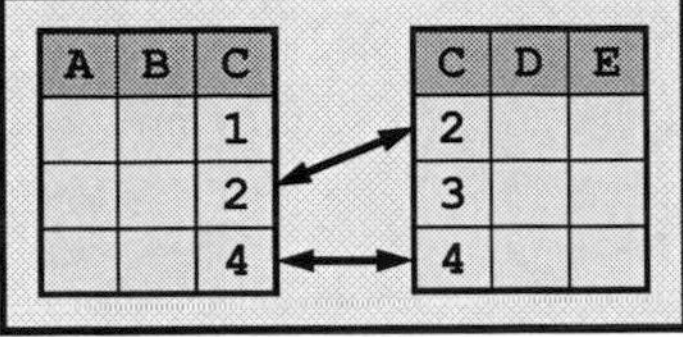

99

Match-Merging

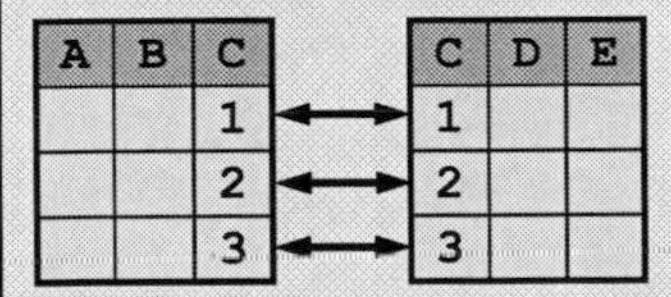

One-to-One

A single observation in one data set is related to one and only one observation from another data set based on the values of one or more selected variables.

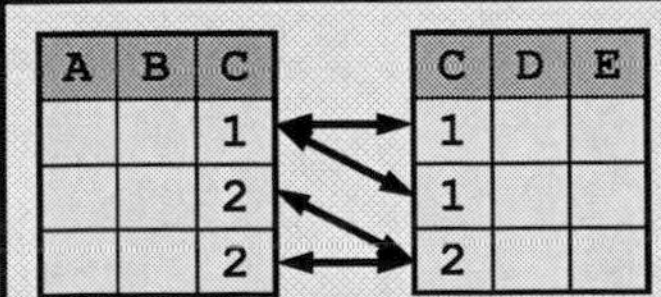

One-to-Many or Many-to-One

A single observation in one data set is related to more than one observation from another data set based on the values of one or more selected variables and vice versa.

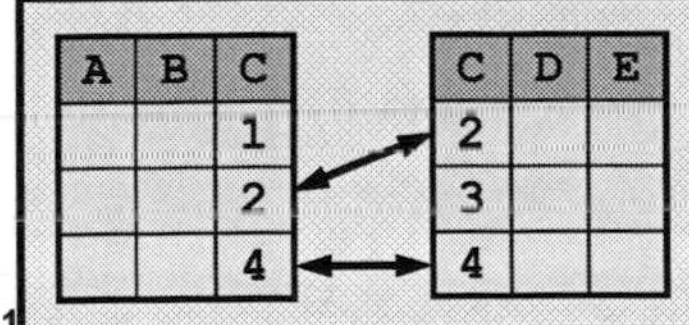

Nonmatches

At least one single observation in one data set is unrelated to any observation from another data set based on the values of one or more selected variables.

1

Match-Merging

In order to perform match-merging, the observations in each data set must be sorted by the one or more common variables that are being matched.

General form of the SORT procedure:

```
PROC SORT  DATA=input-SAS-data-set
           <OUT=output-SAS-data-set>;
     BY <DESCENDING> by-variable(s);
RUN;
```

The *SORT procedure* orders SAS data set observations by the values of one or more variables.

101

The SORT Procedure

```
PROC SORT  DATA=input-SAS-data-set
           <OUT=output-SAS-data-set>;
     BY <DESCENDING> by-variable(s);
RUN;
```

The SORT procedure

- rearranges the observations in a SAS data set
- either replaces the original data set or creates a new data set
- can sort on multiple variables
- can sort in ascending (default) or descending order
- does not generate printed output.

102

10.08 Quiz

Which step is sorting the observations in a SAS data set and overwriting the same SAS data set?

a.
```
proc sort data=work.EmpsAU
          out=work.sorted;
   by First;
run;
```

b.
```
proc sort data=work.EmpsAU
          out=orion.EmpsAU;
   by First;
run;
```

c.
```
proc sort data=work.EmpsAU;
   by First;
run;
```

104

The BY Statement

The *BY statement* specifies the sorting variables.

- PROC SORT first arranges the data set by the values in ascending order, by default, of the first BY variable.
- PROC SORT then arranges any observations that have the same value of the first BY variable by the values of the second BY variable in ascending order.
- This sorting continues for every specified BY variable.

The *DESCENDING option* reverses the sort order for the variable that immediately follows in the statement so that observations are sorted from the largest value to the smallest value.

106

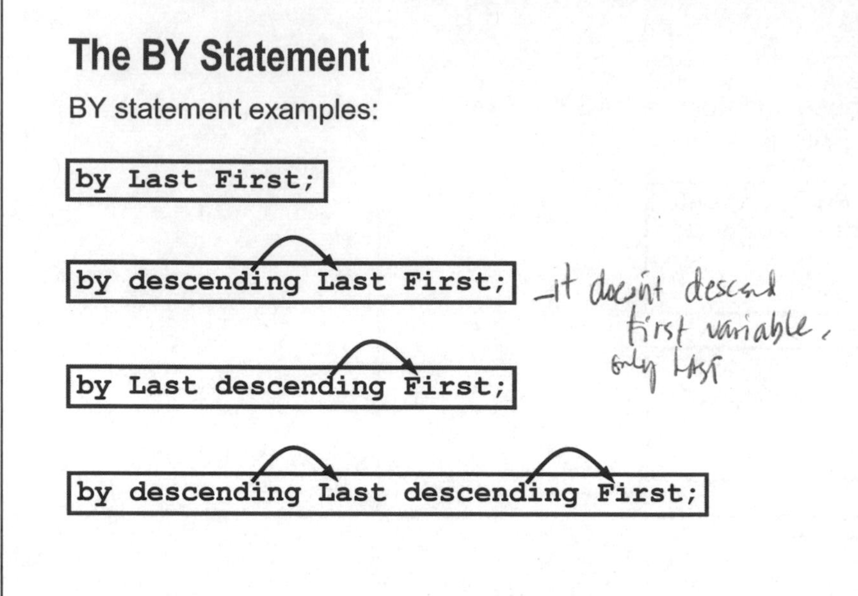

The BY Statement
BY statement examples:
by Last First;
by descending Last First;
by Last descending First;
by descending Last descending First;
107

Setup for the Poll

- Retrieve program **p110a01**.
- Add a BY statement to the PROC SORT step to sort the observations first by ascending **`Gender`** and then by descending **`Employee_ID`** within the values of **`Gender`**.
- Complete the PROC PRINT statement to reference the sorted data set.
- Submit the program and confirm the sort order in the PROC PRINT output.

109

10.09 Multiple Choice Poll

What is the **Employee_ID** value for the first observation in the sorted data set?

a. 120102
b. 120121
c. 121144
d. 121145

110

The MERGE and BY Statements

The *MERGE statement* in a DATA step joins observations from two or more SAS data sets into single observations.

```
DATA SAS-data-set;
    MERGE SAS-data-set1 SAS-data-set2 . . .;
    BY <DESCENDING> by-variable(s);
    <additional SAS statements>
RUN;
```

A *BY statement* after the MERGE statement performs a match-merge.

112

The MERGE and BY Statements

Requirements when two or more SAS data sets are specified in the MERGE statement:

- The variables in the BY statement must be common to all data sets.
- The data sets that are listed in the MERGE statement must be sorted in the order of the values of the variables that are listed in the BY statement.

113

One-to-One Merge

Merge **EmpsAU** and **PhoneH** by **EmpID** to create a new data set named **EmpsAUH**.

EmpsAU

First	Gender	EmpID
Togar	M	121150
Kylie	F	121151
Birin	M	121152

PhoneH

EmpID	Phone
121150	+61(2)5555-1793
121151	+61(2)5555-1849
121152	+61(2)5555-1665

The data sets are sorted by **EmpID**.

```
data EmpsAUH;
   merge EmpsAU PhoneH;
   by EmpID;
run;
```

114

p110d05

Final Results

EmpsAUH

First	Gender	EmpID	Phone
Togar	M	121150	+61(2)5555-1793
Kylie	F	121151	+61(2)5555-1849
Birin	M	121152	+61(2)5555-1665

115

10.10 Quiz

- Retrieve program **p110a02**.
- Complete the program to match-merge the sorted SAS data sets referenced in the PROC SORT steps.
- Submit the program. Correct and resubmit, if necessary.

What are the modified, completed statements?

data work.payadd;
merge addresses
payroll;
by employee-id;

117

run;

Eliminating Duplicates with the SORT Procedure (Self-Study)

The SORT procedure can be used to eliminate duplicate observations.

PROC SORT Statement Options:

- The *NODUPKEY option* deletes observations with duplicate BY values.
- The *EQUALS option* maintains the relative order of the observations within the input data set in the output data set for observations with identical BY values.

120

Eliminating Duplicates with the SORT Procedure (Self-Study)

```
proc sort data=EmpsDUP
          out=EmpsDUP1 nodupkey equals;
   by EmpID;
run;
```

EmpsDUP

First	Gender	EmpID
Matt	M	121160
Julie	F	121161
Brett	M	121162
Julie	F	121161
Chris	F	121161
Julie	F	121163

EmpsDUP1

First	Gender	EmpID
Matt	M	121160
Julie	F	121161
Brett	M	121162
Julie	F	121163

takes out the dup Emp ID from EmpsDUP table

121

p110d04

10.5 Merging Data Sets One-to-Many

Objectives

- Merge SAS data sets one-to-many based on a common variable by using the MERGE and BY statements in a DATA step.

123

One-to-Many Merge

Merge **EmpsAU** and **PhoneHW** by **EmpID** to create a new data set named **EmpsAUHW**.

EmpsAU

First	Gender	EmpID
Togar	M	121150
Kylie	F	121151
Birin	M	121152

PhoneHW

EmpID	Type	Phone
121150	Home	+61(2)5555-1793
121150	Work	+61(2)5555-1794
121151	Home	+61(2)5555-1849
121151	Work	+61(2)5555-1850
121152	Home	+61(2)5555-1665
121152	Work	+61(2)5555-1666

```
data EmpsAUHW;
   merge EmpsAU PhoneHW;
   by EmpID;
run;
```

The data sets are sorted by **EmpID**.

p110d06

124

Execution

EmpsAU

First	Gender	EmpID
Togar	M	121150
Kylie	F	121151
Birin	M	121152

PhoneHW

EmpID	Type	Phone
121150	Home	+61(2)5555-1793
121150	Work	+61(2)5555-1794
121151	Home	+61(2)5555-1849
121151	Work	+61(2)5555-1850
121152	Home	+61(2)5555-1665
121152	Work	+61(2)5555-1666

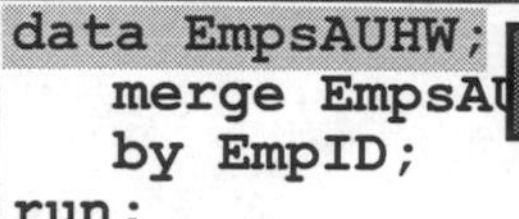

```
data EmpsAUHW;
   merge EmpsAU
   by EmpID;
run;
```

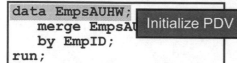

Initialize PDV

PDV

First	Gender	EmpID	Type	Phone
		.		

125 ...

Execution

EmpsAU

First	Gender	EmpID
Togar	M	121150
Kylie	F	121151
Birin	M	121152

PhoneHW

EmpID	Type	Phone
121150	Home	+61(2)5555-1793
121150	Work	+61(2)5555-1794
121151	Home	+61(2)5555-1849
121151	Work	+61(2)5555-1850
121152	Home	+61(2)5555-1665
121152	Work	+61(2)5555-1666

```
data EmpsAUHW;
   merge EmpsAU PhoneHW;
   by EmpID;
run;
```

Do the **EmpID**s match?

PDV

First	Gender	EmpID	Type	Phone
		.		

126 ...

Execution

EmpsAU

First	Gender	EmpID
Togar	M	121150
Kylie	F	121151
Birin	M	121152

PhoneHW

EmpID	Type	Phone
121150	Home	+61(2)5555-1793
121150	Work	+61(2)5555-1794
121151	Home	+61(2)5555-1849
121151	Work	+61(2)5555-1850
121152	Home	+61(2)5555-1665
121152	Work	+61(2)5555-1666

```
data EmpsAUHW;
   merge EmpsAU PhoneHW;
   by EmpID;
run;
```

Reads one observation from each matching data set

PDV

First	Gender	EmpID	Type	Phone
Togar	M	121150	Home	+61(2)5555-1793

127

...

Execution

EmpsAU

First	Gender	EmpID
Togar	M	121150
Kylie	F	121151
Birin	M	121152

PhoneHW

EmpID	Type	Phone
121150	Home	+61(2)5555-1793
121150	Work	+61(2)5555-1794
121151	Home	+61(2)5555-1849
121151	Work	+61(2)5555-1850
121152	Home	+61(2)5555-1665
121152	Work	+61(2)5555-1666

```
data EmpsAUHW;
   merge EmpsAU PhoneHW;
   by EmpID;
run;
```

Implicit OUTPUT;
Implicit RETURN;

PDV

First	Gender	EmpID	Type	Phone
Togar	M	121150	Home	+61(2)5555-1793

128 ...

SAS reinitializes variables in the PDV at the start of every DATA step iteration. Variables created by an assignment statement are reset to missing, but variables that are read with a MERGE statement are not reset to missing.

Before reading additional observations during a match-merge, SAS first determines whether there are observations remaining for the current BY group.

- If there are observations remaining for the current BY group, they are read into the PDV, processed, and written to the output data set.
- If there are no more observations for the current BY group, SAS reinitializes the remainder of the PDV, identifies the next BY group, and reads the corresponding observations.

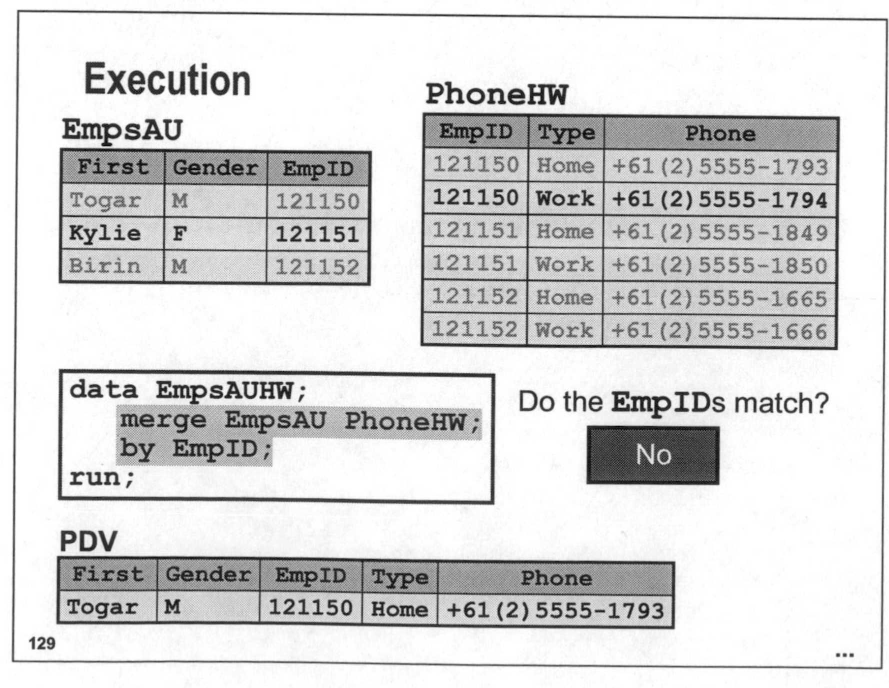

Execution

EmpsAU

First	Gender	EmpID
Togar	M	121150
Kylie	F	121151
Birin	M	121152

PhoneHW

EmpID	Type	Phone
121150	Home	+61(2)5555-1793
121150	Work	+61(2)5555-1794
121151	Home	+61(2)5555-1849
121151	Work	+61(2)5555-1850
121152	Home	+61(2)5555-1665
121152	Work	+61(2)5555-1666

```
data EmpsAUHW;
   merge EmpsAU PhoneHW;
   by EmpID;
run;
```

Is either **EmpID** the same as the **EmpID** currently in the PDV?

Yes

PDV

First	Gender	EmpID	Type	Phone
Togar	M	121150	Home	+61(2)5555-1793

130 ...

Execution

EmpsAU

First	Gender	EmpID
Togar	M	121150
Kylie	F	121151
Birin	M	121152

PhoneHW

EmpID	Type	Phone
121150	Home	+61(2)5555-1793
121150	Work	+61(2)5555-1794
121151	Home	+61(2)5555-1849
121151	Work	+61(2)5555-1850
121152	Home	+61(2)5555-1665
121152	Work	+61(2)5555-1666

```
data EmpsAUHW;
   merge EmpsAU PhoneHW;
   by EmpID;
run;
```

Reads the observation from the appropriate data set

PDV

First	Gender	EmpID	Type	Phone
Togar	M	121150	Work	+61(2)5555-1794

131 ...

Execution

EmpsAU

First	Gender	EmpID
Togar	M	121150
Kylie	F	121151
Birin	M	121152

PhoneHW

EmpID	Type	Phone
121150	Home	+61(2)5555-1793
121150	Work	+61(2)5555-1794
121151	Home	+61(2)5555-1849
121151	Work	+61(2)5555-1850
121152	Home	+61(2)5555-1665
121152	Work	+61(2)5555-1666

```
data EmpsAUHW;
   merge EmpsAU PhoneHW;
   by EmpID;
run;
```

Implicit OUTPUT;
Implicit RETURN;

PDV

First	Gender	EmpID	Type	Phone
Togar	M	121150	Work	+61(2)5555-1794

132

...

Execution

EmpsAU

First	Gender	EmpID
Togar	M	121150
Kylie	F	121151
Birin	M	121152

PhoneHW

EmpID	Type	Phone
121150	Home	+61(2)5555-1793
121150	Work	+61(2)5555-1794
121151	Home	+61(2)5555-1849
121151	Work	+61(2)5555-1850
121152	Home	+61(2)5555-1665
121152	Work	+61(2)5555-1666

```
data EmpsAUHW;
   merge EmpsAU PhoneHW;
   by EmpID;
run;
```

Do the **EmpID**s match?

Yes

PDV

First	Gender	EmpID	Type	Phone
Togar	M	121150	Work	+61(2)5555-1794

133

...

Execution

EmpsAU

First	Gender	EmpID
Togar	M	121150
Kylie	F	121151
Birin	M	121152

PhoneHW

EmpID	Type	Phone
121150	Home	+61(2)5555-1793
121150	Work	+61(2)5555-1794
121151	Home	+61(2)5555-1849
121151	Work	+61(2)5555-1850
121152	Home	+61(2)5555-1665
121152	Work	+61(2)5555-1666

```
data EmpsAUHW;
   merge EmpsAU PhoneHW;
   by EmpID;
run;
```

Is the **EmpID** the same as the **EmpID** currently in the PDV?

No

PDV

First	Gender	EmpID	Type	Phone
Togar	M	121150	Work	+61(2)5555-1794

134 ...

Execution

EmpsAU

First	Gender	EmpID
Togar	M	121150
Kylie	F	121151
Birin	M	121152

PhoneHW

EmpID	Type	Phone
121150	Home	+61(2)5555-1793
121150	Work	+61(2)5555-1794
121151	Home	+61(2)5555-1849
121151	Work	+61(2)5555-1850
121152	Home	+61(2)5555-1665
121152	Work	+61(2)5555-1666

```
data EmpsAUHW;
   merge EmpsAU PhoneHW;
   by EmpID;
run;
```

Reinitialize PDV

PDV

First	Gender	EmpID	Type	Phone
		.		

135 ...

Execution

EmpsAU

First	Gender	EmpID
Togar	M	121150
Kylie	F	121151
Birin	M	121152

PhoneHW

EmpID	Type	Phone
121150	Home	+61(2)5555-1793
121150	Work	+61(2)5555-1794
121151	Home	+61(2)5555-1849
121151	Work	+61(2)5555-1850
121152	Home	+61(2)5555-1665
121152	Work	+61(2)5555-1666

```
data EmpsAUHW;
   merge EmpsAU PhoneHW;
   by EmpID;
run;
```

Reads one observation from each matching data set

PDV

First	Gender	EmpID	Type	Phone
Kylie	F	121151	Home	+61(2)5555-1849

136 ...

Execution

EmpsAU

First	Gender	EmpID
Togar	M	121150
Kylie	F	121151
Birin	M	121152

PhoneHW

EmpID	Type	Phone
121150	Home	+61(2)5555-1793
121150	Work	+61(2)5555-1794
121151	Home	+61(2)5555-1849
121151	Work	+61(2)5555-1850
121152	Home	+61(2)5555-1665
121152	Work	+61(2)5555-1666

```
data EmpsAUHW;
   merge EmpsAU PhoneHW;
   by EmpID;
run;
```

Implicit OUTPUT;
Implicit RETURN;

PDV

First	Gender	EmpID	Type	Phone
Kylie	F	121151	Home	+61(2)5555-1849

137 ...

Execution

EmpsAU

First	Gender	EmpID
Togar	M	121150
Kylie	F	121151
Birin	M	121152

PhoneHW

EmpID	Type	Phone
121150	Home	+61(2)5555-1793
121150	Work	+61(2)5555-1794
121151	Home	+61(2)5555-1849
121151	Work	+61(2)5555-1850
121152	Home	+61(2)5555-1665
121152	Work	+61(2)5555-1666

```
data EmpsAUHW;
   merge EmpsAU PhoneHW;
   by EmpID;
run;
```

Do the **EmpIDs** match?

No

PDV

First	Gender	EmpID	Type	Phone
Kylie	F	121151	Home	+61(2)5555-1849

138 ...

Execution

EmpsAU

First	Gender	EmpID
Togar	M	121150
Kylie	F	121151
Birin	M	121152

PhoneHW

EmpID	Type	Phone
121150	Home	+61(2)5555-1793
121150	Work	+61(2)5555-1794
121151	Home	+61(2)5555-1849
121151	Work	+61(2)5555-1850
121152	Home	+61(2)5555-1665
121152	Work	+61(2)5555-1666

```
data EmpsAUHW;
   merge EmpsAU PhoneHW;
   by EmpID;
run;
```

Is either **EmpID** the same as the **EmpID** currently in the PDV?

Yes

PDV

First	Gender	EmpID	Type	Phone
Kylie	F	121151	Home	+61(2)5555-1849

139 ...

Execution

EmpsAU

First	Gender	EmpID
Togar	M	121150
Kylie	F	121151
Birin	M	121152

PhoneHW

EmpID	Type	Phone
121150	Home	+61(2)5555-1793
121150	Work	+61(2)5555-1794
121151	Home	+61(2)5555-1849
121151	Work	+61(2)5555-1850
121152	Home	+61(2)5555-1665
121152	Work	+61(2)5555-1666

```
data EmpsAUHW;
   merge EmpsAU PhoneHW;
   by EmpID;
run;
```

Reads the observation from the appropriate data set

PDV

First	Gender	EmpID	Type	Phone
Kylie	F	121151	Work	+61(2)5555-1850

140 ...

Execution

EmpsAU

First	Gender	EmpID
Togar	M	121150
Kylie	F	121151
Birin	M	121152

PhoneHW

EmpID	Type	Phone
121150	Home	+61(2)5555-1793
121150	Work	+61(2)5555-1794
121151	Home	+61(2)5555-1849
121151	Work	+61(2)5555-1850
121152	Home	+61(2)5555-1665
121152	Work	+61(2)5555-1666

```
data EmpsAUHW;
   merge EmpsAU PhoneHW;
   by EmpID;
run;
```

Implicit OUTPUT;
Implicit RETURN;

PDV

First	Gender	EmpID	Type	Phone
Kylie	F	121151	Work	+61(2)5555-1850

141 ...

Execution

EmpsAU

First	Gender	EmpID
Togar	M	121150
Kylie	F	121151
Birin	M	121152

PhoneHW

EmpID	Type	Phone
121150	Home	+61 (2) 5555-1793
121150	Work	+61 (2) 5555-1794
121151	Home	+61 (2) 5555-1849
121151	Work	+61 (2) 5555-1850
121152	Home	+61 (2) 5555-1665
121152	Work	+61 (2) 5555-1666

```
data EmpsAUHW;
   merge EmpsAU Ph
   by EmpID;
run;
```

Continue until EOF on both data sets

PDV

First	Gender	EmpID	Type	Phone
Kylie	F	121151	Work	+61 (2) 5555-1850

142

Final Results

EmpsAUHW

First	Gender	EmpID	Type	Phone
Togar	M	121150	Home	+61 (2) 5555-1793
Togar	M	121150	Work	+61 (2) 5555-1794
Kylie	F	121151	Home	+61 (2) 5555-1849
Kylie	F	121151	Work	+61 (2) 5555-1850
Birin	M	121152	Home	+61 (2) 5555-1665
Birin	M	121152	Work	+61 (2) 5555-1666

143

Exercises

Level 1

7. Merging `orion.orders` and `orion.order_item` in a One-to-Many Merge

a. Retrieve the starter program **p110e07**.

b. Submit the two PROC CONTENTS steps to determine the common variable among the two data sets.

c. Add a DATA step after the two PROC CONTENTS steps and prior to the PROC PRINT step to merge **`orion.orders`** and **`orion.order_item`** by the common variable to create a new data set called **`Work.allorders`**.

d. Submit the program and confirm that **`Work.allorders`** was created with 732 observations and 12 variables.

Level 2

8. Merging `orion.product_level` and `orion.product_list` in a One-to-Many Merge

a. Write a PROC SORT step to sort **`orion.product_list`** by **`Product_Level`** to create a new data set called **`Work.product_list`**.

b. Write a DATA step to merge **`orion.product_level`** with the previous sorted data set by the appropriate common variable. Create a new data set called **`Work.listlevel`**.

c. Write a PROC PRINT step with a VAR statement to create the following report:

Partial PROC PRINT Output (First 10 of 556 Observations)

Obs	Product_ID	Product_Name	Product_ Level	Product_ Level_ Name
1	210200100009	Kids Sweat Round Neck,Large Logo	1	Product
2	210200100017	Sweatshirt Children's O-Neck	1	Product
3	210200200022	Sunfit Slow Swimming Trunks	1	Product
4	210200200023	Sunfit Stockton Swimming Trunks Jr.	1	Product
5	210200300006	Fleece Cuff Pant Kid'S	1	Product
6	210200300007	Hsc Dutch Player Shirt Junior	1	Product
7	210200300052	Tony's Cut & Sew T-Shirt	1	Product
8	210200400020	Kids Baby Edge Max Shoes	1	Product
9	210200400070	Tony's Children's Deschutz (Bg) Shoes	1	Product
10	210200500002	Children's Mitten	1	Product

Level 3

9. Joining `orion.product_level` and `orion.product_list` in a One-to-Many Merge

a. Write a PROC SQL step to perform an inner join of **`orion.product_level`** and **`orion.product_list`** by **`Product_Level`** to create a new data set called **`Work.listlevelsql`**. The new data set should include only **`Product_ID`**, **`Product_Name`**, **`Product_Level`**, and **`Product_Level_Name`**.

> Documentation on the SQL procedure can be found in the SAS Help and Documentation from the Contents tab (**SAS Products** ⇨ **Base SAS** ⇨ **Base SAS 9.2 Procedures Guide** ⇨ **Procedures** ⇨ **The SQL Procedure**).

b. Write a PROC PRINT step to create the following report:

Partial PROC PRINT Output (First 10 of 556 Observations)

Obs	Product_ID	Product_Name	Product_ Level	Product_Level_ Name
1	210000000000	Children	4	Product Line
2	210100000000	Children Outdoors	3	Product Category
3	210100100000	Outdoor things, Kids	2	Product Group
4	210200000000	Children Sports	3	Product Category
5	210200100000	A-Team, Kids	2	Product Group
6	210200100009	Kids Sweat Round Neck,Large Logo	1	Product
7	210200100017	Sweatshirt Children's O-Neck	1	Product
8	210200200000	Bathing Suits, Kids	2	Product Group
9	210200200022	Sunfit Slow Swimming Trunks	1	Product
10	210200200023	Sunfit Stockton Swimming Trunks Jr.	1	Product

10.6 Merging Data Sets with Nonmatches

Objectives

- Control the observations in the output data set by using the IN= option.
- Output observations to multiple data sets using the IN= option and the OUTPUT statement. (Self-Study)
- Compare the results of a many-to-many merge based on using the DATA step or the SQL procedure. (Self-Study)

147

Nonmatches Merge

Merge **EmpsAU** and **PhoneC** by **EmpID** to create a new data set named **EmpsAUC**.

EmpsAU

First	Gender	EmpID
Togar	M	121150
Kylie	F	121151
Birin	M	121152

PhoneC

EmpID	Phone
121150	+61(2)5555-1795
121152	+61(2)5555-1667
121153	+61(2)5555-1348

The data sets are sorted by **EmpID**.

```
data EmpsAUC;
   merge EmpsAU PhoneC;
   by EmpID;
run;
```

148 p110d07

Execution

EmpsAU

First	Gender	EmpID
Togar	M	121150
Kylie	F	121151
Birin	M	121152

PhoneC

EmpID	Phone
121150	+61(2)5555-1795
121152	+61(2)5555-1667
121153	+61(2)5555-1348

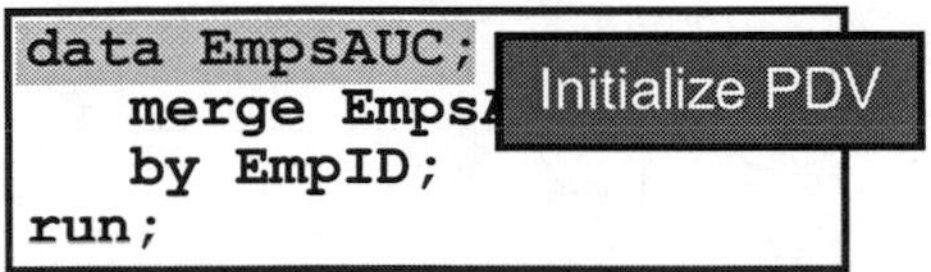


```
data EmpsAUC;
   merge EmpsA
   by EmpID;
run;
```

PDV

First	Gender	EmpID	Phone
		.	

149 ...

Execution

EmpsAU

First	Gender	EmpID
Togar	M	121150
Kylie	F	121151
Birin	M	121152

PhoneC

EmpID	Phone
121150	+61(2)5555-1795
121152	+61(2)5555-1667
121153	+61(2)5555-1348

```
data EmpsAUC;
   merge EmpsAU PhoneC;
   by EmpID;
run;
```

Do the **EmpIDs** match?

PDV

First	Gender	EmpID	Phone
		.	

150 ...

Execution

EmpsAU

First	Gender	EmpID
Togar	M	121150
Kylie	F	121151
Birin	M	121152

PhoneC

EmpID	Phone
121150	+61(2)5555-1795
121152	+61(2)5555-1667
121153	+61(2)5555-1348

```
data EmpsAUC;
   merge EmpsAU PhoneC;
   by EmpID;
run;
```

Reads one observation from each matching data set

PDV

First	Gender	EmpID	Phone
Togar	M	121150	+61(2)5555-1795

151 ...

Execution

EmpsAU

First	Gender	EmpID
Togar	M	121150
Kylie	F	121151
Birin	M	121152

PhoneC

EmpID	Phone
121150	+61(2)5555-1795
121152	+61(2)5555-1667
121153	+61(2)5555-1348

```
data EmpsAUC;
   merge EmpsAU PhoneC;
   by EmpID;
run;
```

Implicit OUTPUT;
Implicit RETURN;

PDV

First	Gender	EmpID	Phone
Togar	M	121150	+61(2)5555-1795

152 ...

Execution

EmpsAU

First	Gender	EmpID
Togar	M	121150
Kylie	F	121151
Birin	M	121152

PhoneC

EmpID	Phone
121150	+61(2)5555-1795
121152	+61(2)5555-1667
121153	+61(2)5555-1348

```
data EmpsAUC;
   merge EmpsAU PhoneC;
   by EmpID;
run;
```

Do the **EmpIDs** match?

No

PDV

First	Gender	EmpID	Phone
Togar	M	121150	+61(2)5555-1795

153 ...

Execution

EmpsAU

First	Gender	EmpID
Togar	M	121150
Kylie	F	121151
Birin	M	121152

PhoneC

EmpID	Phone
121150	+61(2)5555-1795
121152	+61(2)5555-1667
121153	+61(2)5555-1348

```
data EmpsAUC;
   merge EmpsAU PhoneC;
   by EmpID;
run;
```

Is either **EmpID** the same as the **EmpID** currently in the PDV?

No

PDV

First	Gender	EmpID	Phone
Togar	M	121150	+61(2)5555-1795

154 ...

Execution

EmpsAU

First	Gender	EmpID
Togar	M	121150
Kylie	F	121151
Birin	M	121152

PhoneC

EmpID	Phone
121150	+61(2)5555-1795
121152	+61(2)5555-1667
121153	+61(2)5555-1348

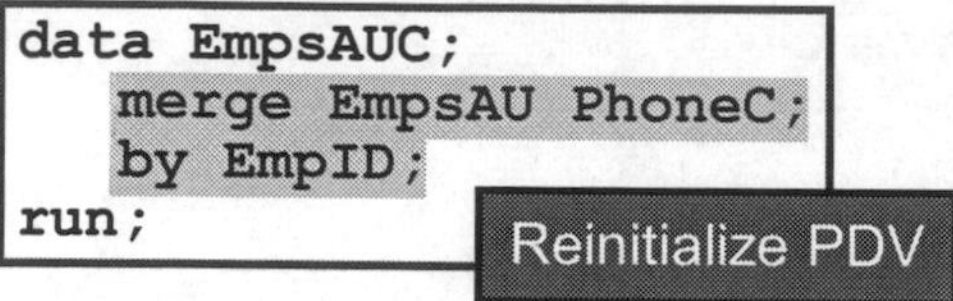

```
data EmpsAUC;
   merge EmpsAU PhoneC;
   by EmpID;
run;
```

Reinitialize PDV

PDV

First	Gender	EmpID	Phone
		.	

155 ...

Execution

EmpsAU

First	Gender	EmpID
Togar	M	121150
Kylie	F	121151
Birin	M	121152

PhoneC

EmpID	Phone
121150	+61(2)5555-1795
121152	+61(2)5555-1667
121153	+61(2)5555-1348

```
data EmpsAUC;
   merge EmpsAU PhoneC;
   by EmpID;
run;
```

Which **EmpID** sequentially comes first?

121151

PDV

First	Gender	EmpID	Phone
		.	

156 ...

Execution

EmpsAU

First	Gender	EmpID
Togar	M	121150
Kylie	F	121151
Birin	M	121152

PhoneC

EmpID	Phone
121150	+61(2)5555-1795
121152	+61(2)5555-1667
121153	+61(2)5555-1348

```
data EmpsAUC;
   merge EmpsAU PhoneC;
   by EmpID;
run;
```

Reads the observation from the **EmpID** that sequentially comes first

PDV

First	Gender	EmpID	Phone
Kylie	F	121151	

157 ...

Execution

EmpsAU

First	Gender	EmpID
Togar	M	121150
Kylie	F	121151
Birin	M	121152

PhoneC

EmpID	Phone
121150	+61(2)5555-1795
121152	+61(2)5555-1667
121153	+61(2)5555-1348

```
data EmpsAUC;
   merge EmpsAU PhoneC;
   by EmpID;
run;
```

Implicit OUTPUT;
Implicit RETURN;

PDV

First	Gender	EmpID	Phone
Kylie	F	121151	

158 ...

Execution

EmpsAU

First	Gender	EmpID
Togar	M	121150
Kylie	F	121151
Birin	M	121152

PhoneC

EmpID	Phone
121150	+61(2)5555-1795
121152	+61(2)5555-1667
121153	+61(2)5555-1348

```
data EmpsAUC;
   merge EmpsAU PhoneC;
   by EmpID;
run;
```

Do the **EmpID**s match?

PDV

First	Gender	EmpID	Phone
Kylie	F	121151	

159

...

Execution

EmpsAU

First	Gender	EmpID
Togar	M	121150
Kylie	F	121151
Birin	M	121152

PhoneC

EmpID	Phone
121150	+61(2)5555-1795
121152	+61(2)5555-1667
121153	+61(2)5555-1348

```
data EmpsAUC;
   merge EmpsAU PhoneC;
   by EmpID;
run;
```

Is either **EmpID** the same as the **EmpID** currently in the PDV?

No

PDV

First	Gender	EmpID	Phone
Kylie	F	121151	

160

...

Execution

EmpsAU

First	Gender	EmpID
Togar	M	121150
Kylie	F	121151
Birin	M	121152

PhoneC

EmpID	Phone
121150	+61(2)5555-1795
121152	+61(2)5555-1667
121153	+61(2)5555-1348

```
data EmpsAUC;
   merge EmpsAU PhoneC;
   by EmpID;
run;
```

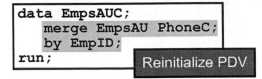

Reinitialize PDV

PDV

First	Gender	EmpID	Phone
		.	

161 ...

Execution

EmpsAU

First	Gender	EmpID
Togar	M	121150
Kylie	F	121151
Birin	M	121152

PhoneC

EmpID	Phone
121150	+61(2)5555-1795
121152	+61(2)5555-1667
121153	+61(2)5555-1348

```
data EmpsAUC;
   merge EmpsAU PhoneC;
   by EmpID;
run;
```

Reads one observation from each matching data set

PDV

First	Gender	EmpID	Phone
Birin	M	121152	+61(2)5555-1667

162 ...

Execution

EmpsAU

First	Gender	EmpID
Togar	M	121150
Kylie	F	121151
Birin	M	121152

PhoneC

EmpID	Phone
121150	+61(2)5555-1795
121152	+61(2)5555-1667
121153	+61(2)5555-1348

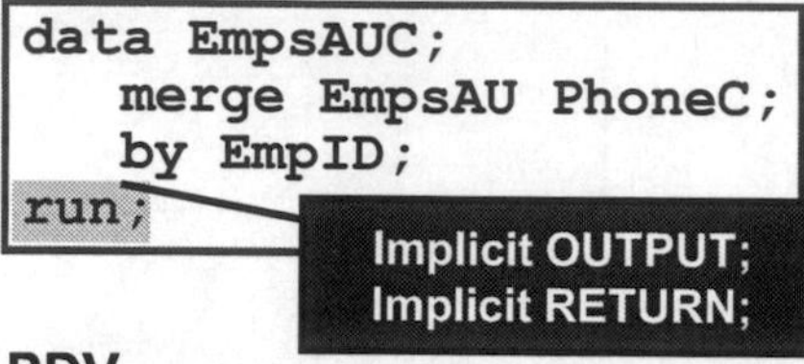
data EmpsAUC;
merge EmpsAU PhoneC;
by EmpID;
run;
Implicit OUTPUT;
Implicit RETURN;

PDV

First	Gender	EmpID	Phone
Birin	M	121152	+61(2)5555-1667

163 ...

Execution

EmpsAU

First	Gender	EmpID
Togar	M	121150
Kylie	F	121151
[EOF] n	M	121152

EOF

PhoneC

EmpID	Phone
121150	+61(2)5555-1795
121152	+61(2)5555-1667
121153	+61(2)5555-1348

```
data EmpsAUC;
   merge EmpsAU PhoneC;
   by EmpID;
run;
```

Is the **EmpID** the same as the **EmpID** currently in the PDV?

No

PDV

First	Gender	EmpID	Phone
Birin	M	121152	+61(2)5555-1667

164 ...

Execution

EmpsAU

First	Gender	EmpID
Togar	M	121150
Kylie	F	121151
n	M	121152

EOF

PhoneC

EmpID	Phone
121150	+61(2)5555-1795
121152	+61(2)5555-1667
121153	+61(2)5555-1348

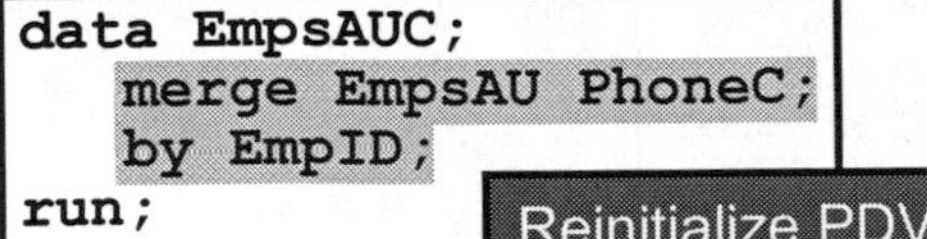

```
data EmpsAUC;
   merge EmpsAU PhoneC;
   by EmpID;
run;
```

Reinitialize PDV

PDV

First	Gender	EmpID	Phone
		.	

165 ...

Execution

EmpsAU

First	Gender	EmpID
Togar	M	121150
Kylie	F	121151
n	M	121152

EOF

PhoneC

EmpID	Phone
121150	+61(2)5555-1795
121152	+61(2)5555-1667
121153	+61(2)5555-1348

```
data EmpsAUC;
   merge EmpsAU PhoneC;
   by EmpID;
run;
```

Reads the observation from the appropriate data set

PDV

First	Gender	EmpID	Phone
		121153	+61(2)5555-1348

166 ...

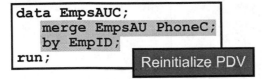

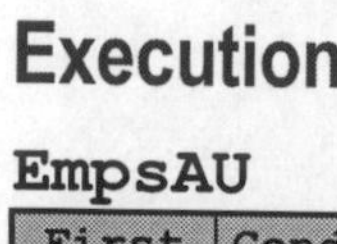

Execution

EmpsAU

First	Gender	EmpID
Togar	M	121150
Kylie	F	121151
EOF n	M	121152

PhoneC

EmpID	Phone
121150	+61(2)5555-1795
121152	+61(2)5555-1667
121153	+61(2)5555-1348

```
data EmpsAUC;
   merge EmpsAU PhoneC;
   by EmpID;
run;
```

PDV

First	Gender	EmpID	Phone
		121153	+61(2)5555-1348

167

Execution

EmpsAU

First	Gender	EmpID
Togar	M	121150
Kylie	F	121151
EOF n	M	121152

PhoneC

EmpID	Phone
121150	+61(2)5555-1795
121152	+61(2)5555-1667
EOF 53	+61(2)5555-1348

```
data EmpsAUC;
   merge EmpsAU PhoneC;
   by EmpID;
run;
```

PDV

First	Gender	EmpID	Phone
		121153	+61(2)5555-1348

168

Final Results

EmpsAUC

First	Gender	EmpID	Phone
Togar	M	121150	+61(2)5555-1795
Kylie	F	121151	
Birin	M	121152	+61(2)5555-1667
		121153	+61(2)5555-1348

The final results include matches and nonmatches.

- Matches are observations that contain data from both input data sets.
- Nonmatches are observations that contain data from only one input data set.

169

10.11 Quiz

How many observations in the final data set **EmpsAUC** are considered nonmatches?

a. 1
b. 2
c. 3
d. 4

EmpsAUC

First	Gender	EmpID	Phone
Togar	M	121150	+61(2)5555-1795
Kylie	F	121151	
Birin	M	121152	+61(2)5555-1667
		121153	+61(2)5555-1348

171

The IN= Data Set Option

The *IN= data set option* creates a variable that indicates whether the data set contributed data to the current observation.

General form of the IN= data set option:

SAS-data-set (IN = *variable*)

variable is a temporary numeric variable that has two possible values:

0	indicates that the data set did **not** contribute to the current observation.
1	indicates that the data set **did** contribute to the current observation.

174

The variable created with the IN= data set option is temporary. Therefore, the variable is only available during the execution phase and is not written to the SAS data set.

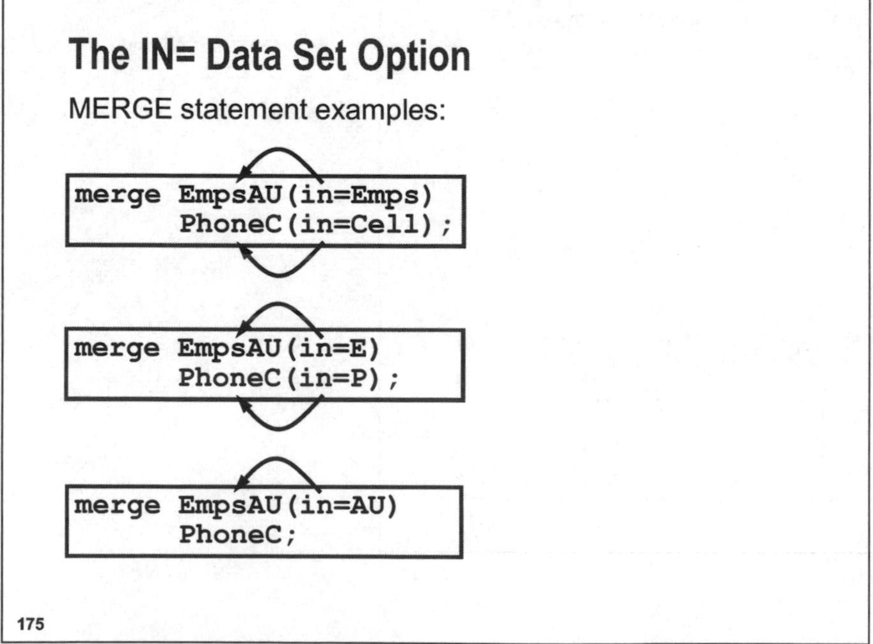

Execution

EmpsAU

First	Gender	EmpID
Togar	M	121150
Kylie	F	121151
Birin	M	121152

PhoneC

EmpID	Phone
121150	+61(2)5555-1795
121152	+61(2)5555-1667
121153	+61(2)5555-1348

```
data EmpsAUC;
   merge EmpsAU(in=Emps)
         PhoneC(in=Cell);
   by EmpID;
run;
```

PDV

First	Gender	EmpID	D Emps	Phone	D Cell
Togar	M	121150	1	+61(2)5555-1795	1

176

p110d07

...

Execution

EmpsAU

First	Gender	EmpID
Togar	M	121150
Kylie	F	121151
Birin	M	121152

PhoneC

EmpID	Phone
121150	+61(2)5555-1795
121152	+61(2)5555-1667
121153	+61(2)5555-1348

```
data EmpsAUC;
   merge EmpsAU(in=Emps)
         PhoneC(in=Cell);
   by EmpID;
run;
```

PDV

First	Gender	EmpID	D Emps	Phone	D Cell
Kylie	F	121151	1		0

177

...

Execution

EmpsAU

First	Gender	EmpID
Togar	M	121150
Kylie	F	121151
Birin	M	121152

PhoneC

EmpID	Phone
121150	+61(2)5555-1795
121152	+61(2)5555-1667
121153	+61(2)5555-1348

```
data EmpsAUC;
   merge EmpsAU(in=Emps)
         PhoneC(in=Cell);
   by EmpID;
run;
```

PDV

First	Gender	EmpID	D Emps	Phone	D Cell
Birin	M	121152	1	+61(2)5555-1667	1

178 ...

10.12 Quiz

What are the values of **Emps** and **Cell**?

EmpsAU

First	Gender	EmpID
Togar	M	121150
Kylie	F	121151
Birin	M	121152

PhoneC

EmpID	Phone
121150	+61(2)5555-1795
121152	+61(2)5555-1667
121153	+61(2)5555-1348

```
data EmpsAUC;
   merge EmpsAU(in=Emps)
         PhoneC(in=Cell);
   by EmpID;
run;
```

PDV

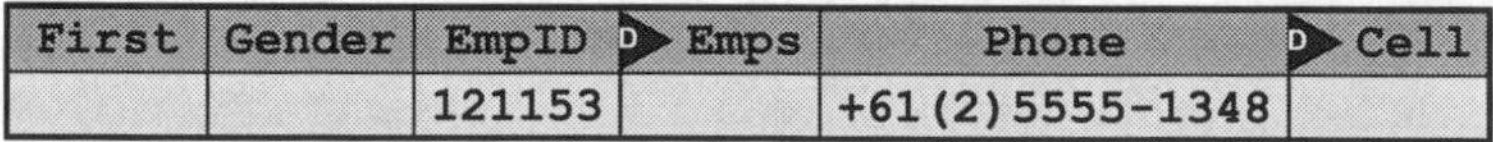

First	Gender	EmpID	D Emps	Phone	D Cell
		121153		+61(2)5555-1348	

180

PDV Results

PDV

First	Gender	EmpID	Emps	Phone	Cell
Togar	M	121150	1	+61(2)5555-1795	1
Kylie	F	121151	1		0
Birin	M	121152	1	+61(2)5555-1667	1
		121153	0	+61(2)5555-1348	1

The variables created with the IN= data set option are only available during execution and are not written to the SAS data set.

182

10.13 Quiz

Which subsetting IF statement can be added to the DATA step to only output the matches?

a. `if Emps=1 and Cell=0;`

b. `if Emps=1 and Cell=1;`

c. `if Emps=1;`

d. `if Cell=0;`

PDV

First	Gender	EmpID	Emps	Phone	Cell
Togar	M	121150	1	+61(2)5555-1795	1
Kylie	F	121151	1		0
Birin	M	121152	1	+61(2)5555-1667	1
		121153	0	+61(2)5555-1348	1

184

Matches Only

```
data EmpsAUC;
   merge EmpsAU(in=Emps)
         PhoneC(in=Cell);
   by EmpID;
   if Emps=1 and Cell=1;
run;
```

EmpsAUC

First	Gender	EmpID	Phone
Togar	M	121150	+61(2)5555-1795
Birin	M	121152	+61(2)5555-1667

186

p110d07

The subsetting IF controls which observations are further processed by the DATA step. In this example, the only processing that remains is the implied output at the bottom of the DATA step. Therefore, if the condition evaluates to **true**, the observation is written to the SAS data set. If the condition is evaluated to **false**, the observation is not written to the SAS data set.

This subsetting IF statement can be rewritten as follows:

```
   if Emps and Cell;
```

Nonmatches from EmpsAU Only

```
data EmpsAUC;
   merge EmpsAU(in=Emps)
         PhoneC(in=Cell);
   by EmpID;
   if Emps=1 and Cell=0;
run;
```

EmpsAUC

First	Gender	EmpID	Phone
Kylie	F	121151	

187 p110d07

This subsetting IF statement can be rewritten as follows:

```
if Emps and not Cell;
```

Nonmatches from PhoneC Only

```
data EmpsAUC;
   merge EmpsAU(in=Emps)
         PhoneC(in=Cell);
   by EmpID;
   if Emps=0 and Cell=1;
run;
```

EmpsAUC

First	Gender	EmpID	Phone
		121153	+61(2)5555-1348

188 p110d07

The subsetting IF statement can be rewritten as follows:

```
if not Emps and Cell;
```

All Nonmatches

```
data EmpsAUC;
   merge EmpsAU(in=Emps)
         PhoneC(in=Cell);
   by EmpID;
   if Emps=0 or Cell=0;
run;
```

EmpsAUC

First	Gender	EmpID	Phone
Kylie	F	121151	
		121153	+61(2)5555-1348

189 p110d07

The subsetting IF statement can be rewritten as follows:

```
if not Emps or not Cell;
```

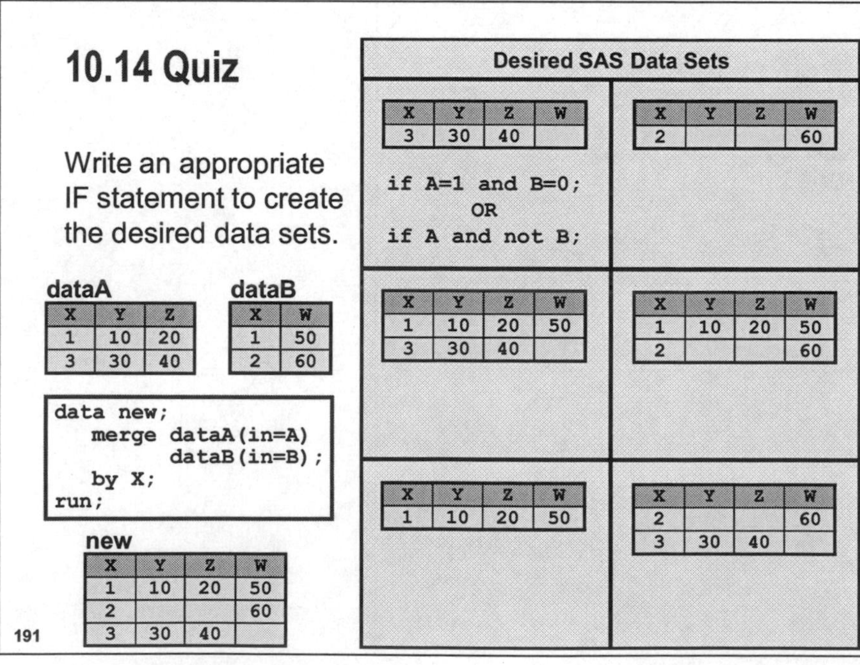

Outputting to Multiple Data Sets (Self-Study)

The DATA statement can specify multiple output data sets.

```
data EmpsAUC EmpsOnly PhoneOnly;
   merge EmpsAU(in=Emps) PhoneC(in=Cell);
   by EmpID;
   if Emps=1 and Cell=1
        then output EmpsAUC;
   else if Emps=1 and Cell=0
        then output EmpsOnly;
   else if Emps=0 and Cell=1
        then output PhoneOnly;
run;
```

194 p110d07

Outputting to Multiple Data Sets (Self-Study)

An OUTPUT statement can be used in a conditional statement to write the current observation to a specific data set that is listed in the DATA statement.

```
data EmpsAUC EmpsOnly PhoneOnly;
   merge EmpsAU(in=Emps) PhoneC(in=Cell);
   by EmpID;
   if Emps=1 and Cell=1
        then output EmpsAUC;
   else if Emps=1 and Cell=0
        then output EmpsOnly;
   else if Emps=0 and Cell=1
        then output PhoneOnly;
run;
```

195 p110d07

Outputting to Multiple Data Sets (Self-Study)

EmpsAUC

First	Gender	EmpID	Phone
Togar	M	121150	+61(2)5555-1795
Birin	M	121152	+61(2)5555-1667

EmpsOnly

First	Gender	EmpID	Phone
Kylie	F	121151	

PhoneOnly

First	Gender	EmpID	Phone
		121153	+61(2)5555-1348

196

Many-to-Many Merge (Self-Study)

Merge **EmpsAUUS** and **PhoneO** by **Country** to create a new data set named **EmpsOfc**.

EmpsAUUS

First	Gender	Country
Togar	M	AU
Kylie	F	AU
Stacey	F	US
Gloria	F	US
James	M	US

PhoneO

Country	Phone
AU	+61(2)5555-1500
AU	+61(2)5555-1600
AU	+61(2)5555-1700
US	+1(305)555-1500
US	+1(305)555-1600

```
data EmpsOfc;
   merge EmpsAUUS PhoneO;
   by Country;
run;
```

The data sets are sorted by **Country**.

197

p110d08

In a many-to-many merge, this note is issued to the log:

```
NOTE: MERGE statement has more
than one data set with repeats of BY values.
```

This message is meant to be informational.

A DATA step that performs a many-to-many merge does not produce a Cartesian product.

Many-to-Many Merge (Self-Study)

DATA Step Results:

EmpsOfc

First	Gender	Country	Phone
Togar	M	AU	+61(2)5555-1500
Kylie	F	AU	+61(2)5555-1600
Kylie	F	AU	+61(2)5555-1700
Stacey	F	US	+1(305)555-1500
Gloria	F	US	+1(305)555-1600
James	M	US	+1(305)555-1600

198

Many-to-Many Merge (Self-Study)

The SQL procedure creates different results than the DATA step for a many-to-many merge.

EmpsAUUS

First	Gender	Country
Togar	M	AU
Kylie	F	AU
Stacey	F	US
Gloria	F	US
James	M	US

PhoneO

Country	Phone
AU	+61(2)5555-1500
AU	+61(2)5555-1600
AU	+61(2)5555-1700
US	+1(305)555-1500
US	+1(305)555-1600

```
proc sql;
   create table EmpsOfc as
   select First, Gender, PhoneO.Country, Phone
   from EmpsAUUS, PhoneO
   where EmpsAUUS.Country=PhoneO.Country;
```

199 p110d08

The SQL procedure is the SAS implementation of Structured Query Language. PROC SQL is part of Base SAS software, and you can use it with any SAS data set. Often, PROC SQL can be an alternative to other SAS procedures or the DATA step.

Many-to-Many Merge (Self-Study)

PROC SQL Results:

EmpsOfc

First	Gender	Country	Phone
Togar	M	AU	+61(2)5555-1500
Togar	M	AU	+61(2)5555-1600
Togar	M	AU	+61(2)5555-1700
Kylie	F	AU	+61(2)5555-1500
Kylie	F	AU	+61(2)5555-1600
Kylie	F	AU	+61(2)5555-1700
Stacey	F	US	+1(305)555-1500
Stacey	F	US	+1(305)555-1600
Gloria	F	US	+1(305)555-1500
Gloria	F	US	+1(305)555-1600
James	M	US	+1(305)555-1500
James	M	US	+1(305)555-1600

200

Exercises

Level 1

10. Merging Using the IN= Option

a. Retrieve the starter program **p110e10**.

b. Add a DATA step after the PROC SORT step to merge **`Work.product`** and **`orion.supplier`** by **`Supplier_ID`** to create a new data set called **`Work.prodsup`**.

c. Submit the program and confirm that **`Work.prodsup`** was created with 556 observations and 10 variables.

d. Modify the DATA step to output only observations that are in **`Work.product`** but not **`orion.supplier`**. A subsetting IF statement that references IN= variables in the MERGE statement needs to be added.

e. Submit the program and confirm that **`Work.prodsup`** was created with 75 observations and 10 variables. The supplier information will be missing in the PROC PRINT output.

Level 2

11. Merging Using the IN= and RENAME= Options

a. Write a PROC SORT step to sort **`orion.customer`** by **`Country`** to create a new data set called **`Work.customer`**.

b. Write a DATA step to merge the previous sorted data set with **`orion.lookup_country`** by **`Country`** to create a new data set called **`Work.allcustomer`**.

In the **`orion.lookup_country`** data set, **`Start`** needs to be renamed to **`Country`** and **`Label`** needs to be renamed to **`Country_Name`**.

Include only the following four variables: **`Customer_ID`**, **`Country`**, **`Customer_Name`**, and **`Country_Name`**.

c. Write a PROC PRINT step to create the following report:

Partial PROC PRINT Output (First 15 of 308 Observations)

Obs	Customer_ID	Country	Customer_Name	Country_Name
1	.	AD		Andorra
2	.	AE		United Arab Emirates
3	.	AF		Afghanistan
4	.	AG		Antigua/Barbuda
5	.	AI		Anguilla
6	.	AL		Albania
7	.	AM		Armenia
8	.	AN		Netherlands Antilles
9	.	AO		Angola
10	.	AQ		Antarctica
11	.	AR		Argentina
12	.	AS		American Samoa
13	.	AT		Austria
14	29	AU	Candy Kinsey	Australia
15	41	AU	Wendell Summersby	Australia

d. Modify the DATA step to store only the observations that contain both customer information and country information. A subsetting IF statement that references IN= variables in the MERGE statement needs to be added.

e. Submit the program to create the following report:

Partial PROC PRINT Output (First 7 of 77 Observations)

Obs	Customer_ID	Country	Customer_Name	Country_ Name
1	29	AU	Candy Kinsey	Australia
2	41	AU	Wendell Summersby	Australia
3	53	AU	Dericka Pockran	Australia
4	111	AU	Karolina Dokter	Australia
5	171	AU	Robert Bowerman	Australia
6	183	AU	Duncan Robertshawe	Australia
7	195	AU	Cosi Rimmington	Australia

Level 3

12. Merging and Outputting to Multiple Data Sets

a. Write a PROC SORT step to sort **`orion.orders`** by **`Employee_ID`** to create a new data set called **`Work.orders`**.

b. Write a DATA step to merge **`orion.staff`** and **`Work.orders`** by **`Employee_ID`**.

Create two new data sets: **`Work.allorders`** and **`Work.noorders`**.

The data set **`Work.allorders`** should include all observations from **`Work.orders`**, regardless of matches or nonmatches from the **`orion.staff`** data set.

The data set **`Work.noorders`** should include the observations from **`orion.staff`** that do not have a match in **`Work.orders`**.

Include only the following six variables: **`Employee_ID`**, **`Job_Title`**, **`Gender`**, **`Order_ID`**, **`Order_Type`**, and **`Order_Date`**.

> Outputting to multiple data sets is mentioned at the end of this section in a self-study section.

c. Using the new data sets, write two PROC PRINT steps to create two reports.

d. Submit the program and confirm that **`Work.allorders`** was created with 490 observations and 6 variables and **`Work.noorders`** was created with 324 observations and 6 variables.

10.7 Chapter Review

Chapter Review

1. What are the three methods for combining SAS data sets? Appending, Concatenating, Merging

2. What data set option enables you to change the name of a variable? Rename

3. What is a requirement of the input SAS data sets prior to match-merging? Sorted

4. Which three statements must be used in a DATA step to perform a match-merge?

   data, merge, by

202

continued...

Chapter Review

5. Which data set option can be used to prevent non-matches from being written to the output data sets in a match-merge?

   the IN = data set option

203

10.8 Solutions

Solutions to Exercises

1. **Appending Like-Structured Data Sets**

   a. Retrieve the starter program.

   b. Submit the two PROC CONTENTS steps.

```
proc contents data=orion.price_current;
run;

proc contents data=orion.price_new;
run;
```

   How many variables are in **orion.price_current**? **6**

   How many variables are in **orion.price_new**? **5**

   Does **orion.price_new** contain any variables that are not in **orion.price_current**? **No**

   c. Add a PROC APPEND step.

```
proc append base=orion.price_current
            data=orion.price_new;
run;
```

   Why is the FORCE option not needed? **The variables in the DATA= data set are all in the BASE= data set.**

   d. Submit the program.

2. **Appending Unlike-Structured Data Sets**

   a. Write and submit two PROC CONTENTS steps.

```
proc contents data=orion.qtr1_2007;
run;

proc contents data=orion.qtr2_2007;
run;
```

   How many variables are in **orion.qtr1_2007**? **5**

   How many variables are in **orion.qtr2_2007**? **6**

   Which variable is not in both data sets? **Employee_ID**

   b. Write a PROC APPEND step.

```
proc append base=work.ytd
            data=orion.qtr1_2007;
run;
```

   c. Submit the PROC APPEND step.

d. Write another PROC APPEND step.

```
proc append base=work.ytd
            data=orion.qtr2_2007 force;
run;
```

Why is the FORCE option needed? **The variable Employee_ID in the DATA= data set is not in the BASE= data set.**

e. Submit the second PROC APPEND step.

3. Using the APPEND Statement

a. Write and submit three PROC CONTENTS steps.

```
proc contents data=orion.shoes_eclipse;
run;

proc contents data=orion.shoes_tracker;
run;

proc contents data=orion.shoes;
run;
```

b. Write a PROC DATASETS step.

```
proc datasets library=orion nolist;
   append base=shoes data=shoes_eclipse;
   append base=shoes data=shoes_tracker force;
quit;
```

c. Submit the PROC DATASETS step.

4. Concatenating Like-Structured Data Sets

a. Write and submit a DATA step.

```
data work.thirdqtr;
   set orion.mnth7_2007 orion.mnth8_2007 orion.mnth9_2007;
run;
```

How many observations in **Work.thirdqtr** are from **orion.mnth7_2007**? **10**

How many observations in **Work.thirdqtr** are from **orion.mnth8_2007**? **12**

How many observations in **Work.thirdqtr** are from **orion.mnth9_2007**? **10**

b. Write and submit a PROC PRINT step.

```
proc print data=work.thirdqtr;
run;
```

5. Concatenating Unlike-Structured Data Sets

a. Retrieve the starter program.

b. Submit the two PROC CONTENTS steps.

```
proc contents data=orion.sales;
run;

proc contents data=orion.nonsales;
run;
```

What are the names of the two variables that are different in the two data sets?

orion.sales	orion.nonsales
First_Name	First
Last_Name	Last

c. Add a DATA step.

```
data work.allemployees;
   set orion.sales
       orion.nonsales(rename=(First=First_Name Last=Last_Name));
   keep Employee_ID First_Name Last_Name Job_Title Salary;
run;
```

d. Add a PROC PRINT step.

```
proc print data=work.allemployees;
run;
```

6. Interleaving Data Sets

a. Retrieve the starter program.

b. Add a PROC SORT step after the PROC SORT step in the starter program.

```
proc sort data=orion.shoes_eclipse
          out=work.eclipsesort;
   by Product_Name;
run;

proc sort data=orion.shoes_tracker
          out=work.trackersort;
   by Product_Name;
run;
```

c. Add a DATA step.

```
data work.e_t_shoes;
   set work.eclipsesort work.trackersort;
   by Product_Name;
   keep Product_Group Product_Name Supplier_ID;
run;
```

d. Add a PROC PRINT step.

```
proc print data=work.e_t_shoes;
run;
```

7. **Merging `orion.orders` and `orion.order_item` in a One-to-Many Merge**

a. Retrieve the starter program.

b. Submit the two PROC CONTENTS steps.

```
proc contents data=orion.orders;
run;

proc contents data=orion.order_item;
run;
```

c. Add a DATA step prior to the PROC PRINT step.

```
data work.allorders;
   merge orion.orders
         orion.order_item;
   by Order_ID;
run;

proc print data=work.allorders;
   var Order_ID Order_Item_Num Order_Type
       Order_Date Quantity Total_Retail_Price;
run;
```

d. Submit the program.

8. **Merging `orion.product_level` and `orion.product_list` in a One-to-Many Merge**

a. Write a PROC SORT step.

```
proc sort data=orion.product_list
          out=work.product_list;
   by Product_Level;
run;
```

b. Write a DATA step.

```
data work.listlevel;
   merge orion.product_level work.product_list;
   by Product_Level;
run;
```

c. Write a PROC PRINT step.

```
proc print data=work.listlevel;
   var Product_ID Product_Name Product_Level Product_Level_Name;
run;
```

9. Joining `orion.product_level` and `orion.product_list` in a One-to-Many Merge

a. Write a PROC SQL step.

```
proc sql;
   create table work.listlevelsql as
   select Product_ID, Product_Name,
          product_level.Product_Level, Product_Level_Name
   from orion.product_level, orion.product_list
   where product_level.Product_Level = product_list.Product_Level;
quit;
```

b. Write a PROC PRINT step.

```
proc print data=work.listlevelsql;
run;
```

10. Merging Using the IN= Option

a. Retrieve the starter program.

b. Add a DATA step.

```
proc sort data=orion.product_list
          out=work.product;
   by Supplier_ID;
run;

data work.prodsup;
   merge work.product
         orion.supplier;
   by Supplier_ID;
run;

proc print data=work.prodsup;
   var Product_ID Product_Name Supplier_ID Supplier_Name;
run;
```

c. Submit the program.

d. Modify the DATA step.

```
data work.prodsup;
   merge work.product(in=P)
         orion.supplier(in=S);
   by Supplier_ID;
   if P=1 and S=0;
run;
```

e. Submit the program.

11. Merging Using the IN= and RENAME= Options

a. Write a PROC SORT step.

```
proc sort data=orion.customer
          out=work.customer;
   by Country;
run;
```

b. Write a DATA step.

```
data work.allcustomer;
   merge work.customer
         orion.lookup_country(rename=(Start=Country
                                      Label=Country_Name));
   by Country;
   keep Customer_ID Country Customer_Name Country_Name;
run;
```

c. Write a PROC PRINT step.

```
proc print data=work.allcustomer;
run;
```

d. Modify the DATA step.

```
data work.allcustomer;
   merge work.customer(in=Cust)
         orion.lookup_country(rename=(Start=Country
                                      Label=Country_Name)
                              in=Ctry);
   by Country;
   keep Customer_ID Country Customer_Name Country_Name;
   if Cust=1 and Ctry=1;
run;
```

e. Submit the program.

12. Merging and Outputting to Multiple Data Sets

a. Write a PROC SORT step.

```
proc sort data=orion.orders
          out=work.orders;
   by Employee_ID;
run;
```

b. Write a DATA step.

```
data work.allorders work.noorders;
   merge orion.staff(in=Staff) work.orders(in=Ord);
   by Employee_ID;
   if Ord=1 then output work.allorders;
   else if Staff=1 and Ord=0 then output work.noorders;
   keep Employee_ID Job_Title Gender Order_ID Order_Type Order_Date;
run;
```

c. Write two PROC PRINT steps.

```
proc print data=work.allorders;
run;

proc print data=work.noorders;
run;
```

d. Submit the program.

Solutions to Student Activities (Polls/Quizzes)

10.01 Quiz – Correct Answer

Which method (appending, concatenating, or merging) should be used for the given business scenario?

	Business Scenario	Method
1	The **JanSales**, **FebSales**, and **MarSales** data sets need to be combined to create the **Qtr1Sales** data set.	**concatenating**
2	The **Sales** data set needs to be combined with the **Target** data set by **month** to compare the sales data to the target data.	**merging**
3	The **OctSales** data set needs to be added to the **YTD** data set.	**appending**

11

10.02 Quiz – Correct Answer

How many observations will be in **Emps** after appending the three data sets?

9 observations

Emps

First	Gender	HireYear
Stacey	F	2006
Gloria	F	2007
James	M	2007

Emps2008

First	Gender	HireYear
Brett	M	2008
Renee	F	2008

Emps2009

First	HireYear
Sara	2009
Dennis	2009

Emps2010

First	HireYear	Country
Rose	2010	Spain
Eric	2010	Spain

22

10.03 Quiz – Correct Answer

How many variables will be in **Emps** after appending the three data sets?

3 variables

Emps2008

First	Gender	HireYear
Brett	M	2008
Renee	F	2008

Emps

First	Gender	HireYear
Stacey	F	2006
Gloria	F	2007
James	M	2007

Emps2009

First	HireYear
Sara	2009
Dennis	2009

Emps2010

First	HireYear	Country
Rose	2010	Spain
Eric	2010	Spain

The base data set variable information cannot change.

25

10.04 Quiz – Correct Answer

How many observations will be in **Emps** if the program is submitted a second time?

15 observations (9 + 2 + 2 + 2)

Be careful; observations are added to the BASE= data set every time that you submit the program.

38

10.05 Quiz – Correct Answer

How many variables will be in **EmpsAll2** after concatenating **EmpsCN** and **EmpsJP**?

EmpsCN

First	Gender	Country
Chang	M	China
Li	M	China
Ming	F	China

EmpsJP

First	Gender	Region
Cho	F	Japan
Tomi	M	Japan

Four variables

First, Gender, Country, and Region

64

10.06 Quiz – Correct Answer

Which statement has correct syntax?

a.
```
set EmpsCN(rename(Country=Location))
    EmpsJP(rename(Region=Location));
```

(b.)
```
set EmpsCN(rename=(Country=Location))
    EmpsJP(rename=(Region=Location));
```

c.
```
set EmpsCN rename=(Country=Location)
    EmpsJP rename=(Region=Location);
```

72

10.07 Multiple Choice Poll – Correct Answer (Self-Study)

Which method would you use if you wanted to create a new variable at the time of concatenation?

a. APPEND procedure

(b.) SET statement

```
data EmpsBonus;
   set EmpsDK EmpsFR;
   if Country='Denmark'
      then Bonus=300;
   else Bonus=500;
run;
```

84

10.08 Quiz – Correct Answer

Which step is sorting the observations in a SAS data set and overwriting the same SAS data set?

a.

```
proc sort data=work.EmpsAU
          out=work.sorted;
   by First;
run;
```

b.

```
proc sort data=work.EmpsAU
          out=orion.EmpsAU;
   by First;
run;
```

(c.)

```
proc sort data=work.EmpsAU;
   by First;
run;
```

105

10.09 Multiple Choice Poll – Correct Answer

What is the **Employee_ID** value for the first observation in the sorted data set?

a. 120102

b. 120121

(c.) 121144

d. 121145

```
proc sort data=orion.sales
          out=work.sortsales;
   by Gender descending Employee_ID;
run;

proc print data=work.sortsales;
   var Gender Employee_ID First_Name
       Last_Name Salary;
run;
```

111

p110a01s

10.10 Quiz – Correct Answer

What are the modified, completed statements?

```
proc sort data=orion.employee_payroll
          out=work.payroll;
   by Employee_ID;
run;

proc sort data=orion.employee_addresses
          out=work.addresses;
   by Employee_ID;
run;

data work.payadd;
   merge work.payroll work.addresses;
   by Employee_ID;
run;
```

118

10.11 Quiz – Correct Answer

How many observations in the final data set **EmpsAUC** are considered nonmatches?

a. 1
(b.) 2
c. 3
d. 4

EmpsAUC

First	Gender	EmpID	Phone
Togar	M	121150	+61(2)5555-1795
Kylie	F	121151	
Birin	M	121152	+61(2)5555-1667
		121153	+61(2)5555-1348

172

10.12 Quiz – Correct Answer

What are the values of **Emps** and **Cell**?

EmpsAU

First	Gender	EmpID
Togar	M	121150
Kylie	F	121151
Birin	M	121152

PhoneC

EmpID	Phone
121150	+61(2)5555-1795
121152	+61(2)5555-1667
121153	+61(2)5555-1348

```
data EmpsAUC;
   merge EmpsAU(in=Emps)
         PhoneC(in=Cell);
   by EmpID;
run;
```

PDV

First	Gender	EmpID	D Emps	Phone	D Cell
		121153	0	+61(2)5555-1348	1

181

10.13 Quiz – Correct Answer

Which subsetting IF statement can be added to the DATA step to only output the matches?

a. `if Emps=1 and Cell=0;`

(b.) `if Emps=1 and Cell=1;`

c. `if Emps=1;`

d. `if Cell=0;`

PDV

First	Gender	EmpID	D Emps	Phone	D Cell
Togar	M	121150	1	+61(2)5555-1795	1
Kylie	F	121151	1		0
Birin	M	121152	1	+61(2)5555-1667	1
		121153	0	+61(2)5555-1348	1

185

10.14 Quiz – Correct Answer

Write an appropriate IF statement to create the desired data sets.

dataA

X	Y	Z
1	10	20
3	30	40

dataB

X	W
1	50
2	60

```
data new;
   merge dataA(in=A)
         dataB(in=B);
   by X;
run;
```

new

X	Y	Z	W
1	10	20	50
2			60
3	30	40	

192

Desired SAS Data Sets

X	Y	Z	W
3	30	40	

```
if A=1 and B=0;
OR
if A and not B;
```

X	Y	Z	W
2			60

```
if A=0 and B=1;
OR
if not A and B;
```

X	Y	Z	W
1	10	20	50
3	30	40	

```
if A=1;
OR
if A;
```

X	Y	Z	W
1	10	20	50
2			60

```
if B=1;
OR
if B;
```

X	Y	Z	W
1	10	20	50

```
if A=1 and B=1;
OR
if A and B;
```

X	Y	Z	W
2			60
3	30	40	

```
if A=0 or B=0;
OR
if not A or not B;
```

Solutions to Chapter Review

Chapter Review Answers

1. What are the three methods for combining SAS data sets?
   - **Append**
   - **Concatenate**
   - **Merge**

2. What data set option enables you to change the name of a variable?
   the RENAME= data set option

204

continued...

Chapter Review Answers

3. What is a requirement of the input SAS data sets prior to match-merging?
   The input SAS data sets must be sorted by the BY variable.

4. Which three statements must be used in a DATA step to perform a match-merge?
   - **DATA**
   - **MERGE**
   - **BY**

205

continued...

Chapter Review Answers

5. Which data set option can be used to prevent non-matches from being written to the output data sets in a match-merge?

   the IN= data set option

206

Chapter 11 Enhancing Reports

11.1 Using Global Statements 11-3

Exercises 11-16

11.2 Adding Labels and Formats 11-20

Exercises 11-29

11.3 Creating User-Defined Formats 11-32

Exercises 11-43

11.4 Subsetting and Grouping Observations 11-46

Exercises 11-52

11.5 Directing Output to External Files 11-55

Demonstration: Creating HTML, PDF, and RTF Files 11-64

Demonstration: Creating Files That Open in Excel 11-77

Demonstration: Using Options with the EXCELXP Destination (Self-Study) 11-80

Exercises 11-83

11.6 Chapter Review 11-88

11.7 Solutions 11-89

Solutions to Exercises 11-89

Solutions to Student Activities (Polls/Quizzes) 11-103

Solutions to Chapter Review 11-109

11.1 Using Global Statements

Objectives

- Identify SAS statements that are used with most reporting procedures.
- Enhance reports by using SAS system options.
- Enhance reports by adding titles and footnotes.
- Add dates and times to titles. (Self-Study)

3

Creating Reports

A procedure step is a primary method for creating reports.

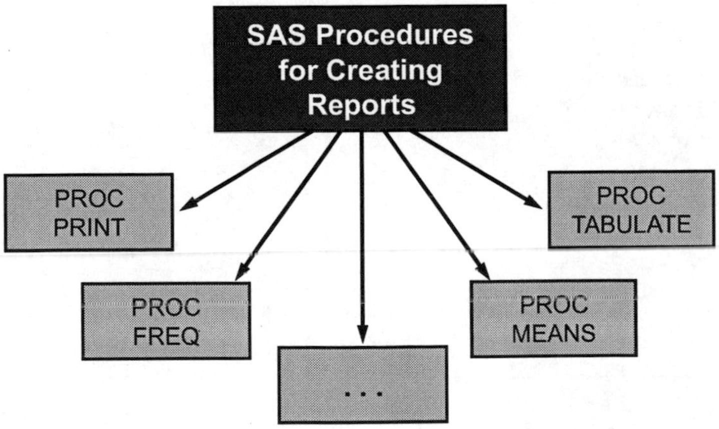

4

Example of a Basic Report

```
proc print data=orion.sales;
   var Employee_ID First_Name Last_Name Salary;
run;
```

Partial PROC PRINT Output

Obs	Employee_ID	First_ Name	Last_Name	Salary
1	120102	Tom	Zhou	108255
2	120103	Wilson	Dawes	87975
3	120121	Irenie	Elvish	26600
4	120122	Christina	Ngan	27475
5	120123	Kimiko	Hotstone	26190
6	120124	Lucian	Daymond	26480
7	120125	Fong	Hofmeister	32040
8	120126	Satyakam	Denny	26780
9	120127	Sharryn	Clarkson	28100
10	120128	Monica	Kletschkus	30890

5 p111d01

Example of an Enhanced Report

option

```
options nocenter;
ods html file='enhanced.html' style=sasweb;
proc print data=orion.sales label;
   var Employee_ID First_Name Last_Name Salary;
   title1 'Orion Sales Employees';
   title2 'Males Only';
   footnote 'Confidential';
   label Employee_ID='Sales ID'
         First_Name='First Name'
         Last_Name='Last Name'
         Salary='Annual Salary';
   format Salary dollar8.;
   where Gender='M';
   by Country;
run;
ods html close;
```

6 p111d01

.rtf = no need for style
→ viewable in word

style = only w/ html

html = filename .xls → can be read in excel (HTML)

– ODS

Example of an Enhanced Report

Partial PROC PRINT Output

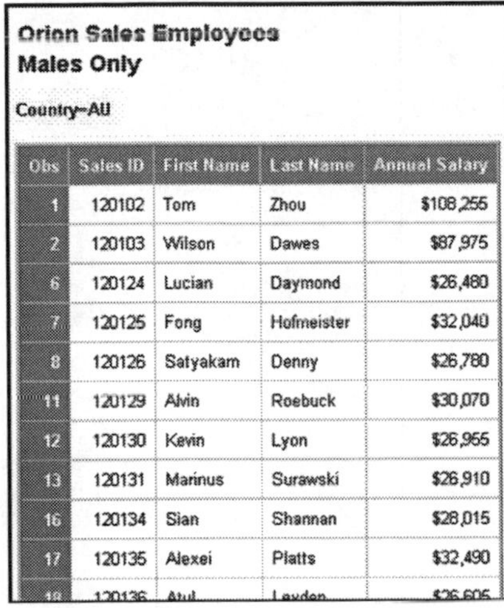

Orion Sales Employees
Males Only

Country=AU

Obs	Sales ID	First Name	Last Name	Annual Salary
1	120102	Tom	Zhou	$108,255
2	120103	Wilson	Dawes	$87,975
6	120124	Lucian	Daymond	$26,480
7	120125	Fong	Hofmeister	$32,040
8	120126	Satyakam	Denny	$26,780
11	120129	Alvin	Roebuck	$30,070
12	120130	Kevin	Lyon	$26,955
13	120131	Marinus	Surawski	$26,910
16	120134	Sian	Shannan	$28,015
17	120135	Alexei	Platts	$32,490
18	120136	Atul	Leyden	$26,605

7

Statements That Enhance Reports

Many statements are used with most reporting procedures to enhance the report.

```
options nocenter;
ods html file='enhanced.html' style=sasweb;
proc print data=orion.sales label;
   var Employee_ID First_Name Last_Name Salary;
   title1 'Orion Sales Employees';
   title2 'Males Only';
   footnote 'Confidential';
   label Employee_ID='Sales ID'
         First_Name='First Name'
         Last_Name='Last Name'
         Salary='Annual Salary';
   format Salary dollar8.;
   where Gender='M';
   by Country;
run;
ods html close;
```

8

Global Statements

The following are global statements that enhance reports:

- OPTIONS
- TITLE
- FOOTNOTE
- ODS

Global statements are specified anywhere in your SAS program and they remain in effect until canceled, changed, or your SAS session ends.

9

The OPTIONS Statement

The *OPTIONS statement* changes the value of one or more SAS system options.

General form of the OPTIONS statement:

OPTIONS *option(s)*;

- Some SAS system options change the appearance of a report.
- The OPTIONS statement is **not** usually included in a PROC or DATA step.

10

SAS System Options for Reporting

Selected SAS System Options:

DATE (default)	displays the date and time that the SAS session began at the top of each page of SAS output.
NODATE	does not display the date and time that the SAS session began at the top of each page of SAS output.
NUMBER (default)	prints page numbers on the first line of each page of SAS output.
NONUMBER	does not print page numbers on the first line of each page of SAS output.
PAGENO=*n*	defines a beginning page number (*n*) for the next page of SAS output.

11

continued...

SAS System Options for Reporting

Selected SAS System Options:

CENTER (default)	centers SAS output.
NOCENTER	left-aligns SAS output.
PAGESIZE=*n* PS=*n*	defines the number of lines (*n*) that can be printed per page of SAS output.
LINESIZE=*width* LS=*width*	defines the line size (*width*) for the SAS log and SAS output.

12

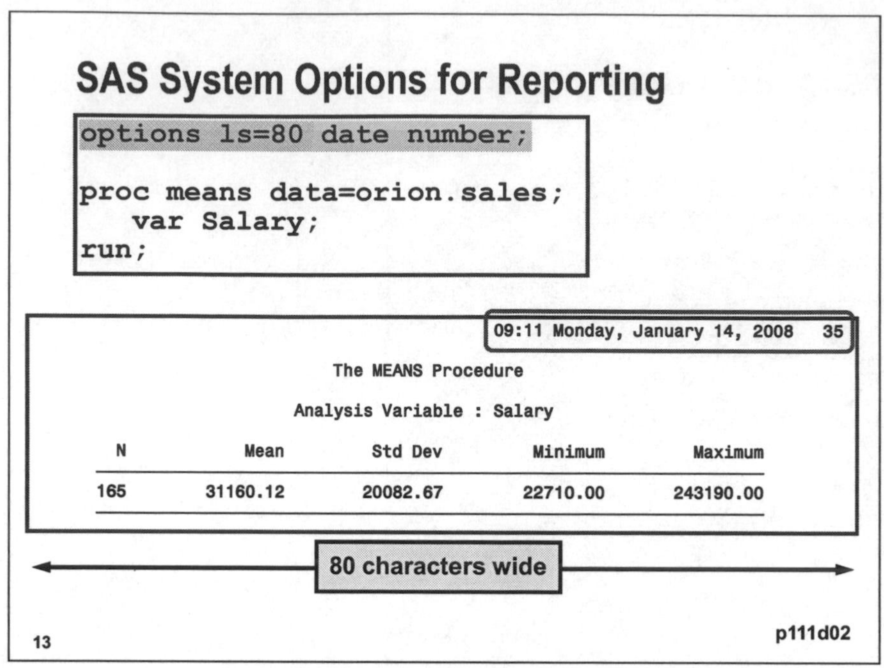
SAS System Options for Reporting
options ls=80 date number;
proc means data=orion.sales;
var Salary;
run;
09:11 Monday, January 14, 2008 35
The MEANS Procedure
Analysis Variable : Salary
N Mean Std Dev Minimum Maximum
165 31160.12 20082.67 22710.00 243190.00
80 characters wide
13
p111d02

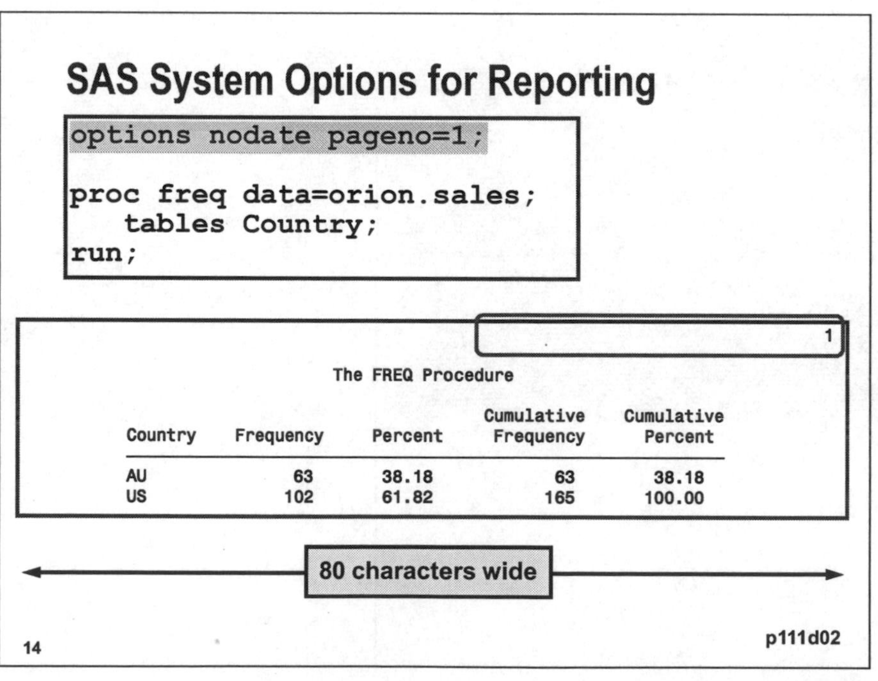
SAS System Options for Reporting
options nodate pageno=1;
proc freq data=orion.sales;
tables Country;
run;
1
The FREQ Procedure
Country Frequency Percent Cumulative Frequency Cumulative Percent
AU 63 38.18 63 38.18
US 102 61.82 165 100.00
80 characters wide
14
p111d02

Setup for the Poll

- Retrieve and submit program **p111a01**.
- Review the results including the date, time, and page number in the top-right corner of each page of output.
- Add the DTRESET system option to the OPTIONS statement.
- Submit the program and review the results.

DTRESET	updates date and time at the top of each page of SAS output.
NODTRESET (Default)	does not update date and time at the top of each page of SAS output.

16

11.01 Poll

Did the date and/or time change?

❍ Yes

❍ No

17

The TITLE Statement

The *TITLE statement* specifies title lines for SAS output.

General form of the TITLE statement:

```
TITLEn 'text';
```

- Titles appear at the top of the page.
- The default title is **The SAS System**.
- The value of ***n*** can be from 1 to 10.
- An unnumbered **TITLE** is equivalent to **TITLE1**.
- Titles remain in effect until they are changed, canceled, or you end your SAS session.

19

The FOOTNOTE Statement

The *FOOTNOTE statement* specifies footnote lines for SAS output.

General form of the FOOTNOTE statement:

```
FOOTNOTEn 'text';
```

- Footnotes appear at the bottom of the page.
- No footnote is printed unless one is specified.
- The value of ***n*** can be from 1 to 10.
- An unnumbered **FOOTNOTE** is equivalent to FOOTNOTE1.
- Footnotes remain in effect until they are changed, canceled, or you end your SAS session.

20

The TITLE and FOOTNOTE Statements

```
footnote1 'By Human Resource Department';
footnote3 'Confidential';

proc means data=orion.sales;
   var Salary;
   title 'Orion Star Sales Employees';
run;
```

21

p111d03

The TITLE and FOOTNOTE Statements

Orion Star Sales Employees

The MEANS Procedure

Analysis Variable : Salary

N	Mean	Std Dev	Minimum	Maximum
165	31160.12	20082.67	22710.00	243190.00

By Human Resource Department

Confidential

22

Changing Titles and Footnotes

TITLE*n* or **FOOTNOTE*n***

- replaces a previous title or footnote with the same number
- cancels all titles or footnotes with higher numbers.

23

Canceling All Titles and Footnotes

- The null TITLE statement cancels all titles.

```
title;
```

- The null FOOTNOTE statement cancels all footnotes.

```
footnote;
```

24

Changing and Canceling Titles and Footnotes

PROC PRINT Code	Resultant Title(s)

`proc print data=orion.sales;`
`   title1 'The First Line';`
`   title2 'The Second Line';`
`run;`
	The First Line
	The Second Line

`proc print data=orion.sales;`
`   title2 'The Next Line';`
`run;`
	The First Line
	The Next Line

`proc print data=orion.sales;`
`   title 'The Top Line';`
`run;`
	The Top Line

`proc print data=orion.sales;`
`   title3 'The Third Line';`
`run;`
	The Top Line
	
	The Third Line

`proc print data=orion.sales;`
`   title;`
`run;`	

35

11.02 Quiz

Which footnote(s) appears in the second procedure output?

a. Non Sales Employees

b. Orion Star
Non Sales Employees

c. Non Sales Employees
Confidential

d. Orion Star
Non Sales Employees
Confidential

```
footnote1 'Orion Star';
proc print data=orion.sales;
   footnote2 'Sales Employees';
   footnote3 'Confidential';
run;
proc print data=orion.nonsales;
   footnote2 'Non Sales Employees';
run;
```

37

Titles with Dates and Times (Self-Study)

The automatic macro variables &SYSDATE9 and &SYSTIME can be used to add the SAS invocation date and time to titles and footnotes.

```
title1 'Orion Star Employee Listing';
title2 "Created on &sysdate9 at &systime";
```

Double quotation marks must be used when you reference a macro variable.

Example Title Output:

```
Orion Star Employee Listing
Created on 11MAR2008 at 15:53
```

39

p111d04

Titles with Dates and Times (Self-Study)

The %LET statement can be used with %SYSFUNC and the TODAY function or the TIME function to create a macro variable with the current date or time.

%LET *macro-variable* **= %SYSFUNC(today(),** *date-format***);**

%LET *macro-variable* **= %SYSFUNC(time(),** *time-format***);**

- %LET is a macro statement that creates a macro variable and assigns it a value without leading or trailing blanks.
- %SYSFUNC is a macro function that executes SAS functions outside of a step.

40

Titles with Dates and Times (Self-Study)

```
%let currentdate=%sysfunc(today(),worddate.);
%let currenttime=%sysfunc(time(),timeampm.);

proc freq data=orion.sales;
   tables Gender Country;
   title1 'Orion Star Employee Listing';
   title2 "Created &currentdate";
   title3 "at &currenttime";
run;
```

Example Title Output:

```
Orion Star Employee Listing
Created March 11, 2008
at 4:09:43 PM
```

41 p111d04

title1 "Report Generated at: %sysfunc(time(), timeampm.)";

– Footnote on each page

–

Exercises

Level 1

1. Specifying Titles, Footnotes, and System Options

a. Retrieve the starter program **p111e01**.

b. Use the OPTIONS statement to establish these system options for the PROC MEANS report:

1) Suppress the page numbers that appear at the top of each output page.

2) Suppress the date and time that appear at the top of each output page.

3) Limit the number of lines per page to 18 for the report. Reset the option value to 52 after the PROC MEANS step finishes.

c. Specify the following title for the report: **`Orion Star Sales Report`**.

d. Specify the following footnote for the report: **`Report by SAS Programming Student`**.

e. After the PROC MEANS step finishes, cancel the footnote.

f. Submit the program to create the following PROC MEANS report:

PROC MEANS Output

```
                         Orion Star Sales Report

                          The MEANS Procedure

     Analysis Variable : Total_Retail_Price Total Retail Price for This Product

       N            Mean         Std Dev         Minimum         Maximum
     ------------------------------------------------------------------
     617     162.2001053     233.8530183       2.6000000         1937.20
     ------------------------------------------------------------------






                   Report by SAS Programming Student
```

Level 2

2. Specifying Multiple Titles and System Options

a. Retrieve the starter program **p111e02**.

b. Limit the number of lines per page to 18 and then reset that option to 52 after both reports are complete.

c. Request that each report contain page numbers starting at 1.

d. Request that the **current** date and time be displayed at the top of each page; not the date and time that the SAS session began.

e. Specify the following title to appear in both reports: `Orion Star Sales Analysis`.

f. Specify a secondary title to appear in the first report with a blank line between the titles:

```
Catalog Sales Only
```

g. Specify the following footnote for the first report:

```
Based on the previous day's posted data
```

> The text specified for a title or footnote can be enclosed in single quotation marks or double quotation marks. Use double quotation marks when the text contains an apostrophe.

h. Specify a secondary title to appear in the second report with a blank line between the titles:

```
Internet Sales Only
```

i. Cancel all footnotes for the second report.

j. Submit the program to create the following PROC MEANS reports:

PROC MEANS Output

```
                         Orion Star Sales Analysis                               1
                                                  16:30 Monday, January 28, 2008
                           Catalog Sales Only

                          The MEANS Procedure

    Analysis Variable : Total_Retail_Price Total Retail Price for This Product

       N            Mean         Std Dev         Minimum         Maximum
      ------------------------------------------------------------------
     170     199.5961765     282.9680817       2.6000000         1937.20
      ------------------------------------------------------------------




                  Based on the previous day's posted data
```

```
                         Orion Star Sales Analysis                               1
                                                  16:30 Monday, January 28, 2008
                          Internet Sales Only

                          The MEANS Procedure

    Analysis Variable : Total_Retail_Price Total Retail Price for This Product

       N            Mean         Std Dev         Minimum         Maximum
      ------------------------------------------------------------------
     123     174.7280488     214.3528338       2.7000000         1542.60
      ------------------------------------------------------------------
```

Level 3

3. Inserting Dates and Times into Titles

a. Use the OPTIONS procedure to verify that the date and time will not be automatically displayed at the top of each page. If the option is not set correctly, change it.

Documentation about the OPTIONS procedure can be found in the SAS Help and Documentation from the Contents tab (**SAS Products** ⇨ **Base SAS** ⇨ **Base SAS 9.2 Procedures Guide** ⇨ **Procedures** ⇨ **The OPTIONS Procedure**). Look for an option in the PROC OPTIONS statement that can display the current setting of a single option.

b. Retrieve the starter program **p111e03**.

c. Add a title with the following text, substituting the current date and time:

`Sales Report as of` ***`4:57 PM`*** **`on`** ***`Monday, January 28, 2008`***

An example of this technique is shown in the self-study material at the end of this section.

d. Submit the program to create the following report:

PROC MEANS Output

```
                     Sales Report as of 4:57 PM on Monday, January 28, 2008

                                   The MEANS Procedure

           Analysis Variable : Total_Retail_Price Total Retail Price for This Product

              N            Mean         Std Dev         Minimum         Maximum
            -------------------------------------------------------------------
            617     162.2001053     233.8530183       2.6000000         1937.20
            -------------------------------------------------------------------
```

11.2 Adding Labels and Formats

Objectives

- Display descriptive column headings using the LABEL statement.
- Display formatted values using the FORMAT statement.

45

Labels and Formats (Review)

When displaying reports,

- a *label* changes the appearance of a variable name
- a *format* changes the appearance of variable value.

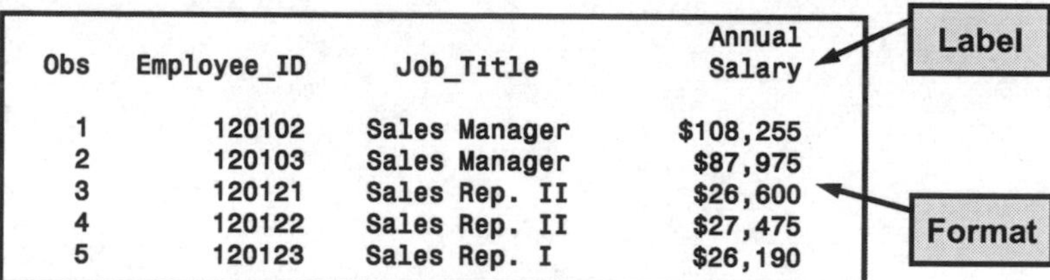

Obs	Employee_ID	Job_Title	Annual Salary
1	120102	Sales Manager	$108,255
2	120103	Sales Manager	$87,975
3	120121	Sales Rep. II	$26,600
4	120122	Sales Rep. II	$27,475
5	120123	Sales Rep. I	$26,190

46

The LABEL Statement (Review)

The *LABEL statement* assigns descriptive labels to variable names.

General form of the LABEL statement:

LABEL *variable* = '*label*'
variable = '*label*'
variable = '*label*';

- A label can be up to 256 characters.
- Labels are used automatically by many procedures.
- The PRINT procedure uses labels when the LABEL or SPLIT= option is specified in the PROC PRINT statement.

47

Assigning Temporary Labels

PROC FREQ automatically uses labels.

```
proc freq data=orion.sales;
   tables Gender;
   label Gender='Sales Employee Gender';
run;
```

The FREQ Procedure

Sales Employee Gender

Gender	Frequency	Percent	Cumulative Frequency	Cumulative Percent
F	68	41.21	68	41.21
M	97	58.79	165	100.00

p111d05

48

Assigning Temporary Labels

PROC PRINT does not automatically use labels.

```
proc print data=orion.sales;
   var Employee_ID Job_Title Salary;
   label Employee_ID='Sales ID'
         Job_Title='Job Title'
         Salary='Annual Salary';
run;
```

Partial PROC PRINT Output

Obs	Employee_ID	Job_Title	Salary
1	120102	Sales Manager	108255
2	120103	Sales Manager	87975
3	120121	Sales Rep. II	26600
4	120122	Sales Rep. II	27475
5	120123	Sales Rep. I	26190

49 p111d05

Assigning Temporary Labels

The LABEL option tells PROC PRINT to use labels.

```
proc print data=orion.sales label;
   var Employee_ID Job_Title Salary;
   label Employee_ID='Sales ID'
         Job_Title='Job Title'
         Salary='Annual Salary';
run;
```

Partial PROC PRINT Output

Obs	Sales ID	Job Title	Annual Salary
1	120102	Sales Manager	108255
2	120103	Sales Manager	87975
3	120121	Sales Rep. II	26600
4	120122	Sales Rep. II	27475
5	120123	Sales Rep. I	26190

50 p111d05

The FSEDIT procedure is another procedure in addition to the PRINT procedure that uses the LABEL option.

Assigning Temporary Labels

Instead of the LABEL option in PROC PRINT, the SPLIT= option can be used.

The *SPLIT= option* specifies the split character, which controls line breaks in column headers.

General form of the SPLIT= option:

SPLIT='*split-character*'

51

Without the SPLIT= option, PROC PRINT can split the headers at special characters such as the blank or underscore or in mixed-case values when going from lowercase to uppercase.

Assigning Temporary Labels

The SPLIT= option makes PROC PRINT use labels.

```
proc print data=orion.sales split='*';
   var Employee_ID Job_Title Salary;
   label Employee_ID='Sales ID'
         Job_Title='Job*Title'
         Salary='Annual*Salary';
run;
```

Partial PROC PRINT Output

```
                           Job           Annual
 Obs     Sales ID         Title          Salary

   1      120102     Sales Manager       108255
   2      120103     Sales Manager        87975
   3      120121     Sales Rep. II        26600
   4      120122     Sales Rep. II        27475
   5      120123     Sales Rep. I         26190
```

52

p111d05

Assigning Permanent Labels (Review)

Using a LABEL statement in a DATA step permanently associates labels with variables by storing the label in the descriptor portion of the SAS data set.

```
data orion.bonus;
   set orion.sales;
   Bonus=Salary*0.10;
   label Salary='Annual*Salary'
         Bonus='Annual*Bonus';
   keep Employee_ID First_Name
        Last_Name Salary Bonus;
run;

proc print data=orion.bonus split='*';
run;
```

53

p111d05

Assigning Permanent Labels (Review)

Partial PROC PRINT Output

Obs	Employee_ID	First_ Name	Last_Name	Annual Salary	Annual Bonus
1	120102	Tom	Zhou	108255	10825.5
2	120103	Wilson	Dawes	87975	8797.5
3	120121	Irenie	Elvish	26600	2660.0
4	120122	Christina	Ngan	27475	2747.5
5	120123	Kimiko	Hotstone	26190	2619.0
6	120124	Lucian	Daymond	26480	2648.0
7	120125	Fong	Hofmeister	32040	3204.0
8	120126	Satyakam	Denny	26780	2678.0
9	120127	Sharryn	Clarkson	28100	2810.0
10	120128	Monica	Kletschkus	30890	3089.0

54

11.03 Quiz

Which statement is true concerning the PROC PRINT output for **Bonus**?

a. Annual Bonus will be the label.
b. Mid-Year Bonus will be the label.

```
data orion.bonus;
   set orion.sales;
   Bonus=Salary*0.10;
   label Bonus='Annual Bonus';
run;

proc print data=orion.bonus label;
   label Bonus='Mid-Year Bonus';
run;
```

56

p111d05

The FORMAT Statement (Review)

The *FORMAT statement* assigns formats to variable values.

General form of the FORMAT statement:

FORMAT *variable(s) format*;

- A *format* is an instruction that SAS uses to write data values.
- Values in the data set are not changed.

59

11.04 Quiz

Which displayed value is incorrect for the given format?

Format	Stored Value	Displayed Value
$3.	Wednesday	Wed
6.1	1234.345	1234.3
COMMAX5.	1234.345	1.234
DOLLAR9.2	1234.345	$1,234.35
DDMMYY8.	0	01/01/1960
DATE9.	0	01JAN1960
YEAR4.	0	1960

61

Assigning Temporary Formats

```
proc print data=orion.sales label;
   var Employee_ID Job_Title Salary
       Country Birth_Date Hire_Date;
   . . .
   format Salary dollar10.0
          Birth_Date Hire_Date monyy7.;
run;
```

Partial PROC PRINT Output

Obs	Sales ID	Job Title	Annual Salary	Country	Date of Birth	Date of Hire
1	120102	Sales Manager	$108,255	AU	AUG1969	JUN1989
2	120103	Sales Manager	$87,975	AU	JAN1949	JAN1974
3	120121	Sales Rep. II	$26,600	AU	AUG1944	JAN1974
4	120122	Sales Rep. II	$27,475	AU	JUL1954	JUL1978
5	120123	Sales Rep. I	$26,190	AU	SEP1964	OCT1985

63

p111d06

Assigning Temporary Formats

```
proc freq data=orion.sales;
   tables Hire_Date;
   format Hire_Date year4.;
run;
```

Partial PROC FREQ Output

The FREQ Procedure

Hire_Date	Frequency	Percent	Cumulative Frequency	Cumulative Percent
1974	23	13.94	23	13.94
1975	2	1.21	25	15.15
1976	4	2.42	29	17.58
1977	3	1.82	32	19.39
1978	7	4.24	39	23.64
1979	3	1.82	42	25.45

64

p111d06

Assigning Permanent and Temporary Formats

Using a FORMAT statement in a DATA step permanently associates formats with variables by storing the format in the descriptor portion of the SAS data set.

```
data orion.bonus;
   set orion.sales;
   Bonus=Salary*0.10;
   format Salary Bonus comma8.;
   keep Employee_ID First_Name
        Last_Name Salary Bonus;
run;

proc print data=orion.bonus;
   format Bonus dollar8.;
run;
```

✎ Temporary formats override permanent formats.

65

p111d06

Assigning Permanent and Temporary Formats

Partial PROC PRINT Output

```
                First_
Obs  Employee_ID  Name        Last_Name       Salary      Bonus

  1      120102   Tom         Zhou           108,255    $10,826
  2      120103   Wilson      Dawes           87,975     $8,798
  3      120121   Irenie      Elvish          26,600     $2,660
  4      120122   Christina   Ngan            27,475     $2,748
  5      120123   Kimiko      Hotstone        26,190     $2,619
  6      120124   Lucian      Daymond         26,480     $2,648
  7      120125   Fong        Hofmeister      32,040     $3,204
  8      120126   Satyakam    Denny           26,780     $2,678
  9      120127   Sharryn     Clarkson        28,100     $2,810
 10      120128   Monica      Kletschkus      30,890     $3,089
```

Exercises

Level 1

4. Applying Labels and Formats in Reports

a. Retrieve the starter program **p111e04**.

b. Modify the column heading for each variable as shown in the sample output that follows.

c. Display all dates in the form ddMONyyyy. If you are running SAS 9.2, specify a width of **11** for the format to obtain the hyphens as shown in the sample output that follows. Otherwise, use a width of **9**; the hyphens will not appear.

d. Display each salary with dollar signs, commas, and two decimal places as shown in the sample output that follows. No salary in the data set exceeds $500,000.

e. Submit the program to produce the following report:

Partial PROC PRINT Output

Employees with 3 Dependents

Obs	Employee Number	Annual Salary	Birth Date	Hire Date	Termination Date
9	120109	$26,495.00	15-DEC-1986	01-OCT-2006	.
11	120111	$26,895.00	23-JUL-1949	01-NOV-1974	.
12	120112	$26,550.00	17-FEB-1969	01-JUL-1990	.
14	120114	$31,285.00	08-FEB-1944	01-JAN-1974	.
18	120118	$28,090.00	03-JUN-1959	01-JUL-1984	.
20	120120	$27,645.00	05-MAY-1944	01-JAN-1974	.
23	120123	$26,190.00	28-SEP-1964	01-OCT-1985	31-JAN-2005
35	120135	$32,490.00	26-JAN-1969	01-OCT-1997	30-APR-2004
47	120147	$26,580.00	19-JAN-1988	01-OCT-2006	.
51	120151	$26,520.00	21-NOV-1944	01-JAN-1974	.

Level 2

5. Overriding Existing Labels and Formats

a. Retrieve the starter program **p111e05**.

b. Display only the year portion of the birth dates.

c. Display only the first initial of each customer's first name. Display the entire last name.

d. Show the customer's ID with exactly six digits, including leading zeros if necessary.

> Documentation on SAS formats can be found in the SAS Help and Documentation from the Contents tab (**SAS Products** ⇨ **Base SAS** ⇨ **SAS 9.2 Language Reference: Dictionary** ⇨ **Dictionary of Language Elements** ⇨ **Formats** ⇨ **Formats by Category**). Look for a numeric format that writes standard numeric data with leading zeros.

e. Modify the column heading for each variable as shown in the sample output that follows. Be sure that the column header for the customer's last name is also split into two lines.

f. Submit the program to produce the following report:

Partial PROC PRINT Output

```
                         Customers from Turkey

                 Customer     First     Last            Birth
          Obs       ID       Initial    Name            Year

           47     000544        A       Argac           1964
           48     000908        A       Umran           1979
           49     000928        B       Urfalioglu      1969
           50     001033        S       Okay            1979
           51     001100        A       Canko           1964
           52     001684        C       Aydemir         1974
           55     002788        S       Yucel           1944
```

Level 3

6. Applying Permanent Labels and Formats

a. Retrieve the starter program **p111e06**.

b. Add permanent variable labels and formats to the **`Work.otherstatus`** data set so that those attributes need not be repeated in subsequent steps.

1) Variable labels:

- **`Employee_ID`** `Employee Number`
- **`Employee_Hire_Date`** `Hired`

2) The format for **`Employee_Hire_Date`** should be displayed in the yyyy.mm.dd form.

> Documentation on SAS formats can be found in the SAS Help and Documentation from the Contents tab (**SAS Products** ⇨ **Base SAS** ⇨ **SAS 9.2 Language Reference: Dictionary** ⇨ **Dictionary of Language Elements** ⇨ **Formats** ⇨ **Formats by Category**). Look for a date format that satisfies the requirements noted above.

c. Override the permanent attributes within the PROC FREQ step so that the hire dates are grouped by calendar quarter in the form yyyyQq and the report explicitly states that the counts are by quarter as shown in the sample output that follows.

> Documentation on SAS formats can be found in the SAS Help and Documentation from the Contents tab (**SAS Products** ⇨ **Base SAS** ⇨ **SAS 9.2 Language Reference: Dictionary** ⇨ **Dictionary of Language Elements** ⇨ **Formats** ⇨ **Formats by Category**). Look for a date format that satisfies the requirements noted above.

d. Submit the program to produce the following reports. Verify that the variable attributes appear in the PROC CONENTS output.

Partial PROC PRINT Output

```
                Employees who are listed with Marital Status=0

                                 Employee
                      Obs         Number           Hired

                        1         120102      1989.06.01
                        2         120117      1986.04.01
                        3         120126      2006.08.01
                        4         120145      1985.06.01
                        5         120149      1993.01.01
```

Partial PROC CONTENTS Output

```
                Employees who are listed with Marital Status=0

                           The CONTENTS Procedure

                 Alphabetic List of Variables and Attributes

 #    Variable                Type    Len    Format         Label

 2    Employee_Hire_Date      Num       8    YYMMDDP10.     Hired
 1    Employee_ID             Num       8    12.            Employee Number
```

Partial PROC FREQ Output

```
                Employees who are listed with Marital Status=0

                             The FREQ Procedure

                               Quarter Hired

      Employee_                                   Cumulative    Cumulative
      Hire_Date    Frequency     Percent           Frequency       Percent
      ----------------------------------------------------------------------
         1974Q1           5        12.50                   5         12.50
         1976Q3           1         2.50                   6         15.00
         1978Q4           1         2.50                   7         17.50
         1981Q1           1         2.50                   8         20.00
         1981Q3           1         2.50                   9         22.50
```

11.3 Creating User-Defined Formats

Objectives

- Create user-defined formats using the FORMAT procedure.
- Apply user-defined formats to variables in reports.

70

User-Defined Formats

A user-defined format needs to be created for **Country**.

Current Report (partial output)

Obs	Sales ID	Job Title	Annual Salary	Country	Date of Birth	Date of Hire
61	120179	Sales Rep. III	$28,510	AU	MAR1974	JAN2004
62	120180	Sales Rep. II	$26,970	AU	JUN1954	DEC1978
63	120198	Sales Rep. III	$28,025	AU	JAN1988	DEC2006
64	120261	Chief Sales Officer	$243,190	US	FEB1969	AUG1987
65	121018	Sales Rep. II	$27,560	US	JAN1944	JAN1974
66	121019	Sales Rep. IV	$31,320	US	JUN1986	JUN2004

Desired Report (partial output)

Obs	Sales ID	Job Title	Annual Salary	Country	Date of Birth	Date of Hire
61	120179	Sales Rep. III	$28,510	Australia	MAR1974	JAN2004
62	120180	Sales Rep. II	$26,970	Australia	JUN1954	DEC1978
63	120198	Sales Rep. III	$28,025	Australia	JAN1988	DEC2006
64	120261	Chief Sales Officer	$243,190	United States	FEB1969	AUG1987
65	121018	Sales Rep. II	$27,560	United States	JAN1944	JAN1974
66	121019	Sales Rep. IV	$31,320	United States	JUN1986	JUN2004

71

FORMAT - instruction for displaying data

User-Defined Formats

To create and use your own formats, do the following:

Part 1 Use the FORMAT procedure to create the user-defined format.

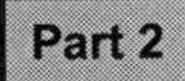

Apply the format to a specific variable(s) by using a FORMAT statement in the reporting procedure.

72

The FORMAT Procedure

The *FORMAT procedure* is used to create user-defined formats.

General form of the FORMAT procedure with the VALUE statement:

```
PROC FORMAT;
     VALUE format-name range1 = 'label '
                       range2 = 'label '
                       . . . ;
RUN;
```

73

The FORMAT Procedure

A *format-name*

- names the format that you are creating
- cannot be more than 32 characters in SAS®9
- for character values, must have a dollar sign ($) as the first character, and a letter or underscore as the second character
- for numeric values, must have a letter or underscore as the first character
- cannot end in a number
- cannot be the name of a SAS format
- does not end with a period in the VALUE statement.

74

Format names prior to SAS®9 are limited to 8 characters.

11.05 Multiple Answer Poll

Which user-defined format names are invalid?

a. $stfmt
b. $3levels
c. _4years
d. salranges
e. dollar

76

The FORMAT Procedure

Range(s) can be

- single values
- ranges of values
- lists of values.

Labels

- can be up to 32,767 characters in length
- are typically enclosed in quotation marks, although it is not required.

78

Character User-Defined Format

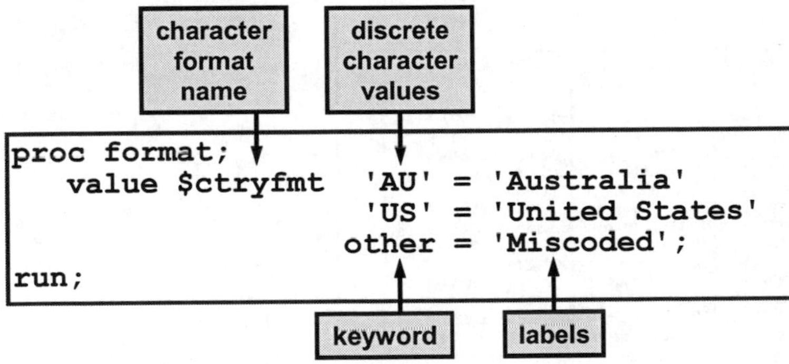


```
proc format;
   value $ctryfmt  'AU' = 'Australia'
                   'US' = 'United States'
                  other = 'Miscoded';
run;
```

The OTHER keyword matches all values that do not match any other value or range.

79

p111d07

Character User-Defined Format

Part 1

```
proc format;
   value $ctryfmt  'AU' = 'Australia'
                   'US' = 'United States'
                  other = 'Miscoded';
run;

proc print data=orion.sales label;
   var Employee_ID Job_Title Salary
       Country Birth_Date Hire_Date;
   label Employee_ID='Sales ID'
         Job_Title='Job Title'
         Salary='Annual Salary'
         Birth_Date='Date of Birth'
         Hire_Date='Date of Hire';
   format Salary dollar10.0
          Birth_Date Hire_Date monyy7.
          Country $ctryfmt.;
run;
```

Part 2

80

Character User-Defined Format

Partial PROC PRINT Output

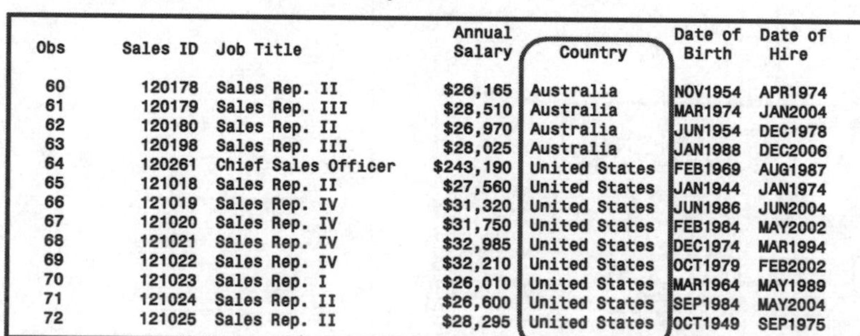

Obs	Sales ID	Job Title	Annual Salary	Country	Date of Birth	Date of Hire
60	120178	Sales Rep. II	$26,165	Australia	NOV1954	APR1974
61	120179	Sales Rep. III	$28,510	Australia	MAR1974	JAN2004
62	120180	Sales Rep. II	$26,970	Australia	JUN1954	DEC1978
63	120198	Sales Rep. III	$28,025	Australia	JAN1988	DEC2006
64	120261	Chief Sales Officer	$243,190	United States	FEB1969	AUG1987
65	121018	Sales Rep. II	$27,560	United States	JAN1944	JAN1974
66	121019	Sales Rep. IV	$31,320	United States	JUN1986	JUN2004
67	121020	Sales Rep. IV	$31,750	United States	FEB1984	MAY2002
68	121021	Sales Rep. IV	$32,985	United States	DEC1974	MAR1994
69	121022	Sales Rep. IV	$32,210	United States	OCT1979	FEB2002
70	121023	Sales Rep. I	$26,010	United States	MAR1964	MAY1989
71	121024	Sales Rep. II	$26,600	United States	SEP1984	MAY2004
72	121025	Sales Rep. II	$28,295	United States	OCT1949	SEP1975

81

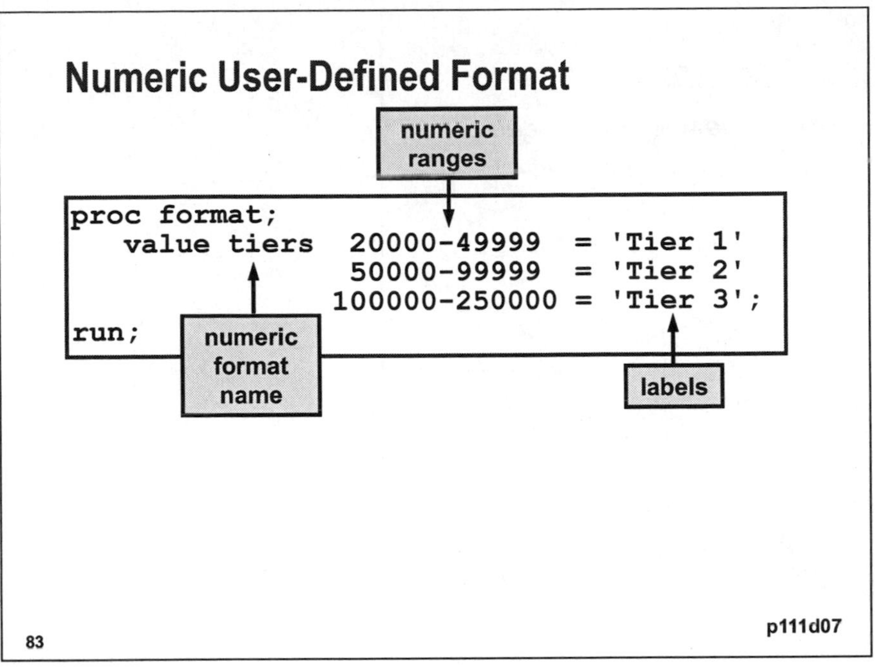

11.06 Quiz

If you have a value of 99999.87, how will it be displayed if the TIERS format is applied to the value?

a. Tier 2
b. Tier 3
c. a missing value
d. none of the above (circled by hand) – SLIPS between the options (handwritten)

```
proc format;
   value tiers  20000-49999   = 'Tier 1'
                50000-99999   = 'Tier 2'
               100000-250000 = 'Tier 3';
run;
```

85

Numeric User-Defined Formats

The less than (<) symbol excludes values from ranges.

- Put < after the value if you want to exclude the first value in a range.
- Put < before the value if you want to exclude the last value in a range.

50000 - 100000	Includes 50000	Includes 100000
50000 - < 100000	Includes 50000	Excludes 100000
50000 < - 100000	Excludes 50000	Includes 100000
50000 < - < 100000	Excludes 50000	Excludes 100000

87

11.07 Quiz

If you have a value of 100000, how will it be displayed if the TIERS format is applied to the value?

a. Tier 2
b. Tier 3
c. 100000
d. a missing value

```
proc format;
   value tiers  20000-<50000  = 'Tier 1'
                50000- 100000 = 'Tier 2'
               100000<-250000 = 'Tier 3';
run;
```

89

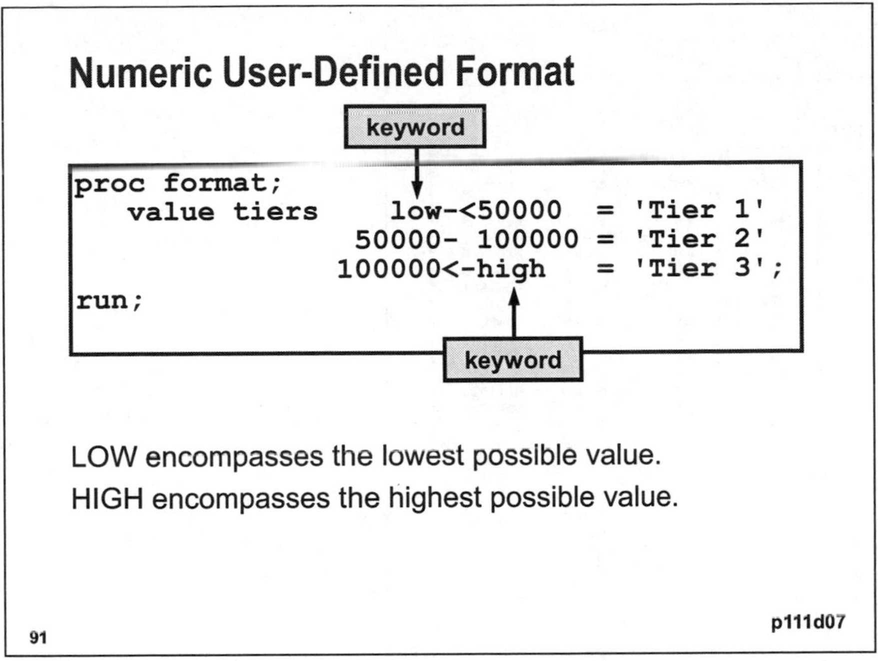

Numeric User-Defined Format
keyword
proc format;
value tiers low-<50000 = 'Tier 1'
50000- 100000 = 'Tier 2'
100000<-high = 'Tier 3';
run;
keyword
LOW encompasses the lowest possible value.
HIGH encompasses the highest possible value.
91
p111d07

Low does not include missing values for numeric variables.

Low does include missing values for character variables.

Numeric User-Defined Format

Part 1

```
proc format;
   value tiers      low-<50000   = 'Tier 1'
                  50000- 100000 = 'Tier 2'
                 100000<-high   = 'Tier 3';
run;

proc print data=orion.sales label;
   var Employee_ID Job_Title Salary
       Country Birth_Date Hire_Date;
   label Employee_ID='Sales ID'
         Job_Title='Job Title'
         Salary='Annual Salary'
         Birth_Date='Date of Birth'
         Hire_Date='Date of Hire';
   format Birth_Date Hire_Date monyy7.
          Salary tiers.;
run;
```

Part 2

92

Numeric User-Defined Format

Partial PROC PRINT Output

Obs	Sales ID	Job Title	Annual Salary	Country	Date of Birth	Date of Hire
60	120178	Sales Rep. II	Tier 1	AU	NOV1954	APR1974
61	120179	Sales Rep. III	Tier 1	AU	MAR1974	JAN2004
62	120180	Sales Rep. II	Tier 1	AU	JUN1954	DEC1978
63	120198	Sales Rep. III	Tier 1	AU	JAN1988	DEC2006
64	120261	Chief Sales Officer	Tier 3	US	FEB1969	AUG1987
65	121018	Sales Rep. II	Tier 1	US	JAN1944	JAN1974
66	121019	Sales Rep. IV	Tier 1	US	JUN1986	JUN2004
67	121020	Sales Rep. IV	Tier 1	US	FEB1984	MAY2002
68	121021	Sales Rep. IV	Tier 1	US	DEC1974	MAR1994
69	121022	Sales Rep. IV	Tier 1	US	OCT1979	FEB2002
70	121023	Sales Rep. I	Tier 1	US	MAR1964	MAY1989
71	121024	Sales Rep. II	Tier 1	US	SEP1984	MAY2004
72	121025	Sales Rep. II	Tier 1	US	OCT1949	SEP1975

93

Other User-Defined Format Examples

```
proc format;
   value $grade       'A' = 'Good'
                  'B'-'D' = 'Fair'
                      'F' = 'Poor'
                  'I','U' = 'See Instructor'
                    other = 'Miscoded';
run;
```

Char

```
proc format;
   value mnthfmt      1,2,3 = 'Qtr 1'
                      4,5,6 = 'Qtr 2'
                      7,8,9 = 'Qtr 3'
                   10,11,12 = 'Qtr 4'
                          . = 'missing'
                      other = 'unknown';
run;
```

numeric

94

→ do not mix uppercase — lowercase

Multiple User-Defined Formats

Multiple VALUE statements can be in a single PROC FORMAT step.

```
proc format;
   value $ctryfmt  'AU' = 'Australia'
                   'US' = 'United States'
                  other = 'Miscoded';
   value tiers     low-<50000  = 'Tier 1'
                 50000- 100000 = 'Tier 2'
                100000<-high   = 'Tier 3';
run;
```

95

p111d07

Multiple User-Defined Formats

```
proc print data=orion.sales label;
   . . .
   format Birth_Date Hire_Date monyy7.
          Country $ctryfmt.
          Salary tiers.;
run;
```

Partial PROC PRINT Output

Obs	Sales ID	Job Title	Annual Salary	Country	Date of Birth	Date of Hire
60	120178	Sales Rep. II	Tier 1	Australia	NOV1954	APR1974
61	120179	Sales Rep. III	Tier 1	Australia	MAR1974	JAN2004
62	120180	Sales Rep. II	Tier 1	Australia	JUN1954	DEC1978
63	120198	Sales Rep. III	Tier 1	Australia	JAN1988	DEC2006
64	120261	Chief Sales Officer	Tier 3	United States	FEB1060	AUG1007
65	121018	Sales Rep. II	Tier 1	United States	JAN1944	JAN1974
66	121019	Sales Rep. IV	Tier 1	United States	JUN1986	JUN2004
67	121020	Sales Rep. IV	Tier 1	United States	FEB1984	MAY2002

96

p111d07

Multiple User-Defined Formats

```
proc freq data=orion.sales;
   tables Country Salary;
   format Country $ctryfmt. Salary tiers.;
run;
```

The FREQ Procedure

Country	Frequency	Percent	Cumulative Frequency	Cumulative Percent
Australia	63	38.18	63	38.18
United States	102	61.82	165	100.00

Salary	Frequency	Percent	Cumulative Frequency	Cumulative Percent
Tier 1	159	96.36	159	96.36
Tier 2	4	2.42	163	98.79
Tier 3	2	1.21	165	100.00

97

Exercises

Level 1

7. Creating User-Defined Formats

a. Retrieve the starter program **p111e07**.

b. Create a character format named **`$gender`** that displays gender codes as follows:

F	Female
M	Male

c. Create a numeric format named **`moname`** that displays month numbers as follows:

1	January
2	February
3	March

d. In the PROC FREQ step, apply these two user-defined formats to the **`Employee_Gender`** and **`BirthMonth`** variables, respectively.

e. Submit the program to produce the following report:

PROC FREQ Output

```
                    Employees with Birthdays in Q1

                         The FREQ Procedure

     Birth                                  Cumulative    Cumulative
     Month      Frequency     Percent        Frequency       Percent
   ------------------------------------------------------------------
   January            44       38.94               44         38.94
   February           34       30.09               78         69.03
   March              35       30.97              113        100.00


   Employee_                                 Cumulative    Cumulative
   Gender        Frequency     Percent        Frequency       Percent
   ------------------------------------------------------------------
   Female              52       46.02               52         46.02
   Male                61       53.98              113        100.00
```

Level 2

8. Defining Ranges in User-Defined Formats

a. Retrieve the starter program **p111e08**.

b. Create a character format named **`$gender`** that displays gender codes as follows:

F	`Female`
M	`Male`
Any other value	`Invalid code`

c. Create a numeric format named **`salrange`** that displays salary ranges as follows:

At least 20,000 but less than 100,000	`Below $100,000`
At least 100,000 and up to 500,000	`$100,000 or more`
missing	`Missing salary`
Any other value	`Invalid salary`

d. In the PROC PRINT step, apply these two user-defined formats to the **`Gender`** and **`Salary`** variables, respectively.

e. Submit the program to produce the following report:

Partial PROC PRINT Output

```
                    Distribution of Salary and Gender Values
                            for Non-Sales Employees

 Obs    Employee_ID    Job_Title                         Salary          Gender

   1       120101      Director                     $100,000 or more    Male
   2       120104      Administration Manager       Below $100,000      Female
   3       120105      Secretary I                  Below $100,000      Female
   4       120106      Office Assistant II          Missing salary      Male
   5       120107      Office Assistant III         Below $100,000      Female
   6       120108      Warehouse Assistant II       Below $100,000      Female
   7       120108      Warehouse Assistant I        Below $100,000      Female
   8       120110      Warehouse Assistant III      Below $100,000      Male
   9       120111      Security Guard II            Below $100,000      Male
  10       120112                                   Below $100,000      Female
  11       120113      Security Guard II            Below $100,000      Female
  12       120114      Security Manager             Below $100,000      Invalid code
  13       120115      Service Assistant I          Invalid salary      Male
```

The PROC PRINT output might not have an invalid **`Gender`** value if the data was previously cleaned.

Level 3

9. Creating a Nested Format Definition

a. Retrieve the starter program **p111e09**.

b. Create a user-defined format that displays date ranges as follows:

Dates through 31DEC2006	Apply the YEAR4. format.
Dates starting 01JAN2007	Apply the MONYY7. format.
missing	Display the text **None**.

> Documentation about the FORMAT procedure can be found in the SAS Help and Documentation from the Contents tab (**SAS Products** ⇨ **Base SAS** ⇨ **Base SAS 9.2 Procedures Guide** ⇨ **Procedures** ⇨ **The FORMAT Procedure**). The documentation for the VALUE statement describes how to use an existing format as the label for a range.

c. Apply the new format to the **Employee_Term_Date** variable in the PROC FREQ step.

d. Submit the program to produce the following report:

> An option is required in the TABLES statement in order to display missing values as part of the main frequency report. Documentation about the FREQ procedure can be found in the SAS Help and Documentation from the Contents tab (**SAS Products** ⇨ **Base SAS** ⇨ **Base SAS Procedures Guide: Statistical Procedures** ⇨ **The FREQ Procedure**).

PROC FREQ Output

Employee Status Report

The FREQ Procedure

Employee_Term_Date	Frequency	Percent	Cumulative Frequency	Cumulative Percent
None	308	72.64	308	72.64
2002	6	1.42	314	74.06
2003	29	6.84	343	80.90
2004	18	4.25	361	85.14
2005	21	4.95	382	90.09
2006	20	4.72	402	94.81
JAN2007	3	0.71	405	95.52
FEB2007	3	0.71	408	96.23
MAR2007	7	1.65	415	97.88
APR2007	3	0.71	418	98.58
MAY2007	4	0.94	422	99.53
JUN2007	2	0.47	424	100.00

11.4 Subsetting and Grouping Observations

Objectives

- Display selected observations in reports by using the WHERE statement.
- Display groups of observations in reports by using the BY statement.

101

The WHERE Statement (Review)

For subsetting observations in a report, the WHERE statement is used to select observations that meet a certain condition.

General form of the WHERE statement:

WHERE *where-expression*;

The *where-expression* is a sequence of operands and operators that form a set of instructions that define a condition for selecting observations.

- Operands include constants and variables.
- Operators are symbols that request a comparison, arithmetic calculation, or logical operation.

102

11.08 Quiz

Which of the following WHERE statements have invalid syntax?

a. `where Salary ne .;`

b. `where Hire_Date >= '01APR2008'd;`

c. `where Country in (AU US);`

d. `where Salary + Bonus <= 10000;`

e. `where Gender ne 'M' Salary >= 50000;`

f. `where Name like '%N';`

104

Subsetting Observations

```
proc print data=orion.sales;
   var First_Name Last_Name
       Job_Title Country Salary;
   where Salary > 75000;
run;
```

Obs	First_ Name	Last_Name	Job_Title	Country	Salary
1	Tom	Zhou	Sales Manager	AU	108255
2	Wilson	Dawes	Sales Manager	AU	87975
64	Harry	Highpoint	Chief Sales Officer	US	243190
163	Louis	Favaron	Senior Sales Manager	US	95090
164	Renee	Capachietti	Sales Manager	US	83505
165	Dennis	Lansberry	Sales Manager	US	84260

106

p111d08

Subsetting Observations

```
proc means data=orion.sales;
   var Salary;
   where Country = 'AU';
run;
```

The MEANS Procedure

Analysis Variable : Salary

N	Mean	Std Dev	Minimum	Maximum
63	30158.97	12699.14	25185.00	108255.00

107 p111d08

Setup for the Poll

- Retrieve and submit program **p111a02**.
- View the log to determine how SAS handles multiple WHERE statements.

```
proc freq data=orion.sales;
   tables Gender;
   where Salary > 75000;
   where Country = 'US';
run;
```

109

11.09 Multiple Choice Poll

Which statement is true concerning the multiple WHERE statements?

a. All the WHERE statements are used.
b. None of the WHERE statements is used.
c. The first WHERE statement is used.
d. The last WHERE statement is used.

110

The BY Statement

For grouping observations in a report, the BY statement is used to produce separate sections of the report for each BY group.

General form of the BY statement:

BY <DESCENDING> *by-variable(s)*;

The observations in the data set must be sorted by the variables specified in the BY statement.

112

Grouping Observations

```
proc sort data=orion.sales out=work.sort;
   by Country descending Gender Last_Name;
run;

proc print data=work.sort;
   by Country descending Gender;
run;
```

113 p111d09

Grouping Observations

Partial PROC PRINT Output

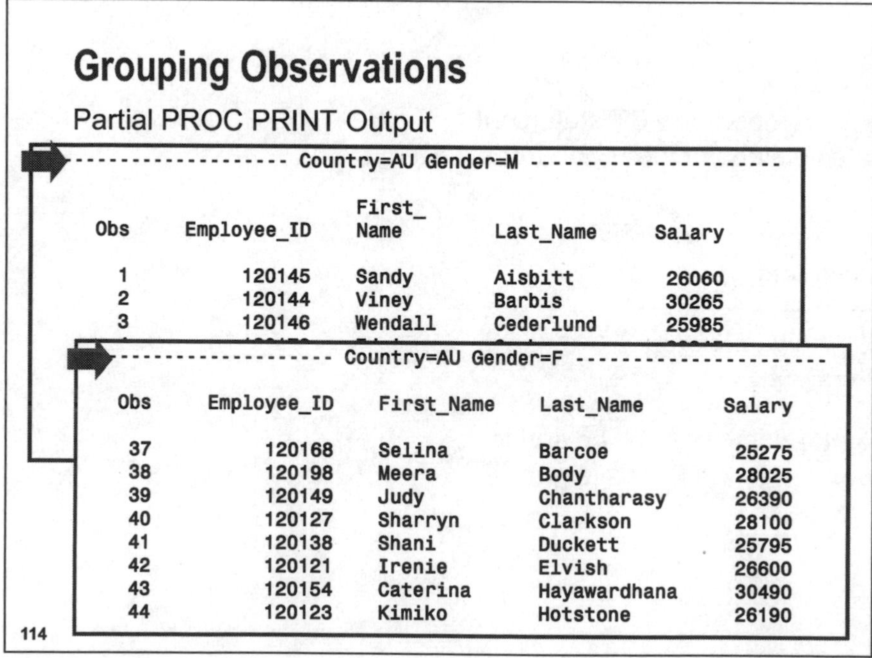

------------------ Country=AU Gender=M ---------------------

Obs	Employee_ID	First_ Name	Last_Name	Salary
1	120145	Sandy	Aisbitt	26060
2	120144	Viney	Barbis	30265
3	120146	Wendall	Cederlund	25985

------------------ Country=AU Gender=F ---------------------

Obs	Employee_ID	First_Name	Last_Name	Salary
37	120168	Selina	Barcoe	25275
38	120198	Meera	Body	28025
39	120149	Judy	Chantharasy	26390
40	120127	Sharryn	Clarkson	28100
41	120138	Shani	Duckett	25795
42	120121	Irenie	Elvish	26600
43	120154	Caterina	Hayawardhana	30490
44	120123	Kimiko	Hotstone	26190

114

11.10 Quiz

Which is a valid BY statement for the PROC FREQ step?

a. `by Country Gender;`

b. `by Gender Last_Name;`

c. `by Country;`

d. `by Gender;`

```
proc sort data=orion.sales out=work.sort;
   by Country descending Gender Last_Name;
run;

proc freq data=work.sort;
   tables Gender;
run;
```

116

Exercises

Level 1

10. Subsetting and Grouping Observations

a. Retrieve the starter program **p111e10**.

b. Add a PROC SORT step to sort the observations in **orion.order_fact** based on the **Order_Type** variable.

> To avoid overwriting the **orion.order_fact** data set, be sure to use the OUT= option to create a new data set containing the sorted observations. Remember to use the new data set in the PROC MEANS step.

c. Restrict the PROC MEANS analysis to two **Order_Type** values: 2 and 3.

d. Modify the PROC MEANS step to generate the summary analysis separately for each selected **Order_Type** value in the sorted data set.

e. Submit the program to produce the following output:

PROC MEANS Output

```
                              Orion Star Sales Summary

------------------------------------- Order Type=2 -------------------------------------

                               The MEANS Procedure

      Analysis Variable : Total_Retail_Price Total Retail Price for This Product

         N            Mean         Std Dev         Minimum         Maximum
       -------------------------------------------------------------------
       170     199.5961765     282.9680817       2.6000000         1937.20
       -------------------------------------------------------------------


------------------------------------- Order Type=3 -------------------------------------

      Analysis Variable : Total_Retail_Price Total Retail Price for This Product

         N            Mean         Std Dev         Minimum         Maximum
       -------------------------------------------------------------------
       123     174.7280488     214.3528338       2.7000000         1542.60
       -------------------------------------------------------------------
```

Level 2

11. Subsetting and Grouping by Multiple Variables

a. Retrieve the starter program **p111e11**.

b. Sort the **orion.order_fact** data set by **Order_Type** (in ascending sequence) and **Order_Date** (in descending sequence).

> Create a new data set containing the sorted observations. Do not overwrite the **orion.order_fact** data set. Remember to use the new data set in the PROC PRINT step.

c. Divide the PROC PRINT report based on **Order_Type** using a BY statement. The orders for each order type should be displayed in reverse chronological order, that is, with more recent orders near the top of the report.

d. Limit the observations in the PROC PRINT report based on the following criteria:

1) Orders placed in the first four months of 2005 (January 1 to April 30)

2) Orders that were delivered exactly two days after the order was placed

e. Add a second title to clarify that filters were applied to the data.

f. Submit the program to produce the following report:

PROC PRINT Output

```
                          Orion Star Sales Details
                 2-Day Deliveries from January to April 2005

---------------------------------- Order Type=2 ----------------------------------

                                          Order_       Delivery_
          Obs         Order_ID              Date         Date

          409        1235611754       27APR2005     29APR2005
          410        1235611754       27APR2005     29APR2005
          411        1235591214       25APR2005     27APR2005
          412        1235591214       25APR2005     27APR2005
          413        1234972570       24FEB2005     26FEB2005
          415        1234659163       24JAN2005     26JAN2005
          417        1234588648       17JAN2005     19JAN2005
          418        1234588648       17JAN2005     19JAN2005
          419        1234538390       12JAN2005     14JAN2005

---------------------------------- Order Type=3 ----------------------------------

                                          Order_       Delivery_
          Obs         Order_ID              Date         Date

          568        1235176942       15MAR2005     17MAR2005
          569        1235176942       15MAR2005     17MAR2005
          570        1234891576       16FEB2005     18FEB2005
```

Level 3

12. Adding Subsetting Conditions

a. Retrieve the starter program **p111e12**.

b. Reorder the variables in the PROC PRINT step's BY statement so that the BY-line displays **`Supplier_Name`**, **`Supplier_ID`**, and **`Supplier_Country`**, in that order. The input data remains grouped, but not sorted, by these variables.

> An option must be added to the BY statement to support the use of grouped, unsorted data. Documentation about the BY statement can be found in the SAS Help and Documentation from the Contents tab (**SAS Products** ⇨ **Base SAS** ⇨ **Base SAS 9.2 Procedures Guide** ⇨ **Procedures** ⇨ **The PRINT Procedure**).

c. Augment the existing WHERE criteria by further restricting the report to product names that contain either the word `Street` or the word `Running`.

> To add clauses to an existing WHERE statement without retyping or editing it, use the SAME-AND operator in a separate WHERE statement within the same step. See the documentation in the SAS Help and Documentation from the Contents tab (**SAS Products** ⇨ **Base SAS** ⇨ **SAS 9.2 Language Reference: Concepts** ⇨ **SAS System Concepts** ⇨ **WHERE-Expression Processing** ⇨ **Syntax of WHERE Expression**).

d. Submit the program to produce the following report:

Partial PROC PRINT Output

```
                        Orion Star Products: Children Sports

--------- Supplier Name=Greenline Sports Ltd Supplier ID=14682 Country=Great Britain ---------

                     Obs      Product_ID            Product_Name

                      50     210200600015     Hardcore Kids Street Shoes


-------------- Supplier Name=3Top Sports Supplier ID=2963 Country=United States --------------

              Obs       Product_ID     Product_Name

               87      210201000169    Children's Street Shoes
               88      210201000174    Freestyle Children's Leather Street Shoes
               91      210201000179    K Street Shoes
               94      210201000187    Mona  C- Children's Street Shoes
               95      210201000189    Mona  J- Children's Street Shoes
              104      210201000205    Torino 2000 K Street Shoes
              107      210201000209    Universe 4 Children's Running Shoes
```

11.5 Directing Output to External Files

Objectives

- Direct output to ODS destinations by using ODS statements.
- Specify a style definition by using the STYLE= option.
- Create ODS files that can be opened in Microsoft Excel.

121

Output Delivery System

Output can be sent to a variety of destinations by using ODS statements.

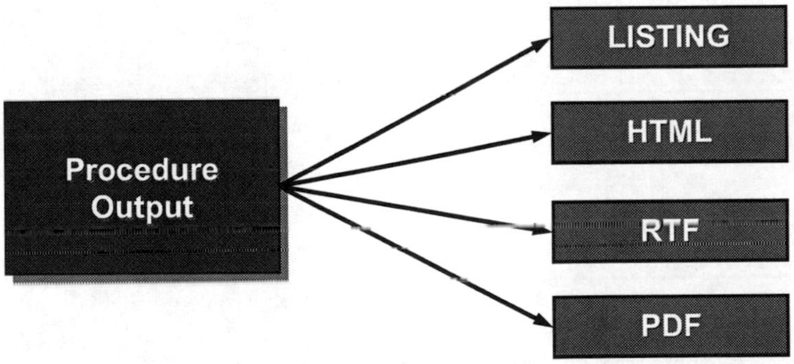

122

Output Delivery System

Destination	Type of File	Viewed In
LISTING		SAS Output Window or SAS/GRAPH Window
HTML	Hypertext Markup Language	Web Browsers such as Internet Explorer
PDF	Portable Document Format	Adobe Products such as Acrobat Reader
RTF	Rich Text Format	Word Processors such as Microsoft Word

123

Default ODS Destination

The LISTING destination is the default ODS destination.

```
ods listing;

proc freq data=orion.sales;
   tables Country;
run;

proc gchart data=orion.sales;
   hbar Country / nostats;
run;
```

124 p111d10

Default ODS Destination

The LISTING destination directs output to the OUTPUT window and the GRAPH window.

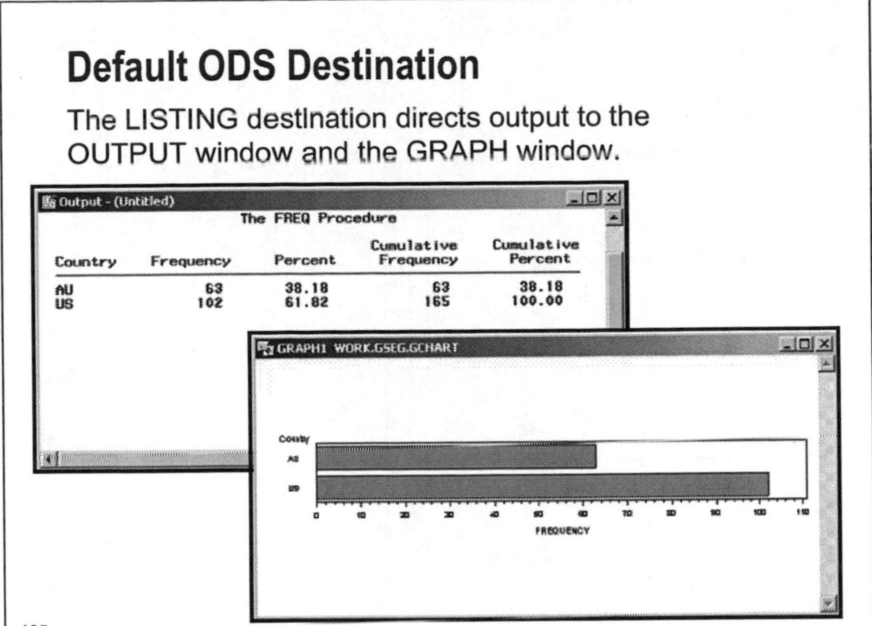

125

Default ODS Destination

The ODS LISTING CLOSE statement stops sending output to the OUTPUT and GRAPH windows.

```
ods listing close;

proc freq data=orion.sales;
   tables Country;
run;

proc gchart data=orion.sales;
   hbar Country / nostats;
run;
```

126

p111d10

Default ODS Destination

A warning will appear in the SAS log if the LISTING destination is closed and no other destinations are active.

Partial SAS Log

```
ods listing close;

proc freq data=orion.sales;
   tables Country;
run;

WARNING: No output destinations active.
NOTE: There were 165 observations read from the data set ORION.SALES.
```

127

HTML, PDF, and RTF Destinations

ODS destinations such as HTML, PDF, and RTF are opened and closed in the following manner:

ODS *destination* FILE = ' *filename.ext* ' *<options>*;

SAS code to generate a report(s)

ODS *destination* CLOSE;

128

The filename specified in the FILE= option needs to be specific to your operating environment.

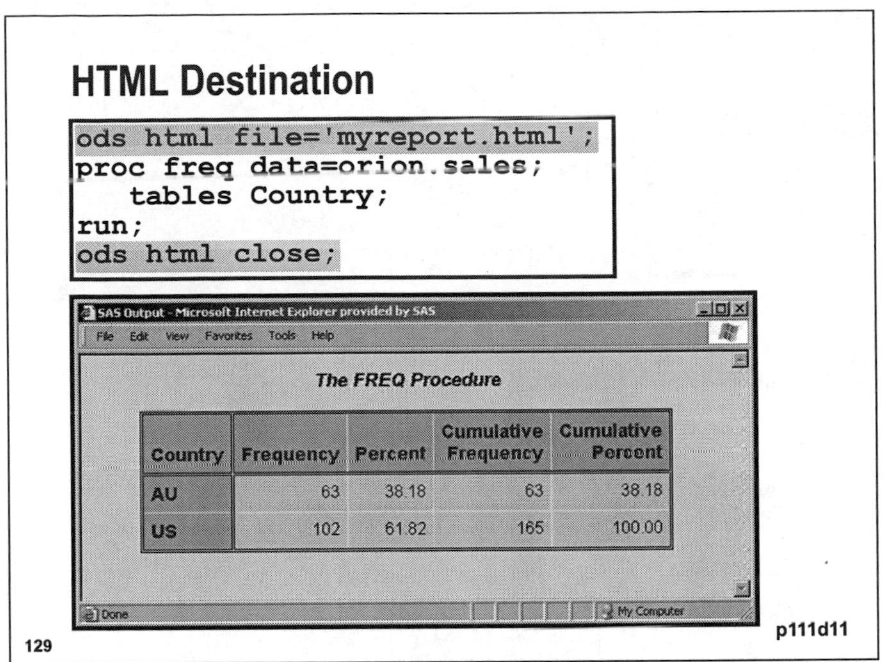

Always terminate steps with an explicit step boundary before closing the destination. Otherwise, the file is closed before the step executes.

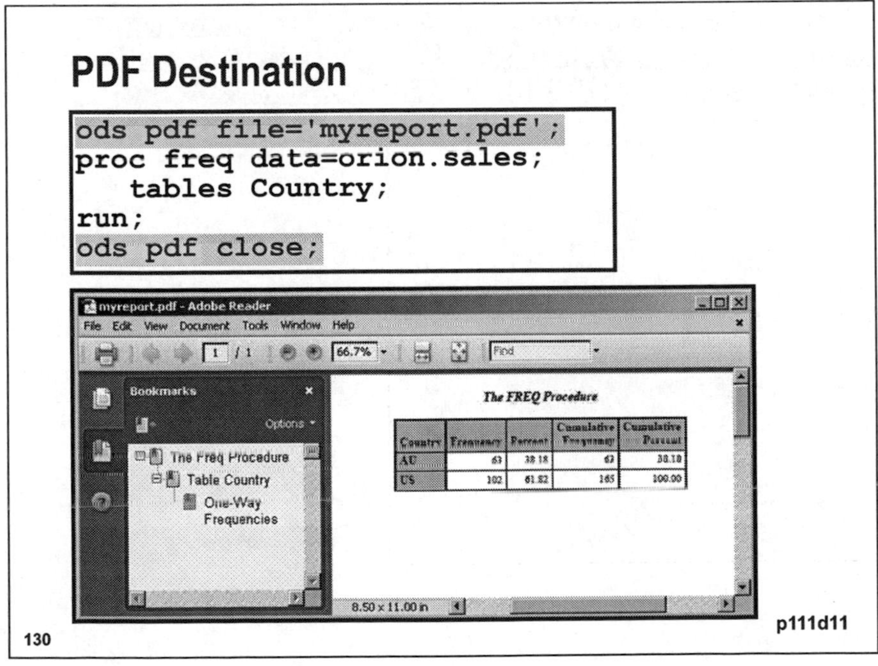

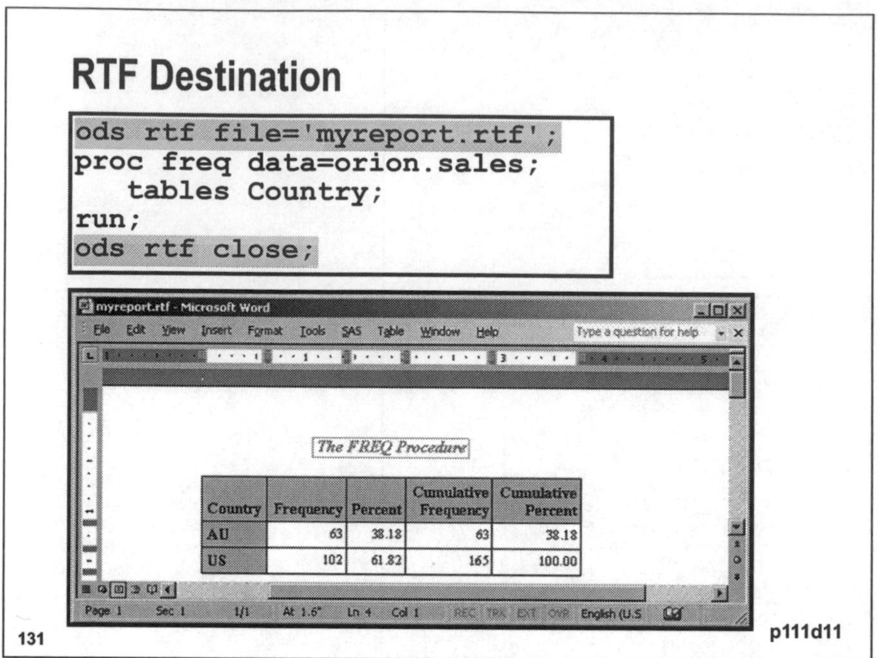

RTF Destination

```
ods rtf file='myreport.rtf';
proc freq data=orion.sales;
   tables Country;
run;
ods rtf close;
```


The FREQ Procedure

Country	Frequency	Percent	Cumulative Frequency	Cumulative Percent
AU	63	38.18	63	38.18
US	102	61.82	165	100.00

131 p111d11

The traditional RTF destination does not control vertical measurement, so page breaking is controlled by the word processor. Starting in SAS 9.2, there is a new destination, TAGSETS.RTF, which does control vertical measurement. Documentation about the TAGSETS.RTF destination can be found in the SAS Help and Documentation from the Contents tab (**SAS Products** ⇨ **Base SAS** ⇨ **SAS 9.2 Output Delivery System User's Guide** ⇨ **ODS Language Statements** ⇨ **Dictionary of ODS Language Statements** ⇨ **ODS TAGSETS.RTF Statement**).

11.11 Quiz

What is the problem with this program?

```
ods pdf file='myreport.pdf';

proc print data=orion.sales;
run;

ods close;
```

133

Single Destination

Output can be sent to only one destination.

```
ods listing close;

ods html file='example.html';

proc freq data=orion.sales;
   tables Country;
run;

ods html close;

ods listing;
```

It is a good habit to open the LISTING destination at the end of a program to guarantee an open destination for the next submission.

135 p111d11

Multiple Destinations

Output can be sent to many destinations.

```
ods listing;
ods pdf file='example.pdf';
ods rtf file='example.rtf';

proc freq data=orion.sales;
   tables Country;
run;

ods pdf close;
ods rtf close;
```

To view the results, all destinations except the LISTING destination must be closed.

136 p111d11

Multiple Destinations

Use _ALL_ in the ODS CLOSE statement to close all open destinations including the LISTING destination.

```
ods listing;
ods pdf file='example.pdf';
ods rtf file='example.rtf';

proc freq data=orion.sales;
   tables Country;
run;

ods _all_ close;
ods listing;
```

137

p111d11

Multiple Procedures

Output from many procedures can be sent to ODS destinations.

```
ods listing;
ods pdf file='example.pdf';
ods rtf file='example.rtf';

proc freq data=orion.sales;
   tables Country;
run;

proc means data=orion.sales;
   var Salary;
run;

ods _all_ close;
ods listing;
```

138

p111d11

File Location

A path can be specified to control the location of where the file is stored.

```
ods html file='s:\workshop\example.html';

proc freq data=orion.sales;
   tables Country;
run;

proc means data=orion.sales;
   var Salary;
run;

ods html close;
```

If no path is specified, the file is saved in the current default directory.

139 p111d11

The path and filename specified in the FILE= option needs to be specific to your operating environment.

Operating Environments

The Output Delivery System works on all operating environments.

z/OS (OS/390) Example:

```
ods html file='.workshop.report(example)'
         rs=none;

proc freq data=orion.sales;
   tables Country;
run;

ods html close;
```

Use the RS=NONE option when you create HTML and RTF files on z/OS (OS/390).

140 p111d11

The RS= option is an alias for the RECORD_SEPARATOR= option.

RS=NONE writes one line of markup output at a time to the file. This enables the file to be read with a text editor. Without the option, the lines of markup output run together.

RS=NONE is not needed with the PDF destination. It is needed with other destinations such as CSVALL, MSOFFICE2K, and EXCELXP.

Creating HTML, PDF, and RTF Files

p111d12

Submit the following program and view the results in the appropriate application. The HTML file can be viewed in a Web browser, the PDF file can be viewed in an Adobe product, and the RTF file can be viewed in a word processor.

```
ods listing close;
ods html file='myreport.html';
ods pdf file='myreport.pdf';
ods rtf file='myreport.rtf';

proc freq data=orion.sales;
   tables Country;
   title 'Report 1';
run;

proc means data=orion.sales;
   var Salary;
   title 'Report 2';
run;

proc print data=orion.sales;
   var First_Name Last_Name
       Job_Title Country Salary;
   where Salary > 75000;
   title 'Report 3';
run;

ods _all_ close;
ods listing;
```

For z/OS (OS/390), the following ODS statements are used:

```
ods html file='.workshop.report(myhtml) rs=none';
ods pdf file='.workshop.report(mypdf)';
ods rtf file='.workshop.report(myrtf)' rs=none;
```

If you are using the SAS windowing environment on the Windows operating environment, the Results Viewer window can be used to view the HTML, PDF, and RTF files.

1. After submitting the program, go to the Results window.
2. Right-click on the word **Results** within the Results window and select **Expand All**.

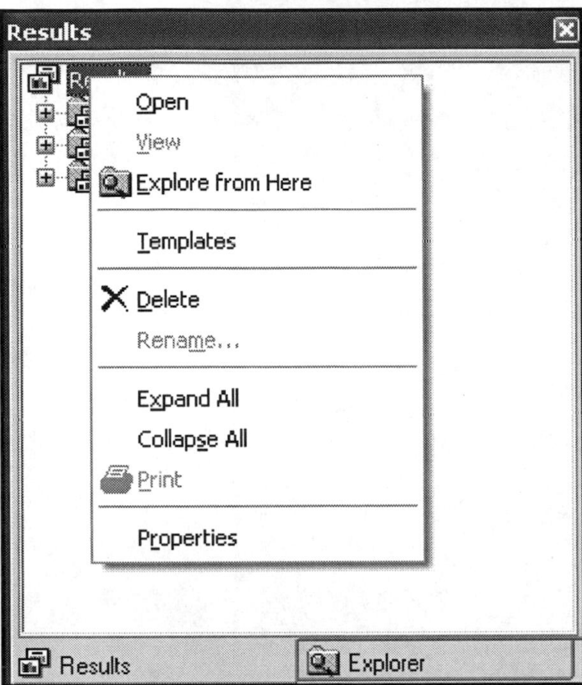

3. Double-click on the HTML file icon, the PDF file icon, or the RTF file icon.

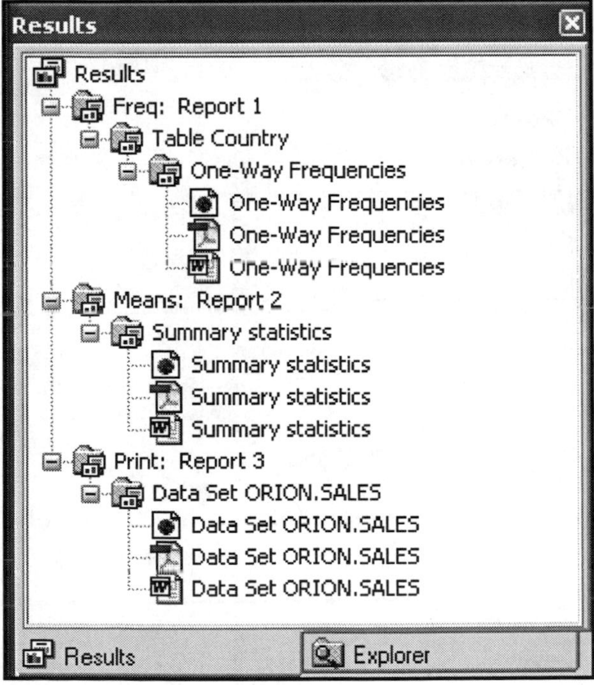

4. View the HTML, PDF, or RTF file in the Results Viewer.

HTML File in the Results Viewer

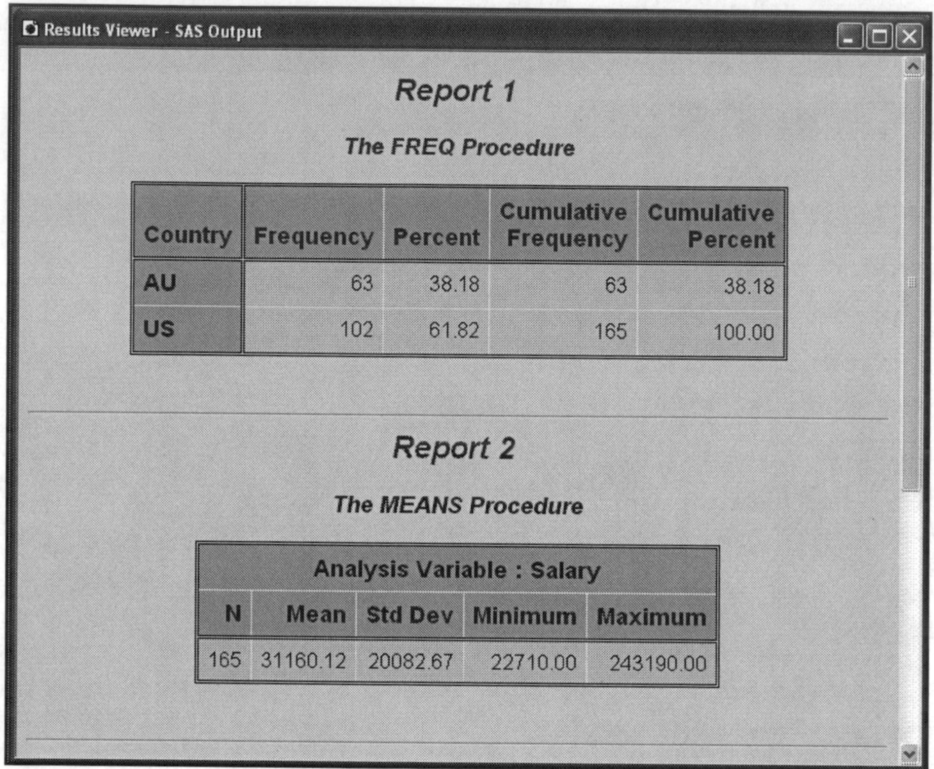

PDF File in the Results Viewer

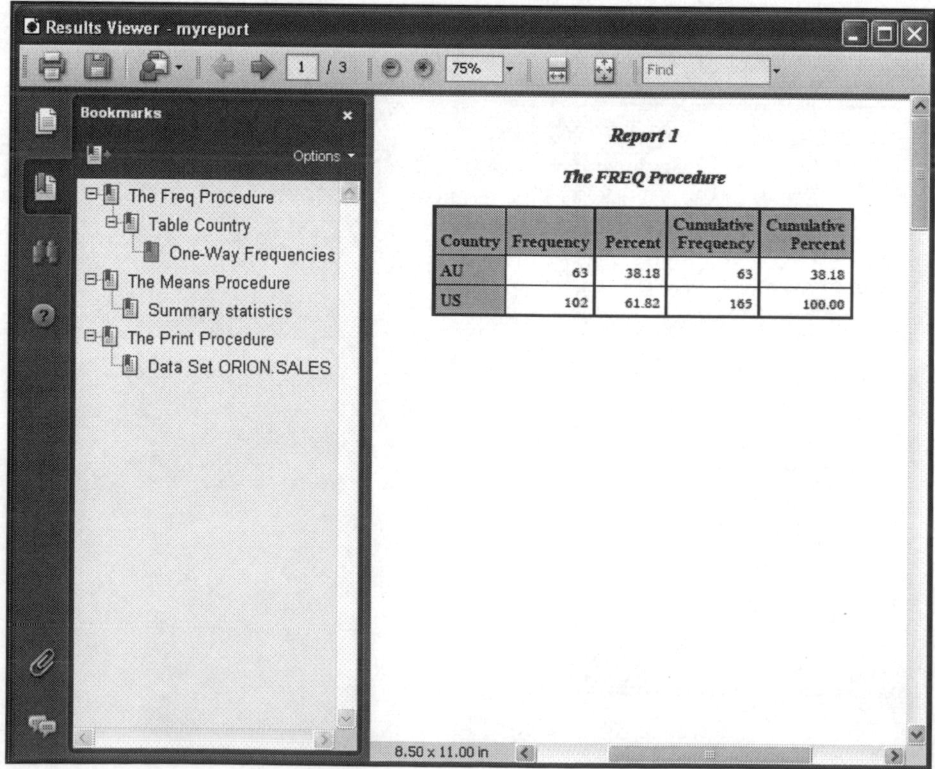

RTF File in the Results Viewer

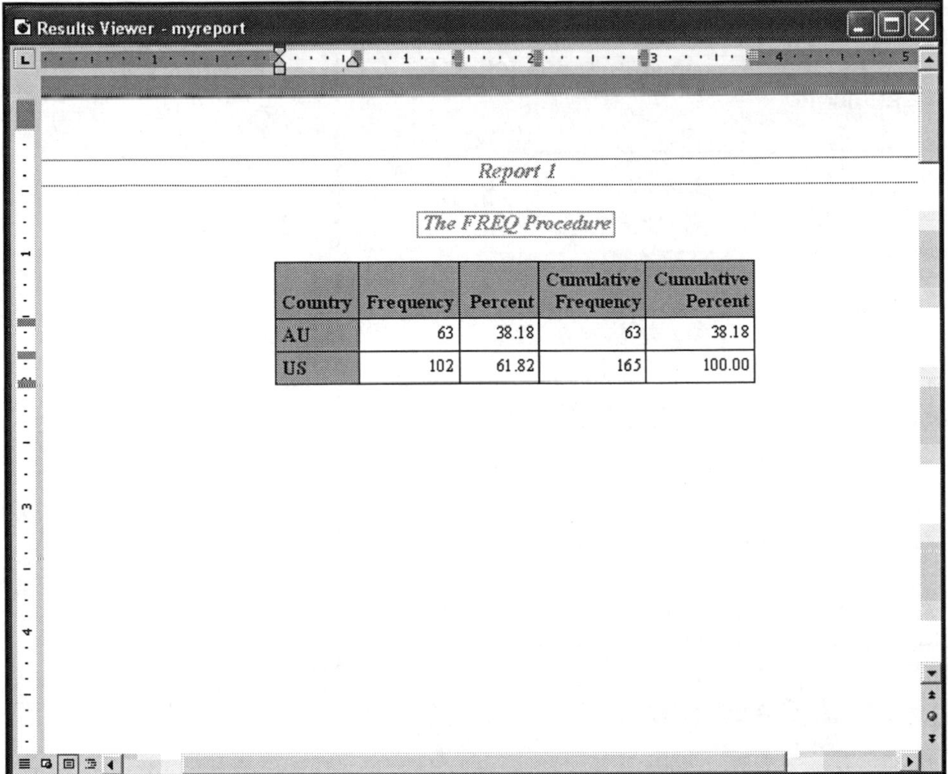

Report 1

The FREQ Procedure

Country	Frequency	Percent	Cumulative Frequency	Cumulative Percent
AU	63	38.18	63	38.18
US	102	61.82	165	100.00

STYLE= Option

Use a STYLE= option in the ODS destination statement to specify a style definition.

```
ODS destination FILE = 'filename.ext'
                STYLE = style-definition;
```

- A *style definition* describes how to display the presentation aspects such as colors and fonts of SAS output.
- STYLE= cannot be used with the LISTING destination.

143

SAS Supplied Style Definitions

Analysis	Astronomy	Banker	BarrettsBlue
Beige	blockPrint	Brick	Brown
Curve	D3d	Default	Education
EGDefault	Electronics	fancyPrinter	Festival
FestivalPrinter	Gears	Journal	Magnify
Meadow	MeadowPrinter	Minimal	Money
NoFontDefault	Normal	NormalPrinter	Printer
Rsvp	Rtf	sansPrinter	sasdocPrinter
Sasweb	Science	Seaside	SeasidePrinter
serifPrinter	Sketch	Statdoc	Statistical
Theme	Torn	Watercolor	

144

SAS Supplied Style Definitions

The following style definitions are new to SAS 9.2:

grayscalePrinter	Harvest	HighContrast
Journal2	Journal3	Listing
monochromePrinter	Ocean	Solutions

145

Some of the style definitions changed between SAS 9.1.3 and SAS 9.2.

- For example, the SAS 9.1.3 Analysis style definition produces different results than the SAS 9.2 Analysis style definition. The SAS 9.1.3 Analysis style definition is similar to the SAS 9.2 Ocean style definition.
- The SAS 9.1.3 Statistical style definition produces different results than the SAS 9.2 Statistical style definition. The SAS 9.1.3 Statistical style definition is similar to the SAS 9.2 Harvest style definition.

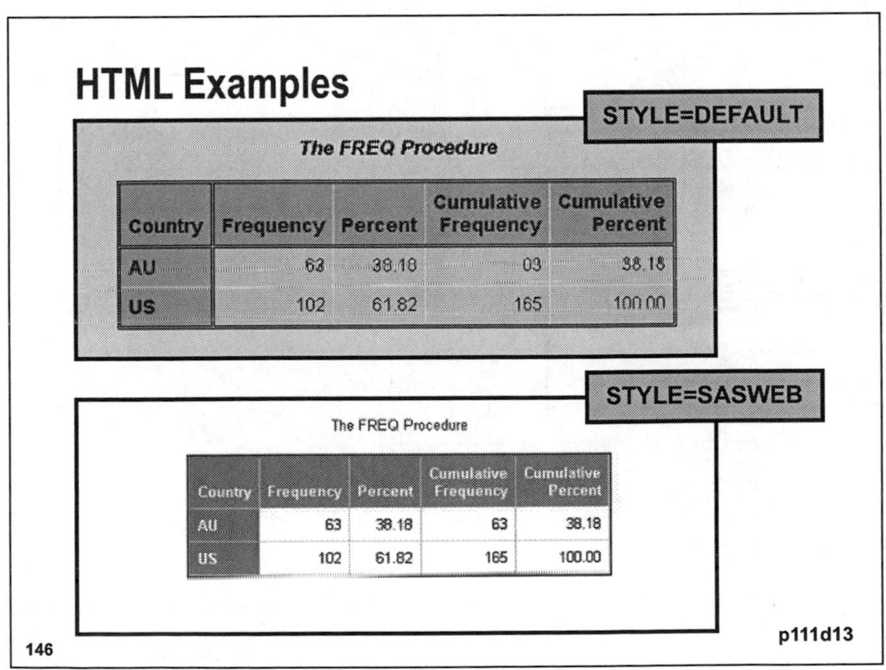

HTML Examples
STYLE=DEFAULT
The FREQ Procedure
Country Frequency Percent Cumulative Frequency Cumulative Percent
AU 63 38.18 63 38.18
US 102 61.82 165 100.00
STYLE=SASWEB
The FREQ Procedure
Country Frequency Percent Cumulative Frequency Cumulative Percent
AU 63 38.18 63 38.18
US 102 61.82 165 100.00
146
p111d13

By default, the HTML destination uses the DEFAULT style definition.

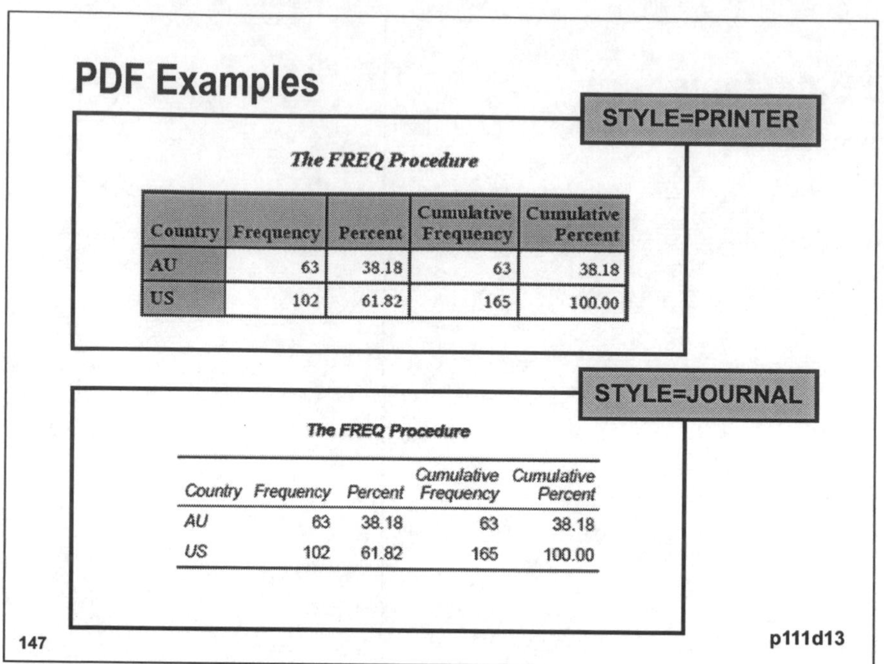

By default, the PDF destination uses the PRINTER style definition.

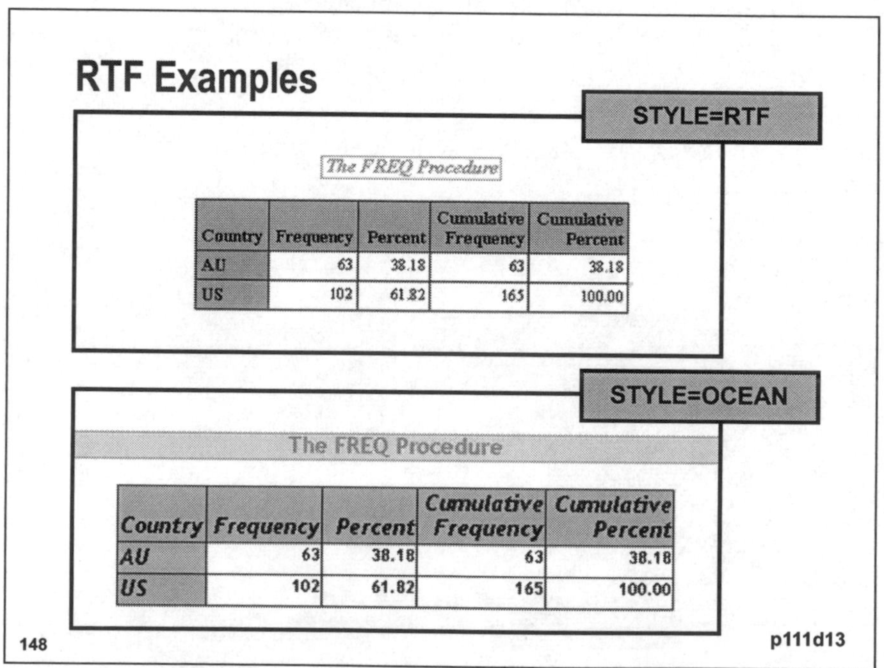

By default, the RTF destination uses the RTF style definition.

Setup for the Poll

- Retrieve **p111a03**.
- Add a STYLE= option to the first ODS statement, and select one of the following style definitions:

HighContrast	Minimal	Listing	Journal3

- Submit the program and review the results.
- Modify the STYLE= option to use one of the following style definitions:

Education	Harvest	Rsvp	Solutions

- Submit the program and review the results.

150

11.12 Poll

Did you notice a difference in the presentation aspects between the two style definitions?

❍ Yes

❍ No

151

Destinations Used with Excel

The following destinations create files that can be opened in Excel.

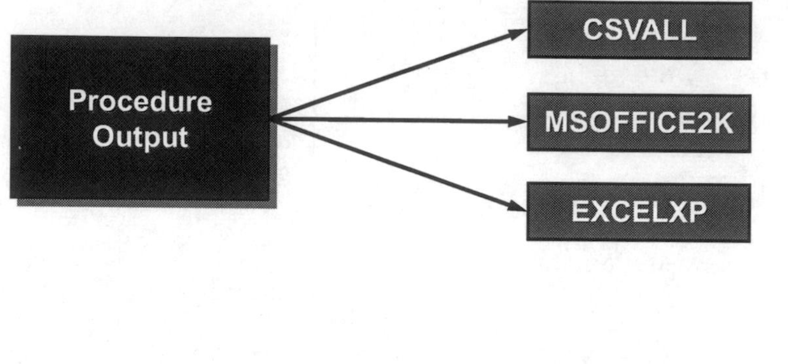

154

Destinations Used with Excel

Destination	Type of File	Viewed In
CSVALL	Comma-Separated Value	Editor or Microsoft Excel
MSOFFICE2K	Hypertext Markup Language	Web Browser or Microsoft Word or Microsoft Excel
EXCELXP	Extensible Markup Language	Microsoft Excel

155

CSVALL Destination

```
ods csvall file='myexcel.csv';

proc freq data=orion.sales;
   tables Country;
run;

proc means data=orion.sales;
   var Salary;
run;

ods csvall close;
```

156 p111d14

CSVALL Destination

CSVALL does not include any style information.

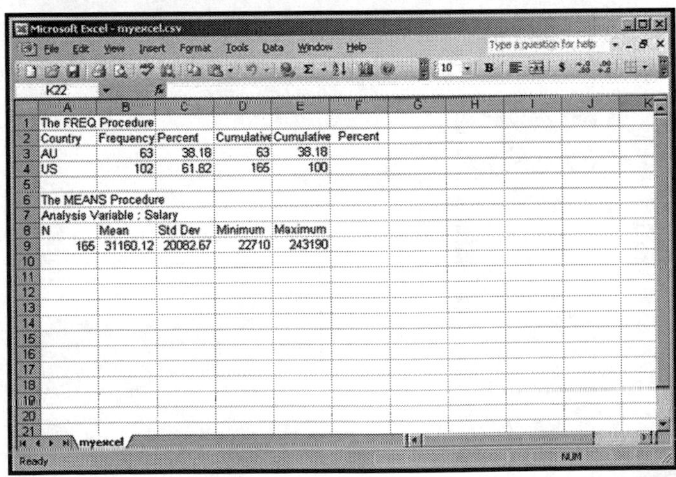

	A	B	C	D	E	F
1	The FREQ Procedure					
2	Country	Frequency	Percent	Cumulative	Cumulative	Percent
3	AU	63	38.18	63	38.18	
4	US	102	61.82	165	100	
5						
6	The MEANS Procedure					
7	Analysis Variable : Salary					
8	N	Mean	Std Dev	Minimum	Maximum	
9	165	31160.12	20082.67	22710	243190	

157

MSOFFICE2K Destination

```
ods msoffice2k file='myexcel.html';

proc freq data=orion.sales;
   tables Country;
run;

proc means data=orion.sales;
   var Salary;
run;

ods msoffice2k close;
```

158 p111d14

Microsoft Excel 97 or greater is needed to open a MSOFFICE2K file.

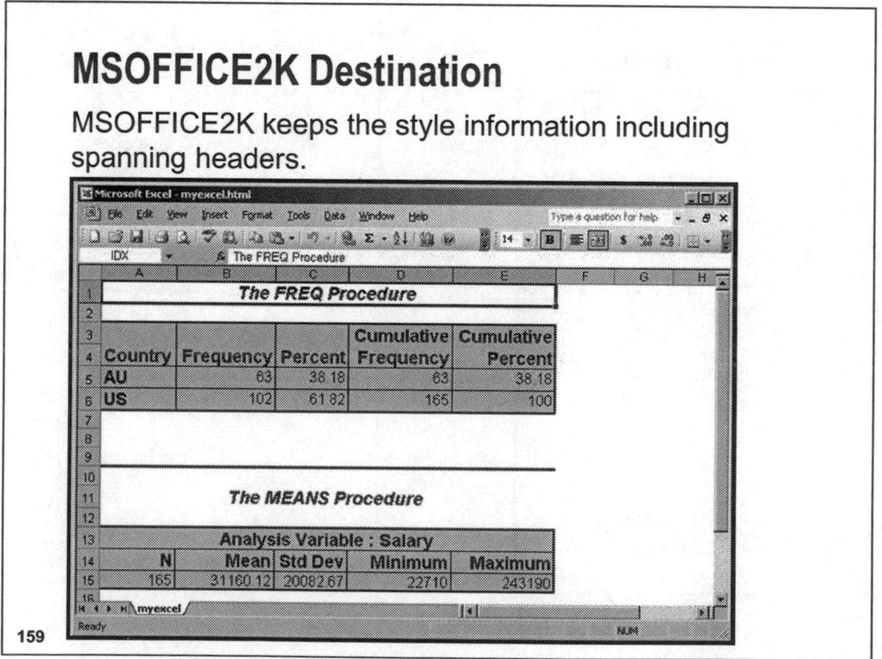
MSOFFICE2K Destination
MSOFFICE2K keeps the style information including spanning headers.
Microsoft Excel - myexcel.html
The FREQ Procedure
The MEANS Procedure
159

Country	Frequency	Percent	Cumulative Frequency	Cumulative Percent
AU	63	38.18	63	38.18
US	102	61.82	165	100

Analysis Variable : Salary				
N	Mean	Std Dev	Minimum	Maximum
165	31160.12	20082.67	22710	243190

EXCELXP Destination

```
ods tagsets.excelxp file='myexcel.xml';

proc freq data=orion.sales;
   tables Country;
run;

proc means data=orion.sales;
   var Salary;
run;

ods tagsets.excelxp close;
```

160

p111d14

Microsoft Excel 2002 or greater is needed to open an EXCELXP file.

EXCELXP Destination

EXCELXP keeps the style information and each procedure is a separate sheet.

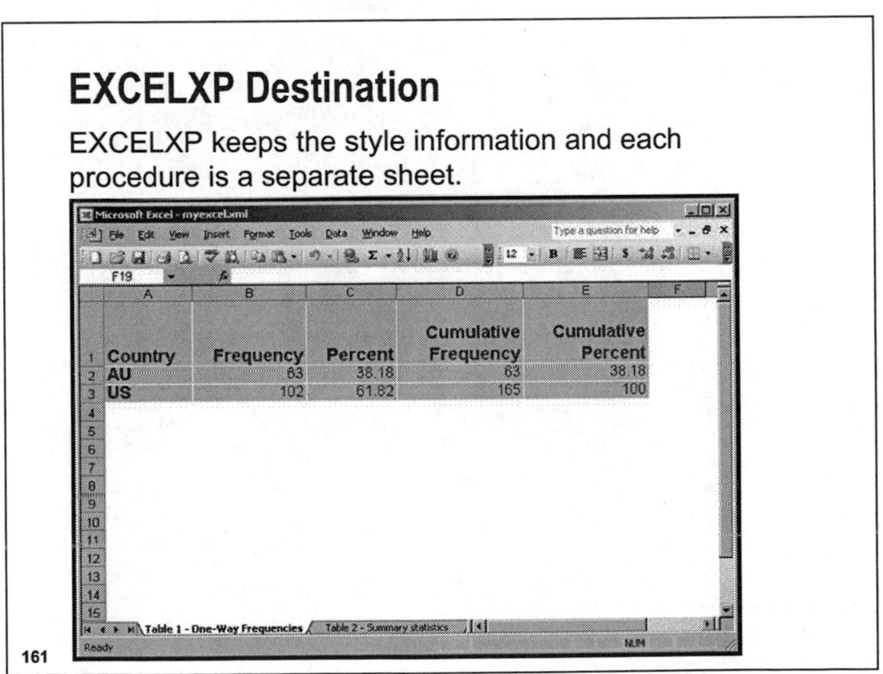

161

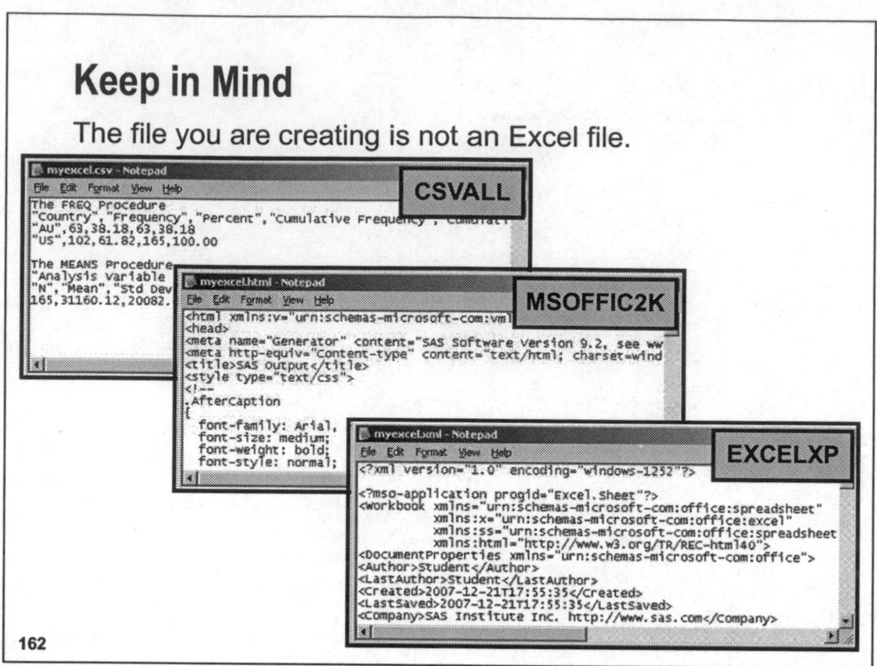
Keep in Mind
The file you are creating is not an Excel file.
myexcel.csv - Notepad
File Edit Format View Help
CSVALL
The FREQ Procedure
"Country","Frequency","Percent","Cumulative Frequency","Cumulat
"AU",63,38.18,63,38.18
"US",102,61.82,165,100.00
The MEANS Procedure
"Analysis Variable
"N","Mean","Std Dev
165,31160.12,20082.
myexcel.html - Notepad
File Edit Format View Help
MSOFFIC2K
<html xmlns:v="urn:schemas-microsoft-com:vml"
<head>
<meta name="Generator" content="SAS Software Version 9.2, see ww
<meta http-equiv="Content-type" content="text/html; charset=wind
<title>SAS Output</title>
<style type="text/css">
<!--
.AfterCaption
{
font-family: Arial,
font-size: medium;
font-weight: bold;
font-style: normal;
myexcel.xml - Notepad
File Edit Format View Help
EXCELXP
<?xml version="1.0" encoding="windows-1252"?>
<?mso-application progid="Excel.Sheet"?>
<Workbook xmlns="urn:schemas-microsoft-com:office:spreadsheet"
xmlns:x="urn:schemas-microsoft-com:office:excel"
xmlns:ss="urn:schemas-microsoft-com:office:spreadsheet
xmlns:html="http://www.w3.org/TR/REC-html40">
<DocumentProperties xmlns="urn:schemas-microsoft-com:office">
<Author>Student</Author>
<LastAuthor>Student</LastAuthor>
<Created>2007-12-21T17:55:35</Created>
<LastSaved>2007-12-21T17:55:35</LastSaved>
<Company>SAS Institute Inc. http://www.sas.com</Company>
162

Creating Files That Open in Excel

p111d15

Submit the following program and view the results in Microsoft Excel.

```
ods listing close;
ods csvall file='myexcel.csv';
ods msoffice2k file='myexcel.html';
ods tagsets.excelxp file='myexcel.xml';

proc freq data=orion.sales;
   tables Country;
   title 'Report 1';
run;

proc means data=orion.sales;
   var Salary;
   title 'Report 2';
run;

proc print data=orion.sales;
   var First_Name Last_Name
       Job_Title Country Salary;
   where Salary > 75000;
   title 'Report 3';
run;

ods _all_ close;
ods listing;
```

For z/OS (OS/390), the following ODS statements are used:

```
ods csvall file='.workshop.report(mycsv)' rs=none;
ods msoffice2k file='.workshop.report(myhtml)' rs=none;
ods tagsets.excelxp file='.workshop.report(myxml)' rs=none;
```

CSV File in Microsoft Excel 2002

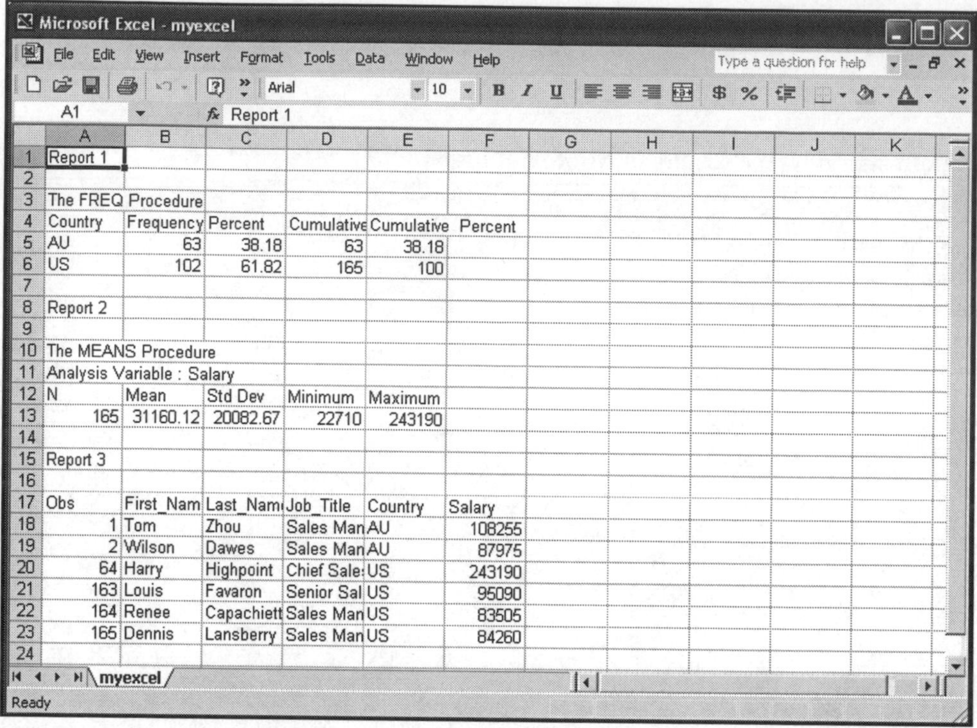

	A	B	C	D	E	F
1	Report 1					
2						
3	The FREQ Procedure					
4	Country	Frequency	Percent	Cumulative	Cumulative	Percent
5	AU	63	38.18	63	38.18	
6	US	102	61.82	165	100	
7						
8	Report 2					
9						
10	The MEANS Procedure					
11	Analysis Variable : Salary					
12	N	Mean	Std Dev	Minimum	Maximum	
13	165	31160.12	20082.67	22710	243190	
14						
15	Report 3					
16						
17	Obs	First_Nam	Last_Nam	Job_Title	Country	Salary
18	1	Tom	Zhou	Sales Man	AU	108255
19	2	Wilson	Dawes	Sales Man	AU	87975
20	64	Harry	Highpoint	Chief Sale	US	243190
21	163	Louis	Favaron	Senior Sal	US	95090
22	164	Renee	Capachiett	Sales Man	US	83505
23	165	Dennis	Lansberry	Sales Man	US	84260

HTML File in Microsoft Excel 2002

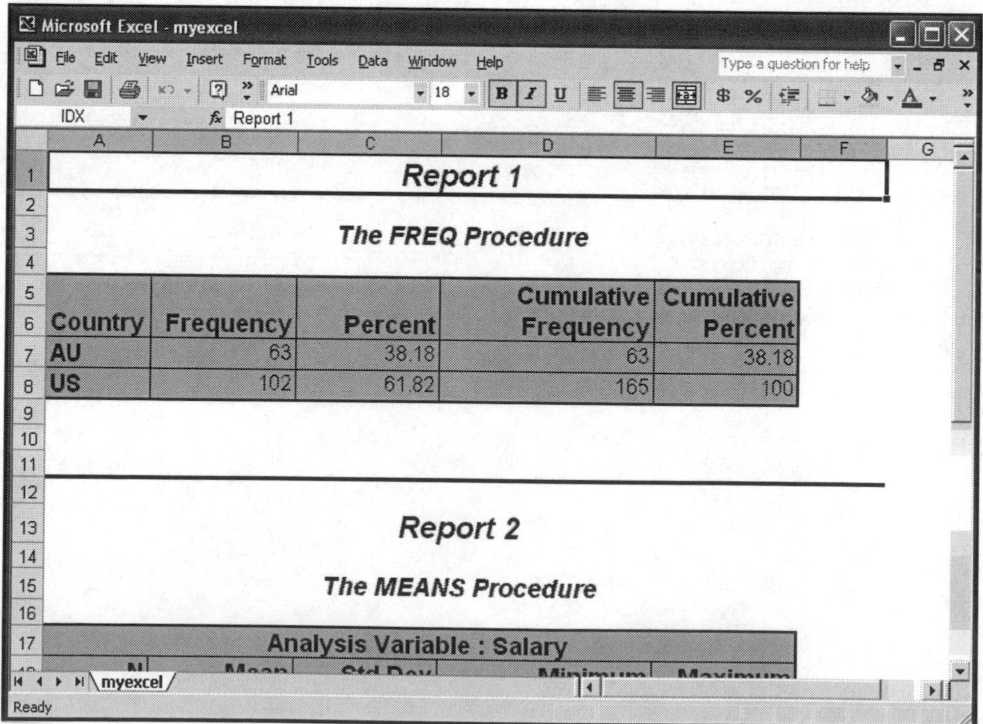

Report 1

The FREQ Procedure

Country	Frequency	Percent	Cumulative Frequency	Cumulative Percent
AU	63	38.18	63	38.18
US	102	61.82	165	100

Report 2

The MEANS Procedure

Analysis Variable : Salary

XML File in Microsoft Excel 2002

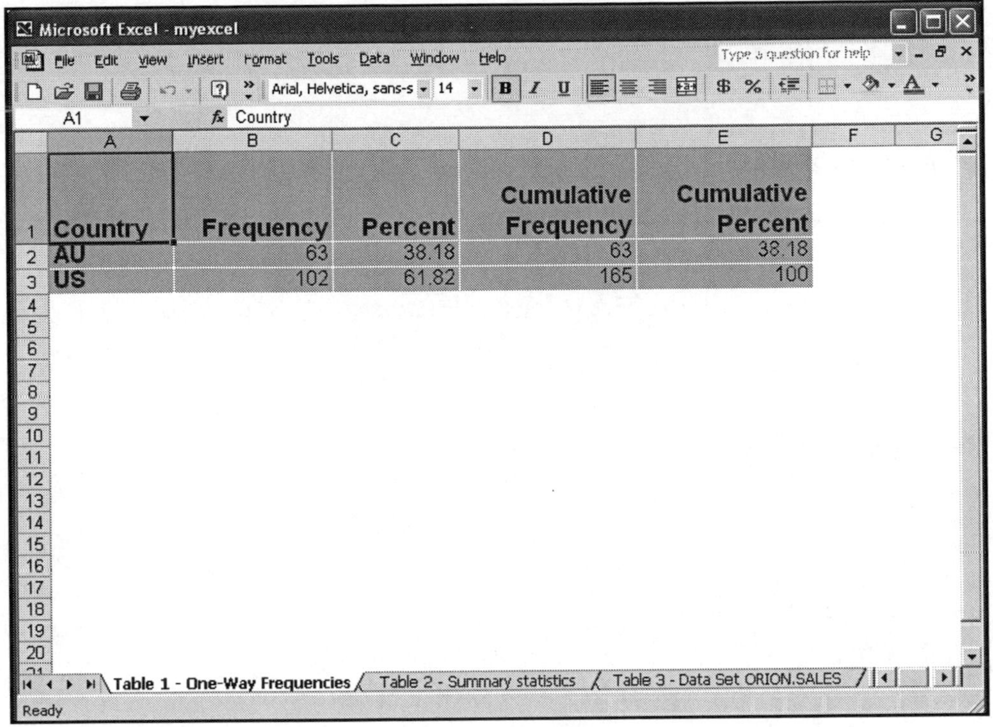

Country	Frequency	Percent	Cumulative Frequency	Cumulative Percent
AU	63	38.18	63	38.18
US	102	61.82	165	100

Using Options with the EXCELXP Destination (Self-Study)

p111d16

Submit the following program and view the EXCELXP documentation in the SAS log and the XML files in Microsoft Excel.

```
********** Documentation Option **********;
ods listing close;
ods tagsets.excelxp file='myexcel1.xml'
                    style=sasweb
                    options(doc='help');

proc freq data=orion.sales;
   tables Country;
   title 'Report 1';
run;

proc means data=orion.sales;
   var Salary;
   title 'Report 2';
run;

ods tagsets.excelxp close;
ods listing;

********** Other Options **********;
ods listing close;
ods tagsets.excelxp file='myexcel2.xml'
                    style=sasweb
                    options(embedded_titles='yes'
                            sheet_Name='First Report');

proc freq data=orion.sales;
   tables Country;
   title 'Report 1';
run;

ods tagsets.excelxp options(sheet_Name='Second Report');
proc means data=orion.sales;
   var Salary;
   title 'Report 2';
run;

ods tagsets.excelxp close;
ods listing;
```

For z/OS (OS/390), the following ODS statements are used:

```
ods tagsets.excelxp file='.workshop.report(myxml1)' rs=none
                    style=sasweb
                    options(doc='help');

ods tagsets.excelxp file='.workshop.report(myxml2)' rs=none
                    style=sasweb
                    options(embedded_titles='yes'
                            sheet_Name='First Report');
```

Partial SAS Log

```
Log - (Untitled)
300  ********** Documentation Option **********;
301  ods listing close;
302  ods tagsets.excelxp file='myexcel1.xml'
303                      style=sasweb
304                      options(doc='help');
NOTE: Writing TAGSETS.EXCELXP Body file: myexcel1.xml
==============================================================================
The EXCELXP Tagset Help Text.

This Tagset/Destination creates Microsoft's spreadsheetML XML.
It is used specifically for importing data into Excel.

Each table will be placed in its own worksheet within a workbook.
This destination supports ODS styles, traffic lighting, and custom formats.

Numbers, Currency and percentages are correctly detected and displayed.
Custom formats can be given by supplying a style override on the tagattr
style element.

By default, titles and footnotes are part of the spreadsheet, but are part
of the header and footer.

Also by default, printing will be in 'Portrait'.
The orientation can be changed to landscape.

The specification for this xml is here.
http://msdn.microsoft.com/library/default.asp?url=/library/en-us/dnexcl2k2/html/odc_xlsr
p

See Also:
http://support.sas.com/rnd/base/topics/odsmarkup/
http://support.sas.com/rnd/papers/index.html#excelxml


Sample usage:

ods tagsets.excelxp file='test.xml' contents='index.xml' data='test.ini' options(doc='He

ods tagsets.excelxp options(doc='Quick');

ods tagsets.excelxp options(embedded_titles='No' Orientation='Landscape');
```

XML Files in Microsoft Excel 2002

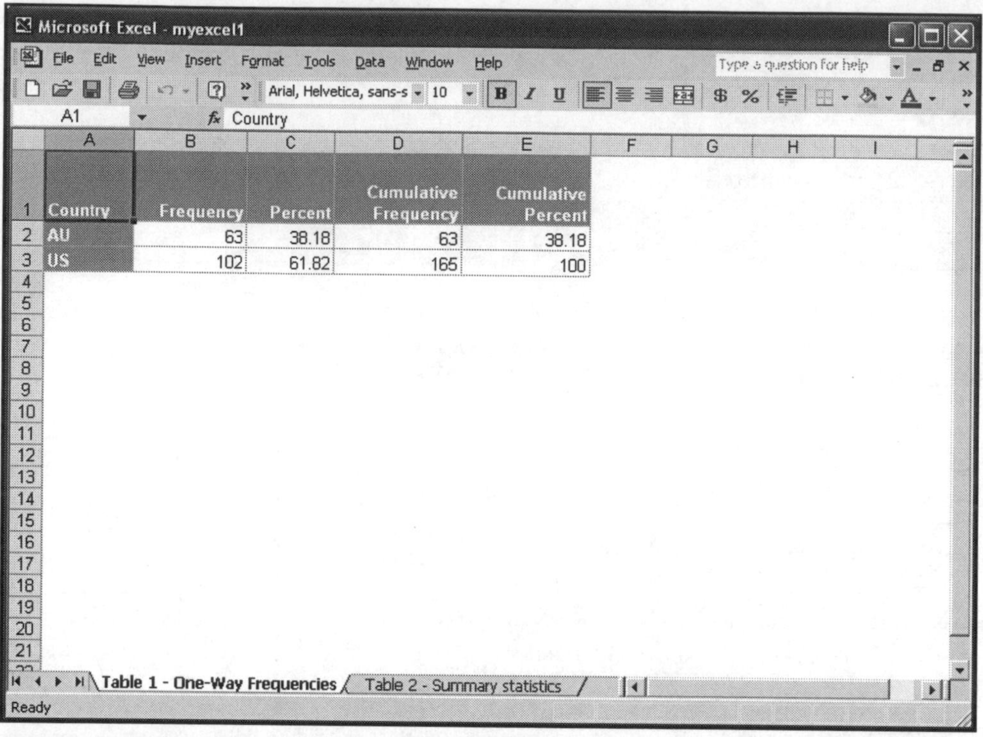

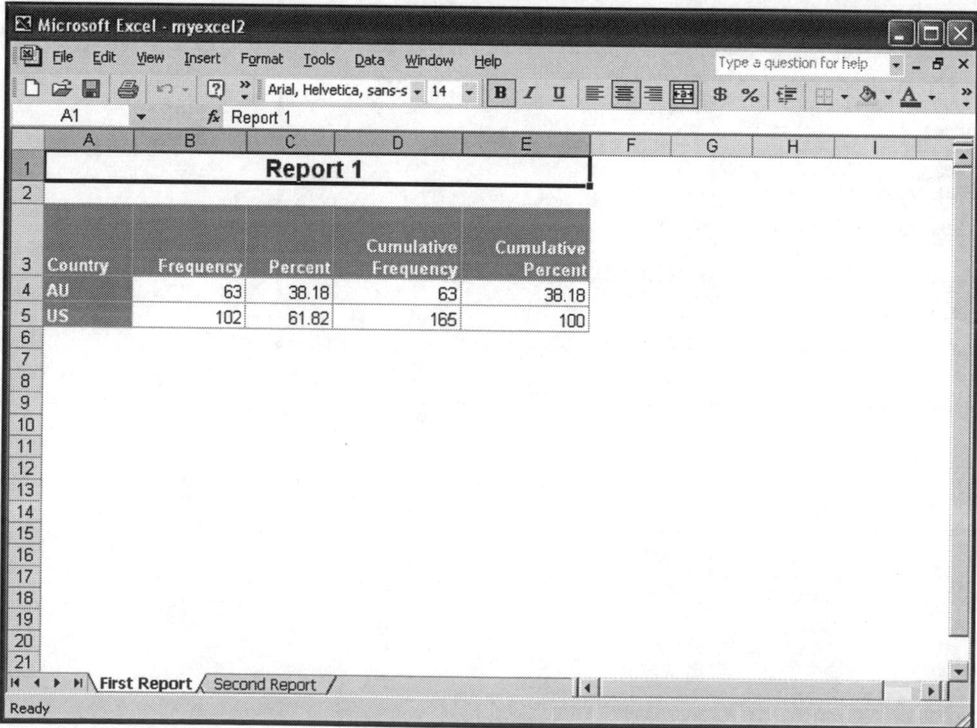

Exercises

Level 1

13. Directing Output to the PDF and RTF Destinations

a. Retrieve the starter program **p111e13**.

b. Create the PDF version of the PROC PRINT report by adding ODS statements.

Use the following naming convention when creating the PDF file:

Windows or UNIX	p111s13p.pdf
z/OS (OS/390)	.workshop.report(p111s13p)

c. Submit the program to produce the following report in PDF form as displayed in Adobe Reader:

Partial PROC PRINT Output

Customer Information

Obs	Customer_ID	Country	Gender	Personal_ID	Customer_Name	Customer_FirstName
1	4	US	M		James Kvarniq	James
2	5	US	F		Sandrina Stephano	Sandrina
3	9	DE	F		Cornelia Krahl	Cornelia
4	10	US	F		Karen Ballinger	Karen
5	11	DE	F		Elke Wallstab	Elke
6	12	US	M		David Black	David
7	13	DE	M		Markus Sepke	Markus
8	16	DE	M		Ulrich Heyde	Ulrich
9	17	US	M		Jimmie Evans	Jimmie
10	18	US	M		Tonie Asmussen	Tonie
11	19	DE	M		Oliver S. Füßling	Oliver S.
12	20	US	M		Michael Dineley	Michael
13	23	US	M		Tulio Devereaux	Tulio
14	24	US	F		Robyn Klem	Robyn
15	27	US	F		Cynthia Mccluney	Cynthia
16	29	AU	F		Candy Kinsey	Candy

Obs	Customer_LastName	Birth_Date	Customer_Address	Street_ID	Street_Number	Customer_Type_ID
1	Kvarniq	27JUN1974	4382 Gralyn Rd	9260106519	4382	1020
2	Stephano	09JUL1979	6468 Cog Hill Ct	9260114570	6468	2020
3	Krahl	27FEB1974	Kallstadtersir. 9	3940106659	9	2020
4	Ballinger	18OCT1984	425 Bryant Estates Dr	9260129395	425	1040
5	Wallstab	16AUG1974	Carl-Zeiss-Str. 15	3940108592	15	1040
6	Black	12APR1969	1068 Haithcock Rd	9260103713	1068	1030
7	Sepke	21JUL1988	Iese 1	3940105189	1	2010
8	Heyde	16JAN1939	Oberstr. 61	3940105865	61	3010
9	Evans	17AUG1954	391 Greywood Dr	9260123306	391	1030
10	Asmussen	02FEB1954	117 Langtree Ln	9260112361	117	1020
11	Füßling	23FEB1964	Hechtsheimerstr. 18	3940106547	18	2030
12	Dineley	17APR1959	2187 Draycroft Pl	9260118934	2187	1030
13	Devereaux	02DEC1949	1532 Ferdilah Ln	9260126679	1532	3010
14	Klem	02JUN1959	435 Cambrian Way	9260115784	435	3010
15	Mccluney	15APR1969	188 Grassy Creek Pl	9260105670	188	3010
16	Kinsey	08JUL1934	21 Hotham Parade	1600103020	21	3010

Compare this PDF output to the equivalent report that appears in the Output window.

d. Modify your ODS statements to create the RTF version of the PROC PRINT report.

Use the following naming convention when creating the RTF file:

Windows or UNIX	p111s13r.rtf
z/OS (OS/390)	.workshop.report(p111s13r)

e. Suppress the default Output window listing before generating the RTF report, and then re-establish the Output window as the report destination after the RTF report is complete.

f. Submit the program to produce the following report in RTF form as displayed in Microsoft Word:

Partial PROC PRINT Output

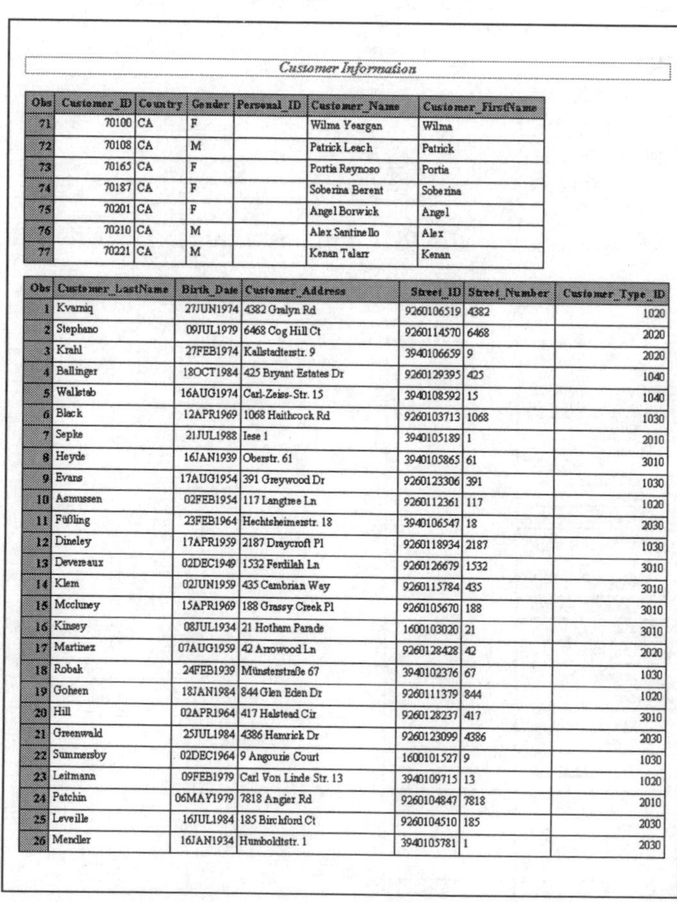

Customer Information

Obs	Customer_ID	Country	Gender	Personal_ID	Customer_Name	Customer_FirstName
71	70100	CA	F		Wilma Yeargan	Wilma
72	70108	CA	M		Patrick Leach	Patrick
73	70165	CA	F		Portia Reynoso	Portia
74	70187	CA	F		Soberina Berent	Soberina
75	70201	CA	F		Angel Borwick	Angel
76	70210	CA	M		Alex Santinello	Alex
77	70221	CA	M		Kenan Talarr	Kenan

Obs	Customer_LastName	Birth_Date	Customer_Address	Street_ID	Street_Number	Customer_Type_ID
1	Kvarniq	27JUN1974	4382 Gralyn Rd	9260106519	4382	1020
2	Stephano	09JUL1979	6468 Cog Hill Ct	9260114570	6468	2020
3	Krahl	27FEB1974	Kallstadterstr. 9	3940106659	9	2020
4	Ballinger	18OCT1984	425 Bryant Estates Dr	9260129395	425	1040
5	Wallstab	16AUG1974	Carl-Zeiss-Str. 15	3940108592	15	1040
6	Black	12APR1969	1068 Haithcock Rd	9260103713	1068	1030
7	Sepke	21JUL1988	Iese 1	3940105189	1	2010
8	Heyde	16JAN1939	Oberstr. 61	3940105865	61	3010
9	Evans	17AUG1954	391 Greywood Dr	9260123306	391	1030
10	Asmussen	02FEB1954	117 Langtree Ln	9260112361	117	1020
11	Füßling	23FEB1964	Hechtsheimerstr. 18	3940106547	18	2030
12	Dineley	17APR1959	2187 Draycroft Pl	9260118934	2187	1030
13	Devereaux	02DEC1949	1532 Ferdilah Ln	9260126679	1532	3010
14	Klem	02JUN1959	435 Cambrian Way	9260115784	435	3010
15	Mccluney	15APR1969	188 Grassy Creek Pl	9260105670	188	3010
16	Kinsey	08JUL1934	21 Hotham Parade	1600103020	21	3010
17	Martinez	07AUG1959	42 Arrowood Ln	9260128428	42	2020
18	Robak	24FEB1939	Münsterstraße 67	3940102376	67	1030
19	Goheen	18JAN1984	844 Glen Eden Dr	9260111379	844	1020
20	Hill	02APR1964	417 Halstead Cir	9260128237	417	3010
21	Greenwald	25JUL1984	4386 Hamrick Dr	9260123099	4386	2030
22	Summersby	02DEC1964	9 Angourie Court	1600101527	9	1030
23	Leitmann	09FEB1979	Carl Von Linde Str. 13	3940109715	13	1020
24	Patchin	06MAY1979	7818 Angier Rd	9260104847	7818	2010
25	Leveille	16JUL1984	185 Birchford Ct	9260104510	185	2030
26	Mendler	16JAN1934	Humboldtstr. 1	3940105781	1	2030

What happens if the RUN statement is moved to the end of the program?

g. Add the STYLE= option to the ODS RTF statement to use a style definitions such as Curve, Gears, Money, or Torn.

h. Submit the program and view the report in RTF form in Microsoft Word.

Level 2

14. Creating ODS Output Compatible with Microsoft Excel

a. Retrieve the starter program **p111e14**.

b. Add ODS statements to send the report to a file that can be viewed in Microsoft Excel. Choose the ODS destination (and use the associated file extension) based on whether you want

1) style information stored in the report output

2) the reports in a single worksheet or multiple worksheets.

If selecting a destination that supports style information, specify the Listing style definition.

Use the following naming convention when creating the file. For Windows or UNIX, choose an appropriate extension for the file depending on the type of file that is created.

Windows or UNIX	p111s14.xxx
z/OS (OS/390)	.workshop.report(p111s14)

c. Submit the program to produce the output file.

d. Open the file with Microsoft Excel. The report should resemble the following results. Your output will look different depending on the ODS destination you choose.

	A	B	C	D	E
1	Obs	Customer_Type_ID	Customer_Type	Customer_Group_ID	Customer_Group
2	1	1010	Orion Club members inactive	10	Orion Club members
3	2	1020	Orion Club members low activity	10	Orion Club members
4	3	1030	Orion Club members medium activity	10	Orion Club members
5	4	1040	Orion Club members high activity	10	Orion Club members
6	5	2010	Orion Club Gold members low activity	20	Orion Club Gold members
7	6	2020	Orion Club Gold members medium activity	20	Orion Club Gold members
8	7	2030	Orion Club Gold members high activity	20	Orion Club Gold members
9	8	3010	Internet/Catalog Customers	30	Internet/Catalog Customers
10					
11					

Table 1 - Data Set ORION.CUSTOM / Table 2 - Data Set ORION.COUNTR

Level 3

15. Adding HTML-Specific Features to ODS Output

a. Retrieve the starter program **p111e15**.

b. Create the HTML version of the PROC PRINT report by adding ODS statements.

Use the following naming convention when creating the HTML file:

Windows or UNIX	p111s15.html
z/OS (OS/390)	.workshop.report(p111s15)

c. Customize the title so that it becomes a clickable hyperlink when displayed in a Web browser. The hyperlink should point to the URL http://www.sas.com (the SAS home page).

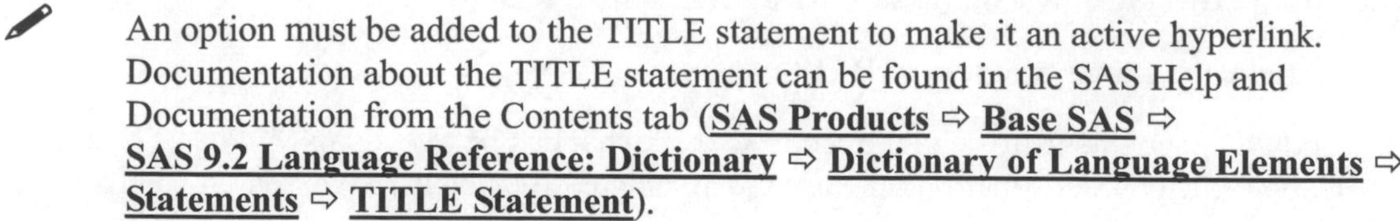

An option must be added to the TITLE statement to make it an active hyperlink. Documentation about the TITLE statement can be found in the SAS Help and Documentation from the Contents tab (**SAS Products** ⇨ **Base SAS** ⇨ **SAS 9.2 Language Reference: Dictionary** ⇨ **Dictionary of Language Elements** ⇨ **Statements** ⇨ **TITLE Statement**).

d. Submit the program to produce the following report in HTML form as displayed in Internet Explorer:

Partial PROC PRINT Output

Customer Information

Obs	Customer_ID	Country	Gender	Personal_ID	Customer_Name	Customer_FirstName	Customer_LastN
1	4	US	M		James Kvarniq	James	Kvarniq
2	5	US	F		Sandrina Stephano	Sandrina	Stephano
3	9	DE	F		Cornelia Krahl	Cornelia	Krahl
4	10	US	F		Karen Ballinger	Karen	Ballinger
5	11	DE	F		Elke Wallstab	Elke	Wallstab
6	12	US	M		David Black	David	Black
7	13	DE	M		Markus Sepke	Markus	Sepke
8	16	DE	M		Ulrich Heyde	Ulrich	Heyde
9	17	US	M		Jimmie Evans	Jimmie	Evans

16. Implementing Cascading Style Sheets with ODS Output

a. Retrieve the starter program **p111e16**.

b. Modify the ODS HTML statement so that the output generated by the program uses a cascading style sheet. The CSS definition applies a yellow background to data cells in the ODS output.

Use the following cascading style sheet:

Windows or UNIX	p111e16c.css
z/OS (OS/390)	.workshop.report(p111e16c)

The syntax required to reference an existing CSS file can be found in the SAS Help and Documentation from the Contents tab (**SAS Products** ⇨ **Base SAS** ⇨ **SAS 9.2 Output Delivery System User's Guide** ⇨ **ODS Language Statements** ⇨ **Dictionary of ODS Language Statements** ⇨ **ODS HTML Statement**). Follow the documentation links for the STYLESHEET= option and its URL= suboption.

c. Submit the program to produce thc following HTML report as displayed in Internet Explorer:

PROC PRINT Output

Customer Type Definitions

Obs	Customer_Type_ID	Customer_Type	Customer_Group_ID	Customer_Group
1	1010	Orion Club members inactive	10	Orion Club members
2	1020	Orion Club members low activity	10	Orion Club members
3	1030	Orion Club members medium activity	10	Orion Club members
4	1040	Orion Club members high activity	10	Orion Club members
5	2010	Orion Club Gold members low activity	20	Orion Club Gold members
6	2020	Orion Club Gold members medium activity	20	Orion Club Gold members
7	2030	Orion Club Gold members high activity	20	Orion Club Gold members
8	3010	Internet/Catalog Customers	30	Internet/Catalog Customers

11.6 Chapter Review

Chapter Review

1. What are some examples of global statements that enhance reports?

2. What is the maximum number of title or footnote lines?

3. How can you force a line break in a column header in PROC PRINT?

4. What is the difference between using a FORMAT statement in a PROC step versus a DATA step?

167

continued...

Chapter Review

5. How can you create a descriptive label for values of a variable such as a department name instead of a department code?

6. What are some examples of ODS destinations?

168

11.7 Solutions

Solutions to Exercises

1. **Specifying Titles, Footnotes, and System Options**

   a. Retrieve the starter program.

   b. Use the OPTIONS statement.

```
options nonumber nodate pagesize=18;
proc means data=orion.order_fact;
   var Total_Retail_Price;
run;
options pagesize=52;
```

   c. Specify a title.

```
options nonumber nodate pagesize=18;
title 'Orion Star Sales Report';
proc means data=orion.order_fact;
   var Total_Retail_Price;
run;
options pagesize=52;
```

   d. Specify a footnote.

```
options nonumber nodate pagesize=18;
title 'Orion Star Sales Report';
footnote 'Report by SAS Programming Student';
proc means data=orion.order_fact;
   var Total_Retail_Price;
run;
options pagesize=52;
```

   e. Cancel the footnote.

```
options nonumber nodate pagesize=18;
title 'Orion Star Sales Report';
footnote 'Report by SAS Programming Student';
proc means data=orion.order_fact;
   var Total_Retail_Price;
run;
options pagesize=52;
footnote;
```

   f. Submit the program.

2. Specifying Multiple Titles and System Options

a. Retrieve the starter program.

b. Limit the number of lines per page.

```
options pagesize=18;
proc means data=orion.order_fact;
   where Order_Type=2;
   var Total_Retail_Price;
run;

proc means data=orion.order_fact;
   where Order_Type=3;
   var Total_Retail_Price;
run;
options pagesize=52;
```

c. Request page numbers starting at 1.

```
options pagesize=18 number pageno=1;
proc means data=orion.order_fact;
   where Order_Type=2;
   var Total_Retail_Price;
run;

options pageno=1;
proc means data=orion.order_fact;
   where Order_Type=3;
   var Total_Retail_Price;
run;
options pagesize=52;
```

d. Request the current date and time.

```
options pagesize=18 number pageno=1 date dtreset;
```

e. Specify a title in both reports.

```
options pagesize=18 number pageno=1 date dtreset;
title1 'Orion Star Sales Analysis';
```

f. Specify a secondary title in the first report.

```
options pagesize=18 number pageno=1 date dtreset;
title1 'Orion Star Sales Analysis';
proc means data=orion.order_fact;
   where Order_Type=2;
   var Total_Retail_Price;
   title3 'Catalog Sales Only';
run;
```

g. Specify a footnote in the first report.

```
options pagesize=18 number pageno=1 date dtreset;
title1 'Orion Star Sales Analysis';
proc means data=orion.order_fact;
   where Order_Type=2;
   var Total_Retail_Price;
   title3 'Catalog Sales Only';
   footnote "Based on the previous day's posted data";
run;
```

h. Specify a secondary title in the second report.

```
options pagesize=18 number pageno=1 date dtreset;
title1 'Orion Star Sales Analysis';
proc means data=orion.order_fact;
   where Order_Type=2;
   var Total_Retail_Price;
   title3 'Catalog Sales Only';
   footnote "Based on the previous day's posted data";
run;

options pageno=1;
proc means data=orion.order_fact;
   where Order_Type=3;
   var Total_Retail_Price;
   title3 'Internet Sales Only';
run;
options pagesize=52;
```

i. Cancel all footnotes for the second report.

```
options pagesize=18 number pageno=1 date dtreset;
title1 'Orion Star Sales Analysis';
proc means data=orion.order_fact;
   where Order_Type=2;
   var Total_Retail_Price;
   title3 'Catalog Sales Only';
   footnote "Based on the previous day's posted data";
run;

options pageno=1;
proc means data=orion.order_fact;
   where Order_Type=3;
   var Total_Retail_Price;
   title3 'Internet Sales Only';
   footnote;
run;
options pagesize=52;
```

j. Submit the program.

3. **Inserting Dates and Times into Titles**

   a. Use the OPTIONS procedure.

```
proc options option=date;
run;
options nodate;
```

   b. Retrieve the starter program.

   c. Add a title.

```
%let currentdate=%sysfunc(today(),weekdate.);
%let currenttime=%sysfunc(time(),timeampm8.);
proc means data=orion.order_fact;
   title "Sales Report as of &currenttime on &currentdate";
   var Total_Retail_Price;
run;
```

   d. Submit the program.

4. **Applying Labels and Formats in Reports**

   a. Retrieve the starter program.

   b. Modify the column heading for each variable.

```
proc print data=orion.employee_payroll label;
   where Dependents=3;
   title 'Employees with 3 Dependents';
   var Employee_ID Salary
       Birth_Date Employee_Hire_Date Employee_Term_Date;
   label Employee_ID='Employee Number'
         Salary='Annual Salary'
         Birth_Date='Birth Date'
         Employee_Hire_Date='Hire Date'
         Employee_Term_Date='Termination Date';
run;
```

   c. Display all dates in the form ddMONyyyy.

```
proc print data=orion.employee_payroll label;
   where Dependents=3;
   title 'Employees with 3 Dependents';
   var Employee_ID Salary
       Birth_Date Employee_Hire_Date Employee_Term_Date;
   label Employee_ID='Employee Number'
         Salary='Annual Salary'
         Birth_Date='Birth Date'
         Employee_Hire_Date='Hire Date'
         Employee_Term_Date='Termination Date';
   format Birth_Date Employee_Hire_Date Employee_Term_Date date11.;
run;
```

d. Display each salary with dollar signs, commas, and two decimal places.

```
proc print data=orion.employee_payroll label;
   where Dependents=3;
   title 'Employees with 3 Dependents';
   var Employee_ID Salary
       Birth_Date Employee_Hire_Date Employee_Term_Date;
   label Employee_ID='Employee Number'
         Salary='Annual Salary'
         Birth_Date='Birth Date'
         Employee_Hire_Date='Hire Date'
         Employee_Term_Date='Termination Date';
   format Birth_Date Employee_Hire_Date Employee_Term_Date date11.
          Salary dollar11.2;
run;
```

e. Submit the program.

5. **Overriding Existing Labels and Formats**

a. Retrieve the starter program.

b. Display only the year portion of the birth dates.

```
proc print data=orion.customer;
   where Country='TR';
   title 'Customers from Turkey';
   var Customer_ID Customer_FirstName Customer_LastName
       Birth_Date;
   format Birth_Date year4.;
run;
```

c. Display only the first initial of each customer's first name.

```
proc print data=orion.customer;
   where Country='TR';
   title 'Customers from Turkey';
   var Customer_ID Customer_FirstName Customer_LastName
       Birth_Date;
   format Birth_Date year4.
          Customer_FirstName $1.;
run;
```

d. Show the customer's ID with exactly six digits.

```
proc print data=orion.customer;
   where Country='TR';
   title 'Customers from Turkey';
   var Customer_ID Customer_FirstName Customer_LastName
       Birth_Date;
   format Birth_Date year4.
          Customer_FirstName $1.
          Customer_ID z6.;
run;
```

e. Modify the column heading for each variable.

```
proc print data=orion.customer split='/';
   where Country='TR';
   title 'Customers from Turkey';
   var Customer_ID Customer_FirstName Customer_LastName
       Birth_Date;
   label Customer_ID='Customer ID'
         Customer_FirstName='First Initial'
         Customer_LastName='Last/Name'
         Birth_Date='Birth Year';
   format Birth_Date year4.
          Customer_FirstName $1.
          Customer_ID z6.;
run;
```

f. Submit the program.

6. **Applying Permanent Labels and Formats**

a. Retrieve the starter program.

b. Add permanent variable labels and formats.

```
data otherstatus;
   set orion.employee_payroll;
   keep Employee_ID Employee_Hire_Date;
   if Marital_Status='O';
   label Employee_ID='Employee Number'
         Employee_Hire_Date='Hired';
   format Employee_Hire_Date yymmddp10.;
run;

title 'Employees who are listed with Marital Status=O';
proc print data=otherstatus label;
run;

proc contents data=otherstatus;
run;

proc freq data=otherstatus;
   tables Employee_Hire_Date;
run;
```

c. Override the permanent attributes within the PROC FREQ step.

```
proc freq data=otherstatus;
   tables Employee_Hire_Date;
   label Employee_Hire_Date='Quarter Hired';
   format Employee_Hire_Date yyq6.;
run;
```

d. Submit the program.

7. **Creating User-Defined Formats**

   a. Retrieve the starter program.

   b. Create a character format.

```
data Q1Birthdays;
   set orion.employee_payroll;
   BirthMonth=month(Birth_Date);
   if BirthMonth le 3;
run;

proc format;
   value $gender
      'F'='Female'
      'M'='Male';
run;
```

   c. Create a numeric format.

```
data Q1Birthdays;
   set orion.employee_payroll;
   BirthMonth=month(Birth_Date);
   if BirthMonth le 3;
run;

proc format;
   value $gender
      'F'='Female'
      'M'='Male';
   value moname
       1='January'
       2='February'
       3='March';
run;
```

   d. In the PROC FREQ step, apply these two user-defined formats.

```
proc freq data=Q1Birthdays;
   tables BirthMonth Employee_Gender;
   format Employee_Gender $gender.
          BirthMonth moname.;
   title 'Employees with Birthdays in Q1';
run;
```

   e. Submit the program.

8. Defining Ranges in User-Defined Formats

a. Retrieve the starter program.

b. Create a character format.

```
proc format;
   value $gender
        'F'='Female'
        'M'='Male'
      other='Invalid code';
run;
```

c. Create a numeric format.

```
proc format;
   value $gender
        'F'='Female'
        'M'='Male'
      other='Invalid code';
   value salrange
                   .='Missing salary'
      20000-<100000='Below $100,000'
      100000-500000='$100,000 or more'
              other='Invalid salary';
run;
```

d. In the PROC PRINT step, apply these two user-defined formats.

```
proc print data=orion.nonsales;
   var Employee_ID Job_Title Salary Gender;
   format Salary salrange. Gender $gender.;
   title1 'Distribution of Salary and Gender Values';
   title2 'for Non-Sales Employees';
run;
```

e. Submit the program.

9. Creating a Nested Format Definition

a. Retrieve the starter program.

b. Create a user-defined format.

```
proc format;
   value dategrp
                        .='None'
       low-'31dec2006'd=[year4.]
      '01jan2007'd-high=[monyy7.]
   ;
run;
```

c. Apply the new format.

```
proc freq data=orion.employee_payroll;
   tables Employee_Term_Date / missing;
   format Employee_Term_Date dategrp.;
   title 'Employee Status Report';
run;
```

d. Submit the program.

10. Subsetting and Grouping Observations

a. Retrieve the starter program.

b. Add a PROC SORT step.

```
proc sort data=orion.order_fact out=order_sorted;
   by order_type;
run;
```

c. Restrict the PROC MEANS analysis.

```
proc means data=order_sorted;
   where order_type in (2,3);
   var Total_Retail_Price;
   title 'Orion Star Sales Summary';
run;
```

d. Modify the PROC MEANS step.

```
proc means data=order_sorted;
   by order_type;
   where order_type in (2,3);
   var Total_Retail_Price;
   title 'Orion Star Sales Summary';
run;
```

e. Submit the program.

11. Subsetting and Grouping by Multiple Variables

a. Retrieve the starter program.

b. Sort the data set.

```
proc sort data=orion.order_fact out=order_sorted;
   by Order_Type descending Order_Date;
run;
```

c. Divide the PROC PRINT report.

```
proc print data=order_sorted;
   by Order_Type;
   var Order_ID Order_Date Delivery_Date;
   title1 'Orion Star Sales Details';
run;
```

d. Limit the observations in the PROC PRINT report.

```
proc print data=order_sorted;
   by Order_Type;
   var Order_ID Order_Date Delivery_Date;
   where Delivery_Date - Order_Date = 2
     and Order_Date between '01jan2005'd and '30apr2005'd;
   title1 'Orion Star Sales Details';
run;
```

e. Add a second title.

```
proc print data=order_sorted;
   by Order_Type;
   var Order_ID Order_Date Delivery_Date;
   where Delivery_Date - Order_Date = 2
     and Order_Date between '01jan2005'd and '30apr2005'd;
   title1 'Orion Star Sales Details';
   title2 '2-Day Deliveries from January to April 2005';
run;
```

f. Submit the program.

12. Adding Subsetting Conditions

a. Retrieve the starter program.

b. Reorder the variables in the PROC PRINT step.

```
proc format;
   value $country
      "CA"="Canada"
      "DK"="Denmark"
      "ES"="Spain"
      "GB"="Great Britain"
      "NL"="Netherlands"
      "SE"="Sweden"
      "US"="United States";
run;

proc sort data=orion.shoe_vendors out=vendors_by_country;
   by Supplier_Country Supplier_Name;
run;

proc print data=vendors_by_country;
   where Product_Line=21;
   by Supplier_Name Supplier_ID Supplier_Country notsorted;
   var Product_ID Product_Name;
   title1 'Orion Star Products: Children Sports';
run;
```

c. Augment the existing WHERE criteria.

```
proc format;
   value $country
      "CA"="Canada"
      "DK"="Denmark"
      "ES"="Spain"
      "GB"="Great Britain"
      "NL"="Netherlands"
      "SE"="Sweden"
      "US"="United States";
run;

proc sort data=orion.shoe_vendors out=vendors_by_country;
   by Supplier_Country Supplier_Name;
run;

proc print data=vendors_by_country;
   where Product_Line=21;
   where same
     and Product_Name ? 'Street' or Product_Name ? 'Running';
   by Supplier_Name Supplier_ID Supplier_Country notsorted;
   var Product_ID Product_Name;
   title1 'Orion Star Products: Children Sports';
run;
```

d. Submit the program.

13. Directing Output to the PDF and RTF Destinations

a. Retrieve the starter program.

b. Create the PDF version of the PROC PRINT report.

```
ods pdf file='p111s13p.pdf';
proc print data=orion.customer;
   title 'Customer Information';
run;
ods pdf close;
```

For z/OS (OS/390), the following ODS PDF statement is used:

```
ods pdf file='.workshop.report(p111s13p)';
```

c. Submit the program.

d. Modify your ODS statements to create the RTF version of the PROC PRINT report.

```
ods rtf file='p111s13r.rtf';
proc print data=orion.customer;
   title 'Customer Information';
run;
ods rtf close;
```

For z/OS (OS/390), the following ODS RTF statement is used:

```
ods rtf file='.workshop.report(p111s13r)' rs=none;
```

e. Suppress the default Output window listing.

```
ods listing close;
ods rtf file='p111s13r.rtf';
proc print data=orion.customer;
   title 'Customer Information';
run;
ods rtf close;
ods listing;
```

f. Submit the program.

What happens if the RUN statement is moved to the end of the program?

The file is empty.

g. Add the STYLE= option.

```
ods listing close;
ods rtf file='p111s13r.rtf' style=curve;
proc print data=orion.customer;
   title 'Customer Information';
run;
ods rtf close;
ods listing;
```

h. Submit the program.

14. Creating ODS Output Compatible with Microsoft Excel

a. Retrieve the starter program.

b. Add ODS statements to send the report to a file that can be viewed in Microsoft Excel.

```
ods csvall file='p111s14.csv';
proc print data=orion.customer_type;
   title 'Customer Type Definitions';
run;

proc print data=orion.country;
   title 'Country Definitions';
run;
ods csvall close;
```

For z/OS (OS/390), thc following ODS CSVALL statement is used:

```
ods csvall file='.workshop.report(p111s14)' rs=none;
ods msoffice2k file='p111s14.html' style=Listing;
proc print data=orion.customer_type;
   title 'Customer Type Definitions';
run;

proc print data=orion.country;
   title 'Country Definitions';
run;
ods msoffice2k close;
```

For z/OS (OS/390), the following ODS MSOFFICE2K statement is used:

```
ods msoffice2k file='.workshop.report(p111s14)' rs=none;
```

```
ods tagsets.excelxp file='p111s14.xml' style=Listing;
proc print data=orion.customer_type;
   title 'Customer Type Definitions';
run;

proc print data=orion.country;
   title 'Country Definitions';
run;
ods tagsets.excelxp close;
```

For z/OS (OS/390), the following ODS TAGSETS.EXCELXP statement is used:

```
ods tagsets.excelxp file='.workshop.report(p111s14)' rs=none;
```

c. Submit the program.

d. Open the file with Microsoft Excel.

15. Adding HTML-Specific Features to ODS Output

a. Retrieve the starter program.

b. Create the HTML version of the PROC PRINT report.

```
ods html file='p111s15.html';
proc print data=orion.customer;
   title 'Customer Information';
run;
ods html close;
```

For z/OS (OS/390), the following ODS HTML statement is used:

```
ods html file='.workshop.report(p111s15)' rs=none;
```

c. Customize the title so that it becomes a clickable hyperlink.

```
ods html file='p111s15.html';
proc print data=orion.customer;
   title link='http://www.sas.com' 'Customer Information';
run;
ods html close;
```

d. Submit the program.

16. Implementing Cascading Style Sheets with ODS Output

a. Retrieve the starter program.

b. Modify the ODS HTML statement.

```
ods html file='p111s16.html' stylesheet=(url='p111e16c.css');
proc print data=orion.customer_type;
   title 'Customer Type Definitions';
run;
ods html close;
```

For z/OS (OS/390), the following ODS HTML statement is used:

```
ods html file='.workshop.report(p111s16)' rs=none
         stylesheet=(url='.workshop.report(p111e16c)');
```

c. Submit the program.

Solutions to Student Activities (Polls/Quizzes)

11.01 Poll – Correct Answer

Did the date and/or time change?

Yes

❍ No

The DTRESET option uses the current date and time versus the SAS invocation date and time.

```
options date number pageno=1 ls=100 dtreset;
```

18

p111a01s

11.02 Quiz – Correct Answer

Which footnote(s) appears in the second procedure output?

a. `Non Sales Employees`

b. (circled) `Orion Star` / `Non Sales Employees`

c. `Non Sales Employees` / `Confidential`

d. `Orion Star` / `Non Sales Employees` / `Confidential`

```
footnote1 'Orion Star';
proc print data=orion.sales;
   footnote2 'Sales Employees';
   footnote3 'Confidential';
run;
proc print data=orion.nonsales;
   footnote2 'Non Sales Employees';
run;
```

38

11.03 Quiz – Correct Answer

Which statement is true concerning the PROC PRINT output for **Bonus**?

a. Annual Bonus will be the label.
(b.) Mid-Year Bonus will be the label.

Temporary labels override permanent labels.

57 p111d05

11.04 Quiz – Correct Answer

Which displayed value is incorrect for the given format?

Format	Stored Value	Displayed Value
$3.	Wednesday	Wed
6.1	1234.345	1234.3
COMMAX5.	1234.345	1.234
DOLLAR9.2	1234.345	$1,234.35
➡ DDMMYY8.	0	01/01/1960
DATE9.	0	01JAN1960
YEAR4.	0	1960

DDMMYY8. produces 01/01/60.

62

11.05 Multiple Answer Poll – Correct Answer

Which user-defined format names are invalid?

a. $stfmt
(b.) $3levels
c. _4years
d. salranges
(e.) dollar

Character formats must have a dollar sign as the first character and a letter or underscore as the second character.

User-defined formats cannot be the name of a SAS supplied format.

77

11.06 Quiz – Correct Answer

If you have a value of 99999.87, how will it be displayed if the TIERS format is applied to the value?

a. Tier 2
b. Tier 3
c. a missing value
(d.) none of the above

```
proc format;
   value tiers  20000-49999   = 'Tier 1'
                50000-99999   = 'Tier 2'
               100000-250000 = 'Tier 3';
run;
```

86

11.07 Quiz – Correct Answer

If you have a value of 100000, how will it be displayed if the TIERS format is applied to the value?

a. Tier 2 (circled)
b. Tier 3
c. 100000
d. a missing value

```
proc format;
   value tiers  20000-<50000  = 'Tier 1'
                50000- 100000 = 'Tier 2'
               100000<-250000 = 'Tier 3';
run;
```

90

11.08 Quiz – Correct Answer

Which of the following WHERE statements have invalid syntax?

a. `where Salary ne .;`

b. `where Hire_Date >= '01APR2008'd;`

c. (circled) `where Country in (AU US);`

d. `where Salary + Bonus <= 10000;`

e. (circled) `where Gender ne 'M' Salary >= 50000;`

f. `where Name like '%N';`

105

11.09 Multiple Choice Poll – Correct Answer

Which statement is true concerning the multiple WHERE statements?

a. All the WHERE statements are used.

b. None of the WHERE statements is used.

c. The first WHERE statement is used.

(d.) The last WHERE statement is used.

```
1000  proc freq data=orion.sales;
1001     tables Gender;
1002     where Salary > 75000;
1003     where Country = 'US';
NOTE: Where clause has been replaced.
1004  run;

NOTE: There were 102 observations read from the data set
      ORION.SALES.
      WHERE Country='US';
```

111

11.10 Quiz – Correct Answer

Which is a valid BY statement for the PROC FREQ step?

a. `by Country Gender;`

b. `by Gender Last_Name;`

(c.) `by Country;`

d. `by Gender;`

```
proc sort data=orion.sales out=work.sort;
   by Country descending Gender Last_Name;
run;

proc freq data=work.sort;
   tables Gender;
run;
```

117

11.11 Quiz – Correct Answer

What is the problem with this program?

```
ods pdf file='myreport.pdf';

proc print data=orion.sales;
run;

ods pdf close;
```

134

11.12 Poll – Correct Answer

Did you notice a difference in the presentation aspects between the two style definitions?

- ❍ Yes (circled)
- ❍ No

The first group of style definitions did not use color.

The second group of style definitions did use color.

152

Solutions to Chapter Review

Chapter Review Answers

1. What are some examples of global statements that enhance reports?
   - **OPTIONS**
   - **TITLE**
   - **FOOTNOTE**
   - **ODS**

2. What is the maximum number of title or footnote lines?
   10

169

continued...

Chapter Review Answers

3. How can you force a line break in a column header in PROC PRINT?
   Use the SPLIT= option in the PROC PRINT statement in combination with the LABEL statement or a permanent label.

4. What is the difference between using a FORMAT statement in a PROC step versus a DATA step?
   A FORMAT statement in a PROC step defines a temporary format. A FORMAT statement in a DATA step defines a permanent format.

170

continued...

Chapter Review Answers

5. How can you create a descriptive label for values of a variable such as a department name instead of a department code?

   Use a VALUE statement in PROC FORMAT to create user-defined formats.

171

continued...

Chapter Review Answers

6. What are some examples of ODS destinations?
   - **LISTING**
   - **HTML**
   - **PDF**
   - **RTF**
   - **CSVALL**
   - **MSOFFICE2K**
   - **EXCELXP**

172

Chapter 12 Producing Summary Reports

12.1 Using the FREQ Procedure **12-3**

Exercises 12-21

12.2 Using the MEANS Procedure **12-27**

Exercises 12-42

12.3 Using the TABULATE Procedure (Self-Study) **12-46**

Exercises 12-60

12.4 Chapter Review **12-65**

12.5 Solutions **12-66**

Solutions to Exercises 12-66

Solutions to Student Activities (Polls/Quizzes) 12-75

Solutions to Chapter Review 12-78

12.1 Using the FREQ Procedure

Objectives

- Produce one-way and two-way frequency tables with the FREQ procedure.
- Enhance frequency tables with options.
- Produce output data sets by using the OUT= option in the TABLES and OUTPUT statements. (Self-Study)

3

The FREQ Procedure

The FREQ procedure can do the following:

- produce one-way to *n*-way frequency and crosstabulation (contingency) tables
- compute chi-square tests for one-way to *n*-way tables and measures of association and agreement for contingency tables
- automatically display the output in a report and save the output in a SAS data set

General form of the FREQ procedure:

```
PROC FREQ DATA=SAS-data-set <option(s)>;
      TABLES variable(s) </ option(s)>;
RUN;
```

4

The FREQ Procedure

A FREQ procedure with no TABLES statement generates one-way frequency tables for all data set variables.

```
proc freq data=orion.sales;
run;
```

This PROC FREQ step creates a frequency table for the following nine variables:

- **Employee_ID**
- **First_Name**
- **Last_Name**
- **Gender**
- **Salary**
- **Job_Title**
- **Country**
- **Birth_Date**
- **Hire_Date**

5 p112d01

By default, PROC FREQ creates a report on every variable in the data set. For example, the **Employee_ID** report displays every unique value of **Employee_ID**, counts how many observations have each value, and provides percentages and cumulative statistics. This is not a useful report because each employee has his or her own unique employee ID.

You do not typically create frequency reports for variables with a large number of distinct values, such as **Employee_ID**, or for analysis variables, such as **Salary**. You usually create frequency reports for categorical variables, such as **Job_Title**. You can group variables into categories by creating and applying formats.

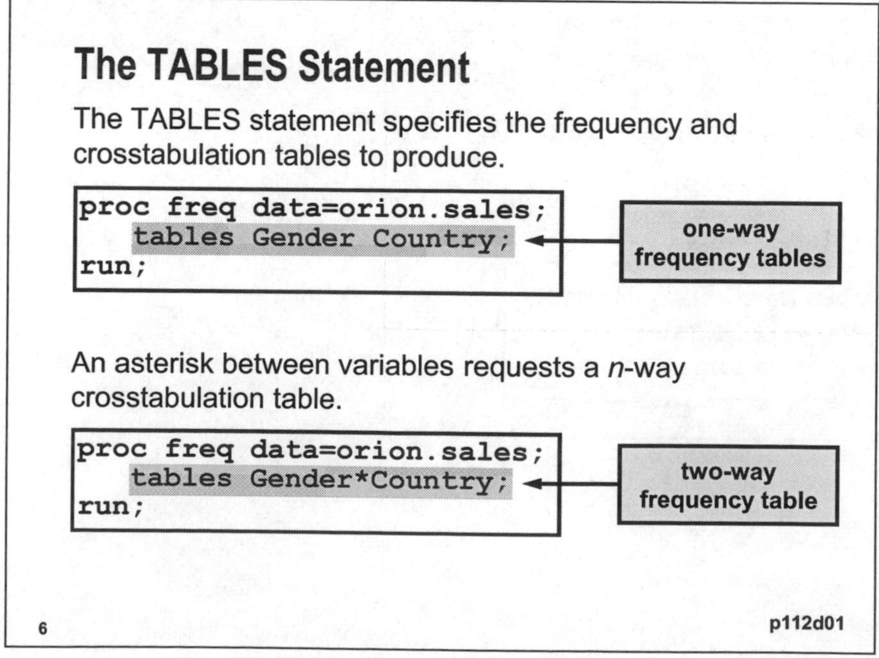

The TABLES Statement
The TABLES statement specifies the frequency and crosstabulation tables to produce.
proc freq data=orion.sales;
tables Gender Country;
run;
one-way frequency tables
An asterisk between variables requests a n-way crosstabulation table.
proc freq data=orion.sales;
tables Gender*Country;
run;
two-way frequency table
6
p112d01

The TABLES Statement

A one-way frequency table produces frequencies, cumulative frequencies, percentages, and cumulative percentages.

```
proc freq data=orion.sales;
   tables Gender Country;
run;
```

The FREQ Procedure

Gender	Frequency	Percent	Cumulative Frequency	Cumulative Percent
F	68	41.21	68	41.21
M	97	58.79	165	100.00

Country	Frequency	Percent	Cumulative Frequency	Cumulative Percent
AU	63	38.18	63	38.18
US	102	61.82	165	100.00

7

The TABLES Statement

An *n*-way frequency table produces cell frequencies, cell percentages, cell percentages of row frequencies, and cell percentages of column frequencies, plus total frequency and percent.

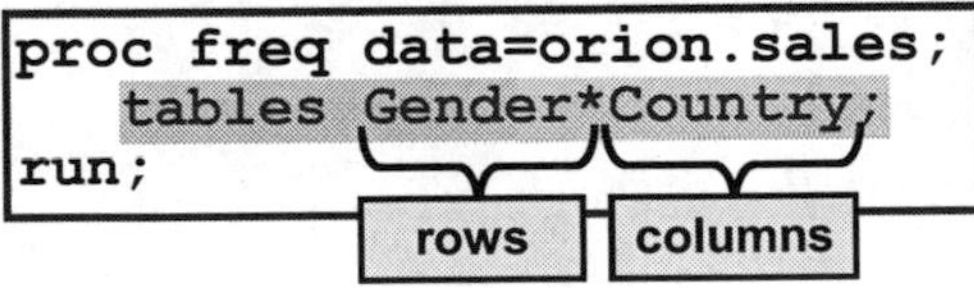
proc freq data=orion.sales;
tables Gender*Country;
run;
rows
columns

8

The TABLES Statement

```
                  The FREQ Procedure

             Table of Gender by Country

        Gender     Country

        Frequency|
        Percent  |
        Row Pct  |
        Col Pct  |AU      |US      |  Total
        ---------+--------+--------+
        F        |     27 |     41 |     68
                 |  16.36 |  24.85 |  41.21
                 |  39.71 |  60.29 |
                 |  42.86 |  40.20 |
        ---------+--------+--------+
        M        |     36 |     61 |     97
                 |  21.82 |  36.97 |  58.79
                 |  37.11 |  62.89 |
                 |  57.14 |  59.80 |
        ---------+--------+--------+
        Total          63      102      165
                    38.18    61.82   100.00
```

9

12.01 Multiple Choice Poll

Which of the following statements **cannot** be added to the PROC FREQ step to enhance the report?

a. FORMAT
b. SET
c. TITLE
d. WHERE

11

Additional SAS Statements

Additional statements can be added to enhance the report.

```
proc format;
   value $ctryfmt 'AU'='Australia'
                  'US'='United States';
run;

options nodate pageno=1;

ods html file='p112d01.html';
proc freq data=orion.sales;
   tables Gender*Country;
   where Job_Title contains 'Rep';
   format Country $ctryfmt.;
   title 'Sales Rep Frequency Report';
run;
ods html close;
```

13 p112d01

Additional SAS Statements

HTML Output

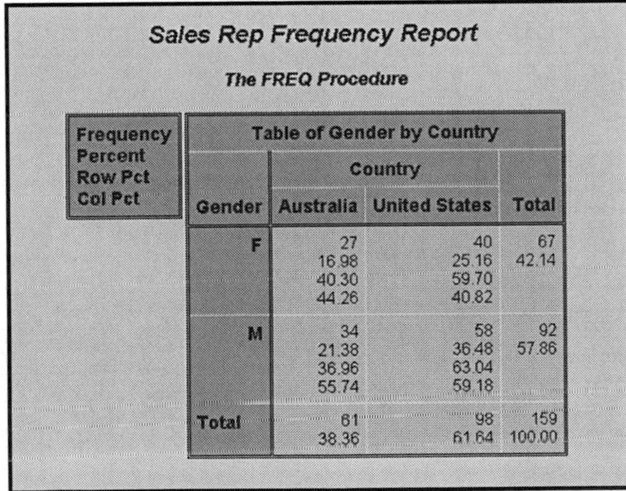

Sales Rep Frequency Report

The FREQ Procedure

Frequency Percent Row Pct Col Pct

Table of Gender by Country			
	Country		
Gender	Australia	United States	Total
F	27 16.98 40.30 44.26	40 25.16 59.70 40.82	67 42.14
M	34 21.38 36.96 55.74	58 36.48 63.04 59.18	92 57.86
Total	61 38.36	98 61.64	159 100.00

14

ods listing close; → turns off ~~output~~ list window

Options to Suppress Display of Statistics

Options can be placed in the TABLES statement after a forward slash to suppress the display of the default statistics.

Option	Description
NOCUM	suppresses the display of cumulative frequency and cumulative percentage.
NOPERCENT	suppresses the display of percentage, cumulative percentage, and total percentage.
NOFREQ	suppresses the display of the cell frequency and total frequency.
NOROW	suppresses the display of the row percentage.
NOCOL	suppresses the display of the column percentage.

15

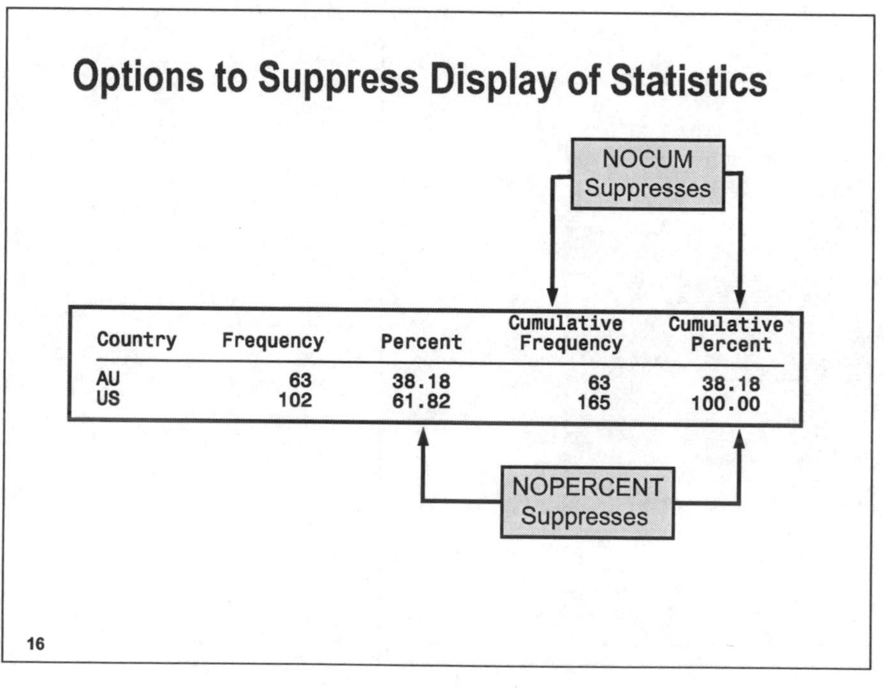

Country	Frequency	Percent	Cumulative Frequency	Cumulative Percent
AU	63	38.18	63	38.18
US	102	61.82	165	100.00

16

Options to Suppress Display of Statistics

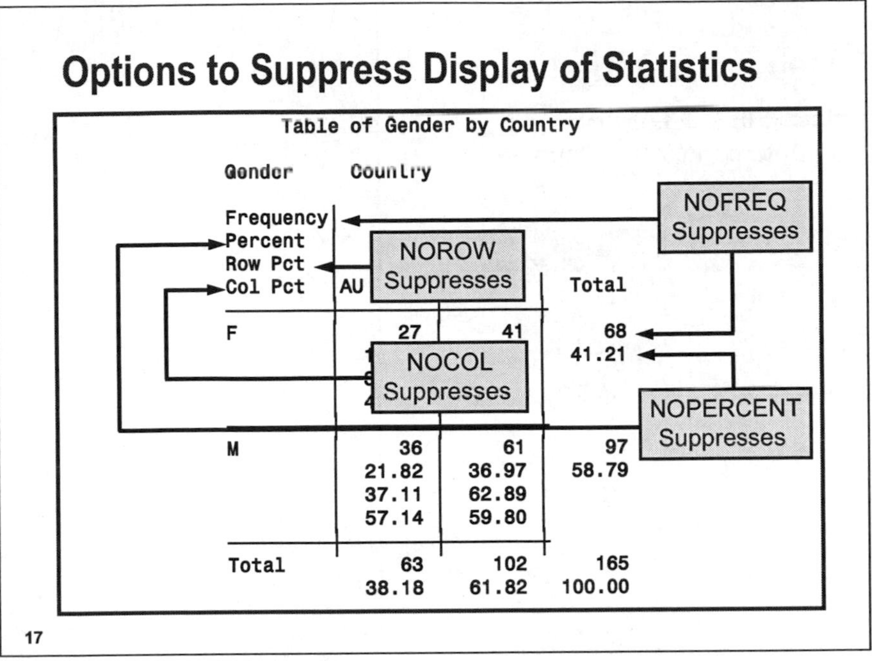

Table of Gender by Country
Gender
Country
Frequency
Percent
Row Pct
Col Pct
AU
Total
NOFREQ Suppresses
NOROW Suppresses
NOCOL Suppresses
NOPERCENT Suppresses
F
27
41
68
41.21
M
36
21.82
37.11
57.14
61
36.97
62.89
59.80
97
58.79
Total
63
38.18
102
61.82
165
100.00

17

12.02 Quiz

Which TABLES statement correctly creates the report?

a. `tables Gender nocum;`

b. `tables Gender nocum nopercent;`

c. `tables Gender / nopercent;`

d. `tables Gender / nocum nopercent;`

The FREQ Procedure

Gender	Frequency
F	68
M	97

19 p112d01

Additional TABLES Statement Options

Additional options can be placed in the TABLES statement after a forward slash to control the displayed output.

Option	Description
LIST	displays *n*-way tables in list format.
CROSSLIST	displays *n*-way tables in column format.
FORMAT=	formats the frequencies in *n*-way tables.

21

LIST and CROSSLIST Options

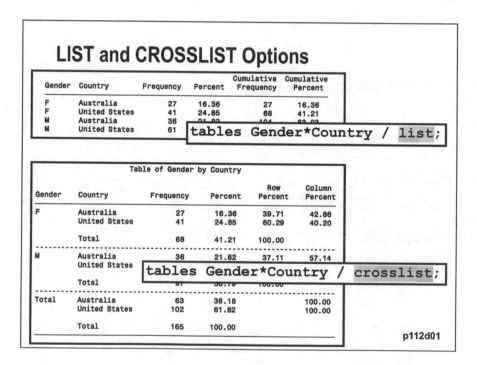

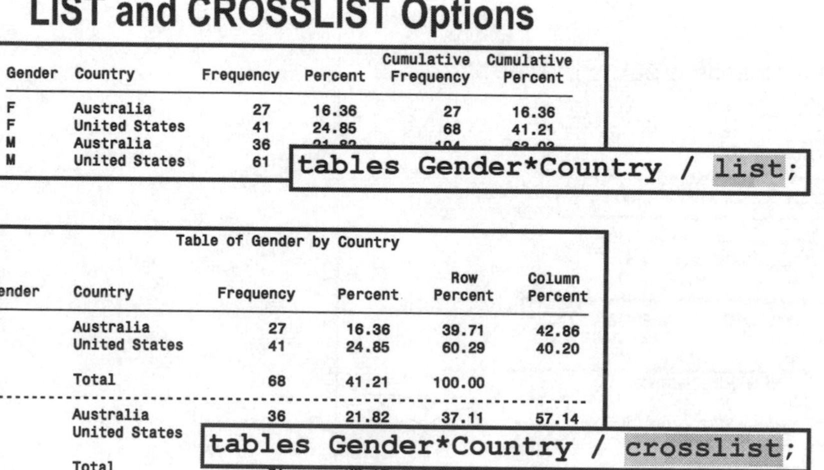

Gender	Country	Frequency	Percent	Cumulative Frequency	Cumulative Percent
F	Australia	27	16.36	27	16.36
F	United States	41	24.85	68	41.21
M	Australia	36	[illegible]	[illegible]	[illegible]
M	United States	61	[illegible]	[illegible]	[illegible]

```
tables Gender*Country / list;
```

Table of Gender by Country

Gender	Country	Frequency	Percent	Row Percent	Column Percent
F	Australia	27	16.36	39.71	42.86
	United States	41	24.85	60.29	40.20
	Total	68	41.21	100.00	
M	Australia	36	21.82	37.11	57.14
	United States	[illegible]	[illegible]	[illegible]	[illegible]
	Total	[illegible]	[illegible]	[illegible]	
Total	Australia	63	38.18		100.00
	United States	102	61.82		100.00
	Total	165	100.00		

```
tables Gender*Country / crosslist;
```

p112d01

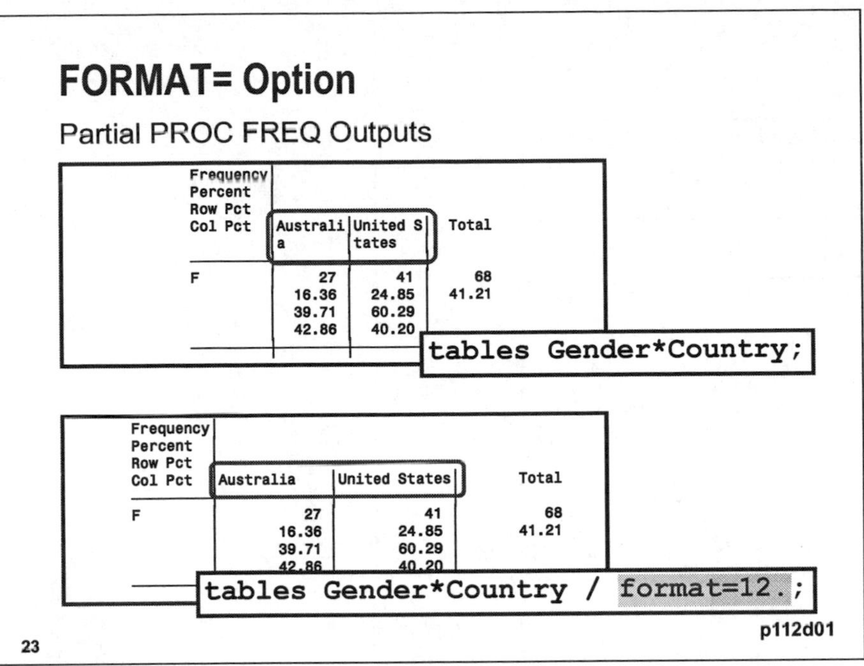

PROC FREQ Statement Options

Options can also be placed in the PROC FREQ statement.

Option	Description
NLEVELS	displays a table that provides the number of levels for each variable named in the TABLES statement.
PAGE	displays only one table per page.
COMPRESS	begins the display of the next one-way frequency table on the same page as the preceding one-way table if there is enough space to begin the table.

24

NLEVELS Option

```
proc freq data=orion.sales nlevels;
   tables Gender Country Employee_ID;
run;
```

Partial PROC FREQ Output

```
                  The FREQ Procedure

               Number of Variable Levels

               Variable          Levels
               ------------------------
               Gender                 2
               Country                2
               Employee_ID          165
```

25 p112d01

To display the number of levels without displaying the frequency counts, add the NOPRINT option to the TABLES statement.

```
proc freq data=orion.sales nlevels;
   tables Gender Country Employee_ID / noprint;
run;
```

To display the number of levels for all variables without displaying any frequency counts, use the _ALL_ keyword and the NOPRINT option in the TABLES statement.

```
proc freq data=orion.sales nlevels;
   tables _all_ / noprint;
run;
```

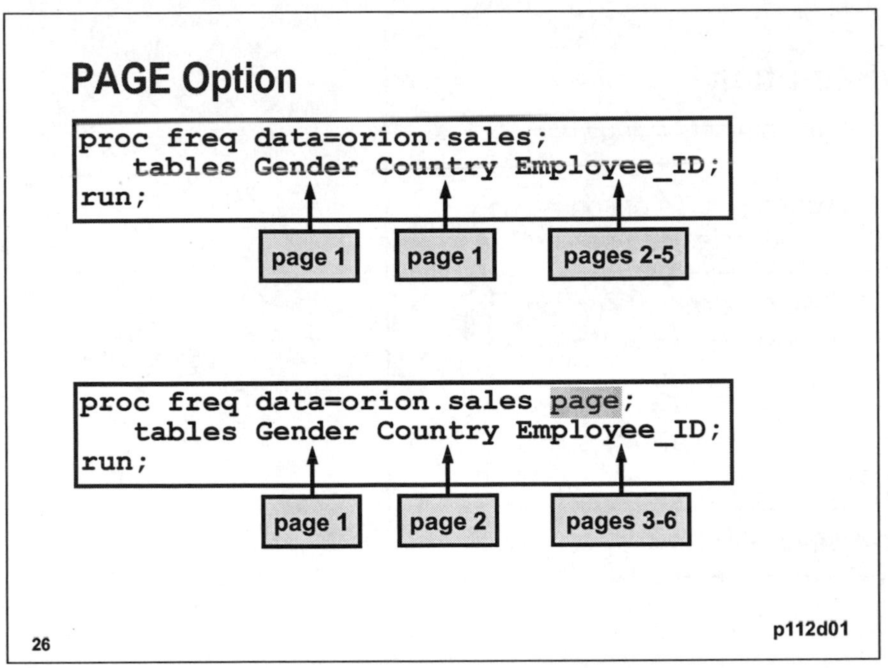
PAGE Option
proc freq data=orion.sales;
tables Gender Country Employee_ID;
run;
page 1
page 1
pages 2-5
proc freq data=orion.sales page;
tables Gender Country Employee_ID;
run;
page 1
page 2
pages 3-6
26
p112d01

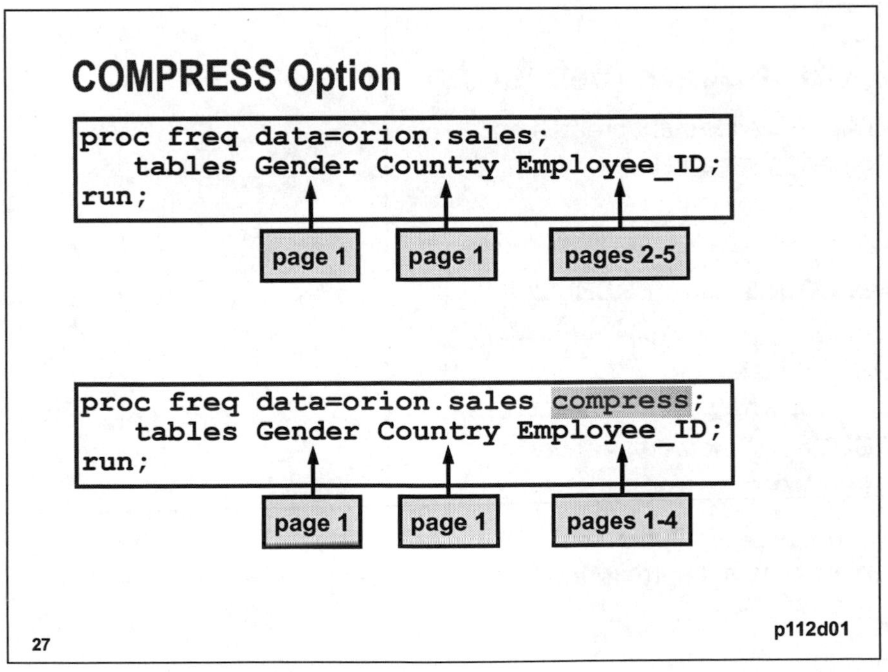
COMPRESS Option
proc freq data=orion.sales;
tables Gender Country Employee_ID;
run;
page 1
page 1
pages 2-5
proc freq data=orion.sales compress;
tables Gender Country Employee_ID;
run;
page 1
page 1
pages 1-4
27
p112d01

Output Data Sets (Self-Study)

PROC FREQ produces output data sets using two different methods.

- The TABLES statement with an OUT= option is used to create a data set with frequencies and percentages.

TABLES *variables* / **OUT=***SAS-data-set* *<options>*;

- The OUTPUT statement with an OUT= option is used to create a data set with specified statistics such as the chi-square statistic.

OUTPUT OUT=*SAS-data-set* *<options>*;

29

TABLES Statement OUT= Option (Self-Study)

The OUT= option in the TABLES statement creates an output data set with the following variables:

- BY variables
- TABLES statement variables
- the automatic variables **COUNT** and **PERCENT**
- other frequency and percentage variables requested with options in the TABLES statement

TABLES *variables* / **OUT=***SAS-data-set* *<options>*;

If more than one table request appears in the TABLES statement, the contents of the data set correspond to the last table request.

30

TABLES Statement OUT= Option (Self-Study)

```
proc freq data=orion.sales noprint;
   tables Gender Country / out=work.freq1;
run;

proc print data=work.freq1;
run;
```

PROC PRINT Output

Obs	Country	COUNT	PERCENT
1	AU	63	38.1818
2	US	102	61.8182

The NOPRINT option suppresses the display of all output.

31 p112d02

TABLES Statement OUT= Option (Self-Study)

```
proc freq data=orion.sales noprint;
   tables Gender*Country / out=work.freq2;
run;

proc print data=work.freq2;
run;
```

PROC PRINT Output

Obs	Gender	Country	COUNT	PERCENT
1	F	AU	27	16.3636
2	F	US	41	24.8485
3	M	AU	36	21.8182
4	M	US	61	36.9697

32 p112d02

TABLES Statement OUT= Option (Self-Study)

Options can be added to the TABLES statement after the forward slash to control the additional statistics added to the output data set.

Option	Description
OUTCUM	includes the cumulative frequency and cumulative percentage in the output data set for one-way frequency tables.
OUTPCT	includes the percentage of column frequency and row frequency in the output data set for *n*-way frequency tables.

33

TABLES Statement OUT= Option (Self-Study)

```
proc freq data=orion.sales noprint;
   tables Gender Country / out=work.freq3
                           outcum;
run;

proc print data=work.freq3;
run;
```

PROC PRINT Output

Obs	Country	COUNT	PERCENT	CUM_FREQ	CUM_PCT
1	AU	63	38.1818	63	38.182
2	US	102	61.8182	165	100.000

34

p112d02

TABLES Statement OUT= Option (Self-Study)

```
proc freq data=orion.sales noprint;
   tables Gender*Country / out=work.freq4
                           outpct;
run;

proc print data=work.freq4;
run;
```

PROC PRINT Output

Obs	Gender	Country	COUNT	PERCENT	PCT_ROW	PCT_COL
1	F	AU	27	16.3636	39.7059	42.8571
2	F	US	41	24.8485	60.2941	40.1961
3	M	AU	36	21.8182	37.1134	57.1429
4	M	US	61	36.9697	62.8866	59.8039

p112d02

35

OUTPUT Statement OUT= Option (Self-Study)

The OUT= option in the OUTPUT statement creates an output data set with the following variables:

- BY variables
- the variables requested in the TABLES statement
- variables that contain the specified statistics.

OUTPUT OUT=*SAS-data-set* *<options>***;**

If more than one table request appears in the TABLES statement, the contents of the data set corresponds to the last table request.

36

If there are multiple TABLES statements, the contents of the data set corresponds to the last TABLES statement.

OUTPUT Statement OUT= Option (Self-Study)

In order to specify that the output data set contain a particular statistic, you must have PROC FREQ compute the statistic by using the corresponding option in the TABLES statement.

```
proc freq data=orion.sales;
   tables Country / chisq;
   output out=work.freq5 chisq;
run;

proc print data=work.freq5;
run;
```

CHISQ requests chi-square tests and measures of association based on chi-square.

37 p112d03

OUTPUT Statement OUT= Option (Self-Study)

PROC FREQ Output

The FREQ Procedure

Country	Frequency	Percent	Cumulative Frequency	Cumulative Percent
AU	63	38.18	63	38.18
US	102	61.82	165	100.00

Chi-Square Test for Equal Proportions

Chi-Square	9.2182
DF	1
Pr > ChiSq	0.0024

Sample Size = 165

38

OUTPUT Statement OUT= Option (Self-Study)

PROC PRINT Output

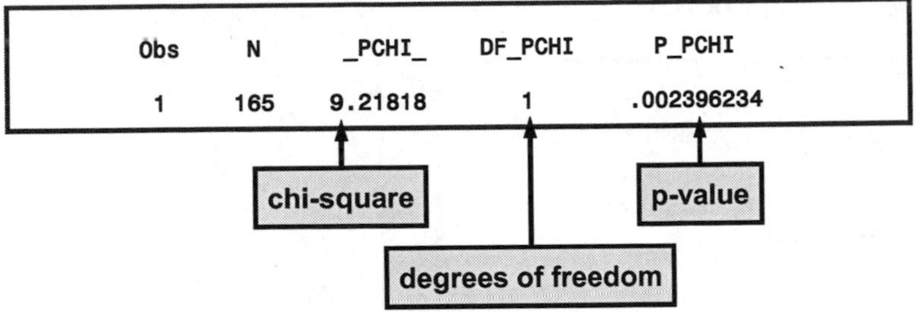

Obs N _PCHI_ DF_PCHI P_PCHI
1 165 9.21818 1 .002396234
chi-square
degrees of freedom
p-value

When you request a statistic, the OUTPUT data set contains that test statistic plus any associated standard error, confidence limits, *p*-values, and degrees of freedom.

39

12.03 Quiz

- Retrieve and submit program **p112a01**.

```
proc freq data=orion.sales;
   tables Gender / chisq out=freq6 outcum;
   output out=freq7 chisq;
run;
proc print data=freq6;
run;
proc print data=freq7;
run;
```

- Review the PROC FREQ output.
- Review the PROC PRINT output from the TABLES statement OUT= option.
- Review the PROC PRINT output from the OUTPUT statement OUT= option.

41

Output Data Sets (Self-Study)

Program **p112d04** is an example of combining multiple PROC FREQ output data sets into one data set.

Obs	Value	Frequency Count	Percent of Total Frequency	Chi-Square	P-Value
1	F	68	41.2121	.	.
2	M	97	58.7879	.	.
3	AU	63	38.1818	.	.
4	US	102	61.8182	.	.
5	Gender	.	.	5.09697	0.023968
6	Country	.	.	9.21818	0.002396

43

Exercises

Level 1

1. Counting Levels of a Variable with PROC FREQ

a. Retrieve the starter program **p112e01**.

b. Modify the program to produce two separate reports:

1) Display the number of distinct levels of **Customer_ID** and **Employee_ID** for retail orders.

a) Use a WHERE statement to limit the report to retail sales by specifying the condition **Order_Type=1**.

b) Display this report title: **Unique Customers and Salespersons for Retail Sales**.

If you do not want to see the counts for individual levels of **Customer_ID** and **Employee_ID**, add the NOPRINT option to the TABLES statement after a forward slash.

2) Display the number of distinct levels for **Customer_ID** for catalog and Internet orders.

a) Use a WHERE statement to limit the report to catalog and Internet sales by specifying the condition corresponding to **Order_Type** values other than 1.

b) Display this report title: **Unique Customers for Catalog and Internet**.

If you do not want to see the counts for individual levels of **Customer_ID**, add the NOPRINT option to the TABLES statement after a forward slash.

c. Submit the program to produce the following reports:

PROC FREQ Output

```
            Unique Customers and Salespersons for Retail Sales

                          The FREQ Procedure

                      Number of Variable Levels

                Variable        Label                Levels
                ---------------------------------------------
                Customer_ID     Customer ID              31
                Employee_ID     Employee ID             100
```

```
            Unique Customers for Catalog and Internet Sales

                          The FREQ Procedure

                      Number of Variable Levels

                Variable        Label                Levels
                ---------------------------------------------
                Customer_ID     Customer ID              63
```

Level 2

2. Producing Frequency Reports with PROC FREQ

a. Retrieve the starter program **p112e02**.

b. Add TABLES statements to the PROC FREQ step to produce three frequency reports:

1) Number of orders in each year: Apply the YEAR4. format to the **`Order_Date`** variable to combine all orders within the same year.

2) Number of orders of each order type: Apply the **`ordertypes.`** format defined in the starter program to the **`Order_Type`** variable. Suppress the cumulative frequency and percentages.

3) Number of orders for each combination of year and order type: Suppress all percentages that normally appear in each cell of an *n*-way table.

c. Submit the program to produce the following output:

PROC FREQ Output

```
                  Order Summary by Year and Type

                       The FREQ Procedure

                 Date Order was placed by Customer

                                             Cumulative    Cumulative
Order_Date    Frequency     Percent     Frequency       Percent
----------------------------------------------------------------
      2003          104       21.22           104         21.22
      2004           87       17.76           191         38.98
      2005           70       14.29           261         53.27
      2006          113       23.06           374         76.33
      2007          116       23.67           490        100.00


                           Order Type

                  Order_
                    Type    Frequency      Percent
                 ---------------------------------
                 Retail           260        53.06
                 Catalog          132        26.94
                 Internet          98        20.00


                Table of Order_Date by Order_Type

          Order_Date(Date Order was placed by Customer)
                    Order_Type(Order Type)

          Frequency|Retail   |Catalog  |Internet|  Total
          ---------+---------+---------+--------+
               2003 |      45 |      41 |     18 |    104
          ---------+---------+---------+--------+
               2004 |      51 |      20 |     16 |     87
          ---------+---------+---------+--------+
               2005 |      27 |      23 |     20 |     70
          ---------+---------+---------+--------+
               2006 |      67 |      33 |     13 |    113
          ---------+---------+---------+--------+
               2007 |      70 |      15 |     31 |    116
          ---------+---------+---------+--------+
          Total          260       132       98      490
```

Level 3

3. Displaying PROC FREQ Output in Descending Frequency Order

a. Retrieve the starter program **p112e03**.

b. Submit the program to produce the following report:

PROC FREQ Output

Customer Demographics

(Top two levels for each variable?)

The FREQ Procedure

Customer Country

Customer_ Country	Frequency	Percent	Cumulative Frequency	Cumulative Percent
AU	8	10.39	8	10.39
CA	15	19.48	23	29.87
DE	10	12.99	33	42.86
IL	5	6.49	38	49.35
TR	7	9.09	45	58.44
US	28	36.36	73	94.81
ZA	4	5.19	77	100.00

Customer Type Name

Customer_Type	Frequency	Percent	Cumulative Frequency	Cumulative Percent
Internet/Catalog Customers	8	10.39	8	10.39
Orion Club members high activity	11	14.29	19	24.68
Orion Club members medium activity	20	25.97	39	50.65
Orion Club Gold members high activity	10	12.99	49	63.64
Orion Club Gold members low activity	5	6.49	54	70.13
Orion Club Gold members medium activity	6	7.79	60	77.92
Orion Club members low activity	17	22.08	77	100.00

Customer Age Group

Customer_ Age_Group	Frequency	Percent	Cumulative Frequency	Cumulative Percent
15-30 years	22	28.57	22	28.57
31-45 years	27	35.06	49	63.64
46-60 years	14	18.18	63	81.82
61-75 years	14	18.18	77	100.00

c. What are the two most common values for each variable?

1) **Country** ________________ ________________

2) **Customer Type** ________________ ________________

3) **Customer Age Group** ________________ ________________

d. Modify the program to display the frequency counts in descending order.

> Documentation about the FREQ procedure can be found in the SAS Help and Documentation from the Contents tab (**SAS Products** ⇨ **Base SAS** ⇨ **Base SAS Procedures Guide: Statistical Procedures** ⇨ **The FREQ Procedure**). Look for an option in the PROC FREQ statement that can perform the requested action.

e. Submit the modified program.

f. What are the two most common values for each variable?

1) **Country** ________________ ________________

2) **Customer Type** ________________ ________________

3) **Customer Age Group** ________________ ________________

Do these answers match the previous set of answers?

Which report was easier to use to answer the questions correctly?

4. Creating an Output Data Set with PROC FREQ

a. Retrieve the starter program **p112e04**.

b. Create an output data set containing the frequency counts based on **Product_ID**.

> Creating an output data set from PROC FREQ results is discussed in the self-study content at the end of this section.

c. Combine the output data set with **orion.product_list** to obtain the **Product_Name** value for each **Product_ID** code.

d. Sort the merged data so that the most frequently ordered products appear at the top of the resulting data set. Print the first 10 observations, that is, those that represent the 10 products ordered most often.

> To limit the number of observations displayed by PROC PRINT, apply the OBS= data set option, as in the following:

```
proc print data=work.mydataset(obs=10);
```

e. Submit the program to produce the following report:

PROC PRINT Output

```
                    Top Ten Products by Number of Orders

                            Product
   Obs     Orders            Number    Product

     1        6        230100500056    Knife
     2        6        230100600030    Outback Sleeping Bag, Large,Left,Blue/Black
     3        5        230100600022    Expedition10,Medium,Right,Blue Ribbon
     4        5        240400300035    Smasher Shorts
     5        4        230100500082    Lucky Tech Intergal Wp/B Rain Pants
     6        4        230100600005    Basic 10, Left , Yellow/Black
     7        4        230100600016    Expedition Zero,Medium,Right,Charcoal
     8        4        230100600028    Expedition 20,Medium,Right,Forestgreen
     9        4        230100700008    Family Holiday 4
    10        4        230100700011    Hurricane 4
```

12.2 Using the MEANS Procedure

Objectives

- Calculate summary statistics and multilevel summaries with the MEANS procedure.
- Enhance summary tables with options.
- Produce output data sets by using the OUT= option in the OUTPUT statement. (Self-Study)
- Compare the SUMMARY procedure to the MEANS procedure. (Self-Study)

47

The MEANS Procedure

The *MEANS procedure* provides data summarization tools to compute descriptive statistics for variables across all observations and within groups of observations.

General form of the MEANS procedure:

```
PROC MEANS DATA=SAS-data-set <statistic(s)> <option(s)>;
     VAR analysis-variable(s);
     CLASS classification-variable(s);
RUN;
```

48

The MEANS Procedure

By default, the MEANS procedure reports the number of nonmissing observations, the mean, the standard deviation, the minimum value, and the maximum value of all numeric variables.

```
proc means data=orion.sales;
run;
```

The MEANS Procedure

Variable	N	Mean	Std Dev	Minimum	Maximum
Employee_ID	165	120713.90	450.0866939	120102.00	121145.00
Salary	165	31160.12	20082.67	22710.00	243190.00
Birth_Date	165	3622.58	5456.29	-5842.00	10490.00
Hire_Date	165	12054.28	4619.94	5114.00	17167.00

49 p112d05

The VAR Statement

The *VAR statement* identifies the analysis variables and their order in the results.

```
proc means data=orion.sales;
   var Salary;
run;
```

The MEANS Procedure

Analysis Variable : Salary

N	Mean	Std Dev	Minimum	Maximum
165	31160.12	20082.67	22710.00	243190.00

50 p112d05

The CLASS Statement

The *CLASS statement* identifies variables whose values define subgroups for the analysis.

```
proc means data=orion.sales;
   var Salary;
   class Gender Country;
run;
```

The MEANS Procedure

Analysis Variable : Salary

Gender	Country	N Obs	N	Mean	Std Dev	Minimum	Maximum
F	AU	27	27	27702.41	1728.23	25185.00	30890.00
	US	41	41	29460.98	8847.03	25390.00	83505.00
M	AU	36	36	32001.39	16592.45	25745.00	108255.00
	US	61	61	33336.15	29592.69	22710.00	243190.00

p112d05

51

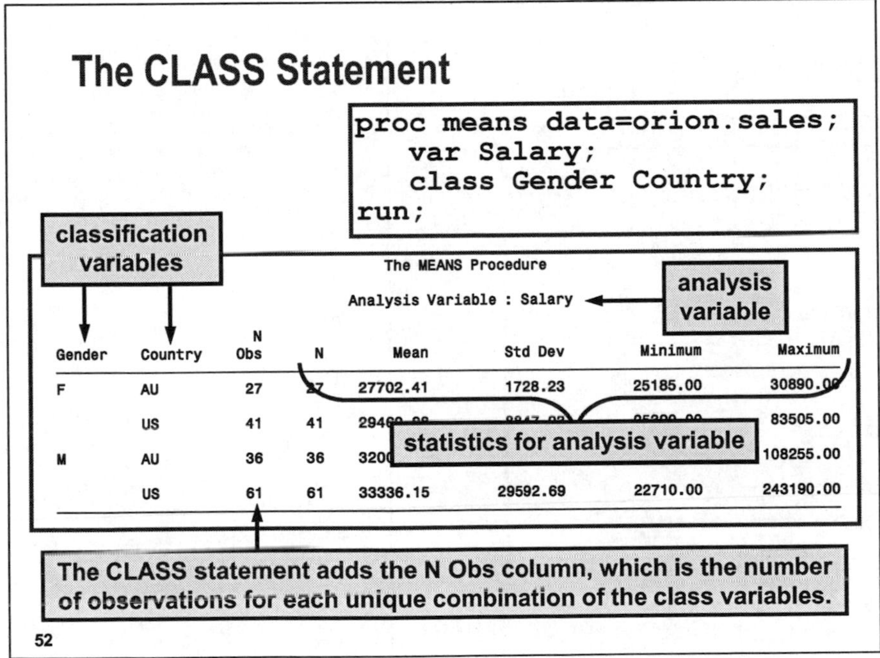

The CLASS Statement
proc means data=orion.sales;
var Salary;
class Gender Country;
run;
classification variables
analysis variable
statistics for analysis variable
The CLASS statement adds the N Obs column, which is the number of observations for each unique combination of the class variables.

52

12.04 Quiz

For a given data set, there are 63 observations with a **Country** value of AU. Of those 63 observations, only 61 observations have a value for **Salary**.

Which output is correct?

a.

Analysis Variable : Salary

Country	N Obs	N
AU	63	61

b.

Analysis Variable : Salary

Country	N Obs	N
AU	61	63

54

Additional SAS Statements

Additional statements can be added to enhance the reports.

```
proc format;
   value $ctryfmt 'AU'='Australia'
                  'US'='United States';
run;

options nodate pageno=1;
ods html file='p112d05.html';
proc means data=orion.sales;
   var Salary;
   class Gender Country;
   where Job_Title contains 'Rep';
   format Country $ctryfmt.;
   title 'Sales Rep Summary Report';
run;
ods html close;
```

56 p112d05

Additional SAS Statements

HTML Output

Sales Rep Summary Report

The MEANS Procedure

Analysis Variable : Salary							
Gender	Country	N Obs	N	Mean	Std Dev	Minimum	Maximum
F	Australia	27	27	27702.41	1728.23	25185.00	30890.00
	United States	40	40	28109.88	1874.39	25390.00	32985.00
M	Australia	34	34	28112.35	2295.81	25745.00	36605.00
	United States	58	58	27775.26	2311.91	22710.00	35990.00

57

PROC MEANS Statistics

The statistics to compute and the order to display them can be specified in the PROC MEANS statement.

```
proc means data=orion.sales sum mean range;
   var Salary;
   class Country;
run;
```

```
                         The MEANS Procedure

                    Analysis Variable : Salary

               N
Country      Obs              Sum            Mean            Range
-------------------------------------------------------------------
AU            63       1900015.00        30158.97         83070.00

US           102       3241405.00        31778.48        220480.00
-------------------------------------------------------------------
```

p112d05

58

PROC MEANS Statistics

Descriptive Statistic Keywords				
CLM	CSS	CV	LCLM	MAX
MEAN	MIN	MODE	N	NMISS
KURTOSIS	RANGE	SKEWNESS	STDDEV	STDERR
SUM	SUMWGT	UCLM	USS	VAR

Quantile Statistic Keywords				
MEDIAN | P50	P1	P5	P10	Q1 | P25
Q3 | P75	P90	P95	P99	QRANGE

Hypothesis Testing Keywords				
PROBT	T			

59

PROC MEANS Statement Options

Options can also be placed in the PROC MEANS statement.

Option	Description
MAXDEC=	specifies the number of decimal places to use in printing the statistics.
FW=	specifies the field width to use in displaying the statistics.
NONOBS	suppresses reporting the total number of observations for each unique combination of the class variables.

60

MAXDEC= Option

```
proc means data=orion.sales maxdec=0;
```

Analysis Variable : Salary

Country	N Obs	N	Mean	Std Dev	Minimum	Maximum
AU	63	63	30159	12699	25185	108255
US	102	102	31778	23556	22710	243190

```
proc means data=orion.sales maxdec=1;
```

Analysis Variable : Salary

Country	N Obs	N	Mean	Std Dev	Minimum	Maximum
AU	63	63	30159.0	12699.1	25185.0	108255.0
US	102	102	31778.5	23555.8	22710.0	243190.0

61

p112d05

FW= Option

```
proc means data=orion.sales;
```

Analysis Variable : Salary

Country	N Obs	N	Mean	Std Dev	Minimum	Maximum
AU	63	63	30158.97	12699.14	25185.00	108255.00
US	102	102	31778.48	23555.84	22710.00	243190.00

```
proc means data=orion.sales fw=15;
```

Analysis Variable : Salary

Country	N Obs	N	Mean	Std Dev	Minimum	Maximum
AU	63	63	30158.96825397	12699.13932690	25185.00000000	108255
US	102	102	31778.48039216	23555.84171928	22710.00000000	243190

62

p112d05

NONOBS Option

```
proc means data=orion.sales;
```

Analysis Variable : Salary

Country	N Obs	N	Mean	Std Dev	Minimum	Maximum
AU	63	63	30158.97	12699.14	25185.00	108255.00
US	102	102	31778.48	23555.84	22710.00	243190.00

```
proc means data=orion.sales nonobs;
```

Analysis Variable : Salary

Country	N	Mean	Std Dev	Minimum	Maximum
AU	63	30158.97	12699.14	25185.00	108255.00
US	102	31778.48	23555.84	22710.00	243190.00

63

p112d05

Output Data Sets (Self-Study)

PROC MEANS produces output data sets using the following method:

OUTPUT OUT=*SAS-data-set <options>***;**

The output data set contains the following variables:

- BY variables
- class variables
- the automatic variables **`_TYPE_`** and **`_FREQ_`**
- the variables requested in the OUTPUT statement

65

OUTPUT Statement OUT= Option (Self-Study)

The statistics in the PROC statement impact only the MEANS report, not the data set.

```
proc means data=orion.sales sum mean range;
   var Salary;
   class Gender Country;
   output out=work.means1;
run;

proc print data=work.means1;
run;
```

66 p112d06

OUTPUT Statement OUT= Option (Self-Study)

Partial PROC PRINT Output

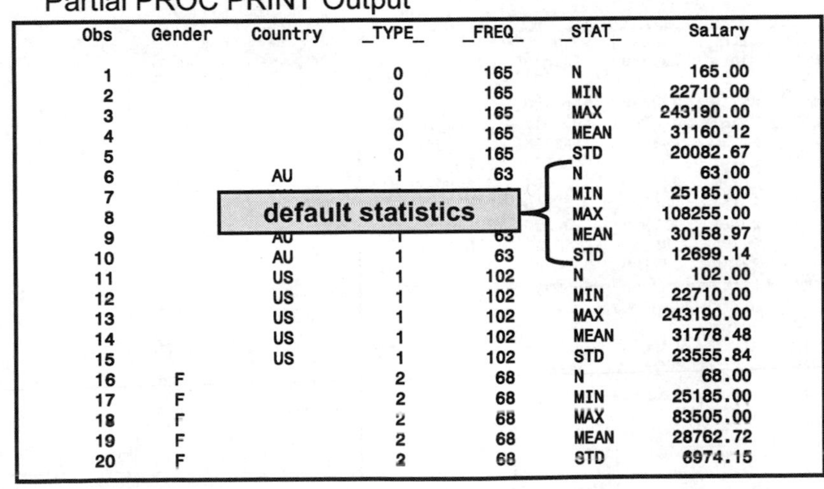

Obs	Gender	Country	_TYPE_	_FREQ_	_STAT_	Salary
1			0	165	N	165.00
2			0	165	MIN	22710.00
3			0	165	MAX	243190.00
4			0	165	MEAN	31160.12
5			0	165	STD	20082.67
6		AU	1	63	N	63.00
7					MIN	25185.00
8					MAX	108255.00
9		AU	1	63	MEAN	30158.97
10		AU	1	63	STD	12699.14
11		US	1	102	N	102.00
12		US	1	102	MIN	22710.00
13		US	1	102	MAX	243190.00
14		US	1	102	MEAN	31778.48
15		US	1	102	STD	23555.84
16	F		2	68	N	68.00
17	F		2	68	MIN	25185.00
18	F		2	68	MAX	83505.00
19	F		2	68	MEAN	28762.72
20	F		2	68	STD	6974.15

67

OUTPUT Statement OUT= Option (Self-Study)

The OUTPUT statement can also do the following:

- specify the statistics for the output data set
- select and name variables

```
proc means data=orion.sales noprint;
   var Salary;
   class Gender Country;
   output out=work.means2
          min=minSalary max=maxSalary
          sum=sumSalary mean=aveSalary;
run;

proc print data=work.means2;
run;
```

The NOPRINT option suppresses the display of all output.

68 p112d06

OUTPUT Statement OUT= Option (Self-Study)

PROC PRINT Output

Obs	Gender	Country	_TYPE_	_FREQ_	min Salary	max Salary	sum Salary	ave Salary
1			0	165	22710	243190	5141420	31160.12
2		AU	1	63	25185	108255	1900015	30158.97
3		US	1	102	22710	243190	3241405	31778.48
4	F		2	68	25185	83505	1955865	28762.72
5	M		2	97	22710	243190	3185555	32840.77
6	F	AU	3	27	25185	30890	747965	27702.41
7	F	US	3	41	25390	83505	1207900	29460.98
8	M	AU	3	36	25745	108255	1152050	32001.39
9	M	US	3	61	22710	243190	2033505	33336.15

69

OUTPUT Statement OUT= Option (Self-Study)

`_TYPE_` is a numeric variable that shows which combination of class variables produced the summary statistics in that observation.

PROC PRINT Output

Obs	Gender	Country	_TYPE_					
1			0					
2		AU	1					
3		US	1					
4	F		2					
5	M		2					
6	F	AU	3	27	25185	30890	747965	27702.41
7	F	US	3					
8	M	AU	3					
9	M	US	3	61	22710	243190	2033505	33336.15

overall summary (_TYPE_ 0)

summary by **`Country`** only (_TYPE_ 1)

summary by **`Gender`** only (_TYPE_ 2)

summary by **`Country`** and **`Gender`** (_TYPE_ 3)

70

OUTPUT Statement OUT= Option (Self-Study)

Obs	Gender	Country	_TYPE_	_FREQ_	min Salary	max Salary	sum Salary	ave Salary
1			0	165	22710	243190	5141420	31160.12
2		AU	1	63	25185	108255	1900015	30158.97
3		US	1	102	22710	243190	3241405	31778.48
4	F		2	68	25185	83505	1955865	28762.72
5	M		2	97	22710	243190	3185555	32840.77
6	F	AU	3	27	25185	30890	747965	27702.41
7	F	US	3	41	25390	83505	1207900	29460.98
8	M	AU	3	36	25745	108255	1152050	32001.39
9	M	US	3	61	22710	243190	2033505	33336.15

TYPE	Type of Summary	_FREQ_
0	overall summary	165
1	summary by **`Country`** only	63 AU + 102 AU = 165
2	summary by **`Gender`** only	68 F + 97 M = 165
3	summary by **`Country`** and **`Gender`**	27 F AU + 41 F US + 36 M AU + 61 M US = 165

71

OUTPUT Statement OUT= Option (Self-Study)

Options can be added to the PROC MEANS statement to control the output data set.

Option	Description
NWAY	specifies that the output data set contain only statistics for the observations with the highest **_TYPE_** value.
DESCENDTYPES	orders the output data set by descending **_TYPE_** value.
CHARTYPE	specifies that the **_TYPE_** variable in the output data set is a character representation of the binary value of **_TYPE_**.

72

OUTPUT Statement OUT= Option (Self-Study)

without options

Obs	Gender	Country	_TYPE_	_FREQ_	min Salary	max Salary	sum Salary	ave Salary
1			0	165	22710	243190	5141420	31160.12
2		AU	1	63	25185	108255	1900015	30158.97
3		US	1	102	22710	243190	3241405	31778.48
4	F		2	68	25185	83505	1955865	28762.72
5	M		2	97	22710	243190	3185555	32840.77
6	F	AU	3	27	25185	30890	747965	27702.41
7	F	US	3	41	25390	83505	1207900	29460.98
8	M	AU	3	36	25745	108255	1152050	32001.39
9	M	US	3	61	22710	243190	2033505	33336.15

with NWAY

Obs	Gender	Country	_TYPE_	_FREQ_	min Salary	max Salary	sum Salary	ave Salary
1	F	AU	3	27	25185	30890	747965	27702.41
2	F	US	3	41	25390	83505	1207900	29460.98
3	M	AU	3	36	25745	108255	1152050	32001.39
4	M	US	3	61	22710	243190	2033505	33336.15

73 p112d06

OUTPUT Statement OUT= Option (Self-Study)

with DESCENDTYPES

Obs	Gender	Country	_TYPE_	_FREQ_	min Salary	max Salary	sum Salary	ave Salary
1	F	AU	3	27	25185	30890	747965	27702.41
2	F	US	3	41	25390	83505	1207900	29460.98
3	M	AU	3	36	25745	108255	1152050	32001.39
4	M	US	3	61	22710	243190	2033505	33336.15
5	F		2	68	25185	83505	1955865	28762.72
6	M		2	97	22710	243190	3185555	32840.77
7		AU	1	63	25185	108255	1900015	30158.97
8		US	1	102	22710	243190	3241405	31778.48
9			0	165	22710	243190	5141420	31160.12

74

p112d06

OUTPUT Statement OUT= Option (Self-Study)

with CHARTYPE

Obs	Gender	Country	_TYPE_	_FREQ_	min Salary	max Salary	sum Salary	ave Salary
1			00	165	22710	243190	5141420	31160.12
2		AU	01	63	25185	108255	1900015	30158.97
3		US	01	102	22710	243190	3241405	31778.48
4	F		10	68	25185	83505	1955865	28762.72
5	M		10	97	22710	243190	3185555	32840.77
6	F	AU	11	27	25185	30890	747965	27702.41
7	F	US	11	41	25390	83505	1207900	29460.98
8	M	AU	11	36	25745	108255	1152050	32001.39
9	M	US	11	61	22710	243190	2033505	33336.15

75

p112d06

12.05 Quiz

- Retrieve and submit program **p112a02**.
- Review the PROC PRINT output.
- Add a WHERE statement to the PROC PRINT step to subset `_TYPE_` for observations summarized by `Gender` only.
- Submit the program and verify the results.

77

OUTPUT Statement OUT= Option (Self-Study)

Program **p112d07** is an example of merging a PROC MEANS output data set with a detail data set to create the following partial report.

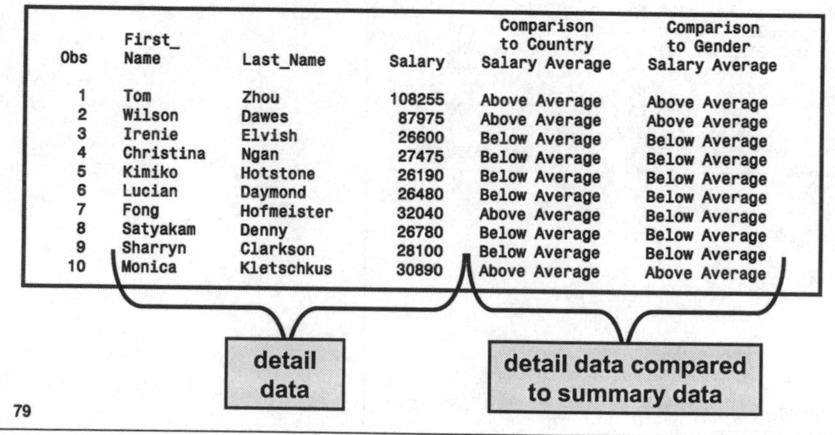

Obs	First_ Name	Last_Name	Salary	Comparison to Country Salary Average	Comparison to Gender Salary Average
1	Tom	Zhou	108255	Above Average	Above Average
2	Wilson	Dawes	87975	Above Average	Above Average
3	Irenie	Elvish	26600	Below Average	Below Average
4	Christina	Ngan	27475	Below Average	Below Average
5	Kimiko	Hotstone	26190	Below Average	Below Average
6	Lucian	Daymond	26480	Below Average	Below Average
7	Fong	Hofmeister	32040	Above Average	Below Average
8	Satyakam	Denny	26780	Below Average	Below Average
9	Sharryn	Clarkson	28100	Below Average	Below Average
10	Monica	Kletschkus	30890	Above Average	Above Average

79

The SUMMARY Procedure (Self-Study)

The SUMMARY procedure provides data summarization tools to compute descriptive statistics for variables across all observations and within groups of observations.

General form of the SUMMARY procedure:

```
PROC SUMMARY DATA=SAS-data-set <statistic(s)>
                                  <option(s)>;
     VAR analysis-variable(s);
     CLASS classification-variable(s);
RUN;
```

80

The SUMMARY Procedure (Self-Study)

The SUMMARY procedure uses the same syntax as the MEANS procedure.

The only differences to the two procedures are the following:

PROC MEANS	PROC SUMMARY
The PRINT option is set by default, which displays output.	The NOPRINT option is set by default, which displays no output.
Omitting the VAR statement analyzes all the numeric variables.	Omitting the VAR statement produces a simple count of observations.

81

Exercises

Level 1

5. Creating a Summary Report with PROC MEANS

a. Retrieve the starter program **p112e05**.

b. Display only the SUM statistic for the **Total_Retail_Price** variable.

c. Display separate statistics for the combination of **Order_Date** and **Order_Type**. Apply the ORDERTYPES. format so that the order types are displayed as text descriptions, not numbers. Apply the YEAR4. format so that order dates are displayed as years, not individual dates.

d. Submit the program to produce the following report:

Partial PROC MEANS Output

```
                Revenue (in U.S. Dollars) Earned from All Orders

                           The MEANS Procedure

     Analysis Variable : Total_Retail_Price Total Retail Price for This Product

                  Date
                 Order
                   was
                placed
                    by    Order        N
              Customer    Type       Obs             Sum
              ------------------------------------------
                  2003    Retail      53         7938.80

                          Catalog     52        10668.08

                          Internet    23         4124.05

                  2004    Retail      63         9012.22

                          Catalog     23         3494.60

                          Internet    22         3275.70

                  2005    Retail      34         5651.29

                          Catalog     33         6569.98

                          Internet    23         4626.40
```

Level 2

6. Analyzing Missing Numeric Values with PROC MEANS

a. Retrieve the starter program **p112e06**.

b. Display the number of missing values and the number of nonmissing values present in the **`Birth_Date`**, **`Emp_Hire_Date`**, and **`Emp_Term_Date`** variables.

c. Suppress any decimal places in the displayed statistics.

d. Display separate statistics for each value of **`Gender`**.

e. Suppress the output column that displays the total number of observations in each classification group.

f. Submit the program to produce the following report:

PROC MEANS Output

Number of Missing and Non-Missing Date Values

The MEANS Procedure

Employee Gender	Variable	Label	N Miss	N
F	Birth_Date	Employee Birth Date	0	191
	Emp_Hire_Date	Employee Hire Date	0	191
	Emp_Term_Date	Employee Termination Date	139	52
M	Birth_Date	Employee Birth Date	0	233
	Emp_Hire_Date	Employee Hire Date	0	233
	Emp_Term_Date	Employee Termination Date	169	64

Level 3

7. Analyzing All Possible Classification Levels with PROC MEANS

a. Retrieve the starter program **p112c07**.

b. Display the following statistics in the report:

1) Lower Confidence Limit for the Mean

2) Mean

3) Upper Confidence Limit for the Mean

c. Change the α value for the confidence limits to `0.10`, resulting in a 90% confidence limit.

d. Display all countries stored in the **`Work.countries`** data set in the report, even if there are no customers from that country.

> Documentation about the MEANS procedure can be found in the SAS Help and Documentation from the Contents tab (**SAS Products** ⇨ **Base SAS** ⇨ **Base SAS 9.2 Procedures Guide** ⇨ **Procedures** ⇨ **The MEANS Procedure**). Look for options in the PROC MEANS statement that can perform the requested actions.

e. Submit the program to produce the following report:

PROC MEANS Output

Average Age of Customers in Each Country

The MEANS Procedure

Analysis Variable : Customer_Age Customer Age

Customer Country	N Obs	Lower 90% CL for Mean	Mean	Upper 90% CL for Mean
AU	8	42.4983854	52.3750000	62.2516146
BE	0	.	.	.
CA	15	31.2270622	40.0000000	48.7729378
DE	10	35.2564025	46.6000000	57.9435975
DK	0	.	.	.
ES	0	.	.	.
FR	0	.	.	.
GB	0	.	.	.
IL	5	30.1150331	40.0000000	49.8849669
NL	0	.	.	.
NO	0	.	.	.
PT	0	.	.	.
SE	0	.	.	.
TR	7	30.5050705	39.4285714	48.3520724
US	28	35.6505942	40.4285714	45.2065486
ZA	4	12.1696649	34.7500000	57.3303351

8. Creating an Output Data Set with PROC MEANS

a. Retrieve the starter program **p112e08**.

b. Create an output data set containing the sum of `Total_Retail_Price` values for each `Product_ID`.

> Creating an output data set from PROC MEANS results is discussed in the self-study content at the end of this section.

c. Combine the output data set with `orion.product_list` to obtain the `Product_Name` value for each `Product_ID` code.

d. Sort the merged data so that the products with higher revenues appear at the top of the resulting data set. Print the first 10 observations, that is, those that represent the ten products with the most revenue.

> To limit the number of observations displayed by PROC PRINT, apply the OBS= data set option, as in the following:

```
proc print data=work.mydataset(obs=10);
```

e. Display the revenue values with a leading euro symbol (€), a period that separates every three digits, and a comma that separates the decimal fraction.

f. Submit the program to produce the following report:

PROC MEANS Output

```
                         Top Ten Products by Revenue

                                 Product
 Obs     Revenue                  Number     Product

   1       €3.391,80        230100700009     Family Holiday 6
   2       €3.080,30        230100700008     Family Holiday 4
   3       €2.250,00        230100700011     Hurricane 4
   4       €1.937,20        240200100173     Proplay Executive Bi-Metal Graphite
   5       €1.796,00        240200100076     Expert Men's Firesole Driver
   6       €1.561,80        240300300090     Top R&D Long Jacket
   7       €1.514,40        240300300070     Top Men's R&D Ultimate Jacket
   8       €1.510,80        240100400098     Rollerskate  Roller Skates Ex9 76mm/78a Biofl
   9       €1.424,40        240100400129     Rollerskate Roller Skates Sq9 80-76mm/78a
  10       €1.343,30        240100400043     Perfect Fit Men's  Roller Skates
```

12.3 Using the TABULATE Procedure (Self-Study)

Objectives

- Create one-, two-, and three-dimensional tabular reports using the TABULATE procedure.
- Produce output data sets by using the OUT= option in the PROC statement.

85

The TABULATE Procedure

The TABULATE procedure displays descriptive statistics in tabular format.

General form of the TABULATE procedure:

```
PROC TABULATE DATA=SAS-data-set <options>;
      CLASS classification-variable(s);
      VAR analysis-variable(s);
      TABLE  page-expression,
             row-expression,
             column-expression </ option(s)>;
RUN;
```

86

The TABULATE procedure computes many of the same statistics that are computed by other descriptive statistical procedures such as PROC MEANS and PROC FREQ.

A CLASS statement or a VAR statement must be specified, but both statements together are not required.

Dimensional Tables

The TABULATE procedure produces one-, two-, or three-dimensional tables.

	page dimension	row dimension	column dimension
one-dimensional			✓
two-dimensional		✓	✓
three-dimensional	✓	✓	✓

87

One-Dimensional Table

Country	
AU	US
N	N
63.00	102.00

- `Country` is in the column dimension.

88

Two-Dimensional Table

	Country	
	AU	US
	N	N
Gender		
F	27.00	41.00
M	36.00	61.00

- **`Country`** is in the column dimension.
- **`Gender`** is in the row dimension.

89

Three-Dimensional Table

Job_Title Sales Rep. I

	Country	
	AU	US
	N	N
Gender		
F	8.00	13.00
M	13.00	29.00

- **`Country`** is in the column dimension.
- **`Gender`** is in the row dimension.
- **`Job_Title`** is in the page dimension.

90

The TABLE Statement

The TABLE statement describes the structure of the table.

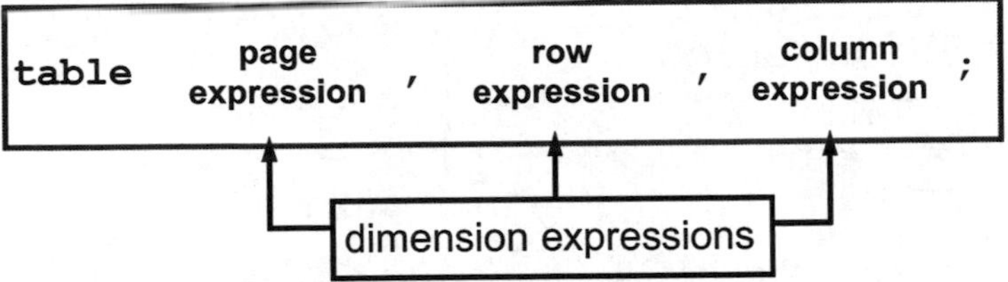

- Commas separate the dimension expressions.
- Every variable that is part of a dimension expression must be specified as a classification variable (CLASS statement) or an analysis variable (VAR statement).

91

The TABLE Statement

```
table   page expression , row expression , column expression ;
```

Examples:

```
table Country;
```

```
table Gender , Country;
```

```
table Job_Title , Gender , Country;
```

92

The CLASS Statement

The CLASS statement identifies variables to be used as classification, or grouping, variables.

General form of the CLASS statement:

CLASS *classification-variable(s)*;

- N, the number of nonmissing values, is the default statistic for classification variables.
- Examples of classification variables:
  Job_Title, **Gender**, and **Country**

93

Class variables

- can be numeric or character
- identify classes or categories on which calculations are done
- represent discrete categories if they are numeric (for example, **Year**).

The VAR Statement

The VAR statement identifies the numeric variables for which statistics are calculated.

General form of the VAR statement:

VAR *analysis-variable(s)*;

- SUM is the default statistic for analysis variables.
- Examples of analysis variables:

  Salary and **Bonus**

94

Analysis variables

- are always numeric
- tend to be continuous
- are appropriate for calculating averages, sums, or other statistics.

One-Dimensional Table

```
proc tabulate data=orion.sales;
   class Country;
   table Country;
run;
```

Country	
AU	US
N	N
63.00	102.00

95 p112d08

If there are only class variables in the TABLE statement, the default statistic is N, or number of nonmissing values.

Two-Dimensional Table

```
proc tabulate data=orion.sales;
   class Gender Country;
   table Gender, Country;
run;
```

	Country	
	AU	US
	N	N
Gender		
F	27.00	41.00
M	36.00	61.00

96 p112d08

Three-Dimensional Table

```
proc tabulate data=orion.sales;
   class Job_Title Gender Country;
   table Job_Title, Gender, Country;
run;
```

97 p112d08

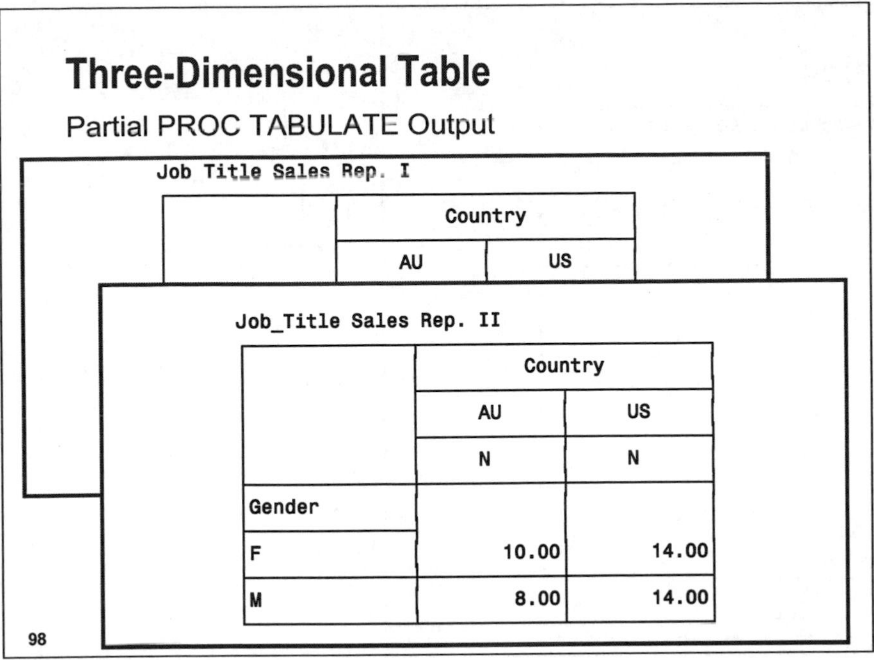

	Country	
	AU	US
	N	N
Gender		
F	10.00	14.00
M	8.00	14.00

Dimension Expression

Elements that can be used in a dimension expression:

- classification variables
- analysis variables
- the universal class variable ALL
- keywords for statistics

Operators that can be used in a dimension expression:

- blank, which concatenates table information
- asterisk *, which crosses table information
- parentheses (), which group elements

99

Other operators include

- brackets < >, which name the denominator for row or column percentages
- equal sign =, which changes the label for a variable or a statistic.

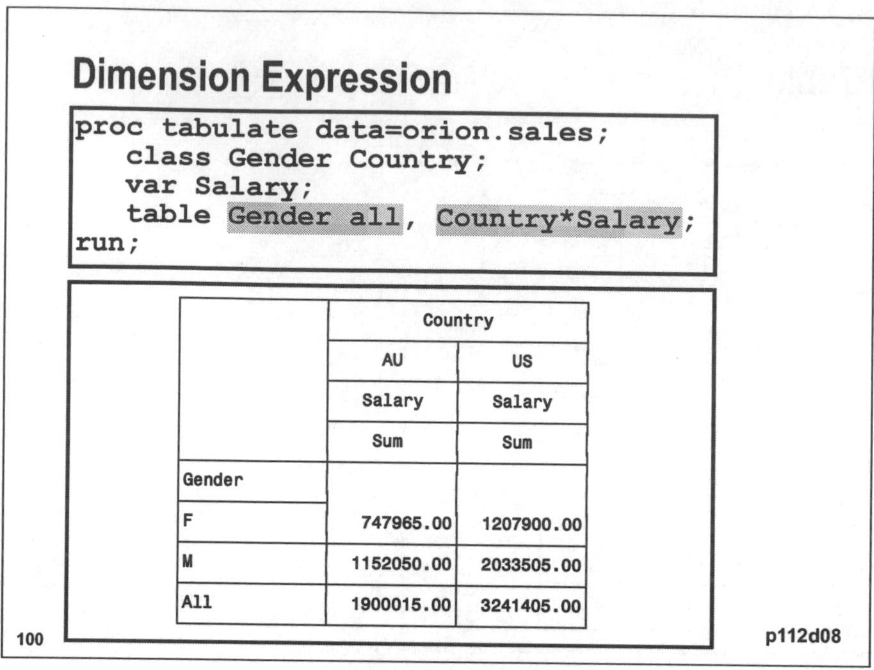

If there are analysis variables in the TABLE statement, the default statistic is SUM.

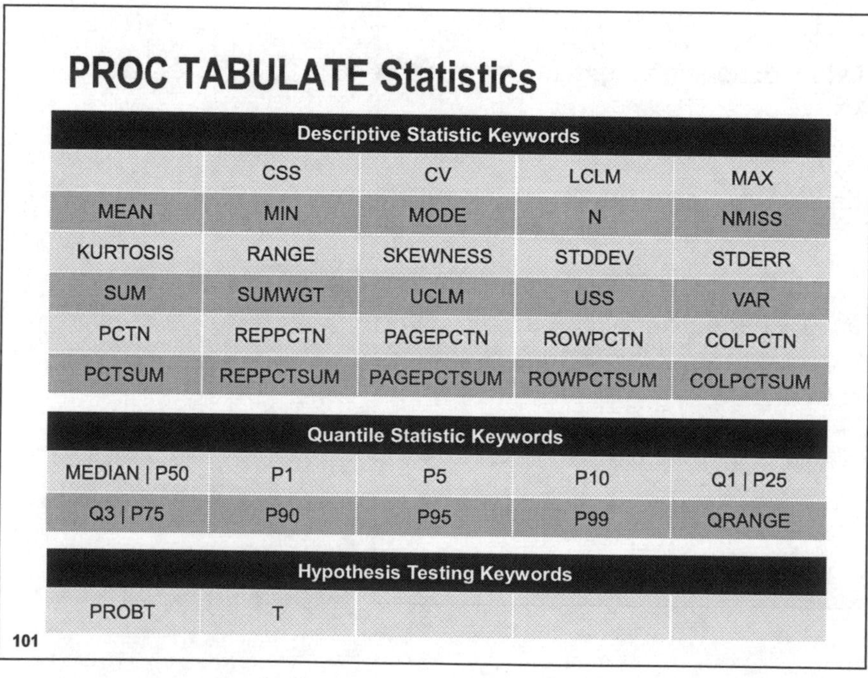

PROC TABULATE Statistics

```
proc tabulate data=orion.sales;
   class Gender Country;
   var Salary;
   table Gender all, Country*Salary*(min max);
run;
```

	Country			
	AU		US	
	Salary		Salary	
	Min	Max	Min	Max
Gender				
F	25185.00	30890.00	25390.00	83505.00
M	25745.00	108255.00	22710.00	243190.00
All	25185.00	108255.00	22710.00	243190.00

Additional SAS Statements

Additional statements can be added to enhance the report.

```
proc format;
   value $ctryfmt 'AU'='Australia'
                  'US'='United States';
run;

options nodate pageno=1;

ods html file='p112d08.html';
proc tabulate data=orion.sales;
   class Gender Country;
   var Salary;
   table Gender all, Country*Salary*(min max);
   where Job_Title contains 'Rep';
   label Salary='Annual Salary';
   format Country $ctryfmt.;
   title 'Sales Rep Tabular Report';
run;
ods html close;
```

p112d08

103

Additional SAS Statements

HTML Output

Sales Rep Tabular Report

	Country			
	Australia		United States	
	Annual Salary		Annual Salary	
	Min	Max	Min	Max
Gender				
F	25185.00	30890.00	25390.00	32985.00
M	25745.00	36605.00	22710.00	35990.00
All	25185.00	36605.00	22710.00	35990.00

104

Output Data Sets

PROC TABULATE produces output data sets using the following method:

```
PROC TABULATE DATA=SAS-data-set
              OUT=SAS-data-set <options>;
```

The output data set contains the following variables:

- BY variables
- class variables
- the automatic variables `_TYPE_`, `_PAGE_`, and `_TABLE_`
- calculated statistics

106

PROC Statement OUT= Option

```
proc tabulate data=orion.sales
              out=work.tabulate;
   where Job_Title contains 'Rep';
   class Job_Title Gender Country;
   table Country;
   table Gender, Country;
   table Job_Title, Gender, Country;
run;

proc print data=work.tabulate;
run;
```

107

p112d09

PROC Statement OUT= Option

Partial PROC PRINT Output

Obs	Job_Title	Gender	Country	_TYPE_	_PAGE_	_TABLE_	N
1			AU	001	1	1	61
2			US	001	1	1	98
3		F	AU	011	1	2	27
4		F	US	011	1	2	40
5		M	AU	011	1	2	34
6		M	US	011	1	2	58
7	Sales Rep. I	F	AU	111	1	3	8
8	Sales Rep. I	F	US	111	1	3	13
9	Sales Rep. I	M	AU	111	1	3	13
10	Sales Rep. I	M	US	111	1	3	29
11	Sales Rep. II	F	AU	111	2	3	10
12	Sales Rep. II	F	US	111	2	3	14
13	Sales Rep. II	M	AU	111	2	3	8
14	Sales Rep. II	M	US	111	2	3	14
15	Sales Rep. III	F	AU	111	3	3	7
16	Sales Rep. III	F	US	111	3	3	8
17	Sales Rep. III	M	AU	111	3	3	10
18	Sales Rep. III	M	US	111	3	3	9

108

PROC Statement OUT= Option

`_TYPE_` is a character variable that shows which combination of class variables produced the summary statistics in that observation.

Partial PROC PRINT Output

Obs	Job_Title	Gender	Country	_TYPE_	_PAGE_	_TABLE_	N
1			AU	001	1	1	61
2			US	001	1	1	98
3		F	AU	011	1	2	27
4		F	US	011	[illegible]	[illegible]	[illegible]
5		M	AU	011	[illegible]	[illegible]	[illegible]
6		M	US	011	[illegible]	[illegible]	[illegible]

0 for **`Job_Title`**, 1 for **`Gender`**, and 1 for **`Country`**

109

PROC Statement OUT= Option

`_PAGE_` is a numeric variable that shows the logical page number that contains that observation.

Partial PROC PRINT Output

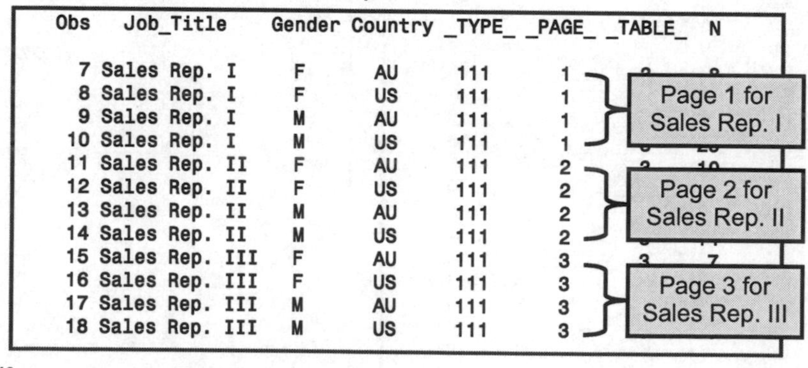

Obs	Job_Title	Gender	Country	_TYPE_	_PAGE_	_TABLE_	N
7	Sales Rep. I	F	AU	111	1	[illegible]	[illegible]
8	Sales Rep. I	F	US	111	1	[illegible]	[illegible]
9	Sales Rep. I	M	AU	111	1	[illegible]	[illegible]
10	Sales Rep. I	M	US	111	1	[illegible]	[illegible]
11	Sales Rep. II	F	AU	111	2	[illegible]	[illegible]
12	Sales Rep. II	F	US	111	2	[illegible]	[illegible]
13	Sales Rep. II	M	AU	111	2	[illegible]	[illegible]
14	Sales Rep. II	M	US	111	2	[illegible]	[illegible]
15	Sales Rep. III	F	AU	111	3	3	7
16	Sales Rep. III	F	US	111	3	[illegible]	[illegible]
17	Sales Rep. III	M	AU	111	3	[illegible]	[illegible]
18	Sales Rep. III	M	US	111	3	[illegible]	[illegible]

110

PROC Statement OUT= Option

`_TABLE_` is a numeric variable that shows the number of the TABLE statement that contains that observation.

Partial PROC PRINT Output

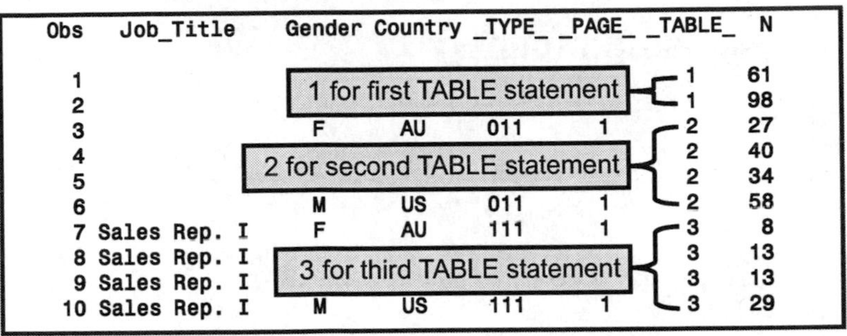

Obs	Job_Title	Gender	Country	_TYPE_	_PAGE_	_TABLE_	N
1						1	61
2						1	98
3		F	AU	011	1	2	27
4						2	40
5						2	34
6		M	US	011	1	2	58
7	Sales Rep. I	F	AU	111	1	3	8
8	Sales Rep. I					3	13
9	Sales Rep. I					3	13
10	Sales Rep. I	M	US	111	1	3	29

111

Exercises

Level 1

9. Creating a Simple Tabular Report with PROC TABULATE

a. Retrieve the starter program **p112e09**.

b. Add a CLASS statement to enable **Customer_Group** and **Customer_Gender** as classification variables.

c. Add a VAR statement to enable **Customer_Age** as an analysis variable

d. Add a TABLE statement to create a report with the following characteristics:

1) **Customer_Group** defines the rows.

2) An extra row that combines all groups appears at the bottom of the table.

3) **Customer_Gender** defines the columns.

4) The N and MEAN statistics based on **Customer_Age** are displayed for each combination of **Customer_Group** and **Customer_Gender**.

e. Submit the program to produce the following report:

PROC TABULATE Output

Ages of Customers by Group and Gender

	Customer Gender			
	F		M	
	Customer Age		Customer Age	
	N	Mean	N	Mean
Customer Group Name				
Internet/Catalog Customers	4.00	49.25	4.00	54.25
Orion Club Gold members	11.00	35.36	10.00	38.90
Orion Club members	15.00	32.53	33.00	47.03
All	30.00	35.80	47.00	45.91

Level 2

10. Creating a Three-Dimensional Tabular Report with PROC TABULATE

a. Retrieve the starter program **p112e10**.

b. Define a tabular report with the following characteristics:

1) **`Customer_Gender`** defines the page dimension.

2) **`Customer_Group`** defines the row dimension.

3) The column dimension should display the number of customers and the percentage of customers in each category (COLPCTN).

> Change the headers for the statistic columns with a KEYLABEL statement. Documentation about the KEYLABEL statement can be found in the SAS Help and Documentation from the Contents tab (**SAS Products** ⇨ **Base SAS** ⇨ **Base SAS 9.2 Procedures Guide** ⇨ **Procedures** ⇨ **The TABULATE Procedure**).

c. Submit the program to produce the following two-page report:

PROC TABULATE Output

```
Customers by Group and Gender

Customer Gender F
```

	Number	Percentage
Customer Group Name		
Internet/Catalog Customers	4.00	13.33
Orion Club Gold members	11.00	36.67
Orion Club members	15.00	50.00

Customers by Group and Gender

Customer Gender M

	Number	Percentage
Customer Group Name		
Internet/Catalog Customers	4.00	8.51
Orion Club Gold members	10.00	21.28
Orion Club members	33.00	70.21

Level 3

11. Creating a Customized Tabular Report with PROC TABULATE

a. Retrieve the starter program **p112e11**.

b. Modify the label for the **`Total_Retail_Price`** variable.

c. Suppress the labels for the **`Order_Date`** and **`Product_ID`** variables.

d. Suppress the label for the SUM keyword.

e. Insert this text into the box above the row titles: **`High Cost Products (Unit Cost > $250)`**. Suppress all titles.

f. Display all calculated cell values with the DOLLAR12. format.

g. Display **`$0`** in all cells that have no calculated value.

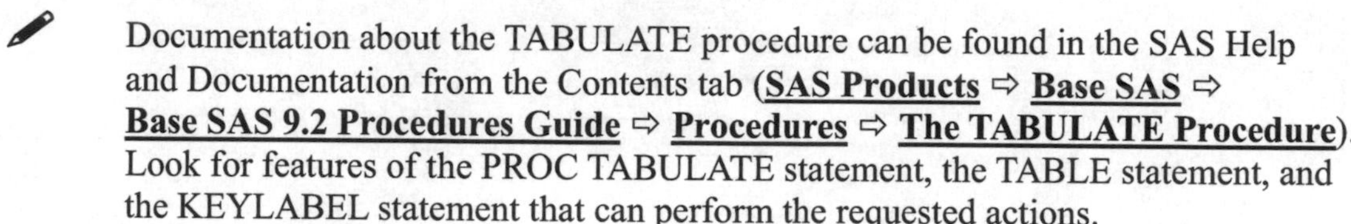

Documentation about the TABULATE procedure can be found in the SAS Help and Documentation from the Contents tab (**SAS Products** ⇨ **Base SAS** ⇨ **Base SAS 9.2 Procedures Guide** ⇨ **Procedures** ⇨ **The TABULATE Procedure**). Look for features of the PROC TABULATE statement, the TABLE statement, and the KEYLABEL statement that can perform the requested actions.

h. Submit the program to produce the following report:

PROC TABULATE Output

High Cost Products (Unit Cost > $250)	Revenue for Each Product			
	230100700008	230100700009	240300100028	240300100032
2003	$0	$0	$0	$1,200
2005	$2,057	$2,256	$0	$0
2006	$0	$1,136	$0	$0
2007	$519	$0	$1,066	$0

12. Creating an Output Data Set with PROC TABULATE

a. Retrieve the starter program **p112e12**.

b. Create an output data set from the PROC TABULATE results. The output data set should contain average salaries for each combination of **Company** and **Employee_Gender**, plus overall averages for each **Company**.

> Creating an output data set from PROC TABULATE results is discussed in the self-study content at the end of this section.

c. Sort the data set by **average salary**.

d. Print the sorted data set. Assign a format and column header to the **average salary** column.

e. Submit the program to produce the following report:

PROC PRINT Output

Average Employee Salaries

Obs	Company	Employee Gender	Average Salary
1	Orion Australia	F	$27,760
2	Orion USA	F	$29,167
3	Orion Australia		$30,574
4	Orion USA		$31,226
5	Orion USA	M	$32,534
6	Orion Australia	M	$32,963
7	Concession	F	$33,375
8	Purchasing	M	$33,462
9	Concession		$33,839
10	Concession	M	$34,650
11	Purchasing		$38,408
12	Logistics	F	$39,055
13	Purchasing	F	$41,556
14	Marketing	M	$42,645
15	Logistics		$43,128
16	Shared Functions	M	$43,428
17	Marketing		$44,390
18	Shared Functions		$44,631
19	Shared Functions	F	$46,016
20	Marketing	F	$47,132
21	Logistics	M	$47,630
22	Board of Directors	F	$68,370
23	Board of Directors		$134,034
24	Board of Directors	M	$212,831

12.4 Chapter Review

Chapter Review

1. What statistics are produced by default by PROC FREQ?
2. How can you produce a two-way frequency table using PROC FREQ?
3. What is the purpose of the VAR statement in PROC MEANS?
4. What is the purpose of the CLASS statement in PROC MEANS?
5. How can you change which statistics are displayed in PROC MEANS output?

114

12.5 Solutions

Solutions to Exercises

1. **Counting Levels of a Variable with PROC FREQ**

   a. Retrieve the starter program.

   b. Modify the program to produce two separate reports.

```
proc freq data=orion.orders nlevels;
   where Order_Type=1;
   tables Customer_ID Employee_ID / noprint;
   title1 'Unique Customers and Salespersons for Retail Sales';
run;

proc freq data=orion.orders nlevels;
   where Order_Type ne 1;
   tables Customer_ID / noprint;
   title1 'Unique Customers for Catalog and Internet Sales';
run;
```

   c. Submit the program.

2. **Producing Frequency Reports with PROC FREQ**

   a. Retrieve the starter program.

   b. Add TABLES statements to the PROC FREQ step.

```
proc format;
   value ordertypes
         1='Retail'
         2='Catalog'
         3='Internet';
run;

proc freq data=orion.orders ;
   tables Order_Date;
   tables Order_Type / nocum;
   tables Order_Date*Order_Type / nopercent norow nocol;
   format Order_Date year4. Order_Type ordertypes.;
   title 'Order Summary by Year and Type';
run;
```

   c. Submit the program.

3. **Displaying PROC FREQ Output in Descending Frequency Order**

   a. Retrieve the starter program.

   b. Submit the program.

   c. What are the two most common values for each variable?

   The top two countries are `US` (United States, 28 customers) and `CA` (Canada, 15 customers).

   The top two customer types are `Orion Club members medium activity` (20) and `Orion Club members low activity` (17).

   The top two customer age groups are `31-45 years` (27) and `15-30 years` (22).

   d. Modify the program to display the frequency counts in descending order.

```
proc freq data=orion.customer_dim order=freq;
   tables Customer_Country Customer_Type Customer_Age_Group;
   title1 'Customer Demographics';
   title3 '(Top two levels for each variable?)';
run;
```

   e. Submit the modified program.

   f. What are the two most common values for each variable?

   The top two countries are `US` (United States, 28 customers) and `CA` (Canada, 15 customers).

   The top two customer types are `Orion Club members medium activity` (20) and `Orion Club members low activity` (17).

   The top two customer age groups are `31-45 years` (27) and `15-30 years` (22).

   Which report was easier to use to answer the questions correctly?

   The ORDER=FREQ option in the PROC FREQ statement sequences the frequency output in descending count order. Because the levels that occur most often appear near the top of each report, the most common data values can be identified more easily.

4. **Creating an Output Data Set with PROC FREQ**

   a. Retrieve the starter program.

   b. Create an output data set.

```
proc freq data=orion.order_fact noprint;
   tables Product_ID / out=product_orders;
run;
```

   c. Combine the output data set with `orion.product_list`.

```
data product_names;
   merge product_orders orion.product_list;
   by Product_ID;
   keep Product_ID Product_Name Count;
run;
```

d. Sort the merged data and print the first 10 observations.

```
proc sort data=product_names;
   by descending Count;
run;

proc print data=product_names(obs=10) label;
   var Count Product_ID Product_Name;
   label Product_ID='Product Number'
         Product_Name='Product'
         Count='Orders';
   title 'Top Ten Products by Number of Orders';
run;
```

e. Submit the program.

5. Creating a Summary Report with PROC MEANS

a. Retrieve the starter program.

b. Display only the SUM statistic for the **Total_Retail_Price** variable.

```
proc format;
   value ordertypes
      1='Retail'
      2='Catalog'
      3='Internet';
run;

proc means data=orion.order_fact sum;
   var Total_Retail_Price;
   title 'Revenue (in U.S. Dollars) Earned from All Orders';
run;
```

c. Display separate statistics for the combination of **Order_Date** and **Order_Type**.

```
proc means data=orion.order_fact sum;
   var Total_Retail_Price;
   class Order_Date Order_Type;
   format Order_Date year4. Order_Type ordertypes.;
   title 'Revenue (in U.S. Dollars) Earned from All Orders';
run;
```

d. Submit the program.

6. Analyzing Missing Numeric Values with PROC MEANS

a. Retrieve the starter program.

b. Display the number of missing values and the number of nonmissing values.

```
proc means data=orion.staff nmiss n;
   var Birth_Date Emp_Hire_Date Emp_Term_Date;
   title 'Number of Missing and Non-Missing Date Values';
run;
```

c. Suppress any decimal places.

```
proc means data=orion.staff nmiss n maxdec=0;
   var Birth_Date Emp_Hire_Date Emp_Term_Date;
   title 'Number of Missing and Non-Missing Date Values';
run;
```

d. Display separate statistics for each value of **Gender**.

```
proc means data=orion.staff nmiss n maxdec=0;
   var Birth_Date Emp_Hire_Date Emp_Term_Date;
   class Gender;
   title 'Number of Missing and Non-Missing Date Values';
run;
```

e. Suppress the output column that displays the total number of observations.

```
proc means data=orion.staff nmiss n maxdec=0 nonobs;
   var Birth_Date Emp_Hire_Date Emp_Term_Date;
   class Gender;
   title 'Number of Missing and Non-Missing Date Values';
run;
```

f. Submit the program.

7. Analyzing All Possible Classification Levels with PROC MEANS

a. Retrieve the starter program.

b. Display statistics in the report.

```
data work.countries(keep=Customer_Country);
   set orion.supplier;
   Customer_Country=Country;
run;

proc means data=orion.customer_dim
          lclm mean uclm;
   class Customer_Country;
   var Customer_Age;
   title 'Average Age of Customers in Each Country';
run;
```

c. Change the α value.

```
proc means data=orion.customer_dim
          lclm mean uclm alpha=0.10;
   class Customer_Country;
   var Customer_Age;
   title 'Average Age of Customers in Each Country';
run;
```

d. Display all countries.

```
proc means data=orion.customer_dim
           classdata=work.countries
           lclm mean uclm alpha=0.10;
   class Customer_Country;
   var Customer_Age;
   title 'Average Age of Customers in Each Country';
run;
```

e. Submit the program.

8. Creating an Output Data Set with PROC MEANS

a. Retrieve the starter program.

b. Create an output data set.

```
proc means data=orion.order_fact noprint nway;
   class Product_ID;
   var Total_Retail_Price;
   output out=product_orders sum=Product_Revenue;
run;
```

c. Combine the output data set with **orion.product_list**.

```
data product_names;
   merge product_orders orion.product_list;
   by Product_ID;
   keep Product_ID Product_Name Product_Revenue;
run;
```

d. Sort the merged data and print the first 10 observations.

```
proc sort data=product_names;
   by descending Product_Revenue;
run;

proc print data=product_names(obs=10) label;
   var Product_Revenue Product_ID Product_Name;
   label Product_ID='Product Number'
         Product_Name='Product'
         Product_Revenue='Revenue';
   title 'Top Ten Products by Revenue';
run;
```

e. Display the revenue values with a leading euro symbol.

```
proc print data=product_names(obs=10) label;
   var Product_Revenue Product_ID Product_Name;
   label Product_ID='Product Number'
         Product_Name='Product'
         Product_Revenue='Revenue';
   format Product_Revenue eurox12.2;
   title 'Top Ten Products by Revenue';
run;
```

f. Submit the program.

9. Creating a Simple Tabular Report with PROC TABULATE

a. Retrieve the starter program.

b. Add a CLASS statement.

```
proc tabulate data=orion.customer_dim;
   class Customer_Group Customer_Gender;
   title 'Ages of Customers by Group and Gender';
run;
```

c. Add a VAR statement.

```
proc tabulate data=orion.customer_dim;
   class Customer_Group Customer_Gender;
   var Customer_Age;
   title 'Ages of Customers by Group and Gender';
run;
```

d. Add a TABLE statement.

```
proc tabulate data=orion.customer_dim;
   class Customer_Group Customer_Gender;
   var Customer_Age;
   table Customer_Group all,
         Customer_Gender*Customer_Age*(n mean);
   title 'Ages of Customers by Group and Gender';
run;
```

e. Submit the program.

10. Creating a Three-Dimensional Tabular Report with PROC TABULATE

a. Retrieve the starter program.

b. Define a tabular report.

```
proc tabulate data=orion.customer_dim;
   class Customer_Gender Customer_Group;
   table Customer_Gender, Customer_Group, (n colpctn);
   keylabel colpctn='Percentage' N='Number';
   title 'Customers by Group and Gender';
run;
```

c. Submit the program.

11. Creating a Customized Tabular Report with PROC TABULATE

a. Retrieve the starter program.

b. Modify the label for the **Total_Retail_Price** variable.

```
proc tabulate data=orion.order_fact;
   where CostPrice_Per_Unit > 250;
   class Product_ID Order_Date;
   format Order_Date year4.;
   var Total_Retail_Price;
   table Order_Date, Total_Retail_Price*sum*Product_ID;
   label Total_Retail_Price='Revenue for Each Product';
   title;
run;
```

c. Suppress the labels for the **Order_Date** and **Product_ID** variables.

```
proc tabulate data=orion.order_fact;
   where CostPrice_Per_Unit > 250;
   class Product_ID Order_Date;
   format Order_Date year4.;
   var Total_Retail_Price;
   table Order_Date=' ', Total_Retail_Price*sum*Product_ID=' ';
   label Total_Retail_Price='Revenue for Each Product';
   title;
run;
```

d. Suppress the label for the SUM keyword.

```
proc tabulate data=orion.order_fact;
   where CostPrice_Per_Unit > 250;
   class Product_ID Order_Date;
   format Order_Date year4.;
   var Total_Retail_Price;
   table Order_Date=' ', Total_Retail_Price*sum*Product_ID=' ';
   label Total_Retail_Price='Revenue for Each Product';
   keylabel Sum=' ';
   title;
run;
```

e. Insert text into the box above the row titles.

```
proc tabulate data=orion.order_fact;
   where CostPrice_Per_Unit > 250;
   class Product_ID Order_Date;
   format Order_Date year4.;
   var Total_Retail_Price;
   table Order_Date=' ', Total_Retail_Price*sum*Product_ID=' '
         / box='High Cost Products (Unit Cost > $250)';
   label Total_Retail_Price='Revenue for Each Product';
   keylabel Sum=' ';
   title;
run;
```

f. Display all calculated cell values with the DOLLAR12. format.

```
proc tabulate data=orion.order_fact format=dollar12.;
   where CostPrice_Per_Unit > 250;
   class Product_ID Order_Date;
   format Order_Date year4.;
   var Total_Retail_Price;
   table Order_Date=' ', Total_Retail_Price*sum*Product_ID=' '
         / box='High Cost Products (Unit Cost > $250)';
   label Total_Retail_Price='Revenue for Each Product';
   keylabel Sum=' ';
   title;
run;
```

g. Display **$0** in all cells that have no calculated value.

```
proc tabulate data=orion.order_fact format=dollar12.;
   where CostPrice_Per_Unit > 250;
   class Product_ID Order_Date;
   format Order_Date year4.;
   var Total_Retail_Price;
   table Order_Date=' ', Total_Retail_Price*sum*Product_ID=' '
         / misstext='$0'
           box='High Cost Products (Unit Cost > $250)';
   label Total_Retail_Price='Revenue for Each Product';
   keylabel Sum=' ';
   title;
run;
```

h. Submit the program.

12. Creating an Output Data Set with PROC TABULATE

a. Retrieve the starter program.

b. Create an output data set.

```
proc tabulate data=orion.Organization_Dim format=dollar12.
              out=work.Salaries;
   class Employee_Gender Company;
   var Salary;
   table Company, (Employee_Gender all)*Salary*mean;
   title 'Average Employee Salaries';
run;
```

c. Sort the data set.

```
proc sort data=work.Salaries;
   by Salary_Mean;
run;
```

d. Print the sorted data set.

```
proc print data=work.Salaries label;
   var Company Employee_Gender Salary_Mean;
   format Salary_Mean dollar12.;
   label Salary_Mean='Average Salary';
   title 'Average Employee Salaries';
run;
```

e. Submit the program.

Solutions to Student Activities (Polls/Quizzes)

12.01 Multiple Choice Poll – Correct Answer

Which of the following statements **cannot** be added to the PROC FREQ step to enhance the report?

a. FORMAT
(b.) SET
c. TITLE
d. WHERE

12

12.02 Quiz – Correct Answer

Which TABLES statement correctly creates the report?

a. `tables Gender nocum;`

b. `tables Gender nocum nopercent;`

c. `tables Gender / nopercent;`

(d.) `tables Gender / nocum nopercent;`

The FREQ Procedure

Gender	Frequency
F	68
M	97

20

p112d01

12.03 Quiz – Correct Answer

The first part of the PROC FREQ output is in the SAS data set that was created with the TABLES statement.

Obs	Gender	COUNT	PERCENT	CUM_FREQ	CUM_PCT
1	F	68	41.2121	68	41.212
2	M	97	58.7879	165	100.000

The second part of the PROC FREQ output is in the SAS data set that was created with the OUTPUT statement.

Obs	N	_PCHI_	DF_PCHI	P_PCHI
1	165	5.09697	1	0.023968

42

12.04 Quiz – Correct Answer

For a given data set, there are 63 observations with a **Country** value of AU. Of those 63 observations, only 61 observations have a value for **Salary**.

Which output is correct?

a.

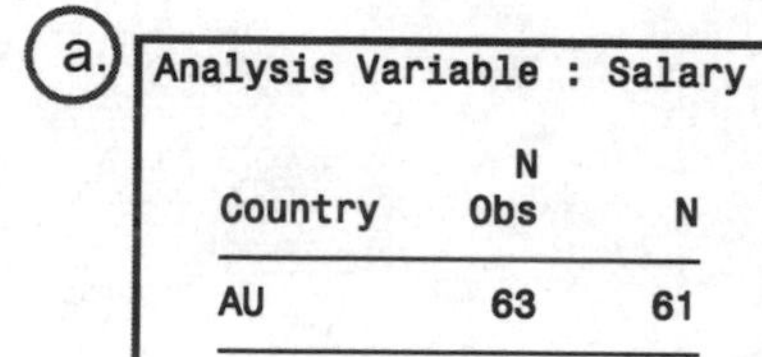

Analysis Variable : Salary

Country	N Obs	N
AU	63	61

b.

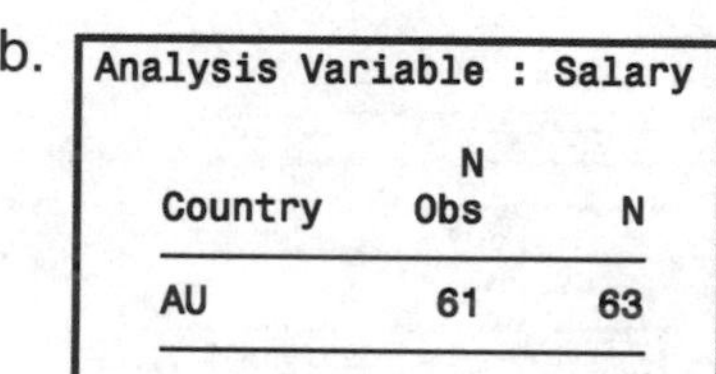

Analysis Variable : Salary

Country	N Obs	N
AU	61	63

55

12.05 Quiz – Correct Answer

```
proc means data=orion.sales noprint chartype;
   var Salary;
   class Gender Country;
   output out=work.means2
          min=minSalary max=maxSalary
          sum=sumSalary mean=aveSalary;
run;
proc print data=work.means2;
   where _type_= '10';
run;
```

Obs	Gender	Country	_TYPE_	_FREQ_	min Salary	max Salary	sum Salary	ave Salary
4	F		10	68	25185	83505	1955865	28762.72
5	M		10	97	22710	243190	3185555	32840.77

78

p112a02s

Solutions to Chapter Review

Chapter Review Answers

1. What statistics are produced by default by PROC FREQ?
   - **Frequency**
   - **Percent**
   - **Cumulative Frequency**
   - **Cumulative Percent**

2. How can you produce a two-way frequency table using PROC FREQ?

   By using an asterisk between two variables in a TABLES statement, you can produce a two-way frequency table in PROC FREQ.

   Example:
   ```
   tables Gender*Country;
   ```

115

continued...

Chapter Review Answers

3. What is the purpose of the VAR statement in PROC MEANS?

   The VAR statement identifies the analysis variables and their order in the PROC MEANS results.

4. What is the purpose of the CLASS statement in PROC MEANS?

   The CLASS statement identifies variables whose values define subgroups for the PROC MEANS analysis.

116

continued...

Chapter Review Answers

5. How can you change which statistics are displayed in PROC MEANS output?

   The statistics to compute and the order to display them can be specified as statistical keywords in the PROC MEANS statement.

   Example:

```
proc means data=orion.sales sum mean;
```

117

Chapter 13 Introduction to Graphics Using SAS/GRAPH (Self-Study)

13.1 Introduction **13-3**

13.2 Creating Bar and Pie Charts **13-9**

Demonstration: Creating Bar and Pie Charts 13-10

13.3 Creating Plots **13-21**

Demonstration: Creating Plots 13-22

13.4 Enhancing Output **13-25**

Demonstration: Enhancing Output 13-26

13.1 Introduction

What Is SAS/GRAPH Software?

SAS/GRAPH software is a component of SAS software that enables you to create the following types of graphs:

- bar, block, and pie charts
- two-dimensional scatter plots and line plots
- three-dimensional scatter and surface plots
- contour plots
- maps
- text slides
- custom graphs

3

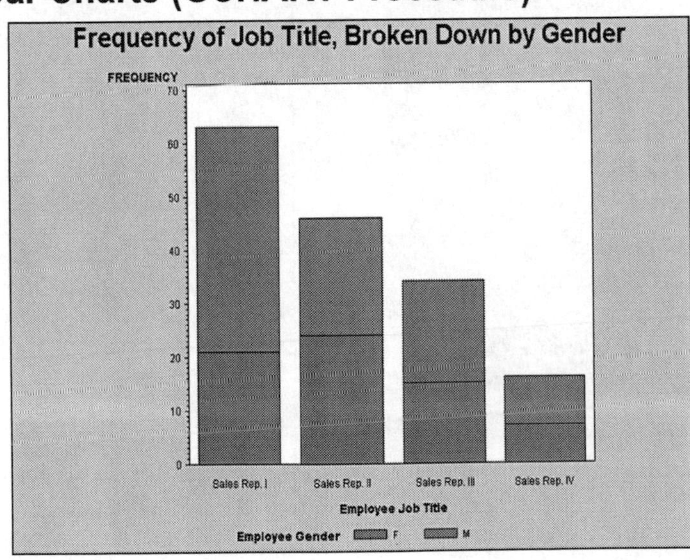

4

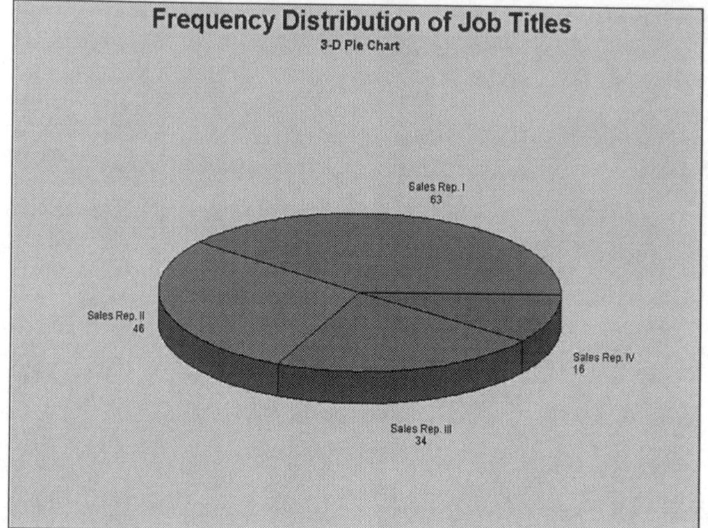

5

Scatter and Line Plots (GPLOT Procedure)

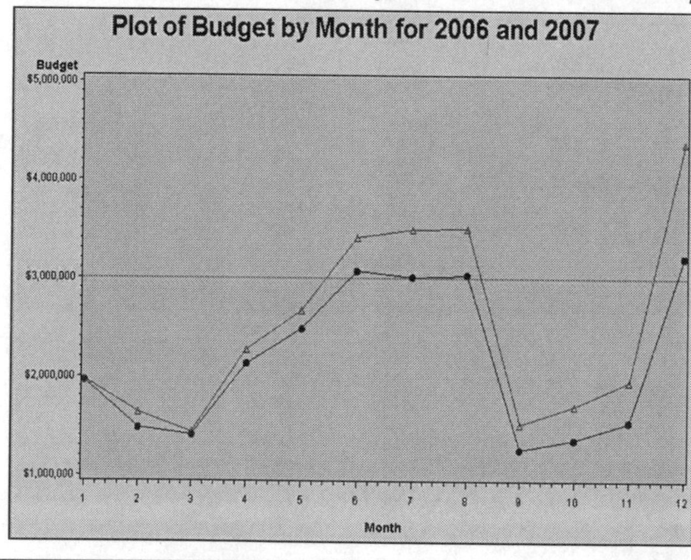

6

Bar Charts with Line Plot Overlay (GBARLINE Procedure)

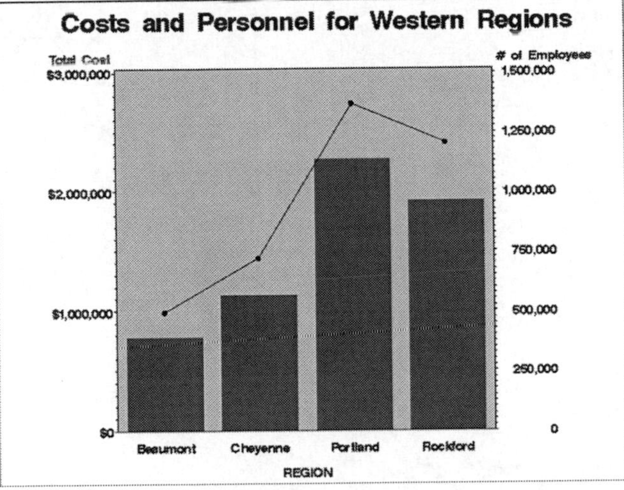

7

Three-Dimensional Surface and Scatter Plots (G3D Procedure)

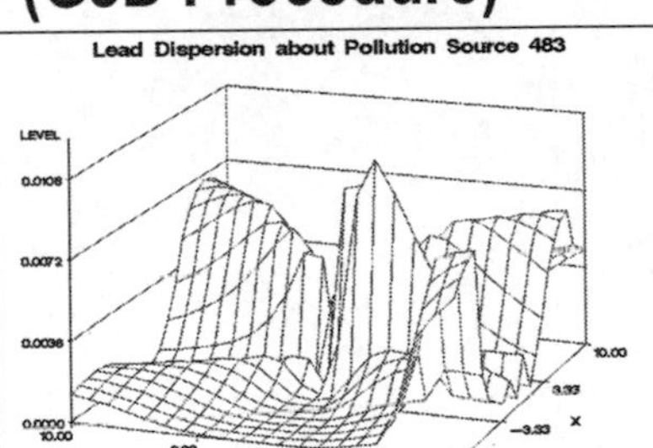

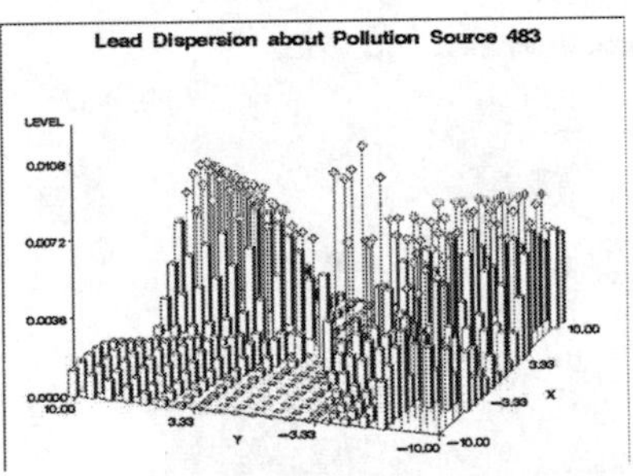

8

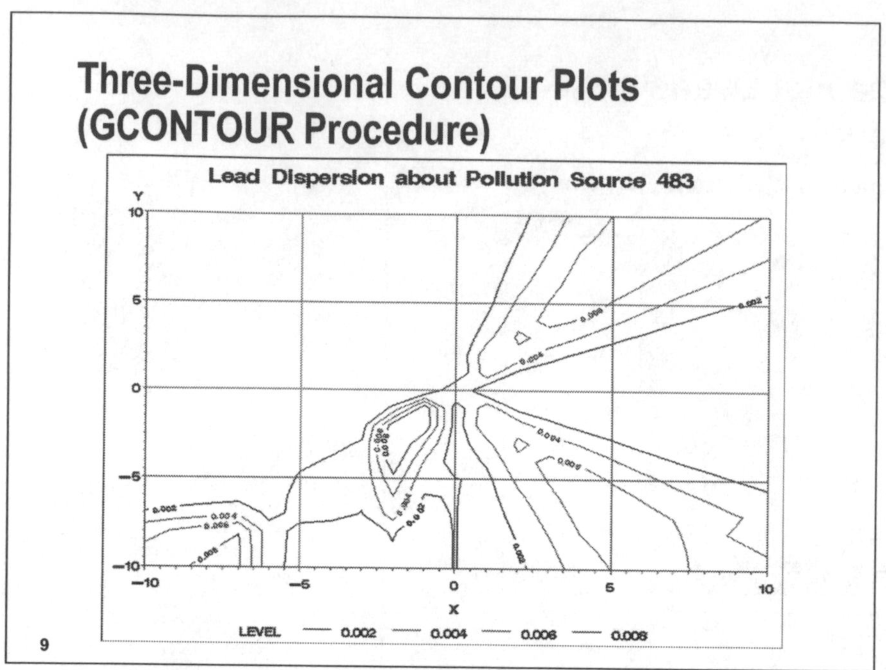
Three-Dimensional Contour Plots
(GCONTOUR Procedure)
Lead Dispersion about Pollution Source 483
Y
10
5
0
−5
−10
−10
−5
0
5
10
X
LEVEL 0.002 0.004 0.006 0.008
9

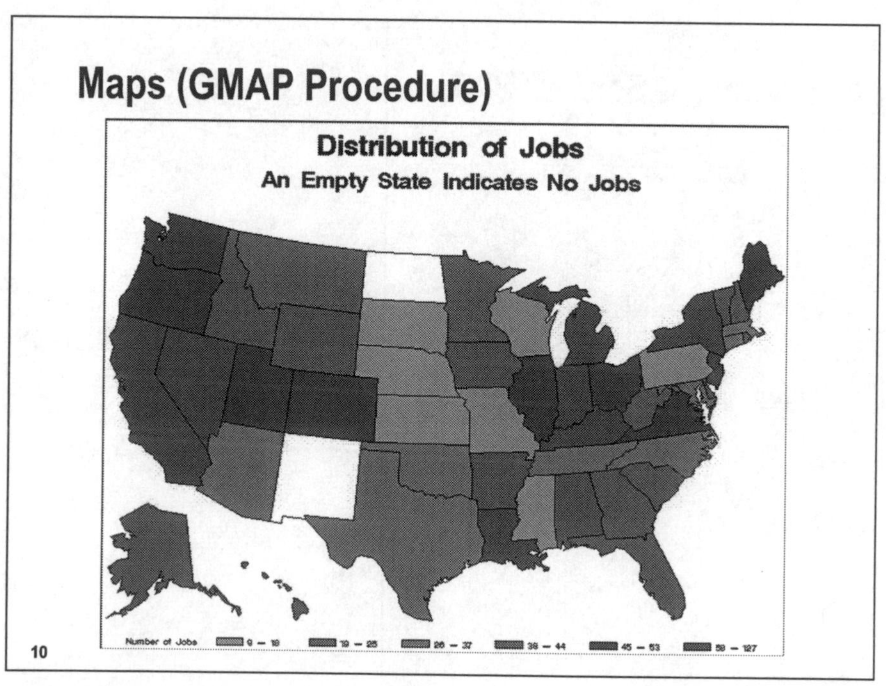
Maps (GMAP Procedure)
Distribution of Jobs
An Empty State Indicates No Jobs
Number of Jobs
45 – 53
10

Multiple Graphs on a Page (GREPLAY Procedure)

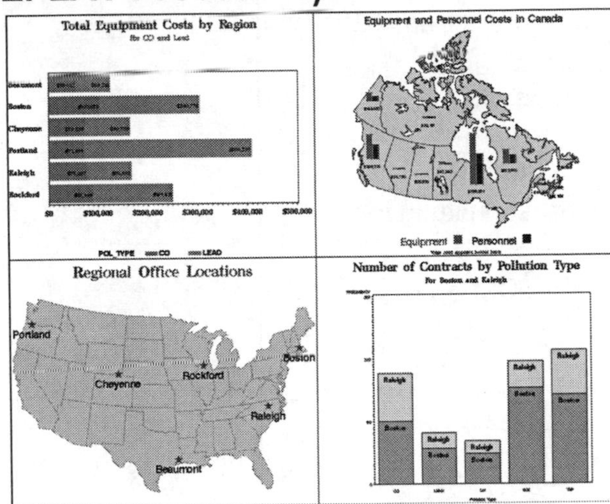

11

SAS/GRAPH Programs

General form of a SAS/GRAPH program:

GOPTIONS *options*;
global statements
graphics procedure steps

For example:

```
goptions cback=white;
title 'Number of Employees by Job Title';
proc gchart data=orion.staff;
   vbar Job_Title;
run;
quit;
```

12

RUN-Group Processing

Many SAS/GRAPH procedures can use RUN-group processing, which means that the following are true:

- The procedure executes the group of statements following the PROC statement when a RUN statement is encountered.
- Additional statements followed by another RUN statement can be submitted without resubmitting the PROC statement.
- The procedure stays active until a PROC, DATA, or QUIT statement is encountered.

13

Example of RUN-Group Processing

```
proc gchart data=orion.staff;
   vbar Job_Title;
   title 'Bar Chart of Job Titles';
run;
   pie Job_Title;
   title 'Pie Chart of Job Titles';
run;
quit;
```

14

13.2 Creating Bar and Pie Charts

Producing Bar and Pie Charts with the GCHART Procedure

General form of the PROC GCHART statement:

PROC GCHART DATA=*SAS-data-set*;

Use one of these statements to specify the chart type:

HBAR *chart-variable . . . </ options>*;
HBAR3D *chart-variable . . . </ options>*;

VBAR *chart-variable . . . </ options>*;
VBAR3D *chart-variable . . . </ options>*;

PIE *chart-variable . . . </ options>*;
PIE3D *chart-variable . . . </ options>*;

16

The chart variable determines the number of bars or slices produced within a graph. The chart variable can be character or numeric. By default, the height, length, or slice represents a frequency count of the values of the chart variable.

Creating Bar and Pie Charts

p113d01

1. Submit the first PROC GCHART step to create a vertical bar chart representing a frequency count.

   The VBAR statement creates a vertical bar chart showing the number of sales representatives for each value of **Job_Title** in the **orion.staff** data set. **Job_Title** is referred to as the *chart variable*. Because the chart variable is a character variable, PROC GCHART displays one bar for each value of **Job_Title**.

```
goptions reset=all;
proc gchart data=orion.staff;
   vbar Job_Title;
   where Job_Title =:'Sales Rep';
   title 'Number of Employees by Job Title';
run;
quit;
```

   The RESET=ALL option resets all graphics options to their default settings and clears any titles or footnotes that are in effect.

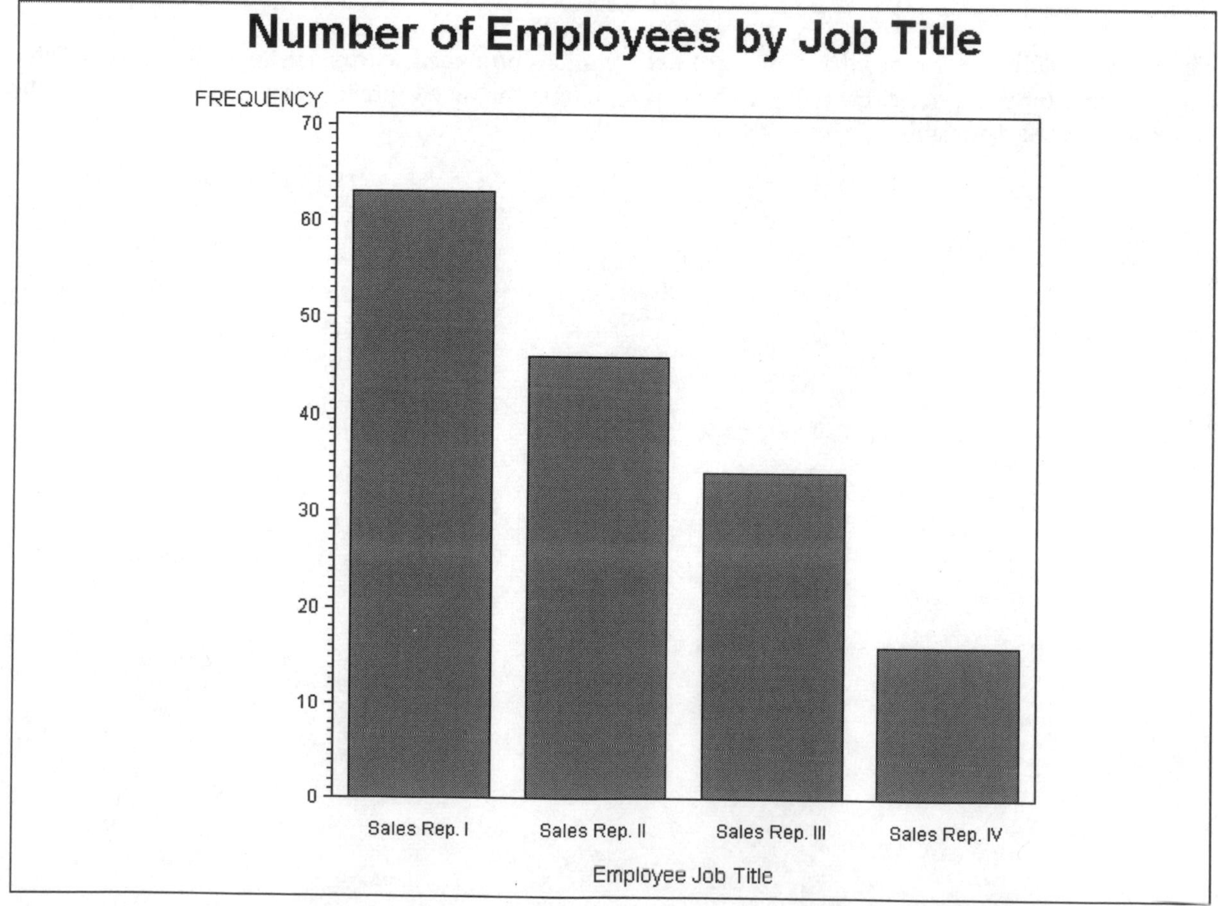

2. Submit the second PROC GCHART step to create a three-dimensional horizontal bar chart.

   The HBAR3D statement creates a three-dimensional horizontal bar chart showing the same information as the previous bar chart. Notice that the HBAR and HBAR3D statements automatically display statistics to the right of the chart.

```
goptions reset=all;
proc gchart data=orion.staff;
   hbar3d Job_Title;
   title 'Number of Employees by Job Title';
   where Job_Title =:'Sales Rep';
run;
quit;
```

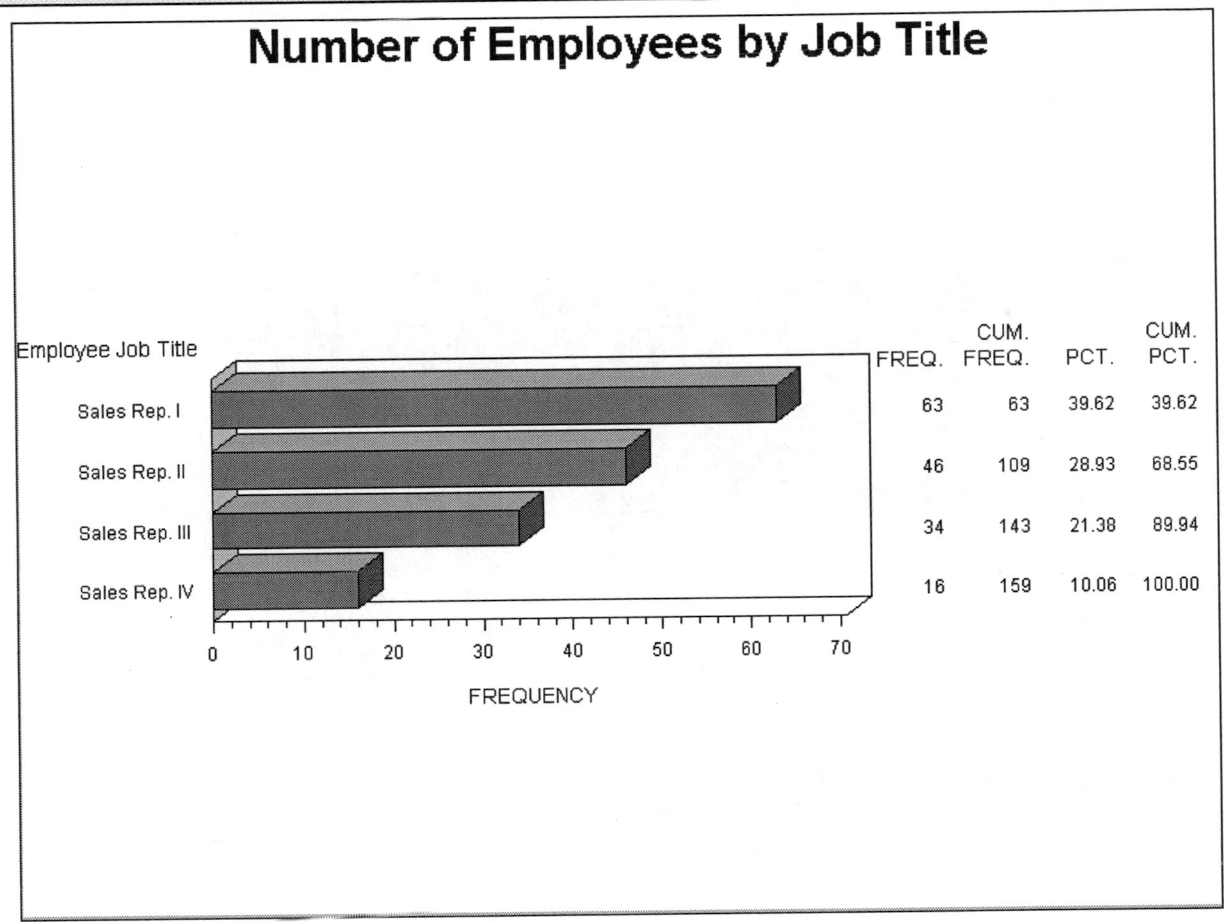

3. Submit the third PROC GCHART step to suppress the display of statistics on the horizontal bar chart.

   The NOSTATS option in the HBAR3D statement suppresses the display of statistics on the chart.

```
goptions reset=all;
proc gchart data=orion.staff;
   hbar3d Job_Title / nostats;
   title 'Number of Employees by Job Title';
   where Job_Title =:'Sales Rep';
run;
quit;
```

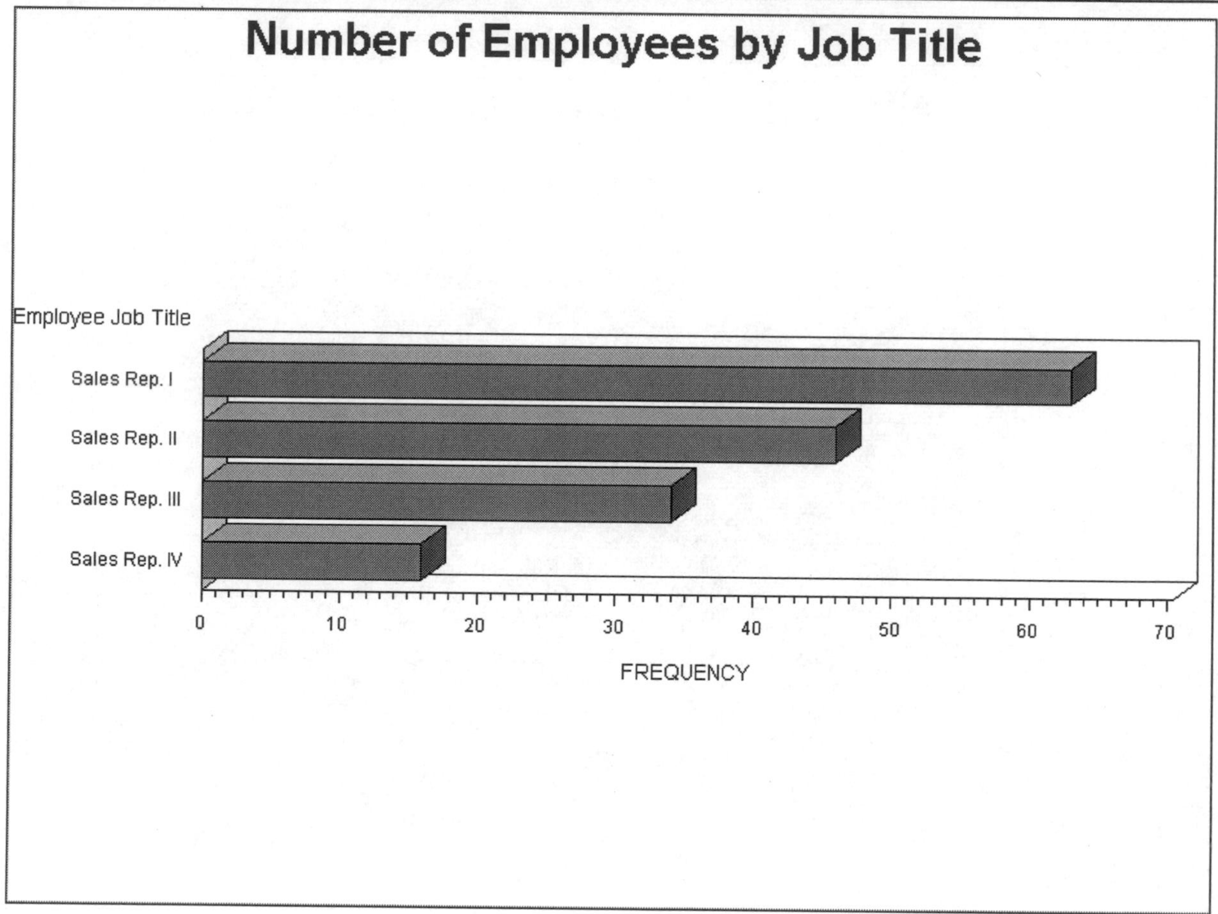

4. Submit the fourth PROC GCHART step to use a numeric chart variable.

   The VBAR3D statement creates a vertical bar chart showing the distribution of values of the variable **Salary**. Because the chart variable is numeric, PROC GCHART divides the values of **Salary** into ranges and displays one bar for each range. The value under the bar represents the midpoint of the range. The FORMAT statement assigns the DOLLAR9. format to **Salary**.

```
goptions reset=all;
proc gchart data=orion.staff;
   vbar3d salary / autoref;
   where Job_Title =:'Sales Rep';
   format salary dollar9.;
   title 'Salary Distribution Midpoints for Sales Reps';
run;
quit;
```

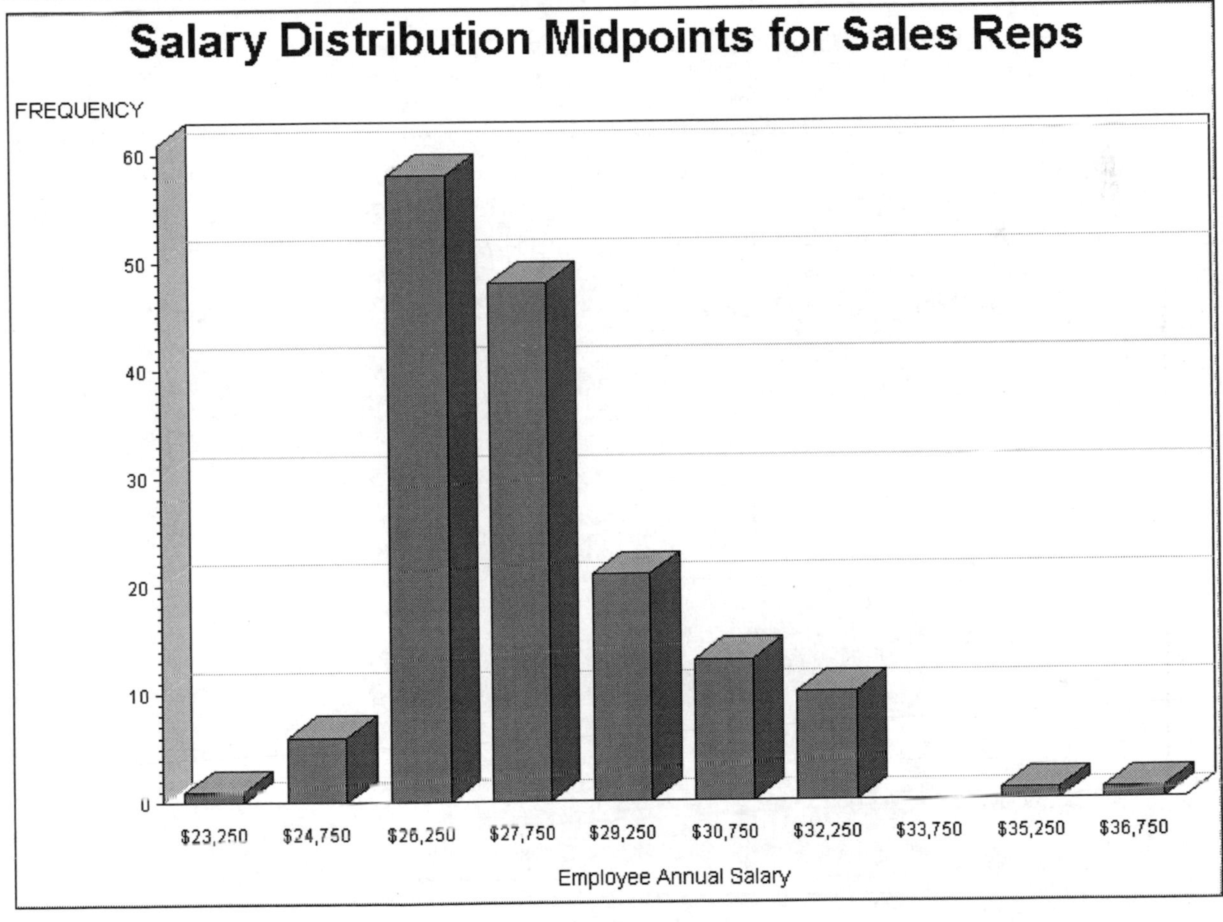

5. Submit the fifth PROC GCHART step to specify ranges for a numeric chart variable and add reference lines.

   The HBAR3D statement creates a three-dimensional horizontal bar chart.

   The LEVELS= option in the HBAR3D statement divides the values of **Salary** into five ranges and display a bar for each range of values.

   The RANGE option in the HBAR3D statement displays the range of values, rather than the midpoint, under each bar.

   The AUTOREF option displays reference lines at each major tick mark on the horizontal (response) axis.

```
goptions reset=all;
proc gchart data=orion.staff;
   hbar3d salary/levels=5 range autoref;
   where Job_Title =:'Sales Rep';
   format salary dollar9.;
   title 'Salary Distribution Ranges for Sales Reps';
run;
quit;
```

   To display a bar for each unique value of the chart variable, specify the DISCRETE option instead of the LEVELS= option in the VBAR, VBAR3D, HBAR, or HBAR3D statement. The DISCRETE option should be used only when the chart variable has a relatively small number of unique values.

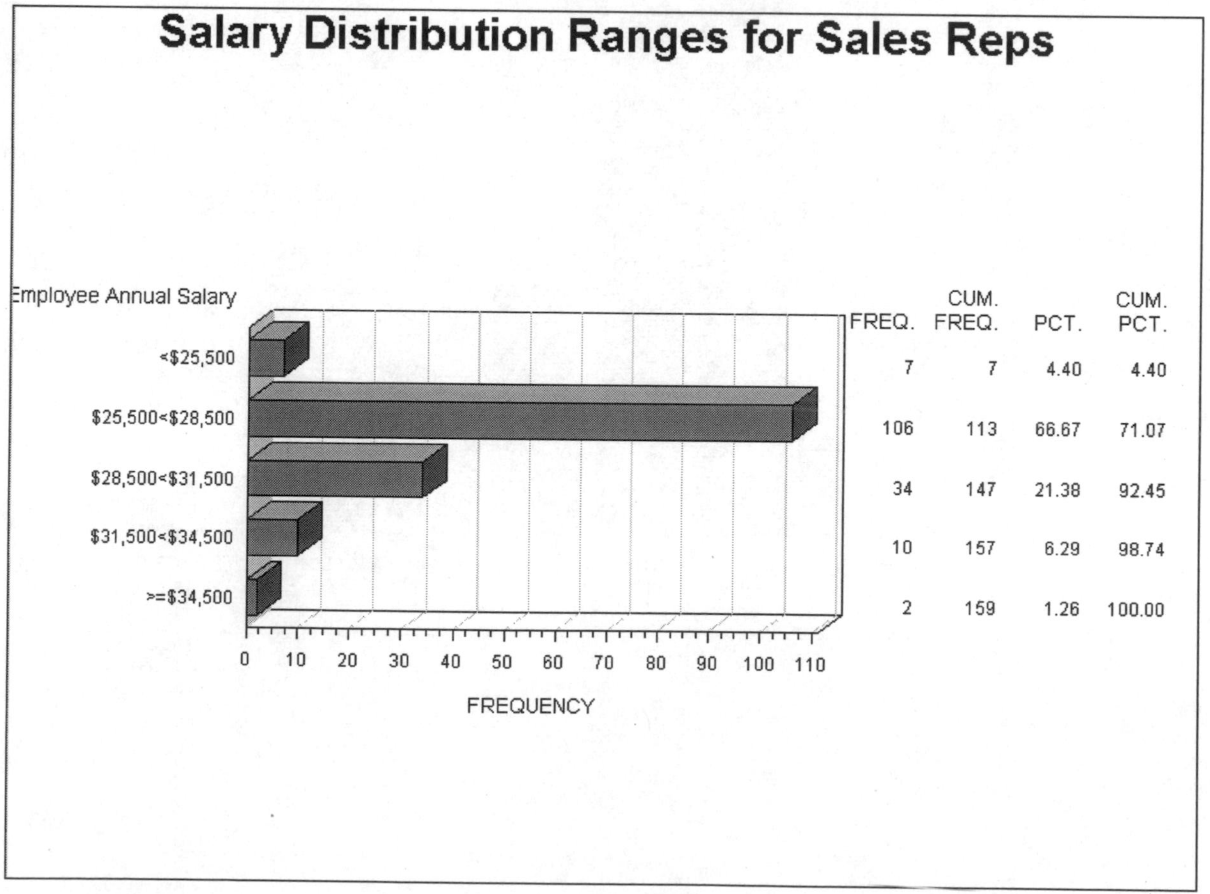

6. Submit the sixth PROC GCHART step to create bar charts based on statistics.

   A vertical bar chart displays one bar for each value of the variable **Job_Title** by specifying **Job_Title** as the chart variable in the VBAR statement. The height of the bar should be based on the mean value of the variable **Salary** for each job title.

   The SUMVAR= option in the VBAR statement specifies the variable whose values control the height or length of the bars. This variable (**Salary**, in this case) is known as the *analysis variable.*

   The TYPE= option in the VBAR statement specifies the statistic for the analysis variable that dictates the height or length of the bars. Possible values for the TYPE= option are SUM and MEAN.

   A LABEL statement assigns labels to the variables **Job_Title** and **Salary**.

```
goptions reset=all;
proc gchart data=orion.staff;
   vbar Job_Title / sumvar=salary type=mean;
   where Job_Title =:'Sales Rep';
   format salary dollar9.;
   label Job_Title='Job Title'
         Salary='Salary';
   title 'Average Salary by Job Title';
run;
quit;
```

   If the TYPE= option is not specified, the default value of the TYPE= option is SUM.

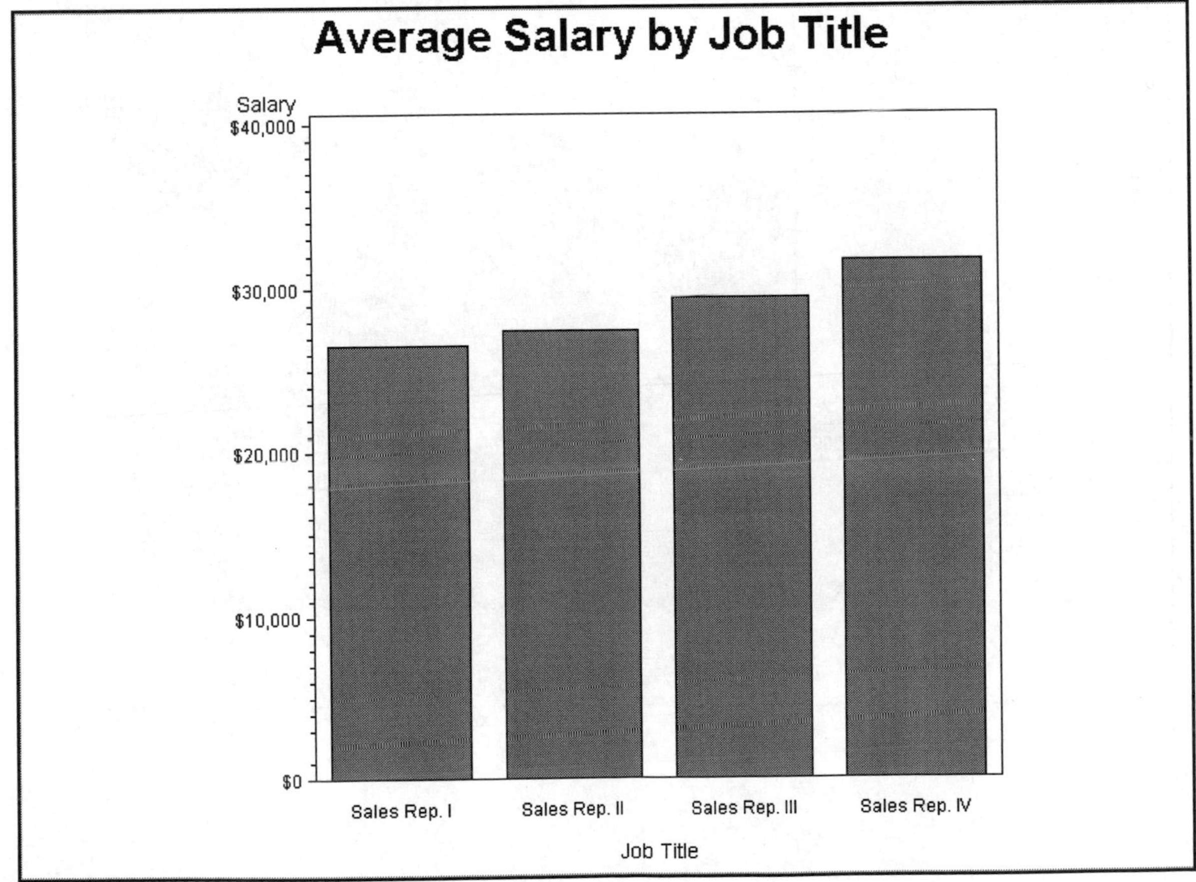

7. Submit the seventh PROC GCHART step to assign a different color to each bar and display the mean statistic on the top of each bar.

   The PATTERNID=MIDPOINT option in the VBAR statement causes PROC GCHART to assign a different pattern or color to each value of the midpoint (chart) variable.

   The MEAN option in the VBAR statement displays the mean statistic on the top of each bar. Other options such as SUM, FREQ, and PERCENT can be specified to display other statistics on the top of the bars.

```
goptions reset=all;
proc gchart data=orion.staff;
   vbar Job_Title / sumvar=salary type=mean patternid=midpoint mean;
   where Job_Title =:'Sales Rep';
   format salary dollar9.;
   title 'Average Salary by Job Title';
run;
quit;
```

   Only one statistic can be displayed on top of each vertical bar. For horizontal bar charts, you can specify multiple statistics, which are displayed to the right of the bars.

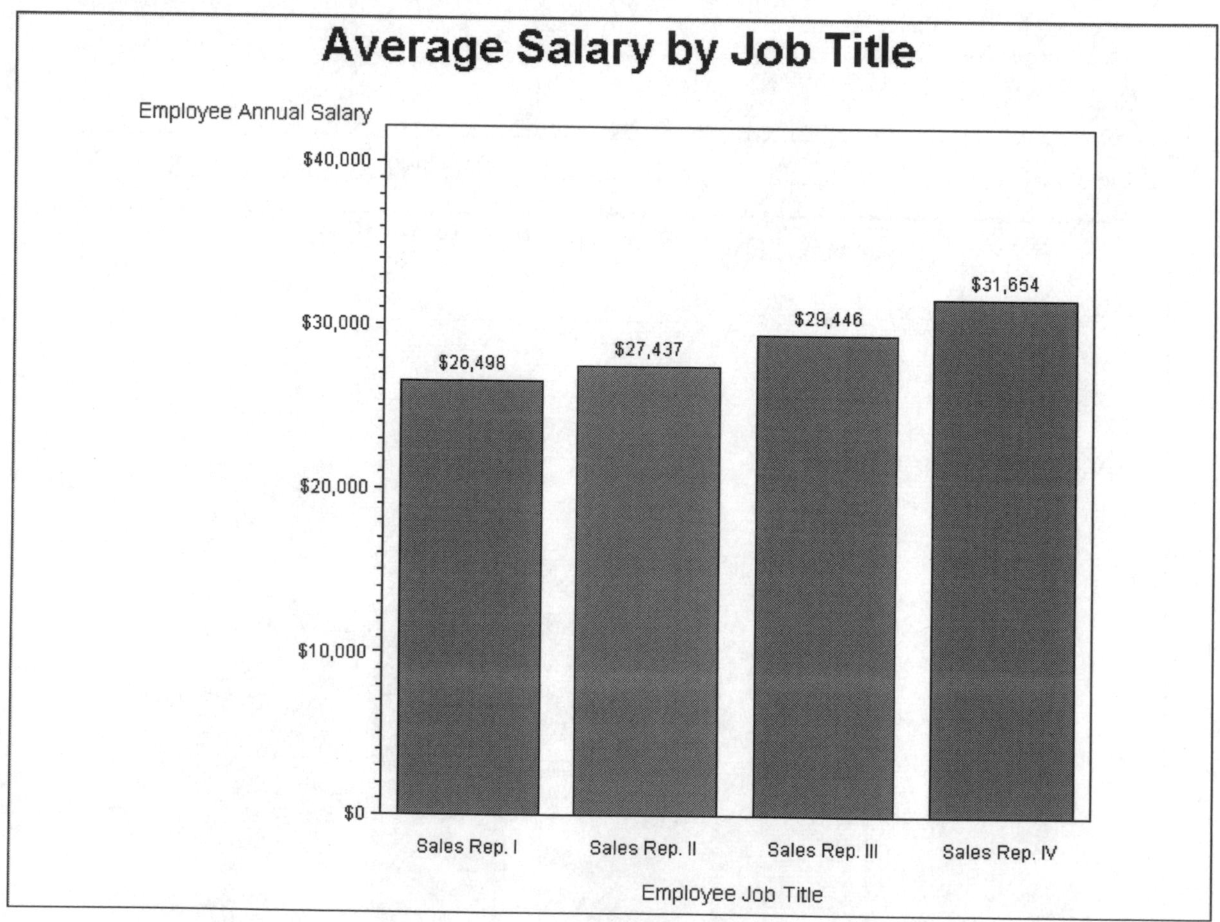

8. Submit the eighth PROC GCHART step to divide the bars into subgroups.

   A VBAR statement creates a vertical bar chart that shows the number of sales representatives for each value of **Job_Title**.

   The SUBGROUP= option in the VBAR statement divides the bar into sections, where each section represents the frequency count for each value of the variable **Gender**.

```
goptions reset=all;
proc gchart data=orion.staff;
   vbar Job_Title/subgroup=Gender;
   where Job_Title =:'Sales Rep';
   title 'Frequency of Job Title, Broken Down by Gender';
run;
quit;
```

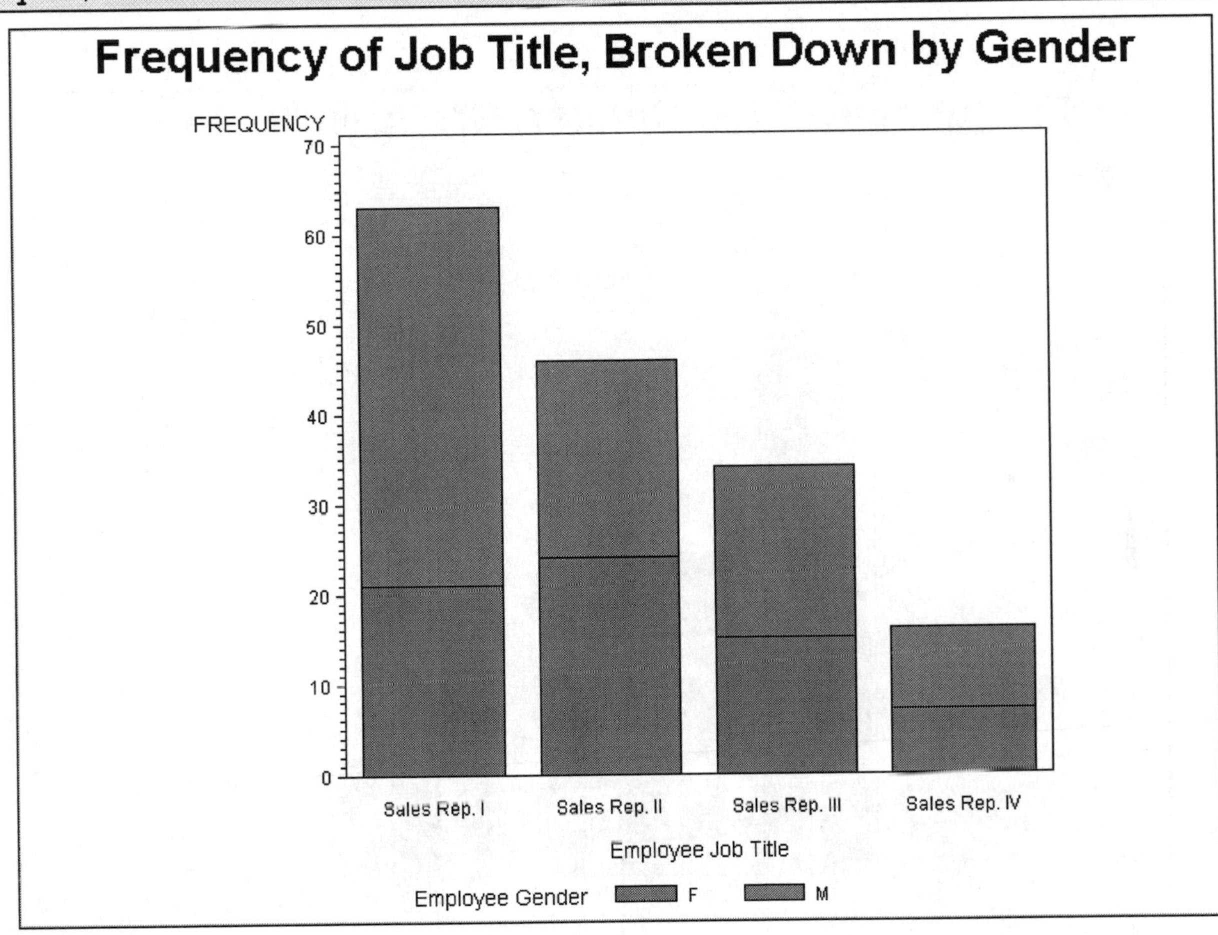

9. Submit the ninth PROC GCHART step to group the bars.

   A VBAR statement creates a vertical bar chart showing the frequency for each value of **Gender**.

   The GROUP= option in the VBAR statement displays a separate set of bars for each value of **Job_Title**.

   The PATTERNID=MIDPOINT option in the VBAR statement displays each value of **Gender** (the midpoint or chart variable) with the same pattern.

```
goptions reset=all;
proc gchart data=orion.staff;
   vbar gender/group=Job_Title patternid=midpoint;
   where Job_Title =:'Sales Rep';
   title 'Frequency of Job Gender, Grouped by Job Title';
run;
quit;
```

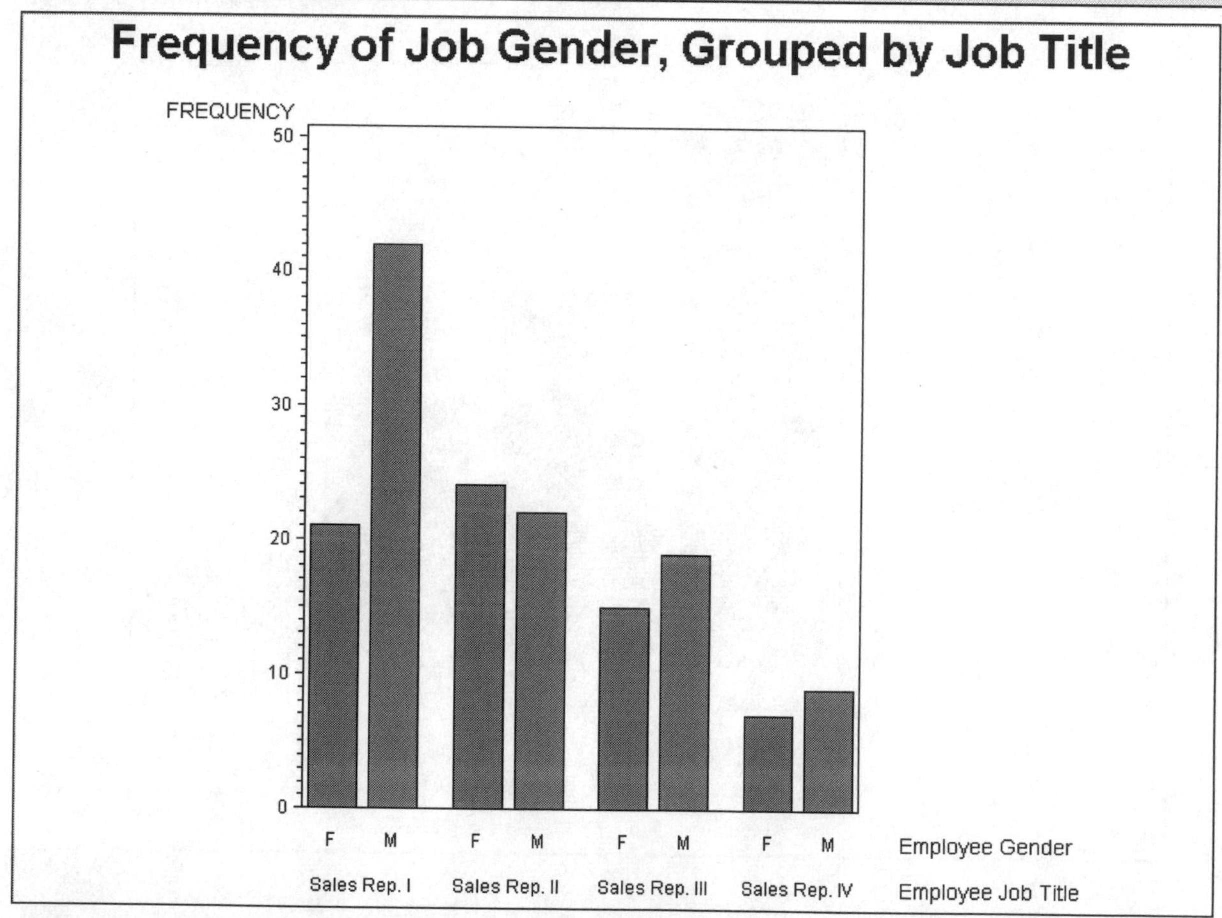

Submitting the following statements (reversing the chart and group variables) would produce a chart with two groups of four bars:

```
proc gchart data=orion.staff;
   vbar gender/group=Job_Title patternid=midpoint;
```

10. Submit the final PROC GCHART step to create multiple pie charts using RUN-group processing.

    A PIE and a PIE3D statement in the same PROC GCHART step produces both a two-dimensional pie chart and a three-dimensional pie chart showing the number of sales representatives for each value of **Job_Title**.

    The TITLE2 statements specify different subtitles for each chart. The NOHEADING option in the PIE3D statement suppresses the FREQUENCY of Job_Title heading.

    Because RUN-group processing is in effect, note the following:

    - It is not necessary to submit a separate PROC GCHART statement for each graph.
    - The WHERE statement is applied to both charts.
    - The TITLE statement is applied to both charts.
    - A separate TITLE2 statement is used for each chart.

```
goptions reset=all;
proc gchart data=orion.staff;
   pie Job_Title;
   where Job_Title =:'Sales Rep';
   title 'Frequency Distribution of Job Titles';
   title2 '2-D Pie Chart';
run;
   pie3d Job_Title / noheading;
   title2 '3-D Pie Chart';
run;
quit;
```

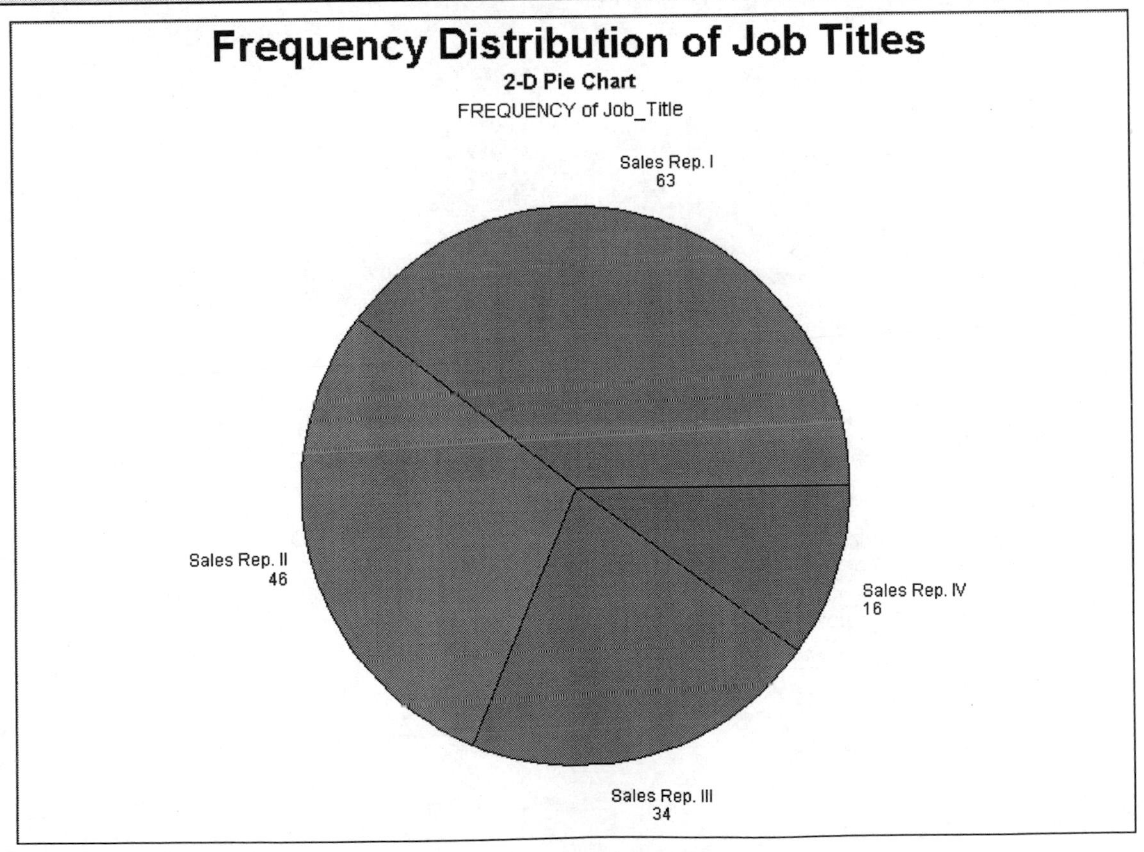

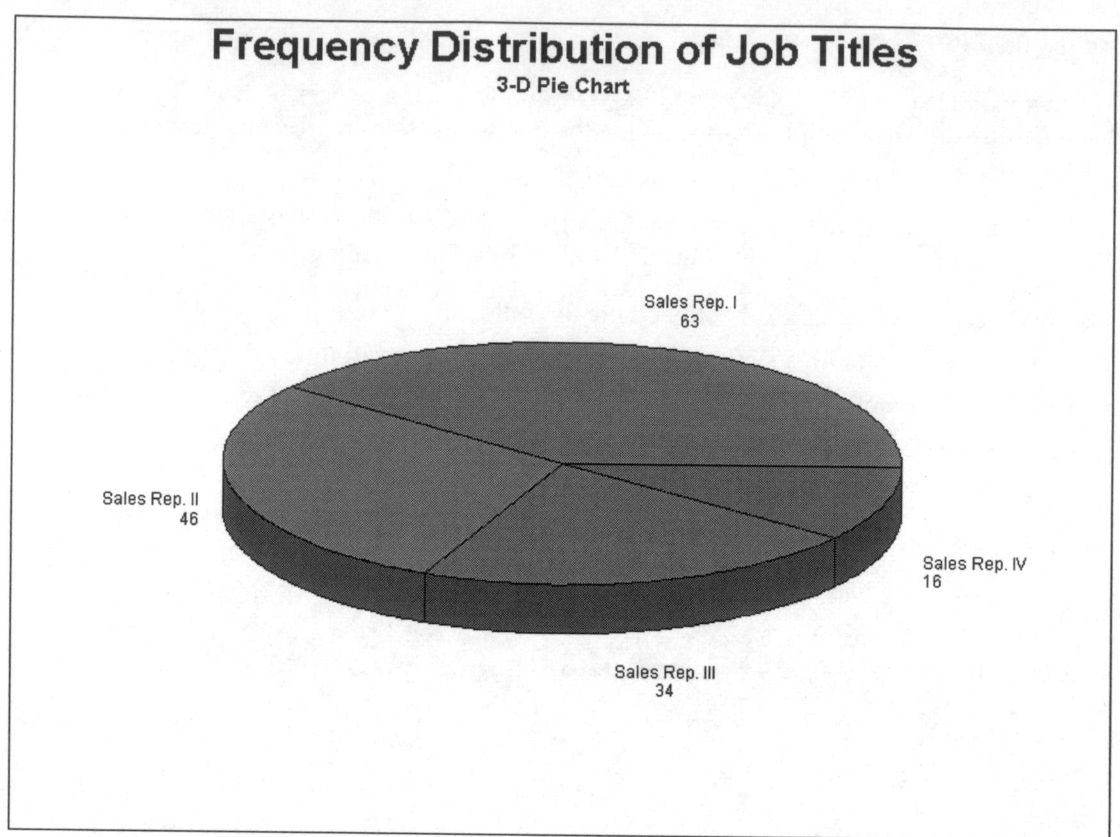
Frequency Distribution of Job Titles
3-D Pie Chart
Sales Rep. I
63
Sales Rep. II
46
Sales Rep. IV
16
Sales Rep. III
34

13.3 Creating Plots

Producing Plots with the GPLOT Procedure

You can use the GPLOT procedure to plot one variable against another within a set of coordinate axes.

General form of a PROC GPLOT step:

```
PROC GPLOT DATA=SAS-data-set;
     PLOT vertical-variable*horizontal-variable </ options>;
RUN;
QUIT;
```

19

Creating Plots

p113d02

1. Submit the first PROC GPLOT step to create a simple scatter plot.

   The PROC GPLOT creates a plot displaying the values of the variable **Yr2007** on the vertical axis and **Month** on the horizontal axis. The points are displayed using the default plotting symbol (a plus sign).

   A FORMAT statement assigns the DOLLAR12. format to **Yr2007**.

```
goptions reset=all;
proc gplot data=orion.budget;
   plot Yr2007*Month;
   format Yr2007 dollar12.;
   title 'Plot of Budget by Month';
run;
quit;
```

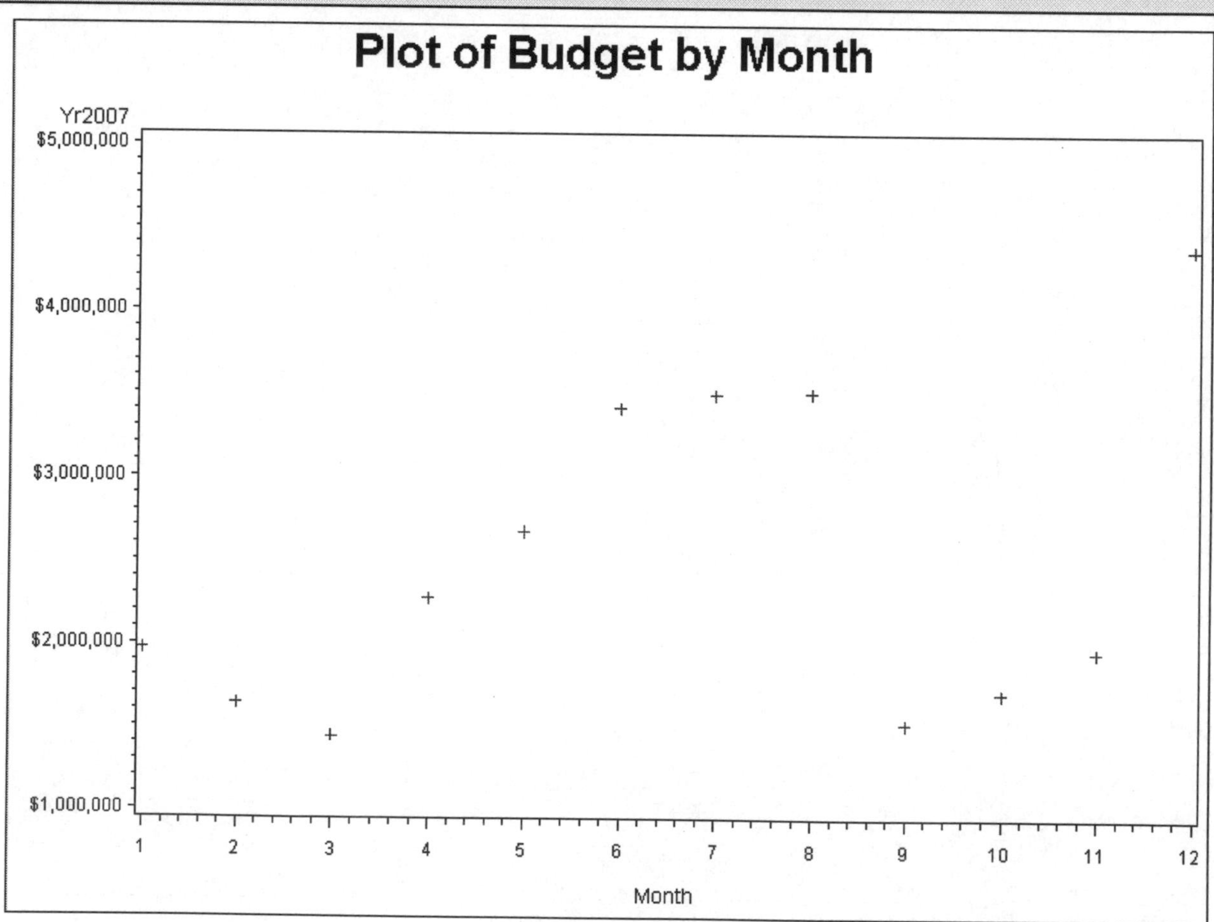

2. Submit the second PROC GPLOT step to specify plot symbols and interpolation lines.

   The SYMBOL statement specifies an alternate plotting symbol and draws an interpolation line joining the plot points. The options in the SYMBOL statement are as follows:

   - V= specifies the plotting symbol (a dot).
   - I= specifies the interpolation method to be used to connect the points (join).
   - CV= specifies the color of the plotting symbol.
   - CI= specifies the color of the interpolation line.

   The LABEL statement assigns a label to the variable **Yr2007**.

```
goptions reset=all;
proc gplot data=orion.budget;
   plot Yr2007*Month / haxis=1 to 12;
   label Yr2007='Budget';
   format Yr2007 dollar12.;
   title 'Plot of Budget by Month';
   symbol1 v=dot i=join cv=red ci=blue;
run;
quit;
```

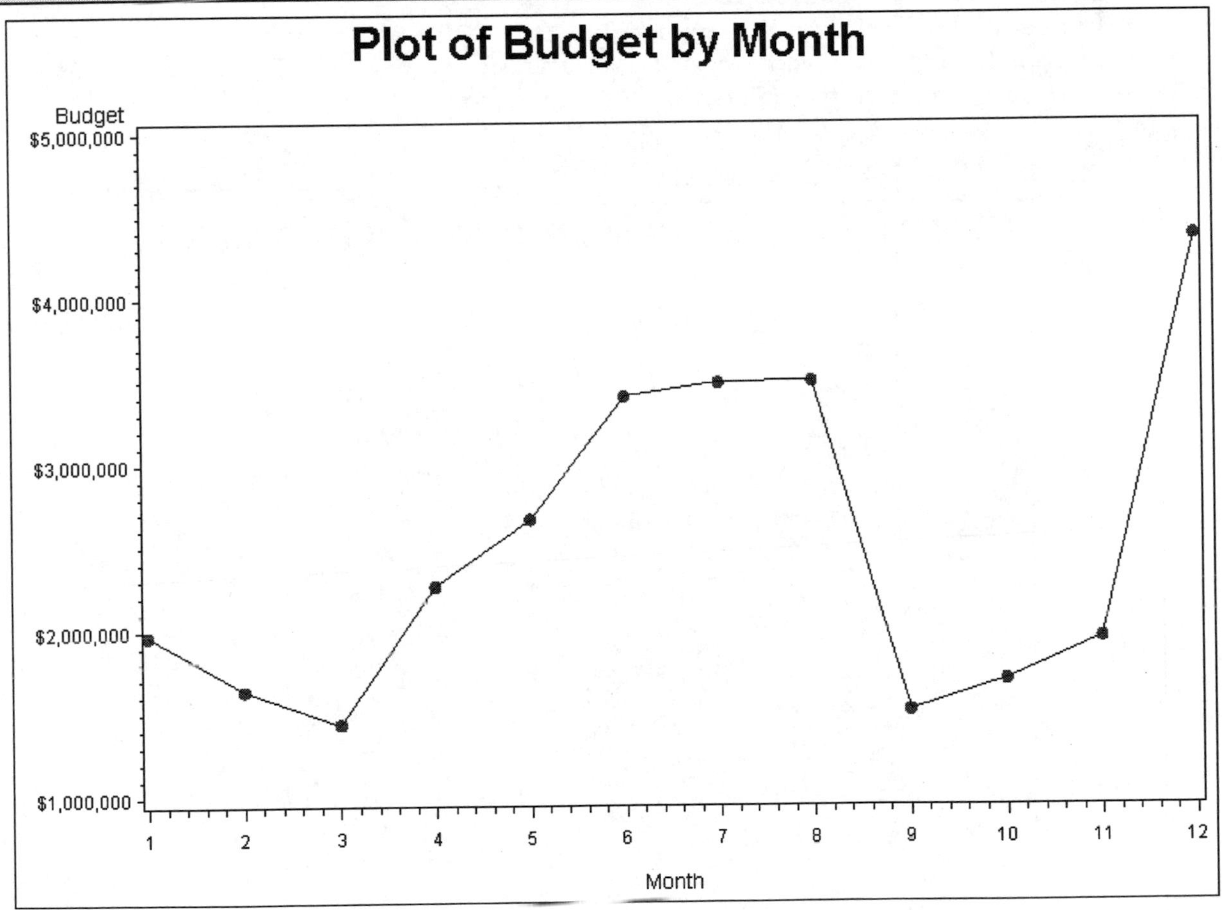

3. Submit the third PROC GPLOT step to overlay multiple plot lines on the same set of axes.

   The PLOT statement specifies two separate plot requests (**`Yr2006*Month`** and **`Yr2007*Month`**), which results in an overlay plot with the variables **`Yr2006`** and **`Yr2007`** on the vertical axis and **`Month`** on the horizontal axis.

   The options in the PLOT statement are as follows:

   - The OVERLAY option causes both plot requests to be displayed on the same set of axes.
   - The HAXIS= option specifies the range of values for the horizontal axis. (The VAXIS= option can be used to specify the range for the vertical axis.)
   - The VREF= option specifies a value on the vertical axis where a reference line should be drawn.
   - The CFRAME= option specifies a color to be used for the background within the plot axes.

```
goptions reset=all;
proc gplot data=orion.budget;
   plot Yr2006*Month yr2007*Month/ overlay haxis=1 to 12
   vref=3000000
   cframe="very light gray";
   label Yr2006='Budget';
   format Yr2006 dollar12.;
   title 'Plot of Budget by Month for 2006 and 2007';
   symbol1 i=join v=dot ci=blue cv=blue;
   symbol2 i=join v=triangle ci=red cv=red;
run;
quit;
```

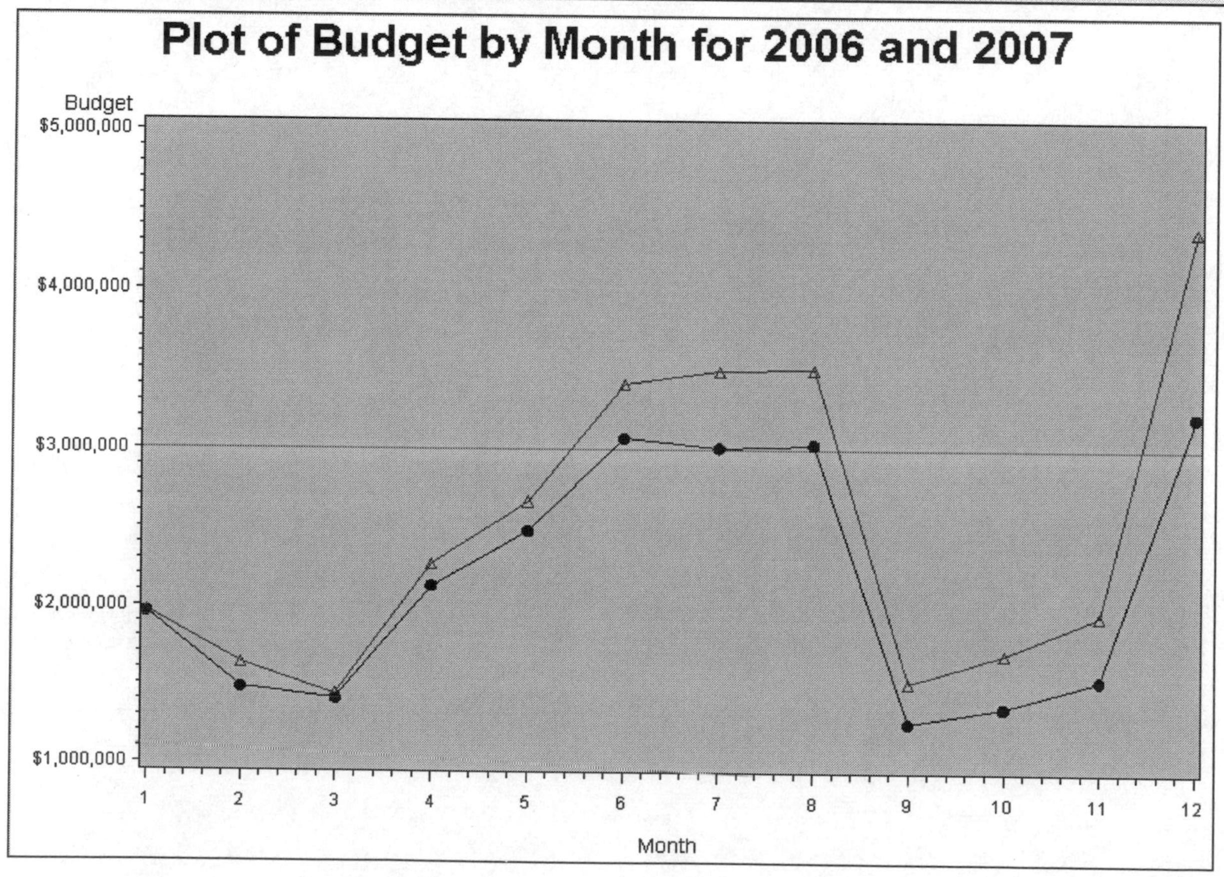

13.4 Enhancing Output

Enhancing SAS/GRAPH Output

SAS/GRAPH uses default values for colors, fonts, text size, and other graph attributes. You can override these defaults using the following methods:

- specifying an ODS style
- specifying default attributes in a GOPTIONS statement
- specifying attributes and options in global statements and procedure statements

22

Enhancing Output

p113d03

1. Submit the first PROC GPLOT step to use ODS styles to control the appearance of the output.

   Specify the style in the ODS LISTING statement with the STYLE= option produces a different ODS style.

```
ods listing style=gears;
goptions reset=all;
proc gplot data=orion.budget;
   plot Yr2007*Month;
   format Yr2007 dollar12.;
   label Yr2007='Budget';
   title 'Plot of Budget by Month';
run;
quit;
```

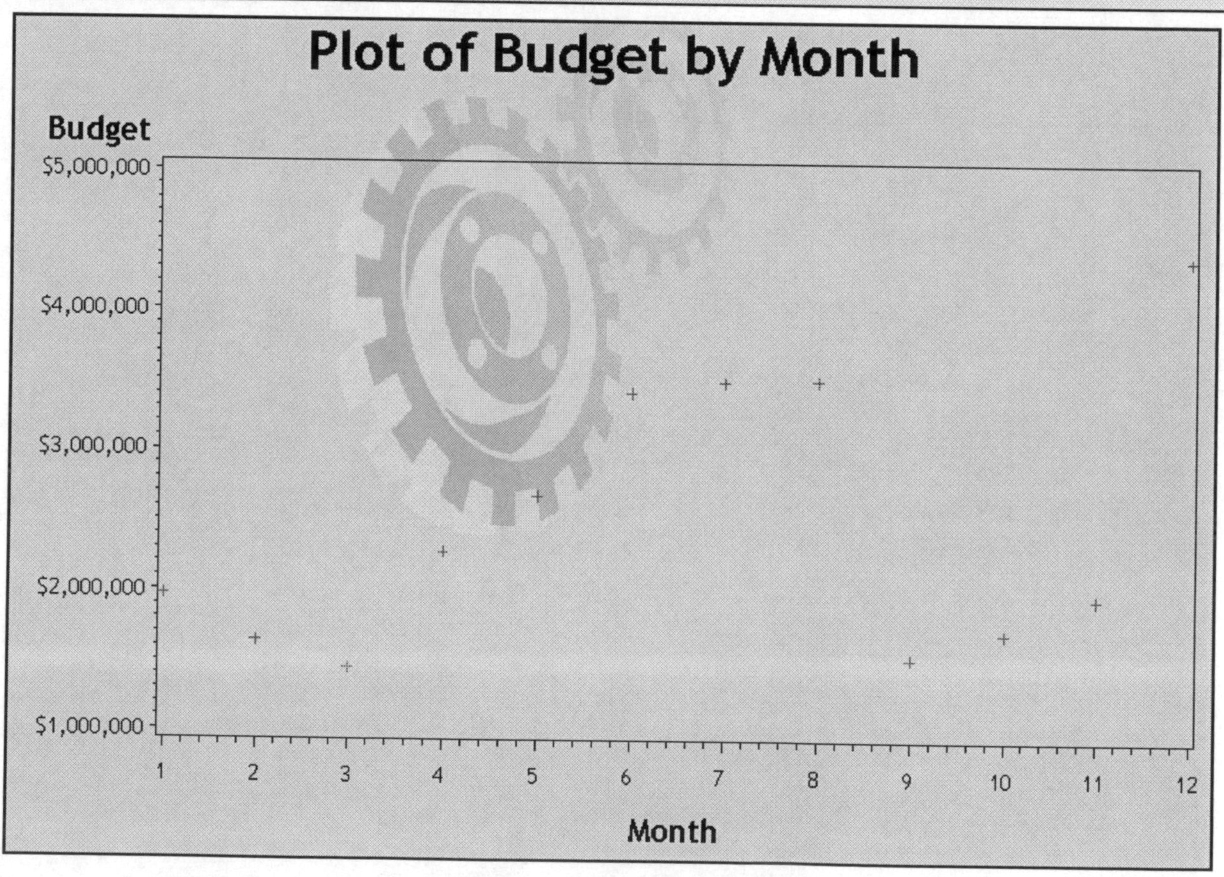

2. Submit the second PROC GPLOT step to specify the options in the TITLE and FOOTNOTE statements to control the text appearance.

   The TITLE and FOOTNOTE statements override the default fonts, colors, height, and text justification. The following options are used:

   - F= (or FONT=) specifies a font.
   - C= (or COLOR=) specifies text color.
   - H= (or HEIGHT=) specifies text height. Units of height can be specified as a percent of the display (PCT), inches (IN), centimeters (CM), cells (CELLS), or points (PT).
   - J= (or JUSTIFY=) specifies text justification. Valid values are LEFT (L), CENTER (C), and RIGHT (R).

   All options apply to text following the option.

```
ods listing style=gears;
goptions reset=all;
proc gplot data=orion.budget;
   plot Yr2007*Month / vref=3000000;
   label Yr2007='Budget';
   format Yr2007 dollar12.;
   title f=centbi h=5 pct 'Budget by Month';
   footnote c=green j=left 'Data for 2007';
run;
quit;
```

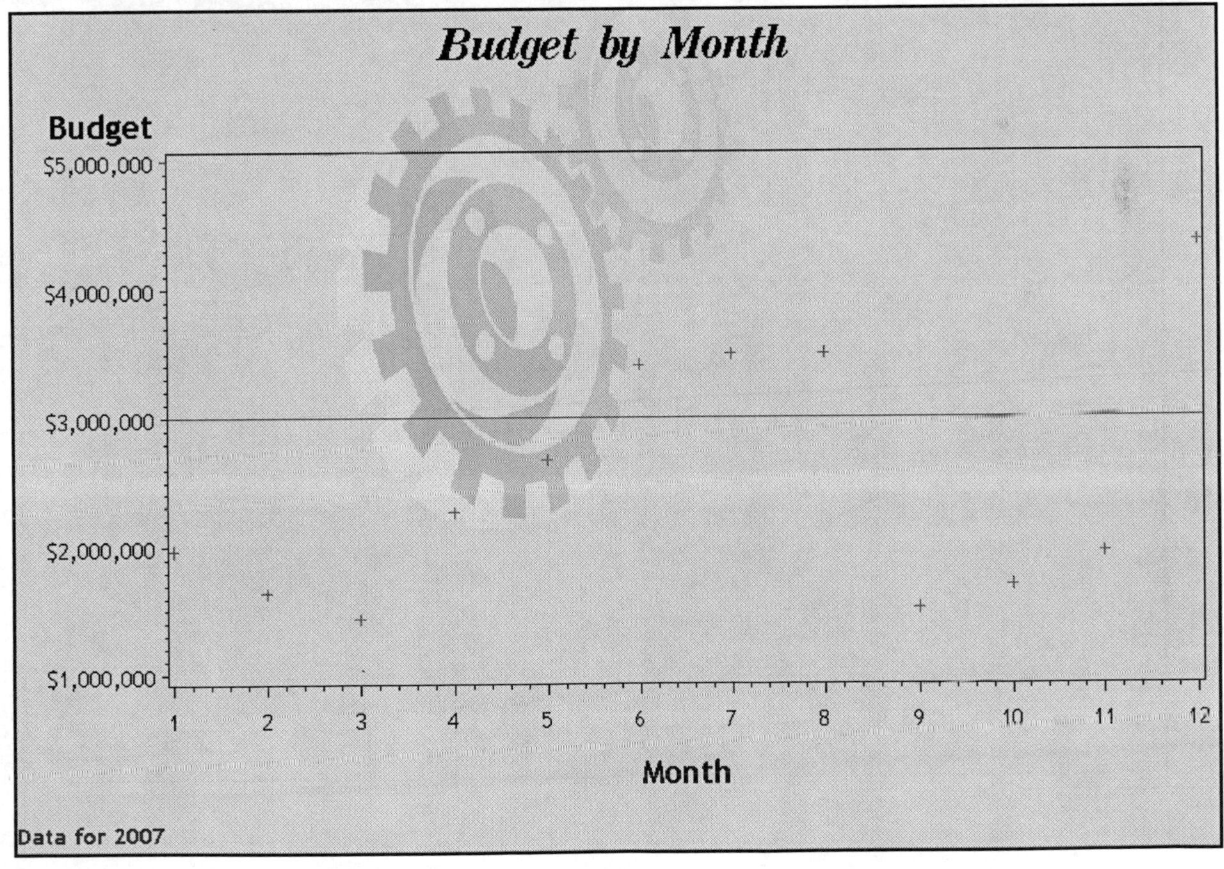

3. Submit the third PROC GPLOT step to use a GOPTIONS statement to control the appearance of the output.

   A GOPTIONS statement specifies options to control the appearance of all text in the graph. The following options are used:

   - FTEXT= specifies a font for all text.
   - CTEXT= specifies the color for all text.
   - HTEXT= specifies the height for all text.

   If a text option is specified both in a GOPTIONS statement and in a TITLE or FOOTNOTE statement, the option specified in the TITLE or FOOTNOTE statement overrides the value in the GOPTIONS statement only for that title or footnote.

```
ods listing style=gears;
goptions reset=all ftext=centb htext=3 pct ctext=dark_blue;
   proc gplot data=orion.budget;
   plot Yr2007*Month / vref=3000000;
   label Yr2007='Budget';
   format Yr2007 dollar12.;
   title f=centbi 'Budget by Month';
run;
quit;
```

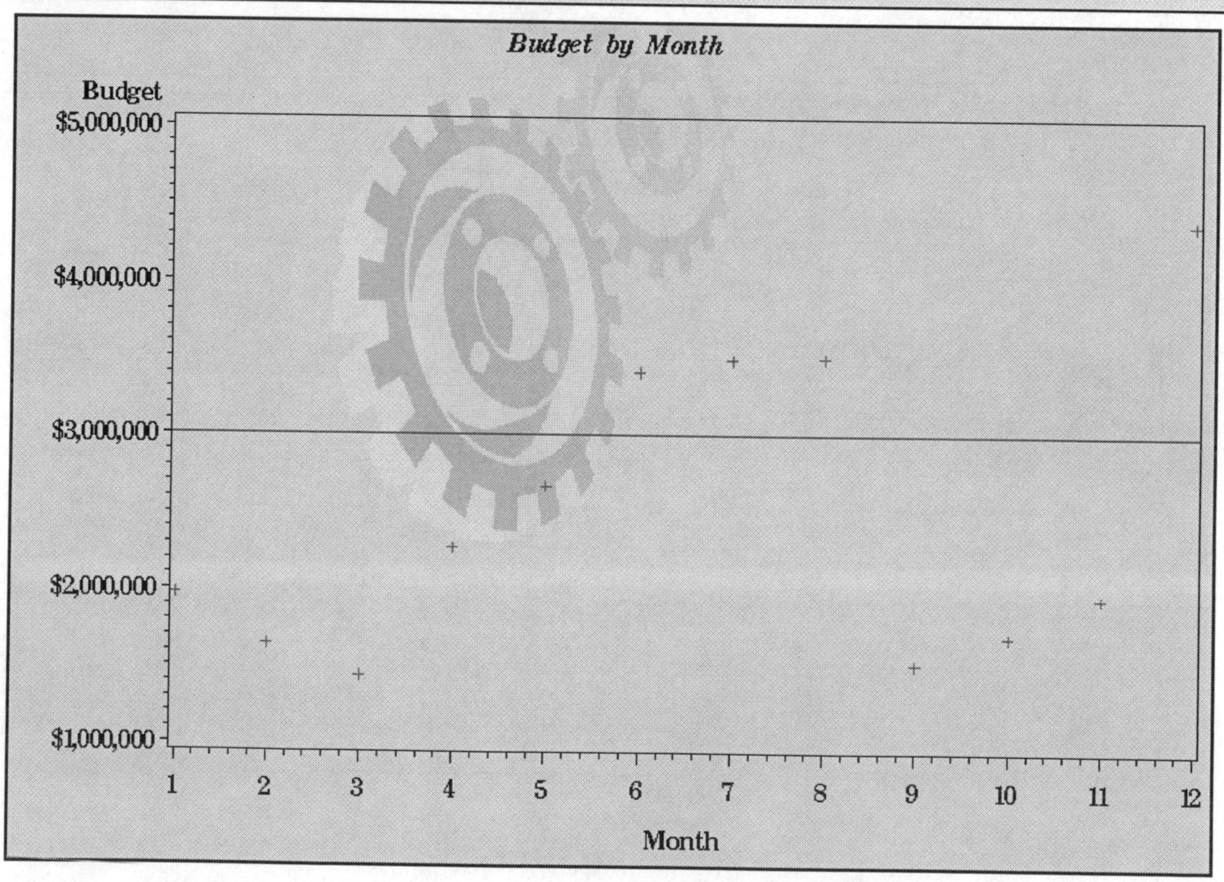

Chapter 14 Learning More

14.1 SAS Resources 14-3

14.2 Beyond This Course 14-6

14.1 SAS Resources

Objectives

- Identify areas of support that SAS offers.

3

Education

Comprehensive training to deliver greater value to your organization

- More than 200 course offerings
- World-class instructors
- Multiple delivery methods: instructor-led and self-paced
- Training centers around the world

http://support.sas.com/training/

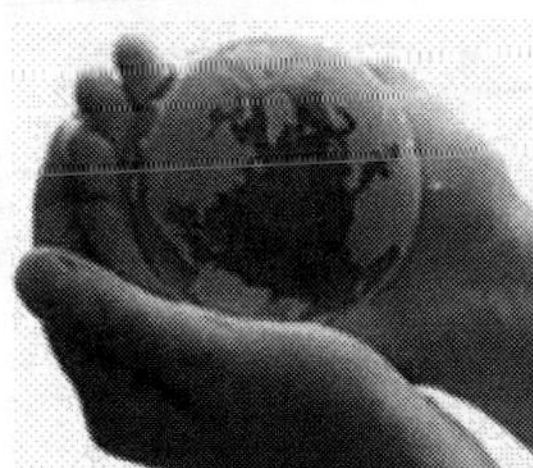

4

SAS Publishing

SAS offers a complete selection of publications to help customers use SAS software to its fullest potential:

- Multiple delivery methods: e-books, CD-ROM, and hard-copy books
- Wide spectrum of topics
- Partnerships with outside authors, other publishers, and distributors

http://support.sas.com/publishing/

5

SAS Global Certification Program

SAS offers several globally recognized certifications.

- Computer-based certification exams – typically 60-70 questions and 2-3 hours in length
- Preparation materials and practice exams available
- Worldwide directory of SAS Certified Professionals

http://support.sas.com/certify/

6

Support

SAS provides a variety of self-help and assisted-help resources.

- SAS Knowledge Base
- Downloads and hot fixes
- License assistance
- SAS discussion forums
- SAS Technical Support

http://support.sas.com/techsup/

7

User Groups

SAS supports many local, regional, international, and special-interest SAS user groups.

- SAS Global Forum
- Online SAS Community: www.sasCommunity.org

http://support.sas.com/usergroups/

8

14.2 Beyond This Course

Objectives

- Identify the next set of courses that follow this course.

10

Next Steps

SAS® Programming 1: Essentials is the entry point to most areas of the SAS curriculum.

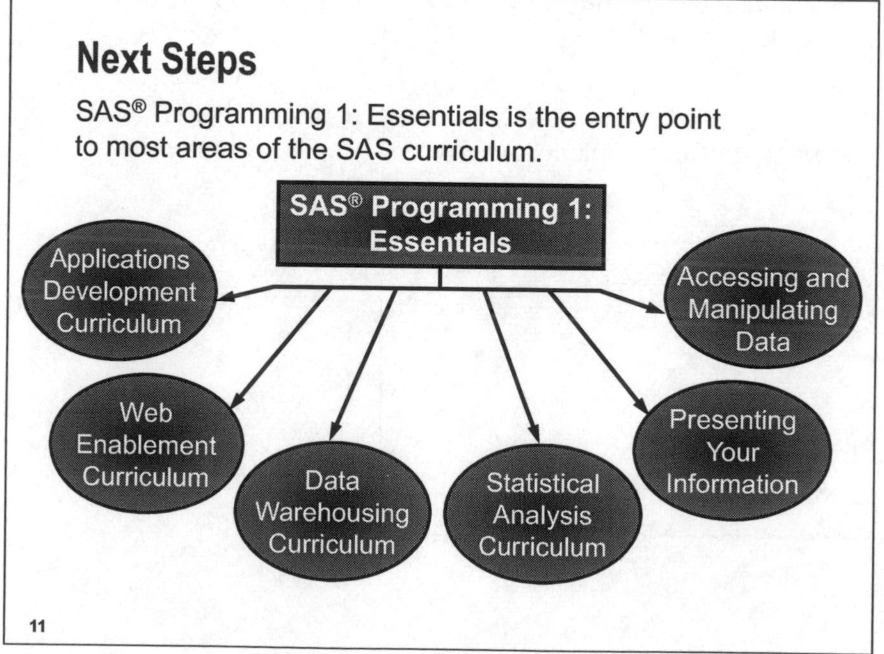

11

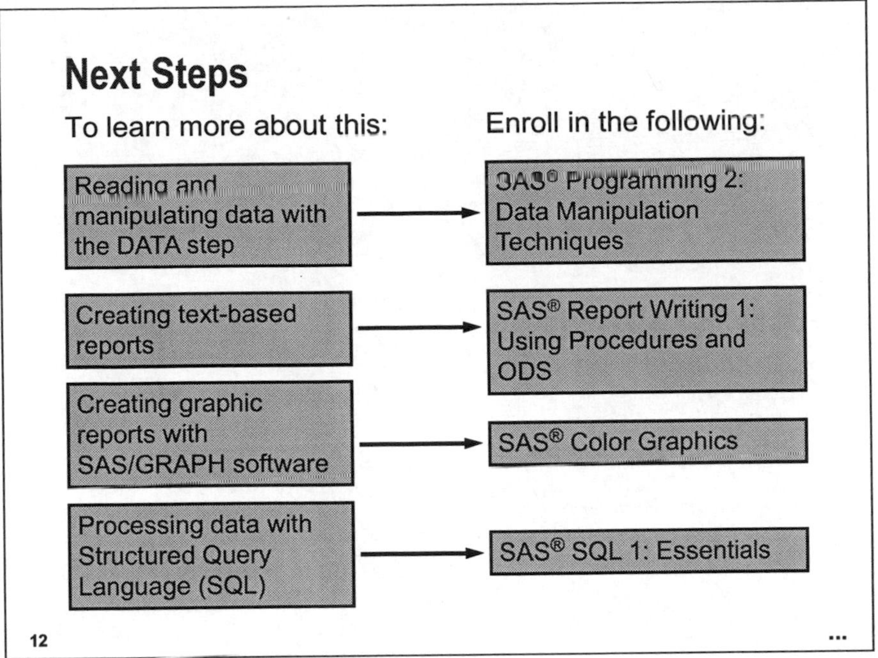

Next Steps
To learn more about this:
Enroll in the following:
Reading and manipulating data with the DATA step
SAS® Programming 2: Data Manipulation Techniques
Creating text-based reports
SAS® Report Writing 1: Using Procedures and ODS
Creating graphic reports with SAS/GRAPH software
SAS® Color Graphics
Processing data with Structured Query Language (SQL)
SAS® SQL 1: Essentials
12

Next Steps

In addition, there are prerecorded short technical discussions and demonstrations called e-lectures.

http://support.sas.com/training/

13

Appendix A Index

_

ALL keyword, 8-28, 12-12

A

accessing SAS data library, 4-16–4-32
APPEND procedure, 10-8, 10-34
appending data sets, 10-7–10-16
  like-structured, 10-11
  unlike-structured, 10-12–10-16
arithmetic operators, 5-15–5-16, 9-6
assignment statements, 8-51–8-55, 9-4–9-5

B

bar charts, 13-3, 13-9–13-20
  with line plot overlay, 13-5
batch mode, 2-9
BETWEEN-AND operator, 5-18
BY statement, 10-47–10-50, 11-49

C

character variables, 4-6
charts
  bar, 13-3
  bar with line plot overlay, 13-5
  creating bar and pie charts, 13-9–13-20
  pie, 13-4
CLASS statement, 12-50
  MEANS procedure, 12-29
  specifying classification variables, 12-50
classification variables
  specifying, 12-50
cleaning data, 8-3–8-8
  programmatically, 8-50, 8-55–8-56, 8-63
  UNIX example, 8-47–8-48
  Windows example, 8-44–8-46
  z/OS (OS/390) example, 8-49
cleaning invalid data, 8-41–8-63
combining data sets, 10-3–10-6
comments
  in SAS code, 3-8
comparison operators, 5-14–5-15
COMPRESS option
  FREQ procedure, 12-11
concatenating data sets, 10-19–10-40
constant operand, 5-14
CONTAINS operator, 5-19
CONTENTS procedure, 4-4–4-5, 6-9–6-10
  browsing a data library, 4-23–4-32
  NODS option, 4-23
CROSSLIST option
  TABLES statement, 12-10

D

data
  browsing with the PRINT procedure, 4-10–4-12
  cleaning invalid, 8-41–8-63
  cleaning programmatically, 8-50
  compilation phase, 7-12–7-16
  errors, 8-4
  execution phase, 7-17–7-23
  missing values, 4-8
  nonstandard, 7-9, 7-30–7-31
  reading, 5-3–5-5
  reading nonstandard delimited, 7-30–7-43
  standard, 7-9–7-10, 7-30
  validating with the FREQ procedure, 8-25–8-29
  validating with the MEANS procedure, 8-33–8-35
  validating with the PRINT procedure, 8-20–8-25
  validating with the UNIVARIATE procedure, 8-35–8-37
  validity and cleaning, 8-3–8-8
data access
  data-driven tasks, 1-6
data analysis
  data-driven tasks, 1-6
data errors, 8-9–8-18
data library
  browsing, 4-22–4-32
  browsing in UNIX, 4-28–4-30
  browsing in Windows, 4-24–4-27
  browsing in z/OS (OS/390), 4-31–4-32
data management
  data-driven tasks, 1-6
data presentation

data-driven tasks, 1-6
data set options
IN=, 10-78–10-84
data sets
adding formats, 5-29–5-40
adding labels, 5-29–5-40
appending, 10-7–10-16
combining, 10-3–10-6
concatenating, 10-19–10-40
eliminating duplicates, 10-52
interleaving, 10-35–10-40
like-structured, 10-20–10-28
match-merging, 10-45–10-46
merging, 10-4
merging one-to-many, 10-53–10-63
merging one-to-one, 10-44–10-52
merging with non-matches, 10-66–10-88
names, 4-9
output, 12-56–12-59
outputting to multiple, 8-17–8-18, 10-85–10-86
renaming with RENAME= option, 10-31
terminology, 4-10
unlike-structured, 10-28
DATA statement, 5-9, 7-6
DROP= option, 9-24–9-26
KEEP= option, 9-24–9-26
DATA step, 5-6–5-11
assignment statements, 9-4–9-5
processing, 7-12
data-driven tasks
data access, 1-6
data analysis, 1-6
data management, 1-6
data presentation, 1-6
date functions, 9-9–9-10
date values, 4-7
delimiter
default, 7-9
dimension expression, 12-53–12-54
DO groups, 9-35–9-37
documentation, 2-24
DROP statement, 5-23, 9-11
processing, 9-14–9-24
subsetting variables, 5-12–5-25
DROP= option
DATA statement, 9-24–9-26
DSD option
INFILE statement, 7-39–7-40

E

Editor window, 2-12
ELSE statements, 9-33, 9-40
Enhanced Editor, 2-12
Excel
creating files that open in, 11-77–11-79
Output Delivery System destinations, 11-72–11-77
Excel worksheets
creating a SAS data set, 6-3–6-16
creating from SAS data sets, 6-20–6-35
reading in Windows, 6-15–6-16
EXPORT procedure, 6-23

F

FILE command, 3-14, 3-18
saving programs, 3-14, 3-18
FOOTNOTE statement
SAS statements, 11-10–11-13
FORMAT option
TABLES statement, 12-10
FORMAT procedure
creating user-defined formats, 11-33–11-42
VALUE statement, 11-33
FORMAT statement, 5-29–5-40
SAS statements, 11-25
formats
assigning permanent, 11-27–11-28
assigning temporary, 11-26–11-28
user-defined, 11-32–11-42
FREQ procedure, 8-7, 12-3–12-20
COMPRESS option, 12-11
NLEVELS option, 12-11
PAGE option, 12-11
TABLES statement, 12-4–12-6
validating data, 8-25–8-29
frequency reports
creating, 12-12
one-way, 12-4
frequency tables
producing and enhancing, 12-3–12-20
FSEDIT window
using to clean data, 8-49
functions
date, 9-9–9-10
sum, 9-8
fundamentals of SAS statements, 3-3–3-9

G

G3D procedure
  SAS/GRAPH software, 13-5
GBARLINE procedure
  SAS/GRAPH software, 13-5
GCHART procedure
  SAS/GRAPH software, 13-3–13-4, 13-9–13-20
GCONTOUR procedure
  SAS/GRAPH software, 13-6
GMAP procedure
  SAS/GRAPH software, 13-6
GPLOT procedure
  SAS/GRAPH software, 13-4, 13-21–13-24
graph
  multiple on a page, 13-7
GREPLAY procedure
  SAS/GRAPH software, 13-7

H

Help facility, 2-24

I

IF-THEN DELETE statements, 9-50
IF-THEN statements, 8-57–8-63, 9-31
IF-THEN/ELSE DO statements, 9-35
IF-THEN/ELSE statements, 9-31, 9-34
IMPORT procedure, 6-29–6-30
Import wizard, 6-23–6-30
IN= data set option, 10-78–10-84
INCLUDE command, 2-17
INFILE statement, 7-6–7-7
  DSD option, 7-39–7-40
  MISSOVER option, 7-42
informats, 7-31–7-33
INPUT statement, 7-7
interleaving data sets, 10-35–10-40
invalid data
  cleaning, 8-41–8-63
IS MISSING operator, 5-19
IS NULL operator, 5-19

K

KEEP statement, 5-23, 9-11
  processing, 9-14–9-24
  subsetting variables, 5-12–5-25
KEEP= option
  DATA statement, 9-24–9-26

L

LABEL statement, 5-29–5-40, 11-21
labels
  assigning permanent, 11-24
  assigning temporary, 11-21–11-23
LENGTH statement, 7-24, 9-38
LIBNAME statement, 4-35–4-39
  assigning a libref, 4-19
  SAS/ACCESS, 6-7–6-8
libref
  assigning, 4-17, 4-19, 4-36
LIKE operator, 5-20–5-21
line plots, 13-4
list input, 7-8
LIST option
  TABLES statement, 12-10
Log window, 2-12, 2-13
logical operators, 5-16–5-17

M

maps
  GMAP procedure, 13-6
match-merging, 10-45–10-46
MEANS procedure, 8-7, 12-27–12-41
  CLASS statement, 12-29
  output data sets, 12-34–12-39
  OUTPUT statement, 12-35–12-39
  validating data, 8-33–8-35
  VAR statement, 12-28
MERGE statement, 10-49–10-50
merging data sets, 10-4
  one-to-many, 10-53–10-63
  one-to-one, 10-44–10-52
  with non-matches, 10-66–10-88
missing data values, 4-8
MISSOVER option
  INFILE statement, 7-42

N

names
  data set and variable, 4-9
NLEVELS option, 8-28–8-29
  FREQ procedure, 12-11
NOCOL option
  TABLES statement, 12-8
NOCUM option
  TABLES statement, 12-8
NOFREQ option
  TABLES statement, 12-8
noninteractive mode, 2-10

NOPERCENT option
TABLES statement, 12-8
NOPRINT option
TABLES statement, 8-28, 12-12
NOROW option
TABLES statement, 12-8
numeric variables, 4-6

O

observations
subsetting, 9-44–9-50
subsetting and grouping, 11-46–11-51
ODS
See Output Delivery System, 11-55
one-way frequency reports, 12-4
operands, 9-5
constant, 5-14
variable, 5-14
operators
arithmetic, 5-15–5-16, 9-6
BETWEEN-AND, 5-18
comparison, 5-14–5-15
CONTAINS, 5-19
IS MISSING, 5-19
IS NULL, 5-19
LIKE, 5-20–5-21
logical, 5-16–5-17
WHERE, 5-18
OPTIONS
SAS statements, 11-6
OUT= option
OUTPUT statement, 12-17–12-19, 12-35–12-39
TABLES statement, 12-14–12-17
TABULATE procedure, 12-56–12-59
output
directing to external files, 11-55–11-82
enhancing with SAS/GRAPH software, 13-25–13-28
output data sets, 12-56–12-59
MEANS procedure, 12-34–12-39
Output Delivery System, 11-55–11-58
creating HTML, PDF, and RTF files, 11-64–11-67
destinations used with Excel, 11-72–11-77
HTML, PDF, and RTF destinations, 11-58–11-60
STYLE= option, 11-68
OUTPUT statement
MEANS procedure, 12-35–12-39
OUT= option, 12-17–12-19, 12-35–12-39
Output window, 2-12, 2-14, 2-18

P

PAGE option
FREQ procedure, 12-11
pie charts, 13-4, 13-9–13-20
plots
creating with the GPLOT procedure, 13-21–13-24
line, 13-4
scatter, 13-4
three-dimensional contour, 13-6
three-dimensional surface and scatter, 13-5
PRINT procedure, 4-10–4-12, 6-11, 8-6
validating data, 8-20–8-25
PROC MEANS statement
computing and displaying statistics, 12-31–12-34
Program Editor, 2-12, 2-17

Q

quotation marks
balanced, 3-16–3-18
unbalanced, 3-16

R

raw data files
errors when reading, 8-9–8-18
reading data, 5-3–5-5
relational database
accessing, 4-35–4-39
RENAME= option, 10-31
reports
creating, 11-3–11-15
enhancing, 11-5–11-15, 11-20–11-28
tabular, 12-46–12-59
RUN-group processing
SAS/GRAPH software, 13-8

S

SAS code
comments, 3-8
SAS data library
accessing, 4-16–4-32
permanent, 4-18
temporary, 4-18
SAS data sets, 4-3

created from delimited raw data files, 7-3–7-26
creating with the DATA step, 5-6–5-11
descriptor portion, 4-4–4-5, 4-6
SAS date formats, 5-36–5-40
SAS date values, 4-7
SAS documentation, 2-24
SAS Enterprise Guide, 2-9
SAS Explorer window
browsing a data library, 4-22
SAS filename
temporary, 4-21
SAS formats, 5-33–5-40
SAS functions, 8-52, 9-8
SAS Help facility, 2-24
SAS informats, 7-31–7-33
SAS names
data set and variable, 4-9
SAS programs
debugging, 3-12–3-14
editor windows, 2-13
examples, 2-4–2-5
fundamentals, 3-3–3-9
including, 2-17
introduction, 2-3–2-9
noninteractive mode, 2-10
running in batch mode, 2-9
saving, 3-14, 3-18
step boundaries, 2-6–2-7
submitting, 2-11–2-14
submitting under Windows, 2-16–2-20, 2-16–2-20
submitting under z/OS (OS/390), 2-25–2-29
SAS sessions
starting, 2-16, 2-21, 2-25, 2-30
SAS statements
BY, 11-49
DROP, 9-11
ELSE, 9-33, 9-40
FOOTNOTE, 11-10–11-13
FORMAT, 11-25
global, 11-3–11-15
IF-THEN, 9-31
IF-THEN DELETE, 9-50
IF-THEN/ELSE, 9-31, 9-34
IF-THEN/ELSE DO, 9-35
KEEP, 9-11
LABEL, 11-21
LENGTH statement, 9-38
OPTIONS, 11-6
SET, 10-20
subsetting IF, 9-46
TITLE, 11-10–11-13
WHERE, 9-45, 11-46–11-48
SAS syntax rules, 3-5–3-7
SAS variable values, 4-6
SAS windowing environment, 2-8, 2-12
SAS/ACCESS
LIBNAME statement, 4-36, 6-7–6-8
SAS/ACCESS Interface for PC File Formats, 6-8
SAS/GRAPH software, 13-3–13-8
enhancing output, 13-25–13-28
G3D procedure, 13-5
GBARLINE procedure, 13-5
GCHART procedure, 13-3–13-4, 13-9–13-20
GCONTOUR procedure, 13-6
GMAP procedure, 13-6
GPLOT procedure, 13-4, 13-21–13-24
GREPLAY procedure, 13-7
RUN-group processing, 13-8
saving programs, 3-14, 3-18
FILE command, 3-14, 3-18
scatter plots, 13-4
SET statement, 5-9, 10-20, 10-34
SORT procedure, 10-46, 10-52
BY statement, 10-47–10-48
specifying classification variables
CLASS statement, 12-50
statistics
computing and displaying with PROC MEANS, 12-31–12-34
TABULATE procedure, 12-54–12-55
SUBMIT command, 2-18
subsetting IF statement, 9-46
subsetting observations, 9-44–9-50
WHERE statement, 5-12–5-25
subsetting variables
DROP statement, 5-12–5-25
KEEP statement, 5-12–5-25
SUM function, 9-8
SUMMARY procedure, 12-41
syntax
diagnosing and correcting errors, 3-10–3-18
syntax rules, 3-5–3-7

T

TABLE statement, 12-49

tables
  creating dimensional reports, 12-46–12-59
  frequency, 12-3–12-20
  suppressing display of statistics, 12-8
TABLES statement
  CROSSLIST option, 12-10
  FORMAT option, 12-10
  FREQ procedure, 12-4–12-6
  LIST option, 12-10
  NOCOL option, 12-8
  NOCUM option, 12-8
  NOFREQ option, 12-8
  NOPERCENT option, 12-8
  NOROW option, 12-8
  OUT= option, 12-14–12-17
TABULATE procedure, 12-46–12-59
  OUT= option, 12-56–12-59
  statistics, 12-54–12-55
terminology
  SAS data sets, 4-10
three-dimensional contour plots, 13-6
three-dimensional surface and scatter plots, 13-5
TITLE statement, 11-10–11-13

U

unbalanced quotation marks, 3-16
UNIVARIATE procedure, 8-8
  validating data, 8-35–8-37
UPCASE function, 8-52
user-defined formats
  creating, 11-32–11-42

V

validating data, 8-3–8-8
VALUE statement
  FORMAT procedure, 11-33
VAR statement, 12-51
  MEANS procedure, 12-28
variable names, 4-9
  assigning descriptive labels, 11-21–11-25
variable operand, 5-14
variables
  character, 4-6
  creating, 9-3–9-26
  creating conditionally, 9-30–9-40
  dropping from output data set, 5-23–5-24
  numeric, 4-6
  writing to output data set, 5-23–5-24
Viewtable window
  cleaning data interactively, 8-42–8-43

W

WHERE operators, 5-18
WHERE statement, 7-36, 9-45, 11-46–11-48
  subsetting observations, 5-12–5-25
  validating data, 8-21–8-23